7/94

P9-AQO-605

with best wishes for your
future success in the
Furniture Industry.

May 26, 1977   Leo Jromile

President Jromile School
Furniture Design and
Technology.

FURNITURE TREASURY

(Mostly of American Origin)

VOLUMES I AND II IN ONE

FURNITURE TREASURY

(*Mostly of American Origin*)

ALL PERIODS OF AMERICAN FURNITURE WITH
SOME FOREIGN EXAMPLES IN AMERICA
ALSO AMERICAN HARDWARE AND
HOUSEHOLD UTENSILS

BY

WALLACE NUTTING

FIVE THOUSAND ILLUSTRATIONS
WITH DESCRIPTIONS ON THE
SAME PAGE

VOLUMES I AND II IN ONE

UNABRIDGED

MACMILLAN PUBLISHING CO., INC.

NEW YORK

COPYRIGHT 1928
BY MACMILLAN PUBLISHING CO., INC.

All rights reserved. No part of this book may be reproduced or transmitted in any form or by any means, electronic or mechanical, including photocopying, recording or by any information storage and retrieval system, without permission in writing from the Publisher.

Thirteenth Printing 1976

Macmillan Publishing Co., Inc.
866 Third Avenue, New York, New York 10022

PRINTED IN THE UNITED STATES OF AMERICA

To

HENRY WOOD ERVING

A STUDENT OF FURNITURE
FOR FIFTY YEARS
WHOSE KNOWLEDGE IS SURPASSED ONLY
BY HIS CHEERFULNESS
IN SHARING IT

EXPLANATORY

A WORK showing 5000 examples of furniture and utensils has proved a prodigious undertaking, but it is hereby humbly presented. Nor let the reader, more or less gentle, suppose that it is only necessary to submit museum examples. Nine-tenths of the work is occupied with private collections, except for those subjects in the collection bearing the author's name, and presented the Wadsworth Atheneum by Mr. J. P. Morgan. Even excluding them, more than 3000 examples are now shown for the first time.

In very rare instances, for completion's sake, subjects have been used which are in the works of other authors, who indeed have also used subjects in this author's former work.

While all the pictures shown are of objects now in America, it is recognized that many looking-glasses and clocks, some chairs and settees, and a few other objects are of foreign origin. Their proportion, however, does not exceed one in twenty of the whole. It has been necessary to include them to afford a rounded view.

The author, in spite of the mass of material presented, does not claim exhaustive treatment. In the matter of cupboards, for instance, he estimates that there are thousands of variations in Pennsylvania alone. But he has presented all the types of furniture which a voluminous work could contain. Particularly, he has thought it better to curtail descriptions than pictures.

Complaint, well warranted, has been made that works on furniture have been restricted to the fine and rare examples. Consequently, the small collector or dealer found difficulty in fixing the period or estimating the merit or rarity of the simpler articles, which, while still available, are by their quaintness and sterling qualities desirable to possess.

This work, while rich in rare and elaborate examples, is designed by its fullness to meet also the hitherto unsupplied needs of the ordinary collector.

About five hundred collectors are represented from twenty-seven states or countries. Thanks are extended, most gratefully, to those who have contributed pictures which the author did not make, and to all who have supplied information, or have otherwise given assistance.

The limit of styles has been fixed at the end of the Empire period, which indeed brings us to the beginning of the degraded styles.

The nearest approximate date is given. The actual date may be ten or occasionally fifteen years earlier or later. All references are to the number of the picture. There are no page numbers to confuse with picture numbers.

That errors have crept in, there is no doubt. The work is too large to escape them. Care has been exercised to exclude the spurious, and the author has personally examined ninety-nine per cent of the objects shown. He here enters, however, a disclaimer of any guarantee of authenticity in regard to the objects themselves, or the descriptions which accompany them.

That an article is included does not mean that it is, therefore, specially meritorious. It may merely register a prevailing taste, and be shown to cover its period fully.

The author knows that readers will be thankful for the arrangement by which in every instance the description of a picture may be read without turning a page. This system has sometimes kept a picture smaller than others not so important, and has cut the description ruthlessly. But any system has its faults. Brevity is not always regrettable.

WALLACE NUTTING.

FRAMINGHAM, MASSACHUSETTS.

CONTENTS

CONTENTS — *Continued*

CONTENTS — *Continued*

FURNITURE TREASURY
(Mostly of American Origin)

Only such descriptions of furniture follow as can be supplied without turning a leaf, and all periods of any class will be shown before another class is illustrated.

Chests are known as early as any form of furniture. Connected with worship we find the ark of the covenant, and all religions used receptacles for their ceremonies. Chests thus early became highly decorated. The coffer of Italy is an article of much beauty and importance. Pronounced in the old way, chist, the word is similar in ancient tongues, and means an enclosed space for a container, like the human chest. So far as this work is concerned, only American chests are shown. They were first of oak. Probably they came with the Pilgrims. They had legs formed by extension of the sides of frame (stiles). The earliest are like architectural fronts, and are carved, three panels in front being usual. The semblance of arches is observed among the first. Carving was never highly artistic, being flat in slight relief. The motives were borrowed from the Gothic, and from Renaissance forms, and were already decadent in our oldest examples.

1. OAK, IMITATIVE ARCHES. BEFORE 1650. C. SANFORD BULL, WATERBURY, WHO OBTAINED IT FROM THE ESTATE OF DR. IRVING W. LYON, THE FIRST AND MOST SCHOLARLY INVESTIGATOR. FOUND IN WINDSOR, CONNECTICUT. IT IS NO. 1 IN HIS BOOK, WHICH HAS NOT BEEN EQUALED IN THOROUGHNESS, BUT CONTAINS ONLY A FEW EXAMPLES. ACANTHUS, LUNETTE, AND IMBRICATED (FISH-SCALE) MOTIVES.

2. Oak, True Arches, with Drawers. Before 1649. Estate of G. H. Buek, "Home Sweet Home," Easthampton, L. I. Restored by Schwartz. Lacks Ornaments at Tops of Stiles. Tulips on Arches, Foliated Scrolls Elsewhere, Rope Mold. Yellow Pine Lid.

3. End of the Above, Scratch Carved.

4. Carving on Cupboard End.

5. OAK. 1640–70. WILLIAM B. GOODWIN, TO WHOM IT CAME FROM DESCENDANTS OF KENELM WINSLOW, COFFIN MAKER OF THE PILGRIMS, AND PERHAPS THE MAKER. TULIPS IN PANELS, EXCEPT THE CENTRAL CLOVER LEAF. OTHER FOLIATIONS DIFFICULT TO DESCRIBE. 27¾ X 47⅜ X 21¾.

6. OAK, SCALLOPED BOTTOM RAIL, LUNETTE AT TOP, ROPE CARVING BELOW. 1650–70. INNER STILES PALMATED. 27½ X 46 X 20. AUTHOR'S COLLECTION. WADSWORTH ATHENEUM.

7. Oak, Four Diamond Panels. Spade Pattern Long Stiles. Arch Mold Top Rail. Lid Incorrect. 32 x 54 x 23. Wadsworth Atheneum.

8. Oak, Five-Panel Front. Lid and Feet Restored. Bottom Should Be. Indentations Above and Below, All Rails and Stiles Notch Carved. 1660–70. George Dudley Seymour.

9. NORMAN TOOTH. OAK. 1670. NAMED FROM VERTICAL ROWS OF SQUARE INCISIONS. DRAWER RESTORED. FEET PIECED. LID OAK. 36 x 33½ x 18. WADSWORTH ATHENEUM.

10. OAK. RUNIC. LID, PANELED OAK. 1660. RAILS OUTLINED FOR FULLER CARVING. FOUND IN PORTSMOUTH, N. H. NOW IN WADSWORTH ATHENEUM. GEORGE DUDLEY SEYMOUR.

11. Tulip Carved. Oak. 1670. Resembles a Hadley, but Carving Better. Similar Two-Drawer Chest in Connecticut Historical Society. 49 x 32 x 18½. H. W. Erving.

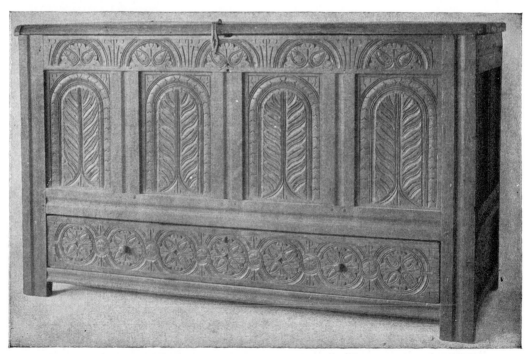

12. Four-Palm Panel. Oak, Pine Lid. 1660. Three-Panel End. Endless Band Rosette Drawer. Legs Since Pieced. Now 52 x 39 x 21. Wadsworth Atheneum.

13. OAK. RENAISSANCE. PINE LID. 1670. ARCH CARVED RAIL. AUCTIONED FROM EFFECTS OF JOSIAH HERRICK, ANTRIM, N. H. 45 x 26½ x 22½. GEORGE DUDLEY SEYMOUR.

14. OAK. MINIATURE. OAK-PANELED LID. 1680. PROBABLY MADE FOR A CHILD. ONLY MINIATURE OF THE SORT. WIDE DENTILS ON LOWER FRONT AND BOTH END RAILS. GEORGE DUDLEY SEYMOUR.

15. Four-Panel Oak, Spade Motive. 1670. Short Stiles Carved Like Inset Split Balls. Bottom Rail Not Chamfered. Shuttle Pattern Lunettes on Top Rail; Lower Rail Scratch Carved. Estate of Wm. G. Erving, M.D., Washington.

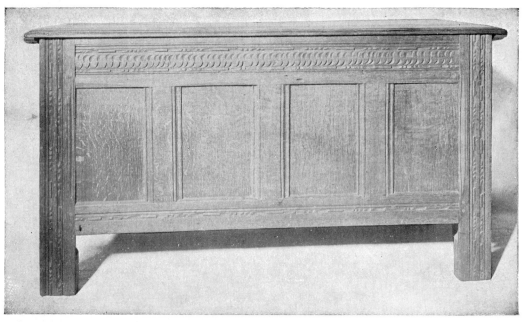

16. Rope-Carved Oak. 1670. Single-Panel Ends. Pencil and Pearl Molds on Leg Stiles. As Usual, Molding on Inside of Leg Stiles Is Worked from the Solid, After the Parts Were Assembled. 47½ x 26½ x 20¼. H. W. Erving.

17. OAK. PINE PANELS. 1680. END PANEL RAISED, CHAMFERED CORNER PANELS. PINE PANELS ARE NOT RARE IN EARLY WORK. 41¾ x 28½ x 18½. H. W. ERVING.

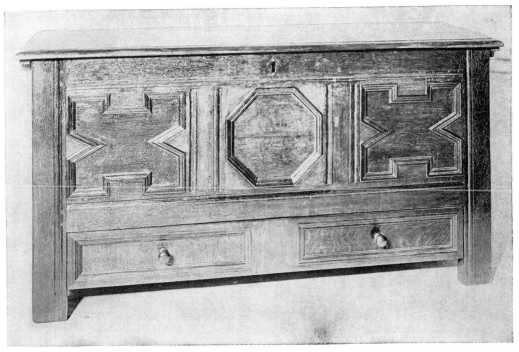

18. OAK. GEOMETRIC PANELS. 1680. NO RAIL BELOW DRAWER. UNUSUAL IN THIS REGARD, LIKE THE PRECEDING. H. W. ERVING.

19. Oak, Identically Carved Panels. 1670. Lid Pine Molded with Bead. Wooden-
Pin Cleat Hinge. 42 x 27½ x 18. Wadsworth Atheneum.

20. Oak, Greek Cross Side Panels. 1670. 43 x 31 x 20½. H. W. Erving.

21. PLAIN PANEL OAK. 1680. LID PINE. THE PECULIAR AND UNDESIRABLE CHAMFER OF FOOT
SEEMS ORIGINAL. 47 X 29 X 20½. WADSWORTH ATHENEUM.

22. MOLDED RAIL. OAK, 1690. DRAWER MOLDS BLEND WITH THE RAILS ABOVE AND BELOW.
DWIGHT BLANEY.

In the earlier American types the hinges either are staples of iron or are wooden pins set in the end of the cleat, enlarged for that purpose. There is never a strap hinge on New England oak. Pennsylvania walnut, or tulip, chests have the strap hinge, often tastefully scrolled. The oldest lid was probably always oak, but the wide pine in quantity very soon induced its use as an ideal material for lids. The lids project about three-quarters of an inch on fronts and ends, this space being occupied at the end by oak cleats. The molding is quite generally that called thumb nail, which is the best and earliest, but an occasional bead is found. Lids sometimes project on the back in oak chests and form a stop to prevent the lifted lid from dropping back too far. The best lids are in one piece. While a paneled oak lid is not a proof of English origin, it is a strong indication of such origin. If the lid is oak boards, it is thinner than the pine.

23. Ball Foot, Oak, Geometric Panel. 1670. The Two Upper Drawers Are False. Back Legs Are Continuations of the Frame. Was Brooks Reed's.

24. Carved Oak, Board, Dated 1698, on Till. Though Not Framed, It Continues an Earlier Tradition in the Carving. Pennsylvania Museum.

25. Painted Oak, Decoration Largely Dimmed, but Imitative of English Lacquer. 1690–1705. From Branford, Conn. George Dudley Seymour. At Wadsworth Atheneum.

26. Oak, Arch Panel. 1680. Oak Lid. Found in New Hampshire. Several Found on North Shore, Mass. American. The Arches Simulate the Architectural. 48 x 31 x 21. Mary M. Sampson, Boston.

27. Oak, Twelve Panel. 1680. Applied Spindles, and Decorated Panels. Triglyphs Opposite Drawer Ends. Mrs. Francis P. Garvan.

28. Oak, Diamond and Arch. 1680. Turned Incised Decorations. Wheels in Diamonds Suggest Gothic Influence. 45¾ x 33½ x 19¾. H. W. Erving.

29. Oak, Diamond Panel, Ball Foot. 1690. Found in New Jersey. Oak Lid. Strap Hinges. Scale and Bead Carving. Thought to Be by a Maker Who Was Trained Abroad before He Immigrated. Wm. B. Goodwin, Hartford.

30. Oak, Ball Foot, Geometric Panel. 1690. Turtle Backs Prominent Feature. Probably Several Lost from Top Rail. Mrs. Hulings Cowperthwaite Brown.

31. Oak, One Arched Panel. 1680. Spindle Ornament Forms Three Crosses. Note Four Sets of Triglyphs; cf. Chest Above. Miss Helen T. Cooke, Wellesley.

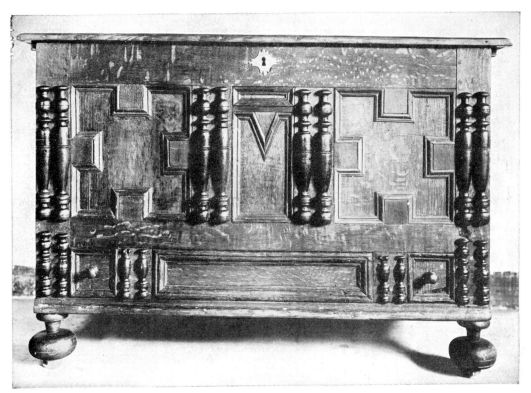

32. Oak, Ball Foot, Spindle Decorated. 1680. One Drawer, Despite Appearances.
Central Panel Mold Forms an M, Possibly for Initial? Spindle Work Puzzling, Possibly
Wrongly Restored.

33. Oak, Painted and Spindled. 1690. A Gaily Decorated Front, with Roses. Paint
Finally Superseded Spindle Ornament. Katrina Kipper, Accord, Mass.

The Gothic chest of boards without frame is earlier than American settlement and not found here. Then came framed chests, carved. Spindle ornament came in strongly about 1665. Painted decorations began in 1680, and were common 1690–1700. Plain panels on simple chests carried through all these periods. After 1700 chests declined rapidly. They appear 1690–1710 in pine with stamped decorations and plain. But the highboy, beginning about 1690, drove chests to the attic by 1710. Spindles at first were added to carving, then with painting and finally were omitted. The carving is almost entirely linear or flat, otherwise called peasant carving. A few very early examples have carving slightly rounded, but there is never high relief or modeling.

34. BALL FOOT, CURVED MOLD. 1680. MOST UNUSUAL. STRAIGHT LINES, HOWEVER SHORT, ALMOST UNIVERSALLY MARK MOLDINGS. THE LONG SPINDLES ARE A DOUBLED MOTIVE, ALIKE AT BOTH ENDS. G. WINTHROP BROWN, BROOKLINE.

35. OAK, SERRATED AND ARCHED PLYMOUTH TYPE. 1670. ALL CHESTS HITHERTO SHOWN HAD LONG DRAWERS. THESE ALWAYS HAVE TWO DRAWERS, END TO END. M. A. NORTON, HARTFORD, AS ALSO THAT BELOW.

36. OAK, SERRATED MULTI-ANGLED PANEL. 1680. MOTIVES SIMILAR TO PRECEDING BUT FRONT FEET TURNED. IT IS BELIEVED THESE CHESTS WERE ALL FROM PLYMOUTH OR ITS NEARBY TOWNS TO THE NORTH, AND THAT KENELM WINSLOW OR JOHN ALDEN OR BOTH WORKED UPON THEM. EIGHT OR TEN ARE KNOWN.

37. OAK, SERRATED. DATED ON TILL 1691. THE BRASS DROP HANDLES ALSO MARK THIS LATE DATE. SEE ORNAMENTS ON FEET, MISSING ON SPECIMEN BELOW. STAMP DECORATED AROUND PANELS AND TILL. 52½ X 34 X 20¼. WADSWORTH ATHENEUM.

38. OAK, SERRATED. 1680. SCRATCH CARVED SERRATIONS ON FEET. PANEL ARRANGEMENT REVERSED FROM THAT ABOVE. THIS CLASS HAS PINE PANELS AS A RULE. WAS B. A. BEHREND'S.

39. Oak, Serrated, Large Foot Turnings. 1680. Oak Panels. The Drawers Are Always Beveled, Like Blocking, by Applied Molds. 50 x 33½ x 21¼. H. W. Erving.

40. Oak, Spindled, Scroll Skirt. 1680. Initials A. B. Ends of Sheathed Paneling; Spindles Partly Restored. 22 x 31 x 19½. Wadsworth Atheneum.

41. OAK, THREE CARVED TULIP PANELS. 1670. FORMERLY IN CAPT. CHAS. CHURCHILL HOUSE, NEWINGTON, CONN. 47 X 26 X 19. GEORGE DUDLEY SEYMOUR.

DROPS OR SPINDLE ORNAMENTS

The long ones are sometimes called banisters or balusters. The oval ones are called turtle backs, eggs, bosses or split balls. These latter are sometimes surrounded by four diminutive split balls, or satellites. The eggs on drawers or front panels are often applied at an angle. The long spindles at their best are very boldly carved, necking at places almost to the vanishing point, and indicating remarkable skill in turning. In some otherwise good chests this turning is degraded. There is a variation in application, but a large spindle on the outside, or leg stile, and pairs of slight spindles on the inner stiles are often found. On drawers or flanking drawer ends delicate spindles appear, ordinarily in pairs. These ornaments are sometimes found even in the feet, like half balls, large, or in small pairs. In certain restorations these have been in error omitted. While the origin of the spindles is not certain, the complete spindles on English livery cupboards may have suggested them. One would say they are not so good as the carving which they supersede.

The spindles are painted black, to represent ebony, which wood we never find. They were of maple, tulip wood, birch, or even pine, but perhaps tulip (white wood) is most common. They are very slightly less than a half section, by thickness of a saw cut. Applied by glue alone, they often dropped off, and sometimes were lost. Sometimes those that stuck were stripped away. Then the whole chest was painted red!

42. OAK, SPINDLE, THREE IDENTICAL PANELS. 1680. MOLDINGS, SPANISH CEDAR. MANY TRIGLYPHS GIVE HEIGHT. 45½ x 30 x 20½. H. W. ERVING.

43. OAK, PLAIN PANELS, SPINDLES. 1680. UNRESTORED. WERE MOLDS ON DRAWER. DWIGHT BLANEY.

44. Oak, Eight-Paneled Front. 1670–1690. Rare in Panel Arrangement. Outside Spindles Possibly Missing. 52½ x 30½ x 28½. Feet Cut Down. Wadsworth Atheneum.

45. Oak, Spindles on Panels. Dated 1693, on Small Central Panel of Drawer, Which Is First Grooved and Then by Insertion of Cross Pieces Given Effect of Small Panels. Wadsworth Atheneum.

Board chests are much inferior to frame chests, and usually later. Finally, in the 18th century all chests were of boards, without frame. It has been held that there are early 17th century board chests, but the author is unable to determine. The Gothic chests were often of boards, centuries earlier.

46. Board, Applied Decoration. Painted. 1700. Some of the Bosses Are Flat.

47. Oak, Spindle and Boss Decoration. 1670-1690. The Triglyphs on Top Rail Are Spaced Wider than Those on Drawer Level. Both Chests Mrs. Francis P. Garvan's.

48. Oak, Ball Foot, Center Block Panels. 1680. Stiles Project beyond Frame, and Then Terminate in Ball Feet. G. Winthrop Brown.

49. Pine, Ball Foot, One Long and Two Short Drawers. 1690. A Delightful Little Chest. 20 x 14 x 25.

50. Oak, Spool-Turned Feet, Small Blocked Drawer. 1690–1705. 33½ x 32 x 21. Both Chests, Mrs. Francis P. Garvan's.

51. Oak, Four Panels, All Carved. 1660. Initials P. W. Strong English Suggestion. Laureling on Short Stiles. Interlaced Straps Surrounding Rosettes on Bottom Rail and Leg Stiles.

52. Oak, Spindles, Geometric Panels. 1680. Crude Triangular Blocks above Long Drops. Heavy Applied Molds. Metropolitan Museum.

53. Oak, Ball Foot, Painted Decoration. 1690. Drawer Lost. Graceful Trees
Were Uncovered by Cleaning Off Paint. 43 x 30¾ x 19. Wadsworth Atheneum.

54. Oak, Sunburst Painted Decoration. 1690. Black and Red Stripes Around
Drawer, Instead of Molding. 43 x 22 x 20½. Wadsworth Atheneum.

55. OAK, SPINDLES, NUMEROUS ROSETTES. 1680. UNUSUAL END PANELS. 48 x 37½ x 20.
JAMES N. H. CAMPBELL, HARTFORD.

THE TULIP MOTIVE

It may be presumed, perhaps, that tulip decoration originated in the Low Countries. But it was rife in America before the Dutch period of furniture came in. We find the tulip on painted work, like loom stools and chests made in Pennsylvania by immigrants from the Palatinate. It is also found in the shapes of iron utensils, on fabrics, and as cutouts on wood. As seen in elevation, as it were, it appears to have three leaves, and a religious motive has been ascribed to it, as to the fleur-de-lis, both being regarded as emblems of the Trinity. At any rate, it became the commonest carved or painted decoration, and appears on the side panels of a large class of Connecticut chests, and as an endlessly repeated figure all over the Hadley chests, and in many other connections. On American chests it is seen, carved, from about 1665 to 1700, and painted from about 1690 to 1800, the later appearances being on Pennsylvania chests. For about twenty years, therefore, the carving or painting may be seen on the same pieces, or separately. There is a great difference in the merit of the carving or painting.

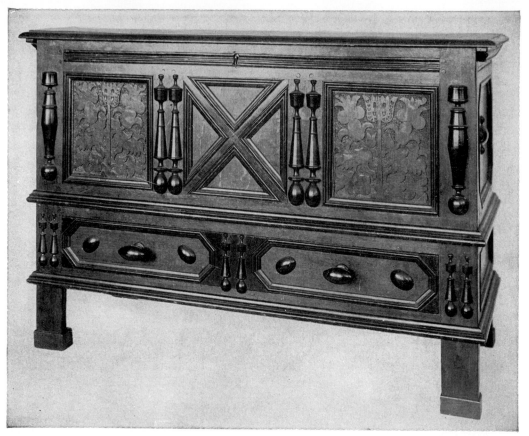

56. Oak, Tulip, and St. Andrew's Cross. 1680. Henry Stearns, New Hartford.

TULIP AND ASTER PATTERNS

A piece loosely called Connecticut chest, which means nothing, as various patterns are found there, is that which has aster, often called sunflower, carving on the central panel, and tulip carving on the side panels. Occasionally a family will aver, if not swear, that their ancestor brought their specimen from England. It is possible. But a good many of these chests are traceable to Hartford County, and so far none have been traced to any other source. The conclusion is obvious that, though one or two specimens may have come from England, they are essentially a local product, though no certain trace of a maker has been found. They have acquired a vogue like the Hadley chests. They are neither better nor older than many other chests, but have become important. They are found with no drawer, very rarely; with one drawer, or with two. Perhaps fifty are known. As in the case of several other styles, similar patterns are found in court cupboards.

57. Oak, Tulip-Carved and Painted. Dated April 5th, 1704, on Painted Center Panel. Drawers Painted. M. A. Norton.

58. A Pine Six-Board Sea Chest. Dated 1677. Initialed Hearts M. S. 53 x 19 x 21. Lunettes Opposed, Star Wheels (Star Fish), and a Crude Foliated Scroll.

59. Tulip and Aster, One Drawer. 1670. 44 x 31 x 19¼. H. W. Erving.

60. Oak, One Carved Panel Initialed W. B. 1680. An Unusual Variant. 44 x 25½ x 18. H. W. Erving.

61. Tulip and Aster, Two Drawer. 1670–1690. Fine Specimen. Lid Yellow (Hard) Pine, Usual. Legs Have Lost about an Inch, Being Now Six Inches. 45 x 40 x 20¼. Wadsworth Atheneum.

62. Tulip and Aster, No Drawer. 1670. 44¼ x 24½ x 18. James N. H. Campbell.

63. Oak, Two-Drawer Hadley. 1690. Initialed H. A. Heart on Bottom Drawer.
44 x 42¾ x 18¾. Wadsworth Atheneum.

In the chest above we have the first of a series much alike. They are always carved all over the front with the tulip, minor motives being sometimes introduced. First named by H. W. Erving from the locality of discovery. Investigations, still incomplete, as to their origin do not make it clear that they were all made in one place, but their provenance is certainly between Hartford and Greenfield, on the Connecticut. A feature is the bevel of the drawer end to correspond with the chamfer of the long leg stile, proving the stile was worked before assembly. They are always initialed as here, or have a full name on the top rail.

64. Oak, One-Drawer Hadley. 1690. Initials H. S. Largely Scratch-Carved with Pig Tails, a Tasteless Decoration. Wadsworth Atheneum.

65. Miniature, Ball Foot, Board. 1700. The Floral Decoration Is Poorly Reproduced. It Consists of Vines with Tendrils and Blossoms. Metropolitan Museum.

66. OAK, ONE-DRAWER HADLEY. INITIALS M. M. 1690. FOUND IN CORNER OF NEW HAMPSHIRE
NEAREST GREENFIELD, MASS. 42½ x 35¼ x 19. WADSWORTH ATHENEUM.

67. PINE, CARVED, SIX BOARD. 1700. THE CENTRAL CARVING MAY BE A SUNFLOWER.
CONNECTICUT ORIGIN. "SHUTTLE" LUNETTES. PENNSYLVANIA MUSEUM.

68. Oak, One-Drawer Hadley. ·1690–1705. Initials M. S. Three End Panels; the Two-
and Three-Drawer Usually Have Four. Henry Ford, Wayside Inn, Sudbury.

69. Miniature, Ball Foot, Pine. The Brass Tear-Drop Handle
Came in about 1690, but Became Common a Decade After. Estate
of J. Milton Coburn, So. Norwalk.

70. OAK, TWO-DRAWER HADLEY, BEFORE 1704. A FINE SPECIMEN. INITIALS E. A. BELIEVED TO STAND FOR ELIZABETH ALLIS. GEO. P. EASTMAN, ORANGE, N. J.

John Allis lived at Hatfield; his daughter Elizabeth married James Bridgman in 1704. In the inventory of his estate is mentioned a "Wainscott Chest." In the same family many generations. There is believed to be connection by marriage between the Allises and the Disbrowes of Hartford. Nich. Disbrowe's name is cut on the interior of a remarkable Hadley, as pointed out by Lockwood. John Allis died 1698, six years after Disbrowe. Elizabeth's brother was in company with a Belden who married the widow of Capt. Allis, and they carried on a cabinet business. This chest has such points of similarity to the Disbrowe chest as to suggest the same or a related maker.

The Reverend C. F. Luther of Amherst has interested himself to delve in the lore of the Hadley chest, and his investigations are still proceeding. But it will never be possible, one would say, to prove that all these chests were made in one town or by one man. The author's casual attention has traced the style as far north on the Connecticut as Hanover. Mr. William B. Goodwin has carefully studied the genealogy of the Belden family, and Mr. Luther has also traced the Hawkes family. Amongst these families coming together at Hadley and Hatfield the origin probably rests.

71. Oak, Two-Drawer Hadley. Dated March 1701. Initials H. B. Widely Divergent in Style. Side Panels Partly in the Round. This Is the Only Hadley Known with Initials Thus Placed. Johnson's Book Store, Springfield.

2. Pine, Carved, Small. The Sunburst Is Partly Repeated in Segments in the Corners. Fuessenich Collection, Torrington, Conn.

73. Pine, Ball Foot, Bail Handles. 1710. Feet Unusual and Good. Mark La Fontaine, Springfield, Vt.

74. OAK, TWO-DRAWER HADLEY. FULL NAME. 1690. FOUND NEAR DEERFIELD, MASS. PHILIP L. SPAULDING.

75. OAK. PINE LID. 1670. OUTSIDE SLIDE OPENS TO TILL. FOUND IN MERRIMAC VALLEY. 29 x 38 x 16. MARY M. SAMPSON.

76. Oak, Three-Drawer Hadley. Initials T. S. 1700. Only Other Known in Deerfield Museum. Flat Bar Inside Locks All Drawers. Mrs. Geo. R. Fearing.

77. Pine Paneled. Spindled. 1690. Initialed I. N. E. Interesting Attempt to Follow Oak Styles. Fluting Stopped for Spindles. Fuessenich Collection.

This chest follows no recognized style, and its origin is therefore hard to determine. Framed pine chests like this and the one below are rare, following as they do the oak tradition, with stile legs. Curious sports are interesting by their very difference.

78. Pine. Oak Stiles. 1790. Mold Not at Base Suggests Building from Memory. 34 x 52 x 22. Mark La Fontaine.

79-80. Large and Small Matched Pine Chests. 1710. Wadsworth Atheneum. Geo. Dudley Seymour.

81. PINE, BOARD. INITIALED R. H. 1710. AUTHOR'S COLLECTION.
WADSWORTH ATHENEUM.

A good example to show construction of the "Six Board" Chest. Edge of ends cut away to allow front to set back flush. Very rarely put together with wood pins; ordinarily frankly nailed. The "boot jack" end is sometimes scrolled to graceful shape, but more often a simple V. Could not be a ship chest, because it has feet.

82. OAK, SIX BOARD. GOUGE CARVED. SHEATHING MOLDS. 1710. WADSWORTH ATHENEUM.

83. Carved Oak Board. 1690. One Drawer. Lunettes, Wheels, Scales, etc.
G. Winthrop Brown.

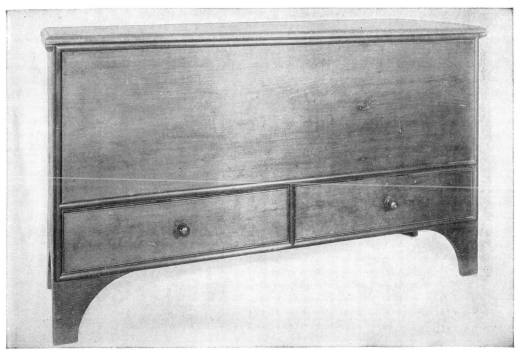

84. Pine. Single Arch Mold. Arched Base. 1710. G. Winthrop Brown.

85. YELLOW PINE. THROUGH MORTISE. CARVED, PANELED. 1700. POSSIBLY UNIQUE. NO HINGES. LID CATCHES IN GROOVE. WADSWORTH ATHENEUM.

86. PINE, BRACKETED, SHEATHED. 42 x 31 x 18. SCROLLED BOOTJACK END. 49 x 24 x 17. WADSWORTH ATHENEUM.

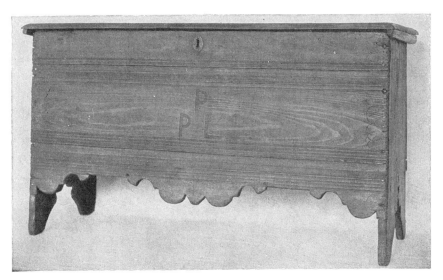

87. PINE, CARVED, INITIALED. SCROLLED BASE. 1700. FUESSENICH
COLLECTION.

The notches, or gouge carvings, on the chest below were a favorite simple motive found not only on a number of pine chests, but often on boxes.

The use of yellow pine, now vanished from our northern forests, and differing from southern pine, was common in oak chest lids and pine chests. The later material was soft white pine.

88. PINE, CARVED, INITIALED. SCROLLED BASE. 1700. MOLDED FRONT. H. H. ARMSTRONG.

89. Pine, Six-Board, Round Panel. 1710. 48½ x 23 x 17. Geo. Dudley Seymour.

90. Pine, on Shoes, Gouged Corner Carving. 1720. Geo. Dudley Seymour.

91. PINE, BALL FOOT, MINIATURE. 1700.
A. W. WELLINGTON, BOSTON.

92. PINE, MAPLE SUGAR CHEST.
WM. B. GOODWIN, HARTFORD.

93. PINE, LATTICE CARVED, SIX BOARD. 1700. FUESSENICH COLLECTION.

94. PINE, CARVED, STAMPED DECORATION. INITIALED H. T. 1673. 22½ x 48¼ x 18½. SIX STYLES OF STAMPS, UNPRECEDENTED NUMBER. FOUND IN WETHERSFIELD. WM. B. GOODWIN.

95. Tulip Wood, Blocked Panels, Six Board. 1700. Mary Miles Lewis Peck, Bristol, Connecticut. Another in Wadsworth Atheneum.

96. Pine, Nine Panel, Bracket Foot. 1720. E. C. Wheeler, Jr., Boston.

97. WALNUT, FIVE DRAWER. PENNSYLVANIA. INITIALED AND DATED.

98. CHERRY, MINIATURE, STAINED, STENCILED. 1820. FOUND IN CONNECTICUT.
$13\frac{3}{4}$ x 15 x $6\frac{1}{2}$. H. W. ERVING.

99. Three Short Drawers, Ogee Bracket Foot. Lid with Lip Mold. Penn-sylvania. Drawers Suggest Tables of Same Region. Howard Reifsnyder.

Drawers with lips came in about 1700. The later simpler New England pine chests did not have lipped drawers. A bracket foot as good as this is very rare on chests. The plain bracket seen below is usual. The finer specimens when not carved, in Pennsylvania, are in walnut. Three end to end drawers are rare.

The origin and date of a chest may be hinted at in the hinge. Decorative hinges are an indicative of the Delaware valley. Pin hinges mean New England. Plain strap hinges mean late New England.

100. Bracket Foot, Two End-to-End Lipped Drawers. Pennsylvania Style. 18th Century. Mrs. Francis P. Garvan.

101. TURNIP FOOT, PINE BOARD. 1690. THE FOOT IS WELL SHAPED. 35 x 39 x 17½.
WADSWORTH ATHENEUM.

102. LATE IMBRICATED FOUR ARCHITECTURAL PANELS. DATED 1776. A SURPRISING REVERSION
TO A TYPE MUCH OLDER. STANLEY A. SWEET.

103. MINIATURE, ROSE, THISTLE, FLEUR DE LIS, CROWN. 1700. BRILLIANT COLOR. 25¼ x 16 x 16¼.
DECORATION WAS HIDDEN BY LATE PAINT. H. W. ERVING.

104. PINE, TULIP PAINTED. BIRDS ON BOTTOM DRAWER.
1700. CHAUNCEY C. NASH.

105. Painted Two Drawer. 1700. Feet Lost. Well Executed. Large Tulip on Ends. 42 x 40 x 20. Formerly in Ives Collection.

106. Pine, Six Board. Slightly Carved. 1710. 32 x 15 x 12½. Wadsworth Atheneum.

107. Painted Tulip Wood. 1700. Frame Oak. Some Score Similar Found Near Guilford.
Ends Also Painted. State of Connecticut. Stone House, Guilford.

108. Pine, Miniature. 1700.   107A. Pine, Miniature, Ball Foot. 1710.

109. Pennsylvania, Tulip Wood, Painted. 1770–90. Heart Motive. $30\frac{1}{2}$ x 51 x 23.
Wm. B. Goodwin.

110. Pennsylvania, Tulip Wood. Late 18th Century. Tulip Decorations.
J. Stogdell Stokes.

111. TULIP AND UNICORN. PENNSYLVANIA. ALL THIS TYPE ARE DATED LATER THAN THEIR STYLE. PENNSYLVANIA MUSEUM.

These chests usually in tulip wood (vulgarly called poplar, west of the Hudson), and rarely in walnut, were popular among the Pennsylvanians of German descent. They are very often dated. The ruling colors are red, black, and brown with white ground, on panels. The body of chest is blue with red molds. The best show structural arches. Often the arches were merely indicated by paint. The designs varied according to the county of origin. The lid is generally decorated; also the ends. Rarely, in early chests, the drawers are flush; usually they overlap. They are short, in a single line. A plain bracket foot is the rule.

112. HEART AND TULIP. DATED 1788. PENNSYLVANIA. 27 X 49 X 23. MRS. FRANCIS P. GARVAN.

113. Square Panels, Decorated. Dated 1805. Brooks Reed.

An unusual chest for the name John Seltzer, the possible painter, scratched through the paint on the vase. Other instances are known. It is not yet determined whether the name represents the owner or the decorator. Of course, if it was a bride chest, the name must be that of the decorator. Found in Dauphin County.

114. Painted Panels, Central Panel Double Arched. 1796. Formerly Clarence W. Brazer's.

Esther S. Fraser has pointed out that this chest by Johann Rank, a pupil of Christian Seltzer, sometimes Selzer, shows good artistic sense. The man, however, was an innkeeper, and farmer, and did not develop new styles.

115. Unicorn Chest. 1797. From Lancaster County. Clarence W. Brazer.

The human figures on the drawer are an amusing variant. The multi-pointed stars over the unicorns are similar to those found on Pennsylvania barns. The unicorn is presumed to be an emblem of maidenly purity.

116. Architectural Arched Panels with Dentil Mold. 1792. Formerly C. M. Heffner's.

This chest is marked by the absence of the usual base mold, and the resting on shoes rather than feet. The base therefore is a mere projecting board. The character of the painting, however, is very much above the average. The carved dentil is also remarkable, perhaps unique, decoration on this class of chests.

117. Two Painted Panels, and Painting to Represent Pillars. 1721. Clarence W. Brazer.

The date on this chest is puzzling, as it is so much earlier than others. The drawer instruction, however, and the molding about it are a very early type. The pillars or banisters are not very successful, but in general the piece is fascinating, particularly the effective drawers and the ornamental human figures.

118. Two Square Panels, No Drawer. Pots with Tulips. 1784. Clarence W. Brazer.

119. Decorated, Ball Foot. 1690.
William B. Goodwin.

120. Angular Roof. 18th Century.
Brooks Reed.

A little white wood chest with pine top. 18 x 29 x 17. The base of the coloring is black. There is a central figure of cock pheasant in color.

This small chest might easily be called a box. The material is pine, and the odd shape may have been a convenience for a catchall. Or it may have been for a child.

CHEST CONSTRUCTION

The frame furniture is that which is formed with mortise and tenon. The joints are held together by white oak pins, driven with a draw bore. That is to say, the hole in the tenon is about one-sixteenth of an inch nearer the shoulder than in the mortise. The result is to draw the tenon and make a lasting tight joint. Pine chests are distinctly inferior, being merely nailed together. Stile legs were about 7½ inches long. If they have lost more than one inch of this length, the probability is that they have been cut off or decayed. The tills were ordinarily of oak, but later of pine. Slots were made to slide the bottom and sides into place. The tills are sometimes decorated and dated. Locks are very often missing. The ball foot is set on with a dowel, the hole being bored with a pod auger, leaving a rounded end, a test for age.

There is no significance in the common term dower chest unless the initials of a lady appear. More chests were acquired after marriage than before.

Practically all carving on American chests is flat, about one-eighth of an inch deep. It is, of course, a declension from the earlier carving in the round. A few examples, very early, have portions carved slightly round. The first chests had no drawer. Then came in succession one and two drawers, and in a few instances three. It was then obvious to the makers that a chest consisting altogether of drawers, without lifting lid, was more convenient. Thus the chests of drawers came in. Oak was the prevailing wood, in the early period. In Pennsylvania walnut occurs. The painted chests are tulip wood, with exceptions. Pine is the latest wood, used in board chests. Rare examples in various other woods are known.

121. Geometric and Conventionalized Foliage. 1670. Dwight Blaney.

122. Oak, Two Carved Panels. 1680. Initial W. Panels Asymmetrical. Geo. W. Seymour.

123. Oak, Banded Imbrications. 1670. 26 x 19½ x 18, without Overhang. Pine Lid and Base.
Wadsworth Atheneum.

124. OAK, HADLEY, PARTLY IN THE ROUND. 1680. WADSWORTH ATHENEUM.

The box is not as old as the initials might suggest. Two other full-depth Hadley boxes are known to the writer. Note top and bottom molds on ends. Pine lid and base, similar molds. Found in Lyme, New Hampshire, settled from Old Lyme, Connecticut.

The box bears the same name in England with the piece of luggage we call a trunk. This is interesting as indicating that these affairs were carried about by travelers of quality. We know that kings, and of course queens who had more gear, carried chests when they made progress, and as many of them, like Queen Bess, kept going, their property got honest marks of wear.

125. PINE, BALL FOOT. 1790. A DESK BOX. FORMERLY B. A. BEHREND'S.

126. PORTICOED OAK BOX. 1660. UNIQUE. H. H. ARMSTRONG.

127. PINE, STAMP CARVED. DATED 1683. $8\frac{3}{4}$ x $25\frac{1}{2}$ x $16\frac{1}{2}$. WM. B. GOODWIN.

128. OAK, ARCHES AND LUNETTES. 1670. 7 x 20 x 14. OAK TILL. WM. B. GOODWIN.

129. GEOMETRIC PANEL. 1680. MRS. FRANCIS P. GARVAN.

130. OAK, FOLIATED VERTICALLY. 1670. FUESSENICH COLLECTION.

131. OAK, FINE ROSETTES, ENDLESS BAND. 1680. FUESSENICH COLLECTION.

132. Oak, Horizontal Foliated Scrolls. 1680. B. A. Behrend.

133. Tulip Carved. 1680. 27 x 10 x 15. H. W. Erving.

134. Oak, Tulip Foliations. 1680. Geo. Dudley Seymour.

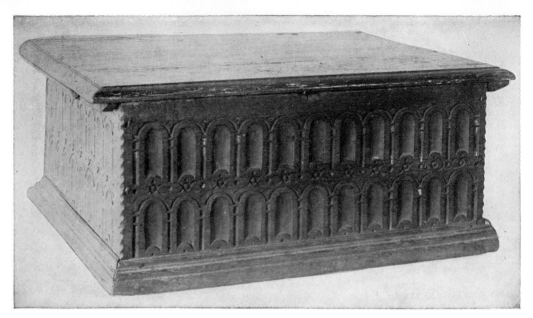

135. OAK, DOUBLED ROW OF ARCHES, CARRIED AROUND ENDS, AS IN ENGLAND. 1670. 23½ x 11¼ x 19. WADSWORTH ATHENEUM.

136. MINIATURE, WITH NORMAN SERRATIONS. 1700.
137. VERTICAL FOLIAGE, OAK. 1680. BOTH, HOLLIS FRENCH.

138. OAK, DAISIES, ROPE BANDED. 1680. 23 x 9½ x 16. WADSWORTH ATHENEUM.

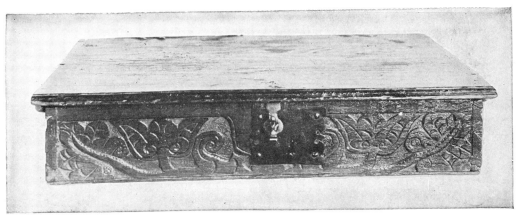

139. OAK, SHALLOW HADLEY. 1690. 25 x 5 x 14. MRS. J. INSLEY BLAIR.

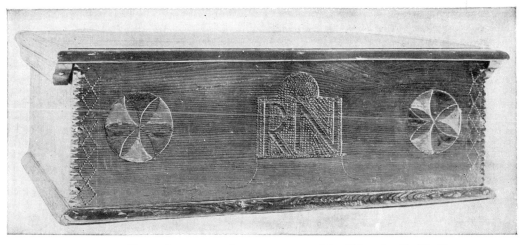

140. PINE, OAK ENDS, GEOMETRIC STARS, 1700, 23½ x 8½ x 18. H. W. ERVING.

141. PINE, STARS AND SERRATED LUNETTES. 1690. GEO. DUDLEY SEYMOUR.

142. WHITEWOOD, PINE AND MAPLE. FRIESIAN. ABOUT 1736. MADE BY DAVID FANNING, NORWICHTOWN. 20⅜ x 6⅜ x 10⅜. GEO. DUDLEY SEYMOUR.

143. PINE, CARVED. 1700. BOTTOM WHEEL CARVED BEFORE MOLD WAS ALLOWED FOR. GEO. DUDLEY SEYMOUR.

144. SMALL DESK. PANELED. 1690.
    J. STOGDELL STOKES.

145. BALL FOOT, DESK. 1690.
    MARY M. SAMPSON.

146. ROSES AND LUNETTES. 1680. RARE MOTIVE. FUESSENICH COLLECTION.

147. ALL PINE, LATTICE CARVED. 1710. 21 x 8⅞ x 11. WADSWORTH ATHENEUM.

148. Curly Maple Desk Box. 1710. 17½ x 13 x 10. Wadsworth Atheneum.

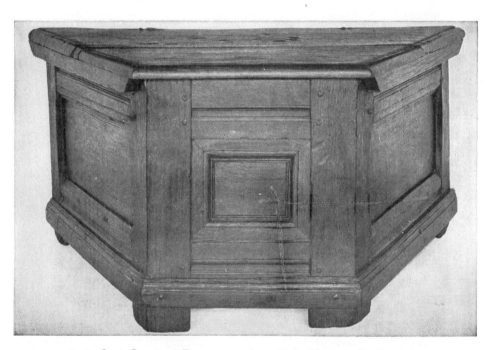

149. Oak, Splayed, Paneled. 1670. Mrs. Francis P. Garvan.

One other such box known. Repaired front of lid and one mold. As is, the box is 12½ inches high. Built like a chest. Molded within on the back. Channel molds in old red. Posts interesting because worked out within by rabbets to fit the angles. Portland.

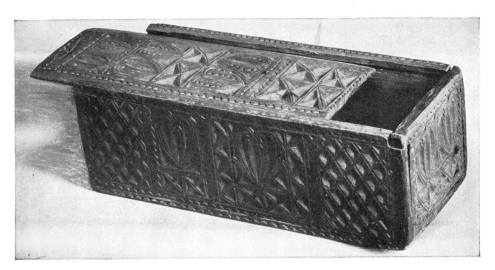

150. Friesian Box, Sliding Cover. 1700. H. V. Weil.

The term Friesian does not mean necessarily that a piece is carved in the Dutch province from which the name comes. These pieces are found from Maine to Pennsylvania, and it is known that some, and believed that all, are native, if long in this country. Similar carving is found on spoon racks and loom stools. Knickerbocker origin.

151. Framed Pine. 1710. Robt. P. Butler, Hartford.

Posts project through the base, and are turned in one piece. Lock early. Butterfly clasp, partly missing. 18½ x 13¼ x 12. Connecticut. Base mold unusual. In all respects a miniature chest.

The drop on the lock is same shape as certain applied spindles, of wood, on chests.

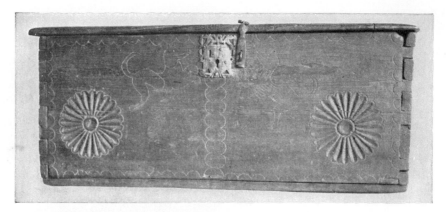

152. Daisy Carved, and Outlined with Animals. Wm. B. Goodwin.

A full-size chest, reduced by error. 18½ x 44½ x 17. The owner regards the date about 1600, since the lock and escutcheon are of fine Spanish design. The origin is the Southwest. Dovetailed corner instead of usual nails. Southern sugar pine.

153. Carved Pine. 1710. 9 x 26 x 17. Mark La Fontaine.

154. Crudely Carved, Birds and Rosette. 1710. Fuessenich Collection.

155. Oak, Lunette and Flute, 1670. 8½ x 27¼ x 14½. H. W. Erving.

156. Oak, Intersecting Lunettes. 1680. 11 x 27¾ x 17. Line of Imbrications, Serrations and Notches. H. W. Erving.

157. All Pine, Lunettes. 8½ x 24½ x 15¼. Late 17th Century.

158. Lunettes, Birds in Spandrels. 1780. Heavy Fluted Lunettes; Good Rosettes. H. W. Erving.

159. Oak, Small Panels and Drops. 1690. 10 x 28 x 17¾. The Peculiar Panels Are Known on Chests. Wadsworth Atheneum.

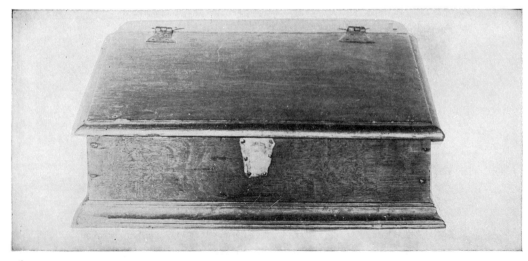

160. Oak Desk Box. 1690. 9¾ x 25 x 19. Fine Butterfly Hinges, Once Called Dovetail Hinges. Wadsworth Atheneum.

161. Oak, Pond Lily, Raised Carving, 1680. 9 x 25½ x 16¾. Rare. H. W. Erving.

162. Oak, Doubled Lunettes. Base Set in. 1660. 7¾ x 24¼ x 14⅝. Wadsworth Atheneum.

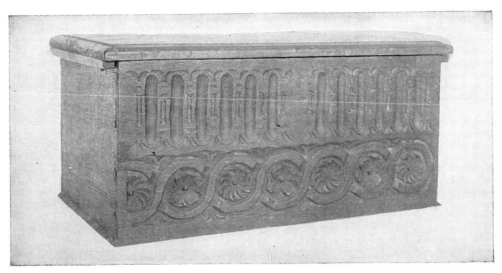

163. Oak, Flutes and Banded Rosettes. 1680. G. Winthrop Brown.

164. Painted Pine. 1710. Fine Painted Vine, not Restored. Molded Base. Geo. Dudley Seymour.

165. Scratch Carved. 1710. 5½ x 10½ x 7. Connecticut Historical Society.

166. Scratch Carved, Pine. Dated 1694. B. A. Behrend.

167. Friesian, Carved from One Piece. 1700. 1½ x 2½ x 4½. Geo. Dudley Seymour.

168. Wall Box. 18th Century. Flayderman & Kaufman.

169. Oak, Scratch Carved. Dated 1677. 9 x 22¼ x 17½. Wadsworth Atheneum.

170. WALNUT, PANELED, LEATHER INSET. 1700. 5⅜ x 9½ x 6¾. WADSWORTH ATHENEUM.

171. WALNUT, TURNED FEET. 1720. 14½ x 19½ x 11½. WADSWORTH ATHENEUM.

172. OAK, FOLIATED. 1670. RESTORED FEET. W. F. HUBBARD, HARTFORD.

173. OAK, CANDLE BOX. 1670–90. HINGE PINS FORMED ON LID. 8 x 16¼ x 7¼.
WM. B. GOODWIN.

174. VENEERED PORTABLE DESK. 19TH CENTURY. ANNA CURTIS, E. LYME.

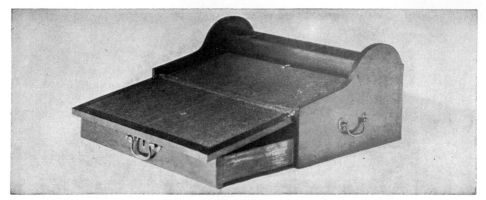

175. PORTABLE, MAHOGANY. 1816. TAMBOUR ROLL. HAS DATED PRESENTATION PLATE. 17¾ x 12. H. W. ERVING.

176. 177. JEWEL CASES. INLAID. 19TH CENTURY. FRANK A. ROBART.

THE NATURE OF THE BOX

A box is ordinarily a mere miniature chest. It has become a fashion to call all such Bible boxes. Boxes with tills and locks were certainly not for Bibles; neither were boxes with slant tops with pigeonholes. We must disabuse our minds of the notion that any container was necessarily made for a specific object. Boxes without locks or inside fittings were no doubt convenient for "The big ha' Bible." Nearly all boxes are nailed together, being the only form of ancient cabinet work so treated. Exceptions are noted of framed or dovetailed boxes. Usually the lid and base were pine, each projecting about seven-eighths of an inch. The earliest sides and ends were oak, then came pine, either carved or plain. The finer specimens are much sought after. One in the Lee Mansion, Marblehead, was probably brought over by the Pilgrims. American boxes only have been shown, as in the case of chests. Strictly, desk boxes belong with desks, but for convenience it has become a custom to place all boxes together.

178. A DAINTY DESK BOX. MIDDLE 18TH CENTURY. MRS. ALEXANDER ARMSTRONG.

A beautiful piece, of peculiar interest also owing to the fine contour of the lower and upper parts. While it is not properly blocked, it is shaped with grace in a series of curves.

Jewel cases in large numbers are found and are perhaps generally foreign. Their principal features are very elegant veneer and a central inlay of a shell or some other object of ornament, which does not come out well in pictures. Their outlines are plain, the ornament being exclusively in the surfaces. They formed an adornment for the parlor tables of the early 19th century, and have been retained up to the last generation. Portable desks in the same style existed in great numbers. In fact, one seldom saw any other desk in a dwelling in the Victorian era.

179. REMARKABLY CARVED, PINE. 1710. BROOKS REED.

180. A BLOCK FRONT. INK WELL. 1761. WM. B. GOODWIN.

This supreme article of its kind has the marks of a craftsman with a strong feeling for beauty. Every part is charming. The base mold is contoured as in the finest John Goddard style, and it is a Rhode Island piece, probably by that master. On the bottom is a brass plate, contemporaneous, "Presented 1761." The elegant brasses seem European, and possibly are. Brasses were often, if not generally, imported. It looks like a jewel case, or tea caddy. Mahogany. 7¼ x 10¾ x 8¼.

180A. A TEA CADDY. MIDDLE 18TH CENTURY. BOMBÉ BASE. VERY ELEGANT CADDIES WERE IN USE AND WERE KEPT IN THE PARLOR. SAMUEL WINECK.

181-2-3. Jewel Cases. Shell or Vase Inlay, 19th Century. Sam Wineck.

184-5-6. Jewel Cases or Caddies, Early 19th Century. Mrs. Francis P. Garvan.

187. A Pipe Box. 18th Century.
Colonial Dames, Wethersfield.

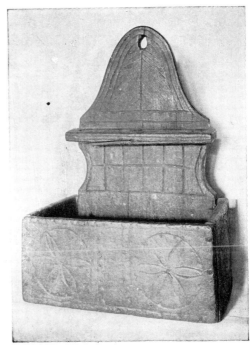

188. A Carved Spoon Rack. 18th Century.
Wheels Suggest the Friesian.
Wadsworth Atheneum.

189–192. PIPE BOXES, WALL BOX, SAND GLASS, AND CHURCH-WARDEN PIPES. ARTHUR WELLINGTON.

The pipe box originated from the need of protecting the long, slender-stemmed clay pipes. A drawer for tobacco is at the bottom. The length of pipe cooled the smoke. The little carved, and often initialed and dated, wall boxes, were before the day of matches. The sand glass, in various sizes was a necessity. It seldom ran an hour.

The sand glass in early patterns was made in two parts, connected by ceiling wax. The collector should note this. Common late glasses in one piece are of no account. The earliest types, somewhat crude, are quite valuable.

The pipe box was sometimes in curly maple. Instances of double partitions are found.

193, 194. WALL BOXES WITH DRAWERS. THEY WERE CONVENIENT FOR CANDLES OF TWO KINDS OR FOR SPILLS (PAPER CANDLE LIGHTERS).

195–197. A Scalloped Edge, a Carved Top, and a Two-Drawer Pipe Box. 18th Century.
Wadsworth Atheneum.

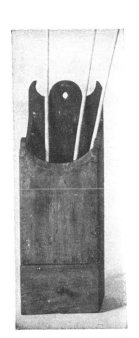
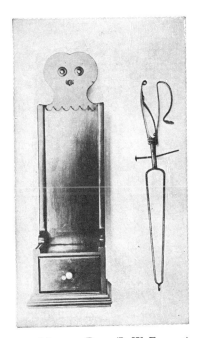

198–201. A Fish-Tail (Metropolitan Museum), an Ordinary, and Molded-Base (L. W. Erving)
Box. Pipe Tongs. 18th Century.

202-3. Knife Boxes. Late 18th Century. H. W. Erving.

American, from Alexandria, Va. Solid mahogany, top and front veneered in crotch grain. Front trimmed with sumach wood. 16¾ inches high. They are not so good, being solid mahogany, as all veneered would have been.

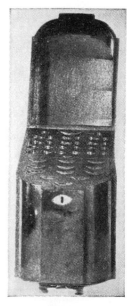

204-206. Knife Boxes, Open. Inlaid Shell on Inside of Top.

207. ARCH AND STAR, URN TURNED. 1670. OAK AND PINE. FINEST KNOWN SPECIMEN. UNRESTORED. TURNINGS RESEMBLE A COURT CUPBOARD. BALL-TURNED DOUBLE-BRACED STRETCHERS IMPORTANT. 35½ x 26½ x 17¾. MAINE. MRS. J. INSLEY BLAIR.

208. Carved and Spindled, Oak. 1670. Was B. A. Behrend's.

These little chests-on-frames are almost the counterpart of the boxes just set forth, except that these always have a drawer, and are set on a frame, made as a unit with the box, with rare exceptions. They are identical in constructive features with large chests. The square stretchers are sharp edged, indicating that they had a shelf, now sometimes lost. The drawers in the older styles have grooved side runs, like chests.

209. Oak, Two Part. 1680. Shelf Probably Replaces a Thinner One. Wadsworth Atheneum.

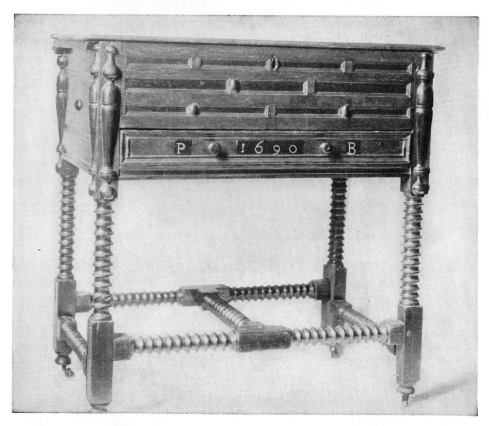

210. Oak, Small Panel. The Initials Are Said to Stand for Polly Bartlett.

She was married about that time. Larger than usual, and the only one known with practically all applied ornaments in place, and these extending around the ends. The date and initials are in a crude inlay. Important. Now at Everett, Massachusetts. Henry R. Davis.

The use of chests-on-frames, often called pilgrim chests, did not differ from that of any small chest. They are always flat-topped. One was called a tabernacle table, perhaps from its holding a Bible. The same name is known as applied to miniature cabinets. Perhaps thirty or forty of these interesting pieces are known. There have been attempts that prove these pieces everything from pulpits to washstands. It is useless to make mystery where none existed. That so few are found, and all rather decorative, suggests that they were made in a limited district, probably the North Shore of Massachusetts, and were used by a few families of taste.

The chests-on-frames must be carefully distinguished from all other classes of furniture. They are always small. They always have one drawer, and a lifting lid. They are in no respect miniature highboys. They are never in mahogany or walnut. In the rare instances when one of them is made in two parts, the top lifting off, one is tempted to say the piece is merely a box on a frame. But the box had no drawer, in the conventional form. Whether these pieces had any considerable vogue abroad, we doubt. The attachment of the hinge is ordinarily by wooden pin through an enlarged end of the cleat under the drawer. Thus the cleat served a double purpose. The prices on furniture change so rapidly that we should make a grave error in naming the worth of anything. We can only say that a good chest-on-frame is not known to be in the market, and that several thousand dollars has more than once been exchanged for a good example, and that the rarity of the article almost insures a still further advance.

211. SMALL PANEL, SPOOL-TURNED BASE. 1690. HERMAN F. CLARKE.

This style of paneling appears in this volume on a chest, a box, and a court cupboard. Channel molds were fitted with applied cross sections forming miniature panels. On the small cross pieces bosses or initials appeared. This sort of slender drop accompanies the style. The brackets and central drop on the frame add grace. New England origin.

This paneling was evidently a specialty with a single cabinetmaker. In all about a dozen pieces have been tallied with this peculiarity. As one is the piece above, which is certainly Massachusetts, and as others have been found from Salem to Concord, New Hampshire, the conviction is forced on one that somewhere from Salem to Newburyport lived the maker of three court cupboards; three, probably four or five, chests; one box; two chests on frame; one court cupboard table, and probably other pieces. A little research, taking the Polly Bartlett piece as a point of departure, should locate the town and perhaps the workman.

212. Oak, Spool-Turned, Applied Spindles. 1690. Back Legs Are Stiles. $37\frac{3}{4}$ x $25\frac{1}{2}$ x 16. Found in Boston. Restorations. Questionable Origin. Wadsworth Atheneum.

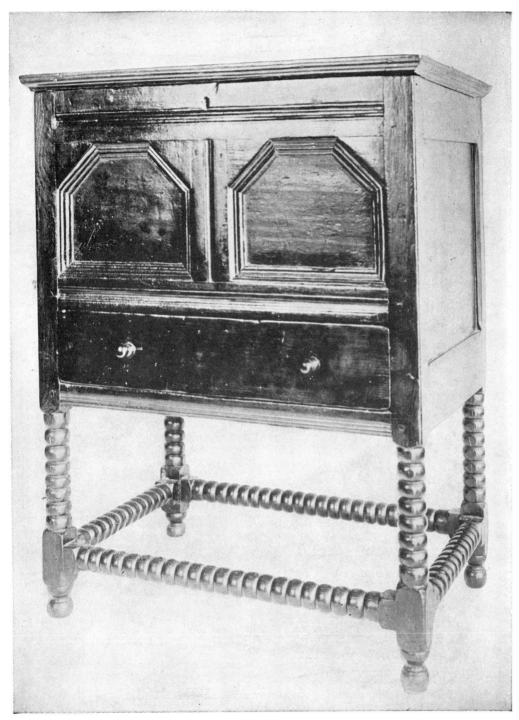

213. Oak, Ball Turned. 1690. Mold on Drawer Since Restored. End Panel Molded
as on Chest. Maple, Turned Stretchers, Deep Drawer. Mrs. F. G. Patterson, Boston.

The maple examples, like this, carried the spray decoration, usually much dimmed. The oak
stiles are earlier. The end cleat, wooden-pin hinge is the more common. Engaged staple hinges,
like those of chests, are next in frequency.

214. MAPLE, SPRAY DECORATION. 1690. SPRAY IN BLACK ON RED GROUND. NEW ENGLAND.
RHODE ISLAND SCHOOL OF DESIGN.

215. Spray Decoration, Turned Stretchers. 1690. Arthur W. Wellington.

216. DEEP DRAWER, TURNED STRETCHERS. 1690. MRS. F. G. PATTERSON.

Here end the small chests-on-frames, according to the usual nomenclature, though we follow with one remarkable sport. After this period the highboy, which occupied little more room, but afforded more storage, came into fashion.

217. DECORATED, EARLY DUTCH. 1700. UNIQUE. METROPOLITAN MUSEUM.

218. A CURIOUS LITTLE BOX, PROBABLY FOREIGN, WITH A TRICK LOCK.
J. STOGDELL STOKES.

219. THREE DRAWER, OAK, BALL FOOT. 1690. MRS. FRANCIS P. GARVAN.

The chest of drawers in oak was of short duration as to style. Between the going out of the chest and the coming in of the highboy there were only about ten years. Hence we do not find so great variety in the oak chest of drawers as in the walnut and mahogany which followed.

There were, however, a number of curious variants which, from the standpoint of the collector, are of the highest interest, always.

The sensible thing would, of course, have been to retain the ordinary four-drawer chest of drawers, because it was convenient for height. But in furniture, as in everything else, the still small voice of sense is the last thing to be heeded. Hence, people forsook for many years the ordinary chest of drawers, and there came in a highboy which required a step ladder. The Philadelphia type had the ceiling as the limit!

220. Oak, Two Part, Ball Foot. 1690. Geo. Dudley Seymour, New Haven.

Said to have been found at Dedham. Restored by Patrick Stevens, the most famous of restorers, who worked in Hartford a generation since, and more, when interest in antiques first revived.

The development from a chest is here evident. The division of the parts should be covered by a mold. Small dowels between the sections engage to keep the parts in place. This example is one of the earliest with teardrop handles.

There was no advance made by 18th-century cabinetmakers, when they abandoned the scheme of frame and panel universal in the 17th century. Particularly in the great highboys and secretaries the wide ends split. How could it have been thought possible, in a glued-up surface twenty-seven inches wide, that anything else would happen? The scheme of dovetailing everything was good, but the abandoning of panels was very unfortunate. The scheme was really the adoption of the board construction scorned in the 17th century. The consequence is today that large mahogany surfaces go to pieces, whereas the old oak goes on forever.

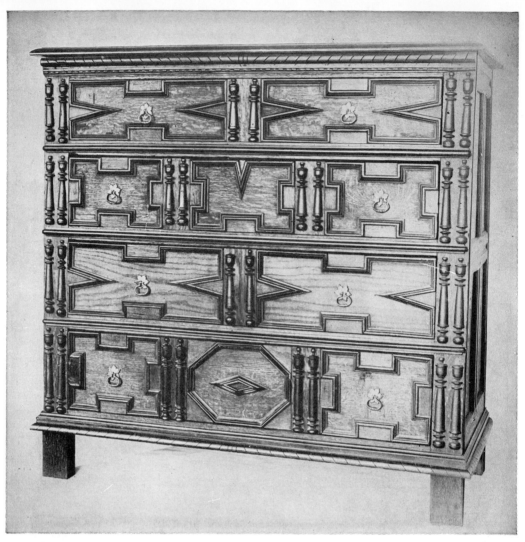

221. Oak, Geometric Panel. 1680. Handles Wrong. Now Changed. Wadsworth Atheneum.

222. Oak, Small, Three Drawer. 1680.
Wadsworth Atheneum.

223. Pine, Three Lip Drawers. 1720.
Wadsworth Atheneum.

224. Oak, Completely Paneled. 1690. From Brooks Reed.

The paneling of the leg stiles is also found on some walnut chests of drawers. These early examples all have grooved drawer ends, which engage with oak strips attached to the end of frame, by rabbet, or nail, or both. The paneling on the ends seems to bear no relation to the style of the front.

225. Two Part, Oak, Mold over Division. 1680. J. Milton Coburn Estate.

The ball mold is an odd feature. It will be noted that the two parts absolutely duplicate one another, and that the two base molds follow around the ends, whereas, as usual, the between-drawer molds stop on the front.

The reader's attention is called to a curious optical delusion. The big ball foot on the 17th century pieces always looks tipped inward. The effect is perhaps caused by the way the light strikes the feet. Perfect specimens, even when photographed, show this apparent defect. The author has repeatedly lined up feet to detect a boring at a wrong angle, but always he has found the error was in the eye. We know that the Greeks noting that a straight roof line looks hollow, crested their ridges. It would really be well to toe out the feet slightly, when they are heavy.

226. OAK, TWO PART, BALL FOOT, PANELED STILES. 1790. MORRIS SCHWARTZ.

227. DECORATED OAK. 1700. 46 X 44 X 20. NEW ENGLAND. MARK LA FONTAINE.

228. Oak, Onion Feet. 1690. 40 x 38 x 20. Bolection Mold on End. Square Section Stile. Henry Stearns.

229. Geometric Panel, Ball Foot. 1680. A Full Size. H. V. Weil, New York.

230. OAK AND WALNUT. 1690. TOP, HALF-INCH WALNUT. ENDS, PINE. GROOVED RUNS.
WADSWORTH ATHENEUM.

231. OAK AND PINE, BALL FOOT. 1690. FINE HANDLES.
NO EVIDENCE OF APPLIED DROPS.

232. ALL WALNUT, PANELED STILES. 1690. 38¼ x 33½ x 21. WADSWORTH ATHENEUM.

233. MINIATURE, BALL FOOT. 1700. SINGLE-ARCH MOLD.
H. V. WEIL.

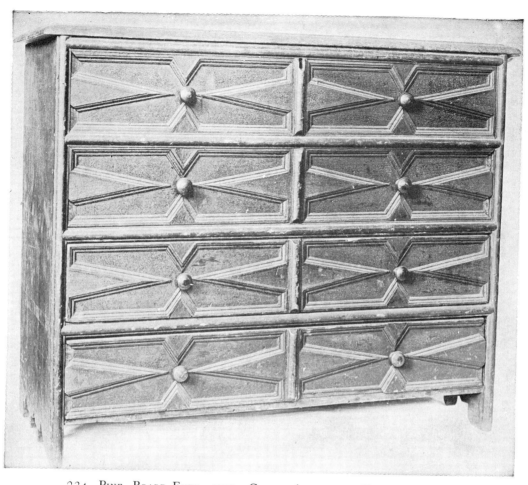

234. Pine, Board Ends. 1700. Gothic Arches for Feet. Koopman.

235. Oak. Initials R. B. and A. P. 1690. Triglyphs Appear to Require Others. Geo. Dudley Seymour.

236. Oak and Tulip-Wood, Decorated. 1690. Described under End View.

237. Small, Pine. 1710. Harry Long, Boston.

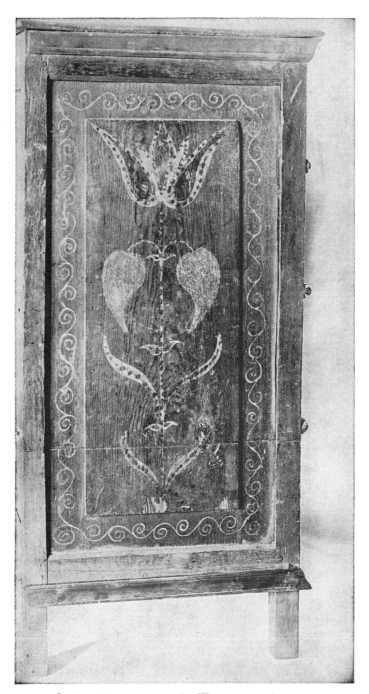

238. END SECTION OF 236. WADSWORTH ATHENEUM.

The decoration reaches its apex in this sort. On the end is an excellent large tulip, with blossom, bud and leaves. The front leaves little to be desired except that the human faces are an unfortunate addition. About a score of these pieces have been found, either as chests or chests of drawers, in the vicinity of Madison, Connecticut. They are distinct in their construction from the Pennsylvania type. The end here shown is pine. It appears that whitewood (tulip), owing to its smooth surface, was found a good material, superior to oak or pine, for decoration. The fashion, however, was ephemeral.

239. Six Drawers, Bandy-Leg Frame. 1730.
N. Cushing, Providence.

240. Walnut, Nine Drawers, Bracket Foot. 1740.
H. C. Valentine & Co., Richmond.

241. Basswood, Turned Foot. 1700.
G. B. Dyer, Greenfield.

242. INLAID, SCROLLED BASE, INITIALED.
HOWARD REIFSNYDER.

243. WALNUT, SCROLLED BRACKET FOOT.
HOWARD REIFSNYDER.

244. MINIATURE, UNUSUAL BRACKET FOOT.
MRS. FRANCIS P. GARVAN.

245. MINIATURE HIGHBOY. 1770.
MRS. FRANCIS P. GARVAN.

246. BALL FOOT, SINGLE-ARCH MOLD. 1690. MRS. FRANCIS P. GARVAN.

247. SERPENTINE, HEAVY CHAMFERED FOOT. CARVED CHAMFER. 1770. 39 x 41 x 22. HANDLES ENGLISH TYPE. EDWARD BRINGHURST, WILMINGTON, DELAWARE.

CONSTRUCTION OF CHESTS OF DRAWERS

The feet of the walnut and early mahogany periods were either the bracket form or the ball and claw. There is very little difference in date, but the bracket foot is in as good style as the ball and claw and is found on the greater part of the more important pieces. In its finer form it is shaped in a double cyma curve, hereafter called ogee. The straight or plain bracket foot is found on the somewhat simpler pieces, including plain block fronts. There is always a pronounced projecting base mold. The usual number of drawers is four. Rarely we find three and not so rarely five. The shapes include serpentine, or its reverse, which is called the oxbow. With the former the finer pieces are swept out to the corner on the ends as well as the front. There is also found the straight front in a greater number of instances. The corners on the oxbow and on the serpentine are sometimes chamfered, and the chamfer is usually fluted or carved.

248. Oak, Ball Feet. 1680. Chas. P. Cooley, Hartford, Conn.

The drawers of mahogany and later periods are invariably done with small dovetails, and ordinarily the backs of the drawers are also finished with the dovetail. The drawers in the serpentine and oxbow are shaped within as well as without. The backs are usually set in by a rabbet. In early examples the drawers are made with a lip. Later they are flush with a very fine half-round molding attached to the frame or the drawer.

This mold varies from three thirty-seconds to an eighth of an inch with a protection of the same dimensions. While it may be better to find this molding on the frame, it occurs in a number of fine pieces on the drawer.

249. SERPENTINE, CARVED CHAMFER, STRAIGHT BRACKET FOOT. 1780. FEET ALWAYS VERY LARGE. MAHOGANY. GEORGIA. VENEERED ON OAK. ROBERT T. SMITH, HARTFORD.

250. SERPENTINE, CHAMFERED CORNER, SCROLLED BRACKET FOOT. 1780. CHAMFER FLUTED. BAILS CHARACTERISTIC. DR. AND MRS. JOHN M. BIRNIE, SPRINGFIELD.

251. Serpentine, Ogee Bracket Foot. 1780. The Top Is Shaped to Follow the Front and the Corners, as Usual. Katrina Kipper, Accord, Mass.

252. Small Oxbow, Ogee Bracket Foot. 1790.
E. B. Leete Co., Guilford.

253. Oxbow, Quarter-Column Corner, Ball-and-Claw Foot. 1760. Cherry. Has Four Claw Feet and Five Drawers. H. W. Erving.

254. Curly, Knee Hole. 1770. Four Instead of Six Feet and a Drawer beyond the Knee Hole Instead of a Door. Simple Plain Bracket. Mrs. Francis P. Garvan.

255. Serpentine, Chamfered Corner, Bracket Foot. 1790. Mahogany Veneer. 37 X 45 X 24. The Urn Handles Are Fine. C. Sanford Bull, Waterbury.

256. Swell Front, Mahogany Veneer, French Foot. 1800. Made in Very Great Numbers with Slight Variations.

257. Mahogany Veneer, Swell Front, French Foot, Ogee Scrolled Skirt. Knob Handles. 1800. Both, the Author's.

258. Very Large, Shaped Front, Ogee Bracket Feet. 1790. 45 x 72 x 21. Fifteen Drawers. A Rare Form. Mahogany. Edward Bringhurst.

259. Straight Front, Ogee Bracket Feet, Quarter-Column Corner. 1780. Molded under the Top. Mrs. Francis P. Garvan.

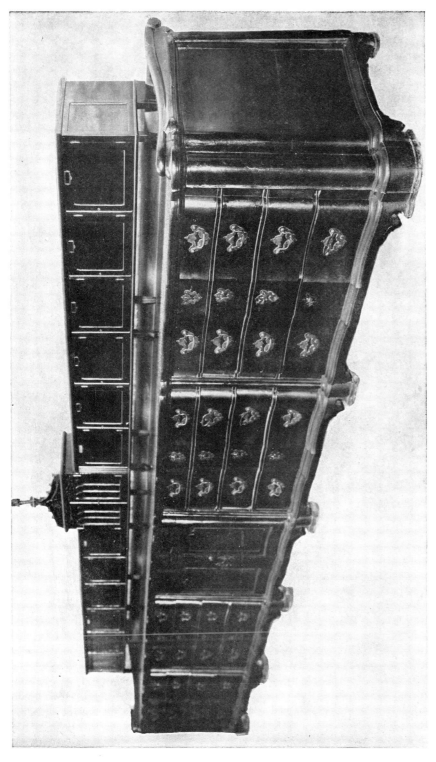

260. SHAPED FRONT, BRACKET FOOT, MAHOGANY, RANGE OF DRAWERS. 18TH CENTURY. PICTURE AND DATA FROM WILLIAM B. GOODWIN.

The statement has been made that this great piece, which is in the cathedral at Havana, may possibly have suggested a block front as made in Newport. The block front is not found in England, but some have thought its inspiration was Dutch. The blocking here is definite at each end of the drawer, but there is an added curve each side of a central flat section. Townsend was doing cabinet making in 1725. John Goddard, the great father of the block front, was his son-in-law, and apprentice. Townsend may have visited the West Indies, for mahogany.

261. Oxbow, Featured Mahogany, Heavy Ball-and-Claw Feet. 1770–80.
Tendency to Depend upon Richer Surfaces as Carving Goes Out.
I. Sack, Boston.

262. Mahogany, Round Block, Plain Bracket, Knee Hole with Door. 1780. Inlaid. This
Variant from the Usual Block Is Occasionally Found. Very High Feet, I. Sack.

263. Scroll Foot, Rare Shaped Front. 1770–80. Possibly Unique. Variant of Block Front. Whole Front May Be Counted as Block. Misses A. and E. P. Foster.

264. Round Block, Knee Hole, Plain Bracket. 1770–80. These Styles Often Called Dressing Tables, or Bureaus. Mrs. Francis P. Garvan.

265. Plain Block, Mahogany. 1770–80. Deep Sweep of Bracket. Scroll on End Differs from Front. These Pieces Are Usually Small. C. S. Bull.

266. Goddard Scroll Foot, Plain Block. 1770–80. Slide under Lid. The Back in a Single Chestnut Board. Unusually Beautiful Handles. I. Sack.

267. Oxbow Front, Spiraled Quarter Column.
Spiraled Engrailing, Ball and Claw Foot. 1770–80.
Mrs. Francis P. Garvan.

268. Goddard Scroll Foot, Conventional Block Front. 1770–80.
Katrina Kipper.

The style is believed to have originated, or at least to have reached its full form, in America, and is undoubtedly the most distinctive and characteristic contribution of America to furniture forms in mahogany. In the plain block there was of necessity a similar contour to the board forming the top of the piece. Where the shell appears the top is straight but is marked by a heavy mold to reënforce it and to give it dignity. The middle shell is concave, and the side shells are convex. The base mold is shaped to agree perfectly with the drawer shape above it. The pieces occur in low and high and double chests of drawers and in knee-hole dressing tables and secretaries. The shell is, in good examples, of one piece with the drawer front, requiring a mahogany plank nearly three inches thick.

269. SHELL BLOCK, GODDARD FOOT, THREE DRAWER. 1770–80. BELONGS IN THE RICH CLASS OF MAHOGANY TRACED TO THE GODDARDS OF RHODE ISLAND. PALMER COLLECTION METROPOLITAN MUSEUM.

The position of the escutcheons on the top drawer is characteristic of the shell type. There was a lock behind one escutcheon only. The attachment of the bail was difficult without marring the beauty of the carving. Sometimes there was a finger hole under the middle block, which dispensed with the brass.

270. A Block Front with Unusually High Ball-and-Claw Feet and Bracket Feet Behind. Unusual Scroll Supporting the Foot. 1770–80. Malcolm A. Norton.

271. Rounded, Plain Block Front, Ball-and-Claw Foot. 1770–80. Courtesy of Pennsylvania Museum of Fine Arts, Philadelphia.

272. Knee Hole, Mahogany, Dressing or Writing Table with Fourth Shell on Knee-Hole
Door. 1770–80. Mrs. Francis P. Garvan.

This piece is marked by the full elaboration of the block-front idea. The entire door in knee hole is
concave. The lining mold is on the frame in what we believe the better manner. It is unusual, however, for the dovetail of the drawer blades, that is, the pieces between the drawers to show. It is usually
made blind. The shell is elaborate, done with a subordinate shell center, scroll, and cross hatching.
An intaglio half-round terminates the edge of the central shell and ends in a small scroll. There is a
slight projection of the bracket foot in the rear, an unusual elaboration. A dovetailed batten is found
with blind ends running across the top on the under side, some inches in from the ends of the top, and
was designed to prevent warping. At the same time the top could come and go. This scheme is also
common on the Pennsylvania library tables, except that they show the end of the dovetail, which always
protrudes or falls short. It will be noted that the piece is small, and they are so found, as a rule. No
accurate estimate can perhaps be made of the number of shell-block examples, but there may be three
score more or less. They are, of course, the supreme pieces of American cabinet work unless, for
courtesy's sake, we except the Philadelphia highboy and lowboy.

273. Block Front, Block Returning on Top Drawer. Modified Goddard Foot. 1770–80. Robert T. Butler, Hartford, Conn.

274. Block Front, Rounded or Segmental Blocking. Date on Back of Bottom Drawer. 1765. Walnut. Massachusetts. H. W. Erving.

275. Mahogany, Block Front, Knee Hole. 1770–80. New England. I. Sack.

276. A Block and Shell, with Three Drawers. Remarkably Quaint. 1760. Wm. B. Goodwin.
Cherry. 36 x 40 x 20. Two Bands of Fretwork Above and Below, on Frame. An Outstanding Connecticut Piece, Inference Favoring New London.

277. Richly Inlaid and Veneered Swell Front, Shaped French Foot. 1800. I. Sack.

278. Small Three Drawer, Quarter Column,
Ogee Bracket Foot. 1770. S. P. Fay.

279. Inlaid and Matched Veneer, French Foot. 1800. Swell Front.
Miss Helen T. Cooke.

280. Late Empire, Carved, Spiraled. 1830.
S. Wolf, New Haven.

281. Sheraton, Corners Shaped over Posts, Maple and Satinwood. 1800–10.
I. Sack.

282. Cupboard, Chest of Drawers, Veneered. 1810. Wadsworth Atheneum.

283. Swell Front, Low French Foot, Two Drawers at Top. 1810. Mrs. Francis P. Garvan.

THE SCHOOL OF SHERATON

The great English cabinetmakers acquired their vogue not so much through their work as through their publications. The genius of Thomas Sheraton is more and more recognized as not inferior to that of any other cabinetmaker in any country whatever. We may challenge his designs as sometimes too delicate. But in the matter of taste the excellence of his line is of the highest order. If we seek for some name subsequent to him, we shall find how far short every one falls from his standard. As distinguished from Chippendale, Sheraton decorated his pieces in every part, leaving few plain surfaces. Chippendale was content with form; Sheraton is notable for both form and color. The world was ransacked for woods of beautiful grain. And even so the makers of this time were not content until they had stained some of their inlays or veneers in colors even richer than nature's. It is true that he held mostly to straight lines, which Chippendale also affected in his frames during the later part of his career. He depended in the legs of his pieces on turnings almost exclusively, whereas Hepplewhite ordinarily used square taper forms, and Chippendale followed curved lines or fluted square posts which did not taper. Sheraton did not work many years in construction, but was always busy as a draftsman and writer. He was a person of good education. His mind loved intricate detail. The work tables, with their numberless contrivances, which he designed, as well as his myriad schemes of ornament, indicate the true artist.

284. Sheraton, Reeded, Carved, Satinwood Veneer. 1810.
Wallace Nutting.

285. SERPENTINE, SHERATON, REEDED, VENEERED. 1810. GEORGE S. PALMER.

286. INLAID AND VENEERED SWELL FRONT. 1800. FRANK H. ROBART.

Sheraton is a term which in America merely indicates a school. The piece below, for instance, immediately suggests his name, though of course he never saw it. The novice should remember this distinction which holds good for all other furniture names, including Phyfe. Anyone who claims that any piece of furniture made in America was by the head of the school, has the burden of proof laid upon him. Pieces by these great makers are simply not for sale once in a blue moon, and then the sale is at Christie's, not in America. In fact, Sheraton's main source of income was, or intended to be, his books of designs. He is a public benefactor, since many cabinetmakers have copied his lines; and if they had only copied them more perfectly, we should have far more beautiful furniture.

287. SHERATON, SWELL FRONT, RICHLY CARVED POSTS. 1810. SOCIETY OF COLONIAL DAMES, WETHERSFIELD.

Born in 1751, Sheraton as a boy began his studies when Chippendale was in his heyday. It was a period of eager creation and deft adaptation. There seems to have been little acknowledgment on the part of anyone of indebtedness to other designers. Thus we shall find in the Sheraton book pieces practically identical in some instances with those of Hepplewhite, who also borrowed — we use a kind word — right and left. There were no copyrights, and art is universal. No moral obliquity attaches to the borrowing, but only to the failure of recognizing the source of inspiration. No designer can be at his best always, but it would appear that Chippendale made more mistakes than Sheraton. If these old makers had devoted all their time to their own proper business and less to lambasting one another, their memory would have been sweeter, especially as every man is in debt to his neighbor.

These pieces are good examples of the last period in tasteful furniture. They belong to a generation sufficiently late, so that they have never really gone out of style. We do not until the 19th century find glasses attached to chests of drawers. By comparison with certain detached shaving glasses in this work, it will appear that the thought now first occurred to furniture makers of attaching the shaving glasses directly to the chest of drawers. The delicacy of these scrolls, finished, as they often were, with little buttons of ivory, is very attractive.

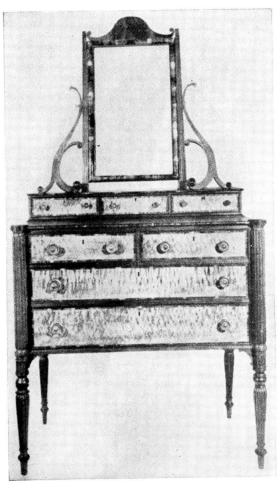 

288 AND 289. A STRAIGHT AND A SWELL FRONT. SHERATON SCHOOL. 1820–30. GLASSES SUPPORTED BY GRACEFUL BRACKETS. I. SACKS.

We repeat that fine dovetailing continued through this and even the following period of rapid declension. That is, the declension was not in the workmanship, but in the style.

The shaped rounded corner over the posts of this period is sometimes varied by allowing the post itself to run up slightly above the surface and to turn it with concentric rings.

At the beginning of this period casters came in. A brass foot was cast to receive the posts in its socket and the caster on the other end. It is, of course, more frequent on tables and chairs than on chests of drawers. A slightly earlier style omitted the caster; the leg finished in a brass ball.

Happily for the collector, a great many pieces of this type, though simpler, yet exist. It will be seen that it is often impossible to distinguish between the Empire and the Sheraton. There was free borrowing of ideas. It is now the fashion to use the term Directoire of what used to be denominated early Empire, and the term is historically correct. Yet there is no suggestion of Empire, in the French sense, here. With this furniture go the round brass knobs, the earlier patterns of which were often dainty.

290. HALF COLUMN CORNERS, SERPENTINE. 1780. CHAS. P. COOLEY, HARTFORD.

291. VERY RARE, COMBINATION DRAWERS AND
WRITING TABLE. THE TOP FALLS OVER ON SLIDES.
1780. FRANCIS D. BRINTON.

292. MINIATURE CABINET, ARCHED DOORS.
18TH CENTURY. FRANCIS D. BRINTON.

293. Painted with Bird Motives. 1830. A. H. Rice, Bethlehem.

The pieces shown on this and the following page were found in a secluded valley in Pennsylvania by that indefatigable searcher, Mr. Rice, who has acquired deserved fame, not only for these curious finds, but for his very extensive discoveries of stove plates and Strasburg pottery.

We do not enter in this work into the exploitation of cast iron. That extensive field has been exhaustively treated by Dr. Mercer, of Doylestown, Pennsylvania, whose museum there to illustrate educative influence of implements is very extensive and unique.

The piece above, with the others following it, retains many features of early construction, as was the habit in Pennsylvania where no good was seen in forsaking a good thing. Thus we have here framed and paneled furniture with turned feet, made well after the 19th century had opened. In fact, the structural features differ little from the manner of more than a hundred years before. The pieces are shown as interesting in themselves and as a curious mark of persistence in their type. They differ from and yet are connected with the painted Pennsylvania chests. They are a specialized development in one neighborhood.

294. Painted and Paneled, Angels and Birds. An Interesting Combination. 1830. A. H. Rice.

295. Painted with Birds and Stars and Fans. 1830. A. H. Rice, Bethlehem.

POVERTY OF INVENTION IN DESIGN

Probably the most characteristic feature of the 19th century was the trend of man's mind away from art to industry. After Phyfe no mind of the first order seems to have considered it worth while to devote himself to interior decoration. A multitude of designs sprang up, but they all hinged entirely on their adaptability to machine production. Even so something passable might have been attained had good men given thought to the matter. Nearly all these productions can be thought of as nothing less than monstrous. Curiously enough the workmanship continued good for three-quarters of the century at least. The old traditions died hard. We refer to such work as was done by hand. The fever to master the physical world took possession of men, and master minds engaged in the vast and unprecedented chemical age which has transformed everything. They were perhaps doing a greater thing, if that is possible, than translating the universe into terms of beauty. We needed the foundation, which these masters have laid for us. It is a fond and perhaps not vain hope to indulge that mentality of the first order may now be devoted to beautifying the modern world.

The only good of collecting and of setting forth fine early forms is the stimulation of a proper taste. Only a very limited number of our citizens can decorate their homes with early pieces. If the fad for collecting continues, the only material to satisfy it will be that left us by the artistically worthless 19th century after 1825. Throughout the west a very large number of pieces even later than degraded Empire are being bought with great avidity. With only a little more knowledge all those purchases will be cast out as junk. Sanity is bound to return sometime. Just now Lincoln's phrase must be modified to run, "You can fool almost all the people all the time."

It has been a favorite thesis that the lack of taste in designs for a hundred years was confined to America. This lack has been equally marked in Europe. Italy, the mother of design, has kept to reproduction very largely. The very gullibility of the English and American buyers has fostered the imitation and attempts to deceive with alleged antiques. A long contemplation of this subject leads to the deliberate judgment that the import of really old pieces from Italy is negligible, that it is almost negligible from France, and that much of the English work, like that of the other origins mentioned, is a clever manufacture from old wood. Of course, dear reader, there is no reference here to your possessions. The fatuous certainty with which the multitude proceed to load themselves up with things which even if original are out of place in America, is only another instance of wealth and fashion advancing more rapidly than knowledge.

The superiority in design of foreign furniture is unquestioned. All the good styles we have here, except the block front and the Windsor chair, are thoroughly English. They are no better in construction than our own work. But the old centers of art and taste were still the source of inspiration throughout all good periods of American furniture. After those good periods had passed it was useless to go abroad for inspiration, for Europe was marked by the same poverty of design as America.

296. Painted, Vines and Birds. 1830. A. H. Rice, Bethlehem.

297. Oxbow Front in Lower Section, Fine Bonnet Top
in Upper Section. 1770–80. I. Sack.

A stately series of pieces called chests-on-chests appeared first in the late Queen Anne time and continued through the Chippendale period, running through all the variations characteristic of the low chests of drawers. The piece above has a breast drawer at the top of the lower section and continues in a modified style on the second section with pilasters, fluted, with carved capitals. The rosettes terminating in the scroll top have a carved spray proceeding from them something in the manner of the rich Georgian mirror. The foot is doubled, the inner section following the curve of the oxbow.

298. STRAIGHT FRONT, OGEE BRACKET FOOT, SCROLLED TOP, FLUTED QUARTER
COLUMN. 1760–80. VERY UNUSUAL IN BASE CONSTRUCTION AND IN THE TWO
SQUARE DRAWERS. MRS. FRANCIS P. GARVAN.

299. Broken Pediment, Fluted Pilasters, Dentils. A Style Attractive but Unusual. 1780. Mrs. Francis P. Garvan.

300. Straight Front, Bracket Foot, Spiraled Quarter Column, Open Fret, Scroll. 1780. Mrs. Francis P. Garvan.

The construction of the chests-on-chests differs in no particular from that of the low chests of drawers. The pieces are made in two parts, with a retaining mold to receive the upper section. Thus that section is smaller by an inch and a half to two inches, the backs ordinarily being flush. Instances, however, are known, in which the back projects about an inch to bear against the wall over the dado of the room finish.

The second piece above is of great interest owing to the unusual quarter columns, which also appear, but in full section in two subsequent pieces under this class. The urns terminate with spikes instead of flames and might well have been more ornate. There is wide variety in the styles of rosettes, but the present example is quite usual. Probably a central urn or carving of some kind is missing.

The cabinet work on 19th century furniture is every bit as good as that on earlier types. The tendency is to over-refinement and to great delicacy. Pieces of merit, however, like these, are deservedly much sought for. The favorite veneer of rich pieces was satinwood. But any beautifully grained wood found its place through the ingenuity and imagination of the cabinetmaker. The student should observe that the fluting of the Chippendale time is ordinarily superseded in the Sheraton period by reeding, so called because, if a bunch of reeds is tied together, the effect is obtained. It is the reverse process of fluting.

301. STRAIGHT FRONT, OGEE BRACKET, BONNET TOP, THREE IDENTICAL FLAMES. 1770-80. BEHIND THE SCROLL THE BONNET IS CLOSED, AS IS SOMETIMES THE FASHION. KATHERINE LORING, WAYLAND, MASSACHUSETTS.

302. (Right.) BLOCK FRONT, STRAIGHT BRACKET, FLUTED PILASTER, BONNET TOP. 1770-80. I. SACK.

It is not unusual to find the blocking stop on the lower section, in which case it returns on the top drawer. We very rarely find a specimen of chests-on-chests with the shell block.

In the construction the bonnet has in this instance two vertical faces boxed in behind the scroll. As a rule, there was no closing of this corridor at the back. It will appear that the pilasters shorten the drawers. We notice here an elaboration of the short drawers at the top by which they are contoured to match the top scrolled mold. This is a harmonious note lacking in the next two examples. The partitions between the top drawers are dovetailed frankly top and bottom. This is a necessary part of good cabinet work. Usually the drawers are divided by blades, showing the dovetail frankly, but sometimes there is a blind dovetail. The runs for the drawers extend in good construction entirely through the board back.

303. STRAIGHT FRONT, PLAIN BRACKET,
BONNET TOP. 1770–80. MRS. FRANCIS P.
GARVAN.

304. BLOCK FRONT, PLAIN BRACKET, BONNET TOP.
1770–80. W. W. SMITH, PROVIDENCE.

We have here a more elaborate shell than the usual pattern. There is an overlapping drawer in both specimens. This overlap ends in a delicate thumb-nail mold, the cabinet makers' term for a narrow fillet followed by a quarter round. When it came to the matter of the shell the style did not call for this ornament on the lower section, but by changing the drawer plan completely, opportunity for that shell was found in No. 298.

The overlapping drawer is an advantage in excluding dust. It also forms a handsome drawer front, giving the effect of a slight blocking. There seems to be no important difference in the merits of the thumb-nail drawer and the drawer edge with a narrow mold. Rare instances are known where the thumb-nail mold is worked on the drawer front without any lip.

In the application of brasses the variation in the width of the drawers gave difficulty. In a convex or concave drawer the brass was bent to conform to the surface.

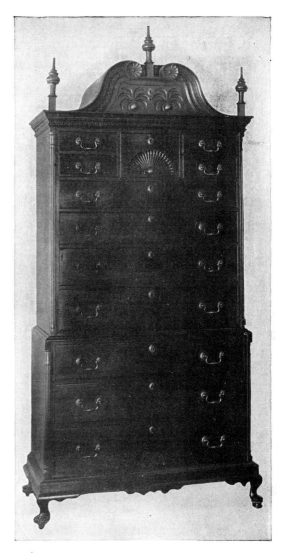

305. Straight Front, Plain Bracket, Fluted Pilasters and Bonnet Top. 1770–80. I. Sack.

306. Straight Front, Dutch Foot, Quarter Columns in Both Sections. Unique Scroll under the Bonnet, I. Sack.

We have the arrangement here of a square top with the bonnet superimposed, and quite different from other examples. The maker evidently thought out a quaint and interesting scheme of decoration, apparently a doubled motive of an apple-shaped fruit with leaves.

There is a rich doubled dentil fret under the straight top mold and also under the bonnet. The rosettes are in the form of daisies. The interesting and peculiar finials are too small to be called urns, and are stilted. The foot being a Dutch cabriole with a shoe or cushion base raises the question of the date, which it will be safer to name with considerable straddle, 1750–70. The handles, however, may or may not bear out this judgment.

The shells as usually carved are recessed, or cut intaglio. In a few instances their edges are raised. It is only by courtesy that they can be called shells. Properly they are the sunrise emblem, called sunburst only when the full circle is shown, as in some examples to appear later. It will be seen in the two pieces before us that where the shell occupies nearly the whole width of the drawer there is no room for an escutcheon plate.

307. STRAIGHT FRONT WITH ARCH IN LOWER DRAWER EXTENDING INTO FRAME. CHAMFERED FLUTED CORNERS IN UPPER SECTION. WILLIAM B. GOODWIN, HARTFORD.

308. SERPENTINE, LOWER SECTION, QUARTER COLUMN. BONNET TOP. 1750–70. FLAYDERMAN AND KAUFMAN.

307. A peculiarity of this piece is the end paneling not found in the American mahogany period. This piece also has a slide at the top of the lower section. Oak, red and white. 74½ x 40 x 20¾. The owner obtained this piece from Massachusetts and gives a very wide spread for the probable date, namely 1680–1750. Its provenance has not been traced farther.

308. The shape of the foot bracket is unusual and the carving on the rosettes is in very low relief. There is a curious effect obtained by a double row of half-round molding separated by a flat space around all the drawers. The quarter columns appear on both sections. In view of the peculiar finial and the lack of an urn below the flame it is difficult to define this variant.

The difficulty of matching the serpentine front with the straight front top was overcome by recessing the top drawer below the top of the lower section. Of course the handles are not original.

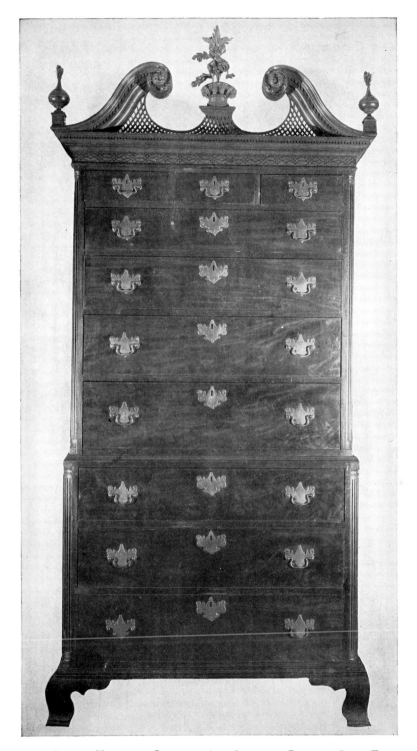

309. Scroll Top with Lattice, All Quarter Column, Ogee Feet. Mahogany. 1750–70. Morris Schwartz. Fine Fret and Dentils and Remarkable Spiraled Scroll. Philadelphia. Mrs. Francis P. Garvan.

310. Lower Section Blocked, Bonnet Top,
Unusual Flames. 1760–80. 87½x38¼x20½.
Original Brasses. Cherry. Dr. and
Mrs. John M. Birnie.

311. Lower Section Blocked, Shell at
Center of Base Mold, Bonnet Top.
1760–70. G. W. H. Smith, Providence.

It will be observed that the left-hand piece has a large bracket foot which is not shaped on the inside to conform to the blocking. This is most unusual. The right-hand piece has a foot somewhat small which starts with a bracket made to conform to the blocking, but does not carry down and end with a scroll, but sweeps in a little in an effort to come to an end. The fluting here ends without a capital below the molding. The cornice, however, breaks forward to form a capital. The two Rhode Island pieces shown without the scroll foot which has acquired the name of Goddard are, nevertheless, regarded as by him. We recognize in those days as at present that some customers called for simplified forms.

It should be noted that the feet behind are shaped only on the base which shows, but on the back are plain. Thus the piece could be set directly against the wall. The construction of the bonnet is clearly shown here. The molding returns at the central opening for several inches, more than its own thickness. It then comes to an end, the entire broken arch being sustained by a box shaped without, but plain and vertical within, and sufficiently back from the face of the return to give good effect to the cornice.

312. Lower Section Blocked, Upper Section Fluted with Capitals, Spiral Flames. 1760–70. F. L. Dunne, Boston.

313. Lower Section Blocked, Knee Hole, Plain Bracket Feet, Carved, Scrolled Pilasters. 1760–70. Cherry. I. Sack.

312. The shaping of the foot bracket, in form of a block, stops about half-way down, and is rounded off in a somewhat doubtful manner quite similar to the piece last described. It may very well be that the idea of carrying this shaping to the very base of the foot and ending in a scroll was a later device of Goddard. Even as he left it at its last estate, it is not absolutely convincing. It was a difficult problem to work out. Whether he ever tried to carry this foot to the floor, completely working out the shape without a scroll, as in some of the straight bracket feet, the author does not know.

313. There are rare and interesting elements in the style. One peculiarity is that the knee-hole door is flanked with pilasters, fluted. The contour of the block is carried completely down to the floor on the foot. The effort to form a capital resulted in a short torus mold returned at both ends, followed by a short plain section of pilaster which connects with the cornice mold. The middle finial is peculiar. A most interesting piece.

314. Lower Section Blocked, Long Straight Brackets. Scrolled
Knee-Hole Door. 1750–70. Warner House, Portsmouth, N. H.
For a Very Long Time in Its Present Ownership.

315. Lower Section Blocked, Sliding Tray. Upper Section, Pilasters and Capitals. Bonnet Top with Carved Rosettes. 1760–70. I. Sack.

A claw-and-ball foot chest-on-chest is extremely rare. The blocking is continued down into the bracket of the foot, and ends harmoniously. Small top drawers shaped to conform to the scroll of the cornice. Center flame varies from others, for what reason is uncertain unless it was so made to gain head room.

316. STRAIGHT FRONT, OGEE FOOT, UNUSUAL SCROLL BRACKET,
FOUR FULL COLUMNS IN THE CORNERS. DENTILED BONNET.
ROSETTES TO CORRESPOND WITH SUNBURSTS IN TWO TOP SIDE
DRAWERS. MIDDLE DRAWER IS CARVED WITH PECULIAR FLUTINGS.
SHELL UNDER CENTRAL URN WHICH IS CUT OFF APPARENTLY FOR
HEAD ROOM. 1730–70. GEO. L. PALMER.

317. Nine Shell, All Blocked, Goddard Foot. Corner
Boxes under Urns. 1760–70. Probably Unique.
Mrs. John R. Gladding.

318. ALL BLOCKED, STRAIGHT BRACKET, SHELL TOP. FOUR FULL-COLUMN CORNERS. 1730–70. TRIPLE ROW OF DENTILS ON CORNICE. CENTRAL SHELL DIVERGENT IN STYLE FROM THE OTHERS. ARTHUR L. SHIPMAN, HARTFORD.

The remarkable piece opposite resembles in some particulars No. 316. Note the scroll of brackets on foot, the spiral columns, the dentils, finials, and top shell. The puzzle about No. 318 is the lapse from full style in the inadequate spiraled rosettes terminating the bonnet. The piece, however, is of greatest rarity, and importance. This slight weakness shown also in the curvature of the scroll is difficult to explain.

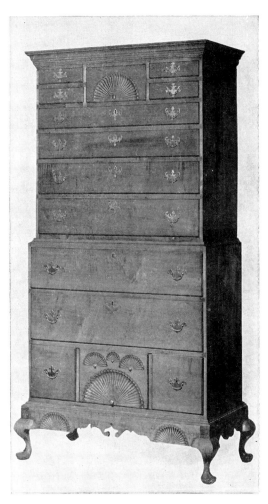

319. Curly, Interesting Variant of Closed Scroll. Chamfered and Fluted Upper Section. 1750–70. I. Sack.

320. Maple, Dutch Bandy Legs, Three Part. 1750–70. Henry V. Weil.

319. A piece indicating what may result when the maker has either forgotten his model or thinks an innovation is an improvement. The scroll is completely closed by the meeting of the two sides on the base for the urn. A very curious feature is that the cornice is chamfered. The author does not remember to have seen anything of the sort previously, with one exception.

320. Several of these or similar pieces have been found in southern New Hampshire. Two lowboys are shown in their section. The curious device of placing two shells in the low frame and three small shells above the large one in the lower middle drawer excite a humorous interest. In another particular the chest is curious in being only three drawers deep in the lower section.

322. Jonathan Gostelowe Chest of Drawers. A Celebrated Maker Just Coming
into Recognition. 1750–80. The Hayloft, Whitemarsh, Pennsylvania.

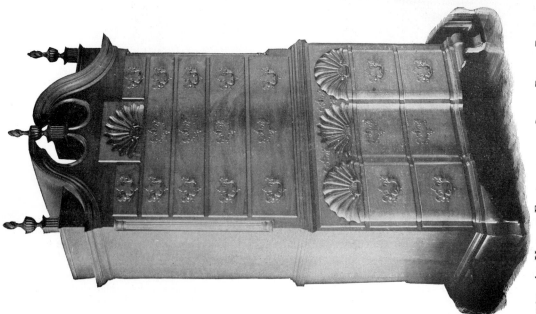

321. An Unique Example with Shell Block Below
and Shell Above. The Boxes under the Corner Urns
Are Found on Two or Three Other Large Pieces, and
Are Also Seen on English and American Clocks.
1760–70. Nathanael G. Herreshoff.

323. BLOCK BELOW, SUNRISE ABOVE, SCALLOPED BASE MOLD. FLUTED PILASTERS WITH CORINTHIAN CAPITALS. DRAWERS IN UPPER SECTION ARE FAINTLY BLOCKED. THE SCROLL OF THE BONNET IS IN A WEAK CURVE. 1760–70. METROPOLITAN MUSEUM.

324. A SALEM CHEST-ON-CHEST. 1790. MIXED MOTIVES. MRS. FRANCIS P. GARVAN.

The base leaves little to be desired if one likes the huge feet resulting from the wide chamfer. Inevitably the feet could not be made moderate size, and with the wide chamfer this effect is emphasized. The top has pillars reminding one somewhat of the Empire period, or Adam design. Supposed to have been made by Samuel McIntire.

325. HEAVY, FIVE-LEG, LOW-FRAME HIGHBOY. UNRESTORED. 1690–1700.
METROPOLITAN MUSEUM.

This and Nos. 328 and 329 are the earliest types. Decorated with painted foliage.

326. Six Legs, Boldly Turned, Low Frame, Two Drawers End to End. 1690.
Metropolitan Museum.

The side runs of the drawers indicate the seventeenth century. Painted in red and black. Unique in the vertical back stretcher. It is quite clear that in the absence of pictures the maker was sometimes stumped!

327. Oak Highboy, Flemish Legs. 1690–1700. Wadsworth Atheneum.

The base is a semi-soft wood, perhaps basswood. There are two other highboys known in this style. The probable origin is Connecticut. The heavy scrolls suggest the origin of the nineteenth century degraded Empire style. Five-legged highboys are rare. The flush drawers and the single arch mold about them suggest the date. 48 x 39 x 21¾.

328. ENGLISH, PANELED. OAK. 1680–90. SHOWN TO INDICATE THAT THE EARLIEST HIGHBOY WAS REALLY AN OAK CHEST OF DRAWERS ON A TABLE FRAME, WHICH PROJECTS MORE THAN THE AMERICAN TYPE. METROPOLITAN MUSEUM.

329. A Five Legger. Walnut. 1690–1700. One Long Drawer in Frame. Early Form of Plate Handle, Stamped Decoration. Chauncey C. Nash.

330. Herringbone Walnut Veneer. Teardrop Handles. 1690–1700. Massachusetts Bay.

331. BURL AND HERRINGBONE WALNUT. 1700–10. MISS HELEN T. COOKE.

The turnings are the so-called trumpet variation. They are much more rare than the cup or bowl turning. This and many walnut highboys are of New England origin. Walnut grew in New England, though it was dark, and there is no reason to suppose it wasn't freely brought here by water from Pennsylvania and Virginia.

332. WALNUT VENEER. BOWL TURNING. 1700–10. EDWARD C. WHEELER, JR.

333. Sycamore and Apple Wood. 1690–1700. Unusual Turnings, Plain Arches. The Hardness and Smoothness of Apple Wood Made It Desirable for Turnings. Horatio H. Armstrong.

334. Country Made, Five Leg, Single Arch Mold. 1700. Mabel Choate.

335. HERRINGBONE WALNUT VENEER. 1700. 62 x 42½ x 23. UPPER SECTION
30¾ x 37 x 20¼. WADSWORTH ATHENEUM.

336. BUTTERNUT. TWO SEPARATED DRAWERS IN FRAME. 1700. WADSWORTH ATHENEUM.

The varying arrangement of the drawers of highboys distinguishes them and makes them interesting. Perhaps the more ordinary arrangement in the frame consists of two deep drawers and one shallow one between. The piece above is perhaps unique in omitting the middle drawer. The earliest design had one long drawer.

337. Bowl Turned. Two Short and Two Deep Drawers in Frame. Torus Drawer
in Top. 1700. Edward C. Wheeler, Jr.

338. Four Legs, Trumpet Turned, Cross Stretcher. 1710-20.

339. FOUR LIGHT LEGS, DOUBLE ARCH MOLD, HIGHLY FEATURED VENEER.
1710. METROPOLITAN MUSEUM.

The construction of this and the preceding piece, in the frame, is like that of the usual lowboy, designed to accompany this piece. That is to say, there is a cross stretcher and four legs. The construction is very weak even with six legs, since the leg was doweled to the frame. For this reason nearly all the old examples were broken beyond repair.

340. CURLY, COUNTRY MADE, FOUR LEGGER WITH EXTRAORDINARY DROPS AND FINIAL.
1720.

In the phrase country made, the meaning is that this was probably constructed away from the centers of manufacture, and hence liable to certain crudities or deviations from fine types. This deviation may not interfere with the collector's ardor if the specimen is sufficiently quaint.

341. Painted White Wood. 1690–1710. 55 x 40 x 21. From Guilford. Fleur de Lis, Thistle and Crown. Other Floral Designs. William B. Goodwin.

342. Cherry, Block Front Highboy. Every Part Original, Including
Handles and Flames. Sections Flush in Front, Top Narrower at Ends.
1740–60.

The only example known to be original throughout. It has stood for generations
where it now is, in New England. It has no Newport connection. A development
of the block with individual features, as the square corners on the returns at top and
bottom of the convex parts.

343. Lacquered. English. The Oriental Lacquer Was Not as Well Done in Europe, Since a Certain Gum Obtained in the East Must Be Used Fresh. The Boston or Other American Attempts Were Not Very Successful. 1710–25. Metropolitan Museum.

344. Maple and Walnut, and White Wood. 1720–30. 67¾ x 41¾ x 21¼.
William B. Goodwin.

Drawer in upper molding. The greater part of the brasses are original. Matched
walnut veneer. Workmanship of the highest quality. Feet pieced.

345. HIGHBOY WITH STEPS. 1750–70. C. SANFORD BULL, WATERBURY, CONNECTICUT.

The use of a series of receding platforms placed on flat-topped highboys for the display of china or other decorative objects is occasionally found. It is a wonder the custom was not general, as the earliest highboys were often less than five, and generally less than six feet high. A highboy so crowned is effective decoration, and is recommended to those who have old pieces. The steps allow one range of articles on the top of the highboy itself, two ranges above, and a final central small step for the major piece of price or beauty.

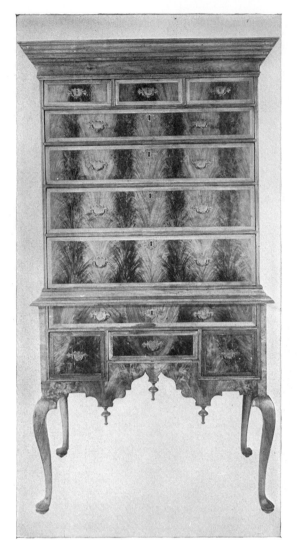

346 AND 347. TWO BURL WALNUT, CABRIOLE LEG HIGHBOYS, 1720-30. I. SACK.

The cornice on No. 346 is seen to be very heavy. That on No. 347 is arranged with a torus molding drawer. The arrangement of the drawers in the lower frame, while not the same, occupies the same space.

THE LINING MOLDING

On many fine highboys except the richly carved, there is a thin applied strip running around the entire contour of the skirt. It was rounded on the face and projected a trifle, a sixteenth of an inch, more or less. This strip gave a good finish and avoided the occurrence in the cabinet work of end wood. Of course, the bends required were sharp, but the strip was very thin and stayed in place well.

THE DROPS ON HIGHBOYS

When the six-legged highboy was abandoned for the four-leg cabriole type, the point at which the extra pair of legs would otherwise have been attached, was finished with an acorn or other tasteful turning. The absence of this drop, if there is a natural place for it, indicates its loss. Sometimes in the course of repairs a small base for this drop is restored and the hole for the dowel is not apparent.

348 AND 349. FULL SUNBURSTS. 1730-50. MRS. FRANCIS P. GARVAN.

The maple highboy on the left is curly, and the feet are three toed, sometimes called drake feet, whereas a plain Dutch (Queen Anne) foot has been called, without warrant in any resemblance, a duck foot. The three-toed foot is a Delaware valley type — a term better than Philadelphia because such types are found in Jersey, Pennsylvania, and Delaware, and farther south, to Baltimore. This example has a shell on the skirt, tiny scrolls at each side of it, shells and scrolls on knees, and a doubled shell in the short top drawer.

The sunbursts, matched, in the frame section are made with a central boss, surrounded by small ornaments. They are convenient for attaching the small drop handles.

No. 349 is a quiet piece with little ornament but no little beauty. Under lowboys will be found its companion. The author confesses to a fondness for the fine sweep of a skirt of this character. There is nothing more graceful than this simple Queen Anne foot. If the lady herself had one as good, it must have attracted admiration.

A singularly graceful base. The two drawers ordinarily found in the top of highboys distinguish these tops from ordinary chests of drawers. Not infrequently the author has been called upon to admire a chest of drawers which was nothing more than the upper section of a highboy. Another method of detecting this delusion, often innocent, is by noticing that chests of drawers had tops finished without a marginal mold. Further investigation will show that the feet are additions. The drops are unusually graceful.

351. (Right.) Curly, Drawer in Cornice, Odd Outward Ramp on Legs. 1730–40.
Mrs. Francis P. Garvan.

The conventional acorn drop here appears.

The curves of skirts on highboys are combinations of many patterns. The more common sort is shown on this page. The highest cut-out in the center is a half circle followed by a flat member (fillet) and an ogee. This brings us to the second flat member, whereon the drops are fastened. On the left-hand piece the ogee repeats as we proceed toward the leg, in the right-hand piece a flat arch carries to the leg bracket. The left-hand piece repeats the ogee against the leg and is more graceful.

Curly maple is the decorative surface peculiarly adapted to American pieces. It always carries a fine flavor of simple early days, more appropriate to our region than mahogany.

353. A Curly Model, with a Heavy Covered Cornice. 1730–50. Frank A. Robart.

352. A Unique Recessed Highboy. 1730–50. Old Inn, So. Woodstock, Connecticut.

One observes two methods of connecting the upper and lower sections. The mold here does not project beyond the frame, as it does in 357.

352. A space was available between the room wall and the chimney, and the scheme carried out (352) was the building of the highboy into the wall, and happily using the same cornice as that on the room and breaking it over the shallow projection of the front. While the idea is perhaps not one to follow, the effect is no end quaint. The wood is cherry, and the piece is contemporaneous with the house.

This type of cornice, common enough on clocks, is very rare in highboys. A modification of it, however, was found the most beautiful possible design for the superb Philadelphia highboy. In the simple form here seen, in 353, it is effective. With a clock in the same room the resemblance would please the eye. The drawer arrangement in the lower section is unusual. More than a score of drawer schemes are found. Above, on the left, there is so nice a graduation of the depths of drawers as at first to escape attention.

354. A New Hampshire Winged Cornice with
Three Tier Lower Part. 1740–70.
Morris Schwartz.

355. Very High, Maple, Three Tier Lower
Section. 1730–50. Rudolph Pauly, Boston.

354. Several of these pleasing designs have come to light. Mrs. DeWitt Howe of Manchester had them.
Above the usual cornice a crowning section is added, pierced with a fret, having a sunrise carving at center
surmounted by a simple scroll, and repeating the same motive at the corners, but cutting it in two so that one
half carries around the end. This half also occurs again on the wall side of the end.

The skirt has paired salamander scrolls, cut through in part at the center, and on either side a shell.
Small scroll brackets on legs missing.

355. There is seldom a highboy found more complete with all original parts and fittings. The sunrise
drawers above and below are virtual duplicates. Curly. Inner scrolls on frame doubles of corner bracket.

356. CHEST ON FRAME, NO DRAWER IN LOWER SECTION. 1720–40. MARY M. SAMPSON.

Chests on frames are usually very small and are shown in a chapter by themselves, but this specimen really belongs with highboys, or is in a class by itself. From Rhode Island. Curly maple. 53½ x 34 x 16. It comes about halfway in size between the 17th century "pilgrim" chests and the 18th century highboys. Drawer in cornice. Amusing variant in leg shape. Repeated ogees on skirt.

357. (Right.) MINIATURE CABINET. SIX LEG HIGHBOY STYLE. SIZE OF DROP HANDLES INDICATES SIZE. 1700. MRS. FRANCIS P. GARVAN.

The turnings are rare, having a small section immediately under the large section. A number of miniatures are said to have been samples which the maker took on his travels, and used to assist the imagination of the buyer. But this specimen has a cabinet above and was intended as a receptacle for my lady's jewels or was designed for a child.

Miniatures are much in request because they are both rare and captivating. They are found in almost every variety of furniture, but are most desirable in pieces of this type and the more usual design of low chests of drawers.

We are now in the era of the willow pattern brasses which run through the Chippendale styles. The name highboy is justified, measurements being 84 x 38½ x 19½. Of seventy highboys shown, No. 355 and No. 352 are the only ones six drawers high in the upper section.

Attractive in several particulars. The bracelet on the ankle will appear on other pieces later. It is a striking variant of the Spanish foot, and increases the importance of a specimen. The mold on the curly edges is almost dazzling, owing to the rich curl. A fishtail under the shallow drawer.

359. (Right.) Curly. Upper Section Four Drawers High. 1740–70. J. Fenimore Cooper, Cooperstown, New York.

With this we enter upon the scrolled, and usually bonnet-topped highboys. They follow after, in date, the flat-top style, though for simple pieces the flat tops continued into the scroll-top period.

It is worth while once to give mold sizes.

Depth of frame, base 20 inches.
Width of frame, base 38¼ inches.
Width of frame upper section 35½ inches.

Thus 2¾ inches difference in width allows 1⅜ inches total projection of mold at top of base. Total height 72½ inches.

Later sheets of detail molds will be given.

The lower section of a highboy appears to have a table top, sometimes with, and again without, a sustaining mold under it. The apparent table top is, however, only a narrow strip on which the top rests.

360. Philadelphia School. Carved Quarter Columns. Spiral Carved
Scroll, Urns with Flowers, Pierced Fret. 1760–70. Courtesy
Pennsylvania Museum, Philadelphia, Memorial Hall.

361. Philadelphia. Mahogany. Richly Carved, Including Quarter
Columns. 1760–70. Rosettes and Finials Missing.
Metropolitan Museum.

362. RICH ROSETTE UNDER CORNICE, KIDNEY ACROTERIUM,
FLAMES SET OUT. FLUTED QUARTER COLUMNS. SHELL DRAWER,
SHELL ON SKIRT. 1760–70. I. SACK.

363. CARVED SKIRT, SHELL DRAWER, CARVED CORNICE, ROSETTES, ACROTERIUM
(ALSO CALLED CARTOUCHE). 1760–70. MRS. FRANCIS P. GARVAN.

364. PHILADELPHIA SCHOOL, QUARTER COLUMNS, SKIRT, DRAWER, LEGS
CARVED. FINE OPEN SCROLL TOP. FEMALE FIGURE RESTORED. 1760–70.
METROPOLITAN MUSEUM.

365. Unusually Delicate, Carved Skirt, Frets on Retaining Mold and Cornice. Dentils, Open Work, Richly Carved Scroll. 1760–70. Mrs. Francis P. Garvan.

366. FRET AND DENTILS. 1760–70. MRS. FRANCIS P. GARVAN.

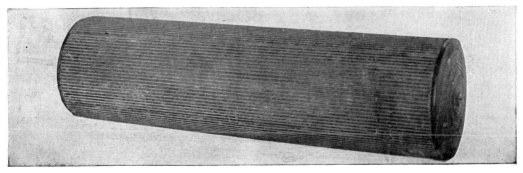

367. A QUIVER. A. M. UHLER, CONCORD, MASSACHUSETTS.

368. Two Carved Drawers, Elaborately Carved Bonnet. Quick Ramp and
Unusual Down Sweep for Rosettes. 1760–70. Morgan B. Brainard.

369. Two Carved Drawers, High Ramp, Small Rosettes, Irregular
Spiraled Flames. 1760-70. Mrs. Francis P. Garvan.

370. Chapin Highboy, Windsor. Two Drawers Carved Charac-
teristically. Fine Spiral Scroll, Open Fret, Open Acroterium.
1760–80. Robert P. Butler, Hartford.

371. Philadelphia, Walnut. Found in Virginia. 1760–70. H. W. Erving. 96 x 43½ x 21. An Elaborate Kidney Centered Cartouche. Two, Similar, Carved Drawers.

The carving on the skirt is a light raised line, with restrained ornament. All corners have fluted quarter columns, the legs being delicately carved. The effect is graceful. The shell under the base of cartouche is good, and unusual. Carving of rosettes comes to sharp points. Irregular spiraling of flames adds to the naturalistic effect.

372. (Right.) All Curly, Shell Knees, Aster Rosettes, Carved Top Drawer Only. 1760–70. J. Fenimore Cooper.

The corners instead of quarter columns have fluted chamfers. Curly pieces, carved, are rare in this size, but at least one other is known. It is a task to carve curly maple, owing to the refractory brittle cross-grain nature of the wood, and ordinarily the curl is allowed to serve as the only ornament. This piece is the only one the author has seen with a carved upper drawer, not matched by a similar drawer below. The unusual curves of the skirt are also distinctive.

373. STRAIGHT FOOT, BALL AND CLAW. BONNET
TOP. CHERRY BASE SECTION, OTHER SECTIONS
PINE. 1760–70. ROBERT P. BUTLER, HARTFORD.

374. CHAPIN MAKE. WINDSOR, CONNECTICUT.
1760–70. MORGAN B. BRAINARD.

373. This is one of those pieces so distinctive as to win instant attention. A lowboy will appear in its section with similar feet. They are carefully carved but entirely without the usual hip, gambrel or cabriole form. Graceful unusual flames. This class has no molding extending beyond the carcass at the intersection of second and third divisions, and the bonnet mold is restored.

374. In this example in cherry, his usual medium, we have slight "urns" hardly true to name; and a remarkable central flame also peculiar to this maker. He seems to have been a lone maker of excellent taste, only lately sought for. The spiral with which he closes his scroll, thus avoiding a rosette, which indeed never looks as if it grew there, is highly successful. Had his urns equalled it, nothing more could be wanted. A dozen of his pieces, more or less, are known. On most the light, graceful central ornament was missing, it being high and delicate and liable to breakage or to be too aspiring for the ceiling. No good lines are missing. The simplicity and lightness of the drawer carving is found quite identical on several examples, as also the half-round fluted base of the top ornament, and the fret. The skirt made up of simple ogee scrolls is not deeply cut, but in good taste. The legs are delicate.

375. DUTCH FOOT, UNIQUE AUGER FLAMES AND CORNER COLUMNS.
1730–60. I. SACK, BOSTON.

The statement concerning uniqueness will no sooner go out than another
will be found. The maker had a fine leg pattern, but his finials were a feat of
memory. The unusual scroll of the skirt and the edges of the shells should
be noted.

376. UNIQUE. CHERRY. CARVING ON KNEES AND BONNET SCROLL, THREE STARS AND A FLEUR DE LIS INLAY. 1750–70. WM. B. BAILEY, HARTFORD.

Said to have been in original Essex House, Salem, later in Newburyport. The straight effect on inside of scrolls arises from the vertical backing of the bonnet, and would not be seen at a little greater distance. Poor blocking out does not do justice to shape of legs. Odd knob scrolls, carved, on skirt.

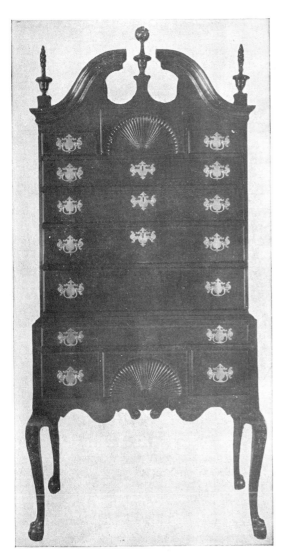

378. (Right.) Queen Anne. Walnut. 1720-40. Mr. and Mrs. George Shipley, Baltimore.

The lighter veneer and the very light-line inlay are effective, especially on the rosettes of cornice. The tasteful blending of herringbone with other surfaces is very satisfactory. The piece is small, and even more narrow in proportion to height, than usual. 73 x 27 x 17 inches, outside all. Height to top of cornice outside, 65 inches. Upper carcass 25¼ inches wide. Original chased brasses. Cornice very simple. Baltimore is rich in its own special variants.

379. MAHOGANY, UNIQUE HORNED CORNICE SCROLL.
1760–70. FROM PHILADELPHIA. 96 x 48 x 24.
MRS. FRANCIS P. GARVAN.

380. QUEEN ANNE. WALNUT. VENEERED.
1730–40. WINGED FINIALS. JACOB MARGOLIS.

379. Two little shells, one on each side of central shell on skirt, appeared on two New Hampshire types. The leg is short, as often occurs on plain or lightly carved Pennsylvania walnut highboys. There is an excellent rosette, bordered, and a narrow ornamental border along the entire length of inside of scroll, Philadelphia pieces having a ruling motive of a low center of the skirt.

380. New England origin. Original brasses. Unusual shell effects. Inlay of the so-called "tree" type, well matched. Very heavy cornice. The position of the outside finials, which we occasionally find so placed, is not counted as good as if the outside base of finial lined with the outside of upper carcass, in the usual fashion. Nevertheless, the effect is striking and of course accords with ancient classical design. The urns lack proper curves.

381. CHERRY. SUNBURST TOP DRAWER, SUNRISE LOWER DRAWER. 1740–50. CONNECTICUT
DESIGN. 80½ x 38 x 19½. ROBERT T. SMITH.

The author has always liked this pattern of scroll on skirt. Though simple, it is pleasing, especially the little doubled ogee, "cupid's bow" at the center. There were never urns at sides.

The use of cherry, the New England mahogany, is frequent, and not confined to Connecticut, though it may occur there on finer pieces than in Massachusetts. No doubt its color made it a favorite substitute for mahogany, though many an old Connecticut craftsman would challenge the word "substitute." He regarded his oak, sycamore, cherry, whitewood, and maple as ample and proper for any demand put on him.

382. (Right.) CURLY. TWO IDENTICAL CARVED DRAWERS. BONNET TOP. 1730–60. 87 x 39 x 20. MR. AND MRS. GEORGE SHIPLEY, BALTIMORE.

The upper carcass is 36 inches high by 18¾ inches deep. Height to top on cornice at side 73 inches. Original brasses. The exigencies to which makers were put in the application of escutcheons appears here. If the keyhole was not made well in from face of lock, there was a tight pinch in applying escutcheons as here, and the tops required bending to fit the thumb-nail edge. Cornice mold returns, and requires no rosettes.

383. SPANISH FOOT WITH BRACELETS. SHELL DRAWER ABOVE. WALNUT. 71 X 41 X 23. FROM PHILADELPHIA. 1720–30. MRS. FRANCIS P. GARVAN.

384. QUEEN ANNE. SWASTIKA CARVINGS. SMALL SUNBURST BELOW MIDDLE URN. 1730–50. I. SACK.

383. This is one of the half dozen or so high or low pieces with this style of leg. The bracelet, or "wrister," is on the outside of the leg only, and is molded carefully with four elements. This type of base for the middle urn is simply sawed out from the face board of the cornice and carries no molded border. The cornice mold, however, is the fully contoured elaborate member found on fine Philadelphia furniture.

384. An excellent illustration of the refinement secured by a very simple ogee skirt, when the curves are rightly combined. There is also just a touch of curvature on the upper part of the leg bracket which serves as good a purpose as the fulled rolled-down scroll.

385. Trumpet Turned Lowboy. New England. 1700–10. Walnut. Drops Lost. 29 x 33 x 22. Stamped Handles. Mrs. Francis P. Garvan.

386. Bowl Turned. Perhaps White Wood. 1700–10. From Wilmington, Delaware. 30 x 30¾ x 19. C. Sanford Bull, Waterbury.

LOWBOYS

A comic, possibly satiric name for a lady's dressing table, made to match the highboy, similarly deriving its name and called in England tallboy. These articles are rare because somewhat slender. They are eagerly sought and approach in desirability the highboys. Their size also wins favor. They came in to supplement the highboy which was obviously impossible as a dressing table, a service formerly rendered by the low chests of drawers.

387. Six-Leg Lowboy. Rare or Unique. Cherry. Stratham, N. H. 1710-20. 30¼ x 34½ x 20. Frame Is 17½ x 29½. Chauncey C. Nash.

Originally owned by Anna Rush, whose monument, erected by the women of Stratham, is in the cemetery. Scroll of stretcher follows, as it should, contour of skirt above.

388. LACQUERED CROSS-STRETCHER TABLE. MAPLE.
LABEL ON DRAWER DATES TABLE 1700. 28 x 24½ x 17¼.
TURNING SOFT, PERHAPS PINE. LACQUER LATE.

389. X-STRETCHER WALNUT LOWBOY. 1700–10. UNUSUAL TURNING. UPPER SECTION DOUBLED
BELOW AND REDUCED. JOHN H. HALFORD, NORRISTOWN, PA.

390. WALNUT AND BIRCH. BOWL TURNED. FINIAL AND FIFTH FOOT. DATED 1724. INLAID TOP. MARQUETRY AND INITIALS. ESTATE OF JAMES CURRAN, PHILADELPHIA.

391. FULL BOWL TURNED, WITH SAUCER FINIAL. 1700-10. ODDLY SUPERFLUOUS HANDLES. WALNUT. PENNSYLVANIA MUSEUM, PHILADELPHIA.

392. WALNUT X STRETCHER TRUMPET TURNED LOWBOY. 1710–20. UNUSUAL FINIAL AND DROPS.
G. WINTHROP BROWN.

393. LIGHT TURNED PINE. 1700–20. PERHAPS WOOD REPORTED IS AN ERROR.
LACKS DROPS. MRS. FRANCIS P. GARVAN.

In addition to those mentioned previously, there is on fine specimens a lining strip, projecting as a minute half-round mold bent about the contour of the bottom of the skirt as in highboys. The cross stretcher was usually adopted partly as a pleasing feature and partly to allow leg room. But we observe that many of these articles were impossible of use as dressing tables because of the forms of the skirt, as instance that on this page where the skirt and drop deny the opportunity offered by the legs. The drawer scheme also varies widely, as in the highboy. The first lowboys came in the walnut age and are not found in oak. They continued rife in the Chippendale period, but are only sporadic later, and of questionable intent, most likely side tables, a term covering all we don't know.

394. Bowl-Turned Lowboy with Drops and Finial. Acorn Pattern. 1690-1710.
Edward C. Wheeler, Jr.

Single arch mold occurs, it is believed, as early as 1690 in rare cases. Double arch mold (about drawers), 1700-25. The feet are always doweled on in this William and Mary type. The construction is not commendable for durability.

Legs on lowboys meet through the stretcher with a long dowel. Th[...]r varies widely. At times its square end, where the legs pierce it, is set at a diagon[...] American and some English pieces are soft wood, ordinarily pine; also drawer [...] ccurs and other woods. The finial is a reverse of the drops, but is modified sor[...]

395. CROSS-STRETCHER, CUP-TURNED LOWBOY OF WALNUT. 1690-1700. WADSWORTH ATHENEUM.

Veneered, with herringbone border. Massachusetts. Drops missing. Though fitted with stamped handles the mold seems to require drops. If these are original, they indicate an extremely early date. If the finial is original, it lacks somewhat in grace by comparison with others.

396. Long Cup Turned, Molded Frame. 1690. 27 x 28 x 18. Walnut.
Mrs. Francis P. Garvan.

397. Daintily Turned, Cup Shaped, Double Arch Mold. Similar to No. 387 in Style
of Leg. 1710–20. W. F. Hubbard, Hartford.

398. "Straight Leg" Queen Anne. Double Arch Mold. 1740–60. 30 x 33 x 21. Ends and Legs Maple; Top Walnut, Front Veneered. E. B. Leete Co., Guilford.

399. Cherry, Queen Anne. Connecticut. 1740–50. 31 x 35 x 21½. Robert T. Smith, Hartford.

400. Veneered, Inlaid Queen Anne. 1740–60. I. Sack.

There is nothing more graceful than a subtly curved cabriole leg. The Queen Anne type was followed long after her day.

401. SCROLLED SKIRT AS ON ONE HIGHBOY. 1740–60. ESTATE OF HARRY W. WEEKS, FRAMINGHAM.

402. SCROLLED TOP. RARE. FINELY SCROLLED SKIRT LIKE ONE HIGHBOY SHOWN. W. A. HITCHCOCK, FARMINGTON.

403. CURLY. CARVED, OUTLINE OF THREE-TOED FOOT. CHAMFERED. 1740–60. MORRIS SCHWARTZ.

404. GRACEFUL LEGS AND SKIRT SCROLL. 1720–50. DOUBLE ARCH MOLD. OWNER'S NAME MISLAID.

405. LARGE BASE, FOR HIGHBOY. SCROLLED LIKE NEW HAMPSHIRE TYPE. SPIRALED FAN AND STAR INLAY. SMALL FANS ON SKIRT. 1740–60. H. N. CAMPBELL, PROVIDENCE.

406. SEVEN DRAWERS. MAPLE. 1730–50. HENRY A. HOFFMAN, BARRINGTON. R. I.

407. CARVED C ON LEG BRACKET. SAME FOUND ON WALNUT EXAMPLES. 1740–60.
AN ATTRACTIVE STYLE. MRS. FRANCIS P. GARVAN.

408. SHELL KNEE, DRAKE FOOT, UNUSUAL SCROLL ON SKIRT.   FROM PHILADELPHIA.
30 x 34 x 20½. WALNUT. ORIGINAL CONDITION. 1740–60. MRS. FRANCIS P. GARVAN.

409. Walnut, from Philadelphia. Full Scroll. 1740–60. Mrs. Francis P. Garvan.

410. Five Drawer Queen Anne. 1740–60. Frank A. Robart.

411. Cherry Frame, 27½ Inches Wide. Good Legs. 1740–50. Connecticut Origin. "Duck" Foot. Unusual Scroll on Skirt. H. W. Erving.

412. Lacquered Lowboy Matching Highboy. English. Early 18th Century. Metropolitan Museum.

413. WALNUT WITH WALNUT VENEER. 1730–50. 31 x 31½ x 18½. BRASSES ORIGINAL.
TOP OLD BUT NOT ORIGINAL. DR. AND MRS. JOHN M. BIRNIE.

414. CHERRY. NEW ENGLAND. 1740–60. SUNBURST MATCHES A HIGHBOY.
MRS. FRANCIS P. GARVAN.

415. DRAKE FOOT, FLUTED QUARTER COLUMN. 1750–70. PLAINVILLE, CONNECTICUT.
THE DRAKE FOOT IS REGARDED AS COMING FROM THE DELAWARE VALLEY.
MRS. FRANCIS P. GARVAN.

416. DRAKE FOOT, COMPLICATED SCROLL ON SKIRT. 1750–70. 28½ x 34. WALNUT.
PHILADELPHIA. MORRIS BERRY.

417. Cherry, from Glastonbury, Conn. 1740–60.
Carved Knee and Foot. Harry L. F. Locke, Hartford.

418. Herringbone Inlay and Walnut Veneer.
Pointed Toe. Lining Mold about Drawers.
1740–60. Morris Schwartz.

419. Curly, Spanish Feet, Bracelets. 1720–40. New Jersey. From Randolph Family; Was in Randolph Mansion, Fairmount Park. James Curran Estate.

420. Swastika Drawer. Matches Highboy. 1730–50.
I. Sack, Boston.

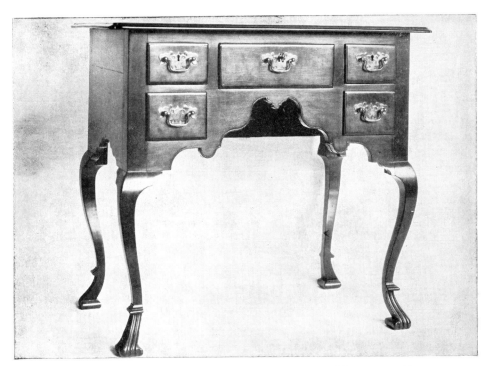

421. SPANISH FOOT. BRACELETS. 1720–30. 31 X 34 X 21. MAHOGANY, PHILADELPHIA.
MRS. FRANCIS P. GARVAN.

422. SPANISH FOOT, BRACELETS. NEW ENGLAND ORIGIN. 1720–30. FRAME 30 INCHES LONG.
MOLD CUT FROM THE SOLID MAHOGANY. H. W. ERVING.

423. MAHOGANY. 1760–70. VERY RICH. PHILADELPHIA. PALMER COL. MET. MUS.

424. WALNUT. PIERCED SCROLLS. CHAMFERED, FLUTED. DRAKE FOOT. PHILADELPHIA
TYPE. 1760–70. 31 X 34 X 20. GEORGE A. PALMER.

425. Rare Foot, Modified Drake. Quarter Column, Fluted. 1750–70. Morris Berry.

426. Curly, Fluted Quarter Column. 1760–70. James Fenimore Cooper.

427. Richly Carved. Philadelphia Type. 1760–70. Mrs. Francis P. Garvan.

428. Great Shell. Curly. 1760–70. Morris Schwartz.

The Philadelphia pieces marked the climax of mahogany carving in America, though the radically different Rhode Island block front was perhaps a piece of work as skilful, but with less wealth of variety and elaboration. These pieces it is now fashionable to attribute to William Savery, but his shop was small, the city was large, wealthy and avid for good forms. Pieces that Savery did not make were as good if not better than his.

429. VERY RICH. FULLY CARVED ENDS AS WELL AS FRONT. CARVED QUARTER COLUMNS. 1760-70. PHILADELPHIA TYPE. NOW IN MINNEAPOLIS INSTITUTION OF ARTS, FROM H. V. WEIL, NEW YORK CITY.

This is the first example with a carved edge on the top, where a dainty twist occurs. The feet on these pieces are large. There is a crosshatch on leg in the portion often left smooth. The carving on the end is found in a very few highboys and even less on lowboys.

One of the most remarkable features of decorative art is the narrow limit, geographically, within which the style was developed. It would appear that there should have been shell-block pieces highly developed in Philadelphia or Baltimore, and similarly it would appear that the fully developed carving on lowboys should be found in New Englamd. Artisans, however, are often prejudiced in favor of their own particular designs, and they are accustomed to develop one aspect of their art to an extreme. Further, nothing is more difficult than to lead the public taste. The consumer is even more prejudiced in favor of certain forms than is the producer.

430. SHELL KNEE, SHELL UNDER SHELL DRAWER. 1760–70. PHILADELPHIA TYPE.
NATHAN CUSHING, PROVIDENCE.

431. ACANTHUS LEG, SHELL AND SCROLL DRAWER, SHELL AND LINE ON SKIRT. 1760–70.
H. N. CAMPBELL, PROVIDENCE.

432. FINE SCROLLS, SHELL DRAWER, FLUTED QUARTER COLUMNS AND HEAVY MOLD UNDER TOP. 1760–70. RHODE ISLAND SCHOOL OF DESIGN.

433. CARVED DRAWER AND LEGS. 1760–70. GEO. S. PALMER. PHILADELPHIA TYPE. FROM I. SACK.

The various degrees of elaboration on the Philadelphia highboy and lowboy cover these points.

1. All have carved feet and knees, the drake foot being occasional, but the ball and claw is usual.

2. All have a carved drawer in frame, a shell, or a shell with a small obverse at its hinge side.

3. Most have a series of scrolled stems each side and below the shell.

4. The richer pieces have carving on the skirt which represents merely lines of beauty rather than anything in nature, except for a small shell or shell-like form in the center.

5. Generally there are fluted quarter columns.

6. The most elaborate have flower patterns instead of fluted columns.

7. In extremely rare cases the carving carries around the ends.

8. The very richest pieces carry a fret or carved band under the top, or on the top edge, or both.

434. CONSUMMATELY RICH; CARVED WHEREVER TASTE ALLOWED, EXCEPT ON END. GREEK SCROLL UNDER TOP. CARVED EDGE OF TOP. 1760–70. MRS. FRANCIS P. GARVAN.

One easily discerns that at least two rival makers sought to outdo one another in the design and execution of these supreme pieces. There is a certain conventional perfection of the form, as the leg. After that, it was every artisan for himself.

The lowboy here displayed delicate features in carving which place it in a class alone. Here is the bird sometimes seen on mirrors but done with a light spiritual grace — a bird better unnamed, but a perfect decoration. At the sides of this exquisite paneled drawer appear uprights with handles, which of course are also sheer fine imaginings, and from the tops of them proceed scrolls and flowers.

435. FULLY CARVED. UNIQUE. IN CUSTODY OF ESTATE OF JAMES CURRAN, PHILADELPHIA. 1765–75. MAHOGANY.

On the skirt the central scheme is a basket with flowers from which two lines of scrolls meander to each side. The leg is daintily done with acanthus motives. A floral scroll decorates the quarter columns. A Greek design alternates with a flower to form the frieze below the top.

The dimensions are the size of a highboy, but no top is known to the author anything like this. That signifies nothing, as discoveries are made every day, and there are still many persons who don't tell all they know.

This piece is unrestored but in excellent condition. There is at present a marble top set within the retaining mold. It is invisible from the point of view of this picture.

Instead of the overlapping drawer there is a thin half-round mold about the drawers.

436. Shells on Knees. Shell Drawer and Fluted Quarter Column. 1760–70. F. L. Dunne.

437. Fully Carved, Unique Skirt. 1760–70. Philadelphia. Metropolitan Museum.

438. Quarter Column. Shells on Knees. 1760–70. F. L. Dunne, Boston.

439. Acanthus Knee. Delicate Scroll on Skirt. Fluted Quarter Columns. 1760–70. F. L. Dunne, Boston.

440. CHAMFERED, CARVED KNEE. PLAIN SKIRT. 1760–70. FORMERLY THE AUTHOR'S.

441. VIRGINIA WALNUT, DRAWER FRONTS SELECTED. 1760–70. SHELL DRAPERY. ACANTHUS KNEE. SHELL DRAWER. TRIPLE CORNER ON TOP. 30¼ x 30 x 19. H. W. ERVING.

In approaching the end of lowboys it should be observed that they were often used as side tables for a variety of purposes, the style brushing aside, on the decorative master-pieces, the element of pure convenience. They became depositaries of documents or valuables of any sort and were found in other rooms than bedrooms, if the fancy of the owner dictated.

442. SHELL DRAPERY, FLUTED CHAMFER. SELECTED WOOD IN SIDE DRAWERS. 1760–70. MRS. FRANCIS P. GARVAN.

The lowboy went out with the incoming of the low chest of drawers. From this point there is rather a rapid decline in styles of furniture. Hepplewhite provided some very elegant chairs, but they did not equal the best of Chippendale. They had a grace of their own. But in cabinet furniture he gave us nothing of the carved sort which at all levels up with the great Philadelphia cabinetmakers. Gostolow is now reckoned superior, by many good judges, to Savery, but there was glory enough for all. Randolph is beginning to gain a great name.

443. ENGLISH LIVERY CUPBOARD, SEVENTEENTH CENTURY. 32 X 29 X 12. OAK.
MRS. FRANCIS P. GARVAN.

The cupboard was the largest piece of cabinet furniture, and on it was expended even more decorative effort than on the chest. We have not anything of the sort shown above, except a grill or two. There is a clear resemblance between the spindles here and those on American cupboards. The important matter to notice is that the split spindles were derived from the fully rounded spindles of the grilled door. They are arranged here in a bad fashion hardly likely to have been original. It is bad taste to reverse a spindle in conjunction with another that is right side up. The split spindle was obviously first thought of as a finish at the side of an opening as here seen on the left side of the doors, and as on some cradles and stair rails.

Having this split spindle in his hand the workman happened to stand it against the front and behold, a new decorative motive.

These cupboards went under various names in England, as almoners, dole, livery (that is, delivery) since they were used by the housewife to dole out the provisions of a day. Thus we perceive that the servants were on rations. The purpose of the opening was to let air at the food, and prevent mold. This is the only English cupboard that is shown, though there may be a little doubt as to one or two others.

Court cupboard is a term variously explained. It is better to say we don't know. The explanation from the French word for short is now regarded askance. That it was a fine piece of furniture adopted first in the court and afterwards by people of wealth and fashion goes without saying, as the same process went on with all changes of style.

444. A Press Cupboard of Remarkable Elaboration. A Recessed Portion on the Lower Section Affords Room for the Fine Bulbous Posts. It Is All in All the Best Piece of Oak Known in America. Size 58 x 48 x 22. Estate of the Late Gen. Charles J. Paine, Weston, Mass. Long in the Family. Believed to Have Been Made in or near Boston. 1660–80. Initials I. K.

Oak drawer ends and bottom ends under an inch thick. Single dovetail on narrow, two on middle drawer.

445. Press Cupboard Base. 1670–1700. Arthur W. Wellington.

This lower section of a press cupboard is shown because it seems likely it was made by the same person who made the preceding. It is owned by a Weston resident, the same town as the preceding. This may be only a coincidence, but at least both seem to be Boston or North Shore pieces. We thus distinguish them from the Plymouth cupboards. The recess between the bottom and top drawers is strikingly similar, as also the little panel left for initials on each. The angular mold on drawers, the bevel of drawers, and the arches are similar.

For the sake of variety the maker placed his pillars, like jars, bottom side up here. Two considerable differences exist. The Paine cupboard has a carved drawer and a saw tooth, or serrated mold under main shelf.

Except on one or two tables, and that in a subdued way, court cupboards offer the only true bulbous turning in American-made furniture.

The drawer bottoms in American cupboards are nearly all pine. They have the side grooves on their oak ends, and the earlier ones are quite often rabbeted rather than dovetailed, an important difference in distinguishing the nationality.

These cupboards are all loosely named court, but it is properly sought to differentiate, and to call those press cupboards which are not open below.

There are two classes of shape of the short cupboard on main shelf, straight front and splayed front.

446. EAMES — NORTH ANDOVER. COURT CUPBOARD. DATED 1684. OAK, GROOVED PANEL DRAWER. FUESSENICH COLLECTION. TORRINGTON, CONNECTICUT.

The great, perhaps supreme importance of this article arises from the fact that the author has succeeded in having the four sets of initials or monograms traced to the original owners, through Gladys M. Salta, in the probate office, Andover, who has a genius for such work. Franklin T. Wood of Rutland, Massachusetts, sold the cupboard to the author. He inherited it from an aunt in North Andover, who found it in a back passage where it was suffering from the weather. It was for long in the Hubbard mansion under the famous elm of the same name in adjoining Boxford. Judge Rollin Harmon (monogram at right), lived there, and apparently had it from his client Hubbard. Robert Eames corresponds with the date (on the little panel). His monogram is on the left. Abigail Poor Foster was Abigail Eames, descendant of Robert (monogram A E at bottom), and married Ephraim Harriman Foster (initials at top). James H. Hubbard must have let Judge Harmon have the piece either as a gift, or more probably it was an unsaleable relic of his estate. They were long close friends, and Harmon administered.

It is unrestored except for the substitution of proper handles, from an old chest, for large late knobs. It still lacks the drops under each meeting of the arches. The traces are clear. One would say it also lacks drops on the top square of the posts.

447. Splayed Concord Court Cupboard. Dated 1689. Philip L. Spaulding, Boston.

The author believes the same person made this and the three pieces preceding, also the Polly Bartlett chest on frame (made 1690), the Samson chest, the Atheneum chest dated 1693, the oak box initialed H. S. (Atheneum), and the court cupboard table shown.

The dates are spread only nine years, and all that are traced at all trace to the North Shore. The Concord cupboard (New Hampshire) once declined at $6, would naturally go up there from eastern Massachusetts. Salem would be the natural place to pitch upon as the origin. There are a few other pieces which have the same earmarks, or should we say hallmarks?

448. Oak Press Cupboard. 1650–60. Very Fully Carved. Pillars Nearly Plain. It Is a Serious Defect that the Doors Are Put on Outside, Like an Afterthought, Spoiling the Architectural Unity. True Arches. Scratch Carved on End Like the Virginia Cupboard. Metropolitan Museum.

In discriminating between American and English oak, these considerations enter in: first, English oak is darker; second, there is a slight difference in the grain which the wise claim to be able to distinguish. The author is not one of them; third, rich elaboration in carving is likely to be foreign; fourth, any pine on an oak piece, as in the drawers or lids, points almost conclusively to America. Conversely, the same is not true, as the sunflower court cupboards and some others have oak interior. Fifth, a wide acquaintance with types found in America is necessary in order to feel the difference when an English piece intrudes. In the last analysis it is a matter of experience and knack. There is at present a cupboard on sale which is obviously English, which the dealer honestly believes to be American. It is a case of lack of experience.

449. "Sunflower" and Tulip Press Cupboard. Yale University. 1660–70.

This corresponds to the chests of the same decoration and with the same provenance, Hartford or Hartford's county. Dentils are cut at an angle and the one at center as a V with a bit of carving. Lacks the drop from center of cornice. Heart motive; applied carving above the four long spindles, very thin. The narrow shelf under pillars on this type is oak about a half inch thick. Seven tulip blocks on cornice. Note the properly long legs. Two doors above, one below. Inside buttons on small knobs. Corner and other blocks and channel molds black. Applied molds, soft wood painted red, or red cedar. Bosses on center of end panels. Small satellites lost. All turnings on court cupboards always black.

450. "Sunflower" and Tulip Press Cupboard. 1660–78. Bought Because It Belonged to the Rev. Jos. Rowlandson, First Minister of Lancaster. He Died in Wethersfield, Connecticut (Next Town to Hartford) Where He Doubtless Acquired the Cupboard before 1678. Found Painted Red, All Over. No Restorations Except Removal of Paint. Very Fine Model for Study of Fat Turnings, Carving and Other Details. All Oak Furniture Was Quartered, as Is Plainly Seen Here. Public Library, Lancaster, Massachusetts.

451. Parmenter Court Cupboard. 1640–60. Wadsworth Atheneum.

Formerly property of the author, like all other pieces credited to the museum, for which the collection was bought by J. P. Morgan, and presented. This beautiful specimen the author pieced, since the bottom was cut off about 1835. The widow of the boy who inherited it, Joshua Parmenter, states that her husband, then a boy of ten, remembered the mutilation. A brass plate bearing his name is kept on the shelf, and is richly deserved. Taken to Sudbury when the Parmenter Tavern was built in 1683. Unique in style. Pine shelves. Carved on ends; no rail under drawers. Inlaid three-eighths of an inch deep. 53¼ x 23 x 52.

While the cupboard opposite is one of the most handsome that below is preferred by some persons. The restorations of the Virginia cupboard are one door (can you tell which?), the drawer, the shelf below, and the tulip carved blocks. A novelist who used this piece in a tale did not know that the drawer was missing, but hinged his plot about the missing door.

452. Virginia Bulbous Court Cupboard. 1640–60. Oak, Southern Pine Shelves and Top. Wadsworth Atheneum.

The full bulbous turning might suggest an English origin were it not for the pine, the top being attached with original pins, and pine interiors. Carving on end as in No. 448. Scalloped rails. Feet partly gone. They were, of course, balls. Found near the estate of Carroll of Carrollton, a remarkable instance of survival. Had probably been given away. Bought a second time by a dealer for a pittance. 48½ x 19 x 48.

453. SPLAYED OAK PRESS CUPBOARD. 1670–90. GEO. DUDLEY SEYMOUR.

On the hood are corbels, often called modillions, which are properly so named only when horizontal and which we have noted on other cupboards. In this case, however, the arrangement is somewhat different. The panel ornaments, on the beveled sides of the cupboard, instead of being in the form of an arch or double arch are here in geometric panel work. On most of the cupboards there is a good deal of channel molding, and this is no exception.

454. STRAIGHT FRONT PRESS CUPBOARD. 1670–90. YALE UNIVERSITY.

This cupboard also was shown in Lyon. He left in his estate another cupboard varying but slightly from this example.

Oak except the drawer bottoms of pine. The parts are made separable as usual. It is interesting to note the statement of Lyon that this cupboard was bought from Durham, Connecticut, the source of No. 465. The origin of the cupboard that Dr. Lyon left in his estate was Madison, Connecticut. 57 x 23¼ x 51½.

455. PRINCE-HOWES PLYMOUTH PRESS CUPBOARD. 1660–70. WADSWORTH ATHENEUM.

The piece that has become celebrated in a suit in which the author was charged with fraud because he bought it for $3000. A two-day trial. The judge, without leaving the bench, gave an opinion destined to be widely used as precedent to the effect that the plaintiff had no case, since the author appeared as a buyer when first asked for advice; since he was taking a chance. It was bought from a small, poor photograph, and the sum paid at the time was in excess of any paid for a piece of American oak. Serrated pattern, traced to Plymouth. Probably made by Kenelm Winslow with the help or knowledge of John Alden. Five or six others exist and several chests.

456. PLYMOUTH COURT CUPBOARD. 1660–70. RESTORED AT BASE, OAK.
METROPOLITAN MUSEUM.

Probably same maker as preceding. As to that we add:

Plymouth in 1660 had but sixty families and the lands were poor. Thomas Prence (spelled also Prince) was Governor when, in 1665, he was called to come to Plymouth to live and continued there in a house, "Plain Dealing," supplied by the colony, till his death in 1673. In his will he devises this cupboard "in my new parlour" to his wife Mary (Howes). She departed for the Cape, and the article was in an old house in Dennis. Pillars interchangeable end for end. Top separates. A number of renewals, including all the ornaments on lower section. Pine drawer bottoms, fronts, and backs. Some believe these parts are spruce in all the series.

457. OAK PRESS CUPBOARD. 1680–90. PILLARS ARE STRAIGHT. JAMES N. H. CAMPBELL, HARTFORD.

These cupboards were the sideboards of their time, and were in the parlor, before that room was differentiated from a dining room. They formed the richer pieces in furniture, and were in many Colonial families of means. Between fifty or sixty are now known, of which the major part are shown. They are now largely in museums. There are a half dozen types, and several unique examples.

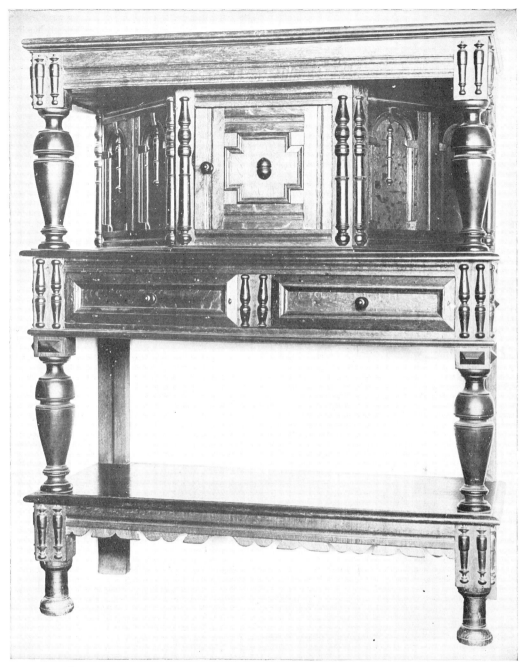

458. SPLAYED OAK COURT CUPBOARD. 1660–90. WAS IN WATERS COLLECTION.

Posts repeated above and below. Resembles in several regards the Eames cupboard, and may have been by the same maker. Somewhat restored. Have never elsewhere seen a horizontal triglyph in this position.

459. SPLAYED OAK COURT CUPBOARD. 1670–80. SAME SLANTED DENTILS AS ARE FOUND ON THE HARTFORD CUPBOARD. PROBABLY SHOULD HAVE TRIGLYPHS ON BOTTOM SQUARE OF POSTS. DRAWER WITHOUT RAIL BELOW, AS OFTEN OCCURS. JAMES N. H. CAMPBELL.

460. Oak Press Cupboard. 1670–90. Dwight Blaney.

Same dentils as on Campbell and Connecticut, aster and tulip pattern. The true arch is not found in American examples, with the exception of a Metropolitan Museum specimen. An amazing number of vertical triglyphs here, twenty-seven.

461. STANTON-CLINTON COURT CUPBOARD. 1660–80. STANTON HISTORICAL HOUSE, CLINTON, CONNECTICUT.

Restored as to its ornaments. One of several in this style found near Clinton, one being in the Brooklyn Museum. Severely plain below. Pillars lack grace. Molding very fully carved and carried around ends. Arched panel on the splay shows indistinctly.

462. SERRATED PLYMOUTH CUPBOARD. 1660–70. HOWARD C. TRACY, PLAINFIELD, NEW JERSEY.

Patience Brewster, daughter of the elder, was aboard the ship "Ann" in 1662. She married Thomas Prence. Their daughter married Stephen Tracy's son John. Stephen came in the "Ann." The cupboard came down in the Tracy family. It varies but little from the Prince-Howes, but has less restoration.

463. Essex Institute Press Cupboard. 1670–90. Oak.

464. Sunflower and Tulip Press Cupboard. 1680–1700. Edwards Dwight Winthrop.

Heirloom in Wheeler family, Fairfield County, Connecticut. Many resemblances to Hartford type, but with the later paneled stiles. Rosettes very attractive feature.

465. DURHAM OAK AND WALNUT PRESS CUPBOARD. 1690–1700. HARTFORD ATHENEUM.

Drawer is beveled like a mold at end, resembling in this the Hadley chest. Restorations in interior and back. Ornaments all walnut, including posts and doweled feet. Large handles new, and wrong.

466. SPOOL-TURNED COURT CUPBOARD. 1690–1700. MRS. J. INSLEY BLAIR.

A light type. Formerly in Historical Society Rooms, New Haven.

467. OAK CARVED CUPBOARD. 1650–70.
METROPOLITAN MUSEUM.

468. ARCHED PANEL CUPBOARD. 1660–80.
METROPOLITAN MUSEUM.

469. INLAID CUPBOARD. 1680–1700.
REV. EDWARD C. STARR, CORNWALL, CONN.

470. WHITE WOOD CUPBOARD. 1690–1710.
(Front View on next page.)

471. Decorated White Wood Press Cupboard. 1690–1710. Drawer with Rail Below. Mrs. G. C. Bryant, Ansonia.

472. CURLY MAPLE PRESS CUPBOARD. 1700. C. W. ARNOLD,
HAVERHILL.

The finest cupboard, not oak, that has come to the author's attention. Pillars are better than the pine press cupboards. An obvious attempt in maple to follow the oak court cupboard. The board construction and all applied molds are the same as in the pine pieces. Eastern New England.

473. Pine Press Cupboard, Applied Moldings. 1690–1710. North Shore or Southern New Hampshire. Wadsworth Atheneum.

No rail below drawer, which would be better made flush with doors. The little posts are probably cherry. There is a wide overhang of top. Simple bootjack ends. Slight traces of decoration, but doubtful. Old butterfly hinges. This is not so good as the other pine and the maple piece. Molds are applied. Section of posts 1½ inches. 51 x 35 x 17. Top is 43½ x 20½. The cupboard lid is molded at the front to match the applied molds.

Of course, the pine court cupboard is a poor relation of its aristocratic oak neighbor. There are those who are very keen for pine. The author never was. It has its place in those sorts of furniture which are naturally made of it, as the ordinary corner or fine shell-top cupboard. But it always suffers when it intrudes on the oak field. A person who prefers it to oak where oak is found indicates a partial taste. The same remarks may apply to maple. An oak chair is not so desirable as one of maple, because maple is the fine American material from which the best chairs of the period 1660–1720 were made.

474. ALL OAK CUPBOARD. 1650–90. OWNED BY THE GLAZIERS OF GLASTONBURY.
F. D. W. GLAZIER IS THE SON.

A truly "fetching" feature in this cupboard is that the lid rises like a chest disclosing a shallow till, the depth of the cornice. The author has never seen another cupboard like this. It stands about shoulder high and is some four feet wide. Evidently a type that has vanished except for this lone example.

This article is in the same house with a Connecticut Sunflower Chest, having the unique feature of an applied mold on the foot, returned on its upper edge.

Regarding the chest just mentioned, it is another case of a traditional importation. Some minor differences from the well-known types are apparent. Philip Doddridge, of theological and musical fame, was an intimate friend of the family and used to write them from England. An inquiry is in progress to learn whether in the quarter whence he wrote there was anything of the kind. It would be notable if the English inspiration of the Hartford chest, certainly made there, should come to light. Perhaps this is the specimen! As we leave court cupboards, a summary may state that they were the great colonial pieces, only rivaled in interest and value by the Goddard secretaries and the Philadelphia highboys.

The construction was largely hewn. The backs and interior of frames and under sides of drawer bottom were left in the rough.

The hinge was a pin into the edge, Egyptian temple door plan! The first were all carved; the next had carving and spindles, and at length there was little, or merely painted ornament.

475. COURT CABINET. 1670–90. MRS. FRANCIS P. GARVAN, NEW YORK.

This piece has been somewhat repaired but is regarded as substantially original. It is believed to be American. It was good enough for the author, at least, to try to obtain. It was long in Albany in the hands of a dealer who is worthy to be written up by the author of Quinneys'.

In the determination of the difference between English and American oak the color is not a sufficient guide. Again, the grain of chestnut is almost precisely like that of some oak. Again, red oak is sometimes used in American furniture; as also bog oak. Live oak has been esteemed in the South for this purpose. There is as much difference in oaks as in men. Some are soft, others hard; some light, others dark; some close, others open. The king of oaks is the white oak for furniture; but when one claims ability to distinguish between American and English white oak, one must prove a good man. A stout insistence is hard to deny. The author is afraid of experts because they are often mistaken. The reputation for knowledge is capital to him who possesses it. One of the keenest judges always claims to know, for why should a judge not be able to render an opinion?

476. Fairbanks House Dresser. Dedham. 1720–50.

This date is named though the house was built in 1636. Built against the wooden partition with no other backing. This wonderful house, our earliest, is public.

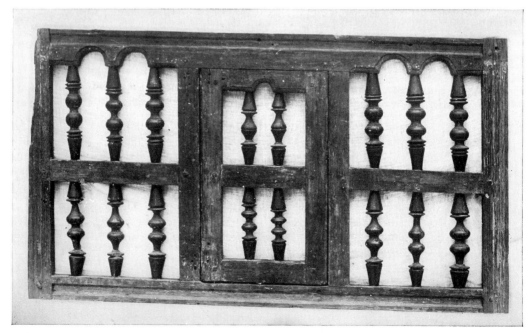

477. Front of Livery Cupboards. 1630–50. George Francis Dow.

Found in the Capen House, Topsfield. Unique American example. Mr. Dow supposes the cupboard was hanging.

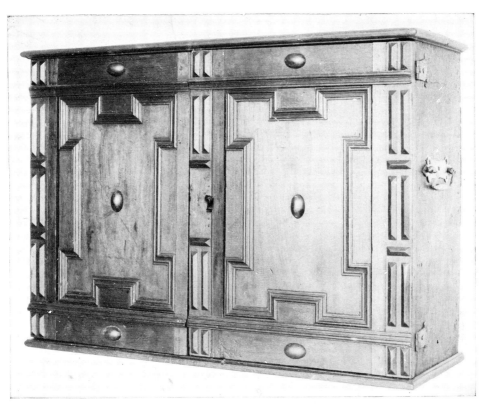

478. Paneled Cabinet. 1680–1700. Apparently Made To Be Set on Table or Frame.
Wadsworth Atheneum.

479. Pine Cupboard. 1700–30. To Hang on Wall.
Hinges Not Original. Formerly the Author's.

480. DECORATED KAS. 1690–1740. KNICKERBOCKER ORIGIN. L. G. MYERS,
NEW YORK CITY.

A very elaborate example. These pieces existed in large numbers up and down the Hudson, but seldom as richly painted. They are marked by immense cornices and feet, and they reach close to the ceiling. Decoration here extends around the ends.

481. Kas. Pine. Said to Have Come from Pennsylvania. Extraordinarily Small Feet.
Curved Cornice. 1710–40. Mrs. Francis P. Garvan.

Handsomely paneled in the period of 1720. Top fine with break and return in the cornice over the stiles, which are paneled with small corner blocks. Oddly enough the base shows four beginnings of pillars and, of course, fails entirely to correspond with the top. This failure to carry through, as the golfers say, is quite a common occurrence in cupboards.

The kas has never been popular as an article to collect. This might not be the case if collectors had great rooms and much bare space. As it is, collectors are jealous of their rooms, which are usually overcrowded anyway.

The hinges were named by the author in a moment of aberration "rat tail," and the name seems to have stuck. It is an unfortunate term in one respect, as there is a spear head at the end of the tail, and I propose here and now to re-christen these "devil tail." It is extremely fashionable to use the devil's name in natural scenery, to which I have always objected. In this case, however, the name seems thoroughly appropriate, and may possibly afford a new element in furniture nomenclature!

This piece is put together entirely with wooden pins. Not only so, but it is arranged as the kas usually is with taper pins to hold the sections together, so that these large pins, or wedges, more properly, may be knocked out and the whole affair disassembled.

482. A Walnut Kas. Diamond Squares Flanking the Ends of the Drawers. The Short Central Mold over the Key-Hole Is Sometimes Designed To Slide, Revealing a Secret Key-Hole. This Example Shows the Extreme to Which the Width and Weight of the Cornice Was Carried. 1710–40. Knickerbocker. Wadsworth Atheneum.

The houses in Pennsylvania being mostly of stone in the early times did not adapt themselves for closets as well as the light interior partition work, common in New England. Hence instead of closets we find large cupboards or wardrobes, and thus their great numbers are explained.

The hinges in the present example are concealed in something the same manner as we find in the court cupboard. The panel work of Pennsylvania is far more elaborate than that of New England. It was quite the thing to cut away from the edge of the face of the panel either a small rabbet-shaped mold, as here shown, or to form scrolls and rounded corners. The same decoration was on occasion applied to the door panels of the dwelling, as may be seen at the Pennsylvania Museum. It is quite frequent to find in Pennsylvania long ranges of cupboard space in the hall, with a series of doors. This was in many ways better than the New England style of plastered partitions for cupboards, and it may even have been more economical. Certainly the results were very satisfactory.

483. Cupboard Built into a Corner. 1745. Benning Wentworth
Mansion, Newcastle, N. H.

The corner post of the house is chamfered and decorated with a finial. The panels are arched at top in Connecticut fashion, and the cupboard is recessed nearly through the thickness of the wall. Unique, so far as known.

The Benning Wentworth house has various features not found elsewhere, since the builder was evidently called upon to do himself proud, and to supply the great Wentworth, a leading political and financial power, with a dwelling that was fit for any governor. There was a huge parlor, the mantel of which we shall show.

 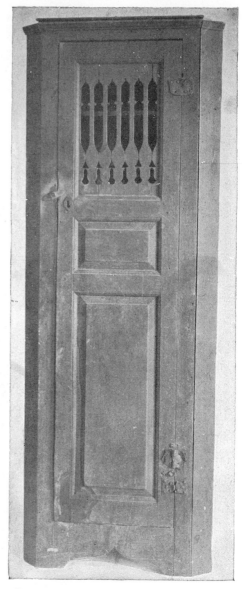

484. HANGING CORNER CUPBOARD. PENN-
SYLVANIA. 18TH CENTURY. J. STOGDELL
STOKES.

485. CORNER CUPBOARD WITH LIVERY
DOOR. 17TH OR EARLY 18TH CENTURY.
FUESSENICH COLLECTION.

(Left.) Hinges are mortised into the door and secured with headed bolts, as is frequent in Pennsylvania, instead of nails. The door panel is formed by grooving out the mold lengthwise and filling in the rails. The door is plain on the inside. The little outside shelf below has a rim about it. The cornice, somewhat heavy, is effective. Owing to its resemblance to cathedral pulpits on pillars, I have named it Pulpit Cupboard. 38 inches long. Pine.

(Right.) A solitary instance, up to the present date, of a door pierced as a reminiscence of the English livery cupboard. Instead, however, of using separated turned spindles, the maker has cut the door into the semblance of series of spindles touching each other. The author considers this a rare and important piece on account of the door. The scheme was carefully thought out so as to allow for half spindles at the sides. Ogee base and the usual small cap-mold.

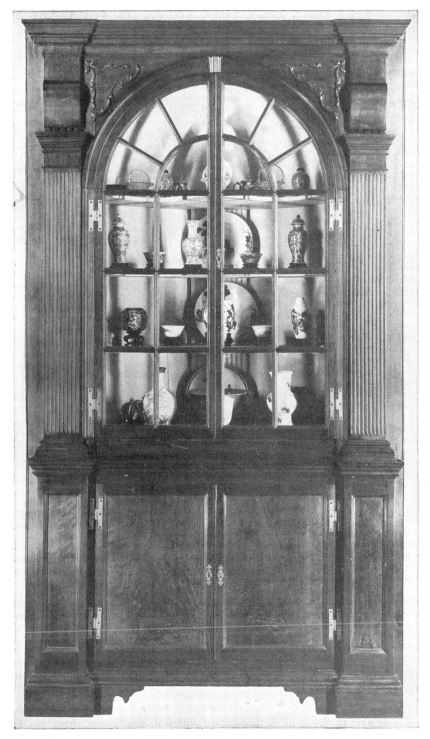

486. Corner Cupboard. Regularly Architectural. Carved Scroll in
Spandrels. Brass H Hinges. Scrolled Bracket at Base. 18th Century.
Howard Reifsnyder.

487. CUPBOARD ON TABLE FRAME. 18TH CENTURY. 61½ x 24 x 12. PINE, PAINTED BLUE. A VERY
RARE INSTANCE OF A STAND MADE FOR A CABINET.

The heavy coved mold of the top is similar to that found on clocks. Somewhat crude cabriole leg may indicate country made. Scrolled frame. The return mold above the drawer affords a proper division.

488. (Right.) NEW ENGLAND CORNER CUPBOARD OF PINE. 1730–50. ROSETTES ABOVE PILASTERS. THE SECOND PAIR OF PILASTERS INSIDE THE CUPBOARD FOLLOW A FASHION QUITE FREQUENT ON PINE PIECES. IT IS USUAL, HOWEVER, TO FIND THEM NARROWER. MRS. FRANCIS P. GARVAN.

It was usual to build the corner cupboard into the room in New England, especially when the back of the piece was rounded. Whether or not this was done, there is found often, as here, a plain flat member back of the pilasters which could meet and continue sheathed paneling in the room.

In the dating of cupboards, the hinges assist, but are not an absolute check. The butt hinge was used from about 1800. Sometimes the H hinge might have been carried over into the 19th century. In this instance the H hinge is scrolled at the ends with a familiar Queen Anne half-round, flanked by horizontals. Door missing on the left.

Another indication of date, of course, is the style of mold. Where, as here, the panel stiles and rail are finished on the inside next the bevel of the panel itself with a quarter-round, either worked on the piece or set in, but preferably the former, we have a type which did not persist after about 1790. A more elaborate mold then came in, but it is not so satisfactory as the earlier type. The base was often arranged to harmonize with the base board around the room. The effect of the built-in cupboard is much more satisfactory. A cupboard built without reference to the room finish never seems quite in place, because cupboards being large must necessarily follow architectural lines. In this respect they differ from all other classes of furniture.

489. CORNER CUPBOARD WITH ANGULAR FRONT, PROTRUDING. OGEE BRACKET FEET. QUEEN ANNE ARCH IN SASH. 18TH CENTURY. H. B. KELLER, LINE LEXINGTON, PA.

The feet of this cupboard would indicate an early date. The cornice could be found at a later date. All in all, the date is somewhat of a puzzle, as the muntins are not the earlier pattern. The piece is peculiar in its obtuse angle front — not a bad idea for gaining depth. It suggests the round fronts, a few instances of which are known. Advantage was taken of this angle by applying a key-stone at the top, although there is no arch. The hinges, apparently original, indicate the close of the 18th century, and therefore the persistence of an earlier style in the foot. Unrestored condition.

490. (Right.) CUPBOARD WITH SPLAYED CORNERS. 18TH CENTURY. MRS. FRANCIS P. GARVAN.

A very complete example. Features of interest are the narrow side panels on the chamfer, which are scrolled at top and bottom. The panels in the doors are similarly scrolled, though the effect is different. The single drawer with doubled panel carries out the scheme. Good ball feet and cornice. The mold covering the meeting of the doors excludes dust as well as the lipped or rabbeted edge of the doors. The devil-tail hinges are so designed to afford an additional brace. It will be seen by the shape of the cornice mold that an endless variety of such molds existed. The bails on the drawers attach directly to wires. The hasp and chain seem old. The feet have been somewhat cut away in the blocking of the plate. They are really a little larger.

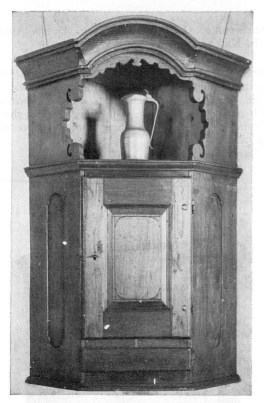

491. HANGING. OPEN. SCROLL TOP. RARE
OR UNIQUE. 18TH CENTURY. J. STOGDELL
STOKES.

492. CUPBOARD. THREE DRAWERS
BELOW. PINE. 18TH CENTURY.
WADSWORTH ATHENEUM.

493. ST. ANDREWS-CROSS DOORS.
CORNICE CUT OFF. 18TH CENTURY.
LUCY A. ROYCE.

494. SPOON RACK AND KNIFE BOX. SCROLLED
AND MOLDED. 23¼ x 13½ x 5¼.
18TH CENTURY.

495. Carved and Scrolled Panel. All Pine. Rare. 1710–40. Edward C. Wheeler, Jr.

496. WALNUT. GOOD KEYSTONE. SCROLLED. PANELED PILASTERS. 18TH CENTURY. PENNSYLVANIA.

498. (Right.) Coved Cupboard. Pine. 18th Century. Edward C. Wheeler, Jr.

Several pieces with this interesting but simple coving of the endboard have been found. It will be noticed that in this instance the coving appears also in the reverse just above the shelf, thus forming an elongated C. The light molding at cornice and base is frequent on New England pieces. The same scroll is sometimes found on a settle. Rhode Island origin.

This peculiar cove is found in a cut of a bed of European 16th century period. It is somewhat surprising that it was not used to greater extent. A practical difficulty has always existed in bringing design and workmanship together in the same person. The 18th century carpenter-architects knew both style and construction and worked with their own hands as foremen of their own crews, but ordinarily dwellings and furniture are built by men who have no access to designs or who are too indolent or conceited to give themselves the trouble to find designs.

499. Beautiful Design. Pateræ and Intaglio Urns. 1720–50.
Sherwood Rollins.

500. LARGE, SCROLL TOP. BUTTON ROSETTES. DENTILS. FLUTED PILASTERS.
18TH CENTURY. THE ODD CAPITALS ARE FORMED BY A SERIES OF SMALL
HOLES OVER THE FLUTED PILASTERS. A. H. RICE, BETHLEHEM, PA.

501. COCKED-HAT CUPBOARD WITH DRAWERS.
18TH CENTURY.

502. HANGING CUPBOARD.   CRUDE SCROLLS.
18TH CENTURY.

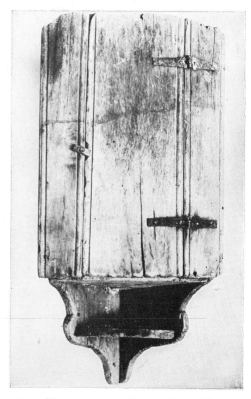

503. HANGING.   HEART-SCROLLED TOP.
18TH CENTURY.

504. HANGING, WITH SCROLL-SHELF BELOW.
18TH CENTURY.

505. Large. Corner. Ogee Scroll.
18th Century. Note Molded Edge.
Morris Schwartz.

506. Wardrobe, with Drawer. Bracket
Feet. 18th Century.
Howard Reifsnyder.

507. Small Wall Cupboard. Very Rare.
1720–50. J. Stogdell Stokes.

508. Rare. Small. Hanging or for Placing
on Side Table. Origin Unknown.

509. FIREPLACE WALL. ROBINSON HOUSE, WETHERSFIELD. 1737.
MANTEL PERHAPS AN ADDITION.

510. PANEL WORK IN METROPOLITAN MUSEUM. FROM CONNECTICUT. 1730–55.

The cupboard opposite has a beautifully scrolled fanlight at the top of the door. The piece was evidently made by a person with a good deal of feeling for style. 48 x 67 x 20½. Semicircular back. In spite of width the sides returning to the wall and the front broken as it is with details, it does not seem broad, but graceful. The four shelves are indented in curve lines in reverse.

511. SIDE LIGHTS. SPOOL DECORATION. DOUBLE DENTILS. ROSETTE. 1750–70. A VERY
BEAUTIFUL AND PERFECT DESIGN. SLIGHT CARVING. HL HINGES. WILLIAM B. GOODWIN.

512. Pine. Unique. Early 18th Century. From Massachusetts. 78 x 52 x 18. Opening 19 x 52. William B. Goodwin.

Top has a curious double cornice. The shell top is carved from a single block over a foot thick. A feature hitherto unknown to the author. Great apparent height is given by the unbroken pilasters. The owner places the date in the late 17th century.

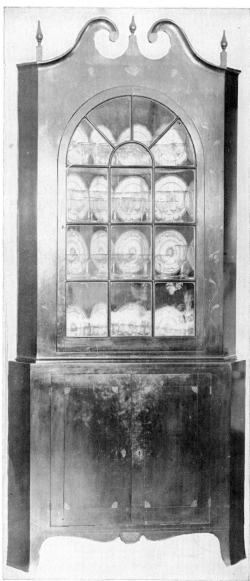

513. (Right.) Inlay on Lower Doors (Very Unusual), on Base Scroll, and Upper Section. Delicate Scrolled Top. 1790–1810. Morgan B. Brainard, Hartford.

We used to see a large number of these cupboards, mahogany, with inlay, in Pennsylvania. They have now been acquired for private collections. But the inlaid scroll at the sides of the door in this specimen is unusually good.

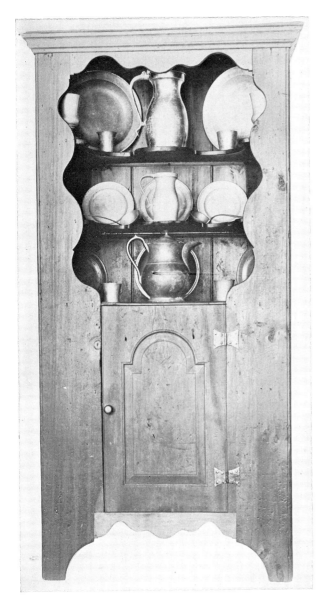 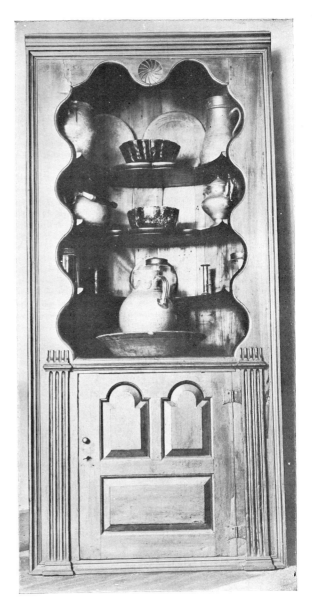

514. Back Corners Chamfered. Wave-Line Opening. Original Hinges. Door Restored. Mid-18th Century. 77½ x 37½. Wadsworth Atheneum.

The name pewter cupboard is getting to be the designation for these narrow, unpainted, open-top cupboards. The probable explanation is that they were not rich enough for china and were in general use before the day when rich china came into use.

515. (Right.) Serpentine Open Top. Queen Anne Panel Below. Spiral Rosette at Top. 1730–70. E. C. Wheeler, Jr.

Architecturally speaking, of course, the stopping of the pilaster is a kind of abortion which might have been overcome by two or three inches more space on each side. There are three ways of finishing the backs of these cupboards — one is to let them run at right angles into the corner, which is unusual; one is to cut off the corners with long chamfers. This is the more usual. One is to make the back a semicircle. This is the style of the fine later pieces, especially of those that are built in.

516 AND 517. PENNSYLVANIA CUPBOARDS ARRANGED ONE ABOVE THE OTHER. 18TH CENTURY.
THE LOWER ONE MAY HAVE SERVED AS A WASHSTAND. IT IS VERY QUAINT. THE UPPER
ONE HAS CHAMFERED AND MOLDED CORNERS. WADSWORTH ATHENEUM.

518 AND 519. PENNSYLVANIA CUPBOARDS. ARRANGED TO CORRESPOND. HINGE ABOVE MORTISED. FINE HINGES BELOW. THIS DECORATION WITH TWO CUPBOARDS IS EFFECTIVE. 18TH CENTURY. WADSWORTH ATHENEUM.

520. (Right.) CORNER FRAME WITH CUPBOARD OVER. 1720–30. METROPOLITAN MUSEUM.

The author is not aware whether this combination was original. If so, it would seem that this beautiful corner table does not perfectly match the chamfered cupboard. Furthermore, the small shelves above are usually below. Is it possible that the doors have been reversed, and that the pieces did not go together? The cupboard itself is one of the best of its kind, and so is the table.

522. Pine. 18th Century. Pennsylvania Museum.

521. Pine Door. Oak Frame. Pennsylvania Museum.

523. Fully Carved around Casing as Well as about the Frame. Same Design Repeated on Both. Pilasters without Logical Termination. 1730–50. Katrina Kipper.

The heart between the upper and lower cupboards is an applied decoration of questionable desirability in this connection, since it is a mere outline not corresponding with any other feature. The break of the inner casing at the top of the lower door, and the widening of the upper over the lower cupboard is an interesting detail. The break in the pilaster is evidently designed to match in spacing the top of the lower door. It is the only example known to the author in which the edges of the shelves are carved. Of course, the hinges below are not original. Four panels in so small a door show careful attention to complete decoration.

524. (Right.) Walnut. 1740–50. One of the Most Beautiful Small Examples. Metropolitan Museum.

Very unusual arrangement in placing the pilasters on the chamfered corner. A nice piece of work in arranging the details as a complete architectural unit. The doors above and below correspond in their tops with the Queen Anne arch, one in wood, one in glass.

525. Shell Carved, Carved Pilasters. Scroll-Top Panels in Door. Finest Specimen Known. 1720–40. Jaffrey House, Portsmouth. House Now Destroyed. Unusual Height. Boston Museum of Fine Arts.

526. SHELL TOP. OUTSIDE DOOR CONNECTICUT CROSS. 1752. COLONIAL DAMES, WETHERSFIELD.

Absolutely original condition. Webb House is public. Door on opposite side of fireplace into passage matches this. Small pilasters within nearly hidden.

527. PINE. 1740–50. 92 x 53 x 15. WILLIAM B. GOODWIN.

The carved tree of life capitals and the twin flowers on stem are extraordinary features. The interior is a frame with hickory laths, plastered, and originally painted a deep blue. The over-board is a restoration. Unique, so far as known.

528. (Right.) UNRESTORED. PINE. THREE ROWS OF SEVEN PANELS EACH CUT FROM THE SOLID. 1730–50.

The author bought this of Wineck in Hartford about 1915. It is a very rare specimen with a crude shell and large rosette. It is now in the Wentworth-Gardner House, Portsmouth, New Hampshire.

Since the cupboard was apparently built in originally and had been removed carelessly, a simple cornice was restored.

529. Wide, with Shell and Connecticut-Type Scrolled Panel Doors. 1730-50. Metropolitan Museum.

The extraordinary width of this piece exceeds that of any shell top that has come to the author's attention. It is probable that the width accounts for the two doors, since one is the rule with shell-top cupboards.

The remarkable panel of the lower doors is found in some other instances. As it seems to suggest a broken arch, it might be challenged by a purist since there is no call for an arch. Yet the effect is pleasing if we forget to ask the origin.

We notice a great many instances in which the pilaster capital gave difficulty with the cornice as here. In some cases the capital stood in mid air supporting nothing. This was evidently a construction for which the makers often lacked a model. In this cupboard the returned or chamfered end, which is built on an angle to strike the wall squarely, is fluted as well as the front pilaster.

The simple rosette on the keystone is effective, and better in this connection than one more elaborate.

530. (Right.) A Shell-Top, Carved Cupboard. With Pilasters and Three Long Upright Panels on Lower Door. 1740-55. I. Sack, Boston.

The student will note that the greater part of the shell cupboards are set behind paneling with a long door. The consequence is a mixture of elements and a hiding of very good features. For instance, in No. 529 a little pilaster each side of the shell is clearly evident. When, however, there is panel work set in front of the cupboards, and a long door, as in No. 526, the effect of this pilaster is lost. It would appear that the fashion of paneling the whole room came in just after the cupboards. The long door covering the whole cupboard is never so good as the arrangement seen on this page. The shell on its face in No. 529 is finished with a raised edge, whereas in No. 530 there is no projection. At the hub or hinge of the shell there was rarely a floral scroll, but more often a smaller applied shell or sunburst above a half-round knob.

531. DINING ROOM OF QUINCY HOMESTEAD. 1730–50. OPEN TO THE PUBLIC. FINE SHELL-TOP CUPBOARD NOT SET CORNERWISE. THIS IS MORE FREQUENT THAN THE CORNER CUPBOARD.

532. OVER-MANTEL CUPBOARD. 1717. THE DRAWING IN OF THE CHIMNEY OVER FIREPLACE AFFORDED SPACE FOR CUPBOARD. WILLIAMS HOUSE, SOUTH EASTON, MASSACHUSETTS.

533. SHELL TOP FORMED BY ATTACHING RIBS OVER PLAIN SURFACE. EXCELLENT MODILLION KEYSTONE. THE CORNICE ABOVE HAS THREE BREAKS AND RETURNS. THE DENTILS ARE COMPOUND AND ARE NARROWER ON THE PROJECTIONS THAN ON THE MAIN CORNICE. THE PILASTERS HAVE STOPPED FLUTES. THE CONSTRUCTION SUGGESTS THE POSSIBILITY OF AN ORIGINAL LONG DOOR. 1735-55. I. SACK.

534. (Right.) PINE. DOUBLE DENTIL ARCH AND DENTIL CORNICE. 1740-70. MRS. FRANCIS P. GARVAN.

It is an excellent feature to arrange the pilaster to follow through to the floor by a break in the base mold as here. There is a misty effort to recollect the compound ogee foot found on some chests of drawers.

The so-called cathedral top door, formed by intersecting arch of the muntin gives some difficulty in dating. The motive was very popular in Sheraton glass-top secretaries. We feel little hesitancy, however, in deciding that the same type of door must have been used for a considerable period before the Sheraton time.

Where the H hinge was used on fine woods it was made of brass. On pine it was of iron and was painted over white. There was no effort to call attention to it, but rather to render it inconspicuous.

535. Parlor of Sparhawk House, Kittery, Maine. 1740–50. Shell Top Each Side of Fireplace.

536. Cupboard on Cupboard. J. H. Halford.

537. Scrolled Back and Ends. 18th Century. I. Sack.

538. Pine. Two Long Doors Arched. 1735. From Eastern Shore, Maryland. The Material, of Course, Is Southern Pine. 99 x 60 x 18. Wm. B. Goodwin.

From the General French Tilghman House. He was on Washington's staff, and inherited the house from his grandmother.

The rare construction is found here of using a wedge-shaped block similar to the keystone to spring the arch from the pillars.

539. (Right.) Cupboard on Cupboard. 18th Century. Pennsylvania. J. H. Halford.

Interesting checker work below the main door and especially three rows on door above. Each checker is reeded, and every other one is horizontal. The same reeding occurs in the cornice above dentils and also flanking the drawers. Whether these cupboards have been used separately we do not know. The drawing in of the molding at the bottom of the top section suggests that it might have been raised in the corner above the other part. It would thus be very effective. There would otherwise seem to be no significance in this base mold, nor in the separation of the two pieces in construction.

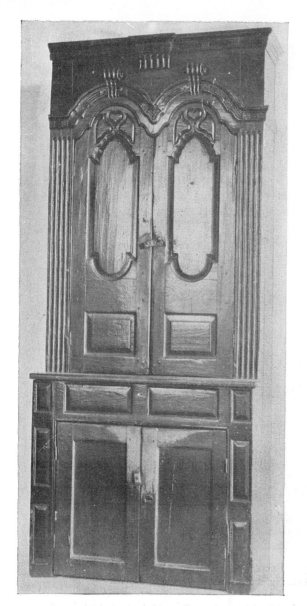 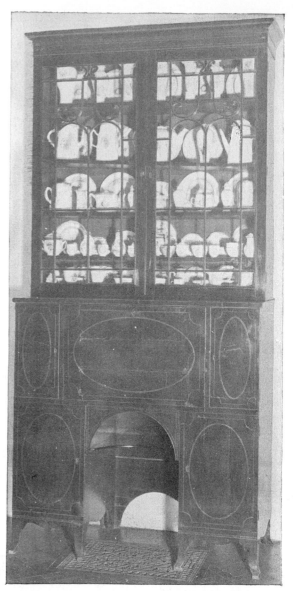

540. Pine. Origin Unknown. 18th Century. Queen Anne Molds, Heart Motive.
Frank A. Robart.

The shape of this mold about the panel is somewhat like that of a piece found in Brattleboro. We are not prepared to name any probable origin. The elaborateness of the work on pine, and especially the keystones, suggest a different center of influence from those with which we are acquainted.

541. (Right.) Hepplewhite. Mahogany Inlay, with Large Ovals. French Foot. 1800.
Mrs. Francis P. Garvan.

The foot suggests a period later than a Hepplewhite. In the piece belonging to the author, with a foot of this description, the date 1803 was found on a drawer. The knee hole in the form of an arch and with a recessed shelf carries out, with the arch against the floor line behind, the suggestion of the ovals of the inlay. The cornices on mahogany pieces of this date were very much restrained.

543. BROKEN PEDIMENT. 1790–1800. CLIFFORD S. DRAKE.

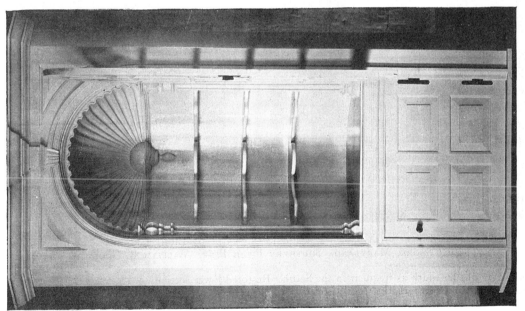

542. SHELL TOP. 1750. MORGAN B. BRAINARD.

On previous page the base of No. 542 is restored. A fine specimen. The piece following it is made in two parts. The blown glass is inserted with a mold having a narrow line of inlay through the center. Line inlay about the entire piece and inlaid medallions or shells and fans.

544. Sunburst or Simple Shell Dome Formed by a Series of Light Grooves. 1735-50. From Eastern Shore, Maryland. Southern Pitch Pine. William B. Goodwin.

Unusual height for width as frequent in the South. Restored lower section. 111 x 50 x 21. The dome is formed by strips of wood radiating from the center. This is a fashion which the author has not seen in the North.

545. (Right.) Walnut. Scroll Top. 1750-70. This Piece, Said To Come from New England, Is Very Beautiful. Mrs. Francis P. Garvan.

The lines of the scroll are excellent, and the inner curve coming down from the rosette and meeting its opposite on the base of the central flame is an excellent device, which requires to be small owing to the narrowness of the piece. The rosette has the kidney center such as is often found on the cartouche. In this position we have not thitherto noticed this. The construction of the top is quite like that of a highboy.

546. APPLIED SPINDLES WITH CROSSHATCHED CENTRAL SECTION. SCROLLED TOP WITH TURNED ROSETTES. 1790–1800. GUY BEARDSLEY, HARTFORD.

The central ornament is carried down with a spindle section on the face of the cupboard. Three incised turned blocks at the bases and the apex of the arch. In the late cupboards we see a reducing in size and a simplifying of the urns. In the crosshatching there is the suggestion of the same molding seen on bed posts.

547. (Right.) SCROLL TOP. FULL SPIRAL COLUMNS BELOW AND ABOVE. 1790–1810. H. W. ERVING.

The columns are exceedingly rare. They end with a little scroll reminiscent of the Ionic capital. The middle finial support is made on the same plan. An incised turned block below this ornament is like that on the previous number. The spiraling comes down from each side on the center ornament ending in V's. The rosettes are carved. It is unusual to find with this late foot so many carved features.

548. Demi-Dome Plastered. 1730. Marsh House,
Wethersfield. Now in Webb House.

549. Pewter Cupboard; Ogee Scroll. 1720–50.
Wadsworth Atheneum.

550. Spinning Attic. 1760.

551. 17th Century Parlor.

552. MAHOGANY, EAGLE INLAY UNDER FLAME. 1780–1800. MRS. FRANCIS P. GARVAN.

553. PINE, HEAVY CHAMFER, DATED 1770. BROOKS REED.

Of course the demand for a mahogany corner cupboard was influenced by the coming in of fine china. Most of these importations occurred after the Revolution. Numerous small cupboards were built purposely to agree with the delicacy of the china. That is to say, we can tell when we look at the cupboard what its purpose was. If it was pine and unpainted, it was for the kitchen, and to hold pewter or ordinary ware. If it was rich or ornate, it belonged in the parlor and was correspondingly used for rare pieces. Old homes would look very much better if owners would bear these facts in mind. The placing of an unpainted pine piece in a richly finished room is obviously inappropriate.

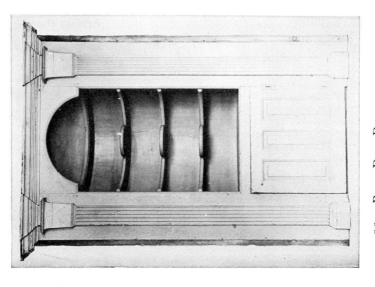

554. Pine, Demi-Dome. 1740-50.

555. (Center.) Pine. 1730-50. 84 x 54 x 22.
Mrs. Francis P. Garvan.

556. Pine. 1740-60. Fine Dentil Work
on This and the Preceding. W. A.
Hitchcock, Farmington, Connecticut.

557. PENNSYLVANIA. 18TH CENTURY.
ARTHUR W. WELLINGTON, WESTON.

558. SCROLL SASH. 1790. MRS. FRANCIS P. GARVAN.

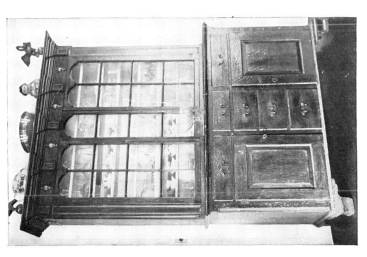

559. PENNSYLVANIA. 18TH CENTURY. GOOD
DESIGN. 89 x 58 x 19. C. R. MORSON.

560. INLAID, DECORATED TOP. 1790. THIS PIECE IS INTERESTING BECAUSE THE TOP LOOKS LIKE A CRENELLATED CASTLE WITH EMBRASURES. STYLES SOMETHING LIKE THIS ARE COMMON IN ENGLAND. THE CHIEF CHARACTERISTIC IS A VERY LARGE GEOMETRICAL SCROLL OR OVAL OUTLINE OF INLAY, AND FILLED ON EACH SIDE WITH PARTI-COLORED VENEERS. PALMER COLLECTION. I. SACK.

561. (Right.) INLAID AND VENEERED, FRENCH FOOT. 1790–1800. HELEN T. COOKE.

This piece and its compeers depend mostly upon the figure in the inlay and veneer. The piece is very gay in appearance and makes its presence felt. In this instance the contrasts are very strong and effective. It is necessary in pieces of this sort, even though they be antique, to keep the surface in perfect condition, since the beauty depends on surface rather than line. Of course, the advantage in early pieces was, since the work was all done by hand, it was never necessary to make two pieces alike. In fact, it was part of the pride of the cabinetmaker to vary his work for the sake of individuality.

562. PINE. 18TH CENTURY.
NEW ENGLAND. 33 x 21½ x 12.
MRS. FRANCIS P. GARVAN.

563. 18TH CENTURY. SCROLLS RESEM-
BLE NOTHING FAMILIAR. FLAYDERMAN
AND KAUFMAN.

564. BALL FOOT, ARCH TOP. 18TH CENTURY.
W. F. HUBBARD, HARTFORD.

565. SILVER CABINET. ALEXANDRIA, VA.
CHERRY. 26 x 22. SECRET DRAWER.
H. W. ERVING.

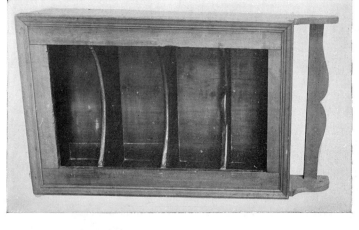

568. WATER BENCH, PENNSYLVANIA. 18TH CENTURY OR EARLY 19TH. SCROLL TOP, THREE DRAWERS. DRAWERS BEVELED.

567. PINE. 18TH CENTURY. PENNSYLVANIA. THE BAR STANDS FREE FROM WALL; USED AS HANGER.

566. WALNUT. 18TH CENTURY. CUT-AWAY SCROLLS ON PANELS. ORIGINAL HINGES. PENNSYLVANIA. WADSWORTH ATHENEUM.

The water bench is a peculiar feature of Pennsylvania whence it penetrated somewhat into southern New York. The one shown above is better than usual, with some little attempt at decoration. It has attained a considerable vogue among collectors of pine as a sort of small dresser, on which pewter or pottery may be set forth. Really it belongs in a kitchen or the wash room.

We ought to distinguish between age and style, and not consider a thing is of any importance unless it has at least some element of decoration. An instance came to the author's attention of the sale of an absolutely plain board cupboard, cut off square at the top and bottom, with modern butt hinges and lacking any feature whatsoever of design or decoration. Yet the buyer thought she had an antique because she had heard that cupboards were desirable. It was precisely such a piece as a carpenter builds today, and for a fraction of the collector's investment. In collecting one must either have some feeling for style or, merely desiring to be in fashion, must have the advice of one who does have that feeling.

The fatuous direction to the person who answers newspaper correspondents, "consult an expert" leads nowhere. Where is the expert? If he is a dealer he is selling his own goods. If he is not a dealer, the question is embarrassing, because, unless he takes time to make certain regarding the antiquity of the piece, he is likely to be running into serious trouble for the future. There is no professional appraiser of antique furniture, though some persons act in that capacity on occasion. An instance recently occurred of the appraisal of a Hadley chest at $100. Even then it was worth $2000. On the other hand, had an expert in antiques appraised, he would very likely have been a prospective customer. Letters come to the author daily wanting to know what an article is worth. He steadfastly declines to give any opinion. It is a most thankless task. Almost always the inquirer is disappointed.

571. Spice Cupboard, Hanging. 18th Century. Sunburst with Miniature Repetition Below of the Same. Such Pieces Are Very Desirable for Wall Decoration. They Have not Received Adequate Attention. Francis D. Brinton, W. Chester, Pa.

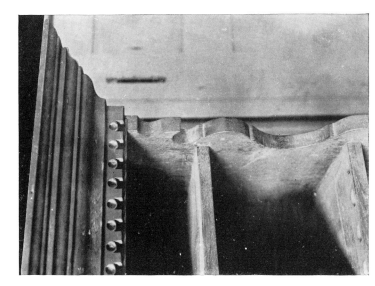

570. Detail. Pennsylvania Dresser. Dentil Ornament and Molding Contour Very Clear. The Conventional Scroll Consists of a Series of Curves Alternately Reversed. With a Short Plain Section. This Motive Is Found North and South. A. H. Rice, Bethlehem.

569. Queen Anne Cabinet. 1720–40. Walnut. Fine Decorated Panel. Cut from the Solid. There Were Two Locks. Found in Virginia. Scroll Partly Restored. Probably a Jewel Case. Small. Sets on a Chest of Drawers. Wallace Nutting.

572. DRESSER. 1730–90. A FINE PENNSYLVANIA TYPE. SCALLOPED CORNICE. GUARD RAILS. PROPER LARGE KNOBS BELOW. SCROLLED ON CORNICE SECTION. CHARACTERISTIC. ARTHUR W. WELLINGTON.

573. Dresser. Scrolled Cornice and End Boards. Rests on Shoes. This Type Is in Two Parts Ordinarily. Spoon Rack on Lower Shelf. 1740–80. Shreve, Crump and Low.

574. NORTH SHORE DRESSER. CORNICE WITH PLAIN EDGE AS USUAL IN NEW ENGLAND. KNOBS ALWAYS SMALL IN THAT REGION. 1740–90. OFTEN BUILT IN. THESE DRESSERS WERE SOMETIMES MOVABLE. IN THAT CASE THEY WERE SMALL, AS A RULE. HINGES SHOULD BE H OR IN VERY EARLY EXAMPLES EXTREMELY RARE, BUTTERFLY. WADSWORTH ATHENEUM.

575. PINE. LARGE. 1740–90. HINGES MODERN AND, PRESUMABLY, PULLS ALSO. SHELVES WITH MOLDED EDGE. SPOON RACKS SCARCELY FOUND IN NEW ENGLAND. CORNICE END NOT ORIGINAL OR PROPER. MAIN CORNICE GOOD EXAMPLE OF FULL DEVELOPMENT. BOARDS OF BACK USUALLY SHIP LAPPED, SOMETIMES TONGUED AND GROOVED. BROOKS REED.

576. North Shore Dresser. 1730–70. Drawers with Lips. Slide over Right Door. Top Said to Have Been Found in Attic. Top Scroll Board Somewhat Suspicious. Poorly Designed at Center. Wadsworth Atheneum.

577. Pine Wardrobe. Middle Panel Carved from the Solid. Rare. 1720–40.
Shape of Narrow Panels at Top of Door Suggest the Date, Which May Be Named
Too Early. Edward C. Wheeler, Jr.

578. Combined Wardrobe and Chest of Drawers. Walnut. 1730–80. The Two Arched Doors, One Long, One Short, Suggest, in Their Queen Anne Type, the Earlier Date. A Very Large Specimen and Perhaps Unique. If the Handles Are Original, of Course the Piece Cannot Belong to the Earlier Date. J. H. Halford. At Fred Allen's Jeffersonville Hotel, Norristown, Pennsylvania.

579. WARDROBE FROM PENNSYLVANIA. 1730–70. THE STYLE WOULD ALMOST WARRANT THE DESIGNATION OF A KAS. BUT THE LINES ARE A LITTLE LIGHTER, AND THE DENTILS ADD GRACE. C. C. LITTLEFIELD, NEWFIELDS, NEW HAMPSHIRE.

581. Pine Cupboard from Westtown, Chester County, Pennsylvania. Late 18th Century. Gertrude S. Camp, Whitemarsh, Pennsylvania.

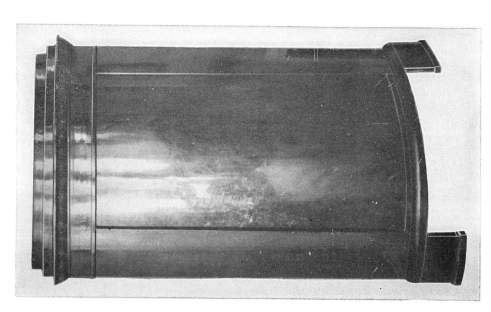

580. Mahogany Corner Wardrobe. Carved Cornice. Late 18th or Early 19th Century. Adolph G. Breitenstein, Providence.

582–86. Parlor Lee Mansion, Marblehead. Corner Cupboard, Box on Table Brought by Pilgrims, Fine Mantel, Dutch Chairs.

587. Pine Desk. Maple Frame. 1680–1700. Original Butterfly Hinges. Heavy Early Type. The Piece Is Small. Probably Reversed on Base, as Wear on Stretcher Comes on Wrong Side Stretchers Molded. Dovetails Very Obvious. Very Rare. Rhode Island School of Design.

588. PINE WITH MAPLE MIDDLE STRETCHER. 1710–30. BOOK REST ON THIS AND PREVIOUS PIECE. OPENING IN BOOK REST WAS FOR THE HASP, NOW LOST, WHICH CONNECTED WITH THE LOCK. ORIGINAL BUTTERFLY HINGES. THE MIDDLE STRETCHER MUCH MORE CONVENIENT BECAUSE IT GIVES LEG ROOM. 38½ x 29¼ x 22¾. WADSWORTH ATHENEUM.

589. WALNUT MIDDLE STRETCHER DESK. TURNING, BETWEEN THE SPOOL AND THE BALL STYLES. TOP REMOVABLE. HANDLES TOO LATE. 1710–30. I. SACK.

A lid opening upward does not give leg room. These pieces are too high to use with an ordinary chair. The turning suggests Pennsylvania style, but the same turnings have been found in New England. They resemble those on the next piece, except that the latter required longer legs and another element was added. The rests for the lid are molded to correspond with the mold of the drawer. The interiors of pieces of this era show very simple cabinets, scarcely worth detailing.

590. WALNUT, STRETCHER FRAME, FROM PENNSYLVANIA. EXCELLENT LOCAL TURNINGS. 1700–30. PLAIN INTERIOR. LID REST HAS LIP ALL AROUND WHICH WOULD SCAR LID UNLESS PULLED OUT FULL LENGTH.

591. WALNUT, QUEEN ANNE, BALL FEET. 1700.

592. PINE. MAPLE FRAME. 1700.

593. Turned Outside Stretchers. Stamped Brasses. Butterfly Hinge. Double Arch Mold about Drawer. 1710–20. Chauncey C. Nash.

Some desks are built with table frame, as this on which the desk box is set. In other desks the frame runs through the top. There is perhaps no choice. The box here is nailed together, and the piece is precisely like the so-called Bible box type. Where the frame is one with the desk a heavy dovetail is usual. It will be seen that the turning of the stretchers is a precise duplication of that of the legs.

594. A Cross Stretcher with Onion, or, as They Are Called in England, Bun Turnings. 1690–1700. Original Hinges. Pine. Single Arch about Drawer and Frame. The Turning Which Resembles the Next Number and That of a 17th Century Table Known to Be of New England Origin, Also Closely Resembles a Chair Table with Cross Stretchers Which, However, Is of Jersey Origin. Frame 29¾ x 19¼. The Whole Piece 33½ x 31¾ x 19¾. Edward C. Wheeler, Jr., Boston.

Attention is called in Lyon to the ancient spelling of box backward, scob, the c standing for x, to denote a desk. The French scriptoire is a name having the advantage of defining itself, like our more awkward writing desk. Our word bureau is a direct borrowing from the French, and with an erroneous application to a chest of drawers. A bureau is properly a writing desk, and originated the use of the word in connection with an office in charge of important work.

The use of the quill pen was universal during the period of all our desks, and it is shown on some of them. Of course the pen knife got its name from its use in "mending" the pen, that is, cutting back the nib to form a new point.

595. Walnut, Cross Stretcher. Single Arch Mold about Drawer. 1690–1700. Dovetailed Frame. Butterfly Hinges. This Piece Is so Like the Preceding in Turning as to Indicate That One Is a Copy of the Other, Although This Piece Is the Larger. Wadsworth Atheneum.

There was often but not always a finial attached at the intersection of the cross stretchers. A large dowel sawed off can often be detected at this point, and indicates the loss of a finial, since it was not required to bind the cross together. In the previous piece the stretcher end is rounded as we have not elsewhere seen it where it is pierced by a dowel for the feet. A large dowel runs from the foot through the stretcher and up into the leg. The shape of the stretcher end on the piece above is observed to be angular, as usual. The resemblance between these pieces and the highboy bases is striking especially in one instance, the construction is strong enough when the corner post is in one piece, but here as always in this type the leg appears to be attached with a dowel, and the pieces become shaky in time.

It is probable that the small number of these pieces is accounted for from the desire for greater drawer space. We therefore find the William and Mary and Queen Anne types with frames running close to the floor and filled entirely with drawers. The lid opening outward, a thought which apparently did not occur to builder until about seventeen hundred, there was abundant leg room. From this time on we find more elaborate examples, but in every case the heavy turned foot persists, until we have passed the Queen Anne period.

596. QUEEN ANNE DESK ON FRAME. 1730–40. FRAME SCROLLED IN THE STYLE OF A HIGHBOY BASE. S. PRESCOTT FAY, BOSTON.

597. STANDARD DESK. J. S. STOKES.

598. INLAID. 1790. CLIFFORD S. DRAKE.

599. BALL FOOT, SLANT TOP, TEARDROP HANDLE. CABINET WITH SCROLL FRONTS IN PART.
1700–10. HORATIO H. ARMSTRONG, HARTFORD, CONNECTICUT.

It will be noted that there is a kind of shoe or cushion under the ball foot with an enlarging taper as the floor is approached. Apparently this was a device to secure greater height, though it may be that the maker thought the turning added to the grace of the piece.

These pieces mostly have a blind drawer at the top just under the slant lid writing section. In this case access is had by a sliding lid which is part of the floor of the cabinet. The characteristic of the ball-foot pieces is a heavy base mold returning on the ends to the back. The cabinet, while straight in the central portion, has a scrolled division at each end slanting backward to agree with the general slant of the lid. The drawers outside these divisions are scrolled. But the scroll is never in the form of a block in this period.

600. BASE TURNED LIKE LOWBOY. 1700. I. SACK.   601. MAPLE. 1700–30. MARY M. SAMPSON.

602. PENNSYLVANIA. WALNUT. WILLIAM AND MARY. 1710-20. J. STOGDELL
STOKES.

603. Button Feet. 1700–30. W. F. Hubbard.

604. Dutch Feet. 1700–30. J. Stogdell Stokes.

605. Straight Ball Feet. 1730–60.
Morris Schwartz.

606. Button Feet. Scalloped. 1700–30.
Geo. S. Palmer.

607. CABRIOLE, TASTEFUL SCROLL. BUTTON FEET BEHIND. 1730–50. GEO. S. PALMER.

608. UNIQUE. FIVE SHELLS. CLAW FOOT. CARVED BASE.
1750–70. SAM WINECK.

609. BANDY LEG. LOW FRAME. SCROLLED SKIRT.
1730–60. MRS. HARRY L. F. LOCKE.

610. FIVE BALL FEET. UNIQUE. WALNUT. 1710–20. HOWARD REIFSNYDER.

611. OGEE FOOT. BLOCK RETURNING ON TOP DRAWER. 1760–70.

612. KNEE HOLE. STRAIGHT BRACKET. 1760–70. MAHOGANY. 44 x 23 x 21¾. FINELY
PARTITIONED. SECRET COMPARTMENT. ALL ORIGINAL. JAMES DAVIDSON.

613. KNEE HOLE. OGEE FEET. FLUTED QUARTER COLUMNS. 1760–70. RARE, OWING
TO INTERIOR QUARTER COLUMN. J. W. BERRY & SON, BALTIMORE.

614. BLOCK, RETURNING ON TOP DRAWER. OGEE FEET. MAHOGANY. 1765–75. 42 X 41 X 22.
H. W. ERVING.

615. CURLY. OGEE FOOT. 1760–70. MADE BY DANIEL SILMORE. NEW HAMPSHIRE.
CHESTER E. DIMICK.

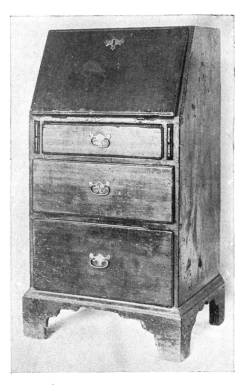

616. MIDDLE STRETCHER DESK. 1720-40. BROOKS REED.   617. SMALL PINE. 1720-50.

618. DESK ON FRAME. 1720. PLAIN STRETCHER.
FUESSENICH COLLECTION.

619. WALNUT. DRAKE FOOT. FINE SCROLL. 1740-70.
HOWARD REIFSNYDER.

620. Oxbow. Breast Drawer. Claw Foot. Mahogany. 1740–60. Rudolph Pauly.

621. Table Desk. All Original. Mahogany. Fluted. 1770–80.
Wallace Nutting.

622. OXBOW. 1760-70. MAHOGANY. 44 x 41¾ x 20½. FROM NORTH CAROLINA. ROBERT T. SMITH.

623. OXBOW. OGEE FOOT. THREE SHELLS. 1750-70. MRS. ALEX. ARMSTRONG, BALTIMORE.

624. CURLY. ODD SCROLL FOOT. 1750–70. E. C. HALL, LONGMEADOW.

625. MINIATURE. CURLY. 26 x 24 x 12. 1750–70. RUDOLPH PAULY.

626. Open Form of No. 628. The Drawer Pulls out and Swings Down. Perhaps Unique in This Period and Type. Plain Blocks both Obverse and Reverse Appear on the Cabinet. On the Finest Pieces the Cabinet Partitions Are Slotted into Ends of the Piece. That Is To Say, There Is not the Thin Frame Running All around the Cabinet.

There are five drawers in a row in the cabinet, three of them are concave and two convex, carrying out the spirit of the exterior. There are, however, no shells on the interior, as one would expect. The probable reason is that the space was limited vertically.

The shape of the mold on the base is quite generally the same, being an ogee terminated at the top by a horizontal, and at the base by a vertical.

One notes in most secretaries a shallowness of the bookcase, so that only books of small size could be accommodated. In the patterns, however, of the oxbow type, bookcases have been noted ten inches deep, which is ample.

One wonders at the "secret" drawers, because a person of moderate intelligence can open them at once, especially since a great number were made in the same pattern. But logic is, of course, the last thing to be looked for. We may be glad that structural beauty was uppermost in the minds of the makers. We can get on without hidden treasure, but beauty we must have.

Early mahogany is hard and very heavy. The sources of this wood in San Domingo were exhausted by the 19th century. The wood was drawn by oxen to the shore. Beyond four or five miles the oxen would, as the saying goes, "eat their heads off."

627. BLOCK, FOUR SHELLS, KNEE HOLE. 1770. MAHOGANY. JOHN C. TOLAND, BALTIMORE.

Attributed to John Goddard of Newport. 25 x 41 x 21. The fretwork is a rare enrichment. It is the only desk that has come under the writer's observation, with knee hole and four quarter columns with stop flute. Further, it should be noted in addition to the usual detail of the foot attributed to Goddard there is also a leaf carving on the corners of the feet, and a series of raised reeds across the front.

It should be noted that the scroll on the foot is shown on the front only, as is customary. Also that the top is finished with an under-mold where the top drawer is shell carved.

In relation to the bases and capitals of the quarter columns these were imitated at a later date in brass on clock construction. In the usual New England clocks, especially the Willard, collectors would hardly know what to make of wood in this connection. Nevertheless, wood is better and earlier, and as proof of this it is found in the richest of the Goddard and Philadelphia clocks. There can be no doubt that clocks were made to harmonize with the larger cabinet pieces of the period.

The color of the wood is as light as maple, but is not maple. The wood is supposed to have come from South America. The middle shell is finished at the edge with a slight half-round scroll incised, and stopping on the mold about the drawer, or seeming to. The molds about the drawer made on a frame. The novice would suppose these feet somewhat large, but the knee-hole style was a somewhat small piece. The opening requires four feet, and these are invariably of good size, the brackets nearly meeting, and in some cases actually meeting. The dovetail of the drawer blades shows on the front. The door in the cupboard under the knee hole is paneled with the usual feather edge.

629. BLOCK FRONT. BLOCK RETURNING ON TOP DRAWER. SHELL SLANT TOP. 1775. MAHOGANY.
FROM PALMER COLLECTION. METROPOLITAN MUSEUM.

We make the date thus late because the piece is understood to have been made for Brigadier General Ebenezer Huntington, of Norwich, Connecticut. As he was born in 1754 and died in 1834, he would have been only twenty-one years old in 1775.

The foot is very large, the secondary portion of bracket under the block, being carried through to the floor. On this block bracket there is a raised border scroll running to the base and carried round on the base of the foot to the end of the front portion. Whether or not this was a Goddard production it was at least made under the inspiration of that master.

The spandrels on the lid are somewhat reduced in size by carrying the shells so high. Hence, instead of the usual escutcheon matching those below, there are small oval escutcheons with covers.

Lining of drawers is on frame and the blades between the drawers. The lid rest has the proper small brass knob.

It is quite unusual to block the lid rather than the top drawer. It will be observed that in the block fronts there is not only the usual graduation of drawers with the deepest at the bottom, but that the top drawer is always quite shallow.

630. BLOCK FRONT WITH SHELL ON TOP DRAWER. ONLY THREE DRAWERS DEEP.
1760–70. PICTURE SUPPLIED BY MORRIS SCHWARTZ.

The cabinet shows an unusual feature in the central bottom drawer by grooving resembling the outside of the shell work, but with the lines horizontal and fading away, on the flat portion of the drawer. These richer cabinets had a scrolled contour carrying out the block idea, and with a general concave effect. The pillar drawers are delicately reeded. Some secret compartment is usual in the fine desks. Generally the central portion has a spring release with miniature drawers behind.

Next page shows a secretary with the same drawer enrichment.

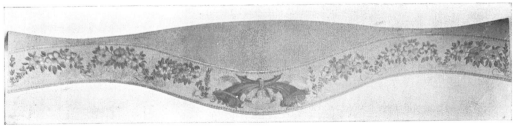

631. A PAINTED WINDOW CORNICE. ONE OF SEVERAL. LATE 18TH CENTURY. JAMES DAVIDSON.

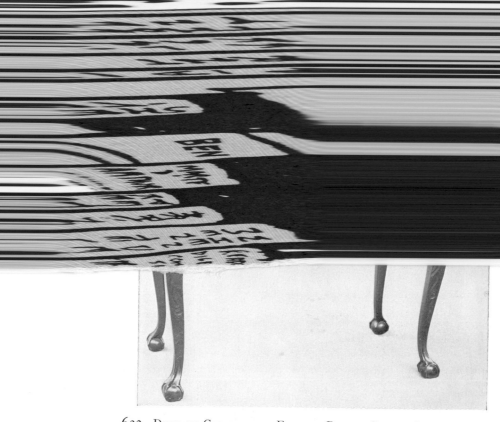

632. Desk on Chippendale Frame. Richly Carved Leg. Ball and Claw. 1760–70. Beautiful and Rare. Metropolitan Museum.

633. Heavy Claw Foot. Block Front. 1760–70. Mrs. Alexander Armstrong.

634. Queen Anne. Apple Wood. 1710–20. Met. Mus.

635. Claw Foot. Block, Shell Below. Three Cabinet Shells. 1770. Met. Mus.

...rise carving, but ...served that, when ...ay or may not show ...erse cove. There is a

It will of course be understood by the novice that the brackets are separate pieces from the foot block, and are ordinarily of horizontal grain while the foot block is of vertical grain. The block in all good construction carries through the mold of the base and the bracket.

The end board of desk frames has a slight triangular piece either cut upon it or attached, to harmonize it with the raised slant lid. Where a secretary top is to be set above the desk portion there is a blind dovetail on top. In the earlier pieces before mahogany the dovetail is not blind, but shows on the end as well as the top.

Some of the features of the block front, not already enumerated are: the central block is usually lower than the outside edges of the drawer, but it is sometimes flush with it. A block is sometimes round but usually flat. The overlap of the drawers is less frequent than the small half-round mold about them. It is curious that on some of the finest desks and secretaries the cabinet was simple. The material is usually mahogany and occasionally maple or cherry. The most regretful fact concerning them is that their vogue was so brief, it being, probably, confined to thirty years.

637. STRAIGHT FRONT, OGEE BRACKET. THREE DRAWERS HIGH. 1760–70. SHELLS ON THREE TOP DRAWERS. LID SUPPORTS ARE POCKETS, BEING MADE WIDER THAN USUAL, FOR DOCUMENT DRAWERS. A. D. BARNEY, FARMINGTON, CONNECTICUT.

This interesting piece is perhaps unique in having three drawers in place of the one usual under the slant lid. Further, these drawers were made deeper than usual, being the same as the bottom drawer, so that the middle drawer is less than either. The outside shells resemble sunrise carving, whereas the simpler shell resembles the carving on block fronts except that there are less convolutions.

In the bracket foot the maker forgot the rule by which the inside scroll follows the outside scroll. Instead of turning the interior of the foot outward, he turned it inward. The base mold is simpler than usual. It is probable that the piece was made away from the centers of manufacture.

John Goddard of Newport has the distinction of having popularized and developed the block front, if he did not invent it. He also developed the ogee foot more specially than any who preceded him. On his low chests of drawers he seems to have taken the initiative in using thin lids or tops, which he reinforced by a supporting mold. He was succeeded by his son Thomas. He was preceded in the cabinet business by his father-in-law, Townsend. Goddard's great grandson thinks that he came from England and returned there at the outbreak of the Revolution. He died there also in the neighborhood of the year 1785. Lockwood states that he was born in Newport 1724, son of David and Mary Goddard, and that he married August 6th, 1746, Hannah Townsend, daughter of Job, from whom he was supposed to have learned his trade. He died insolvent, one of his sons named for his father-in-law, being his executor. It would appear, therefore, that he worked nearly thirty years in Newport before the outbreak of the Revolution. As somebody must have invented the block front with shell, there is no reason to doubt that this great designer was the man. Among his numerous children, others besides Thomas became cabinetmakers. One of them was found in Providence. A John Townsend, a generation later than Job, appears by a label in a chest-on-chest owned by George D. Pratt.

638. STRAIGHT FRONT. LID SUPPORTED BY SQUARE DRAWERS. 1760–70. FRANCIS D. BRINTON, WEST CHESTER, PENNSYLVANIA.

Rare drawer construction. Fine Interior. Five concave shells surrounded by a line of dot decoration. Stop fluted pillar drawers, sometimes called document drawers. 43 x 40½ x 20.

While the block fronts have also been traced to Hartford, where cherry is the usual base, John Goddard used the supreme examples. On the lids of some of his secretaries the convex block was finished with a depressed curved cove, which gave the block greater relief, and simplified the difficulty of stopping a shell on a perfectly plain surface. It is believed that none of his pieces fails to show distinguished workmanship. To state, as has been done, that none of them had quarter columns is at once refuted by the most distinguished piece of all, namely, the nine-shell secretary with three raised panels in the cornice. His great grandson believes that he learned his trade in England, possibly from Thomas Chippendale. His son at least had Chippendale's book, and as the edition was that of 1762, of course Goddard was familiar with it. The block front seems to have died as it started, with John. The carving was a highly technical matter, which only the finest workman could undertake. For some of these effects we are indebted to Lockwood, for some to Dyer, in *Antiques*.

639. STRAIGHT FRONT. STRAIGHT BRACKET WITH UNUSUAL SCROLL. BEAUTIFUL AND RARE INTERIOR. 1760-70. COLLECTION OF EDWARD SANDERSON, NANTUCKET.

The cabinet is unique. The third shell is in a short bottom drawer. There is the unprecedented number of four document drawers, each fronted by a fluted half column in excellent taste. The lower drawer section is straight, the upper section is blocked.

640. STRAIGHT. PLAIN BRACKET. INLAID. VIRGINIA WALNUT. PROBABLY PENNSYL-
VANIA. 1750–70. 45 x 28 x 21½. CABINET. BLOCK FRONT. ROBERT P. BUTLER,
HARTFORD.

641. MINIATURE. PINE. 1700. 29 x 22½ x 15.
MRS. F. P. GARVAN.

642. LIFTING TOP. 1800. N. CUSHING.

643. Maple Desk on Low Separate Frame. 1730–60. 42¼ x 36 x 16½. The Curious Small Ball Feet Are Finished without Any Attached Bracket. Feet Behind Are Duck. Mary M. Sampson.

644–48. "John Alden House" Parlor, Duxbury. Panel Work 1720–40.

Interior has the well, that is, a shallow receptacle reached by a slide in the table. The molding about the frame is a rare feature, known to the writer in one other instance. It is doubtless the survival of the separate desk box on frame. Mold on the lid as a book rest with return. The brasses are restored.

The date is set early, because of the style of mold. This is not the true herringbone, but one-half of it. The desks three drawers deep are, like this, more usually terminated with two narrow drawers at the top. In investigations concerning the block front dogmatism is out of place. While John Goddard was the master, a few sporadic instances are known of the block work being continued as late as 1783. It is thought that some of the shell blocks or arc blocks were made on the north shore of Massachusetts.

650. CURLY, DUTCH FOOT. BLOCKED CABINET. 1760-70. I. SACK.

651. WASHINGTON'S TABLE. CITY HALL, NEW YORK. STOPPED FLUTES. FALSE DRAWERS ALL
SIDES EXCEPT FRONT.

652. DESK END. 1800. SANDERSON COLLECTION.   653. EMPIRE. 1820. WALLACE NUTTING.

654. TAMBOUR SECRETARY.   BIRCH, SATINWOOD. $40\frac{1}{2}$ x 46 x $19\frac{3}{4}$.   1790.
HARRY W. WEEKS.

655. TAMBOUR. 1790. 41½ x 37½ x 19½. FINE BRACKET AND INLAY. I. SACK.

656–60. BRYCE HOUSE PARLOR, ANNAPOLIS. RARE CARVED CHIPPENDALE TABLE, PEMBROKE, AND INLAID HEPPLEWHITE CHAIRS.

661. TAMBOUR, MAHOGANY. PERHAPS UNIQUE. 1790. HENRY W. WEIL, NEW YORK.

662. TAMBOUR, RICH INLAY. 1790. RARELY BEAUTIFUL. I. SACK, BOSTON.

663-68. ATTIC OF WEBB HOUSE, WETHERSFIELD, 1752, WITH CART, BARREL TRUNK, TWO LANTERNS, AND TACKLE.

669. Tambour. Spade Feet. Inlay. Very Rich. 1790. I. Sack.

670–72. Cross-Stretcher Room. 1690. Wadsworth Atheneum.

673. Tambour. Spade Foot. 1790. Delicately Figured Front. Carved Brackets. Line of Carving on Base of Frame. Folding Lid Is Inlaid on Edge. The Sections of the Tambour Are in Beautifully Marked Curly Wood.

This piece and several others preceding of similar type are among the most delicate and dainty examples of the last years of the 18th century. The taper leg and spade foot would class them in the Hepplewhite period. The inlay is of the richest and most tastefully selected character.

One feature is the slender pilasters at the center and at each side of the tambour opening. Nothing was neglected that could add elegance.

Owned by Mr. and Mrs. George A. Cluett.

674–77. ORIGINAL PANELS. 1690. CHEST OF DRAWERS, MIRROR, CAST ANDIRONS.
LEONARD P. GOULDING, SUDBURY.

678–80. WINDSOR TABLE, PLAIN DRESSER. SEVERAL OF THESE TABLES ARE KNOWN.

681. WALNUT, BALL-FOOT SECRETARY. 1690–1700. LID PINE. SINGLE-ARCH MOLD. ACCESS TO SPACE UNDER LID BY SLIDE. HEAVY BALL FEET. WADS-WORTH ATHENEUM.

682. Walnut, Queen Anne. Double-Arch Top. 1720–40. J. Stogdell Stokes, Philadelphia.

The door in the cabinet has also a panel of the earliest 18th century sort. Cabinet round blocked. Side drawers advanced. Candle slides in base of top and large door panels in ogee scrolls. This and the following are the rarest type of secretaries, except the preceding. The cabinet is extraordinary for the date.

683. (Right.) Walnut, Queen Anne. Double-Arch Mold. 1720–40. Edward Bringhurst, Wilmington, Delaware.

This shows slight variations from the preceding, it having ogee bracket feet, and a cornice mold much more condensed in the heavy coved member. Owing to shallowness the lids on these pieces stand at a sharp angle to give room for the top section. Panels on both pieces are identical. Suggestion is that both are work of the same maker. Handles can hardly be correct, or a later date should be named. Thumb-nail drawer.

684. SECRETARY CABINET. SLIDING TRAYS WITHIN LOWER DOORS. PROBABLY FOR GENTLEMEN'S WARD-
ROBE. SKELETON DENTILS ON CORNICE. UNUSUAL DENTILS ON SCROLL TOP, WHICH ENDS WITH SPIRAL
ROSETTES. TRUE PANELS BUT CORNERS OF STYLE ADOPTED LATER IN THE FORM OF OUTLINES. 1770–80.

685. (Right.) DUTCH. BANDY LEG. SUNBURST ROSETTES. 1740–60. PICTURE FROM MORRIS SCHWARTZ.

686. (Opposite.) DOORS BELOW: SLIDING TRAYS WITHIN. OGEE SCROLLS WITH FOLIAGE. TOP, RICH
FRET. TWO DESIGNS CARRIED AROUND ENDS. SPIRAL ROSETTES. 1760–70. METROPOLITAN
MUSEUM. PALMER COLLECTION.

This is the fullest rosette development with incipient wings. The ogee bracket feet are carved, and a
raised band runs down the inside of their brackets.

Comparison with the comparatively humble No. 684 shows the same skeleton dentils under cornice
and same plain dentils under the scroll. Disconnected frets on the four upper stiles. Pine finish within.
Mold will be shown also elsewhere.

687. Broken Pediment, Kettle Base, Carved Ogee Foot. Doors
Paneled, Ogee Curves, Carved Edges. Pilaster Swings Made as Pent
of Door. Capital Carved with Leaf Like a Modillion. Carved Edges
of Lower Part Run Also Up the Face of the Slant. 1760–70.
Metropolitan Museum.

is a curious study. This one looks a little like Shakespeare. Classical characters representing ideal figures, or poets, or an owl, for wisdom, were also used.

688. Interrupted Pediment. Sharp Pitch. Ball Foot, Ogee Scrolled Panels, Fluted Pilasters. Large Shell on Center of Lid, and Half Shell in Every Corner. Curious Knob on Claws. 1760–70. Susan Wentworth, Portsmouth, N. H.

689. (Right.) Claw Foot, Oxbow, Ogee Scroll Panels, Bonnet Top, Return Mold without Rosette. 1760–70. 96 x 42 x 25. Plain Opening. No Restorations. New England. Mrs. Francis P. Garvan.

690. Cherry, Oxbow, Breast Drawer. Claw Feet, Long, Simple Ogee Scroll Panels. Pierced Scroll Top. Small Curved Rosettes. 1760–80. E. B. Leete Co., Guilford.

All original, including handles. Secret slot in the left pull that supports the lid. 90 x 42 x 22; top 12 inches deep. Dentil compound, Connecticut origin. This type of skeletonized scroll is dainty, but probably a little later development than the heavy type.

691. (Right.) Plain Bracket Foot. Panel Conformed to Bonnet, which is a Little too Rampant. Rosettes with Four Leaves. Flames Unusual. Curious Indentations on Inside of Scroll which Is Bordered by a Carved Raised Line, not Applied, but Formed by Cutting Away the Surface Below It. Candle Slides. Evidently Made with Care but Away from the Centers of Cabinet Work. 1760–80. Morris Berry.

692. BLOCKED, CLAW FOOT, OGEE SCROLL PANELS.
1760–70. SCROLL TOP WOULD SEEM TO BE CALLED
FOR, BUT THIS FORM IS NOT UNIQUE. N. CUSHING.

693. OGEE FOOT, ROUND-PANEL TOP, BLOCKED INTERIOR.
1740–60. FOOT NOT DEVELOPED TO GODDARD PERIOD.
JAMES DAVIDSON, NEW LONDON.

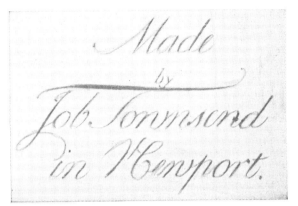

694. LABEL IN METROPOLITAN MUSEUM PIECE.

695. LABEL IN PIECE ABOVE.

696. BLOCKED, PILASTERS PART OF DOOR. SHELLS BEHIND DOORS. 1760–70. THIS SECRETARY SHOWN CLOSED ON THE RIGHT, NEXT PAGE. MRS. FRANCIS P. GARVAN.

697. Blocked Mold, Running through Foot, Pilaster Carved in Scroll, Round-Topped Panels, Bonnet Mold Returns Instead of Rosette. 1760–70. Malcolm A. Norton.

A similar scrolled pilaster is known on another piece. At first thought the bonnet scroll being worked back on the apex of its rise did not seem to be so rich as a rosette, yet familiarity with these pieces gives the sense that this is a very chaste and handsome arrangement. The rosettes often made difficulty in harmonizing them with the molding. Probably this example is more classical than the rosette.

698. (Right.) Plain Blocks on the Lid. Round-Top Panel Doors. Bonnet Top with Rosette. Middle Finial with Unique Spiraled Ball. 1760–70. The Ball Feet and the Simplicity of the Lid May Indicate a Date Slightly Subsequent to the Bracket Foot. Mrs. Francis P. Garvan.

The offset hinges in the finer examples were made with a right-angled turn on the door or jamb when a pilaster was used. No such hinges are now commercially made. They were finished with a daintily turned ball at top and bottom.

700. A Lowboy Desk. Three Part. About 90 High, 40 Wide
Below, 36 or 38 Wide in the Center, 36 Wide in Upper Section. 1750-75. Francis D. Brinton.

699. Blocked, Fine Flames. 1760-70.
Morgan B. Brainard, Hartford.

701. Fully Blocked with Shells, Lines Carried Through
the Top Panels Above Doors. Only Known Instance. Top
Corner Boxes Seen Rarely Except on Clocks. 1760–70.
Highest Importance. Brown & Ives.

702. BLOCKED, BALL FEET, UNIQUE PIERCED SCROLL IN THE HOOD, FAN
ON SPANDREL. 1760–70. UNIQUE DRAPERY ON FRAME.
MRS. C. F. RICE, WORCESTER.

703. BLOCKED, THROUGH BASE MOLD. CLAW FEET, CABINET BLOCKED, THREE SHELLS. RAISED PANEL DOORS, LARGE CONCAVE SHELLS BACK OF DOORS. FINE LINES. 1765–75. MAHOGANY. NEW ENGLAND. 94 x 42. H. W. ERVING.

704. PANELED LID, BROKEN PEDIMENT, FRETS AND DENTILS, THREE BLOCKS IN CABINET. 1760–70. ESSEX INSTITUTE, SALEM, MASSACHUSETTS.

705. Blocked, Document Drawers with Flames. Carved Shells Behind Long Doors. Carved Urns, Shell in Spandrel. 1760–70. 96½ Inches High. Lower Section 43 Inches High. Helen T. Cooke.

707. "Animal" Foot. Panel Scrolled at Top. Dentils, Fluted Pilasters, Carved Bonnet Rosettes. 1760–70. Found Near New York City, H. V. Weil.

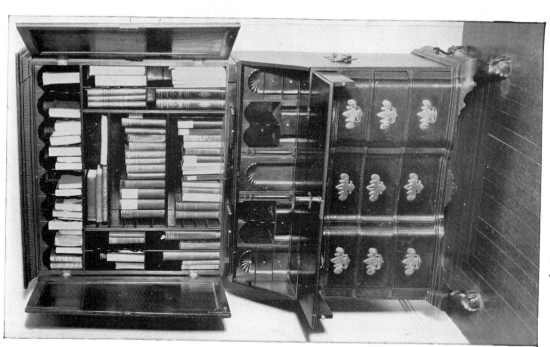

706. Rare, Flat Top. John H. Buck.

708. Triple Doors, Quarter Columns, Goddard Foot, Carved Urns. Compare with No. 701. 1760–70. Quarter Column in Base Not Found in This Type. Escutcheon Bent to Fit Mold on Door. Square Supports for Urns Fluted as Usual. Applied Mold Around Arched Opening. Mrs. Francis P. Garvan.

709. (Right.) Cherry, Full Spiral Column Below, Full Fluted Column Above, Which Acts as a Hinge, a Column Being Attached to the Door and with a Swinging Dowel Above and Below. 1760–75. Instead of Glass the Panes Are Filled with Beveled Panels. Perhaps Originally so Built. Rare Scalloped Base. C. Sanford Bull.

In the richer pieces raised panels appear under the scroll top, and the last member of the cornice mold is carried around the opening, which sweeps from the rosette to the base of the middle finial.

710. Broken Pediment. Quarter Circle Corners on Door Panels. 1760–70. 95 x 42 x 23. Solid Mahogany, Finely Marked. Interior Has Fourteen Drawers, Six Pigeonholes, and Compartment Back of Middle Door. Secret Spring on Both Document Doors. Found in Greenville, South Carolina. H. C. Valentine & Company.

711. (Right.) Plain Block Extending over Lid, Claw Foot, Bonnet with Molded Return. Round Top Panels on Door. Carved Female Figures. 1760–70. Bolles Collection. Metropolitan Museum.

Interior blocked. The attractive shell at top is of unusual form. Small shell in base, candle slides. The inner arch of the bonnet ends with a small knob like an embryonic rosette.

Many of these two-part secretaries had great brass handles on the ends of each part. They were so made with a heel on the bail as to stop the bail from rising above the horizontal. Their absence on many of the pieces apparently indicated a reluctance to mar the broad plain surface.

The distinction between this piece and the Rhode Island pattern is marked.

It is a questionable device to make the pilaster a part of the door, but we find it so here and frequently. The pilaster is also doubled on the inner side so that each door is complete with its flanking supports.

712. ARC BLOCK. MAHOGANY, ALL TURNED URNS, 1770. 95 x 45¾ x 23½. CONNECTICUT ORIGIN. WM. B. GOODWIN.

Secret drawer in shell carved drawer above door. Contour of blocking resembles the Spanish cabinet in cathedral at Havana, except that that is incomplete. Made for Saltonstall family in New London. In fine condition. Original patina, as well as all hardware. Good sunflower rosettes. Carved detail on support of middle urn. Round-top doors do not conform to the cornice shape.

713. SHELLS BEHIND DOORS, UNUSUAL URNS, ALL TURNED. 1760–70. H. V. WEIL, NEW YORK CITY.

In these pieces having shells on the inside of the top section, the pigeonholes, of course, require to be shaped to agree with the demi-dome. This was achieved by cutting away the upper part of the scrolled partition more or less until it met the dome.

So far as the author has noted, the inner shell, in this case not fully carved, takes the place of a block shell without. This to say, we do not find a block shell without and a shell on the interior.

714. Broken Pediment. Arched Glass. Hinges Should Be Removed. 1760–70. Cherry. Stanton House, Clinton, Connecticut.

715. Oxbow, Breast Drawer. Broken Pediment, Brass Urns. 1760–70. W. W. Smith, Providence.

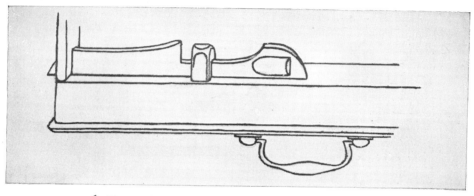

716. Detail Drawer Catch. Job Townsend, Secretary.

717. KETTLE BASE, BALL AND CLAW FEET, CARVED KNEES AND DRAPERY. THREE-SHELL CABINET. FRET ABOVE AND BELOW, SCROLL DOORS, RICHLY CARVED. BROKEN ARCH CORNICE. 1760–70. I. SACK.

718. Oxbow, Breast Drawer, Heavy Claw Foot, Cathedral Glass Top, Sheraton Cornice. 1770–90. F. L. Dunne.

This specimen has a base which seems to keep to earlier lines than the top. The cornice is a series of miniature arches ending in acorns, which is characteristic of the McIntire time. Attention is called to the difference between this breast drawer and that on No. 715, here the stop in the curve occurs on a heavy line, and there it is softened.

719. (Right.) Oxbow Front, Prominent Breast Drawer, Claw Foot, Fluted Half-Round Pillars Surmounted by a Handsome Fret, and Cornice Breaking over Pilasters. 1760–70. Clifford S. Drake, North Hampton.

The fret is light and dark wood, half of the point being dark. The columns taper. Matched grain doors resemble a flame or plume. Eighteen drawers in cabinet.

720. Small Ogee Bracket Foot. Panels with Quarter-Circle Corners. Broken Arch, Dentils and Spiral Rosettes. Finely Pierced Lattice. Excellent Unusual Acroterium. 1760–70. Morgan B. Brainard, Hartford.

721. STRAIGHT FRONT, OGEE FOOT, CABINET WITH BLOCKS AND THREE SHELLS. INTERIOR OF TOP REMARKABLY FINE. PLAIN DEMI-DOMES. TIER OF BLOCKED DRAWERS SURMOUNTED BY SHELL, AND FLANKED BY SECRET DOCUMENT DRAWERS. BELOW THEM ARE TWO DRAWERS WITH HORIZONTALLY MOLDED OGEE CONTOURS. SIMPLE BONNET TOP. CANDLE SLIDE SHOWN IN USE. THESE ARE SO OBVIOUS THAT MENTION HAS OFTEN BEEN OMITTED. ALL TURNED SIMPLE URNS. 1760–70. G. W. H. SMITH, PROVIDENCE, RHODE ISLAND.

722. (Right.) OGEE FOOT. QUARTER COLUMNS BELOW AND ABOVE. DENTIL CORNICE UNDER WHICH IS A FRET. PLAIN PANEL DOORS. 1760–70. NEWARK, DELAWARE. J. R. ERNEST.

The so-called Philadelphia type which is a better and truer word than Savery type, extended to Wilmington and Baltimore. At Baltimore was made some of the finest furniture, especially chairs. While we do not find the highboy developed to the supreme point reached at Philadelphia, we do find many of the rich features on some that are peculiar to Baltimore.

725. Oxbow Base. Attenuated Broken Arch. Rich Grain. 1760–70. Essex Institute.

724. Bonnet Top, Demi-Dome Interior. Square Drawer in Spandrel. One Block and Shell in Cabinet. Central Drawer with Fluted Ends. 1760–70. Colonial Dames, Webb House, Wethersfield.

723. Simple, Late. Early 19th Century. Scroll Top. 1800–10. Mrs. Francis P. Garvan.

727. Maple. Queen Anne. Rolling-Wave
Top. 1740-50. Mrs. Francis P. Garvan.

726. Mahogany. Fall Front. Pierced Scroll Top.
1800. Metropolitan Museum.

The writing table slides outward, and the main portion of it then swings upward, the whole device reminding us strongly of Sheraton's ingenious contrivances. The lid or cover is a quarter circle built solid and rolling in its groove. The very long French feet are connected by an ogee scroll.

729. (Right.) Tambour. 1790–1800. Same Owners.

This example resembles one other shown in that it has the double set of tambour doors, one below the writing drawer of the table and one above the table. The lower set is decorated at each side by a quarter round resembling the tambour slats. This tambour section is scrolled. The upper section is straight, but both are flanked by handsome stiles with inlay. The glass is plain diamond pattern. The handles on this piece are correct, while those on the preceding are apparently Victorian substitutes, probably for brass knobs.

732. MAHOGANY. MAPLE. 1790. GEO. SHIPLEY.

731. MAHOGANY. 1800. H. C. VALENTINE & CO.

730. MAHOGANY. 1800. S. PRESCOTT FAY.

of the glass. No.

three drawers below, as often in this period. One long drawer below the bookshelves is made to appear as three. Reeded pilasters. 94 x 42½ x 22. ｜No. 732 has inlaid cornflower legs and the finial bases are surrounded by beautiful checker inlay, which also appears above the doors. 71 x 36 x 18¼ (does not include finials).

733. SHERATON. BRASS FINIALS. WELL-SCROLLED BASE. DRAWERS BORDERED AS USUAL WITH ³⁄₃₂ INCH HALF-ROUND MOLD. 1800. KATHERINE N. LORING, WAYLAND, MASSACHUSETTS.

734. (Right.) HEPPLEWHITE. 1790. MAHOGANY AND SATINWOOD MAPLE. CLIFFORD S. DRAKE.

Small drawers have maple fronts with cross-band veneer mahogany, light and dark, with hair-line inlay divisions. Legs finely inlaid, at top to resemble a small pillar. Sash, satinwood inlay. Small drawers are simulated to cover pigeonholes. Origin, Boston.

735. MAHOGANY. BIRD'S-EYE MAPLE. 1800. 97 x 45 x 22. TOP 13¾ INCHES DEEP. ORIGINAL BRASSES WITH SHOOTING SCENE. S. PRESCOTT FAY.

This graceful French foot was a prime favorite in the period. The cabinet is especially rich in the beauty of its veneer. From Hingham, Massachusetts.

736. (Right.) FRENCH FOOT. MOLDED EDGE DRAWERS. RICHLY MATCHED BRANCH GRAIN VENEER OF GREAT BEAUTY. THE FALL FRONT UNDER THE GLASS DOORS SHOWS AN EXQUISITE FEATURED PANEL. 1800. I. SACK.

Confusion and even discord often arise from the attempt to name this style in furniture. It is far better to name a date. There was a confluence, an overlapping, and even an interlacing of styles. Empire elements appeared very early, and it would often be as correct to name a piece early Empire as Sheraton. It would be far better to keep the name Sheraton for those chairs and dainty stands which are the special exponents of his genius. There is positively no limit to the variety of the design of this period. Whatever the experience of others, the author has never seen two pieces precisely alike.

737. MAHOGANY WITH INLAY. SHERATON TYPE. BAD HANDLES LIKE THESE SHOULD BE REMOVED
FOR PROPER RESTORATIONS. 1800. METROPOLITAN MUSEUM.

The inlay on the small drawers is beautiful as also on the spandrels. Reeded legs under reeded pilasters.

738. (Right.) HEPPLEWHITE WITH ARCHED KNEE HOLE. ROLL TOP WITH SLIDING WRITING TABLE. 1790.
HOWARD REIFSNYDER, PHILADELPHIA.

Exquisite paterae, on legs, and equally good foliage inlay on spandrels of knee-hole arch and around all
drawers. Shuttle-shape inlays under the finials. Cross-section inlay about doors.

739. Hepplewhite School. 1790. Mahogany. Inlaid with Cornflower Decoration on the Spade-Foot Legs. Attenuated Oval Line Inlay on Drawers and Upper Sections of Legs. Curved Stretchers. Metropolitan Museum.

740. Hepplewhite. 1790. Mahogany with Featured Grain. All Corners with Fan Inlay. Recessed Scroll Center. The Particular Feature Is the Diagonal Setting of the Central Pair of Legs. H. V. Weil, New York.

741. SHERATON SCHOOL. 1800. POSTS ABOVE FLUTED AND STOPPED; REEDED BELOW. CARVED DAINTILY. THE TOP SHAPED OVER POSTS. SERPENTINE FRONT. FRANK A. ROBART.

This sideboard refutes the view that the later boards had rounded ends. That might have been general, but by no means a rule.

742. SHERATON SCHOOL. 1790–1800. MAHOGANY. OXBOW FRONT. LEGS TURNED AND REEDED. UPPER SECTION FLAT. 72 x 40½ x 24. ROBERT T. SMITH, HARTFORD.

The usual distinction made between the Hepplewhite and the Sheraton sideboard is that the Sheraton legs are turned. Whereas the Hepplewhite are taper square. But, as previously stated, the name often counts for little.

743. An Exquisite Example of the Hepplewhite School. 1790. Pair of Legs Near Center Set Angularly to the Board and Followed by the Same Contour on the Top. The Inlay Is Exceedingly Rich, Running Down the Legs as a Cornflower with a Change to a Vine below the Frame. Around Every Drawer and Door There Is Beautiful Banded Inlay, and a Lining Mold about the Drawers. Harry V. Weil.

744. Inlaid Mahogany. 1790. Sheraton Influence. The Term Is Used Because of the Intricacy of the Inlay, Which Would Have, of Course, Applied to the Preceding. The Oval Brass Is Quite Usual on All Sideboards Except the Latest. Metropolitan Museum.

745. Inlaid Mahogany. 1790. Fans in All Door Corners. The Contour of the Central Drawer, as Is Quite Common in the Case of the Finer Specimens, Varies from That of the Doors Below. This Design Is Supposed To Beautify the Front by Breaking up Similar Surfaces. Octagonal Handles.

746. A Purely English Setting. 1780. The More Massive Construction without Drawer Marks the Sideboard Table, Which Comes before the Sideboard And Is Attributed to the Influence of Adam and Chippendale. The Massive Wine Coolers with Their Ornate Pedestals Flank the Board at Either End. Mrs. Francis P. Garvan.

747. HEPPLEWHITE. 1800–10. MAHOGANY. 72 INCHES LONG BY 26 INCHES DEEP. RECESSED CUP-
BOARD. OGEE FRONT AT ENDS. CONNECTICUT ORIGIN. IF THE DATE IS CORRECT, IT WOULD
INDICATE THAT THE HEPPLEWHITE TYPE PERSISTED INTO THE 19TH CENTURY. H. W. ERVING.

748. HEPPLEWHITE. 1790. CONTOUR OF THE FRONT SOMEWHAT SIMPLE, ONE LONG SWEEPING
ELLIPTIC UNDER DRAWERS. RICHLY FEATURED VENEER. HARRY V. WEIL, NEW YORK.

749. A Beautiful Example with Shield-Shaped Design, Unhappily not Visible in the Picture. Tambour Cupboard. Unusual Foot. 1790–1800. L. B. Plimpton Estate.

750. Sheraton School. 1800. Unusual in Possessing a Dainty Shelf for the Entire Length Sustained on Slight Turned Columns, Twelve in All. Back of the Shelf There Is a Fret Interrupted by a Central Medallion with a Floral Design. Tambour Cupboard. A Similar but not Identical Floral Medallion Is Set in the Center of the Middle Drawer. Upper Handles in Diamonds; Those Below in Circles. Mrs. Francis P. Garvan.

751. Hepplewhite. 1790. One of the Very Few Known with Sorting Shelf Which Slides Forward. 41½ x 68 x 26. New England Origin. Concaves between the Outer Pair of Legs; Convex Middle Drawer. Serpentine below Sorting Tray. Katherine N. Loring, Wayland.

752. Chest of Drawers, or Sideboard, Made in Two Tiers of Four Drawers Each with Turned Legs. A Very Rare Construction, Now Used in the Dining Room, but Equally Proper as a Chest of Drawers in a Bedroom. 1800–10. Palmer Collection. J. Sack.

753. SMALL SIDEBOARD. 1790. A VERY BEAUTIFUL PIECE WITH FANS AND THE CORNFLOWER. BEAUTIFUL BRANCH VENEER. COURTESY OF THE PENNSYLVANIA MUSEUM.

754. SERPENTINE FRONT. ALL LEGS SQUARE TO THE BACK LINE. FANS AND INLAYS AND LOVELY VENEERS COMPLETE AN IMPRESSIVE WHOLE. 1790. I. SACK.

755. SERPENTINE. HEPPLEWHITE SCHOOL. 1790. 61½ x 38 x 25. THE DIFFERENCE BETWEEN THE GREATER AND THE SMALLER DEPTH IS 6½ INCHES, SHOWING THE SWEEP OF THE SERPENTINE. COMPANION PIECE TO A MIRROR ALSO SHOWN. EAGLE INLAY ON ALL POSTS. MR. AND MRS. GEORGE SHIPLEY. BALTIMORE.

756. BUTLER'S SIDEBOARD. SERPENTINE. THE LARGE MIDDLE DRAWER LETS DOWN, DIS-CLOSING A DESK. DEEP BOTTLE DRAWERS. LINE INLAY ONLY. 1790. WALLACE NUTTING.

757. A Serving Table or Small Sideboard. 1790. A Table Flanked by Deep Drawers with Rounded Tops. Delicate Inlay, with Satinwood. A Rare Design. The Table Section Is Closed by a Tambour Roll. Metropolitan Museum.

758. Serving Table or Small Sideboard. 1790. Inlaid with Quarter-Circle Panel Outlines. Estate of Harry W. Weeks.

759. Hepplewhite. Semi-Circular. 1790. Mahogany with Ebony and Light Wood Inlay. 78 x 39¼ x 28½. Came from Salem and Thought To Have Been Designed by McIntire or Someone under His Influence. Remarkable for Cornflower Carving down the Posts, Instead of the Usual Inlay. The Shape Also Is Rare. One Board 27 Inches Wide Forms Nearly Entire Top. The Carving Is Extended along the Edge of This Board, Being a Series of Alternating Triglyphs and Blossoms. Clifford S. Drake.

760. A True Block Front Sideboard. A Startling Adoption of the Goddard Idea with a Hepplewhite Leg. Yet the Time Varies Little from the Last Blocks of Newport. 1780. J. K. Beard, Richmond, Virginia.

761. HEPPLEWHITE PLAIN SWELL FRONT. 1790. UNUSUAL IN HAVING END HANDLES, AND BRACKETS ON CORNER LEGS. HELEN T. COOKE, WELLESLEY.

762. DEEP CUPBOARD TYPE. SQUARE TAPER LEGS. SERPENTINE CENTER. 1800–10. WE ARE NEARING THE PERIOD OF A SOLID-BUILT CABINET NEARLY TO THE FLOOR. F. D. W. GLAZIER.

763. Small, with Arch Center. Light Sheraton Legs Reeded, and Ringed. Reeding on the Square Above. 1800–10. N. Cushing, Providence.

764. Swell Front. Sheraton Type. 1800. A Well-Executed Leg Beginning with a Turned Top Followed by Vase Carving and Reeding. The Handles Are of the Correct Style for the Period. Flayderman & Kaufman.

765. EMPIRE. 1810–20. SWELL FRONT. POST CARVED AS PINEAPPLE FOLLOWED BY SPIRAL REEDING, AND THEN BOLD TURNING. THIS EXAMPLE IS A RARE ADAPTATION OF THE PINEAPPLE CARVING WITH SO SLENDER A POST, AND SUGGESTS THE RELATION OF THE PINEAPPLE BED. 43 X 54 X 23. RUDOLPH P. PAULY, BOSTON.

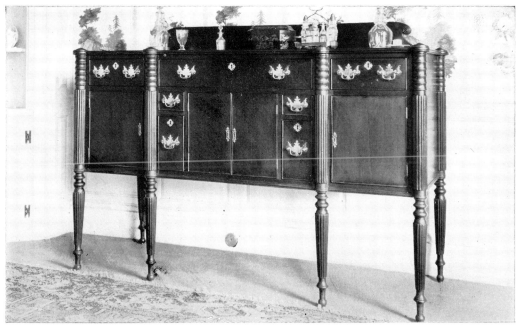

766. SHERATON TYPE WITH SPOOL TURNING FOLLOWED BY REEDING. POSTS PROJECT THROUGH TOP AND END IN A TURNED-BUTTON EFFECT. 1790–1810. UNFORTUNATE RESTORATION OF HANDLES, WHICH SHOULD BE OVAL OR KNOB BRASSES. 69⅜ X 43⅜ X 25. PYNCHON HALL, SPRINGFIELD, CONNECTICUT VALLEY HISTORICAL SOCIETY.

767. BEAUTIFULLY FEATURED. DINING ROOM OR CHAMBER PIECE. WHAT APPEAR TO BE END
DRAWERS SWING SEPARATELY BY HINGES, FROM THE BACK. 1800. BIGELOW COLLECTION.

768. EMPIRE. 1820–30. POSTS CARVED. D. E. HARLLEE, HIGH POINT, NORTH CAROLINA.

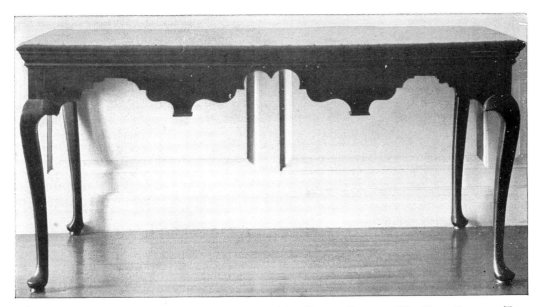

769. QUEEN ANNE SIDEBOARD TABLE. 1720–40. THE FINEST EXAMPLE WE HAVE SEEN OF THIS EARLY TYPE. SIDEBOARD OF COURSE DERIVED ITS NAME FROM THIS TYPE, WHICH HISTORICALLY PRECEDED IT. THE SCROLL ON THE SKIRT HERE ON WHICH PENDANTS SHOULD HANG IS ANALOGOUS TO THE SCROLL OF THE HIGHBOY OF THE SAME PERIOD. THESE TABLES ARE USUALLY IN WALNUT, AND OFTEN, AS HERE, THERE IS A MARBLE TOP, WITH OR WITHOUT A RETAINING MOLD. MISS HELEN T. COOKE.

770. ENGLISH SIDEBOARD TABLE. FLUTED LEGS WITH BASES. OPEN SCROLLED BRACKET. BEAUTIFUL CHINESE FRET ON FRAME. MARBLE TOP. 1760–75. FORMERLY THE AUTHOR'S.

771. Chippendale Period with Bracket. Stone Top. Finest Known Wall
Paper Panel Behind. Hot-Plate Basket Below.

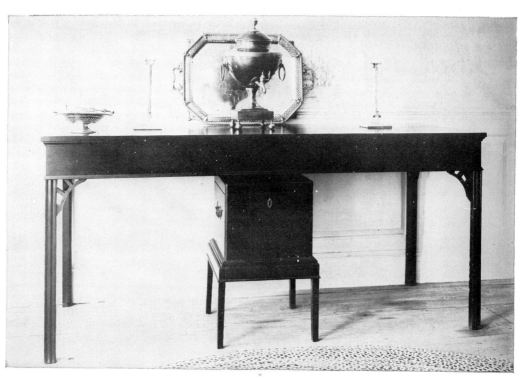

772. a, b, c, d, Chippendale Period. Wine Cooler Below. Tea Urn and Sheffield Tray
and Candlesticks. Wood Top.

773. OPEN CURVED BRACKET. NOTICE THAT THE LEGS NEVER TAPER. THEY BELONG TO THE CHIPPENDALE PERIOD. THESE TABLES WERE USED NOT ONLY IN THE DINING ROOM, BUT ALONG THE SIDE OF A LARGE HALL. THEY ARE NEVER FINISHED ON FOUR SIDES.

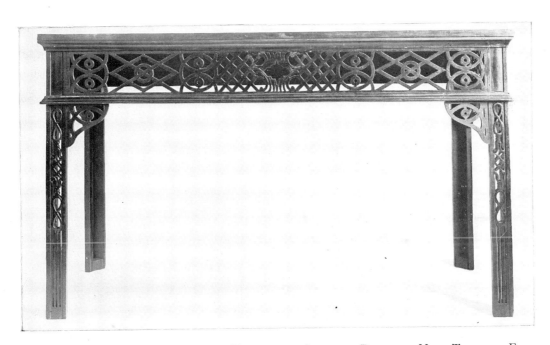

774. CHINESE FRET, INCLUDING OPEN FRET IN THE LEGS AND BRACKET. NOTE THAT THE FEET ARE BEVELED OFF INSIDE LIKE A CHIPPENDALE CHAIR. ENGLISH. THE LOWER MOLD OF THE FRAME IS CARRIED TO THE WALL ON EACH END. BOTH FORMERLY THE AUTHOR'S.

775. RARE SIDEBOARD TABLE. HEPPLEWHITE SCHOOL. SERPENTINE. 1790. DELICATELY INLAID. WOOD TOP. HOWARD REIFSNYDER, PHILADELPHIA.

776. RARE. TOP SHAPED ON ALL SIDES. BALL AND CLAW FEET. BELONGING TO THE FABENS-MANSFIELD FAMILIES, SALEM, ANCESTORS OF MRS. BELKNAP BEACH. 1755. 29½ x 53¾ x 27½. IMPORTANT. MR. AND MRS. T. BELKNAP BEACH, HARTFORD.

777. HEPPLEWHITE SERVING OR SIDEBOARD TABLE. 1790. ORIGIN, MARYLAND. MAHOGANY. INLAID PANEL AT TOP OF LEGS AND ON FRAME PANEL. DRAWER AND LEGS, STRING INLAY. H. W. ERVING.

778. SMALL SERVING OR SIDEBOARD TABLE. CHINESE FRET CUT IN RELIEF. CHIPPENDALE SCHOOL. ENGLISH. 1750. FORMERLY THE AUTHOR'S.

779. WALNUT. HUNTER'S SIDEBOARD TABLE. SLIGHTLY CARVED ON LEG SCROLL. RARE. WOOD TOP. TOP 22 x 42. HEIGHT 32½. EXCELLENT LINES. 1730–40. WALLACE NUTTING.

780. MEDIUM SIZE. DUTCH LEG, CARVED. MARBLE TOP. QUARTER-ROUND CORNERS. THE TWO BRACKETS ON THE SKIRT PROBABLY REPRESENT THE EVOLUTION OF THE PIECE. 1730–40. I. SACK.

781. RICHLY CARVED CABRIOLE LEG. BALL AND CLAW FOOT. ENGRAILED SKIRT BELOW A TORUS MOLD, WHICH IS FULLY CARVED WITH A FRET AND FOLIAGE. FINE ACANTHUS KNEES. STONE TOP. PHILADELPHIA SCHOOL. 1760–75. METROPOLITAN MUSEUM.

782. MAHOGANY. EXQUISITELY CARVED. DOLPHIN FEET. SCROLLS WITH FOLIAGE. CHILD'S FIGURE AT CENTER, SHAPED ENDS AND SIDES. PERHAPS PHILADELPHIA SCHOOL. 1760–75. METROPOLITAN MUSEUM.

783. LARGE. WALNUT SOUTHERN, BALL-AND-CLAW-FOOT SIDE TABLE. 1760–75.
FLAYDERMAN & KAUFMAN.

784–89. OLD PANELING. FINE POLE SCREEN. ANDIRONS. SCONCE-MIRRORS. WING CHAIR AND
CARD TABLE. PIE-CRUST TABLE, CARVED PEDESTAL. HIGHEST TYPE OF CHIPPENDALE CARD
TABLE. A NOTABLE ROOM. PHILADELPHIA MUSEUM.

790. A Bookcase with Drawers and Doors Below. 1760–75. Ætna Life Insurance Co.,
Hartford, Connecticut.

Very few of these rich cases were made in the North. Baltimore was noted for rich examples, and it is
presumed that this piece was made in that vicinity. It is a curious fact that massive articles like these
were largely imported from England and apparently ever have been. They are so difficult to move that
one would presume they would always be made here. This example has ogee feet which are doubled at
the forward break of the central portion. The carving extends along the scrolled base, and the rich fret,
dentils, and carved edge of the cornice suggest the Philadelphia and southern type. The effigy of the owl
stands for wisdom.

791. A Massive Bookcase of Great Size, but without Feet, the Base Coinciding with That of the Room, or Intended to Do So. 1760–75. Mrs. Francis P. Garvan.

The length is 25 feet more or less, and it could be placed only in a very stately room. The panels are lined with carving, the foliage clusters are placed in the corners. A cartouche occupies the center of a large panel at the top and is surmounted by an elaborate finial.

792–96. Library in the Warner House, Portsmouth. 1760–75. Bookcase with Original Brass Handles. A Rich Wing Chair on the Right and a Good Ball-Foot Table, Chippendale Chair, and Hepplewhite High-Back Chair on the Left.

797. A Contoured Front, the Serpentine Line Being Generally Followed. The Upper Section Has Doors with Geometrical Sash, and the Cornice Is Crowded by an Open Light Scroll. 1780–1800. Mrs. Francis P. Garvan.

This bookcase is somewhat later in date than the preceding, and lighter in outline and suggests the smaller American secretaries. Featured mahogany veneers are found throughout the piece.

Surmises as to reason for the rarity of such pieces suggest that their size and richness account for it. Others would unkindly say that the lack of libraries was responsible. There may be something in both suggestions, but perhaps our fathers made up in thorough knowledge of a few books the lack of a greater number.

798. HEPPLEWHITE. 1790. BRASS ORNAMENTS LIKE THOSE USED ON CLOCKS, WHICH ALSO FIX THE DATE AS BETWEEN 1790 AND 1800. THOUGH ON CLOCKS THE BRASSES WERE ALSO USED LATER. BEAUTIFULLY INLAID WITH MATCHED BRANCHING GRAIN. THE GLASS IN A SERIES OF POINTED OVALS. MRS. FRANCIS P. GARVAN.

799. SHERATON MOTIVE. TURNED FEET. STRONGLY FEATURED VENEERS AND INLAYS. THE GLASS AT TOP HAS A SERIES OF CLASSICAL SUBJECTS RESEMBLING THOSE ON MIRRORS. THE USUAL BREAKING FORWARD OF THE MIDDLE SECTION FOR TWO OR THREE INCHES TO GIVE GREATER GRACE. 1790–1810. MISS HELEN T. COOKE.

800–02. One of the Few Pilgrim Period Boards with Trestles. Was in the Richardson Tavern in Millis, Massachusetts. Board 25 x 84 Originally. One End Cut Off a Little. Base Hard Wood, Perhaps Maple. Sustained from Sagging by Two Spindles on the Truss Instead of a Third Trestle. Early 17th Century. Not to be Confounded with the Shaker Trestles. Tin Candle Holder at Right. Long Scouring Board at Left.

803. Walnut. Pennsylvania Trestle. 64 x 28. 17th Century. An Independent Development of the Trestle Design. Trusses with Wedges. Shoe Base. Top Attached by Pins in Conventional Pennsylvania Manner. Very Important. J. Stogdell Stokes.

804. "Sawbuck" or X Frame. Oak. Walnut Top. Foot Rest. Massive. Had Drawer with Side Runs. Late 17th or Early 18th Century. J. Stogdell Stokes.

805. Trestle with Vertical Board Truss. Pine Top 59 x 30. Oak Frame, Maple and Beech. Height 28 Inches. 17th Century. Mark La Fontaine, Springfield, Vermont.

806–08. Trestle and Stools. Stools Are Primitive Windsors. Harry Long, Boston and Cohasset.

809. Trestle Table with Leaves Sustained by Tongue, Swiveled at Center, and
Serving Both Sides. Possibly Unique. 1690–1710. Mrs. Dewitt Howe,
Manchester, New Hampshire.

810. A "Sawbuck" or X Stretcher. Delaware Valley.
Early 18th Century. Willoughby Farr, Edgewater,
New Jersey.

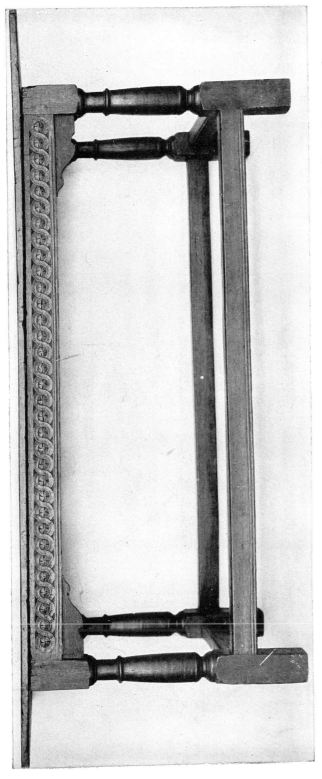

811. Communion Table, Carved, All Original Except Brackets. 1650–60. Oak, Including Top. From First Church at Salisbury, Massachusetts. Hartford Atheneum. Wallace Nutting Collection (as always where Atheneum is named).

This table is confessedly the most important in America. The carving in an endless band said to symbolize eternity is on one face alone. The two planks forming the top were loose and the dealer took off a shaving to make a closer joint between them. Otherwise than that and the addition of brackets, there is no restoration. The height of the table indicates that there could not have been balls on the feet. 89 x 34¼ x 28¾. The top is 1⅜ inches thick. The frame is 26 x 71¼. Posts 3½ inches square. Square of posts at bottom 11¼ inches, and 6 inches below the stretchers. At top square is 7 inches long. Upper frame 4 x 1½. Bottom frame 3 x 2¼. This table undoubtedly stood on a dais, one step higher than the congregation. The carving is confined to the visible side, and was obvious, it being higher than the eyes of persons sitting.

Regarding the design of the carving, the straps surround an indefinite four-leafed design. The mold below the carving runs out at each end, proving that it was done after the frame was assembled, as on old chests. The mortise hole found in the posts on this side only and the broken-off nail at the other end indicated the size of the bracket, which varies almost not at all on a number of tables of this date.

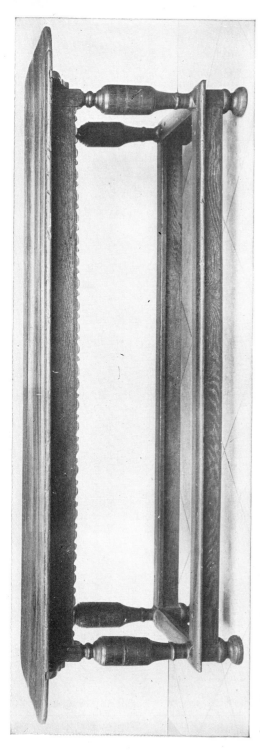

812. Pennsylvania German Origin. 18th Century. Scalloped Frame, Two-Part Stretcher, Turnings Typical of Region. Dovetailed Cleat Permits Movement of Top. Pennsylvania Museum. J. Stogdell Stokes.

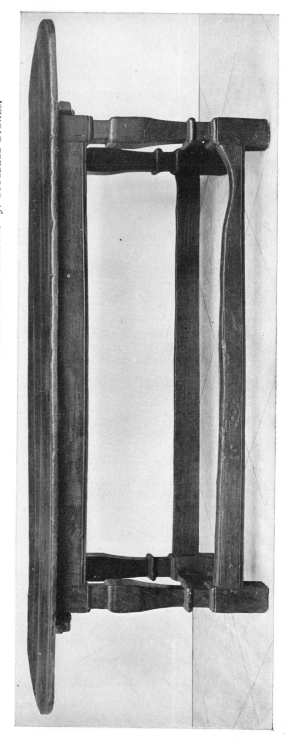

813. "Square" Turnings. Refectory Is a Term Applied to All Long, Heavy Tables. Late 17th or Early 18th Century. J. Stogdell Stokes.

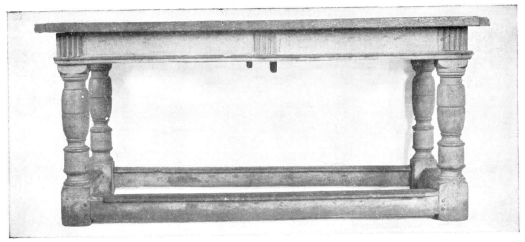

814. MASSIVE DRAWING TABLE. WHITE OAK. MID 17TH CENTURY. ONLY AMERICAN EXAMPLE. LEAVES MISSING. 33 x 35½ x 72⅞. CONNECTICUT HISTORICAL SOCIETY, HARTFORD, CONNECTICUT.

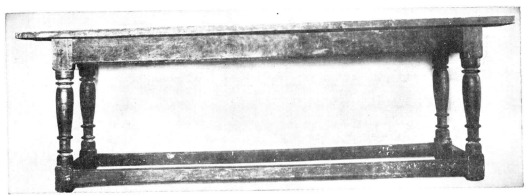

815. COMMUNION TABLE. MAPLE OR BIRCH AND PINE. 1660–90. I. SACK.

Most New England tables of this sort with heavy turnings were communion tables. The author has never seen a very heavy example, which he believes to have been for any other purpose. Before the loss of feet was about 34 inches high.

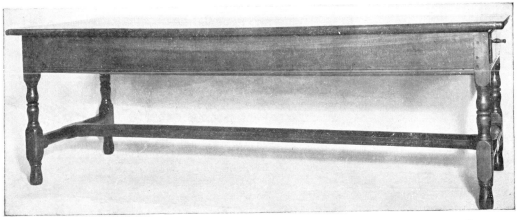

816. TRUE REFECTORY TABLE. LATE 17TH OR EARLY 18TH CENTURY. PINE TOP. NEW ENGLAND. CHAMFERED STRETCHERS. MRS. FRANCIS P. GARVAN.

817. HADLEY TABLE. 1680–1710. UNIQUE. OAK AND MAPLE. 141 INCHES LONG, 34⅜ INCHES HIGH, 37³⁄₁₆ INCHES WIDE. UNIQUE BRACKET.

A fragment from which this restoration was made was found in attic of old tavern in Hatfield where it had been used for the front of a bar and later as a rail for the attic landing. The fragment was a center leg and end leg connected to a carved apron to which three of the original brackets were still attached. The length of the frame was, of course, easily made out by spacing the new leg at an equal distance with the original leg from the center. Side mortises in the legs showed that the frame was part of a table with the carved motive found on the Hadley chest. Ordinarily features so largely restored should not be illustrated, but the great rarity and interest connected with this remarkable piece make it necessary to give it careful attention. Wm. B. Goodwin, of Hartford, the owner, has a large mass of data regarding it. The author restored the top and the feet, which were a puzzle. He is persuaded that the fragment was a part of a table, and that the restoration is legitimate. The Hadley elements therefore are now extended to one more article of furniture being formerly found in chests, boxes, court cupboards.

818–22. KITCHEN, PENNSYLVANIA MUSEUM. UNIQUE. COMBINED CHIMNEY TREE AND MANTEL CARVED FROM THE SOLID, FOUND IN PENNSYLVANIA HOUSE. WE REGARD THIS MANTEL AS THE MOST IMPORTANT FIND OF AN ARCHITECTURAL CHARACTER IN AMERICA. ANDIRONS, REMOTE CHAIR, CRANE, KETTLE, NOT ELSEWHERE SHOWN. FURNITURE PRESENTED BY J. STOGDELL STOKES.

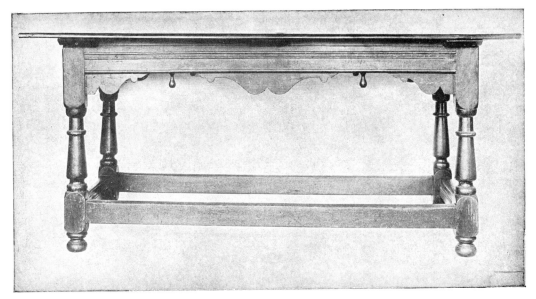

823. Heavy Table with Brackets, from Grant Family, East Windsor Hill. Oak. $32\frac{3}{4}$ x 70 Top; Frame 32 x $58\frac{1}{2}$; Height 31 Inches. 17th Century. Mrs. John Marshall Holcombe, Hartford.

824. American White Oak. Bulbous Turned. Square. 1670–90. Found at 59 Central Street, Andover, Massachusetts, in a Very Ancient House. Top Removable. Shallow Mortises, Tenoned Posts. Slight Restorations. Eight Inch Overhang. $31\frac{1}{2}$ x $45\frac{1}{2}$ x 46. Square of Leg $2\frac{3}{4}$ Inches, Largest Turning $4\frac{1}{8}$ Inches, Smallest Turning $1\frac{3}{8}$ Inches. Wadsworth Atheneum.

825. Quartered-Oak Top of Preceding. Note Device for Avoiding End Wood.

826-27. 17th Century Drawer Ends. At Right Appears Rabbet Construction Generally Found on 17th Century Cupboards. At Left the First Form of Single Dovetail.

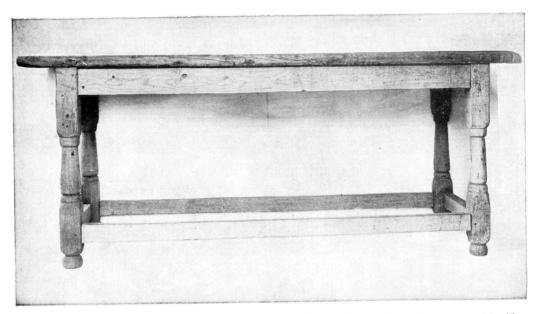

828. SUDBURY COMMUNION TABLE. WHITE OAK. PINE TOP. 1655. TOP 29 x 84½. THE HEIGHT IS 33¼ INCHES, FROM WHICH PROBABLY ¾ OF AN INCH IS LOST. END OVERHANG 6½ INCHES. SIDE OVERHANG 2¾ INCHES FROM FRONT. ¾ INCHES BEHIND. POSTS 3½ INCHES SQUARE. STRETCHERS 2 x 2¾. FRAME PIECES FROM THE TOP 2¾ TO 1½ INCHES ON SIDES. POSTS EXTEND ¼ INCH ABOVE FRAME TO LET INTO SHALLOW MORTISE IN THE TOP. ALL ORIGINAL. SHOULD HAVE HAD BRACKETS; APPARENTLY NEVER DID.

829. PANELED FRAME TABLE. 17TH CENTURY. CONTAINS A BOX OR HUTCH, ACCESS TO WHICH WAS MADE BY SLIDING THE TOP. THE IRON HANDLES SUGGEST ENGLISH ORIGIN, BUT THE QUESTION HAS BEEN DEBATED. THE HEAVY MOLD COMES TOO NEAR THE EDGE OF THE PANEL. METROPOLITAN MUSEUM.

830. Refectory Type. Late 17th Century. Has Lost Ball of Feet. End Stretchers Worn Away so That Middle Stretcher Mortise Edge Shows. Rare Bracket on Frame Formed by Cutting Away. George B. Dyer, Greenfield, Massachusetts.

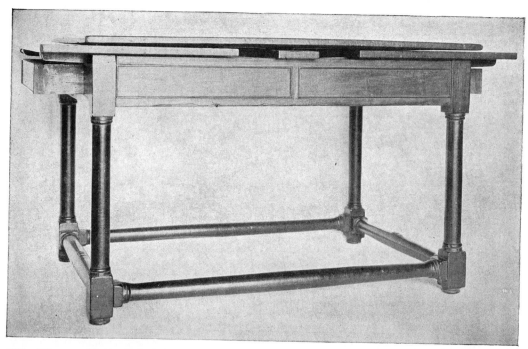

831. Walnut Turned Drawing Table. 18th Century. 28 x 32 x 44. When Extended, 84 Inches Long. The Lining Mold about Drawers (False at Sides) Indicates 18th Century. Origin Unknown to the Author. Edward Bringhurst, Wilmington, Delaware.

832. BRACKET AND DROP. REFECTORY OR PARLOR TABLE. TOP ORIGINAL. 1670–90. WITH ONE EXCEPTION THE BRACKETS ON THESE TABLES ARE OF ALMOST IDENTICAL CONTOUR AND ARE MORTISED AT ONE END AND NAILED AT THE OTHER. MRS. G. C. BRYANT, ANSONIA, CONNECTICUT.

833. ALL-SPLAY LEG. SCROLLED OGEE SKIRT. LEAVES SUSTAINED BY SLIDES. 1690–1710. TOP 44 x 52. HEIGHT 30 INCHES. ORIGIN UNCERTAIN; PROBABLY NEW ENGLAND. PIECE OF UNUSUAL DESIGN AND MUCH INTEREST. OWING TO THE GREAT OVERHANG THERE IS ABUNDANT LEG ROOM.

834. Pennsylvania Kitchen Table. Legs Maple, Other Members Pine. Drawers not Paired. Large Knob Characteristic. 1710–50.

835. Heavy High Stretcher. Ball and Ring Turnings. 1660–80. Frame $23\frac{7}{8}$ x $18\frac{1}{4}$. Top $36\frac{3}{8}$ x $33\frac{3}{4}$. Square of Leg $2\frac{1}{2}$ Inches. Height $26\frac{1}{2}$ Inches. $12\frac{1}{4}$ Inches to Top of High Stretcher and $4\frac{1}{2}$ Inches to Top of Medial Stretcher. Metropolitan Museum.

836. Walnut, Pennsylvania, Scalloped Skirt, End Drawer. Turnings Bold, Almost Bulbous. Feet Characteristic. 1700–40.

837. Pennsylvania Type. Parlor or Refectory Table. Early 18th Century. The Excellent Turnings and Delicately Outlined Scallop Indicate a Probable Decorative Use as for a Parlor. Two Bottom Stretchers Formed by a Vertical and Horizontal Member, Which Latter Is Applied above the Mortised Stretcher. Howard Reifsnyder.

838. Pennsylvania German, Walnut. "Square" Turnings. Splayed Legs. Late 17th or Early 18th Century. J. Stogdell Stokes.

839–41. Splay Leg. Somewhat Resembling No. 833, but with Turned Stretchers. Wooden Utensils, Especially Two Larger with Handles. Origin of Table, Western Massachusetts. 25½ x 43½ x 44. Walnut. About 1700. Mary A. Sampson.

842. Pennsylvania, Walnut, "Library." 1700–30. Tops as Here Generally Cleated with a Dovetail Slot. Three Drawers. Top 31 x 66. Frame 25 x 53. Height 29¾ Inches. Hartford Atheneum.

843. Pennsylvania Library Table. Scalloped Skirt. Walnut. 1700–30. Two Unequal Drawers. Wadsworth Atheneum.

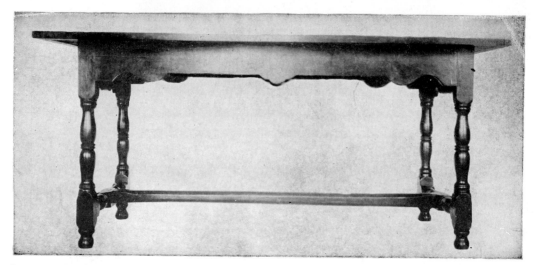

844. MEDIAL STRETCHER. BRACKETS AND ORNAMENT ON THE CENTER OF THE FRAME. TOP AND RAILS PINE. STRETCHER ASH. TOP 32¾ x 64 x 27¾ HIGH. FRAME 24½ x 54¾. 1690–1710. ESTATE OF WILLIAM G. ERVING, M.D., WASHINGTON.

845. PENNSYLVANIA, WALNUT. OUTSIDE STRETCHERS. THREE DRAWERS. 18TH CENTURY. THE SOMEWHAT LIGHTER TURNINGS HERE ARE AN UNUSUAL FEATURE OF PENNSYLVANIA TABLES. MRS. FRANCIS P. GARVAN.

846. Light Mahogany or Bay Wood. Carved Frame. Extends on All Sides and All Legs Alike. Simulated Drawer on Opposite Side. Top Contoured at Corners. 32 Inches High. Frame 30 x 49½. Top 32¼ x 57¾. Picture Supplied by Francis D. Brinton, West Chester.

847-49. Corner of Great Room Discovered in Pennsylvania and Built into Pennsylvania Museum. Original and Probably Unique Oak Stair. Beveled Square Banisters. The Door Also Is Most Remarkable. Fine Hinges of the Moravian Pattern. An American Origin Is Claimed for the Chair with Heart Motive in Center of Back. 17th Century.

850. Library Table, with All Four Legs in a Modified Dutch Foot, with Edge Something Like Drake Foot. 1730–60. Sanderson Collection, Nantucket.

851. Sideboard Table in the Palmer Section, Metropolitan Museum. Richly Carved. Raised Central Panel. Foliated Scroll on Frame and Carved Husk on the Leg, with Rosettes for Capitals. Marble Top. 1770–80.

852. TAVERN TABLE. WITH ODD BRACKETS. FEET MISSING. FRAME OAK. 1670–90. MOLDED FRAME.

853. HEAVY TURNED SPLAY LEG. MOLDED FRAME AND STRETCHERS. FRAME OAK. TOP PINE. 20 x 34. THE FRAME AT TOP IS 10½ x 22¼; JUST BELOW STRETCHERS IS 22 x 14¼, SHOWING A SPLAY ONE WAY ONLY. 1670–90. WADSWORTH ATHENEUM.

854. FINELY DESIGNED, HIGH STRETCHER. SKIRT DRAPERY FORMED BY CENTRAL PIECE DOUBLING THE BRACKETS. LIGHT PERFECT TURNINGS, BALL TYPE WITH VASE CENTERS. 1680–90. WADSWORTH ATHENEUM.

855. UNIQUE TAVERN TABLE; TOP APPARENTLY ORIGINAL. TWO LEAVES. RARE TURNING. 18TH CENTURY. FRANK A. ROBART.

856. OCTAGON, SCROLL SKIRT. PLAIN STRETCHER. 1690–1700. BOUGHT AT PLYMOUTH AND FOUND NEAR THERE. RARELY GOOD. ALL ORIGINAL AND UNTOUCHED. WADSWORTH ATHENEUM.

The section of Massachusetts about the old colony has been searched until it is the least likely of any region to yield old furniture. As a rule the North Shore was a better picking ground, as its communities were richer. The descendants of the Pilgrims for the most part forsook Plymouth to settle the balance of America.

857. HIGH STRETCHER, SCROLLED SKIRT. 1690–1700. UNUSUAL IN THE APPLIED MOLDING RUNNING AROUND THE FRAME. SKIRT IS FORMED BY DOUBLING IN THE CENTER THE LEG BRACKETS, AND IS MADE IN ONE PIECE. TOP 13¾ x 33¾. HEIGHT 25 INCHES. EDWARD C. WHEELER, JR.

858. LIGHT TURNED TAVERN TABLE, ONE LEAF. 18TH CENTURY. WADSWORTH ATHENEUM.

859. All Turned, Scrolled Skirt. 1690–1710. Frame Maple, Top Pine.

860. Walnut, Scrolled Frame, Middle Stretcher.
1710–30.

861. Oak Frame, Pine Top. 1690–1700. Wadsworth Atheneum.

862. Small, Oak, Feet Lost. Top Restored. 1650–90. Wadsworth Atheneum.

863. CROSS STRETCHER. LATE 17TH CENTURY.
WALNUT. DIAMETER 29 INCHES. L. G. MYERS,
NEW YORK.

864. HIGH STRETCHER WITHOUT MIDDLE STRETCHER.
1680–1700. TOP 28½ x 37½.

865. BALL TURNED, SPLAY LEG. 1660–90. VERY RARE. CHAUNCEY C. NASH.

866. Splay Leg, Oval Top. 1680–1700. Top 18¾ x 25¼. Height 21⅜ Inches.
Edward C. Wheeler, Jr.

867. Small, Heavy Turned. Feet Lost. 1660–70. Frame Oak. 14¾ x 8¾ and, as
It Stands, 21 Inches High. H. W. Erving.

868. Maple, Pine Top. Turned Stretchers. Good Lines. 1700–1720.
Wadsworth Atheneum.

869. Turned, with Medial Stretcher. Portion of Ball of Foot Lost. 1700–30.
Wadsworth Atheneum.

870. HIGH STRETCHER, BALL TURNED, PIERCED BRACKET. 1680–90. CHAUNCEY C. NASH.

871. TURNED STRETCHERS. UNUSUAL SCROLL ON FRAME. FEET LOST. 1680–1710.
FORMER IVES COLLECTION.

872. Birch Frame, Ball and Ring Turned. 1660–80. Found in Milford, Massachusetts. Extreme Overhang of Top 17 Inches. Was B. A. Behrend's.

873. Spiraled Oak. 17th Century. Spiral Turning Used to be Considered Foreign. This Example, However, Is a Remarkable American Survival. G. A. Goss, Waterbury, Connecticut.

874. Medial Stretcher, Bracket on Frame, not Separate. Drawer Restored. 1690–1710. Original Pine Top. Frame 21 x 31; Top 27¾ x 40⅝. Height 25¼ Inches. Portion of Ball of Foot Lost. Wadsworth Atheneum.

875. Small, with Old Black Paint. All Original. Light Turnings. 1700–30. Wadsworth Atheneum.

876. Heavy, Plain Stretchers. 1680–90. Top 29 x 41¾; Frame 21 x 32; Height 28 Inches.
Turnings Very Rare. Estate of William G. Erving, M.D., Washington.

877. Heavy, Bracket and Drop. Large Stretchers Molded at Top. Lacks Cleats on
Ends of Top. 39½ x 41. Height 29 Inches. 1660–90. Mrs. J. Insley Blair.

878. Very Heavy Walnut. Pennsylvania Type. No Stretchers. Rare.
Feet Restored. Posts Project beyond Frame and Have Quarter-Round
Molds at Corners. 18th Century. Wallace Nutting.

879. Turned Medial Stretcher, Waved-Line Scallop. 18th Century.
Oak Frame, Pine Top. 25 x 30. Pennsylvania German.
J. Stogdell Stokes.

880. HIGH STRETCHERS, WAVED-LINE TURNING ON POSTS, VASE TURNING ON STRETCHERS. ALL
WALNUT. 1680–1700. MRS. J. INSLEY BLAIR.

881. DRESSING TABLE STYLE. THREE ARCHES IN FRONT. OTHERWISE LIKE TAVERN
TABLE. MAPLE, PINE TOP. 26½ x 30¼ x 18½. 1700–30. MARY M. SAMPSON.

882. Oak, Scroll Skirt. Balls of Feet Lost. Pine Top. Very Early
Turnings. 1660–80. Fuessenich Collection.

883. Small Oval, Painted Black, All Original. Top
$21\frac{1}{2}$ x 24, Height 23 Inches. Frame, Just under Stretcher,
$12\frac{1}{2}$ x $15\frac{1}{2}$. 1700–30. Wadsworth Atheneum.

884. Cross Stretcher, Scrolled Edge, Finial Missing. 1690–1700.
Fuessenich Collection.

885. Dutch Foot. Good Bracket Cut on Frame. Top Scrolled All
Around. 1720–40. N. Cushing.

886. Oak, Maple Top. 1680–90. Found in Connecticut. New Drawer. 26 x 47 x 29½, Unusual Size. Painted Indian Red When Found in the Rough. Wide End Overhang. Brackets on All Four Sides. Rare. Wm. B. Goodwin.

887. All Turned, Frame Scrolled in an Unusual Manner. Feet Lost. Original Top. 1680–1710. We Are Purposely Showing a Great Many Variants because Only Thus Can Proper Comparison Be Made.

The tavern table, otherwise called taproom table, was so named because it was placed before a person at an inn for special service wherever he happened to be sitting, as in England today. But the tables are not confined to that use, since there was large demand for them in dwelling houses as occasional tables. To merit the name the table should be small and light. When any under this classification are shown which do not meet these specifications it is because it seems difficult to find any other class for them. The heavier examples might have been used as small dining tables in taprooms or elsewhere.

889. A Chippendale Tavern Table, of a Careful Design. The Legs Have a Stop Flute, a Term Used to Designate a Fluting Changed to a Reeding. That Is, if a Reed Is Set into Each Flute the Effect Is Obtained, and the Phrase Stop Flute Indicates This Process, Which Is Sometimes Used in Clocks by Inserting Round Brass Rods. Mahogany One-Piece Top. 27 Inches High, 24 Inches Wide. Refinished, but not Otherwise Restored. 1750–70. E. B. Leete Co., Guilford.

888. In This and the Following Number We Have an Exceedingly Rare Table Which Seems to Classify as to Style and Use as a Tavern Table. It Is, However, in the Straight Fluted Leg Style and the Chippendale Period but without Stretchers. This Example Has a Clover-Leaf Top. It Was Found in Worcester, Massachusetts, and Is in Maple, Curly. 26¾ x 32½ x 27. Chester E. Dimick, Gales Ferry, Conn.

890. Pennsylvania Bread Tray. Unusually Good Turnings. Larger Families of Pennsylvania Seemed to Call for These Large Articles. Possibly the Baking Was Done at Long Intervals. 18th Century. J. Stogdell Stokes.

891. A Kneading Trough or Bread-Tray Table with X Stretcher. Carving on the Drawer. Put Together Like a Trestle Table with Wedge through Truss. The Author Has Been Informed that This Piece Is Foreign, but Is Not Certain.

892. Butterfly Table, Original Top, 1700. Top 40½ x 45¾. Middle Board of Top 14½ Inches Wide; Height 25¾ Inches. Possible Ball on Foot Missing. Wadsworth Atheneum.

893. Rare Table with Half-Moon Handhole Openings in Leaf Bracket. 1700. Legs Hickory. Top, Wings, and Stretcher Yellow Pine. 26 x 16 x 29. Ball of Feet Missing. Perhaps Unique. C. R. McKenrick, Baltimore.

894-99. EMPIRE DINING TABLE. STRAIGHT-FRONT EMPIRE SIDEBOARD, URN, SPOON RACK, CON-
STITUTION MIRROR, FIDDLE-BACK DUTCH CHAIR. QUINCY HOMESTEAD.

900. CURLY BUTTERFLY TABLE WITH CRANE BRACKET. 1700. THE AUTHOR DOES NOT KNOW THE
ORIGIN. FOUND IN BOSTON MUSEUM OF FINE ARTS. ESTATE OF MRS. REINHOLT FAELTEN.

901. Unique Butterfly with Swivel Brackets Operating Either Side. Top of Brackets
Shut into Frame as with Gate Legs. 1690–1700. Top 33 x 37. H. W. Erving.

902. Vertical-Legged Butterfly. Wing Doweled into
Frame. 1700. Formerly the Author's.

903. Very Large, with Heavy Leather Connection at Base of Brackett. 48 Inches Long with the Grain. Found Near Haverhill. There Is no Occasion to Challenge the Leather Connection. Another Table, Small, Was Found in the Same House with the Same Construction and at Least One Other Is Known. 1700. The Hayloft, Whitemarsh, Pennsylvania.

904. All Turned, Framed and Turned Mortised Bracket. Partly Restored. 1700. This Bracket Is One of the Most Interesting Known, and the Table Is Important. Ogee on Ends of Frame. Fuessenich Collection.

905–10. Lean-To, Restored. L. P. Goulding House. About 1690. The Summer Beam Is Paneled. Fireplace with Brass Ball Andirons. Large Brass Kettle as Wood Box. Chippendale Chair at Right. Two Ball-Foot Chippendale Tables. Corner Cupboard. Dutch-Foot Table.

911. Butterfly Trestle Table. Late 17th or Early 18th Century. Top 31 x 26. Height 25½. Wadsworth Atheneum.

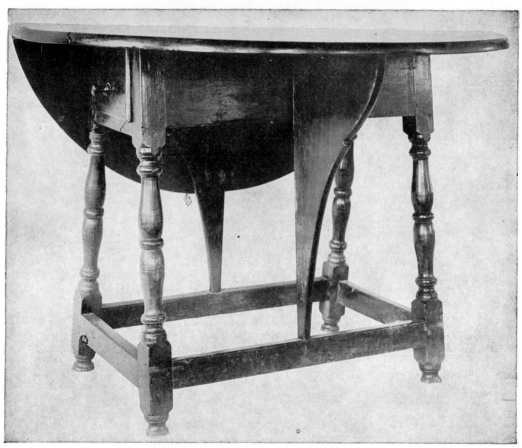

912. Heavy Turned, Drawer with Thumb-Nail Mold Lap. Late 17th or Early 18th Century. Formerly the Author's.

913. Large, Square Cornered. Round Cut Out in Bracket. While the Top Is Claimed to be Original, the Author Feels Uncertain. Late 17th or Early 18th Century. Formerly the Author's.

914. Heavy Turned, Interesting, Unusual Scroll of Butterfly Bracket. Late 17th or Early 18th Century. Drawer Never Had Handle. From Captain Churchill House, Newington, Connecticut. George Dudley Seymour.

915. Small Butterfly, Light Turning. Late 17th or Early 18th Century. H. W. Erving.

916-17. Rare Cupboard, Small, Ball Feet. Triangular Blocks in Molded Panel. Origin Unknown. Small Butterfly Table, Plain Curve on Bracket. Late 17th or Early 18th Century. Rhode Island School of Design.

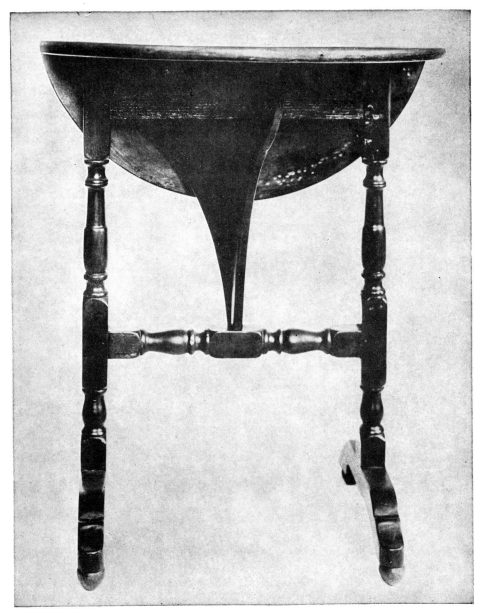

918. BUTTERFLY TRESTLE. LATE 17TH OR EARLY 18TH CENTURY. THE SHOE BASE IS
SHAPED WITH A COMPOUND CUTOUT AND IS FINISHED WITH CONICAL BALLS. THE AUTHOR
DOES NOT UNDERSTAND THEM. THE BRACKET IS CONTOURED LIKE THE USUAL BUTTERFLY
TABLE. DWIGHT BLANEY.

The term "Butterfly" refers to the shape of the supporting brackets and has no reference to the hinges.
However, incidentally, the original hinges are often of the butterfly pattern. The bracket as a rule is
engaged by a dowel cut on itself and entering into a socket on the frame and socket above into the table
top itself, so placed as to allow clearance for the turning of the bracket.

919. RARE OR UNIQUE TRESTLE BASE, WITH CENTRAL POST TURNED LIKE THE ENDS BUT CARRYING BRACES WHICH ACT AS BRACKETS AND SHUT INTO THE SINGLE FRAME. LATE 17TH OR EARLY 18TH CENTURY. FUESSENICH COLLECTION.

920. UNIQUE BUTTERFLY, RESEMBLING THAT ABOVE, BUT WITH FOUR TURNED STRETCHERS AND THE BRACKET TURNING ON A TURNED POST. LATE 17TH OR EARLY 18TH CENTURY. FEET LOST. FUESSENICH COLLECTION.

The edge of the butterfly table top was usually slightly rounded. Sometimes the round was worked forward somewhat as it progressed downward.

THE SHAPE OF THE BUTTERFLY TABLE

The author does not remember to have seen a round butterfly. To use an Hibernian expression, the top is longer the shorter way. That is to say, the table is broader across the grain than along the frame, owing to the shape of the leaf which is very strongly ovaled, in most instances. There is a projection of the central part of the top on each side of the frame, in order to allow the leaf to drop perpendicularly without leaning on the frame. Sometimes, however, this detail is not followed, and the leaf slopes even when down.

The bracket is almost invariably thin, a half an inch being common, and more than five-eighths being unusual. It is found in pine and maple, and a thick bracket is considered a detriment. A very elaborate scroll to the edge of the bracket is often the cause of suspicion.

922. VERTICAL LEG, CRANE BRACKET. LATE 17TH OR EARLY 18TH CENTURY. FOUND AT WESTBORO, MASSACHUSETTS. THIS VARIANT IS KNOWN IN SEVERAL EXAMPLES, ALL PAINTED BLACK AND PLAIN TURNED WITHOUT A TAPER, THE BRACKET SHUTS INTO THE FRAME AS IN GATE LEGS. THE EXAMPLES THE AUTHOR HAS SEEN ARE ALL OF ·MASSACHUSETTS ORIGIN. HARRY LONG, BOSTON AND COHASSET.

THE ORIGIN OF THE BUTTERFLY TABLE

These tables were formerly supposed to be confined to a Connecticut origin, but that supposition is no longer tenable. Something like these bracket-tables is known abroad. Massachusetts is also certainly the home state of some examples, and perhaps southern New Hampshire.

Of late these tables have come into great request, and have run to extraordinary figures. Other things being equal, the curly tables are the more sought after. Also the absence of a drawer detracts from the value. Delicacy of turning or any special feature adds to the value.

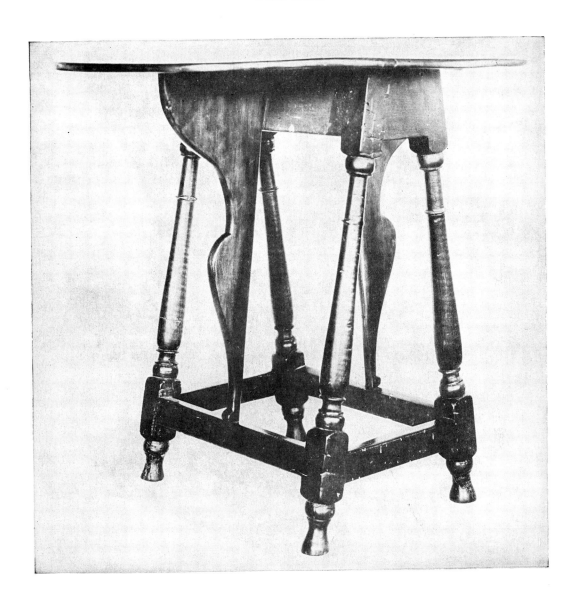

THE SHAPE AND ATTACHMENT OF THE DRAWER

The drawer of the butterfly table is always built on a bevel to conform to the straddle of the frame, and is, therefore, always wider at the bottom than at the top. There is usually a lath-like support placed just under the drawer. Occasionally cleats are attached to the sides of the frame for support. The drawers are nearly always of soft pine, and never have a metal pull, but always a small knob. The drawer is generally about two-thirds the length of the frame, and in the better examples is dovetailed. One should note that the bracket must be cut on the bevel at the top because the inside edge stands at a bevel with the perpendicular.

924-33. Stone Fireplace. Late 17th or Early 18th Century. In L. P. Goulding's, Sudbury. A Deep-Skirted Chair Table, a Bench of the Type Originally Used in America. There also Appear a Large Bellows, Gun, and Powder Horn. Tin Lanterns with Holes, a Boot-jack and Long-Legged Boots, and a Wooden Latch with String. Other Articles not Enumerated.

934. Butterfly with Extreme Overhang, and a Carved Top Running Entirely Around. Late 17th or Early 18th Century. Mr. Erving Pronounces This Carving Either Original or Nearly Contemporaneous. Carving Is Sufficiently Clear so That Every Man May Designate the Fruit for Himself. Guy E. Beardsley, Hartford.

935. Gate-Leg Tables in Their Largest Form Have Two Gates on a Side. Late 17th or Early 18th Century. In the English Type the Gate Often Swung from the Center, Giving the Appearance of an Eight-Pointed Star. The Only Known Example in America Is the One in the Albany Historical Society. Often Illustrated. Above Appears a Walnut Four-Gate in the Southern Style, So Called from the Plain Stretchers. Chauncey C. Nash.

936. Walnut Four-Gate, Beautifully Turned in the Conventional Northern Pattern. Late 17th or Early 18th Century. Top not Original. Now Replaced in Oval Form with Old Walnut. Wadsworth Atheneum.

937. Folding Gate Leg. Grooved Scroll Trestles. Late 17th or Early 18th Century.

938. Folding Gate Leg. Late 17th or Early 18th Century. Height 27½ Inches. Top of Stretcher 5⅝ Inches from the Floor. Center Board of Top 6½ x 43. Leaves 10½ Wide. Frame 35¼ Long. Shoe Now 9 Long and 2½ Square. Very Rare. Metropolitan Museum.

939. FOLDING OR TUCKAWAY GATE. LATE 17TH OR EARLY 18TH CENTURY. TOP SWINGS
TO VERTICAL POSITION. 20 x 26½ TOP. HEIGHT 26¼ INCHES.
THE LONG WAY IS UP AND DOWN.

940. A NEW ENGLAND MAPLE GATE LEG OF USUAL SIZE, MUCH REDUCED IN PHOTOGRAPH.

One notices that to harmonize the main posts with those which swing it was necessary to shorten the turnings. The same is to be said of the horizontal sections. The upper stretcher of the swing frame is not turned in this or the previous example.

THE ORIGIN OF GATE LEGS IN AMERICA

These tables often found in England were made in America from Maine to Virginia and probably farther south. The so-called conventional gate-leg turning seen to perfection in No. 936 and No. 949, and various others, is a multiple of vase and ball motives. In New England maple construction was frequent, but walnut is found in a good number of examples. In Pennsylvania walnut is general, and in the South said to be the exclusive material. The tables are in great request, partly from their beauty, partly from their adaptability.

942. CHERRY, TRESTLE END. THIS SHAPE IS SOMETIMES SEEN IN ENGLAND, BUT CHERRY IN THESE TABLES IS CONSIDERED TO ESTABLISH THE AMERICAN ORIGIN. THERE MAY BE EXCEPTIONS. 1680–1700. WADSWORTH ATHENEUM.

The large vase turning here is identical above and below with the exception of one ring at the top and a consequent shortening of the vase. A board connects the trestles, and the gate is in all its members flat, and molded. Several of these examples have been found in Maine, New Hampshire, and Massachusetts, possibly elsewhere.

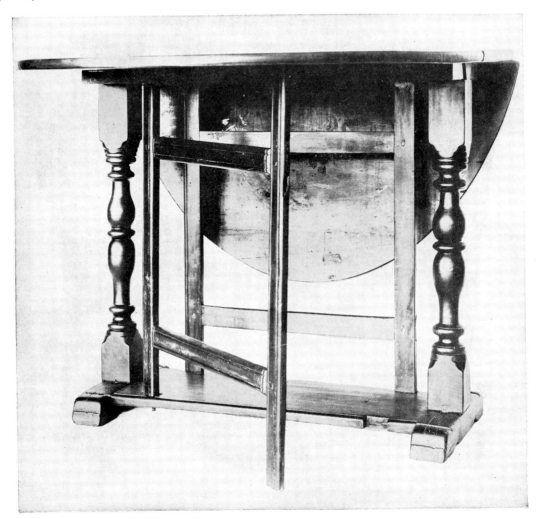

Gate leg or other early tables with leaves have groove joints where the leaf and top connect, similar to but shallower than modern matched boards. A construction with three or four engaging tenons and mortises is supposed to indicate English origin. The later gate legs often had the rule joint which makes a handsome job, and was a later invention and a decided improvement. The groove joint is preferred on account of age. Various examples are known with the square joint, plain. The burden of proof is always with him who endeavors to prove that such tops are original. If the top is pine with square edge, it is at once ruled out. There is no way of establishing the fact that a top is original. If the top is removed and only one set of pinholes is found, the presumption is in favor of originality, though it is easy enough to put a new top on, using the old pinholes.

943. Gate Leg with Flat Swing Frame. This Rare Turning or Some Turning Different from the Conventional Is Usually Found with the Trestle Gate or the
Flat Gate. Walnut. 1690–1710. Wadsworth Atheneum.

944. Triangular Frame, Single Gate. When Leaf Is Raised Table Is Square. Feet Have
Lost Full Contour of the Ball. The Author Does not Know Whether the Top Is
Original. He Has Seen Another Base Like This with a Restored Round Top.
31 x 31 x 27. 1680–1710.

945. Unusually Long Squares and Deep Cuts in the Gate Section. 1690–1710.
Mrs. Francis P. Garvan.

946. Triangular Frame. Bracket Leg Pulls Out, Guided by
Slots. At Least One Other Example Is Known. 1690–1710.
Diameter 31 Inches. Height 25 Inches. The Sliding Leg Is
Smaller than the Others. Found in Sudbury.
L. P. Goulding.

947. Unusually Slender Turnings. Small. Early 18th Century.
Miss Helen T. Cooke.

948. Split Gate. Triangular Frame, Making Round Table When
Open. c. 1700. Howard Reifsnyder.

949. Very Perfect Turnings. Small. 1690–1720. Walnut. Top 24½ x 28¾; 27½ Inches High. Leaves 10 Inches Wide. Wadsworth Atheneum.

950. Trestle Gate with Two Swinging Legs. Rare Form. 1680–1700. Fuessenich Col.

951. WELL TURNED, SMALL. LIP DRAWER. GROOVE JOINT, OBVIOUS. 1690–1720. FINE
EXAMPLE. G. WINTHROP BROWN.

952–53. SPLIT GATE LEGS. ONE AND TWO GATES RESPECTIVELY. 1680–1710. THESE FORMS ARE
KNOWN IN SPAIN. THE AUTHOR IS NOT PREPARED TO DECLARE THE ORIGIN OF
THESE TABLES.

954. HEAVY TURNINGS, FEET MISSING. MAPLE, INCLUDING THE TOP, AS USUAL. 1680–1720. WADSWORTH ATHENEUM.

955. GATE WITH CROSS STRETCHER. EARLY 18TH CENTURY. THE AUTHOR CANNOT SPEAK FOR THIS TABLE AS HE HAS NOT SEEN IT, BUT THE TOP AT LEAST WOULD NOT BE ORIGINAL. THE FEET ARE LOST. WAS J. H. STILES', YORK, PENNSYLVANIA.

956. LARGE GATE, STRONGLY TURNED. EARLY 18TH CENTURY. BEAD ON LOWER EDGE OF END FRAME. METROPOLITAN MUSEUM.

957-58. TWO EXAMPLES IN METROPOLITAN MUSEUM. LIGHT TURNINGS. EARLY 18TH CENTURY.

All gate legs look better closed, as the cutaway of the leg in the frame is not then visible. There is usually one drawer running two-thirds of the length. The pull is a small wooden knob. The better construction has dovetailed drawer, which is of pine, except the face. Very large tables may have a drawer in each end.

959. Unique. Two Gates on One Side. Probably for Official Use in a Court, Wear of Stretchers Being on Back Only. Legend on Back Rail "Chas. Hosmer. Hartford, Conn." He Has Been Called the Father of the Historical Society in Hartford. Legend Is Probably a Shipping Direction. His Date Was 1785–1871. 78 x 30. Legs 3½ Inches Square. Back Stretcher 2½ x 3½.

960. Four Gates. Walnut. 1690–1730. Mrs. Lewis Sheldon Welch, New Haven.

961. Small, Well-Turned Walnut Gate Leg. 1690–1730. Frame 11 x 29. Top 41¼ (with the Grain) x 39½. Unusual. Southern New Hampshire.

962. A Side Gate, Unique. Two Gates on One Side. Rare Turning. 1690–1730. J. Stogdell Stokes, Philadelphia.

963. SPANISH FOOT. OTHERS ARE KNOWN. TOP OLD, BUT NOT ORIGINAL. 1680–1720. FRAME 14 x 33, 27½ INCHES HIGH. HAS DRAWER. WADSWORTH ATHENEUM.

964. HEAVY, TURNED, SOUTHERN STYLE. WALNUT, FRAME SCROLLED AT ENDS. GROOVE JOINT AND ORIGINAL HINGES. 1690–1720.

965. Ball Turned. Split Gate. Yellow Pine or, as Some Would Say, Piñon. Perhaps
Spanish. 1690–1730.

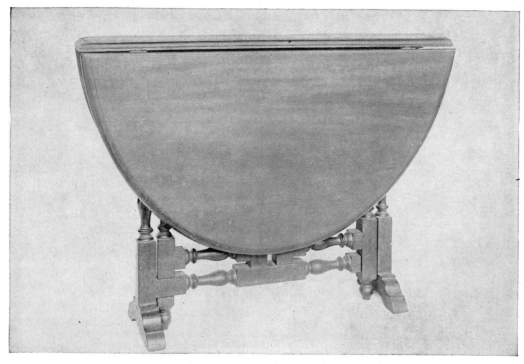

966. Walnut. Folding Gate Leg. 1720–30. Southern. Top 35 x 42¾. Very Strong
Oval. Height 24½ Inches. Thumb-Nail Mold. Rare. Wadsworth Atheneum.

967–70. DELICATE LIGHT GATE OF GREAT BEAUTY. HALE MANSION, SOUTH COVENTRY, CONNECTICUT. TOP 41 x 52½. TABLE ON RIGHT CALLED A WINDSOR. BENCH IN CENTER. ANDIRONS WITH TURNED BALLS. GEORGE DUDLEY SEYMOUR.

971–74. PARLOR HARWOOD MANSION, ANNAPOLIS. LATE EMPIRE TABLE. CLAW-FOOT WING CHAIR. HIGH BRASS ANDIRONS. RICH MANTEL. DOOR AND ROOM CORNICES. HOUSE IS NOW PUBLIC AND IS RICHLY FURNISHED.

975. DINING OR REFECTORY TABLE. MODIFICATION OF THE DRAW TABLE. 1690–1710. GEORGE DUDLEY SEYMOUR.

Instead of a trestle or draw, very wide leaves depend from the ends. It represents the evolution from the trestle table, showing that the original idea was to extend the table lengthwise rather than to make it square.

It was the habit a generation since of housewives to remove the dining table to the side of the room, letting down the leaves. This was a holdover from the original custom of removing the trestle and board except during meal time.

976. KITCHEN TABLE WITH SLIDE. ONE DROP END AND DRAWER IN THE OTHER END. PLAIN TURNINGS LIKE THE PLAIN-TURNED BUTTERFLY. 18TH CENTURY. MRS. F. GORDON PATTERSON.

977. Large Dutch Foot below Straight Legs. 1730–40. Red Walnut. Virginia or Maryland. Six Legs. 29¼ x 61 x 59½. This Walnut with Proper Finish Has a Close Resemblance to Mahogany. Wm. B. Goodwin.

978. Six Legs, Ball and Claw. 1760–70. The Finer Examples in the Larger Size Were Made with Six Legs for Great Stability and Elegance. Thus the Four Legs on the Corners Were Fixed, and the Swing Legs Had a Shorter Frame Member, So that the Effect, Whether Open or Closed, Is Fine.
Palmer Collection. I. Sack.

979. Drake Foot, with Flutes Running Well Up on the Ankle. A Southern Type. 1720–40. 29 x 47 x 54. Walnut. Mrs. Francis P. Garvan.

Said to have been found in Massachusetts. Whether brought there from the South is not known. The connection by sea of New England with the South ought not to be overlooked. Walnut could easily come back on ships sailing light. Products were freely interchanged.

980. Ball and Claw Foot. Small Size. Ogee Scroll on Ends of Frame. 1750–70. Frank A. Robart, Newton, Massachusetts.

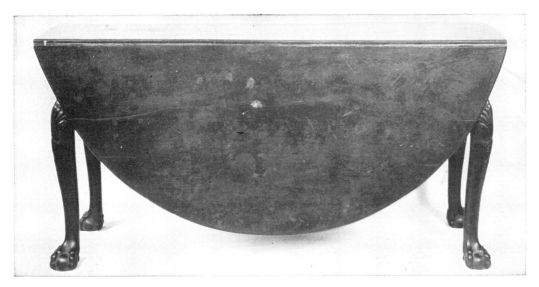

981. Great Southern Walnut Dining Table. On Account of Size Perhaps the Ankle Was Left Somewhat Heavy. Shell Carved Knee. Carving Is Most Unusual in This Position. 1750–70. Flayderman & Kaufman.

In using the phrase "Southern" we are probably open to the charge of indefiniteness. The phrase is supposed to include anything in Baltimore or south of it, and has often been applied in New England to Philadelphia. We are seeking at least to avoid that designation.

982. Well-Shaped Leg. 1750–70. H. N. Campbell, Providence, Rhode Island.

It will be noted that there is a difference in treatment of the leg. Some are worked from a square almost round by the time the ankle is reached. Others, as here, merely have the corner softened.

983. CHIPPENDALE. BALL AND CLAW. LEGS A LITTLE TOO STRAIGHT FOR THE BEST STYLE.
THE SQUARE TOP IS COMMON IN THESE TABLES, SINCE THEY WERE OFTEN USED IN PAIRS AS
DINING TABLES. TOP ORIGINAL. 1750–70. WALLACE NUTTING.

984. PAIR OF HEPPLEWHITE TABLES WITH HUSK AND LINE INLAY. BRASS FEET AND CASTERS.
TWO VERY BROAD LEAVES WHEN LIFTED FORMED AN EFFECTIVE LARGE DINING TABLE. FOUND
IN BOSTON. MAHOGANY. 29½ x 49½ x 96. LEAVES 21½ INCHES WIDE. FRAME 5½ INCHES
WIDE. CROTCH MAHOGANY. BANDED WITH AN INLAY OF DARKER COLOR, SET INTO LEG AT THE
BASE OF THE FRAME. BOUGHT FROM THE ORIGINAL FAMILY OF OWNERS BY
CLIFFORD S. DRAKE, NORTH HAMPTON, NEW HAMPSHIRE.

985. Simple Hepplewhite, but Interesting as Showing Eight Legs, Two Swinging to Either Side, a Fashion Followed in Large Tables. 1790. Flayderman & Kaufman.

986. Eight-Legged Sheraton. The Reeding Is Doubled in the Number of Reeds Three-Quarters of the Way up the Leg. This Table Is Said To Have Been Used by Washington, Who Was Such a Remarkable Sleeper and Eater. 1790–99. Mrs. Francis P. Garvan.

987-89. THREE-PART HEPPLEWHITE TABLE. END SECTIONS WITHOUT LEAVES. ABOUT 9 FEET LONG EXTENDED. HEPPLEWHITE CHAIRS AND FIREPLACE SCREEN OF THE SAME PERIOD. A PARLOR OF THE CUTLER-BARTLET HOUSE, NEWBURYPORT.

This is one of a chain of five houses formerly furnished by the author. They followed correct periods throughout in their sixty rooms, covering the entire era from the Pilgrim date to 1800. These houses now are mostly in the hands of museums or patriotic or historical societies.

990. A THREE-PART HEPPLEWHITE TABLE, SPADE FEET. INLAY WITH PATERAE ON LEGS. BANDED INLAY ALL ABOUT ON THE BASE OF THE FRAME. AN IMPRESSIVE FOREST OF LEGS, FOURTEEN OF THEM. 1790.

991. THREE-PART SHERATON TABLE. LEGS REEDED WITH A SLIGHT BULGE. 1800–10. MAHOGANY. No Restorations. 29 x 48 x 105. THE CENTER SECTION WITH LEAVES UP IS 48 x 62. THE HALF-ROUND ENDS ARE 21½ x 48. THE CASTERS OF THIS PERIOD WERE SET IN BRASS SOCKETS FITTED TO THE END OF THE LEG AND SECURED BY A SCREW. ROBERT T. SMITH, HARTFORD.

992. EMPIRE, SPIRAL TURNED. TWO PART. EACH WITH ONE BROAD LEAF AND FIVE LEGS. ORIGINAL FINISH. 1810–20. MRS. C. L. BROWNELL, JACKSONVILLE, FLORIDA.

993. Chippendale Three Part. Middle Section Has Four Legs. These Elegant Tables Are Mostly from England. This One Is Carved on the Knee with the Acanthus, and It Has Ball-and-Claw Feet. Carving of the Toes Well Together. These Tables Are Found with Even More Sections. 1750–70. The Sections Are about 3½ Commonly Called Rat's Claw. Feet Wide and 4 Feet Long. Katherine Loring.

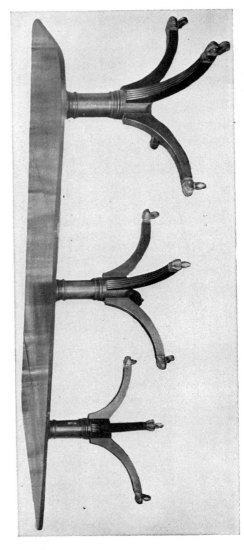

994. Three Part, Empire, with Standards. Brass Feet. 1800–20. I. Sack.

995. Two Part, Empire. Note That This Style Is Reeded on the Upper Edge of the Leg Which Is Cut as an Ogee. Also That There Are Four Legs Instead of Three. The Base Is Much More Secure with This Construction. 1800–20. Metal Bolts with Corresponding Sockets under the Leaves Were Used to Fasten the Sections Together. Morris Berry.

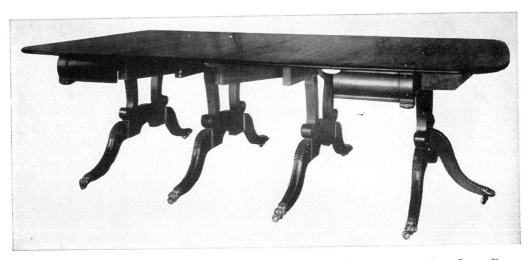

996. Empire Table. Carved Knee. Four Frames, the Inner Having Two Legs Each and the Outer Having Three. Heavy Ogee Mold on the Frame Showing Continuously When the Extension Is Removed. The Outward Scroll of the Standards Coming Down from the Frame to Rest upon the Legs Is the Beginning of the Late Empire Style So Familiar to the Past Generation. I. Sack.

The mahogany from which all these dining tables were built from Chippendale time down was heavy San Domingo. The tops and leaves were always in one piece. In the earliest period less attention was paid to grain than in the later time.

997. The Great Table Which Belonged to Thomas Jefferson. It Is Now a Part of the Furniture of the Directors' Room, Ætna Life Insurance Company, Hartford, Connecticut.

The furniture of this room was assembled by the late Governor Morgan G. Bulkeley. The table represents the complete development of the late Empire style. The heavy spiraled scroll ends with turned rosettes. A massive central ornament with cross-hatching like a pineapple in the upper part surmounts each pedestal. There are animal feet, a term which seems to have been synonymous with quadruped in the mouths of the old makers. An acanthus leaf curved like a C finishes the leg and a supporting scroll bracket beneath the pedestal is extended by a floral scroll. The great spiraled supports are similarly carved. A rich pair of ball-foot andirons decorates the fireplace. It will be remembered that Thomas Jefferson himself had a great love of architecture and designed many pieces of furniture which were made for him, as well as his dwelling, Monticello, which has now been purchased as a public monument.

We are, of course, ready to admit that we do not regard the late Empire style as the highest type, nor even as a high type. This, however, can be said of it: the workmanship of the cabinetmakers was faithful, and the pieces held together. We should, perhaps, comfort ourselves that the decline of taste was not confined to America. We should also recollect that some elements of the style still commend themselves, like the pineapple.

998. A Late Empire Parlor Table with Four Straight Standards Rising from a Platform below Which Are Four Carved Feet. 1820–30.
Mrs. Charles P. Cooley, Hartford.

999. Empire with Some Resemblance in the Scrolls to the Jefferson Table. 1820–30.
F. D. W. Glazier, Glastonbury, Connecticut.

1000–3. Empire Table, Philadelphia Make, 18 Feet Long When Fully Extended. The Third Leg of the End Section Is Turned Inward. 1800–20. An Eight-Leg Sideboard, a Small Four-Leg Sideboard, and a Set of Queen Anne Chairs. The Room Is Wonderfully Done with Modern Walls Painted from Old Whaling Scenes. Sanderson Collection, Nantucket.

1004. EMPIRE DINING TABLE. AN EXTENSION TO SUPPORT THE DROP LEAF BY SWINGING OUT A PAIR OF LEGS. THE PILLARS OF THE FRAME ARE TAPER TURNED WITH RAISED RINGS. 1810. FRANK A. ROBART, NEWTON, MASSACHUSETTS.

The magnificent mahogany which came in about 1800, and permitted the working of boards 26-inches wide, is no longer available except at rare intervals.

1005. CARVED, TWO PART. ANIMAL FEET. 1800–20. THE DISTINCTION IN STYLE BETWEEN A PIECE OF THIS SORT AND THAT WHICH FOLLOWS MAY BE MADE WITHOUT THE ASSISTANCE OF AN EXPERT. C. R. MORSON.

1006. Duncan Phyfe Side Table. Lyre Standard. Legs Ending in Spiral Scroll. Exquisite Inlay below the Lyre and on the Frame. If All Empire Examples Were Done with the Same Grace, There Would Be No Objection to the Style. 1800–10. I. Sack.

1007. Spiral Shaft. Reeded Legs, Terminating in Brass. 1800–10. Mahogany Top Is in One Piece 26 Inches Wide. S. Prescott Fay.

1008. Duncan Phyfe. 1800–10. A Trestle Style Affording Room on Two Shelves below the Top. Metropolitan Museum.

1009. Work Table. Empire. 1800–10. Edward Bringhurst, Wilmington, Delaware.

1010. Serving Table with Leaves at End. Trestle Form. 1810. Morris Berry, Plainville, Connecticut.

CARD TABLES

These tables must be of very ancient use because the game for which they stand is so. Although they bear the name, there is no law against their adaptation to any other use for a small table. Their usual characteristic is a top, one-half of which folds over on the other half. The outline is usually semicircular or elliptical. The outline, however, may be a square when open, or it may be varied by curves. The tables were in use through all epochs of American furniture, although there is very little to show for it in Pilgrim period. Card playing was not indulged by the Pilgrims or Puritans, mostly for the reason that it would have been a bore to them. A couple of examples, however, have been discovered in America which, we may charitably hope, were used as breakfast tables.

1011. A So-Called Card Table in the Court Cupboard Style. It Agrees Perfectly with the Turnings of Several Court Cupboards Which Originated Apparently on the North Shore and Probably in Salem. 1660–80. Mrs. J. Insley Blair.

The example above was found near Manchester, Massachusetts, and was presumably made to accompany one of the court cupboards referred to. Another similar table was found recently near Hartford. The wood is oak. The fifth leg is a true gate, long before its time. It is, however, very much smaller than the other legs. It is believed that all parts of this piece are original except that the drawer has been removed and only the face of it remains on the front. The drop below it served as a pull. Diameter of posts about 3½ inches. The author saw a similar table at Sulgrave Manor in England. The caretaker stated that museum people in London regarded the table as rare or unique.

1012. A Dutch-Foot Table with Drawer. Ogee Scroll on Apron. These Are Called the Salem Type. The Outlines Are Graceful. 1730–60. Flayderman & Kaufman.

1013. A Very Beautiful Piece with Outswept Corners Which Does Not Give the Effect of the Shape from the Point Seen. A Drawer with Lining Mold. Dutch Feet. 1730–50. C. P. Cooley, Hartford.

1014. A Carved Acanthus-Leaf Leg and Ball-and-Claw Foot, with an Ornamental Bracket below the Drawer. There Is Also a Carrying About of the Backing of the Small Scroll of the C Curve around the Inside of the Posts. 1750–70. Katrina Kipper, Accord, Massachusetts.

1015. Chippendale, Shaped Frame, Ball-and-Claw Feet. 1750–70. Formerly the Author's.

1016. BALL AND CLAW IN FRONT, DUTCH FOOT BEHIND. SAID TO BE A CONNECTICUT FEATURE. CARVED LEG. VERY HIGH FOOT, LIKE AN EGG SET ON END. FRAME SWEEPS DOWNWARD IN AN OGEE CURVE BEFORE THE PLAIN CENTER IS REACHED. 1750–70. FLAYDERMAN & KAUFMAN.

1017. BOLDLY SHAPED LEG, CARVED. CARVED BRACKET AND CARVED SCROLL COMING WELL UP ON THE FRAME. STRONGLY SHAPED FRAME WITH SEMICIRCULAR PROJECTION OVER THE LEGS. BALL-AND-CLAW FEET. 1750–70.

1018. Richly Carved Leg. The Effect Proceeding from a Spiral on the Bracket Sweeping Upward, Outward, and Downward on the Leg Is Suggestive of the Winged Foliated Decoration Proceeding from the Rosettes of Georgian Mirrors. The Frame Is Carved with a Series of Scrolls Ending in Spiral Rosettes. There Is a Drawer with a Lining Molding. The Posts Stand under a Half-Circle Projection on the Frame, and the Top Is Contoured To Agree with It. There Are Four Ball-and-Claw Feet. 1750–70. I. Sack.

It will be observed that the Queen Anne tables shown quite generally have a drawer; that the Chippendale tables frequently have a drawer, and that the later types, Hepplewhite and Sheraton almost never have a drawer.

In all the mahogany or walnut types so far shown there are four legs, one of which swings out to support the thrown-over top. An exception to this shown on the next page where two legs appear at the center in the rear. Both these legs throw out so that the table when open is symmetrical and stable, having a leg on each corner.

1019–20. QUEEN ANNE TYPE WITH PADDED FOOT. WALNUT. FRONT IN LONG SWELL AND CONTINUOUS CURVES TO THE CONCAVED ENDS. C CARVING BELOW THE BRACKETS. A TEA CADDY OF ELABORATE WORKMANSHIP RESTS ON TOP. 1730–50. FORMERLY THE AUTHOR'S.

1021. RED WALNUT, FROM PHILADELPHIA. 1750. HAS A LIPPED DRAWER AND BALL-AND-CLAW FOOT. ALSO A SCROLLED FRAME. 32½ INCHES HIGH. 16½ INCHES DEEP WHEN CLOSED. H. W. ERVING.

1022. Elegant Lines. Ball-and-Claw Feet. Tastefully Scrolled Carving on Leg, and on the Drawer, Which Is Shaped Below. 1750–75. Chippendale Type. The Author Has Seen a Precise Duplicate. 30 High. 13½ Deep. H. W. Erving.

1023. A Sideboard Table with One Leaf. Queen Anne Type. The Top and Sides Do Not Vary Much from Those of a Card Table, but the Shaping of the Frame, Especially on the End, Removes It from That Class. Placed Here for Convenience. 1730–50. A Rare Example. H. L. Locke, Hartford.

1024. A Rich Straight-Leg Table. Drawer in End. More Probably a Sideboard Table. Made by John Townsend, Rhode Island. A Tasteful Pierced Bracket. A Band of Inlay on the Bottom of Frame below an Applied Mold. 1750–70. Metropolitan Museum.

1025. Fine Lines. Mid 18th Century. Essex Institute, Salem.

1026. (Right.) Richly Carved with Round Tray Corners and Four Pockets. A Shell-Carved Knee Backed by Cross-Hatching. Carved Bracket. 1750–70. Howard Reifsnyder.

1027. Mahogany. Shell-Carved Knee. Ball-and-Claw Feet. Back of the Bottom of the C Scroll a Band Runs around the Two Inside Squares of Legs. 28 High, 34 Wide, 32 Deep When Open. On the Back Cut in the Wood Is: "J. S. Ingraham," Probably the Maker. 1740–60. Clifford S. Drake.

1028. Fluted Leg. Open Scrolled Bracket. Carved Mold at Base of Frame. Lip Drawer. An Elegant Simple Design. 1750–60. Howard Reifsnyder.

1029. CHIPPENDALE. FLUTED LEG, WITH DELICATE ROPE DOWN THE CENTER. EN-
GRAILED FRAME. OPEN SCROLLED BRACES. SERPENTINED ON FRONTS AND SIDES. MOLDED
EDGE. 1760–75. METROPOLITAN MUSEUM.

1030. HEPPLEWHITE, ADAM INFLUENCE. SQUARE TAPER LEGS. ELEGANT PATERAE.
CORNFLOWER DRAPERY. RICH VENEER PANELS WITH DELICATE LIGHT EDGES. SHAPED
FRAME. THE INLAID GRIFFIN CHAINED. 1790–1800. HOWARD REIFSNYDER.

1031. MAHOGANY INLAID SERPENTINE FRONT, SHERATON. REEDED LEGS BELOW A CARVED
FOLIAGE. 1800. SAM WINECK.

1032. SHERATON. EXQUISITE PLUME INLAY WITH CENTRAL PANEL. SERPENTINE.
1790–1800. MISS HELEN T. COOKE.

1033. Hepplewhite. Inlay of Pot with Flowers. Banded Inlay on Edges and Lines on Frame and Leg. 1790. Origin Portsmouth, Virginia, the Campbell Family. M. A. Norton.

1034. Inlay of Husks, Drops, and Lines. 1790. Sanderson Coll.

1035. Shaped Frame. 1790. Pennsylvania Museum.

1036. Posts at Top with Floral Inlay. Oval Center Featured Mahogany.

1037. SIMPLE, HEPPLEWHITE WITH PEG FOOT. EDGE OF TOP POSTS AND FRAME WELL INLAID. 1790.

1038. A SERVING TABLE IN THE SHAPE OF A CARD TABLE. WITHOUT LEAF. A SCALLOPED GALLERY. ENDS OF FRAME REEDED LIKE A TAMBOUR. DRAWER. HEPPLEWHITE LEGS. 1790–1800. S. PRESCOTT FAY, BOSTON.

1039. EXQUISITELY INLAID WITH PLUMED GRAIN. LEGS OUTSTANDING, SPOOL TURNED ABOVE. TAPER REEDED BELOW. CURIOUS BUTTON-LIKE ORNAMENTS ON BOTTOM OF FRAME AND EDGE OF TOP. 1800. PENNSYLVANIA MUSEUM.

1040. ALL CURLY MAPLE. HEPPLEWHITE. 1790. FRANK McCARTHY, CHESHIRE, CONNECTICUT.

1041. DELICATE OUTSTANDING REEDED AND SPOOL-TURNED LEG. INLAID PANELS. 1800. S. PRESCOTT FAY.

1042. HEPPLEWHITE. SPADE FOOT. LEGS DIAMOND SHAPE TO AGREE WITH THE SER-
PENTINE CONTOUR OF THE FRONT. 1790. FORMERLY THE AUTHOR'S.

1043. TAPERED FLUTE LEG. OPEN SCROLL BRACKET. VENEERED AND BANDED
FRONT. 1790. S. PRESCOTT FAY.

1044. LATE EMPIRE. REEDED. REEDING RETURNED AND ROUNDED AT TOP. POSTS
CARVED ON FRAME. 1820. ONE OF A PAIR. CLIFFORD R. WELD, ROCK,
MASSACHUSETTS.

1045. ATTRIBUTED TO PHYFE. REEDED LEG. FINE FEATURED INLAY. 1800.
SANDERSON COLLECTION, NANTUCKET.

1046. Ogee Ends, Bow Front, Inlay at Center Panel. Eagle. 1790.
Connecticut. American Hepplewhite. H. W. Erving.

Inlays and veneers on Hepplewhite are often on mahogany. In looking-glasses the inlays are on pine.
The cheaper Hepplewhite might be veneered on some semi-hard wood. When veneers were done on legs a
hardwood base was needed for strength.

1047. Quarter-Round Ends. Straight Front. Banded Inlay. 1790. The Author's.
1048. (Right.) Concave Front. Quarter-Round Ends. Inlaid Simply. 1790. The Author's.

1049. SEVEN LEG. FRONT, SIDEBOARD STYLE. STRING INLAY ON DRAWER AND LEGS, OVAL PANEL TOP OF LEGS. SIX STATIONARY LEGS, THE SEVENTH SWINGS. CHERRY. CONNECTICUT. 1790. H. W. ERVING.

1050. MAHOGANY. WITH INLAY. THREE PANELS, LIGHT GRAIN, BRANCH MAHOGANY OUTLINED WITH MAPLE. LEGS INLAID WITH BELLFLOWER AND DROP. PROBABLY FROM PORTSMOUTH. 1790. 30½ x 34½ x 17¾. CLIFFORD S. DRAKE.

1051. (Right.) HALF ROUND. BELLFLOWER AND DROP. 1790. THE AUTHOR'S.

1052. DUNCAN PHYFE. FOLDING-TOP TABLE. CONCAVED LEGS, CARVED, SUSTAIN A PEDESTAL CONSISTING OF A HALF GLOBE ON WHICH IS POISED AN EAGLE WITH OUTSTRETCHED WINGS. THE FRAME EDGE IS IN A RICH CLOUDED GRAIN VENEER. THE CORNERS ARE CUT OFF WITH A PLAIN CHAMFER. A GROTESQUE FACE IS CARVED ON THE BASE OF THE PEDESTAL BETWEEN THE LEGS. MRS. FRANCIS P. GARVAN.

THE WORK OF DUNCAN PHYFE

This maker was the most celebrated of the exponents of the Empire style in New York, or in America, for that matter. More and more anything that savors of pieces he is known to have built, is called by his name. He was a thorough artist, and his work is in excellent taste. But it will soon be or now is so that all good Empire work will be named Phyfe. He undoubtedly did a large amount of cabinet work. Any rich piece seeming to date from 1800 to 1820 and conforming to his refined, delicate taste may be attributed to him. In this work a good number of pieces are known to be his, and others are attributed to him with good reason. As to many others it is probably no honor to him to name him as the maker. The widest-spread piece of humor regarding antiques was the recent advertisement of a dealer that he had returned from England with a very large quantity of Duncan Phyfe furniture!

1053. Dressing Table. Sheraton Mode. 1800. From Connecticut. Mahogany.
34 Inches Long. Shaped Front. Drawers Curly Maple. H. W. Erving.

1054-58. The Parlor of the Pringle Mansion, Charleston, South Carolina. Regarded as the Finest House in the City, and Perhaps the Best South of Virginia. The Fireplace Is in Marble with a Raised Panel with Sculpture in Relief. The Over-Mantel and Cornices Are Rich. Late Empire Table Appears on the Right, a Side Chair with a Chippendale Base and Amazingly Intricate Back, Probably French, Near Where the Ladies Stand. The Armchairs Are of the Ornate Spanish Period Corresponding with Charles II in England. A French Clock on the Mantel.

1059. Phyfe Table. Lyre Standard. Carved Very Perfectly. Legs Carved. Brass Feet.
Inlay of the Most Beautiful Character. Rosettes at the Corners of the Table Frame.
30 x 35 x 18. Left in the Will of Member of Bartlett Family of Roxbury to T. Belknap
Beach. 1805. An Example as Fine as Any Known to the Author.

1060. Empire. Legs Swept Upward to the Sides of the Standard Rather Than Beneath
and in a Single Curve, Whereas the One above It Is a Complete Ogee. Rosettes on Legs,
Carving on Standard. Panel on Frame. 1800–10. One of Pair. Part of Trousseau of
Mrs. Beach's Grandmother, Mrs. Nathaniel Brookhouse Mansfield, of Salem.

1061. PHYFE, TRESTLE FORM. POSTS HEXAGONAL. CARVED ABOVE AND BELOW. TRESTLE ALSO CARVED WITH AN ANTHEMION. CORNER OF FRAME CHAMFERED. 1810. THIS AND THE FOLLOWING, EDWARD CROWNINSHIELD'S, STOCKBRIDGE.

1062. CONSISTS OF SERIES OF CURVES. A RING-SHAPED STANDARD INTERSECTED BY A SEMICIRCULAR SUPPORT FOR THE TABLE. BASE WITH AN IRREGULAR SCROLL AT ONE END AND BRASS FEET AT THE OTHER. TABLE FRAME WITH A PANEL AND ROUNDED CORNERS. 1810.

1063. TRIANGULAR FRAME, QUEEN ANNE TYPE. ONE LEG SWINGS,
MAKING SQUARE TOP. CORNERS INDENTED. 1730–50. I. SACK.

1064. SMALL QUEEN ANNE TABLE. GROOVED-JOINT LEAF.
1730–60. MORRIS BERRY.

1065. SEMICIRCULAR SIDE TABLE OF RARE FORM WHEN WITH LEGS OF THIS TYPE. FRAME PLAIN. WAS NOT PART OF ANY OTHER TABLE. 1760–70. CLIFFORD R. WELD, ROCK, MASSACHUSETTS.

1066. MAHOGANY DROP LEAF, BANDY LEG, BALL-AND-CLAW FEET, OVAL TOP. SMALL OF ITS KIND. 35 x 36 TOP. NEW ENGLAND ORIGIN. c. 1725. H. W. ERVING.

1067. Legs of Great Beauty and Grace. Richly Carved. Serpentine
Frame. Rounded Corners. Stone Top. A Pier or Side Table. 1760–70.
Pennsylvania Museum, Philadelphia.

1068. Ball and Claw, Cabriole Leg. One Leaf Only, Forming a Square, 33½ Inches.
Height 27¼ Inches. 1740–70. Dr. and Mrs. J. M. Birnie, Springfield.

1069. A Side Table with Three Drawers and a
Slide. Very Rare Form. Round Indented Corner
of Top. 1750–70. Morris Berry.

1070. Side Table. Three Drawers. Straight Legs.
Beaded Corner. 1750–70.
J. W. Berry & Son, Baltimore.

1071. Small Side or Dressing Table, Sheraton.
Dining Room or Boudoir. 1800. Arch Knee
Hole. Harry V. Weil.

1072. SHERATON SERVING TABLE. MAHOGANY. CONNECTICUT ORIGIN. 36¾ HIGH. 36½ WIDE. 16½ DEEP. THE HEIGHT INDICATES USE OF TABLE. 1790. ROBERT T. SMITH.

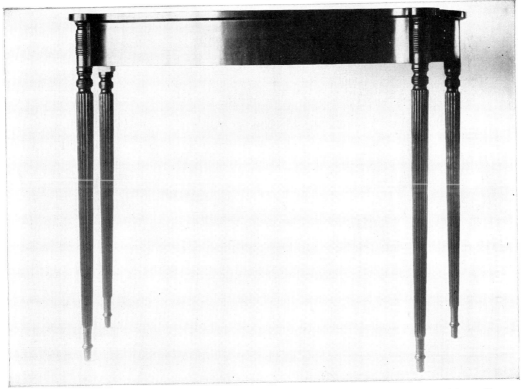

1073. WALL OR SERVING TABLE. CONNECTICUT ORIGIN. MAHOGANY LEGS AND TOP. CURLY MAPLE FRAME, REEDED LEGS. 1800. H. W. ERVING.

1074. Beginning the Class of Pembroke Tables, the Sample Above Has a Scrolled Top and a Somewhat Straight Dutch Foot. Bracket on Frame. 1725–40. Frank A. Robart.

A Pembroke table may be defined as a small drop-leaf table, nearly square when extended. In style it runs from the Queen Anne through the Hepplewhite. A more or less mythical explanation of the name is that a Countess of Pembroke first ordered a table built on these lines.

1075. Queen Anne with Pad under Foot and Plain Vertical X Stretcher. 1730–50. Formerly the Author's.

1076. A Dainty Pembroke, Vertical Pierced Cross
Stretchers. Chippendale Fluted Leg. Fine Open
Scroll Bracket, Engrailed Frame, Clover-Leaf Scroll.
Used as Card Table. Rounded Corners Serving for
Counters. 28½ x 37 x 30. 1750–75. Philadelphia
Origin. Wm. B. Goodwin.

1077. Mahogany. Flat Pierced Cross
Stretcher. Pierced Bracket. Plain Top.
28¾ x 37 x 28. George S. Palmer.

1078. Chippendale, Scrolled Top. Molded Foot. 1750–70.
H. C. Valentine & Company.

1079. Room in Cutler-Bartlet House, with Pembroke, Vertical Stretcher, Pierced, and Exquisite Hepplewhite Chairs. Table, 1760. Chairs, 1790.

1080. Spade Foot, Hepplewhite, Scrolled Top, Mahogany. Top 30 x 39. Molded Edge. String Inlay on All Sides of Leg and Foot. New England Origin. 1780–90. H. W. Erving.

1081. Pembroke, Effective, Simple Cross Stretcher, Characteristic Serpentine Top. Hepplewhite Taper Leg. 1790. Formerly the Author's.

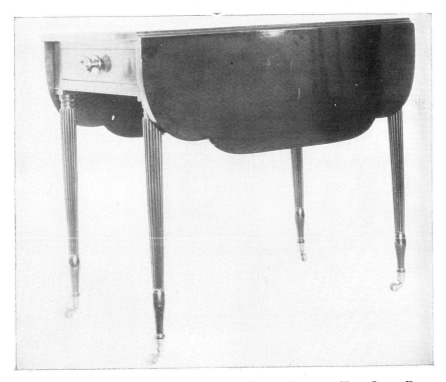

1082. Sheraton. Reeded. Scalloped Top. Rare in This Late Form. 1790–1800. 28½ x 41 x 23¾. Robert T. Smith.

1083. Shaped Top. Molded Edge. Finely Carved Frame. Ends Alike. Drawer in One End. Mahogany. 1790–1800. Top 38 x 31. Probably English. H. W. Erving.

1084. Oval Top. Edge Molded. Band of Inlay Near the Edge. Hepplewhite Mode. 1790. Top 32 x 40, the Smaller Dimension Always Indicating the Length, Closed. Connecticut Origin. H. W. Erving.

1085. Curly Maple. Hepplewhite. Richly Inlaid Top. 1790. Metropolitan Museum.

1086. Hepplewhite, Oval Top. Husk Inlay on Leg under Patera. Spade Feet. 1790. M. A. Norton, Hartford.

1087. Oval Top. Cut Away Sufficiently To Allow for Patera on Two Sides of Leg, above the Husk Inlay. 1790. Miss Helen T. Cooke.

1088. Hepplewhite, Black and White Banded Inlay of Posts at Top,
Followed by Unusual Design Below. Oval. Edge with Line Inlay as
Well as Legs. 1790. Alan Wright, Gloversville, New York.

1089. Long Elliptic Inlay on Frame and Legs.
Line Inlay at Bottom of Frame and on Legs.
1790. H. C. Valentine & Company, Richmond.

1090. Rectangular, Rounded Corners. Richly
Inlaid on Legs. Cross-Banded Border of Inlay.
Drawer. 1790. Helen T. Cooke.

1091. WALNUT TEA TABLE, WITH STONE TOP, VENEERED PANELS. OCTAGON SHAPE. TOPS MADE PERHAPS IN SWITZERLAND. BASES NATIVE.

1092. WHOLE TABLE OF WHICH ABOVE IS TOP. TRUMPET TURNED. KNOB AT CROSS STRETCHER. DOVETAILING OF FRAME OBVIOUS. 1690–1700. PICTURE FROM BROOKS REED.

1093. WALNUT TRUMPET TURNED. DOUBLE LYRE STRETCHER. OUTSWEPT SPIRAL SCROLL FOOT WITH TURNED BUTTON. SOLD THE AUTHOR BY THE DEALER AS AMERICAN, BUT OF COURSE FOREIGN. 1690–1700. WADSWORTH ATHENEUM.

1094. TOP OF ABOVE TABLE. THE STONE WAS USUALLY A VERY THIN SHEET OF SLATE.

1095. Turned with Gate-Leg Motive. The Theory of Protecting the Top by Slate Was Good, but the Veneered Margin Was Especially Liable to Injury by Liquids and Is Always Found in Bad Condition. 1690–1700. Antiquarian Society, Worcester.

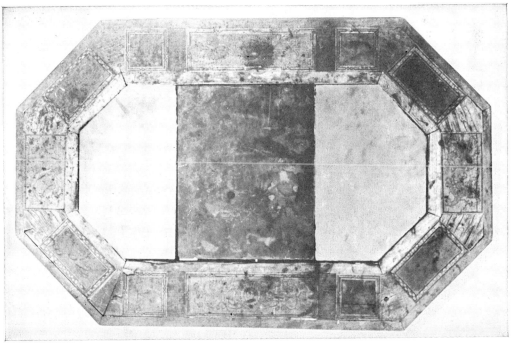

1096. Top of Table Above. One Section of Slate New. Original Slate Always in One Piece.

1097. Well-Turned Vase and Ring Pattern. Waved Line Scallop on Frame. 1690–1700. Fine Condition. Daniel Staniford, Boston.

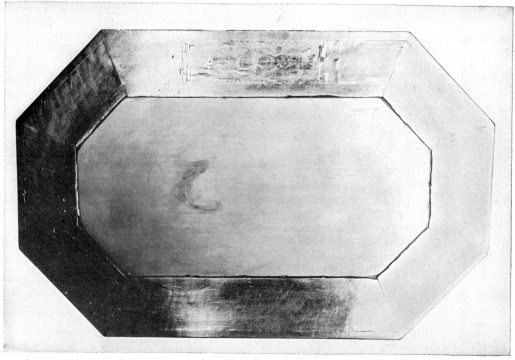

1098. The Top of Table Above. Better Condition than Is Usually Found. Inlay on One Side Only.

1099. DUTCH FOOT. RECTANGULAR TRAY TOP. SCROLLED EDGE ON FRAME. A FEATURE OF THESE DUTCH TRAY TOPS IS THAT THE BRACKET OFTEN RUNS DOWN TO THE LEG WITHOUT A SPECIAL SCROLL. MOLD ON FRAME IS EMBELLISHED BY ADDITIONAL MOTIVES ON THIS AND THE FOLLOWING. THESE TABLES ARE FAR MORE RARE THAN THE ROUND TRAY TOPS. THESE ARE EXTENSIVELY COUNTERFEITED BY APPLYING A TRAY RIM ON OLD TABLES. THE DETECTION OF THIS FRAUD IS DIFFICULT FOR THE LAYMAN. 1730–50. ROBERT P. BUTLER, HARTFORD.

1100. A NEW ENGLAND DUTCH TYPE WITH FINE APRON SCROLL. NO RESTORATIONS. MAHOGANY. RAISED MOLD AROUND DEEP FRAME. 1730–50. MRS. FRANCIS P. GARVAN.

1101. APPLE WOOD. SPANISH FOOT. GOOD OGEE SCROLL ON FRAME.
1690–1710. FORMERLY THE AUTHOR'S.

1102. GRACEFULLY SCROLLED LEG, WITH SMALL BRACKET. COMPOUND SCROLL
ON FRAME. 1730–50. S. PRESCOTT FAY.

1103. Dutch Style, Connecticut Origin, Walnut Frame. 36 x 20. 1730–50. Bold and Handsome Frame Scroll. H. W. Erving.

1104. Chippendale Tray with Gallery. 1750–70. Wallace Nutting.

1105. Deep Frame. Dutch Leg. 25 x 29½ x 18. 1730–50. T. Belknap Beach.

1106. Dutch, with Simple, Effective Scroll on Deep Frame. 1730–50.
John H. Buck, Hartford.

1107. Chippendale Type. Carved Knee, the Scroll Proceeding from the Center of a
Rosette. Ball-and-Claw Foot. Sliding Tray under Main Tray. 1740–70. Met. Mus.

1108. Regarded as English, Like All Those with the Open Gallery. The Carving Is Very Rich. 1750–70. I. Sack.

Entering on the class of tip-and-turn carved tripod tables of the Chippendale period, we reach the richest development in tables as regards carving and style. This class is also very popular and much sought for. Single good examples have lately brought many thousands of dollars. The best are counted those that are about 33 inches in diameter and made of one board, with pie-crust edge. The name is derived from the raised carved edge of the tray top, since our grandmothers sometimes decorated the edges of their pies with a scrimshaw implement. In good examples there is always carving on the hip of the leg, and the foot is a ball and claw. The shaft is also more or less carved. The contrivance at the top of the shaft is called a crow's nest, and consists of a whirling square with four posts at the corners with another square above them on which the top is hinged.

1109. Tip-and-Turn Tray Top, Usually Called Pie Crust. Carved Foliage. Carved Base of Shaft. Bought in Trenton, N. J., About 1914, from a Dealer-Collector Who Had Had It Many Years. 1760–75.

Trenton is counted in the Philadelphia district as regards style. There is a great variety in the rich patterns of these tables. At once one notes that the carving is always on the solid wood and never applied. By merely passing by and touching the hand inside the carving, the spurious may often be detected by the thinness of the wood. It indicates that a plain top has been turned down to leave a raised edge. In an original pie crust the wood is very thick to permit of this turning down. The cleats are also an infallible method of detection. If an ordinary top has been turned down, it must also be beveled underneath near the edge, and the cleats must be cut off somewhat. It is impossible to refinish the ends of the cleats to look like the old finish. The old tables are also smaller in diameter across the grain than with the grain. There are several other methods of detection, but the above are sufficient.

1110. Flute and Foliage Carving. 1770. Mrs. A. Armstrong.

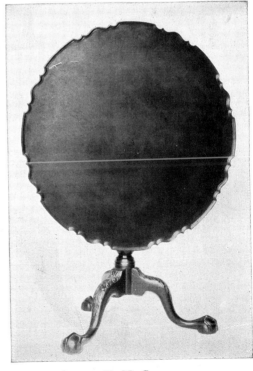

1111. Spiral and Carved Standard. Small. 1760–75. H. N. Campbell.

1112. (Right.) One Board Crotch Mahogany, 35 In. Philadelphia. c. 1760. H. W. Erving.

1113. Mahogany. 28½ High by 29½ Wide. Carved Shaft. 1760–75. Geo. S. Palmer.
1114. (Right.) Pie Crust with Shells. H. 30. W. 29. 1770. The Misses Foster, Hartford.

1115. English. Elaborately Carved. It Is Quite Unusual in American Tables
To Carry a Separate Carving Motive down the Sides of the Legs. 1760–65.
Metropolitan Museum.

1116. Rare Example, Since No Carving on Knee. 1760–75.
Metropolitan Museum.

1117. Very Beautiful and Elaborate Leg. Carved down the Sides. Shaft Fully
Carved, Ending with a Spiral. 1760–75. Metropolitan Museum.

1118. Fully Carved. Upper Shaft Fluted. 1770–75. Metropolitan Museum.

1119. English. 28 x 21. E. B. Leete.

1120. Back of No. 1109. To Show Cleats.

1121. Spiraled Bowl of Shaft Reeded. Vertical Fluting Above. 28 In. High, 29½ Inches Diameter. 1760–70. S. Prescott Fay.

1122. Beautifully Carved Bowl of Shaft. 1760–70. The Misses Foster.

1125. 29¼ x 29⅝ Diameter. Crow's Nest 3¾ High by 6¾ Square. 1770. James Fenimore Cooper.

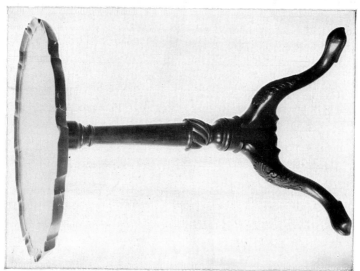

1124. Small Spiraled Bowl. Modified Dutch Foot with Shoe. Rare Foot. 1760–70. Formerly the Author's.

1123. Unusual Edge. Plain Shaft. 28 x 26. 1760–70. Bellflower below Oval on Leg. Edward Bringhurst.

1126. UNUSUAL EDGE. CARVED SHAFT. 1760–70.
MRS. ALEXANDER ARMSTRONG.

1127. SHELL AND SCROLL EDGE. CARVED
SHAFT. 1760–70. SAME OWNER.

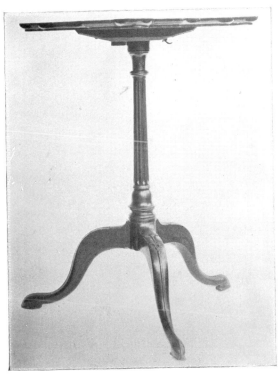

1128. FROM OLD TAVERN, NEW LONDON, "RED
LION." KEPT BY NATHANIEL BOIT. BOUGHT
FROM DESCENDANTS BY JAMES DAVIDSON.

1129. EXQUISITE CARVING. TOP WARPED.
30 INCHES HIGH. 32½ INCHES DIAMETER.
THE MISSES FOSTER.

1130. Carved Bowl and Base. Fluted Shaft. 1760–70. American. All
Original. Mrs. Francis P. Garvan.

1131–38. Parlor, Captain Brown House, Concord, Massachusetts. Tray-Top and Plain-
Top Tables. Hepplewhite Settee. Chippendale Chair. Oxbow Secretary. Spinet.
French Clock and Sand Glass. House Open to the Public. Antiquarian Society.

1139-40. Tip-and-Turn Tables. The Latter Carved. 1760-70. Howard Reifsnyder.

1141. Long, Fluted Shaft. $27\frac{3}{4}$ x $34\frac{1}{2}$. H. W. Weeks.

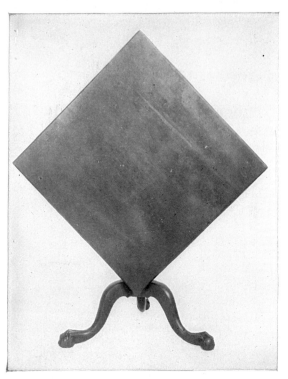

1142. A Square Tip Table. Mahogany.
1770–80.

1143. A Scrolled Square Top. 1770–80.

1144. Plain Tray Top. Dutch Foot.
1750–70.

1145. Plain Tray Top. Ball Foot.
1770–80.

1146. CARVED KNEE. LARGE. 1760–70.
GEORGE S. PALMER COLLECTION.

1147. CARVED KNEE. UNUSUAL SHAPE.
INLAID TRAY EDGE. 1760–70.
H. N. CAMPBELL.

1148. SMALL, TASTEFUL. WELL-SHAPED
SHAFT. BALL AND CLAW. 1760–70.
MRS. FRANCIS P. GARVAN.

1149. EMPIRE. REEDED BASE AND SINGLE-CURVED
LEG. 1800–10. MRS. FRANCIS P. GARVAN.

1150. HEPPLEWHITE. SPADE
FOOT. REEDED BASE. OCTA-
GON. 1790. KATRINA KIPPER.

1151. HEPPLEWHITE. TURNED DEC-
ORATION IN CORNERS. 1790.
T. BELKNAP BEACH.

1152. GOOD, UNUSUAL SHAFT. ODD
FOOT. 1760–70.
SANDERSON COLLECTION.

1153. CHERRY. TOP 14 x 21.
REEDED STANDARD. 1790.
H. W. ERVING.

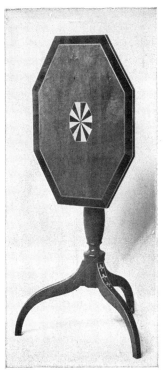

1154. WITH INLAY. 1790.
ALAN WRIGHT.

1155. SPADE FOOT. OCTAGON.
1790. ROBERT T. SMITH.

1156. FRUIT WOOD TOP.
28½ x 19¼ x 14½.
CHESTER E. DIMICK.

1157. GOOD DUTCH LEGS.
CHERRY. 18 INCHES LONG.
H. W. ERVING.

1158. DUTCH FOOT. GRACEFUL.
1750. T. BELKNAP BEACH.

1159. ARCHITECTURAL INLAY.
1800. CLIFFORD S. DRAKE.

1160. BEDSIDE. GALLERY WITH HANDHOLES.
1760–70. SCROLLED BASE. DELICATE LINES.
METROPOLITAN MUSEUM.

1161. HEART HANDHOLES. SCROLLED GALLERY.
DUTCH FOOT. 1750–80. MAHOGANY. PROBABLY
ENGLISH. 24½ x 17½ x 12. H. W. ERVING.

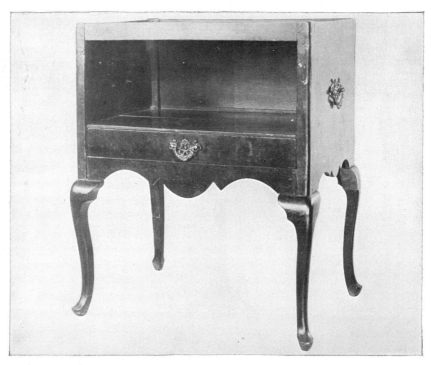

1162. SCROLLED BASE. DUTCH FEET NOT DEVELOPED. HANDLES ENGLISH
AND PROBABLY THE PIECE. TRAY TOP NOT VISIBLE. 1740–70.

All the bedside tables shown on this page have flush drawers and the same general dimensions and style.

1163. TOP CHERRY. BASE PINE. 24½
INCHES HIGH. PENNSYLVANIA WORKTABLE.
TOP 19 X 13. 18TH CENTURY.
E. B. LEETE COMPANY.

1164. HUDSON VALLEY. WORKTABLE.
QUAINT TRESTLE AND CONNECTION. HAND-
HOLE CUBBY. TOP RAISED THREE SIDES.
18TH CENTURY. WADSWORTH ATHENEUM.

1165. TRESTLE WITH
WEDGE TRUSS. VASE
ENDS ON SHOES.
PLAIN FRAME.
THUMB-NAIL MOLD
TOP. SCROLLED
TRUSS. PINE. CON-
NECTICUT ORIGIN. NO
RESTORATIONS.
29 X 25¾ X 16½.
CHESTER E. DIMICK,
GALES FERRY, CON-
NECTICUT.

The fascinating
worktables on this
page are among the
rare but simple and
appealing small pieces
dear to the heart of a
collector. There is a
flavor about them
which gives a small
room done in pine
proper atmosphere.

1166. BAG TABLE. TWO DRAWERS.   1167. TWO DRAWERS AND TRAY.

These work stands nearly all Sheraton type with an occasional Hepplewhite and dating 1790–1800.

1168. ALL SIDES SHAPED, RARELY GOOD.
F. A. ROBART.

1169. "MARTHA WASHINGTON." LEGS CURVE
OUTWARD. I. SACK.

1170. CHAMFERED CORNERS. OUTSTANDING
POSTS. F. L. DUNNE.

1171. DAINTILY TURNED AND REEDED.
FOUR SIDES SHAPED. I. SACK.

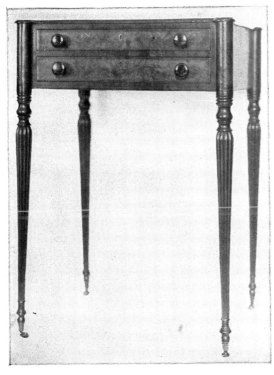

1172. VERY DELICATE POSTS. OUTSTANDING.
S. PRESCOTT FAY.

1173. MAHOGANY. BOLD TURNING. CHAM-
FERED CORNER. 28 x 20 x 18.
E. B. LEETE COMPANY.

1174. RARE BAG TABLE. ARCHED STRETCHERS WITH
SPIRAL FINIAL. LINE INLAY.
MRS. FRANCIS P. GARVAN.

1175. OUTSTANDING POSTS. CHAMFERED
CORNERS. EMPIRE HANDLES.
F. A. ROBART.

1176. CROSS STRETCHER WITH ROUND
SHELF. DRAWER ON CURVE. OUTCURVED
LEGS.

1177. CHAMFERED CORNER. FEATHER-GRAIN
VENEER. LEGS SET UNDER FRAME.
HELEN T. COOKE.

ALL ON PAGE DATE 1790–1800.

1178. Cherry. Frame Rabbeted. Top
Lifts Off. $26\frac{5}{8}$ x $16\frac{1}{4}$ x 16.
Robert T. Smith.

1179. Hepplewhite. Feather-Grain
Veneer. Scalloped Shelf.
F. A. Robart.

1180. Empire. Carved Standard.
Multi-Partitions.
Pennsylvania Museum.

1181. "Martha Washington." Chamfered
Corners. Samuel Wineck, Hartford.

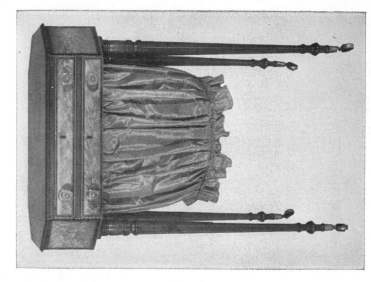

1184. Chamfered Corners. Legs Under as in No. 1182 instead of Extending to the Top. Feather Grain. Attenuated Turnings.

1183. Phyfe Attribution. Tambour. Chamfer. Featured Grain. 1810. Harry V. Weil.

1182. Two Drawers and Bag Drawer. Bent Stretchers. Feathered Grain. Very Dainty. Drawers with Lining Mold.

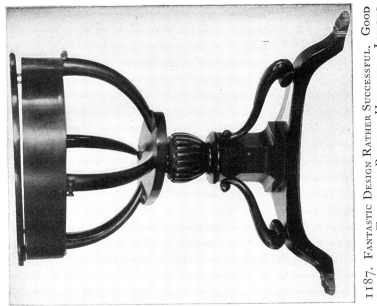

1187. Fantastic Design Rather Successful. Good Scrolls on Triangles Below. Hexagon. Lifting Top. 1820–30. Charles P. Cooley.

1186. Late Empire. Unusually Good Design for Period. Brass Feet. 1830–40. Sanderson Collection, Nantucket.

1185. "Lady's Companion." Corner Shaped over Reeded Posts. Good Veneer. 1800. Opens as Desk. Has Slide Shelf at End. Mahogany. Estate of Harry W. Weeks.

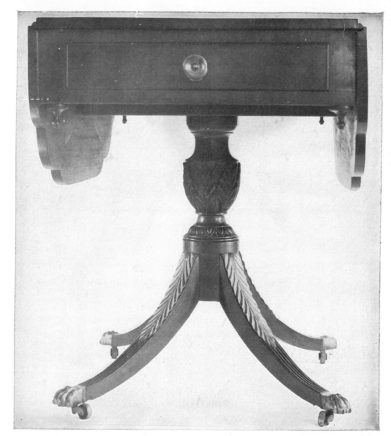

1188. DUNCAN PHYFE. PARLOR OR OCCASIONAL TABLE. DROPS AT CORNERS. BRASS FEET. CONCAVED CARVED LEGS AND CARVED STANDARD. THIS TYPE WAS SOMETIMES CALLED A SOFA TABLE. 1800–15. SANDERSON COLLECTION.

1189–92. KITCHEN OF FOWLER HOUSE, DANVERS, MASSACHUSETTS. OWNED BY PRESERVATION SOCIETY. OVEN FOR SPIT, MISNAMED DUTCH. 1790. BUILT-IN SIDEBOARD. "CRICKET." BALL-HEAD BANDY-LEG ANDIRONS.

1193. LATE EMPIRE ANIMAL FOOT. CARVED CHAMFERED CORNER. 1810. 30¾ x 23½ x 17½.
VIRGINIA. SEWING COMPARTMENT AND WRITING DESK IN TOP. ROBERT T. SMITH.

1194. (Right.) SIMPLE LATE EMPIRE. 1820–30. WALLACE NUTTING.

1195. LATE EMPIRE. MAHOGANY. TOP VENEERED ON MAHOGANY, 18½ x 40½. LEGS LION'S
FEET AND ACANTHUS CARVING. ORIGIN CONNECTICUT. H. W. ERVING.

1196. Trestle Stand. Maple, Pine Top. Top One Piece, 18½ x 30. Shoes 15½ Long. Height 25¼. Connecticut. Important and Rare. 1770–90. Wadsworth Atheneum.

1197–1203. Tap Room of Wayside Inn, Sudbury. Henry Ford. Chair Table at Left. Pilgrim Chair Next. Carved Candle Box Over. Warming Pan. Bulb and Ring Andirons.

In this work where rooms are shown, only those articles are enumerated that are not shown in any other place. The author has hundreds of pictures of interiors that are not included in this work. He is persuaded from the consensus of opinion that the room settings will prove of interest and value to readers. An effort has been made to conform the period of the room as nearly as possible to the period of the articles connected with it, shown in detail.

1204. TRESTLE STAND OR TABLE. THE CLEAT IS CUT TO FORM A PART OF THE FRAME, BEING MORTISED WITH A CHAMFER. DR. MARK L. MINER, OF GREENFIELD, MASSACHUSETTS.

These small tables or large stands might have been used as tavern tables or side tables in the home. They are rare and found in three sorts. No. 1196 had plain stretcher at top. This has both stretchers turned. Nos. 1205 and 1208 have but one stretcher.

1205. TRESTLE STAND, NOTCHED CARVED BASE. 1690. FUESSENICH COLLECTION, TORRINGTON, CONNECTICUT.

1206. TRESTLE STAND, BOARD ENDS. PIERCED WITH HEARTS AND DIAMONDS. 18TH CENTURY. FUESSENICH COLLECTION.

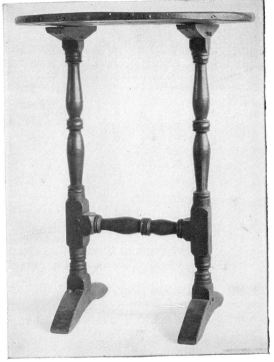

1207. STAND WITH SWINGING INSET GATE FRAME. PINE. TOP DECORATED. TOP 28 x 21. HALF-MOON FEET. EARLY 18TH CENTURY. J. STOGDELL STOKES.

1208. TRESTLE STAND. ONE STRETCHER. ALL TURNED. HALF-MOON FEET. 1690. FUESSENICH COLLECTION.

1209. TRESTLE, BOARD ENDS. 18TH
CENTURY. REVERSIBLE.
CHAUNCEY C. NASH.

1210. TRESTLE STAND WITH CUBBY UNDER LIFTING
TOP. EARLY 18TH CENTURY.
OWNERSHIP LOST TO AUTHOR.

1211. TRESTLE STAND, SCROLL FEET. LATE 17TH CENTURY.
FUESSENICH COLLECTION.

1212–13. TRESTLE STAND WITH LAN-
TERN. 17TH CENTURY.
WAS B. A. BEHREND'S.

The reader will be lenient with us in the matter of classification when we state that a great deal of effort has been expended on that branch of the subject, with the consequence that the individuality of the pieces and the variation in sizes from the largest to the smallest, and the mixture of elements almost make it impossible to find a name and a place that are clearly appropriate. The greatest difficulty seems to occur with stands. Nobody has yet made a law defining size of a tavern table or stand. The division must, therefore, be arbitrarily made. So long as all the animals are gathered into one ark we must be content, even if a little squabbling results.

1214. Light Turned Stand with Plain Stretchers. Vase and Ring Turning with Ogee Scrolled Frame. Oddly Enough There Is No Drawer, but a Drawer Pull. 1690–1720. Edward C. Wheeler, Jr.

In the earliest period no thought seemed to be given to weight. Perhaps the Pilgrim housewives swept round an article which they could not move. When they had had about a century of that sort of thing, they evidently demanded lightly turned furniture. The universal demand for stands is easily understood when we remember that all the lights were one candle power. In case of any illumination which could do more than make darkness visible, several candlesticks were required in each room. We should, of course, except the room where the sparking was done, where a bowl, with oil and a floating wick, was called a sparking lamp, and was about as illuminating as a white bean.

1215. A Splay-Leg Stand with Cross Stretcher. 1690–1710.
Harry V. Weil, New York City.

We quite mistake our fathers if we take it for granted that they thought only of utility. The elaboration, beauty, and expense of many of the garments, even those worn by the men, should effectually refute any such supposition. The same is true of their furniture, on which in many instances pure ornament was lavish to a great extent. The author, in restoring one piece which looked pretty well covered with knobs and drops as it was, was obliged to add thirty-three more. A year or two after he was persuaded that at least a dozen more should have been added. A poor country is never without its decorations. The American Indian expended more on ornament in proportion to necessities than his white brother.

1216. A Stand with All Turned Stretchers.
c. 1700. Very Decorative.
Edward C. Wheeler, Jr.

1217. A Light Stand Easily Suggesting the
Term Applicable to Its Weight and Use.
1700. Same Owner.

1218. Raked Leg. Strongly Shaped. Cut-Out Bracket
Frame. 1690–1720. Present Ownership Unknown.

1219. MAPLE SPLAY-LEG TABLE. PINE TOP. 25½ x 30¼ x 18. TOP ¾ INCH THICK. SPREAD OF LEGS AT BASE 16½ INCHES SQUARE. AT TOP 12½ INCHES. ALL ORIGINAL. 1730–50. A VERY FINE EXAMPLE. CLIFFORD S. DRAKE, NORTH HAMPTON, NEW HAMPSHIRE.

1220–23. SPLAYED. GOOD OGEE SCROLL. ALSO A NOGGIN, FIRKIN, AND A SMALL TUB.

1224. DAINTY CHERRY TABLE. PENNSYL-VANIA. DRAWER ON SIDE RUNS. 1700 OR BEFORE. L. G. MYERS.

1225. Splayed, Walnut Table. Frame Suggesting Highboy Lines. Excellent. 1690–1700. Wadsworth Atheneum.

1226. Walnut, Pennsylvania. Slight Inlay. 1700–40. Formerly the Author's.

1227–28. Well-Turned Stand. Pewter Plate and Pitcher. 1700–30. Was B. A. Behrend's.

1229–30. Well-Turned Stand, with Turned Stretchers. 1700. Hat Box Is Swedish and Closes with a Snap.

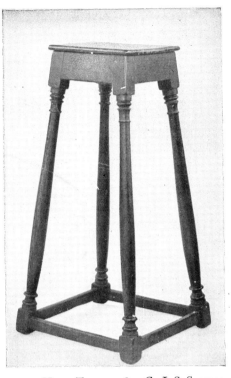

1231. BALL-TURNED STRETCHERS. 17TH C. FUESSENICH COLL.   1232. HIGH, TAPER. 18TH C. J. S. STOKES.

1233. PLAIN STRETCHER. OVAL MAPLE TABLE, FEET LOST. 1690–1700. TOP 18¾ x 27¾.
HEIGHT NOW 20¾ INCHES. WAS PROBABLY 23 INCHES. EDWARD C. WHEELER, JR.

1234-36. Fire Frame. Rare and Excellent Design. A Broadax and Bootjack Are Barely Visible. Clifford R. Weld, Rock, Massachusetts.

1237. Well Turned. Middle Stretcher. 1690–1720. J. J. Sullivan, Woodbury, Connecticut.

1238. Heavy-Turned Splayed Stand, Stretchers Staggered. 1690–1730. J. Stogdell Stokes.

1239. All Turned. Splayed Both Ways. Bracket
Cut on Frame; Round Top. 1690–1700.
Wadsworth Atheneum.

1240. Maple Leg, Pine Top and Frame. Massachusetts Bay. 26½ x 24 x 20. 1730.
Rudolph P. Pauly.

1241. Chamfered Posts. Top Gouge Carved. 1700.
From Churchill Family. Newington, Connecticut. At
Wadsworth Atheneum. George Dudley Seymour.

1242. MIDDLE STRETCHER, ALL-TURNED TABLE. VERY RARE. CURLY MAPLE. NO RESTORATIONS. FOUND NEAR PHILADELPHIA. 29 x 31 x 23½. RARE TURNINGS AND RARE SCROLL AT FRAME. 1730–50. FRANCIS D. BRINTON, WEST CHESTER, PENNSYLVANIA.

1243. SPLAYED CROSS-STRETCHER STAND. 1690–1730. FUESSENICH COLLECTION.

1244. DUTCH-FOOT STAND. CURVE ALL AT THE BOTTOM. 1730–50. MORRIS BERRY.

1245. SPLAYED TABLE. PRESUMABLY WALNUT. FEET LOST. ODDLY SCROLLED SKIRT.
18TH CENTURY. PENNSYLVANIA MUSEUM. MEMORIAL HALL, PHILADELPHIA.

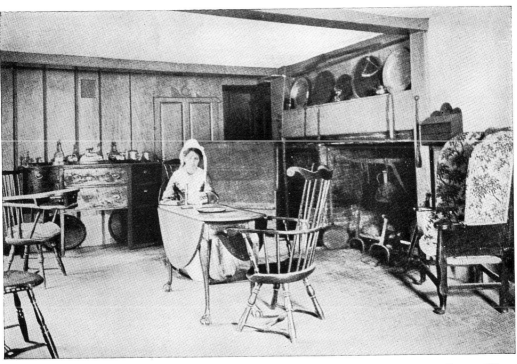

1246–49. ANTIQUARIAN SOCIETY, CONCORD. WRITING CHAIR USED BY EMERSON. UNIQUE WING
CHAIR ON RIGHT. WINDSOR CHAIR WITH EXTREME EARS. ROUND-END SIDEBOARD, STRAIGHT FRONT.

1250. Maple, Oak, and Pine. Feet Missing. Reputed Property of Mother of Nathan Hale, on Farm in Coventry. 18th Century. James Danielson, New London.

1251. (Right.) Stand with Very Small Base, Possibly Unique. 1690–1720. Fuessenich Collection.

1252. Two-Story Stand. Feet Wrong. Possibly Unique. 18th Century. Clifford R. Weld.

1253. (Right.) Stand, with Doubled Turnings, Squares Between. Maple, Pine Top. 17½ Inches Square. 18th Century. Pennsylvania. J. Stogdell Stokes.

1254-55. Two Stands of Similar Type. Plain Stretchers. 1690-1720. That on the Left Has Oval Top, and Is 21¾ Inches High, but Both Have Lost Their Feet. Top 21 x 31. That on Right Is 19 Inches High. Slant One Way. Top 20 x 18. Edward C. Wheeler, Jr.

The plain square stretcher is probably older than the turned stretcher type. Novices should note that it is a habit of scamps to wear down the stretchers in order to give an appearance of age. The pins used in old work, or good new work, are never round, but square, and get a rounded shape by driving home. A round pin will not hold as well. All joints are always pinned.

1256. Heavy Turned Table with Dutch Feet.
Early 18th Century. Morris Berry.

1257. Walnut. Drawer on Side Runs. Fluted
Turnings. 27 x 26½ x 16. Eastern Massachusetts.
18th Century. Nearer Date Uncertain. Unique.

1258. Cross-Stretcher Stand. Cut Corners.
Finial and Fifth Leg. Rare. 1690–1720.
Morris Schwartz.

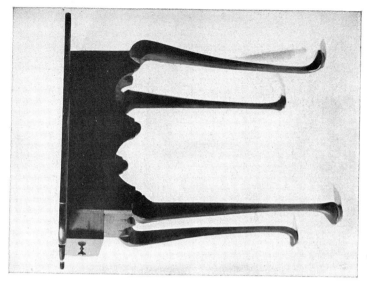

1261. Queen Anne, Deep Frame, Scrolled. Full of Contrast and Style. Shaped Top. 1720-40. W. F. Hubbard, Hartford.

1260. Medial Stretcher, Maple, Pine Top. 24 x 14½ x 13½, on Frame. Dr. and Mrs. J. M. Birnie.

1259. Dutch. Curly. Legs Drawn In, Curved Only at Bottom. Connecticut Origin. 1720-40. James Davidson, New London.

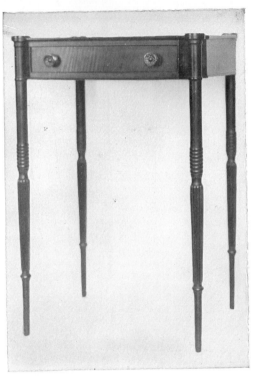

1262. STAND WITH SLIDE. STANTON HOUSE.
CLINTON, CONNECTICUT. 1790–1800.

1263. ATTENUATED TURNINGS. OUTSTANDING
LEGS. CURLY. 1790. S. PRESCOTT FAY.

1264–68. PARLOR, WAYSIDE INN, SUDBURY. RARE STENCILED CRADLE, AS IF FOR TWO DOLLS
FOOT TO FOOT. TRANSITION CHIPPENDALE CHAIR ON RIGHT. TRANSITION DUTCH CHAIR ON
LEFT. SMALL, BRASS BALL ANDIRONS AND FENDER. HENRY FORD.

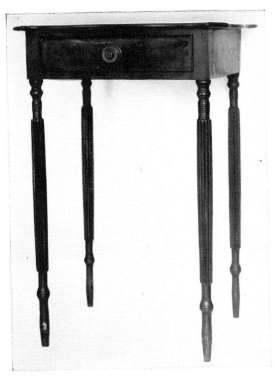

1269. RECTANGULAR STAND, REEDED. 1790.
S. PRESCOTT FAY.

1270. SQUARE HEPPLEWHITE STAND. INLAID.
SIMPLE. 1790. ROBERT T. SMITH.

1271. HEPPLEWHITE PEG FEET. CHAMFERED.
LEGS SET UNDER. 1790. S. PRESCOTT FAY.

1272. OVAL. HEPPLEWHITE. 29 x 15 x 23.
TOP ⅜ INCH THICK INLAID.
CLIFFORD S. DRAKE.

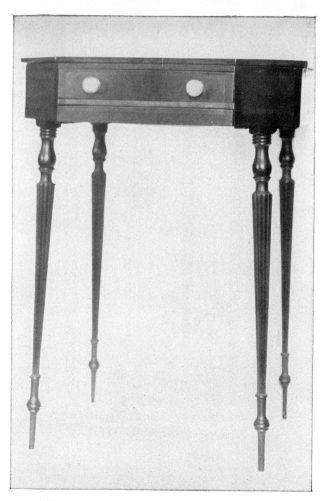

1273. Beautifully Carved. 1790. S. Prescott Fay.　　1274. Reeded. Sharp Taper. 1790. S. Prescott Fay.

1275-79. Wayside Inn. Chair Table, Chippendale Mirror, Andirons, Windsors, Fire-Box.

1280. WINDSOR TABLE. PINE TOP. RARE. 1770–90.
FORMERLY THE AUTHOR'S.

1281–84. HAZEN HOUSE KITCHEN. HAVERHILL. 1690. PINE CRADLE ON RIGHT. SPANISH
CHAIR LEFT. WINDSOR FOOT STOOL. TRIVET IN FIREPLACE. BANISTER BACK, ARCHED TOP RAIL.

1285. Unique, Triangular, Queen Anne Stand from Virginia. 1720–40. J. Stogdell Stokes.

1286. (Right.) Three-Leg Windsor Stand. Maple, Pine Top. From Connecticut. 27 x 24 Diameter. 1780. Mary M. Sampson.

1287. Three Leg, Octagon Table. Three Corners Finished with Drop, Corresponding to Leg Turning. Perhaps Unique. 1710–40. Harry V. Weil.

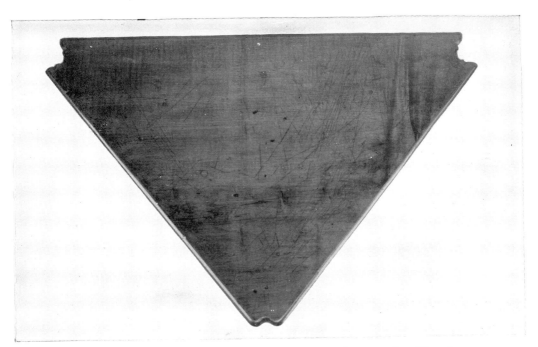

1288. TOP OF STAND NO. 1285. NOTE THAT THE CORNERS ARE NOT ALIKE.

1289. HEAVY, TRIANGULAR, SPLAY-LEG STAND. ALL ORIGINAL. 1720–50.

1290. Triangular Frame, Round Top. 25 x 28¾ Diameter. 1700–30. Balls of Feet Lost. Chauncey C. Nash.

1291–1294. (Right.) Triangular Splayed Stand. Double Betty Lamp, Candlestick with Odd Handle, Sand Glass. 1700–40. Was B. A. Behrend's.

1295. Triangular Frame, Round Top, Swiveled. Three Drop Leaves Which Fall When Top Is Swung. Ball Feet Double. 1700–30. Metropolitan Museum.

1296. (Right.) Stand with T Stretcher. Molded. Very Rare. 1720–50. J. Stogdell Stokes.

1297. A—B. Folding Table, Cabriole Legs. Rare or Unique. Top 26 Inches in Diameter. Height 24¾ Inches. Tray Top. Maple. Mid 18th Century. Stephen Van Rensselaer, Peterboro, New Hampshire.

1298. Hard Pine, Triangular, Round Top. Perhaps Southern. 18th Century. Formerly the Author's.

1299. (Right.) Triangular Rake-Leg Stand, Staggered Stretchers. Chamfered. 22½ x 14¼ Inches Diameter. 18th Century. Frederick A. Gaston, New York.

1300–02. Kitchen, Wentworth-Gardner House. 1760. Portsmouth, New Hampshire.
Always Tiles from Fireplace Out. Blunderbus and Rapier. Goose-Neck Andirons.

1303. Three-Legged Windsor Table.
Dish Top. Late 18th C. J. Stogdell Stokes.

1304. Light Turned, Tray-Top Windsor.
Very Delicate. Francis D. Brinton.

1305. Triangular Stand. Maple,
Cherry Top. 26¾ x 19¼ on Frame.
Early 18th Century.
Dr. and Mrs. J. M. Birnie.

1306. Raked Leg, Curly Maple, Molded
Drawer. 18th Century. Mold on Stretchers
and Frame. J. Stogdell Stokes.

1307. Shoe on Foot, with Carved Toe.
1740–60. N. Cushing.

1308. Carved Toe. 1740–60.
S. Prescott Fay.

1309. Dutch Foot. Drawer Moved
Both Ways through Frame. 1730–60.
Morris Schwartz.

1310. Ball Foot, Spiral Vase, Scalloped
Pendant. Rare. 1750–70.
Morgan B. Brainard.

1311. Odd Claw Feet, Spiral
Shaft, Reversed. 28 x 15. Walnut.
1750–70. Mary M. Sampson.

1312. Whirling Tray Top, on an X Crow's
Nest. 1740–60.
W. A. Hitchcock, Farmington.

1313. DIAMETER 17½ INCHES. BALL
AND CLAW. GADROONED EDGE. FINELY
SHAPED LEGS. 1750–60. H. W. ERVING.

1314. DUTCH FEET. HOLLOW TRIANGLE WITH RECESS
AND DOOR. FLUTED CORNERS. 1740–60.
MALCOLM A. NORTON.

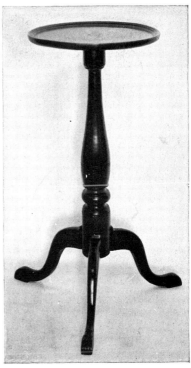

1315. WELL-TURNED STANDARD. DRAWER RUNS
BOTH WAYS. CHERRY, BIRCH TOP. 26½ x 15¼.
BEADED EDGE IS CHERRY. 1740–50. ROBERT T. SMITH.

1316. DUTCH FOOT, CARVED TOES.
1740–60.
MRS. FRANCIS P. GARVAN.

1317. WORK STAND, CHERRY, 18TH C.
TOP 15½. TOP FRAMED INTO CORNER
POSTS. H. W. ERVING.

1318–19. PAIR VERY HIGH, DELICATELY TURNED
CURLY CONCAVED LEG CANDLE STANDS. 1790.
JAMES FENIMORE COOPER.

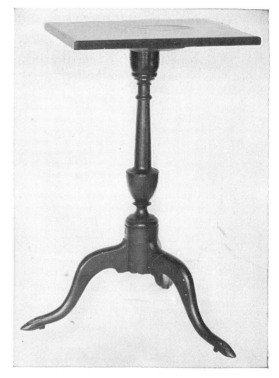

1320. CONVEX LEGS, ODDLY TURNED
SHAFT, HEXAGONAL TOP. 1790.
MRS. FRANCIS P. GARVAN.

1321. WELL-TURNED STAND WITH SHOE IMITA-
TIVE OF LEATHER. NOTE HEEL. 1740–60.
HELEN T. COOKE.

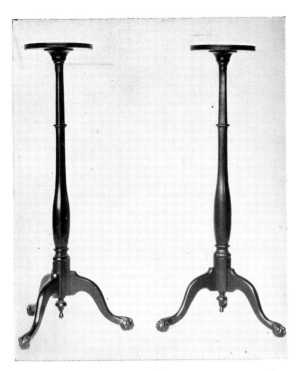

1322–23. Pair Torchères. 1750–75. Ma-
hogany. 39 Inches High. Ball and Claw.
Hollow Molds on Triangular Pillars.
H. W. Erving.

1324–25. Torchères. Feet with Rosettes.
Concave Molded Standards, Top Square with
Broken Extended Corner Squares. 1780–90.

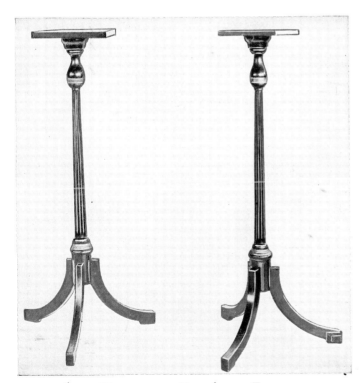

1326–27. Hepplewhite Torchères. Fluted. 1790.
Morgan B. Brainard.

1328. One of Pair. 1790.

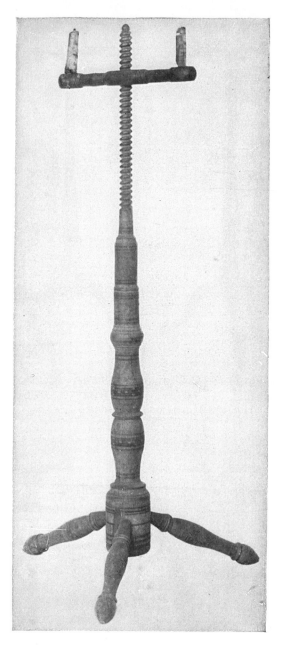

1329. SCREW CANDLE STAND, WITH SCREWS TO PUSH
UP CANDLES AS THEY BURN. ALL MAPLE. ONE
OTHER KNOWN. 18TH CENTURY. SWIVEL TABLE WITH
SLIGHTLY RAISED RIM. WADSWORTH ATHENEUM.

1330. TRIPOD STAND WITH CROSS BAR. THE
FRATERNITY WHOSE PROFESSION IS TO DECEIVE
IS SAID TO MAKE THEM UP FROM OLD BED-
POSTS AND SPINNING WHEELS.

The kind of wood proper for a piece of furniture is not regulated wholly by the period. A chest of drawers, for instance, is properly made in pine, during the maple turned period. Persons who refer to pine tables should refer to the tops alone. The bases would never be strong enough in common pine. There is no pine period, and no maple period. The periods were one. The wood used depends upon the use. Thus a Windsor chair requires hickory in the spindles, but should avoid it in the seat to save weight. The legs also should be maple, as that is the best material.

1331. SCALLOPED TOP. SHAPED BASE.
CROOKED LEGS. 18TH CENTURY.
FRANCIS D. BRINTON.

1332. TABLE STAND FOR BETTY LAMP.
13 INCHES HIGH. 18TH CENTURY.
J. STOGDELL STOKES.

1333. HEIGHT 34 IN.
MARY M. SAMPSON.

1334. T BASE. ONE TURNED FOOT.
18TH CENTURY. J. STOGDELL STOKES.

1335. X BASE.
KATRINA KIPPER.

1336. A Crude Stand with Odd Feet. The Screw Carries a Whirling Table and a Bar with Holes for the Candle. 18th Century. Present Ownership Unknown.

These small stands were sometimes called cobblers' lights, and of course cobblers used them, but they were universally in use for reading or sewing, because they were so small that they could be brought directly to the workers' hand. They come under the class of folk furniture, despised in elegant volumes, but beloved of collectors. It is for this reason that this work shows hundreds of such things at the same time increasing the number of elegant pieces.

 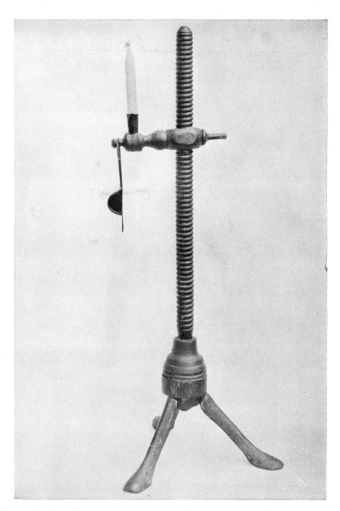

1337. (Right.) Screw Stand with Crude Dutch Feet, Attached to a Hub. Arranged for One Candle Only. A Pair of Wrought Snuffers Depends from the Knob. 18th Century. J. Stogdell Stokes.

The snuffers were a very necessary article as the wick in a few minutes would grow a long charred end which smoked. In great houses a servant was employed who did nothing in the evening but go about and snuff candles. These candles were, in the earlier time, dipped in hot tallow and required numerous immersions as that which adhered from each dipping hardened. Later on, molds came into use, commonly tin, but in good examples batteries of many pewter molds, one of which was recently offered for sale for a sum that reached three figures. The candle wicking was run through the point of the mold and tied. At the upper end it was tied to a long crossbar, which, when the tallow had set, lifted out the entire row.

1338. Cross Base. 17th Century. Henry V. Weil.

1339. Massive Post. Cross Base. Chamfered. 17th or 18th Century.

1340-41. Ratchet Stand. Blocked Base. A Pawl Engages the Ratchet. Standard of Red Clay with Coarse Black Glaze. West Virginia. H. W. Erving.

1342. Ratchet and Pawl. Mrs. J. Insley Blair.

1343. STICK LEGS. TABLE AND CANDLE BAR.

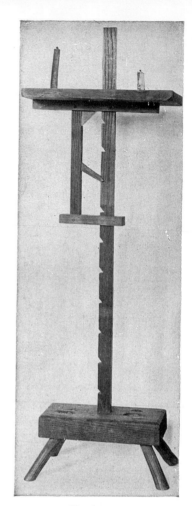

1344. RATCHET STAND.

1345-1346. FUESSENICH COLLECTION.

1347. CRANE. WM. B. GOODWIN.

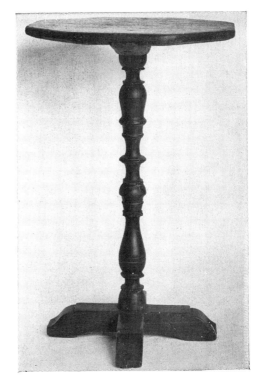

1348. Adjustable Post. H. V. Weil.

1349. Well Turned, X Base.
Mary M. Sampson.

1350. Tip Top, Odd Base. 18th
Century. Pocket.
Howard Reifsnyder.

1351–52. Posts with Screw Between, and
Posts with Slot and Pin.
Fuessenich Collection.

1353-54. Two Fine Cross Base Stands. That at Right Has Fluted Column Set on Diagonally. Late 17th or Early 18th Century. Wadsworth Atheneum.

1355-58. Four 18th Century Stands. Formerly B. A. Behrend's.

1360. (Right.) RATCHET AND PAWL STAND WITH A BASE FORMED FROM THE SECTION OF A SLAB INTO WHICH THE POSTS WERE MORTISED. AN ARRANGEMENT SEEN IN ONLY ONE OTHER INSTANCE IS THAT OF THE PODS OR SLOTS INTO WHICH THE CANDLES SLIP. THESE SOCKETS HAVE BEEN BORED OUT AND AN ADJUSTABLE MOVING BASE WITH A HANDLE HAS BEEN FITTED IN, SO THAT THE CANDLE CAN BE LIFTED AS IT BURNS. 18TH CENTURY. WADSWORTH ATHENEUM.

An important use of a work like this is to bring to light fine rare, odd, or important articles of furniture. The mere statement that a piece is unique, which means, of course, to the knowledge of the author or his friends, is a motive to call out information and in this manner the search for such articles is stimulated.

1361-63. CROSS BASE STAND, TAPERING BASE. ON IT SETS A CARVED SPOON RACK WITH SLOTS FOR PEWTER SPOONS. THESE WERE A FAVORITE DECORATION IN KNICKERBOCKER KITCHENS. THE OLDEST PEWTER SPOONS HAD A ROUND BOWL AS SHOWN. 18TH CENTURY. B. A. BEHREND.

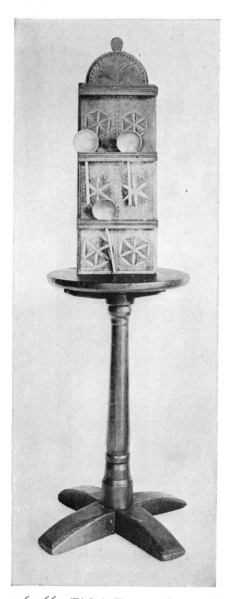 

1364-66. (Right.) DEEPLY TURNED STAND. ON IT RESTS A PIPE BOX WITH A DRAWER. THERE ARE THREE HEART CUT-OUTS AND A SWASTIKA. THE DRAWER WAS FOR TOBACCO. THE RARE STANDARD FOR THE BETTY LAMP HAS A DOUBLE BASE, ONE DISHED DOWN, ANOTHER DISHED UP, THE SECOND BEING TO CATCH THE DRIP. THE LAMP IS ADJUSTABLE BY MEANS OF A SPRING, AND THE STAND ENDS AT THE TOP IN A RING. G. WINTHROP BROWN.

The variety of these wooden stands is endless. The author saw in one shop twelve different patterns, all of them new, all purporting to be old. Good patterns were rare, and the demand always finds itself met by a certain sort of supply.

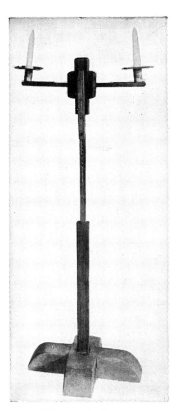

1367. Hollis French.

1368. B. A. Behrend.

1369–70. With
Hook on Candle.

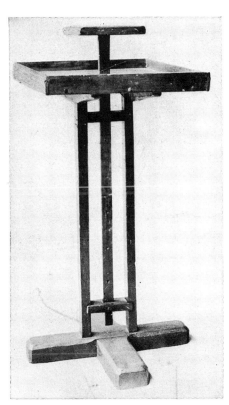

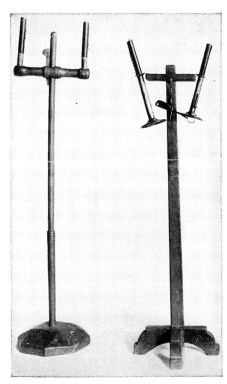

1371. Double Top. Post Adjusted
by Pin. Henry V. Weil.

1372–73. Edward C. Wheeler, Jr.

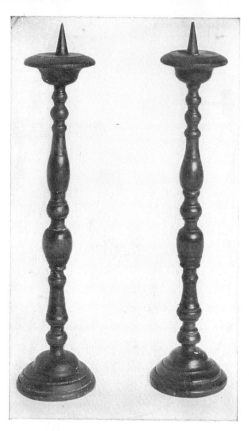

1376. WIND SHIELD
E. B. LEETE COMPANY.

An important device in a
draughty house. It took the
place of the great glass globe
often used over candles.

1374-75. STANDARDS WITH SPIKE.
MARY M. SAMPSON.

1377-78. STANDS WITH CONTOURED FOOT. 18TH CENTURY.
WADSWORTH ATHENEUM.

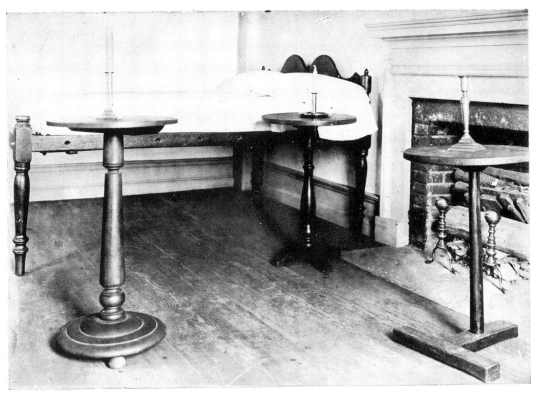

1379–83. THREE STANDS, HIRED MAN'S BED, AND SAUCER-BASE CANDLESTICK. 18TH CENTURY.
NATHAN HALE BIRTHPLACE, COVENTRY, CONNECTICUT. GEORGE DUDLEY SEYMOUR.

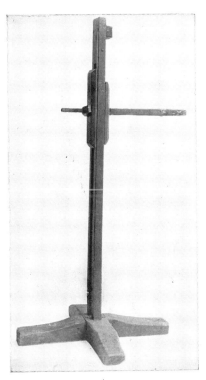

1384. JAMES DAVIDSON.

1385. F. D. BRINTON.

1386. FOSTER DISINGER.

1387. TABLE STAND FOR BETTY.
J. STOGDELL STOKES.

1388. OCTAGON, HEPPLEWHITE.
WAS THE AUTHOR'S.

1389-90. THESE STANDS OF CURIOUS DESIGN ARE SAID BY SOME TO BE FOUND IN WESTERN NEW YORK, AND BY SOME IN CANADA. THEY ARE CERTAINLY A QUAINT CONCEIT. THE RIGHT-HAND ONE HAS A KIND OF BASKET IN WHICH YARN MIGHT HAVE BEEN PLACED. IT IS IMPOSSIBLE TO DATE THEM. FRANK A. ROBART.

1391. A Screw Stand with Crossbar and Rotary Table of a More Decorative Character Than Usual. There Being a Good Acorn at the Top and the Hub Being Hexagonal with a Slight Carved Decoration on Top. 18th Century. Formerly in Ives Collection.

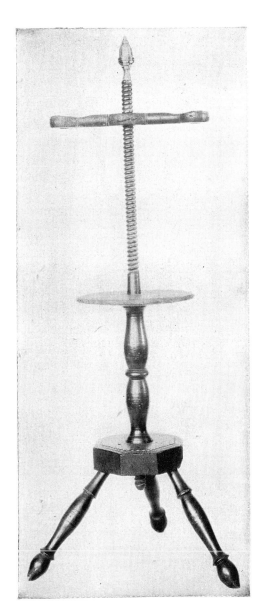 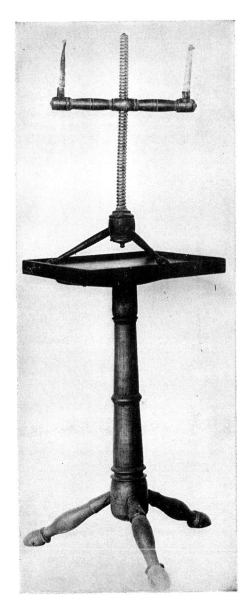

1392-93. (Right.) A Floor and Table Stand. Formerly in Same Collection.

These table stands were very convenient because the writer still remembers that an ordinary candle placed on a table did not illuminate it well, particularly on a dining table or to throw light abroad in a room. The effect of a wall sconce was obtained by these low stands placed on other articles of furniture.

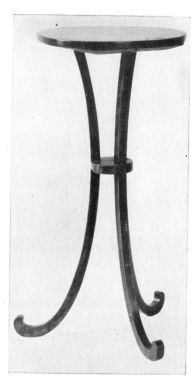

1394. A Standard with Tilted Table Which May Be Let Down, Meeting a Similar Table. Between the Two Are Swing Brackets for the Candlesticks. 1740. Solid Mahogany. Said to Have Belonged to the Gardners, of Gardner Island. James Davidson, New London.

1395. (Right.) Scrolled Tripod Stand. Robert T. Smith.

1396. Slant Base with Cleat for Book or Music. Katrina Kipper.

1397. Mahogany Tilt Stand with Drawers, and Swing Candle Rests. 31 x 22 x 16. Edward Bringhurst.

1398. Screen, Dutch Feet, Large Tapestry Panel. 1740–70. Katrina Kipper, Accord, Massachusetts.

The apparent simplicity of the base is deceiving, like all good Dutch lines, for they are subtle, and a slight deviation from the line of grace is fatal.

Most fine screens are English. The earlier types, of the Dutch and Chippendale school, are rare anywhere, and in this country those found are for the most part later.

1399. (Right.) Covered with Early Paint; Apparently Maple or Cherry. Found at Norwich, Connecticut. 39 Inches High; Frame 15¼ x 15¾. 1750–70. Chester E. Dimick, Gales Ferry, Connecticut.

A frame surrounded the decorative piece, to hold it in place. In this case the fine quaint design stands out from the plain ground effectively.

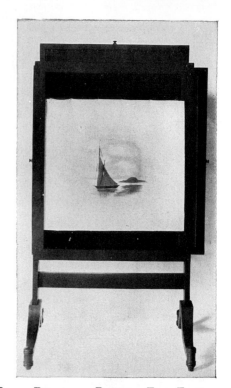

1400–01. Dutch Mode, the Foot of That on Right Being the Better. Fine Floral Spray at Left, Chinese Garden at Right. 1750–70. H. W. Erving.

1402. (Right.) Late Empire, Trestle Base, on Spool Feet. Three-Part Sliding Top. 1825–40. The Author's.

1403. Empire, Brass Feet, Reeded Trestle. Three-Part Sliding. 1820–30. Morris Berry.

1404. (Right.) Three Part, Empire. Fine Fabric. 1820. T. Belknap Beach.

1405. Lamp Screen.

1406. Wadsworth Atheneum.

1407. Lamp Screen.

Nos. 1405 and 1407, the First in Curly Maple, Are to Place upon a Table in Front of a Light. 18th or Early 19th Century. Mrs. Francis P. Garvan.

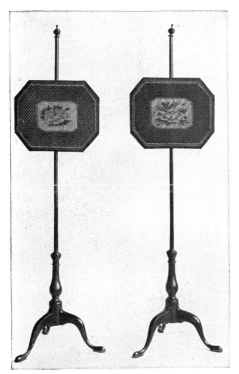

1408-09. Pair, Dutch Foot. 18th Century. T. Belknap Beach.

1410. 17th or 18th Century. James Davidson.

1411. 18th Century. L. P. Goulding.

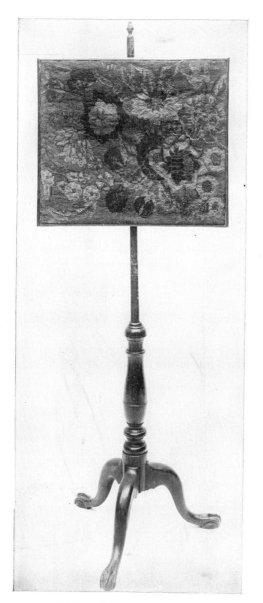

1413. (Right.) A Very Dainty Screen, Fully Carved Feet, Carved Knee and Two Spirals on the Shaft, above Which There Is a Fluting. As to the Origin of These Two Pieces, No. 1412 May Be American or May Not. It Has Been Long in This Country. No. 1413 Is, We Believe, English. 1750–70. The Sliding Panel Itself Is 22½ x 19½. The Misses A. and E. P. Foster.

1414. An Oval Screen, Dutch Foot. Beautifully Worked Floral Design; Graceful, Simple Shaft. 1740–80. S. Prescott Fay, Boston.

1415. (Middle.) A Dutch-Foot Screen, Pointed Toe. Floral Design. 1740–80. Mrs. Francis P. Garvan.

1416. (Right.) Dutch Foot. With Needlework in Silk: Crane, Swallow, Lilies. Formerly the Author's.

The pole screen was an object on which the young ladies of the family exercised their skill. The object of it was to protect the face from the open fire. For this reason the height was made adjustable. The pieces were light and graceful and very decorative.

1417. Eagle Ornament for Ship's Stern. 18th or Early 19th Century. Edward P.
Sanderson Collection, Nantucket.

This eagle is very well done. There is a wide divergence of merit in these. Now that the day of the sailing ship has passed, these objects are highly decorative for colonial homes. They are especially appropriate in the old coast towns, where the better houses were those of sea captains or merchants whose calling was connected with the sea.

1418. A Ship Model.

What we have said above of the eagle applies equally to figure heads, although these are better adapted for garden ornaments. The ship model is much sought for and is excellent for mantels in old houses.

1419. Scrimshaw Ornaments, Made by Sailors, of Bone or Ivory, Are Endless in Their Variety. There Is a Great Collection of Them at the Dartmouth Historical Society, New Bedford.

1420. A Good Type of Tavern Table with a Middle Stretcher.

1421. A Pair of Late Windsor Chairs. All on This Page from Sanderson Collection.

1422–23. A Room in Iron Works House, Saugus, Built about 1646. It Shows a Great Chimney Girt with a Molded Edge. The Floor Timbers Are Frankly Open as in the Earliest Time. The Only Article of Furniture to Which Attention Is Now Called Is the Three-Cornered Chair in Which the Lady Sits. It Is English, Such as Was Sought for by Walpole, and Is Probably of Scandinavian Origin, so Far as Style Is Concerned.

1424–28. Great Room of Ipswich Historical Society. Probably the Best in This Country. There Is a Cross Summer Beam. The Objects Illustrated Are the Reel on the Right, the Hank of Flax, the Three Mortars with Pestles, and the Birch Broom.

1429. A Carved Cake Board. This Was Used To Make an Impression on Cake Dough, Especially Hard Gingerbread. The Author Had Another Which Showed the Full Figure of a Queen in Full Regalia. They Are Foreign and of the 18th and Perhaps the 17th Century, The Size Is Large. Brooks Reed, Boston.

1430. A Baby Walker, of Amusing Crudity in the Base. The Contrivance Which Held the Wheels Swung About. There Is, of Course, a Round Opening in the Top on Which the Baby Rested Hands. While It Is Impossible To Date This Unique Affair, It Is as Early as the 18th Century or Perhaps the 17th. Fuessenich Coll.

1431-34. A Fireplace and Paneled Room, Original. In Pynchon Hall, Springfield, Erected for the Connecticut Valley Historical Society. The Article in the Distance Is a Baby Pen of Very Quaint Construction. It Was Not to Push About. The Andirons Are Cast. The Bellows Are Large, with Turning on the Face.

1435-36. The Splayed Recessed Fireplace in Kitchen Chamber of the Wentworth-Gardner House, Portsmouth, New Hampshire, Which the Author Sold for the Use of the Metropolitan Museum through the Generosity of R. T. H. Halsey. All the Work Is Original. The Passage on the Left Gave Access to a Small Room with Another Door into the Front Chamber. These Small Passages Were Used as Closets for Clothing or Powdering Wigs. A Pair of Simple Chippendale Chairs and a Crude Transition Chair on the Left.

1437-39. Pennsylvania Pottery. At the Left a Lamp with Outlets for Two Wicks. At the Center a Frame for Roasting. At the Right an Ink Well. All Rare. Collection of J. Stogdell Stokes, Philadelphia.

1441-43. A Mantel with Delicate Attenuated Paired Pillars. The Work Belongs to the McIntire Time. Andirons with Oval Balls. Serpentine Fire Screen. 1790.

1440. The Carved Mantel in the Great Parlor of the Benning-Wentworth Mansion, Newcastle, New Hampshire. It Is Perhaps the Most Elaborate of Its Period. 1730-45.

1444-46. A Mantel of 1790-1800. In the Henry Stearns' Place at New Hartford, Connecticut.

Done in composition ornament so far as the festoons are concerned. The dentils and all other work are in carved wood. The fireplace formed the center of decoration in all colonial rooms. The lack of it in any modern house can in no way be supplied. This example shows a good pair of andirons in brass and a serpentine screen pierced with spiral openings and decorated at the center with medallions. The feet also are in brass imitative of animal feet. These brass fenders were mostly English. They form a fine decoration and finish for any fireplace except that in the kitchen. They should never be used with iron andirons. In the kitchen there were invariably iron andirons and never very tall. The English type rather lofty and decorative is entirely out of place in those American kitchens or dining rooms which are transformed kitchens.

The old houses were really built around the chimney and the amplitude of the fireplace dates a house within about thirty years. Even in the earliest time chamber fireplaces were small, some of them very small. The 17th century fire room or kitchen, however, had a fireplace probably never less than seven feet, and from that running up to twelve feet. The parlor fireplaces were in size between the kitchen and the chamber fireplaces. It was not before about 1720 that decorative mantels were built, and they did not meet their full flower of decoration till the latter part of that century. The highest type in taste, however, were those with simple large molding of about 1750. Some of this date have appeared under the caption shell top cupboards, which coincided in date with the best mantels. Later will appear fireplaces full of kitchen contrivances.

1447. Crewel Work Bed. Colors Very Rich, Especially Greens and Reds. Texts or Poems around Upper Valance. The Owner's Own Picture of This Piece, the Only Good One. 1745. York Jail, Maine, Museum.

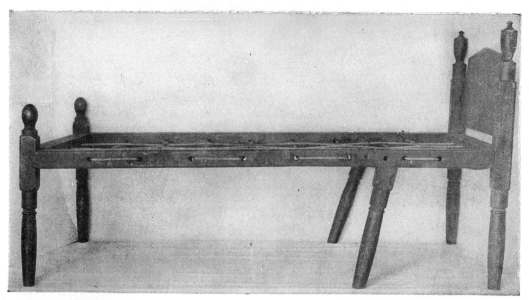

1448. FOLDING PRESS BED. 18TH CENTURY. TOP SWINGS BEYOND THE UPRIGHT POSITION TO ALLOW FOR USE IN A LARGE CLOSET WITH TWO DOORS.

1449. PANELED HEAD, TRUNDLE BED. 18TH CENTURY.

In the daytime it was pushed beneath a large bed. Those with paneled heads are rare. Our ancestors had more pieces of convertible furniture than we do. They used press beds, trundle beds, settle beds, chair tables, settle tables, folding chairs, and various other contrivances.

1450–56. An Oak
Bed with Double
Arch Headboard.
Oak Beds Are
Rare. The Chair
in the Rear with
Three Slats Is of
White Oak. 17th
Century. The
Last on the Right
Is a Simple Four
Back on Which
the Rockers May
Be Original. The
Rugs Are Date-
less. They Have
Probably Been
Made for Hun-
dreds of Years
from Braided
Rags. Chest on
Left, Not Else-
where Shown,
Has Very High
Blocked Panels.
The Spinning
Jenney Is Shaped
Like a Chair
Frame, but Open
at One Side.

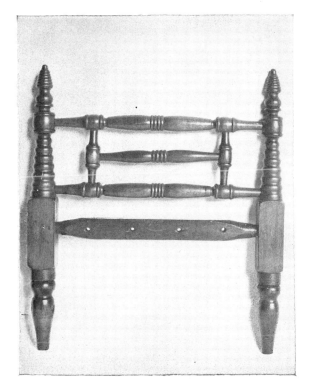

1457. A New
York State Bed.
18th or Early
19th Century.
Mrs. Francis P.
Garvan.

1458–61. A Bed with Original Canopy, but Open at the Foot as in the Second Period. 18th Century. A Small Mirror in a Leather Frame. An All-Turned Child's Chair; a Mushroom Four Back Chair.

1462–63. Canopied Bed with Ogee Arch. This Shows How Unimportant the Posts Were, Being Invisible and Therefore Styleless and Difficult To Date. A Simple Queen Anne Mirror. The Upper Section Cut with a Figure. 18th Century.

1464–66. A Bed in Which the Pole Disjoints. Possibly Suggesting the Term Tent Bed, Although That Pattern Is Usually Round Top. A Fine Early Round Table without Stretchers, by the Bedside. A Mirror of About 1700. Other Articles Shown Elsewhere.

The earliest beds by no means always had canopies. The beds of the poor, those of the hired men, placed in the attic, and even some rich beds, were without canopies. But the canopy seemed to be called for in the spirit of the age, and even after it ceased to be used, as a room was set apart for a bed, the old tradition of the high post continued.

1467. A Settle End Folding Bed. Perhaps Unique. 18th Century.
Wadsworth Atheneum.

1468–71. Heavy Bed, Square Section Below. Octagoned Above. In John Alden House, Duxbury. A Beautiful Wrought Canopy. The Chair at the Foot Is the Turned Banister Back. Hooked Rugs. In the Corner One Sees a Gun Stock Post with a Chamfered Corner, Which Was Very Likely Wrought by John Alden Himself. The House Was Built by His Grandson, but as He Was a Carpenter and Lived Here with Priscilla the Last Thirteen Years of His Life, It Is Reasonable To Suppose That His Services Were Enlisted.

It is a great pleasure to state that this house belonging to the Alden Family Association is in the custody of Charles Alden, a man of taste and of proper feeling towards the founders of his family in America. He has interested himself to see that proper furniture adorns the house and that it is conducted without a commercial tone.

The bedroom of John and Priscilla is that off the kitchen. Some of the original shingles are undoubtedly on the side walls of this house. House dates about 1653. John Alden was at that time about 53 years old. Bed, 18th century.

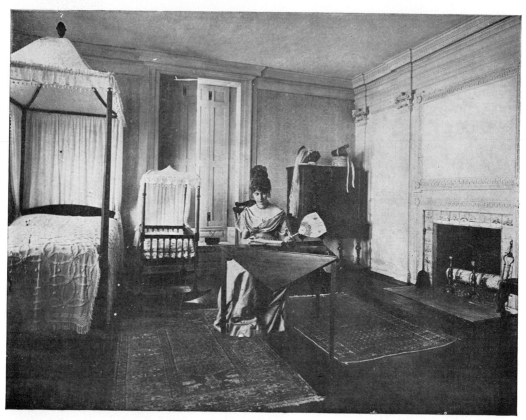

1472-74. Bed with Fluted Posts, Molded Foot, and Double Curve or Ogee Frame. The Crib Which Did Not Have Rockers Originally Is One of the Most Delightful Pieces of Furniture. The Three-Cornered Table Is Rare. 18th C. Wentworth-Gardner House.

1475-77. A Bed with Molded Foot and Large Netted Canopy. Good Dutch Chair with Fan Carving. Rag Carpet. Dutch Chair in Distance with Wide Fiddle Back. 1770-1800. Washington's Bedroom, Webb House, Wethersfield. Colonial Dames of Connecticut.

1478. A Ball and Claw Foot with Well-Carved Knee and Taper Fluted Posts. The Best Type of Rich Bed, Which, It Should Be Observed, Has a Post Always Tapering from the Frame. A Netted Fringe on the Counterpane Which Is in Candle Wicking Not Cut. 1760–75. Howard Reifsnyder.

1479. A SHERATON BED. WELL CARVED ON THE URN ABOVE THE POST. OGEE CANOPY FRAME. 1790–1800. I. SACK.

1480–81. A CHIPPENDALE BED, FORMERLY THE AUTHOR'S. MIRROR NOT SHOWN ELSEWHERE. 1670–75.

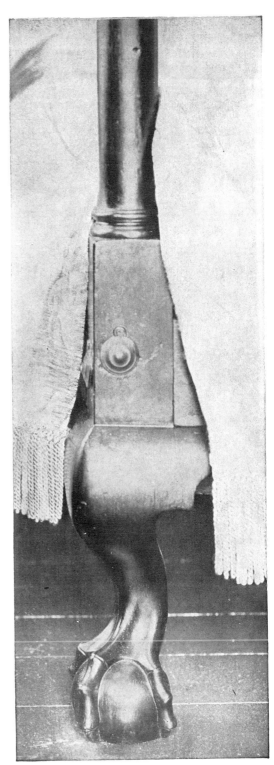

1482. DETAIL OF POST NO. 1478.
HOWARD REIFSNYDER.

1483. DETAIL POST. CHIPPENDALE.
1770. SANDERSON COLLECTION.

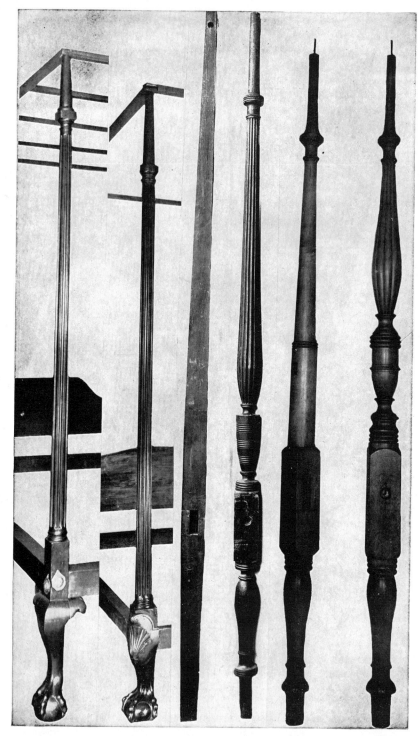

1484–87. The First and Second Are the Chippendale Time. The Third and Fourth Are Sheraton. Rhode Island School of Design, Left. I. Sack, at Right.

1488–90. Bed with Molded Foot, the Canopy of Which Is Attached by a Ring to the Ceiling. The Comfortable Was Made Sufficiently Large To Serve as a Valance. The Mirror Is Not Shown Elsewhere. Half-Round Chippendale Table at Left.

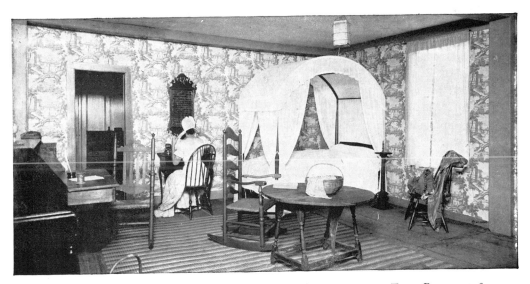

1491–92. Kitchen Chamber of Webb House, Wethersfield. Tent Bed of 1780. Chippendale Mirror of 1760.

1493–94. Voluminously Carved Foot and Wide Bracket. Chippendale Motive.
89 x 62 x 79. Note that the Decoration Is Massed. The Covers of the Bolts Are
in the Shape of Escutcheon Covers. Bed Furniture in Crimson Silk. Valance on
Inside of Frame. Chippendale Chair at Left. 1760–75. Edward Bringhurst,
Wilmington, Delaware.

1495. A REMARKABLE SPORT. BALL-AND-CLAW FOOT AND CARVED KNEE, BUT SHORT POSTS. NOTE THAT USUALLY THROUGH THE CHIPPENDALE PERIOD THE HEAD POSTS WERE SIMPLE. THE CANOPY PERSISTED AT THE HEAD WITH ITS CURTAINED DRAPERIES, WHILE THE FOOT POSTS WERE EXPOSED. THIS BED MADE WITHOUT CANOPY IS AFTER THAT ANALOGY. 1760–75. MISS SELMA ERVING. WASHINGTON, D. C.

1496. A CHIPPENDALE BED RICHLY CARVED WITH SPIRALED URNS AND ACANTHUS LEAF, AND A CANOPY WITH A GREEK MOTIVE, BORDER BACKED BY A CHIPPENDALE SCROLL WITH ROSETTES.

1497. (Right.) A RICHLY CARVED DETAIL. CHIPPENDALE POSTS. 1760–75. NOTE THAT THE CARVING EXTENDS ABOVE THE FRAME. THIS BLOCK WAS REMOVABLE. FORMERLY THE AUTHOR'S.

1498–99. A Press Bed Designed To Remain Always in the Same Position. To Modern Thought the Doors Would Seem Superfluous. A Small 18th Century Mirror.

1500. Richly Carved with Elaborately Carved and Painted Canopy. 1790–1800. Metropolitan Museum.

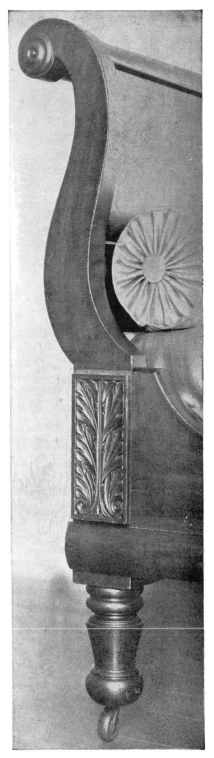

1501. FULLY CARVED POST. PRESUMABLY ENGLISH. 1760–75. IN THIS CASE ALL FOUR POSTS
WERE ALIKE.

1502. (Middle.) CHIPPENDALE BED. RHODE ISLAND SCHOOL OF DESIGN. THE HEAD IS BELIEVED
TO BE NOT ORIGINAL.

1503. (Right.) A SO-CALLED SLEIGH BED WITH A CARVED PANEL. ROSETTE AT TOP. MADE UP
WITH ROLLED BOLSTERS. 1800–20. EDWARD F. SANDERSON COLLECTION, NANTUCKET.

1504–08. Bed of Oak. Wing Chair. Silhouette. Late Windsor. Wadsworth Atheneum.

1509–12. Hepplewhite Bed, Spade Foot, Crane, Bandbox, Hepplewhite Mirror, Etc.

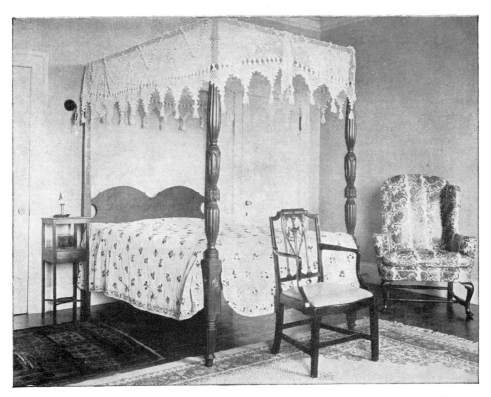

1513–15. Sheraton Bed, Carved. Double Arch Headboard. Three-Shelf Candle Stand. Sheraton Chair, Unusual Square Legs. 1790. I. Sack.

1516–18. Bedroom, Ipswich Historical Society. Tent Bed. Early Canopy, Netted. Cradle of 1790.

1519–21. A Press Bed Built To Stand in the Room. Six Legs. When Folded the Spread Was Pulled Down over All. Dutch Clock. Simple Pine Blanket Chest, 18th Century.

1522. Square Posts. Molded Foot. Posts Chamfered Above. 18th Century.
A Good Example of the Middle Period While the Head Was Still Draped and the
Foot Posts Were Cleared of All Drapery.

Logically there was no reason to retain the canopy at the head and coming down against the wall after it had been removed from other portions of the bed. The fashion shown here is only another mark of the slowness with which ideas moved. The canopy, of course, was first a convenience, and later it appears it was thought of as a decoration. Observe the eight-sided posts at the foot of this bed. Their plain contour indicates that they were certainly made to be closed in with drapery.

Most colonial beds, the term being strictly used, were very plain — mere poles to hold the canopy. The use of press beds to shut in closets was frequent, to save room. The elaborate beds of England are not found at all here, of the 17th century type. The commonest bed with any pretension to style was a Sheraton with reeded posts. It is not as good as the slightly earlier fluted posts. The ball-and-claw foot was always rare, as it required a great deal of labor and skill in construction. The pineapple bed of early 19th century came after the good period.

1523–25. 18th Century Bed with Double Netting. Chair at Foot, Late 18th Century. Large Hooked Rug on Right.

1526–28. Hepplewhite, Spade Foot, Carved Urn Bed. A Round Hepplewhite Table. Mirror About 1820 with Reeded Pillars.

1529-30. SHERATON BED WITH FINE SUNBURST SPREAD. 1790. QUINCY HOMESTEAD. RARE 17TH CENTURY TABLE, HEAVILY TURNED. FIRE FRAME. GOOSE CHASE PATTERN QUILT IN THE MAKING. NOTE THE HEAVY SUMMER BEAM AND THE OGEE CANOPY ON BED.

1531-35. LOW BED. DOUBLE ARCHED HEADBOARD. TRUNDLE BED. WALL SHELVES MADE WITH ROPE. WICKER BIRD CAGE. TURNED BANISTER-BACK SIDE CHAIR. 18TH CENTURY.

1536–38. Bedroom, Quincy Homestead. Sheraton Bed. Constitution Mirror. Bandbox Papered Originally To Agree with the Room. Note that the Earliest Beds Did Not Have Turned Feet, but Were Square from the Frame to the Floor with or without a Base Mold.

1539–40. Very High Frame Bed. Sheraton. The Urns Were Placed above the Canopy Frame. Good Mirror on Left.

1541. Sheraton Bed. Handsomely Carved on Urn with Reeded Top, and Good Furniture. Headboard Also Carved. Edward F. Sanderson Collection. Nantucket.

1542-43. Wayside Inn Bedroom, Henry Ford. Sheraton Bed of 1790-1800. Chair at Right, Square Post, Modified Dutch Back. 1740.

1544-46. Sheraton Bed. Canopy Unique to the Author, Arches from All Sides. Very Effective. Simple Mirror. 1820. Chippendale Dutch Transition Chair against Curtain. 1750.

1547. Detail of Headboard of No. 1493. The Eagle Is in Two Parts. The Head Being Projected Far in Front of the Headboard. This Example Is Interesting as Appearing on a Chippendale Bed Far Earlier than the Ordinary Flat Carved Eagle Motive.

1548. Detail Gooseneck Bed. A Variation of the Sleigh Bed Pattern. The Larger Piece Shows the Post. In This Instance We Have What Is Called a Side Bed. That Is To Say, There Are Only Two Finished Posts, and the Bed Was Pushed against the Wall. A Rare Single Bed. The Back Posts Lack the Carved Decoration. The Second Smaller Gooseneck Carving Is the Bracket on the Rail of the Same Bed.

1549–51. Bed with Molded Foot. Fluted Post. Simple but Effective. Ogee Canopy. Good Pembroke Table. Eight-Centered Braided Rug. Good Small Brass Andirons. 1760.

1552–53. Hepplewhite Type Bed with Arched Mahogany Canopy as a Flat Surface with Small, Half-Round Molds on Edge. Unusual Jacobean Chair against Window. Gothic Chippendale Chair in Front of Bed. This and Many Others Not Designated Were in the Furniture of the Author's Chain of Houses,

1554. Eagle Carved Headboard. 1790–1810. J. J. Sullivan, Woodbury, Connecticut.

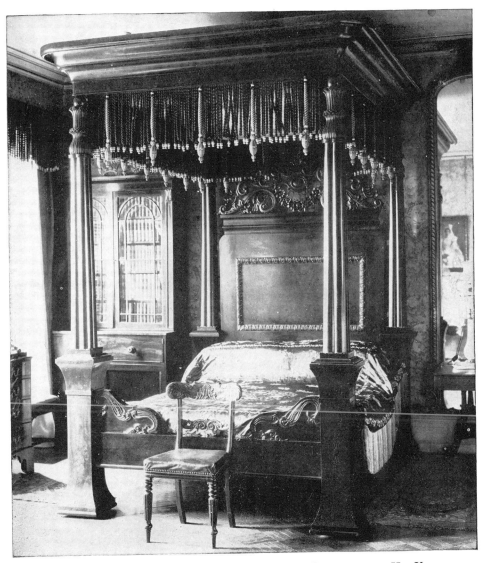

1555–57. A Late Bed Said To Have Been Built for Lafayette on His Visit about 1825. Shows the Massive Nature of Beds of That Period, with Clustered Columns and Huge Canopies and Posts. Chair Late Empire, Carved Back. Barrel Desk. Edward Bringhurst, Wilmington, Delaware.

1558–60. Canopied Bed on Curtain Sticks, Trundle Bed, Clock.

1560A. Bed Steps. About 1800. Very High Box, Carpeted in a Panel. H. W. Erving.

The student will note that the earlier the bed the less decoration appeared in the headboard for the reason that when the bed was made up the headboard was invisible, and the canopy was draped behind, coming down below the top of the pillow. Good beds, therefore, are found with pine or plain mahogany, coming up to an obtuse angle, and without any decoration.

1561. BED STEPS. EARLY VICTORIAN. H. W. ERVING.

The use of bed steps of course indicates a very high bed frame which was inconvenient for the aged or sick without the use of steps.

1562. OPEN FRAME BED STEPS. SHERATON PATTERN. ONE NOTES THAT THE TURNINGS ARE PRECISELY LIKE THOSE OF SOME SHERATON CHESTS OF DRAWERS. H. W. ERVING.

1563. (Right.) 19TH CENTURY BED STEPS. BOX FOR SHOES, ETC. ROBERT T. SMITH.

1564. MOST REMARKABLE CRADLE THAT HAS COME TO LIGHT IN AMERICA. THE AUTHOR WAS DIRECTED TO IT BY HIS FRIEND STEPHEN ALDEN, OF BROCKTON. IT WAS IN ABINGTON, MASSACHUSETTS. OWNED IN THE CUSHMAN FAMILY WHO HAD MARRIED INTO THE FULLER FAMILY.

Samuel Fuller came over in the "Mayflower," and the cradle had the reputation of having been brought over in her. In fact, the great painting in Pilgrim Hall of the landing of the "Mayflower" shows a sailor with his leg over the ship's rail tugging this cradle aboard. It was a good artistic motive, but Samuel Fuller was not married when he came to America, and he would scarcely have brought the cradle unless he had been a man of very great faith, even for a Pilgrim. Furthermore, the side panels and the lid of the hood are of American pine.

The cradle was made by a chest maker. It has half spindles on the sides of the panels. Undoubtedly of Plymouth origin and used in the family of Samuel Fuller, who mended his ways and took a wife after reaching Plymouth. The Channel molds are precisely like those used on chests. So are the chamfers on the rails. There is a gouge mold and a scratched hackling around the lid. All original except the rockers.

THIS CRADLE, WHICH HAS THE SPIRIT OF THE PILGRIMS IN EVERY LINE, IS IN THE WALLACE NUTTING COLLECTION, PRESENTED BY J. P. MORGAN TO THE HARTFORD ATHENEUM.

1565. Oak. Gouge Carved Panels. Cap Missing. Foot Posts Almost Gothic. Reputed To Have Come From Wethersfield. 38½ x 30 x 16¼. Posts 2⅜ x 1⅞. 17th Century.

1566. The Wood Appears To Be Beech. Head Formed Like Five Sides Of An Octagon. 1680–1710. Brantford Public Library, Connecticut. Plant Family, from Mill Plain District In That Town. Traced To Jonathan Barker. Born 1705.

1567. Galleried Cradle, Cap Missing. Reported Found Near Abington, Massachusetts. Sides Vertical. Rhode Island School of Design, Providence.

1568. Walnut. Pennsylvania. Good Brackets and Scrolled Ends with Heart Handhole. 18th Century.

1569. Suspended Cradle, Swinging from T Truss. Found on North Shore. 18th Century.

1570. Pennsylvania Stenciled Type. The Bottom Is Roped Like a Bed. 18th Century.

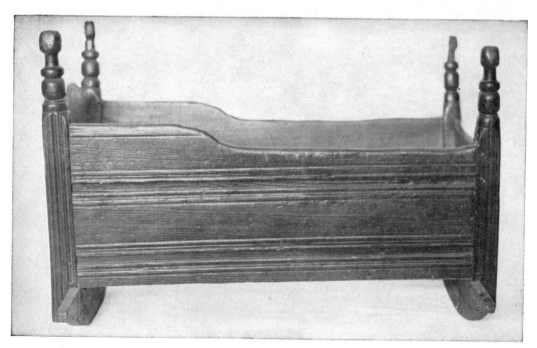

1571. CHANNEL MOLD CRADLE. THE POSTS HAVE SURVIVED VERY WELL THE WHITTLING PROPENSITIES OF MANY GENERATIONS OF CHILDREN. 17TH OR 18TH CENTURY. N. CUSHING.

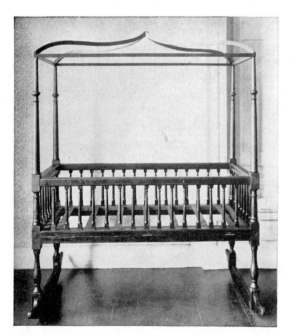

1572. A REMARKABLE CRIB. PROBABLY WITHOUT ROCKERS ORIGINALLY. SIDE LETS DOWN. A VERY FASCINATING SPECIMEN. FORMERLY THE AUTHOR'S.

1573. (Right.) DOLL'S CRADLE. DOUBLE. HUNG LIKE A SWING. WELL-SCROLLED TRESTLE FEET AND POSTS AND CONNECTING STRETCHER AT THE TOP. 18TH CENTURY. MRS. FRANCIS P. GARVAN.

1574. Windsor Cradle, Bamboo Turning. Head and Foot Have
Suggestion of Chair Backs. Late 18th Century. Arthur Leslie
Green, Weaver House, Newport, Rhode Island.

1575. Bow Head and Foot. Ends Alike. Very Rare. Late 18th Century. J. Stogdell Stokes,
Philadelphia.

1576. SUSPENDED CRADLE. SOMETIMES CALLED BARREL CRADLE. THE T-SHAPED TRUSS RE-
SEMBLES, ON THE FLOOR, THAT OF TRESTLE STAND. THERE IS A SIMILAR PIECE IN THE SAME ROOM.
18TH CENTURY. ESSEX INSTITUTE, SALEM.

1576A. A PINE CRADLE FRAME. A SOMEWHAT LATE FORM OF THE JACOBEAN CRADLE. AMERICAN.

1576B. (Right.) AN OAK CRADLE WITH WINGS AT THE HEAD TO KEEP THE DRAUGHT FROM THE
CHILD, THE IDEA BEING THAT AIR WAS DANGEROUS, AS IN A VERY COLD HOUSE IT MIGHT HAVE
BEEN. THE POST AT THE FOOT WOULD SEEM TO HAVE BEEN CONVENIENT FOR ROCKING THE CRADLE.
THE GOOD HOUSEWIFE, HOWEVER, USED HER FOOT ON THE ROCKER AND USED HER HANDS TO KNIT.

1577. A Spinet with Fine Long Spanish Feet. These Instruments Were Made Abroad, but It Is Thought That the Bases Were Made in This Country. The Top or Instrument Portion Was Removable and Was Kept from Slipping by Small Brads in the Frame. The Example Above Was Owned by the Author. 1690–1700.

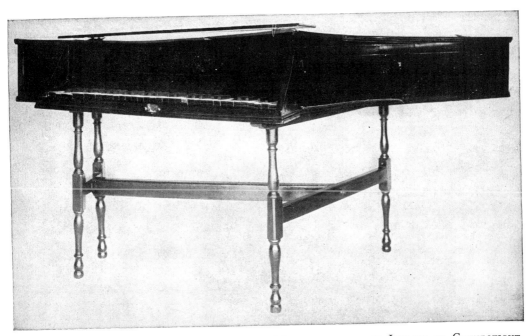

1578. Formerly Owned by David Brainard, Missionary to the Indians in Connecticut. Bought in Old Haddam by the Author and Now in His Possession. 1690–1700.

1579–81. Harpsichord in the Parlor of the Benning Wentworth Mansion, Newcastle, New Hampshire, and Two Chairs, Originally Caned, with Carved Stretchers and Rails.

1582. Spinet in Essex Institute. "Samuel Blyth, Salem Massachusetts Fecit." These Instruments Were Often Numbered, and in One Instance, at Least, the Number Has Been Taken for the Date. Early 18th Century.

1583. A Piano in the Adam or Hepplewhite Style with Brasses Attached Where a Carved or Inlaid Patera Usually Is Found. The Instrument Is One of Clementi's, London. A Carved Lattice at Each End of the Nameboard. Inlay with Diagonal Woods of Two Colors. Long Shelf Underneath for Music. Late 18th Century. Mrs. Francis P. Garvan.

1584-85. An Early Piano Formerly Owned by the Author. Four Legs in Front with Knee Hole and Drawer. 1810. Sheffield Brass and Glass Lighting Fixtures.

1586. A Spanish Foot Day Bed. In England Often Called a Couch, and in France a Chaise Longue. The Feet Here Are of Two Sorts; Four End Feet Are Alike, and the Side Feet Are Otherwise Shaped. It Would Seem that the Analogy of the Chair Would Be Properly Carried Out if the Feet at the Head Were Not Carved. Walnut. 1690–1700. Martin Gay, Hingham.

1587. All Spanish Feet, Second and Third Pair Being Carved on Three Sides. 1690–1700. Mrs. Francis P. Garvan.

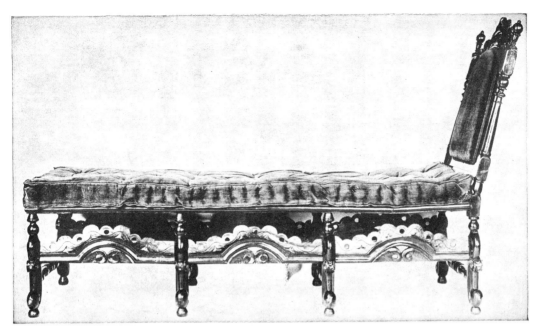

1588. FLEMISH DESIGN, FULLY CARRIED OUT IN LEGS AND BACK. IN A PERFECT STYLE, HOWEVER, IT WOULD SEEM THAT THE LEGS AT THE HEAD AND FEET SHOULD HAVE ANGLED. 1680–1700. MRS. ROGERS, HINGHAM.

1589. QUEEN ANNE TYPE WITH STRONGLY SCROLLED AND DOUBLED STRETCHERS. SHELL BETWEEN EACH PAIR OF LEGS. 1720–30. HELEN T. COOKE.

1590. Turned Feet, Flemish Stretchers. 1680–1700. The Chaise Longue Regularly in the Earlier Types Has a Swinging Head. It Was Let Down by a Chain. The Lower Part of the Head Frame Was Doweled into the Posts To Form Hinges. Metropolitan Museum.

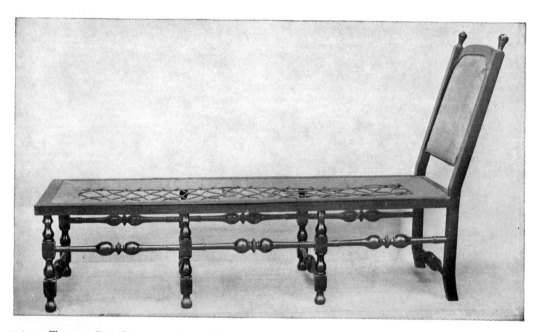

1591. Turned Day Bed with Laced Canvas. 1700–1710. The Finer and Earlier Beds Were Caned. Later They Were Arranged Like the Above for a Cushion or Were Rushed. The Author Has Never Seen Upholstery as an Original Finish, in the Earlier Type. Metropolitan Museum.

1592-95. A Third Storey Chamber with Late Empire Bed and an Odd Pembroke with
Large Dutch Feet and Straight Legs. Simple Pembroke in Background.

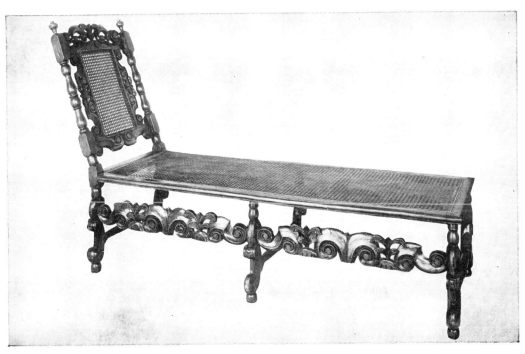

1596. A Flemish Day Bed with Six Legs. 1690-. I. Sack.

1597–99. REMARKABLE DAY BED, FLEMISH. FEET MODIFIED SPANISH. ARM AND SIDE CHAIR, AND CHILD'S CHAIR, THE LAST WITH PIERCED SPLATS. ANTIQUARIAN SOCIETY, CONCORD. 1690.

1600. SIMPLY TURNED. HEAD FIXED. 1700–20. OWNER NOT KNOWN.

1601. QUEEN ANNE, EIGHT LEGGER. 1730–50. THE LENGTH IS 62 INCHES. SCALLOPED FRAME. THE SWINGING HEAD HALVES INTO THE HEADPOSTS. WOOD IS BEECH. PROVENANCE, NEW ENGLAND. H. W. ERVING.

The couch with eight legs is considered much more desirable than that with six. In period the couches range from about 1680 to 1770, but the earlier dates are more frequently found. The turned specimens are the most numerous.

1602. ALL TURNED, THE HEADPOSTS VERTICAL, WITHOUT A BEND. 1690–1710. BROOKS REED.

1603. Turned with Head Built Like Back of Chair in What We Consider the Better Style. 1690–1710. Edward C. Wheeler, Jr., Boston.

1604. Turned with One Set of Spanish Feet at the Foot. The Name Pasted on the Stretcher, Clarissa Griswold, Killingworth, Connecticut. 74 x 21¾ x 37½. The Frame Is 14 Inches High. Head Swings. The Upholstery Is Not Original. Wadsworth Atheneum.

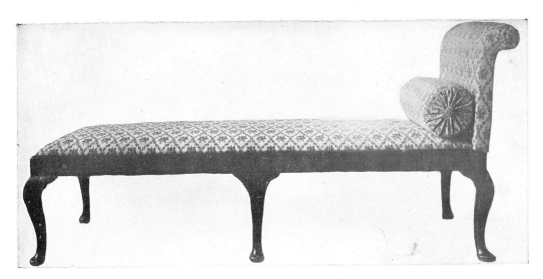

1605. Six Leg without Stretchers. Head Fixed. Queen Anne Type. 1730–50. Formerly the Author's. The Propriety of the Roll Is Somewhat Doubtful. It Would Seem that That Was a Little Later and Belonging to Empire Furniture.

When the wood is not named it is to be regarded as that of the period. Above, the piece being in the Dutch period, is walnut. On the other hand, a Chippendale piece is mahogany unless mention is made that it is cherry.

1606. Chippendale Straight Leg. Which Apparently Had a Slip Seat. Cherry. 76 x 26 x 17. Head 38½ Inches. This Is a Very Long Piece. The Head Shows Still One More Chair Pattern. 1750–70. H. W. Erving, Hartford.

1607. A Six Leg, Queen Anne Foot with Extraordinary Heavy Bracket and Fixed Head.
The Head Is Pure Chippendale. 1750–70. Brooks Reed, Boston.

1608–09. A Dutch-Foot Couch with Head Corresponding. The Scroll of the Frame Is
Similar to That of Mr. Erving's. A Handsome Pierced Brass Fender Is Seen in the Rear.
Couch, 1730–50. Edward F. Sanderson Collection.

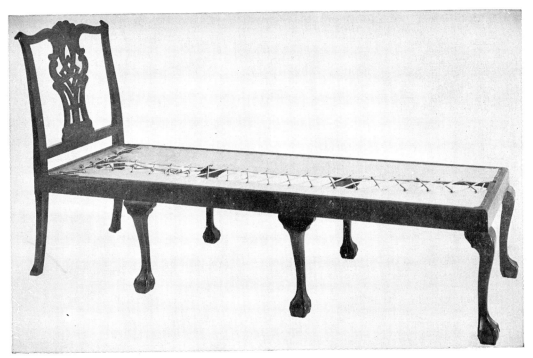

1610. A Very Rare Example, There Being Only One Other Known of a Chippendale Ball-and-Claw Couch. The Post at the Head Ends with a Knob on the Floor, as Often Seen on Chairs and Couches. One Should Notice that the Side Legs Have Not the Curvature of Those on the Corner, Which Latter Are Set at an Angle. That Is To Say, that the Side Legs Line with the Side of the End Leg. 1760–75. H. W. Erving.

1611–12. A Wing Chair of the Hepplewhite Type with a Short Couch or Long Stool Arranged Together as a Duchesse. 1790. The Mantel Shows the Raised Medallion of the Same Period. Edward F. Sanderson Collection, Nantucket.

1613. A COUCH WITH UNUSUAL IF NOT UNIQUE TURNINGS. EIGHT LEGS WITH STRETCHERS. NOTE
THERE ARE PLAIN TURNED STRETCHERS ON THE TWO INTERMEDIATE STRETCHERS TO BRACE THE
COUCH JUST UNDER THE TOP, AGAINST THE STRAIN OF THE RUSHING. THIS IS A NECESSITY OF
CONSTRUCTION. 1690–1710. MORGAN B. BRAINARD.

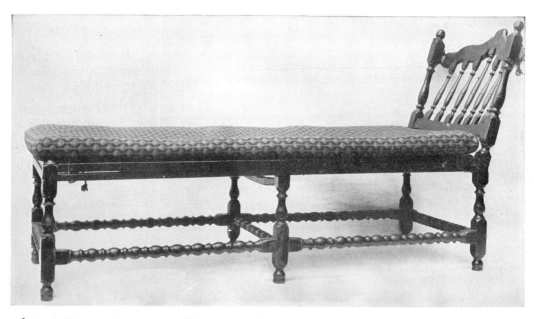

1614. A WALNUT COUCH WITH HANDSOMELY TURNED BALL AND RING STRETCHERS. SIX LEGS.
THE HOLLOWED STRETCHER BETWEEN THE MIDDLE PAIR OF LEGS JUST UNDER THE FRAME WAS
THUS MADE IN ORDER NOT TO MAKE ITSELF FELT THROUGH THE UPHOLSTERY. 64 x 23 x 16. THE
HEAD CONSISTS OF A LIGHT REPETITION OF THE POST TURNING IN SEVEN SPLIT SPINDLES. THE
HEADRAIL IS SCROLLED. 1690–1710. EDWARD BRINGHURST.

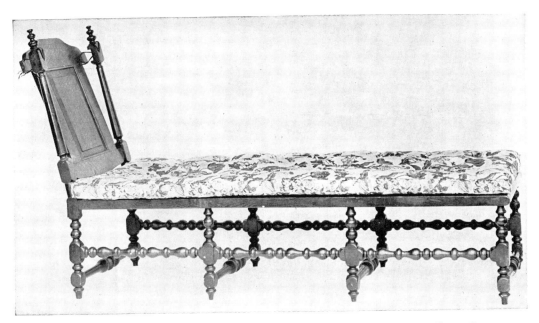

1615. All Turned, Including Stretchers. Note the Usual Position of the Cross Stretchers Is Low, and in This Instance Very Low Like the Next Example. This Was in Part To Gain Strength and To Avoid Cutting into the Post with Three Mortises on One Level. The Head Has One Plain Panel. 1690–1710. L. G. Myers, New York.

1616. A Six-Leg Turned Couch, with Head in the Dutch Manner. 72 x 26¾ x 16¾. The Head Is 36¾ Inches High. Estate of William G. Erving, Washington, D. C.

1617. A Couch with Absolutely Plain Turning. The Central Set of Stretchers Is Staggered. The Head Is Just as It Always Has Been, and Possibly a Cloth or Leather Back Might Have Been Fitted around the Posts at One Time, but There Never Was Any Other Wood Construction. 18th Century. Fuessenich Collection, Torrington.

1618. A Pennsylvania Day Bed. In Some Examples the Feet Are Bulbous. The Head Is Composed of Reeded Banisters, and an Arch Corresponding to Certain Pennsylvania Chairs Which Will Be Shown. 1710-40. Hollis French, Boston.

1619. An Unusual Type with Fixed Head Having Seven Plain Turned Spindles. The Head Is Crowned Like a Knickerbocker Dutch Chair. Stretchers Scrolled Below and Plain Above. 1710–50. Estate of J. Milton Coburn, South Norwalk, Connecticut.

1620. A Day Bed without Stretchers but with a Frame Sufficiently Wide To Secure All Needed Stiffness. The Head Consists of Six Plain Spindles Run into a Saddle-Shaped Rail. 1720–50. Fuessenich Collection, Torrington.

1621. An Oddly Scrolled Short Pine Settle. The Seat Board of the Settle Is Hinged To Form a Wood Box or Other Receptacle. 18th Century. Mrs. DeWitt Howe, Manchester, New Hampshire.

1622. A Knife Tray Prettily Scrolled, and with Dovetails. 18th Century.

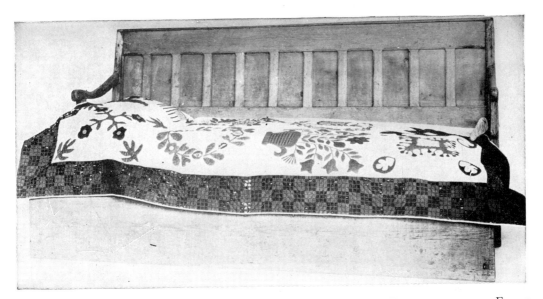

1623. A Settle Bed Made Up. 1720. The Seat Swings Out and Down so that the Front Panels Rest on the Floor. The Ends of the Swinging Portion Are Boxed In, so as To Leave a Complete Box When Made Up. The Material Is Largely Pine, Some Hard, Some Soft. Arms Are Wainscot Chair Type. Feather Beds Were Used. Such Types Are Well Known in Ireland. This Was Found on the North Shore.

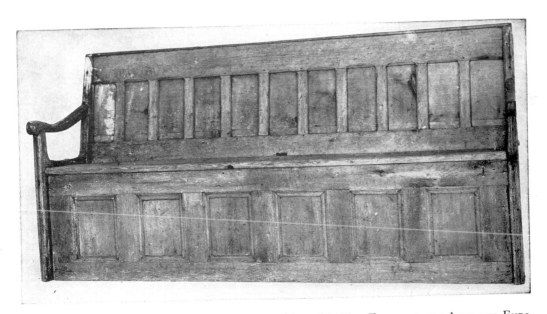

1624. Settle Bed Arranged as Settle. 74 x 36¾ x 17¾. The Frame at the Arms and Ends Is 1⅝ Inches Thick. Wadsworth Atheneum.

1625. Settle with More Than the Usual Features, Namely, Heavily Molded Top Rail in Addition to the Hood. 18th Century. Pine. From South Jersey. Francis D. Brinton, West Chester, Pennsylvania.

1626–27. A Short, Built-In Settle in the 17th Century House at Wrentham. The Wooden Latch Appears as Original, and the House Has a Good Many Features of the Original Period Still in Place.

1628. A Large, Pine Paneled Settle. Hood and the Usual Knoblike Terminals of the Scrolled Board End. The Board behind the Feet Usually Ran to the Floor To Keep Off the Wind. 18th Century. Rhode Island School of Design.

1629. Framed Maple and Pine Settee. The Only One of the Sort Known to the Author. The Special Features Are the Fifth Leg, the Wainscot Chair Arm. The Back Sill Is of Oak. Connecticut Origin. 75 x 50½ x 27. Width of Seat 20½ Inches. Height 20¼ Inches. Square of Posts 2¼ Inches. Back Posts 1¼ x 2½. Wadsworth Atheneum.

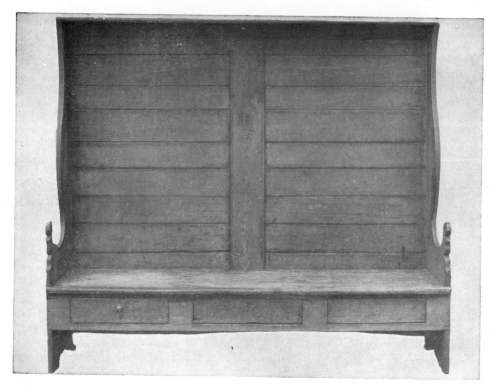

1630. A SOUTH JERSEY SETTLE WITH THREE DRAWERS UNDER THE SEAT. VERY RARE OR UNIQUE. IT WAS ABOUT 6 FEET LONG, AND ABOUT 5½ FEET HIGH. FRANCIS D. BRINTON.

1631-32. A CHILD'S SETTLE AND WING CHAIR. THE THREE BORINGS FOR FINGER HOLES AND THE TYPES OF ARMS INDICATE THE PIECES WERE MADE TO GO TOGETHER. ONE SEES HERE THAT THE SETTLE WAS THE OUTGROWTH OF A CHEST. THE SETTLE WAS PROBABLY USED AS A PUNG SEAT. WADSWORTH ATHENEUM.

1633. A Curved-Back Settee. At About the Same Time that This Was Discovered Another Came to Light in Massachusetts. 18th Century. Fuessenich Collection.

1634. A Walnut Settee of Very Good Dimensions. It Was Arranged As a Bed, the Seat Swinging Out. The Hasps Securing It Are Plainly Seen. Owner's Name Mislaid.

1635. TRIPLE BOW BACK WINDSOR SETTEE. THE RAREST TYPE. WELL TURNED.
MIDDLE BOW NINE SPINDLES, SIDE BOW SEVEN SPINDLES. 1760–80.
VICTOR A. SYKES, HARTFORD, CONNECTICUT.

1636. TRIPLE BOW BACK, EIGHT-LEG WINDSOR. VERY WIDE SEAT. 1760–80.
THE MISSES MABEL AND ELEANOR JOHNSON, HARTFORD.

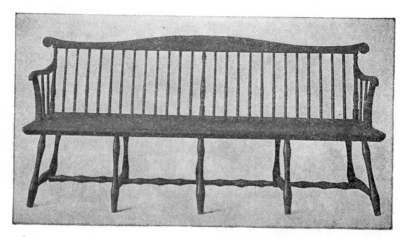

1637. SCROLL BACK WITH EARS, TEN LEG. BASE IN BAMBOO STYLE.
1790–1800. WAS THE AUTHOR'S.

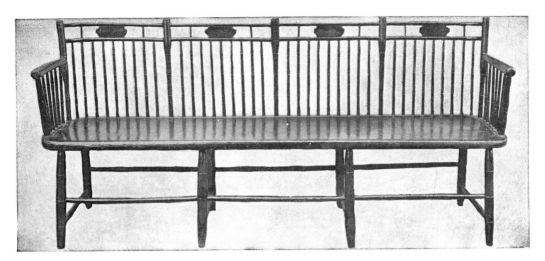

1638. Eight-Leg Sheraton Type. Late Windsor. Stretchers on the Outside Indicate the Late Period. In All Forms and Any Period They Are Much Sought After. Francis D. Brinton, West Chester, Pennsylvania.

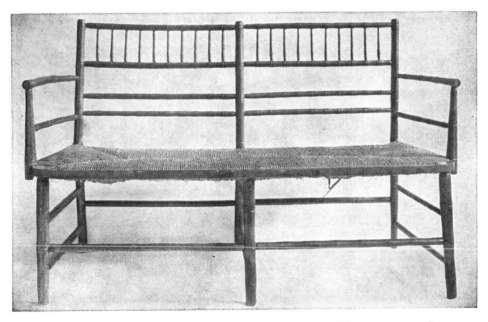

1639. Sheraton Type, Six Legger. Posts Attached in the Manner of the Chairs of the Period. Naturalistic Bamboo Turning. 1800–10. C. R. Morson.

1640. An Eight Legger, Sheraton Type with Wide Seat. Stretchers Staggered. Central Section of Back Higher, for Appearance and Strength. 1800–10. Howard Reifsnyder, Philadelphia.

There was a parallel development of the Windsor chair along with richer types of furniture. Thus in the first Windsors we have a Queen Anne stretcher. We later find an arm carved in the Chippendale style. Finally we reach Sheraton elements.

1641. Ten-Legger Settee with Three Divisions in the Back. Compare This with No. 1638, Which Has Four Sections at the Back, but Only Eight Legs. Bamboo Patterns. Sheraton Influence. 1800. Howard Reifsnyder, Philadelphia.

1642. Four-Leg Settee, or Love Seat. Otherwise Called a Courting Chair, or John and Priscilla Chair, or Double Windsor. Simple Stick Legs in the Earliest Style. Shaped Seats. 1740–70. Arthur Leslie Green, Weaver House, Newport.

1643. A Six Legger, Pennsylvania Style. Well-Shaped Arm and Rolled Back. 1740–60. J. Stogdell Stokes, Philadelphia.

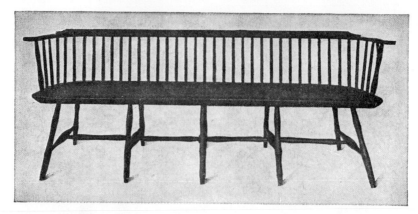

1644. Ten Legger, Bamboo Turning, 1770–90. Formerly the Author's.

1645. A Twelve Legger. Unique in the Author's Experience. Good Arm, and Back. Strongly Turned Spindles. Stretchers Maple, Legs and Seat Oak. Doubling of Rail, Walnut. Bent Portions, Hickory. 1770–95. Francis D. Brinton.

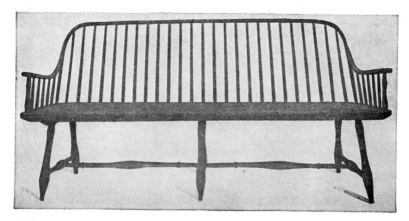

1646. A Six-Leg, Continuous Arm Settee. Rare Type. 1780–1800. Thomas B. Clarke, New York City.

1647. Love Seat, Plain Board. Four Legs. Single Stretcher. The
Bow Follows the Analogy of a Common Type in the Armchair. 1760–80.
Arthur Leslie Green, Weaver House, Newport.

1648. Sheraton Type Six Legger. Mortised Arm. This Construction
Is Likely To Be Weak. 1800. Rhode Island School of Design.

1649. Humped Back, Six Legger. Unique Construction. Arm Mortises into Posts on the Side. Bamboo Turning. 1780-90. J. Stogdell Stokes. (All on Page.)

1650. Short, Late, Love Seat. Sheraton Influence. 1800-10.

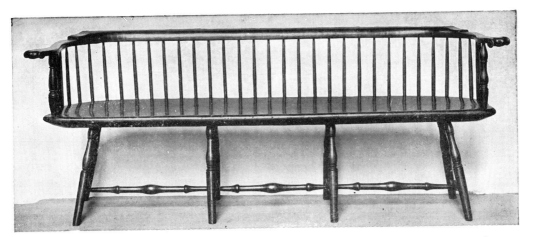

1651. An Eight Legger, Low Back. Strong Knuckle Arm. 1760–80. J. Stogdell Stokes.

1652. Eight Legger, Sheraton Influence. Shuttle Spindle. 1800. Howard Reifsnyder.

1653. Small Love Seat. The Bow Mortising into the Arm. 1760–80. J. Stogdell Stokes.

1654. Comb-Back Love Seat. The Ears Are Rather Unceremoniously Rounded Down. Love Seats with Comb Backs Are Extremely Unusual. 1750–1800. Mrs. William Raedeke, Providence, Rhode Island.

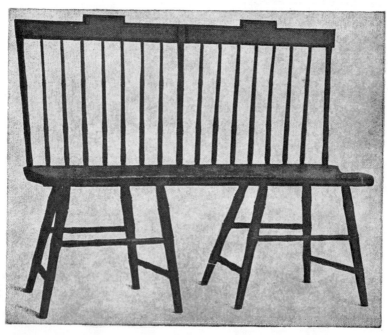

1655. Unique, Late, Sheraton Seat, without Arms. Base Like Two Separate Chairs. 1810. C. R. Morson.

1656. QUEEN ANNE SETTEE, C SCROLL ON LEGS, AND SLIGHT CARVING. 1720–40. HELEN T. COOKE.

1657. CHIPPENDALE LOVE SEAT, BALL AND CLAW, CARVED LEGS, FRAME, ARMS AND TOP RAIL.
1760–75. I. SACK.

1658. The Best Settee in America. English, Attributed to Grinling Gibbons. Further Descriptions under Chairs of the Set and Details Shown under Moldings. 1720–40. Pendleton Collection, Rhode Island School of Design.

1659. Walnut. Philadelphia Style. 1750–70. Gertrude H. Camp, Whitemarsh, Pennsylvania.

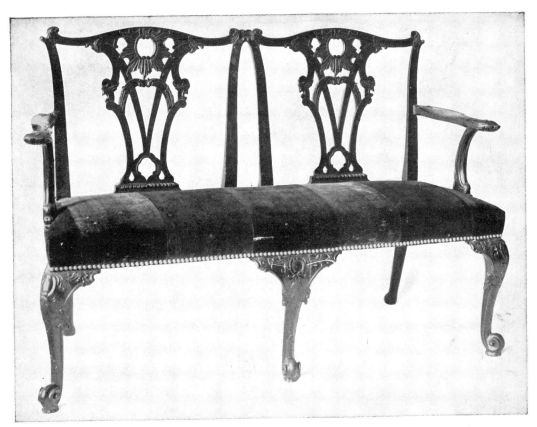

1660. LOVE SEAT, TWO-CHAIR-BACK CHIPPENDALE. LEGS CARVED IN THE SCROLL SUPPOSEDLY ENGLISH FROM A FRENCH MOTIVE. THE ARMS AND ARM SUPPORTS ARE GRACEFUL. 1750–75. RHODE ISLAND SCHOOL OF DESIGN.

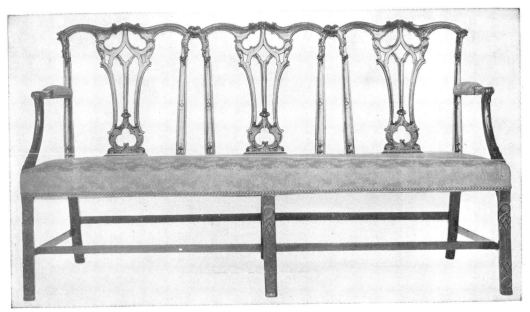

1661. THREE-BACK CHIPPENDALE. CHINESE FRET ON LEGS. UPHOLSTERED ARM. DAINTILY CARVED. 1760–75. THE MISSES A. AND E. P. FOSTER, HARTFORD.

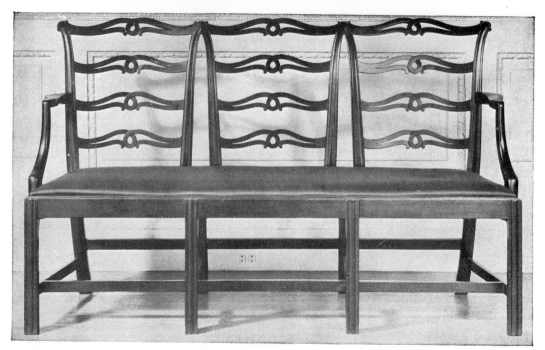

1662. Three Ladder-Back Settee. Straight Fluted Legs and Fluted Backs. 1760–75. Courtesy of the Pennsylvania Museum, Memorial Hall, Philadelphia.

1663–64. Parlor Wentworth-Gardner House. Three-Back Chippendale Settee, English. 1760–75. A Fine Pair of Andirons with Chamfered Squares.

1665. CHIPPENDALE SETTEE, BALL AND CLAW, RICH ACANTHUS CARVING, CARVED BACK, SIAMESE CONNECTION. 1760–75. MORGAN B. BRAINARD, HARTFORD.

1666. SETTEE, CHIPPENDALE BACK, DUTCH FEET. ONLY FOUR LEGS. 56¼ x 36¾ x 20. 1760–75. ESTATE OF HARRY W. WEEKS, FRAMINGHAM.

1667. Love Seat, Plain Chippendale Legs. 1760–75. Morris Berry.

1668. Hepplewhite. Eastern Shore, Maryland. Bigelow Collection.

1669. FOUR-BACK SHERATON, EIGHT LEGS, TAPER SQUARE. 1790–1800. MORRIS BERRY, PLAINVILLE.

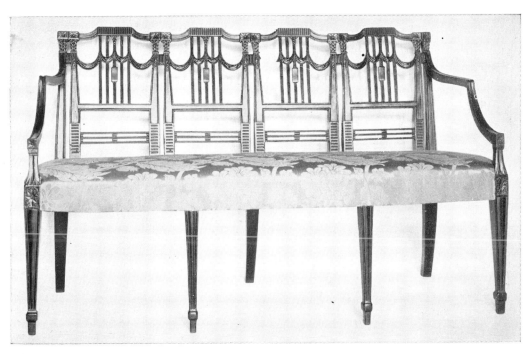

1670. FOUR-BACK SHERATON. VERY ELABORATE. CARVED PATERAE. FLUTED TAPER LEG. SPADE FOOT. BACKED WITH SERIES OF REEDED BANISTERS CONNECTED BY CARVED FESTOONS. 1790. EDWARD BRINGHURST, WILMINGTON, DELAWARE.

1671. HEPPLEWHITE EIGHT-LEG SETTEE. SUGGESTION OF ADAM INFLUENCE. FLUTED FRONT RAIL AND LEGS. RAISED CARVED EDGES ON BACK SCROLLS. THE CANE SEAT ASSISTS IN THE DATING OF THIS PIECE. 1790–1800. F. L. DUNNE, BOSTON.

1672. UNIQUE SIX-BACK HEPPLEWHITE SETTEE, ROUNDED TO FIT SPACE IN THE HALL OF THE PIERCE-NICHOLS HOUSE IN PORTSMOUTH. THIS CELEBRATED PIECE WAS OBVIOUSLY BUILT TO ORDER. THE THREE RIBS IN EACH BACK ARE CARVED, AS ARE ALSO THE THREE FLOWERS IN THE SPANDRELS ABOVE. ALL THE SHIELD BACKS ARE FLUTED. THE PIECE IS ALSO UNIQUE IN THE ARM ARRANGEMENT BY WHICH ONE OF THE BACKS IS REPEATED TO FORM AN ARM. 1790.

1673. HANDSOME SHERATON FOUR-CHAIR BACK, WITH SAME DRAPERY IN CARVING AS SHOWN ON A CHAIR. LEGS ARE IN HEPPLEWHITE FASHION. 1790. BIGELOW COLLECTION.

1674. SETTEE ATTRIBUTED TO DUNCAN PHYFE. 1800–15. WE ARE SEEKING TO ESTABLISH A DISTINCTION THAT A SETTEE IS NOT UPHOLSTERED IN THE BACK AND A SOFA IS. THIS PIECE IS TO ALL INTENTS A SOFA. THE PIECE IS IN MAHOGANY. IT HAS THE SAME FLUTING ON THE BACK THAT A PIECE RECENTLY SHOWN HAD ON THE RAIL. FLUTED LEGS WITH BRASS BALL FEET NOT DESIGNED TO CARRY CASTERS. REEDED ARMS, POSTS, AND LOWER BACK RAIL. METROPOLITAN MUSEUM.

1675. An Interesting Specimen with Its Deviation from Type. The Back Consists of Five Transition Pierced Splats. The Legs Are Good. The Criticism Would Be Directed to the Extreme Rake of the Arms and the Method of Attachment. There Is an Amusing Spreading Fan-Wise of the Back Splats Increasing from the Center Outward. 1800. Mrs. Alexander Armstrong, Baltimore.

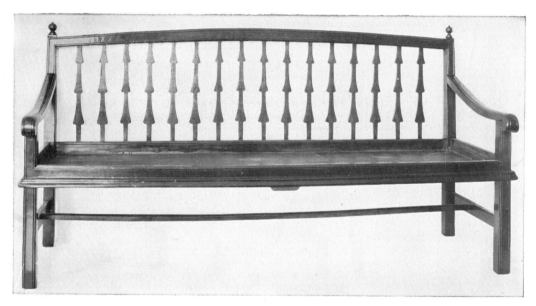

1676. Long Four-Leg Settee with a Simple Rail as Stretcher. Seat in Squab Style. Legs, Arms, and Back with a Double Mold Like a Bead. Probably Country Made. The Period Is Difficult To Fix; Perhaps We Had Better Say Merely 18th Century. Frank A. Robart.

1677. MAPLE SETTEE, LATE SHERATON TYPE. FOLLOWS THE LINES OF THE HITCHCOCK CHAIRS. THE SLIGHT FORWARD BEND AT THE BOTTOM OF THE LEG AND THE SHUTTLE-SHAPED SECTION OF THE BACK ARE FAMILIAR IN THOSE CHAIRS. IN BLACK, GILT, AND RED. $34\frac{1}{2} \times 73\frac{1}{2} \times 20\frac{3}{4}$. GRACEFUL OUTLINE. 19TH CENTURY. WILLIAM B. GOODWIN, HARTFORD.

1678. EIGHT-LEG SETTEE. GRACEFULLY SPIRALED BACK RAILS AND CUT-OUT FRET. RAIL BELOW. THE FRONT FEET ARE THOSE OF THE HITCHCOCK CHAIR OF THE EARLY TYPE. THE ARM ALSO FOLLOWS THE BETTER EARLIER TYPE OF THE HITCHCOCK AND IS VERY CLOSE IN ITS RESEMBLANCE TO THAT ON THE TOP OF THE PAGE. EARLY 19TH CENTURY. MRS. FRANCIS P. GARVAN.

1679. Eight Legger. Straight Stenciled Back Rail and Single Straight Rail Below. Straight Turned Front Legs. The Top Rail Is Stenciled, and the Lower Rail Is Lined. The Seat Rail Is Reeded. Arm of the Hitchcock Type. 19th Century. Howard Reifsnyder.

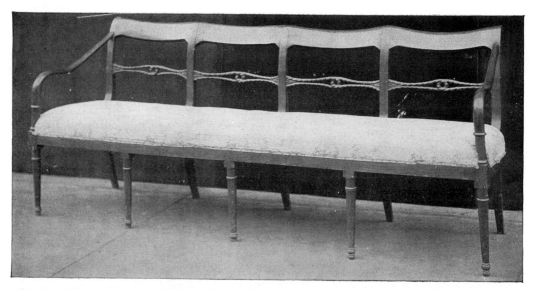

1680. Ten-Leg, Late Empire Settee, with Light, Carefully Carved Lower Back Stretcher. The Upper Stretcher Is Shaped. The Turnings of the Legs Strongly Resemble Those of a Piece Recently Shown. The Arm Would Be Better if It Engaged the Post Lower Down. Light-Colored Mahogany, Appearance of Walnut. Featured Grain. 36 x 78 x 23. 1820. H. C. Valentine & Company.

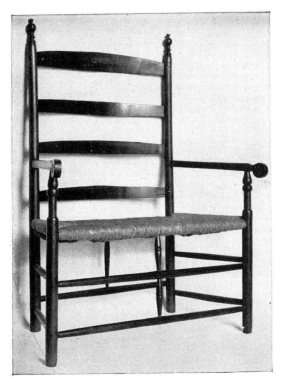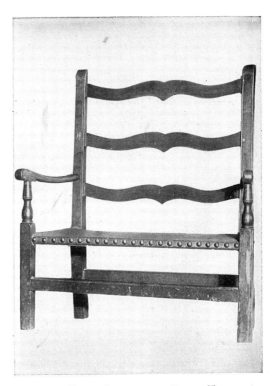

1681. SHORT SETTEE WITH STAR CARVED ON ARM SCROLL. FOUR SLATS WITH POSTS TURNED LIKE CHAIRS OF 1730. SMALL SUPPORTING SPINDLES AT THE CENTER. FOUND IN NEW HAMPSHIRE. MAPLE AND OAK. 36 x 44 x 16. 1730–40. MARY M. SAMPSON.

1682. (Right.) CHILD'S SETTEE. STRAIGHT DUTCH STYLE. SCROLLED BACK LIKE DUTCH CHAIRS OF 1730. STRAIGHT LEGS WITH CORNER BEAD WHICH ALSO FOLLOWS EACH SIDE OF THE POST BEHIND. A DELIGHTFUL LITTLE PIECE OF THE SORT WHICH ATTRACTS BY ITS ODDITY AND ITS SMALL SIZE AND ITS GOOD LINES. 1730. HARRY V. WEIL, NEW YORK CITY.

1683. ATTRACTIVE, SIMPLY TURNED, EIGHT-LEG SETTEE WITH A SPINDLE MIDWAY UNDER EACH ARM. CANE BOTTOM AND BACK. THE SUPPORTING INTERMEDIATE SPINDLE DOES NOT FOLLOW THE LINES OF THE OTHER TURNED PORTIONS, BUT IS GRACEFUL. STRETCHERS ALL PLAIN. 1790–1810. FRANK A. ROBART.

1684. A Sofa of the Jacobean Type. Many Generations in America. Ball Turning with a Ring at the Center. Upholstered Arm, Seat, and Back. 1650–60. Essex Institute.

The tradition is that this piece was brought from abroad, perhaps from the continent. It follows precisely the lines of some American chairs, but of course is to be accepted as foreign unless something to the contrary can be proved. The turning and the design interest the cabinetmaker, but the upholstery is the greatest interest for the decorator. It is in turkey work, and the detail can be fully studied by examining the piece, since the openwork weave of the base is clearly discernible and the method of hooking. While we have used the term Jacobean, the type is really a variation called Cromwellian.

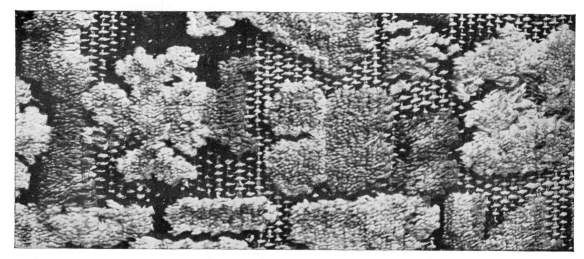

1685. Turkey Work Was Made Especially for Chairs and Settees in Patterns of the Right Size and Imported into England, and Possibly into This Country.

1686. SOFA WITH SCROLLED BACK AND SIX LEGS. THREE BALL-AND-CLAW FEET. PENNSYLVANIA
MUSEUM, MEMORIAL HALL, PHILADELPHIA. IN THE UPHOLSTERY IT IS NOTICED THAT THE LINES
OF BRASS TACKS ARE SET IMMEDIATELY AGAINST ONE ANOTHER. THE UPHOLSTERY OF THESE
PIECES IS CAREFULLY MATCHED TO BRING FIGURES IN THE CENTER. THE BACK HERE LOOKS
AS IF IT WERE WOVEN FOR THE POSITION IT OCCUPIES. 1760–75.

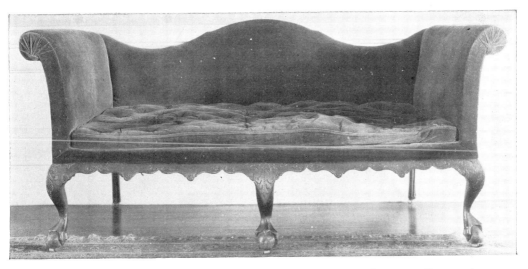

1687. A SOFA WITH THREE CARVED BALL-AND-CLAW FEET AND A SCROLLED SKIRT. ACANTHUS
LEAF ON LEGS. RAISED BAND ON SKIRT. 1760–75. HELEN T. COOKE.

1688. Three Dutch Feet Carved, Solid Upholstered Back. 1765–75. English. 40½ x 55 x 23. The Sharp Curve of the Arm Where the Hand Touches Is a Style Mark. C. Sanford Bull, Waterbury.

1689. A Chippendale Love Seat or Short Sofa with Legs Carved in an Elaborate and Unusual Pattern. It Will Be Noted that the Wings of These Sofas Follow the Style of the Wing Chair of the Same Period. Undoubtedly the Wing Chair Was Often Made To Go with the Sofa. 1760–75. Pennsylvania Museum, Philadelphia.

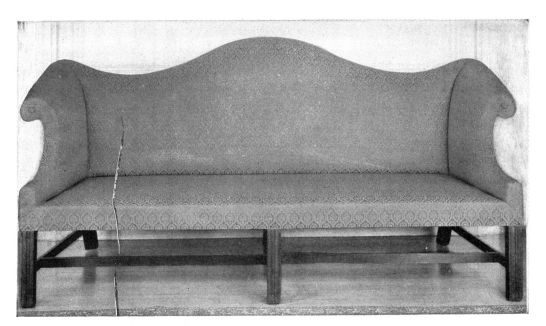

1690. Chippendale Six-Leg Sofa. Straight Fluted Leg. It Is Interesting To Note that the Upholstering on This Piece, Whether by Design or Otherwise, Is the Same as That Seen in Some Chippendale Frets. The Stretchers on These Pieces Are Not Placed Halfway between Front and Back, but About a Quarter of the Way Back so as To Afford Room To Draw in the Feet. 1760–75. Howard Reifsnyder.

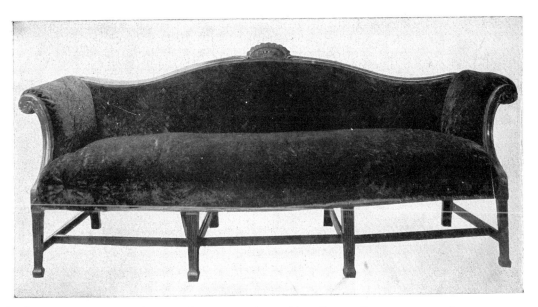

1691. An Eight Legger with Fluted and Spade Foot Legs. Carving on the Scroll of the Arm, and Shell Carving at the Center at Back. 1760–75. Samuel Wineck, Hartford.

1692. SHORT WALNUT SOFA. DRAKE FOOT WITH SHELL CARVING. ONLY TWO LEGS IN FRONT. ARM PRECISELY THE SHAPE OF THAT ON THE BEST WING CHAIR. A VERY GRACEFULLY SCROLLED BACK. PROBABLY OF SOUTHERN ORIGIN, THAT IS, PHILADELPHIA OR BALTIMORE. 1750–75. METROPOLITAN MUSEUM.

1693. EIGHT PLAIN LEGS WITH PLAIN STRETCHERS. SIMPLE LONG SCROLLED BACK. CHIPPENDALE TYPE. MAHOGANY. 76½ INCHES LONG. SEAT 16 INCHES HIGH BY 26 INCHES DEEP. 1760–75. DR. AND MRS. J. M. BIRNIE, SPRINGFIELD.

1694. RICH ENGLISH; FIVE BALL-AND-CLAW FRONT LEGS. SHOWS THE DIGNITY AND MASSIVENESS OF THE GREAT CARVED SOFAS. RAM'S HORN ARM IS UNEXPECTED, BEING EARLY. RHODE ISLAND SCHOOL OF DESIGN.

1695. EIGHT LEGS. TAPER FLUTE. STAGGERED STRETCHERS. TRANSITION CHIPPENDALE. 1780. I. SACK.

It is obvious that pieces completely upholstered as these sofas must derive their charm chiefly from the elegance of the material, rather than from the woodwork.

1696. Sheraton, Reeded Leg and Back with Festoons in the Middle Back Panel. American, Mahogany. 1790–1800. Mrs. Francis P. Garvan.

1697. Shaped Front, Sheraton. Veneered on Squares of Posts with Mahogany of a Different Grain. The Post Is of an Attenuated Vase Shape above the Rail. Turned and Reeded. 1790–1800. I. Sack.

1698. Eight-Leg Sheraton in the Style Frequently Found Which Shows the Post and the Slight Curve of the Arm above It, beyond Which All Is Upholstered. 1790–1800. The Estate of Harry W. Weeks, Framingham.

1699. Detail of Back of Sheraton Sofa. Attributed to Duncan Phyfe. Edward F. Sanderson, Nantucket.

1700. Carved Leaf Panel from Phyfe Dining Table. 1800–20. In the Metropolitan Museum.

1701. SIX-LEG SHERATON SOFA. MAHOGANY. EASTON, MASSACHUSETTS. OVAL PANELED BACK INLAID WITH BRANCH SATINWOOD AND OUTLINE IN SATINWOOD AND EBONY. REEDED POSTS BELOW GROOVED ARMS. SEAT BOWS AN INCH AND A HALF IN FRONT OF STRAIGHT LINE. 37 x 68 x 21. 1790. CLIFFORD S. DRAKE, NORTH HAMPTON, NEW HAMPSHIRE.

1702. GRACEFUL SHERATON TYPE WITH ADAM SUGGESTION. LEG REEDED AND ABOVE THE SQUARE A SLENDER VASE SHAPE CARVED. ALSO CARVED AT TOP OF POST AND CORNERS OF BACK. RAISED CARVED CENTER OF BACK. 1790–1800. HELEN T. COOKE.

1703. Unusual in that the Mahogany Frame Is Followed Closely All about the Arm and Back by the Upholstery. Legs Carved Near the Feet, Which Are Shaped Somewhat Like the Spade Foot. Carving at and above the Rail. 1790–1800. Morris Berry, Plainville.

1704. Sheraton. Light, Graceful Frame with Arms Standing Free from the Square Upholstered Section behind It. Inlaid at Square of Posts, Apparently with Satinwood. White Outlines on Frame. 1800–10. Pennsylvania Museum, Philadelphia.

1705. A Carved Panel in the Back and Carved Scroll Each Side of It. Carved Rosettes Intersected with Flutings across the Whole Back. Foliations down the Arm Rail. Reeded Legs without Carving. 1800. Metropolitan Museum.

1706. Handsomely Carved Sheraton Eight Legger. A Narrow Panel on the Back Rail Is an Urn or Fruit Dish Flanked by Festoons Which Are Repeated in a Smaller Form at Each Side. Carved Vase or Urn on the Posts and Foliage on the Roll of the Arm and Back. The Back Has a Rosette Intersected by Fluting Repeated for the Whole Length. 1790–1800. Pennsylvania Museum.

1707. SHERATON SOFA, CARVING ON THE TURNINGS OF THE LEG FOLLOWED BY REEDING. REEDED VASE ABOVE THE SEAT ENDING WITH A ROSETTE. MAHOGANY. 36 x 67 x 20. 1790. EDWARD BRINGHURST, WILMINGTON, DELAWARE.

1708. DUNCAN PHYFE SOFA IN THE SHERATON MODE. CARVED POSTS AND REEDED ARMS. FESTOONED BACK. NOTE THAT THE ARMS CURVE INWARD. 1800–10. THE MISSES A. AND E. P. FOSTER, HARTFORD.

1709. EIGHT-LEG SHERATON WITH FINE FOLIAGE CARVING AT THE TOP OF THE LEG, FOLLOWED BY A CARVED TURNING AND REEDING. REEDED BACK, STRAIGHT. 1790–1810. HOWARD REIFSNYDER, PHILADELPHIA.

1710. LATE EMPIRE ANIMAL FOOT. FOLIAGE BRACKET AND ARM AND DOWNWARD CARVED SCROLL TERMINATING THE BACK ROLL. 1823–33. H. N. CAMPBELL, PROVIDENCE.

1711. EMPIRE SOFA WITH FAN OR CORNUCOPIA-SHAPED ARM. 1810–20. 31½ x 72. MR. AND MRS. T. BELKNAP BEACH.

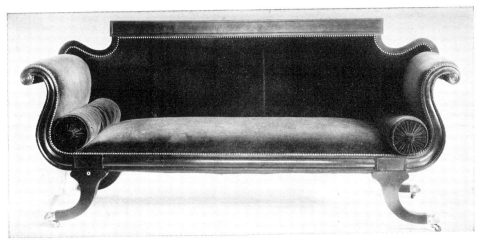

1712. An Empire Sofa in the Phyfe Style. Arms Designed To Take Roll as Seen. Formerly Owned by Mrs. Beach's Mother, Mrs. Nathaniel Brookhouse, Mansfield. 38 x 83. Mr. and Mrs. T. Belknap Beach, Hartford.

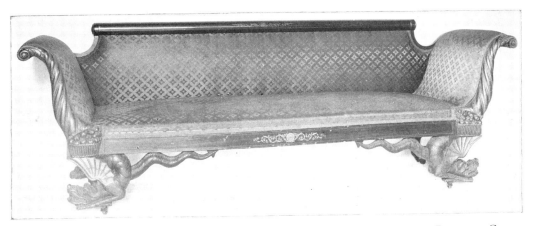

1713. Empire Sofa of an Early High-Class Carving. Dragon Motive Done in Green Gilt. For Late Empire the Merit of the Piece Is High. 1800–10. G. W. H. Smith, Providence.

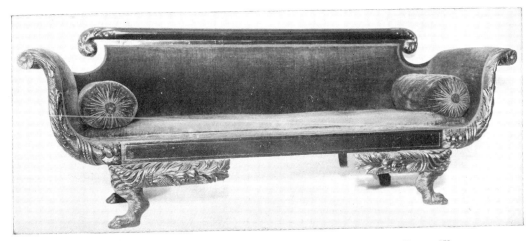

1714. Empire with Very Long Bracket. 1810–20. C. Sanford Bull, Waterbury.

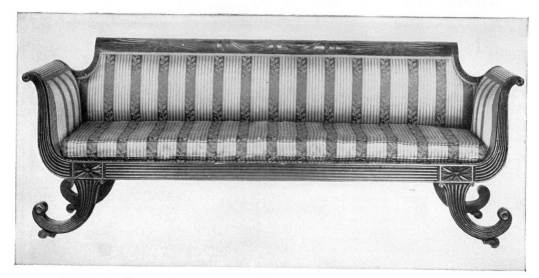

1715. An Empire Sofa. 1800–10. Pennsylvania Museum, Philadelphia.

1716. A Late Empire Sofa, Fully Carved. Swan End, the Bill Supporting the Tassel.

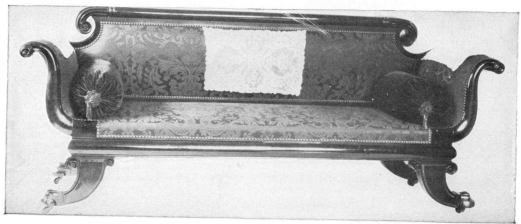

1717. Graceful Arm. Mahogany, from Connecticut. 1800–20. Robert T. Smith, Hartford.

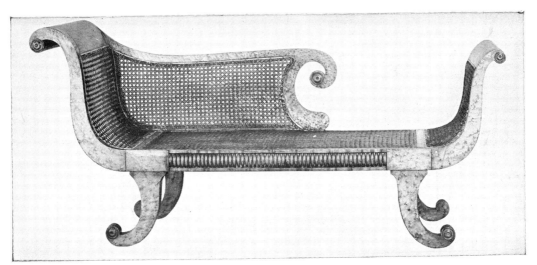

1718. A Bird's-Eye Maple, Late Empire Couch. Possibly We Should Use the Plebeian Word Lounge. 1810–20. Pennsylvania Museum, Philadelphia.

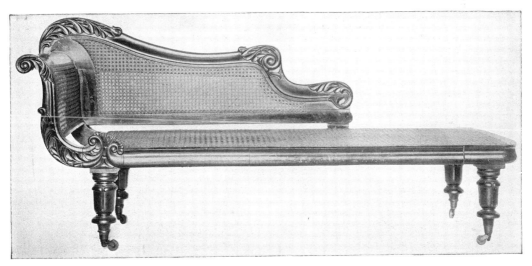

1719. Sofa or Couch. Late Empire with Back at One End Only. Very Strongly Curved Foot Rail. Carved Leg and Rosettes. 1820. Mrs. Alexander Armstrong, Baltimore.

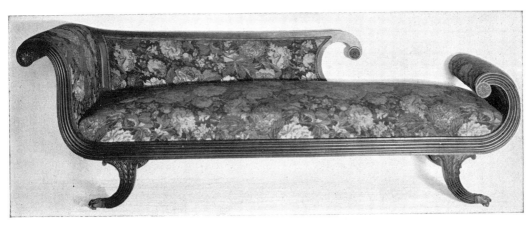

1720. A Mahogany Couch or Lounge. The First Shown with One Arm. Cane Seat. 78 x 24 (Wide) x 35 (High). 1830. Edward Bringhurst, Wilmington, Delaware.

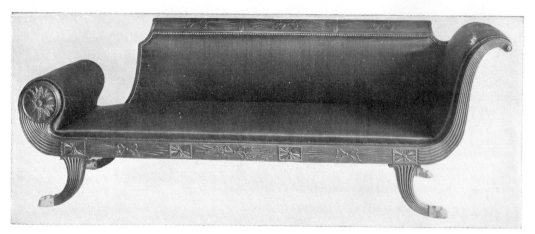

1721. Duncan Phyfe Sofa. Very Large Rosette Terminating the Foot Scroll. Carved Rail. Reeded Legs and Ends. Back Carved To Correspond with Rail. 1800–20. Mr. and Mrs. George L. Cluett.

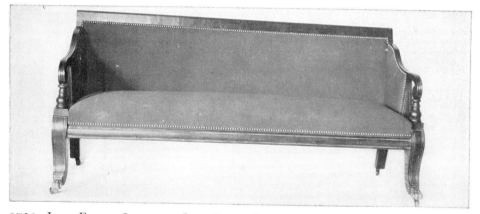

1722. A Late Empire Sofa of the Plain Type. 1840. Curly Maple. Cane Seat. S. Wolfe, New Haven.

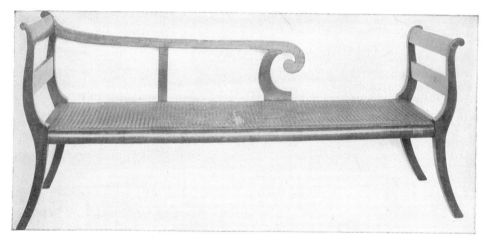

1723. Late Empire Sofa with Legs Swept Forward instead of toward the Ends. 1820–40. Pynchon Hall, Connecticut Valley Historical Society, Springfield.

1724–26. The Above Are Sheraton Sofa Ends. The First Is Attributed to Phyfe. Sanderson Collection. Note the Concave Arm. The Second Is a Detail of a Sofa Belonging to Mr. Howard Reifsnyder, with Excellent Carving. The Third Is Also a Detail from the Sanderson Collection. The Brass Foot Is Missing.

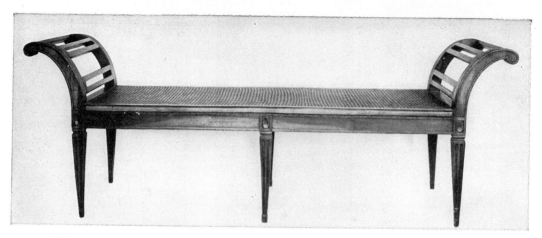

1727. WINDOW SEAT WITH ADAM SUGGESTIONS. THIS BEAUTIFUL LITTLE PIECE FORMERLY OWNED BY THE AUTHOR. THE ONLY CRITICISM REGARDING IT WOULD BE THE TOO RAPIDLY TAPERING LEGS. A WINDOW SEAT MAY BE DEFINED AS A BENCH WITH ENDS ALIKE BUT WITHOUT BACK. THEY ARE ALMOST NEVER FOUND OF AMERICAN MANUFACTURE. THIS MAY BE BECAUSE THE THIN WOODEN WALLS OF AMERICAN HOUSES DID NOT LEAVE RECESSES FOR THESE ARTICLES. 1780–1800.

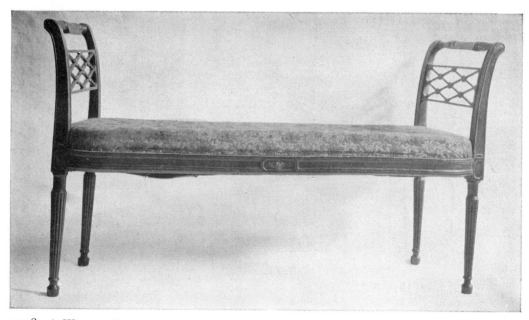

1728. A WINDOW SEAT PRESUMABLY ENGLISH IN THE ADAM STYLE. THE SHAPE OF THE TOP RAIL MAY INDICATE THE INSPIRATION OF THE MAKER OF THE HITCHCOCK CHAIR. CHINESE FRETS UNDER THE TOP RAIL, REEDED LEGS TERMINATING IN PLAIN TURNED FEET. 1800–10. C. R. MORSON, NEW YORK.

1729. Rolled Arm Upholstered. Chippendale. 21 x 50. Mahogany. Penna. Joe Kindig, Jr.

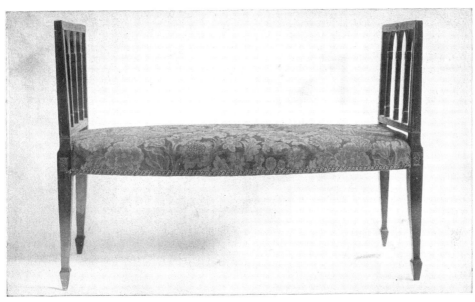

1730. Sheraton Vertical Ends. Carved Rails. 1800. C. R. Morson.

1731. The Size of a Bed. Used by Ancestor of Nathaniel Herreshoff, 1795–1805.

1732. A Small Window Seat with Sheraton and Adam Suggestions. Provenance: Connecticut. Material: Mahogany. There Is Good Carving on the Top Rail Like That Found on Sheraton Sofas. Duncan Phyfe, in the Sheraton Mode. 1800–10. H. W. Erving.

1733. Early Empire. Rosettes on Arms and Frame Are Brass. Reeded on the Edges of the Long Sweeping Lines. If One Prefers the Name Late Sheraton, There Is No Objection. 16 x 45. Joe Kindig, Jr. York, Pennsylvania.

1734. Window Seat Presumably Made by Lemuel Adams of Hartford, for the Old State House. The Style Is Hepplewhite with Inlay. They Probably Belong to the Same Period as the Famous Senate Chairs. Picture Supplied by William B. Goodwin.

1734A–B. The Former Is Phyfe with Turnings above the Post. The Latter a Bamboo Sheraton. A Somewhat rare Use of the Bamboo Motive in That Period. A Very Light and Graceful Article. 1800–1810. Bigelow Collection.

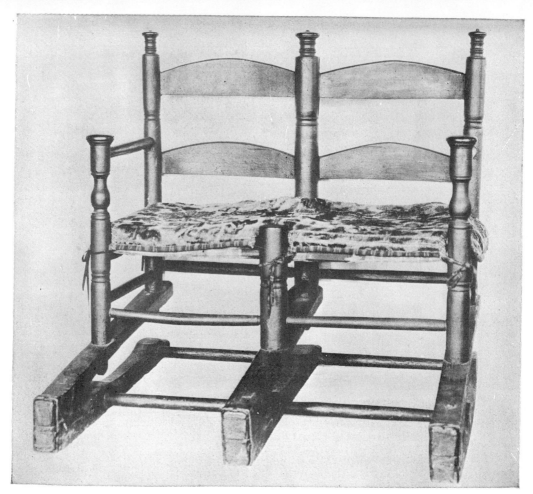

1735. A Spring Wagon Seat with Unusually Good Turnings. 18th Century. The Construction Makes It Obvious that This Was Primarily Intended for a Wagon. Samuel Wineck.

1736-38. A Wigwag Churn, an Excellent Wall Cupboard in the Style of 1780. A Glass Sconce.

1739. WINDOW SEAT WITH SPINDLES ALTERNATELY SET ON DIAGONALS. 18TH CENTURY.
RUDOLPH P. PAULY.

1740. ARROW-BACK WAGON SEAT. IN THE RUSHING IT WAS NECESSARY TO HAVE TWO RUNGS
SIDE BY SIDE IN THE CENTER AS SEEN. 1800. FLAYDERMAN & KAUFMAN.

1741. (Right.) A SETTLE ON ORIGINAL ROCKERS WITH CONCAVED FOOT REST. PENNSYLVANIA.
1780–1820. WAS B. A. BEHREND'S.

1742–43. Wagon Seat Is Shown as Placed Indoors. A Dutch Table.

1744. A Conventional Wagon Seat. These Are Found in New York State and to a Limited Extent in Northern Pennsylvania and Western Connecticut. The Middle Posts Are Always Much Larger than the End Posts. This Was To Accommodate Two Rungs Side by Side for the Rush. 1780–1820. Rudolph P. Pauly.

1745. A Fully Carved Ball-and-Claw Foot Dumb Waiter. English. 1760–75. Palmer Collection. I. Sack.

1746. (Right.) Dutch-Foot Dumb Waiter with Urn Top. Both of These Pieces Have a Raised Rim on the Whirling Tables. Also Called Lazy Susan. 1740–70. F. A. Robart.

1747–48. On the Mantel a Scalloped Chippendale Tray. These Were Similar to the Small Pie-Crust Table. A Chippendale Dining Table, and in the Distance a Dutch-Foot Dining Table.

1749. A Bootjack in Walnut Arranged To Use by Steadying Oneself on the Handle. Those Who Presume that Our Ancestors Lived Simple Lives Would Revise Their Opinions Were They Acquainted with Their Garments and Their Furniture. Monroe Tavern, Lexington.

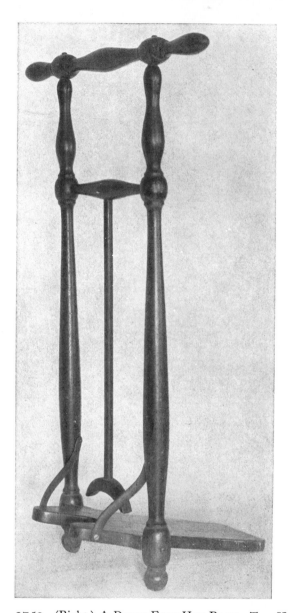 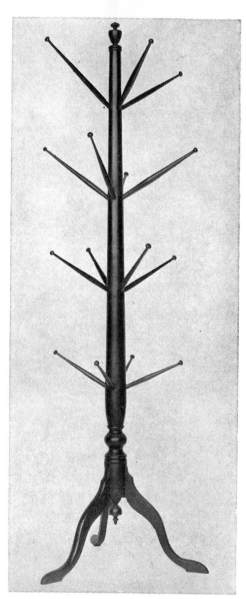

1750. (Right.) A Dutch-Foot Hat Rack. The Hanging Sticks Are Arranged in Lines and Angles about the Piece, Reminding One of a Young Pine Tree. Urn at Top and Bottom. 1750 or Later. Provenance: Connecticut. Material: Maple. 67½ Inches High. Pins Shaped Like Wheel Pins and in Graded Lengths. H. W. Erving.

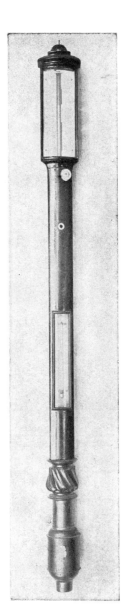

1751. A Barometer on a Gimbal of Course Arranged for Ship's Use. Finely Wrought Instruments Like These Were Especially Loved by Ship Masters and Were Considered Elegant Gifts. Mahogany, Spiraled Reeding. Brass Fittings. 18th Century. H. N. Campbell, Providence.

1752. (Middle.) A Combined Aneroid, a Thermometer, and Other Devices Ornamental and Useful. This Sort Seems To Have Been Made in Large Numbers at Preston, England. 18th Century. Flayderman & Kaufman.

1753. (Right.) Another Type of Barometer of About the Same Date, and Also Perhaps Imported, Belonging to the Estate of Harry W. Weeks, Framingham, Massachusetts.

These instruments are highly decorative, and add a sense of completion to the furniture of a dwelling. They are designed with a great deal of artistic feeling. Notice, for instance, the delicate scrolled top on the central example.

1754. A Washstand in the Chippendale Mode. Two Little Triangular Drawers. Pointed Dutch Foot. 1750–70. Howard Reifsnyder.

1755. The Top of This Stand Lifts. Mahogany Side and Top and Oval Panels. Bird's-Eye Maple Doors. 1790. S. Prescott Fay.

1756. Round Front. Drawer in Frame. Fourth Leg. Reeded. Very Delicate. New England. 1790–1800. H. W. Erving.

1757. Round Front, Fourth Leg, Cross Stretchers. Inlaid. 1790–1800. James Curan Estate.

1758. WINE COOLER. MAHOGANY. HEPPLEWHITE.
MRS. FRANCIS P. GARVAN.

1759. WINE COOLER. MAHOGANY. ENGLISH.
I. SACK. PALMER COLLECTION.

1760-64. ROOM AT THE "HAYLOFT," WHITEMARSH, PENNSYLVANIA. THE SIDEBOARD WITH KNIFE
BOXES, THE VENEERED TWO-PART DINING TABLE, THE ODD STYLE CARD TABLE AGAINST WALL, AND
THE CHAIRS ALL DIFFER FROM OTHERS SHOWN. 1760-90.

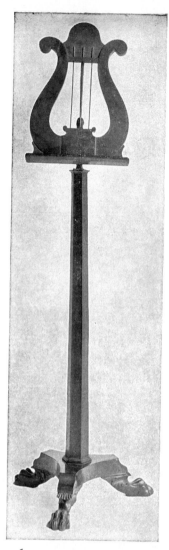

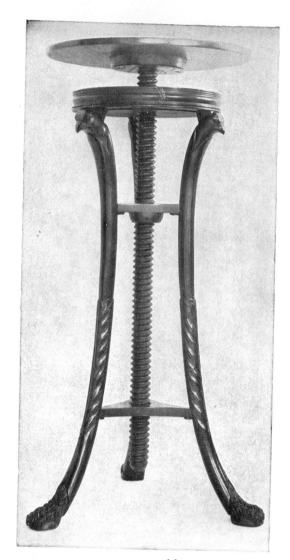

1765. A Music Stand. Empire Style Top in Form of a Lyre. Hexagon Post. Mahogany. Collection of Edward P. Sanderson, Nantucket.

1766. A High Adjustable Stand with a Wood Screw. Carved as Bird's Head with Foliage on Foot. Late Empire, 1830–40. For Artists' Colors. Used by Thomas Sully, American Artist. Sanderson Collection.

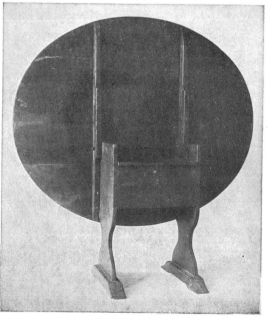

1767. (Right.) Chair Table, Found on North Shore. Trestle Base. 18th Century.

1768. AMERICAN, PINE, PANELED, GOTHIC CHAIR TABLE. FOUND BY THE AUTHOR IN FREEPORT, MAINE. WONDERFULLY QUAINT. PROBABLY MADE SOON AFTER AMERICAN SETTLEMENT, FOLLOWING A LOST ENGLISH MODEL. 17TH CENTURY.

1769. American, Oak, Cross-Stretcher Chair Table. Finial Restored from Original Picture. The First Finial Was "Lost" in Transit. Unique. Probably from New Jersey or the Delaware Valley. Wadsworth Atheneum.

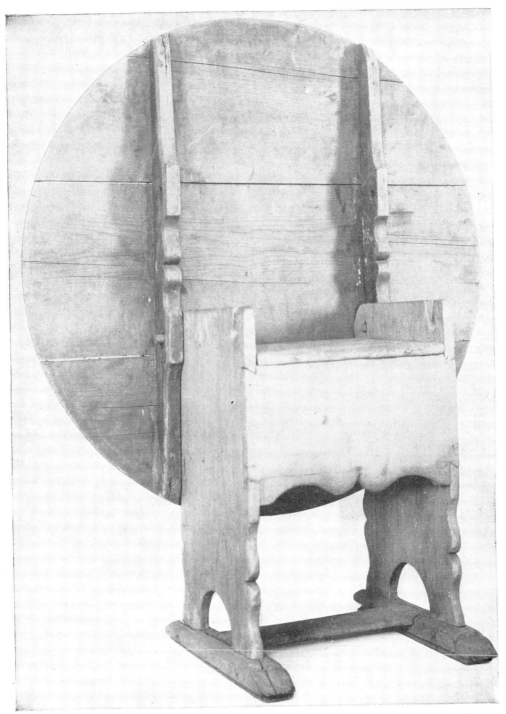

1770. Pine Chair Table. More Properly Hutch Table on Shoes. Dovetailed Front and Back Boards. Was in Ives Collection. Present Owner Unknown. 18th Century.

1771. CHAIR TABLE WITH SLIDING TOP. FOUND IN VIRGINIA. PERHAPS UNIQUE. A SLOT PERMITS THE TOP TO BE DRAWN TO THE CENTER WHEN IT IS RAISED. 17TH OR 18TH CENTURY. J. STOGDELL STOKES, PHILADELPHIA.

1772. (Right.) BALL-TURNED CHAIR TABLE WITH ARM RAILS ALSO TURNED. SQUARE STRETCHERS. FEET MISSING. 17TH OR EARLY 18TH CENTURY. HOWARD REIFSNYDER, PHILADELPHIA.

1773. UNIQUE CHAIR TABLE IN THE DUTCH MANNER. OGEE FRAME. TOP ATTACHED IN THE PENNSYLVANIA STYLE. 1730–50. WADSWORTH ATHENEUM.

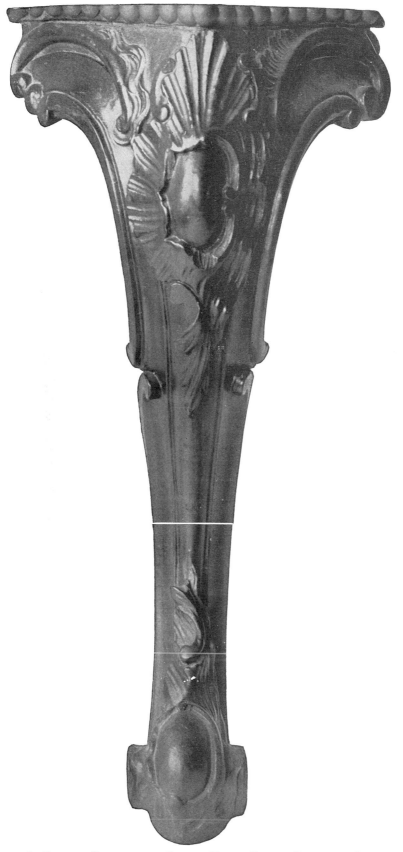

1773 A. Leg of Chippendale Chair. Rhode Island School of Design.

1773 B. Carved Head of a Chippendale Sofa Crest, Rococo. Rhode Island School of Design.

1774. Carved Three-Legged Chair. Reputed To Have Been Brought from France, but Claimed To Be Made of American Woods. Carving and Molds Resemble Those on Chests. 17th Century. William B. Goodwin, Hartford.

1775. THREE-LEGGED CHAIR, RUNG MISSING. SIMPLE TYPE. SEAT SET IN AS PANEL. 17TH CENTURY. FUESSENICH COLLECTION.

1776. (Right.) STYLE OF CORNER CHAIR, BUT WITH FOUR LEGS. 17TH OR 18TH CENTURY. FLAYDERMAN & KAUFMAN.

1777-79. KITCHEN OF WEBB HOUSE, WETHERSFIELD. TWO CHAIR TABLES. QUAINT WALL SHELVES WITH ROPE. EARLY 18TH CENTURY. COLONIAL DAMES.

1780. Cromwellian. Term Applied to Chairs with This Back. 1650–60. William B. Goodwin.

1781. (Right.) Cromwellian. Covered with Original Turkey Work. 1650–60. Mrs. Francis P. Garvan.

1782. Cromwellian. New Leather. Small Finials a Puzzle. Formerly the Author's.

1783. (Right.) Cromwellian. Unusual Turnings. Besides Turkey Work, These Chairs Were Upholstered in Leather or Fabric. 1650–60. Wadsworth Atheneum.

1784. "Two Back" Turned Chair, Matches a Mushroom Arm. Restored Feet. 17th Century. Wadsworth Atheneum.

1785. (Right.) All Turned. Carver and Brewster Elements. 17th Century. Connecticut Historical Society, Hartford.

1786. Unique Chair Found on Cape Cod. 17th Century. Dr. Irving Lyon, Buffalo.

1787. (Right.) Wainscot, Carved Back. King Philip Chair. 17th Century. Martin House.

1788. Robinson Wainscot, Guilford, Connecticut. Seat New, Tape Loom Cut in Back Subsequent to Date of Chair. The Earliest Turnings. 1630–50. Wadsworth Atheneum.

1789. Rector Pierson Wainscot. Yale University. 1640–60.

1790. Governor Leete Wainscot. Wainscot Means Wagon Oak,
and Refers to the Paneling of the Earliest Chairs. 1640–60.
Stone House, Guilford.

1791. WAINSCOT, BANISTER BACK. THIS IS THE ONLY AMERICAN CHAIR SHOWN WITH TWO PANELS UNDER THE ARM. STRONG RESEMBLANCE OF ALL WAINSCOT ARMS. 17TH CENTURY. FRANCIS D. BRINTON.

1792. (Right.) WALNUT. UNIQUE ARM. PENNSYLVANIA CHAIRS, 17TH CENTURY TYPE, QUITE DIFFERENT FROM ANY OTHERS FOUND. J. STOGDELL STOKES.

1793. OAK, ONE NEW ARM. LONG ISLAND. 17TH CENTURY. WADSWORTH ATHENEUM.

1794. (Right.) CARVED OAK. POSSIBLY AMERICAN. 17TH C. DANVERS HISTORICAL SOCIETY.

1795. Wainscot, "Square Turning." Found in Virginia. American White Oak. Feet and Crest Restored. Only Example from the South. Before 1650. William B. Goodwin.

1796. (Right.) Side Wainscot. Cromwellian Except for Panel. 17th Century. J. Stogdell Stokes, Philadelphia.

1797. Upholstered Arm and Back, Scrolled Ears. Difficult to Date. J. Stogdell Stokes.

1798. (Right.) Wainscot. Dulled Decoration on Top Rail. 17th Century. J. Stogdell Stokes.

1799. Most Perfect Brewster Type. There Are Only One or Two Others. Posts More Than 2½ Inches in Diameter. 1640–60. Mrs. J. Insley Blair.

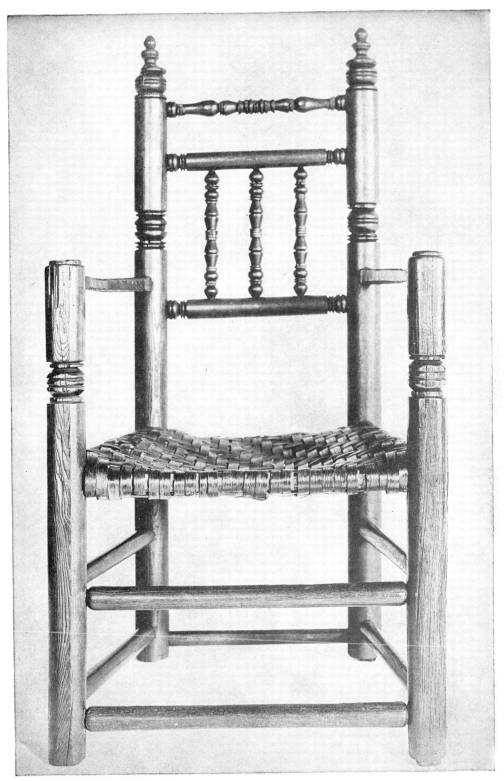

1800. Governor Carver, Good Finials and Spindles. Ash. Balls on Front Posts Lost.
43½ Inches High. Posts Large Diameter, 1⁹⁄₁₆ Inches. 1640–60.
Wadsworth Atheneum.

1801. Great Carver, Best Back Known. 1640–60.
Wadsworth Atheneum.

1802. "Brewster," Original Balls. The Term Brewster Is Applied to Chairs Having Spindle Work below the Seat. 45½ Inches High, 23½ Inches Wide. Outside Width of Back 17⅜ Inches. Most Such Chairs Found in Massachusetts or Connecticut. 1640–60. Wadsworth Atheneum.

1803. A Slant-Back Carver, All Original. 1640–60. Pilgrim Chairs Were First in Ash, Then in Maple. George Dudley Seymour. Wadsworth Atheneum.

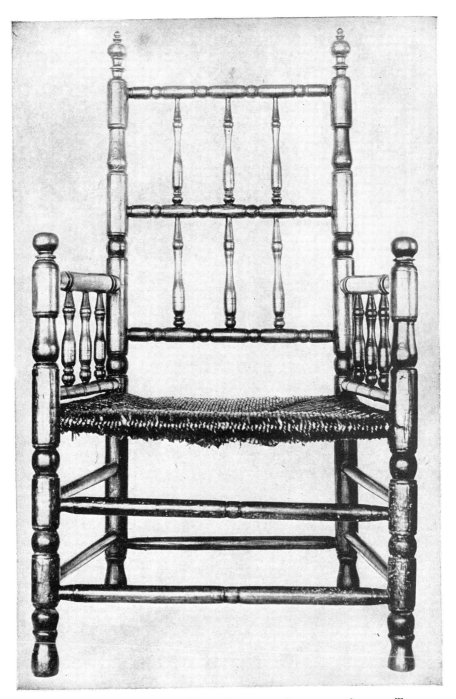

1804. Transition Brewster. Posts Somewhat Smaller. 1670–90. Turning below Seat not Found in the First Period in America. Present Ownership Unknown.

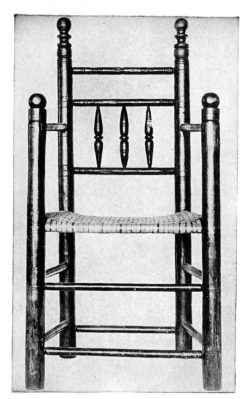

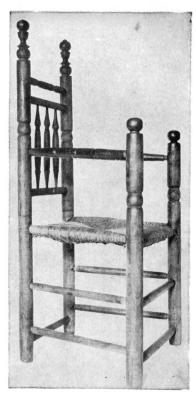

1805. CARVER OF MEDIUM WEIGHT. SOUTH SHORE. BALLS RESTORED. 1650–70.
WADSWORTH ATHENEUM.

1806. (Right.) HIGH-POST CARVER. WESTERN MASSACHUSETTS. 48½ x 25. THESE ASH
SPINDLES ARE SHAKY. 1650–70. WADSWORTH ATHENEUM.

1807. A LIGHT CARVER. BALLS REPLACED. 1670–80. WADSWORTH ATHENEUM.

1808. (Right.) LIGHT CARVER. ALL ORIGINAL. 1680–90. WADSWORTH ATHENEUM.

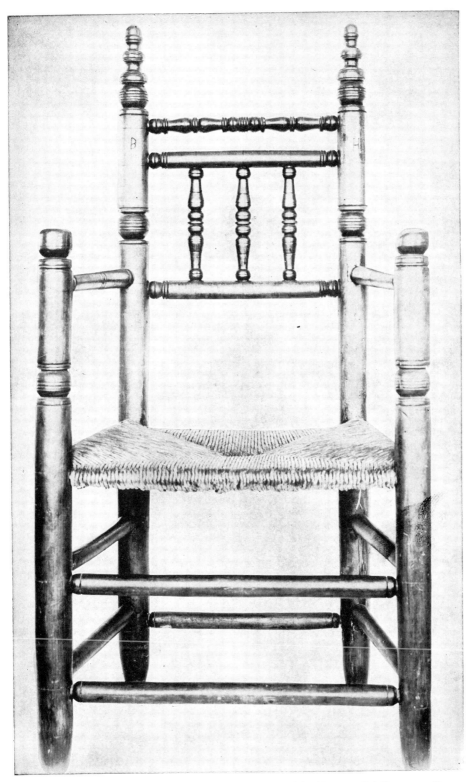

1809. HEAVY, INITIALED CARVER. MAPLE. 47 x 24½. BACK 18½ INCHES. DEPTH
16 INCHES. 1640–60. WADSWORTH ATHENEUM.

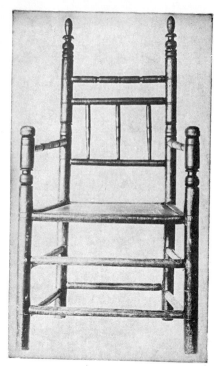

1810. SIDE CARVER. SPOOL-TURNED TOP RAIL. AUTHOR FOUND A SIMILAR CHAIR IN ENGLAND. 1660–80. WAS B. A. BEHREND'S.

1811. (Right.) LIGHT CARVER, POORLY SPACED SPINDLES. 1660–80. WADSWORTH ATHENEUM.

1812–13. PAIR OF SIDE CARVERS. 1665–80. CHAUNCEY C. NASH.

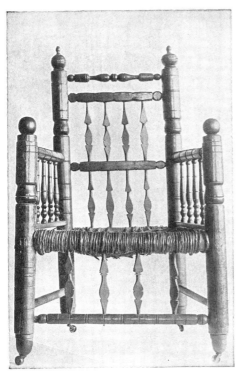
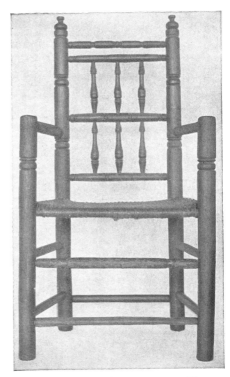

1814. "Miles Standish" Brewster. Badly Restored as to Feet and Balls in Front. 1630–40. Posts' Largest Diameter 2¹¹⁄₁₆ Inches. Flattened Spindles. Side Spindles Not Original. Mrs. F. H. Lincoln, Hingham.

1815. (Right.) Two Tiers of Spindles. 1640–70. Balls Lost. Fuessenich Collection.

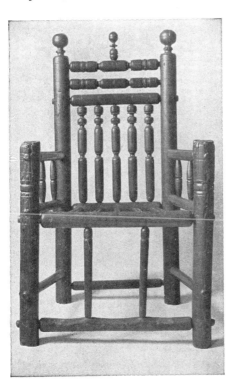

1816. Brewster Type, Dowels Run Through and Show as Knobs. 1630–50. Seat Composed of Spindles. Fuessenich Collection.

1817. (Right.) Double Tier of Spindles. 1640–70. Fuessenich Collection.

1818-19. A Pair of Side Carvers. Unusual Finials. 1650-70. J. Stogdell Stokes.

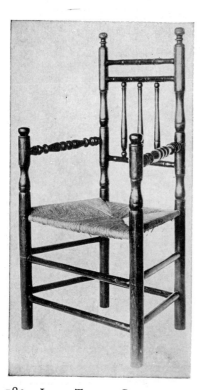

1820. Light Turned Carver. 1650.   1821. A Brewster. Dowels Protrude. 1640.

Wadsworth Atheneum.

1822. Great Slat Back, Winged. Flat Arm Rail. Turnings below the Seat Indicate Later Date Than the Carver. 1670-90. Dwight Blaney.

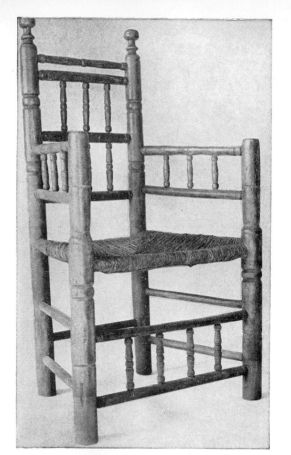

1823. SEMI-BREWSTER. FEET PIECED. 43½ x 26½. 1640–60. WADSWORTH ATHENEUM. (ALL ON PAGE.)

1824. (Right.) PILGRIM SLAT BACK. FINE FINIALS. 43½ INCHES HIGH. POST DIAMETER 2½ INCHES.

1825-26. MUSHROOM PILGRIM SLAT BACKS. THE LEFT A CHILD'S CHAIR, THE RIGHT A SEMI-BREWSTER. ORIGINAL TYPE OF MUSHROOM. 1640–60.

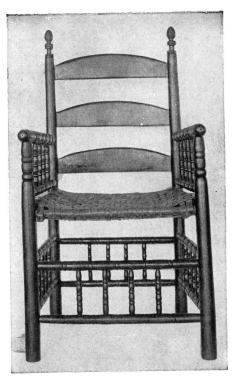
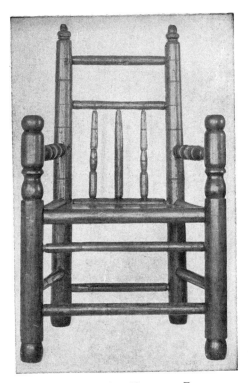

1827. Pennsylvania Semi-Brewster. Probably of Later Date than New England Examples, Owing to the Lighter Turnings and Later Settlement. 17th Century. J. Stogdell Stokes.

1828. (Right.) Spindles Running into Seat. Feet Wrong. Author Cannot Speak with Certainty Regarding This Chair. 17th Century.

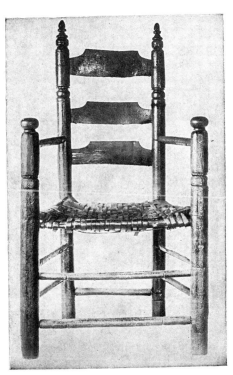
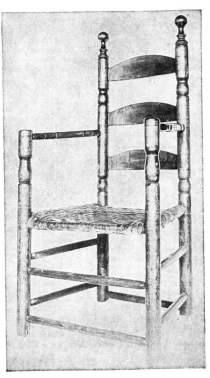

1829. Pilgrim Slat Back. 1650–70. Wadsworth Atheneum.

1830. (Right.) Pilgrim Slat Back. Lighter, Later. 1680–1710. Wadsworth Atheneum.

1831. Heaviest, Perhaps Earliest Pilgrim Side Slat Back. New Hampshire. 1630–50. Wadsworth Atheneum.

1832. (Right.) Pilgrim Slat Back. Finials Probably Missing, Paneled Seat. 1640–60. John C. Spring, Boston.

1833–34. Pair of Side Pilgrim Slat Backs. 1680–1710. Wadsworth Atheneum.

1835. TURNED CORNER CHAIRS ARE NOW ENTERED UPON. A FINE EXAMPLE HERE WITH LARGER TURNINGS IN THE UPPER THAN IN THE LOWER STRETCHER. 1700–1720. MARK HENDERSON, NORWALK, CONNECTICUT.

In leaving the Pilgrim chairs, it is understood that the reason for the use of ash was that the turning could be roughed out by splitting from this wood. The material, however, was inferior to maple, and this fact was soon observed. The material of chairs of this period in England was generally oak. It has been found rarely in American Pilgrim chairs.

Maple is the most admirable wood for turning because it is strong and smooth. But much, if not most of the early maple was soft, growing in the lowlands. The sugar (rock) maple is stronger and harder and is much used today. But the softer maple answered all purposes and was easier to work. Apple wood supplies the finest material for smooth turnings, and was used for tool handles. But it is very hard, difficult to work, heavy, and often gnarled.

1836. A Turned Corner Chair with an Attached Drinking Arm Which Swings Down. 1700–30. Clifford S. Drake, North Hampton, New Hampshire.

1837. (Right.) Corner Chair with a Double Lap, and a Wide Flattening of Arm. Reported as from New England. Maple Except Oak Top Rail. 1700–20. J. Stogdell Stokes.

1838. Corner Chair, Unusual. All Original. 1700–20. Mark LaFontaine, Springfield, Vermont.

1839. (Right.) Corner Chair with Crude Dutch Feet. A Scrolled Slat Back. Most Interesting. 1710–30. William F. Hubbard, Hartford, Connecticut.

1840. ROUNDABOUT. ONE SPANISH FOOT. UPPER BACK IS PURE DUTCH. 1720. HARRY V. WEIL.

1841. (Right.) CORNER OR ROUNDABOUT WITH COMB. IN ENGLAND WOULD BE CALLED BARBERS' CHAIR. 1700–20. G. WINTHROP BROWN.

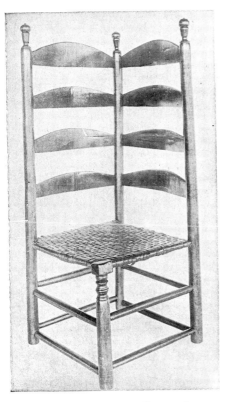
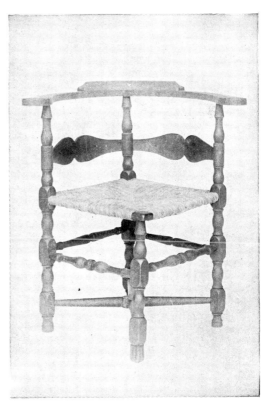

1842. TWO BACKS AT RIGHT ANGLES. COURTING CHAIR. 1700–20. ARTHUR W. WELLINGTON.

1843. (Right.) X STRETCHER. THE COMBINATION OF OUTSIDE AND CROSS STRETCHERS MAY BE UNIQUE. 1700–20. L. G. MYERS.

1844. One Spanish Foot. 1720. H. W. Erving.   1845. Foreign. 17th Century. Geo. S. Palmer.

1846. Burgomeister, Walnut, 25 x 33. 17th or 18th C. Mrs. Francis P. Garvan.

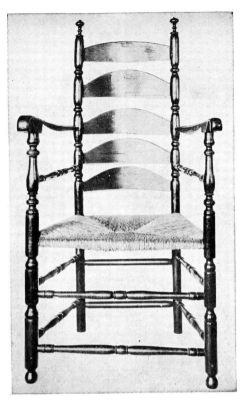

1847. Five Back, Maple. Rolled Arm. 1710–20. Estate of J. Milton Coburn.

1848. (Right.) Five Back, Rolled Arm, Intermediate Spindle. 1710–20. Henry S. Stearns.

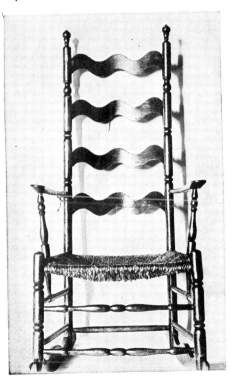
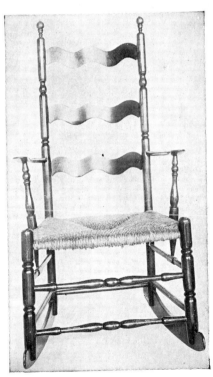

1849–50. Serpentine Backs. Double Bearing Arm. Connecticut Type. 1710–40. Left, Estate of J. Milton Coburn; Right, G. Winthrop Brown.

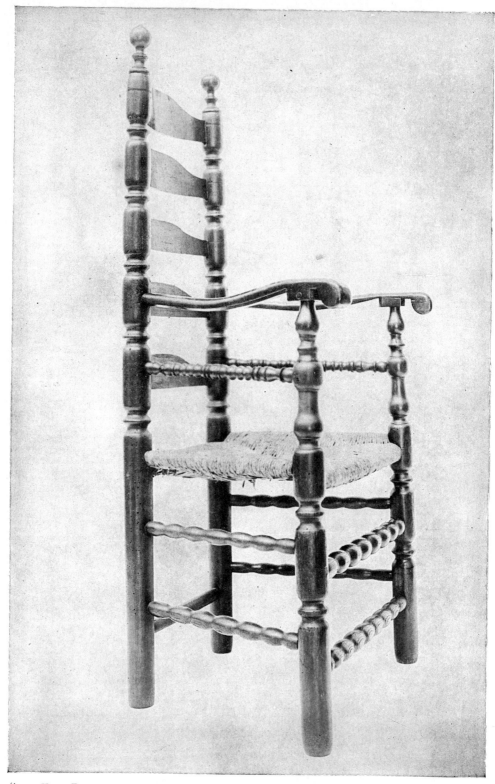

1851. Five Back, Sausage and Ball Turned. A High Type. Delicate Intermediate Spindle. 1710–30. George Dudley Seymour.

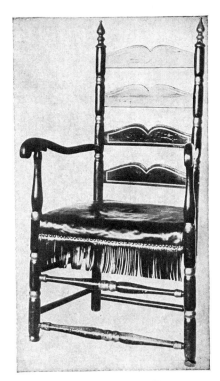

1852–53. Sausage Turned, Rolled Arm, Five Back. Followed by Four Back with Scrolled Slats. 1700–20. Wadsworth Atheneum.

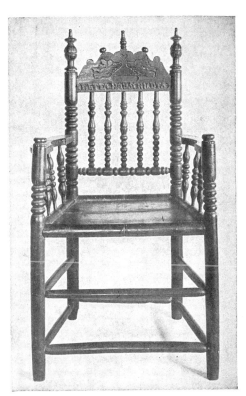

1854. Three Slat, Designed for Rollers Behind. Front of Arms Apparently Cut Off. 1700–20. Was B. A. Behrend's.

1855. (Right.) A Name Chair with Cherub Carving and Applied Knobs on Back. Foreign or Pennsylvanian. Early 18th Century.

1856. A Well-Turned Five Back. Flat Arm Rail. Balls instead of Rolled Arm. 1700–10.

1857. (Right.) Four Back. Candle Posts. Tin Caps Restored. 1710. Wadsworth Atheneum.

1858–59. Webb House, Wethersfield. Fine Ball Foot, Pennsylvania, Parlor Table.

The author thought it a fine plan to perpetuate celebrated Connecticut houses in the wall paper. Because this was a bit different from the conventional, the present owners have obliterated the work.

1860. Square Posts, Tenoned Rungs. Date Uncertain, Also Origin.

1861. (Right.) Sausage Turned, Four Back, Intermediate Spindle. 1700–20.
Wadsworth Atheneum.

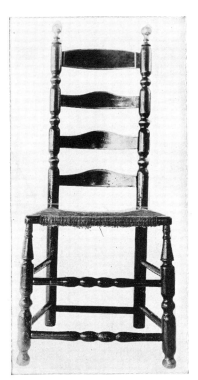
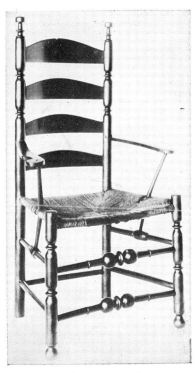

1862. Turned Four Back, Side. Fine Finials. 1710–20. Wadsworth Atheneum.

1863. (Right.) Double Bearing Arm, Probably Connecticut. 1710–30.
Wadsworth Atheneum.

1864. MAPLE AND ASH, SEAT PINE. SOUTHERN CONNECTICUT. 34¾ x 20¼ x 16.
PERHAPS EARLY 18TH CENTURY. CHESTER E. DIMICK, GALES FERRY, CONNECTICUT.

1865. (Right.) SHORT BANISTERS, SIDE CHAIR. ORIGIN AND DATE DOUBTFUL.

1866. ORIGINAL ROCKER, WITH POSTS TURNED FOR THAT PURPOSE. EARLY ROCKERS
ALWAYS PINNED, NOT NAILED. 1700–25. WADSWORTH ATHENEUM.

1867. (Right.) HIGH DESK CHAIR. FOUR SETS OF RUNGS INCLUDING SEAT. 1710–40.
WADSWORTH ATHENEUM.

1868. Four Slat Back with Drinking Arm, Which Tilts. A Hollow Box
Which Swings Carries Arm. 1720–30. R. P. Pauly.

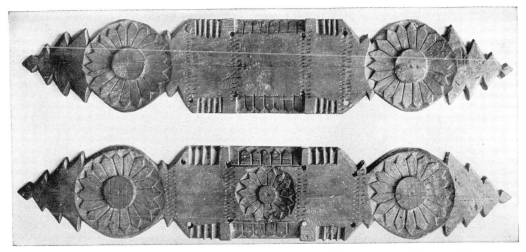

1869–70. Carved Embroidery Yarn Holder To Be Connected by Ropes. Hickory.
1680–1700. Wadsworth Atheneum.

1871-72. New England Slat Backs. The Turning Is the Same in the Posts with Very Slight Variation. Stretchers on Chair at Right, Sausage Turned. 1700-20. George Dudley Seymour.

1873. A Potato Boiler. H. W. Erving.

1874. Heavy Cast Griddle. Pennsylvania.

1875–76. A Five Back, Very High. Sausage Turning. On the Right a Four Back with Graduated Spacing. Sixteen Identical Stretchers. 1700–10. Formerly the Author's.

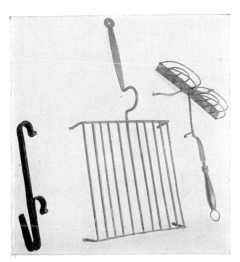

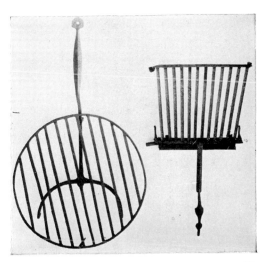

1877–81. Gooseneck Broiler, Swivel Broiler, Broiler with Hollowed Grids and Spout To Save Juices. Whirling Toaster, Double Pothook.

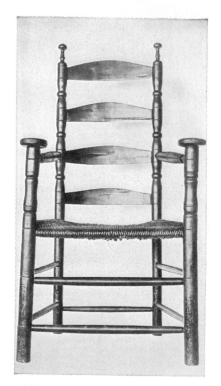

1882. Large Mushroom, Finials Too Small. Arms Slightly Slanting. 1700–20. Wadsworth Atheneum.

1883. (Right.) Slant of Arm Very Marked. 1700–25. Wadsworth Atheneum.

1884. Grouping of Author's Collection. Wadsworth Atheneum.

1885. Great Mushroom Chair, Posts in One Piece, Tops 4½ Inches Diameter.
Giant Size. Connecticut Origin. 1700-20. Wadsworth Atheneum.

1886. SMALL MUSHROOM. THE POSTS ARE ALWAYS TURNED IN ONE PIECE, THE MUSHROOM NEVER BEING DOWELED ON. SUCH A DOWEL WOULD RENDER A CHAIR SUSPICIOUS. 1700. MRS. W. B. LONG, BOSTON.

1887. Three Wide Slats. Onion-Shaped Mushrooms. Two Other Chairs
Like It Are Known. Also a Side Chair, All Probably by the Same Maker.
Mrs. J. Insley Blair.

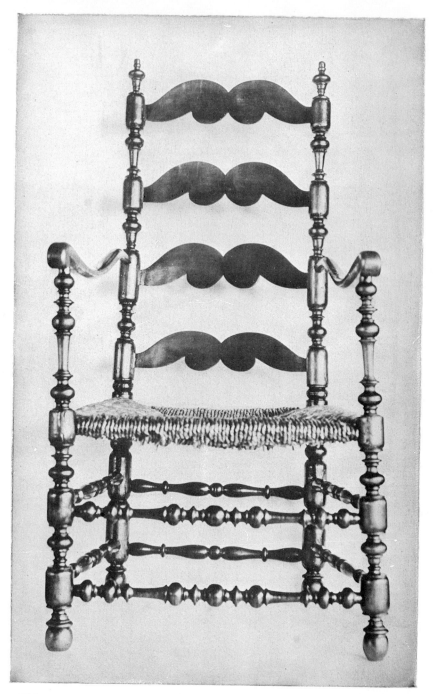

1888. Elaborately Turned. Salamander Back. Origin: This Style Found in Canada, Vermont, and New Hampshire. Rare; Sought After. 1720-30, Mark M. Henderson, Norwalk, Connecticut.

1889. CHAIR WITH ELEMENTS OF NO. 1888. TWO BEARING ARM. 18TH CENTURY. I. SACK.
1890. (Right.) FIVE-BACK PENNSYLVANIA ARM. ROCKERS NOT ORIGINAL. 1710–40.

1891. LOOM STOOL WITH REEL, PENNSYLVANIA. THE HEAD IS SHOWN
IN ANOTHER PICTURE. TULIP DECORATION. WILLIAM B. MONTAGUE,
NORRISTOWN.

1892. Light Pennsylvania Arched Slat Back. Bulbous Feet Restored Properly. 1720–50. Author's Former Collection.

1893. FIVE SCROLLED BACKS. BALLS OF FEET RESTORED. 1710-30. FRANCIS D. BRINTON.
1894. (Right.) FIVE SCROLLED BACKS. SIDE. THIS TYPE HAS GOOD FRONT STRETCHERS. FEET HAVE LOST PART OF BALLS. 1710-30. NEWARK, DELAWARE.

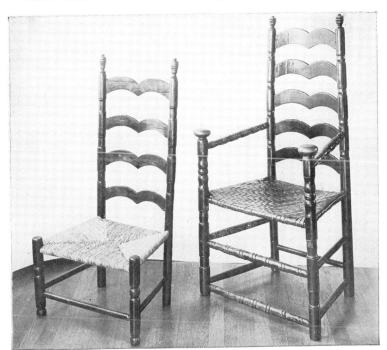

1895-96. AN ARM AND A SIDE CHAIR MADE TO MATCH. ARM HAS MUSHROOM. PROBABLY NEW ENGLAND. 1710-30. HARRY L. F. LOCKE, HARTFORD.

1897–98. Beautiful Examples, Four and Five Backs. The Former with Somewhat More Brilliant Turnings. Pure Delaware Valley Type. 1720–30. J. Stogdell Stokes.

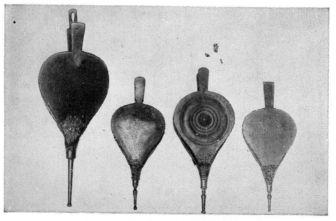

1899–1902. Four Pairs of Bellows, Stenciled or Decorated with Turning. 18th Century.

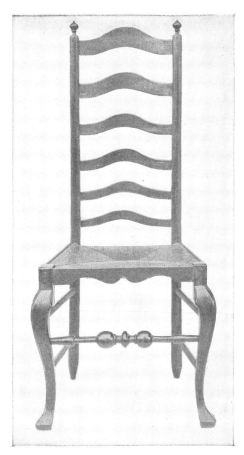

1903. Fine Type Pennsylvania Six Back. Cabriole Legs in Front. These Were Made without Brackets. 1720–30. J. Stogdell Stokes, Philadelphia.

1904. (Right.) Side Chair, Probably by Same Maker, and Made To Match the Preceding. Exceedingly Rare. 1720–30. Francis D. Brinton, West Chester, Pennsylvania.

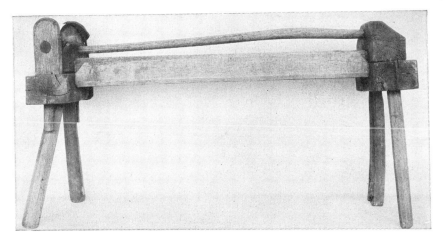

1905. A Flax Breaker. 18th or Early 19th Century. Used To Loosen the Fibers of the Flax before Hatcheling. Wadsworth Atheneum.

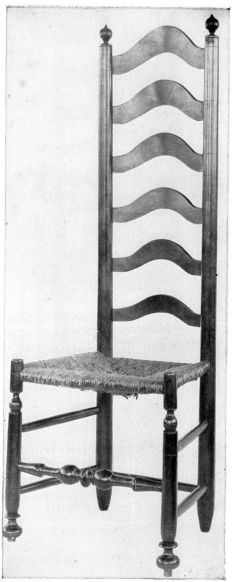

1906. CHAIR WITH TREADLE FOR OPERATING FLY SWITCH. LATE 18TH CENTURY. CONTRIV-
ANCE FOUND IN OTHER INSTANCES. THOUGHT TO HAVE BEEN INVENTED BY FRANKLIN.
1907. (Right.) FINE PATTERN, PENN. SIX BACK. BOTH, J. STOGDELL STOKES.

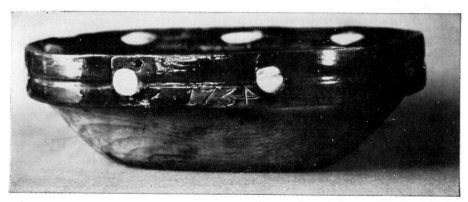

1908. A BOWL DATED 1734; TURNED WOOD WITH DECORATIVE INSERTS. W. B. MONTAGUE.

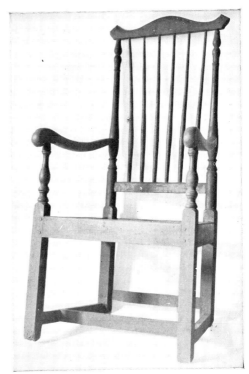

1909. A Five Back, Two Bearing Arm, Original Rocker. Placed Here for Convenience. The Author's. Early 18th Century.

1910. (Right.) Rolled Arm, Square Post, Spindle Back. Apparently in a Class by Itself. 18th Century. W. F. Hubbard, Hartford.

1911. Mushroom Banister Back. Turned Arm. 1700–20. Wadsworth Atheneum.

1912. (Right.) Banister Back Mushroom, Arm Strongly Slanted, and Turned. Fine Type. 1700–20. Dr. and Mrs. J. M. Birnie.

1913–14. Spanish Foot Banister Back. Not a Pair. Large Front Stretcher Is a Mark
of Style. 1700–10. Wadsworth Atheneum.

1915–17. A Toaster, a Loaf Sugar Cutter, and a Huge Pair of 17th Century Oak Hinges.
Wadsworth Atheneum.

1918. Reversed Banister Back. 1700–10. Mrs. John M. Holcombe, Hartford.
1919. (Right.) Banister Back, Dutch Carved Top Rail. 1700–1725. N. Cushing.

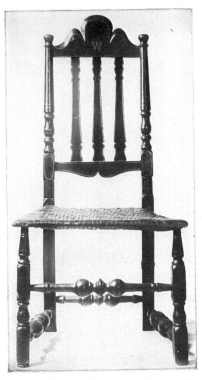

1920. Three Banister Back, Feet Missing. Beveled Top Rail. Initial W.
Maple. 1710. 40½ x 19½ x 13½. Katherine N. Loring, Wayland, Mass.
1921. (Right.) Attractive Connecticut Type. Reeded Banister, Arched Bottom
Rail; Wild Rose Top Rail. 1710–30. Fuessenich Collection, Torrington.

1922. SPANISH-FOOT SIDE CHAIR, CARVED STRETCHERS IN TOP
AND BOTTOM RAILS DIFFERING IN STYLE. WELL CARVED IN
MOLDED SCROLLS. 1700–20. FORMERLY THE AUTHOR'S.

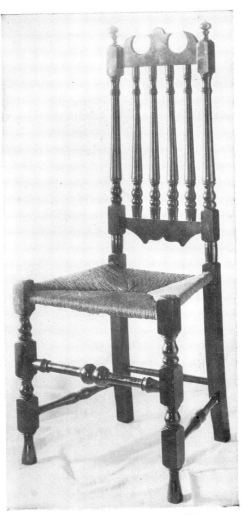

1923. SPANISH FOOT, CARVED TOP RAIL. THE FEET OF SPANISH CHAIRS USUALLY HAVE GLUED-ON TOES, AS IT WAS PRACTICALLY IMPOSSIBLE TO WORK THE LEG OTHERWISE. 1700-10. WAS B. A. BEHREND'S.

1924. (Right.) REVERSED BANISTER BACK. 1710-30. GEORGE S. McKEARIN, HOOSICK FALLS, NEW YORK.

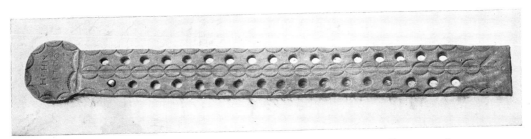

1925. AN ARTICLE WHOSE USE IS NOT CERTAIN. PERHAPS FOR SPIT BEARING. INITIALED AND DATED 1799. WM. B. GOODWIN HAS A SIMILAR IRON. WADSWORTH ATHENEUM.

1926. BANISTER BACK; ROCKERS SHOULD BE REMOVED. STAR CARVING ON ROLL OF ARM. 1700–30. MRS. NILES LEWIS PECK, BRISTOL, CONNECTICUT.

1927. (Right.) FIVE BANISTERS, CARVED RAIL, SPANISH FEET. RAM'S HORN ARM. 1700–10. HELEN T. COOKE, WELLESLEY.

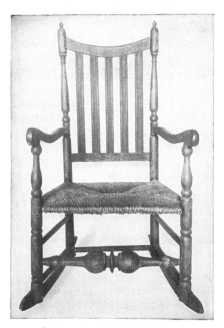

1928. SADDLE BACK, REEDED BANISTER ARM. NOT ORIGINALLY A ROCKER. FINE LARGE STRETCHER. 1710–20. FORMERLY THE AUTHOR'S.

1929. (Right.) A SPINNING CHAIR. SEAT VERY HIGH. 18TH CENTURY. FORMERLY THE AUTHOR'S.

1930-31. A Well-Turned Reeded Banister, and Neatly Turned Four Back with Doubled Foot. 1700-10. J. Stogdell Stokes.

1932. Ball and Chain. The Stone Has Spiral Strips Welded about It. Probably for a Gate or a Bucket Balance. Unique. Fuessenich Collection.

1933. Heart and Crown Reeded Banister, Intermediate Spindle. A Good Type. 1700–30.
George Dudley Seymour, Wadsworth Atheneum.

1934. Reversed Banister Back. Less Comfortable, but Perhaps Thought More Decorative. 1700–20. Side Chairs To Match. E. C. Hall, Longmeadow, Massachusetts.

1935. (Right.) Banister Back, Double Bearing Arm. 1710–30. Mark LaFontaine.

1936. Banister Back, Scalloped Top Rail, Spiraled Arm. 1710–30. Geo. S. McKearin.

1937. (Right.) Five Reeded Banisters, Heart and Crown Rail. Arm, Which Looks as if Superimposed, but Probably Original. 1710–30. James Davidson, New London.

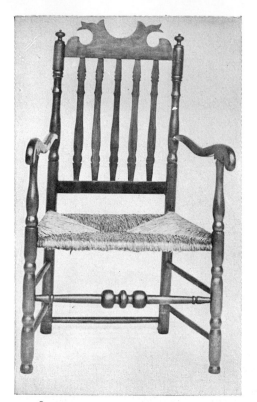

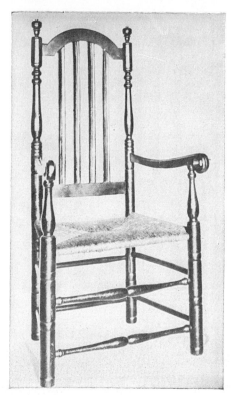

1938. Five-Banister Back, Rolled Arm, Winged Top Rail. 1710–30. L. G. Myers.

1939. (Right.) Banister Back, Pierced Arm Roll. 1710–30. James N. H. Campbell.

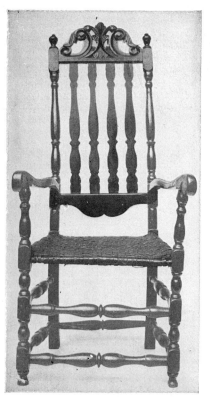

1940. Banister, Carved Rail. 1700–10. The Split Spindle Should Line with and Duplicate the Post, as Here. Brooks Reed.

1941. (Right.) Five Banister, Rolled Arm, Ogee Top Rail. 1710–20. Was B. A. Behrend's.

 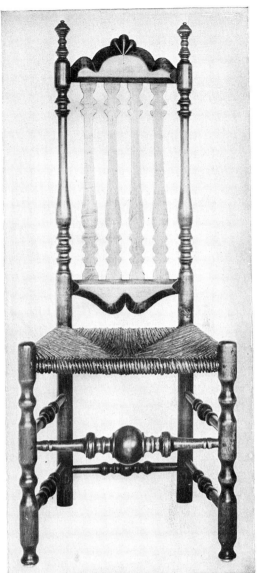

1942. SIDE BANISTER, DAY BED BACK. 1700. ARTHUR W. WELLINGTON, WESTON.

1943. (Right.) BEVELED RAILS, STRONGLY TURNED BANISTERS. FINE STRETCHER. 1700.
G. WINTHROP BROWN.

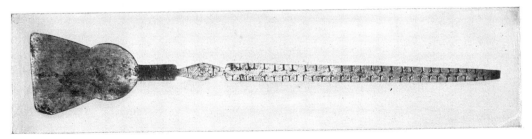

1944. DECORATIVE FLAPJACK TURNER. PENNSYLVANIA. 18TH CENTURY. WADSWORTH ATHENEUM.

1945. SADDLE-BACK, REEDED BANISTER, INTERMEDIATE STRETCHER. PIERCED ARM ROLL. CONNECTICUT TYPE. 1700–20. J. STOGDELL STOKES.

1946. (Right.) BANISTER WITH SUNRISE TOP RAIL. GOOD FINIALS. 1700–20. RHODE ISLAND SCHOOL OF DESIGN.

1947–52. TWO WOODEN TRENCHERS. LARGE AND SMALL. A DOUBLE-FACED PLATE FOR THE MEAT AND DESSERT COURSE. A GOPHERING IRON. TWO COVERED DRINKING MUGS BUILT OF STAVES. WADSWORTH ATHENEUM.

1953. REEDED BANISTER. DAY BED BACK, GRACEFUL ARM, GOOD STRETCHER. THIS CHAIR AND THE NEXT ARE FROM THE SAME SET, AND THEIR CRESTS FOLLOW EXACTLY THE TYPE OF THE PENNSYLVANIA DAY BED. THE INFERENCE IS THAT THEY WERE MADE TO ACCOMPANY A BED WITH THE SAME TURNINGS.

1954. (Right.) SIDE CHAIR, SAME DESIGN. 1710–25. BOTH, J. STOGDELL STOKES.

1955. A DOUBLE-ENDED CULINARY FORK, TWISTED HANDLE. AT AN ANCIENT INN SOUTH OF BETHLEHEM. 18TH CENTURY.

1956. Walnut, "Square Turned" Post. Pennsylvania. Late 17th C. J. Stogdell Stokes.

1959. Rayed Spindles above Banisters. 1720-40. J. Stogdell Stokes.

1960. (Right.) Side Banister, Unique Carved Rail. Was in First Church of Framingham. 1700. Maple and Ash. The Edgell Chair. Stanton D. Loring.

1961. Hatchel Block on a Stand with Cover. Late 17th or Early 18th Century. Katrina Kipper.

1962. (Right.) Turned Frame with Tilting Board, Adjustable. Use Not Known. Flayderman & Kaufman.

1957. (Opposite.) Winged Scrolled Back. Shaped Arm. The Hayloft, Whitemarsh, Pennsylvania.

1958. (Opposite.) (Right.) Oak, Paneled Seat. The Type of This Chair Is Very Much Like the Wainscot or Cromwellian, Except for the Back. 17th Century. New Jersey. J. Stogdell Stokes.

It should be generally understood that the turned chairs of which we have shown many dating from 1690–1720 are maple, unless we have specified to the contrary. Maple was the readily available and excellent wood for this purpose. We get into walnut or fruit wood for fine chairs about 1700. And before 1690 ash persisted to some extent, though maple is usual after 1650.

 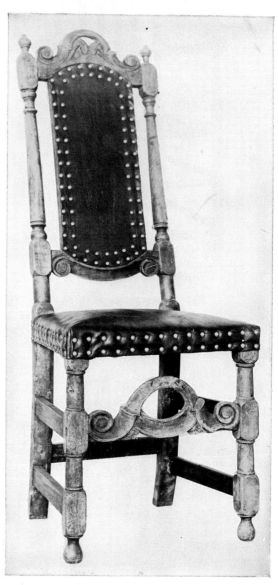

1963. Leather Back. Built in the Style of the Cane Chairs, except for the Upholstery. 1700–25. Wadsworth Atheneum.

1964. (Right.) Leather Back with Rabbeted Curved Recess To Take Leather Back. 1690–1710.

1965. Walnut, Five Leg with Finial. Said To Have Been Made by Early Knickerbocker Craftsmen. 1690–1700. J. Stogdell Stokes.

1966. (Right.) High and Middle Stretcher Well Turned, as Well as Posts and Side Stretchers. A Large Chair, Peculiar Arm. 1690–1700. J. Stogdell Stokes.

1967. Graceful Arms and Peculiar Stretchers. None in Front. Face of Arms Is Molded. Not in Leather. 1690–1700. Howard Reifsnyder, Philadelphia.

1968. (Right.) Spanish Foot, Side Chair. 1700. Flayderman & Kaufman.

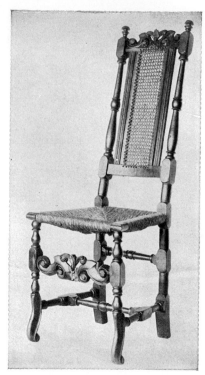

1969. LEATHER BACK, CARVED TOP RAIL. 1690–1700. WADSWORTH ATHENEUM.
1970. (Right.) CANE, BACK AND SEAT ORIGINAL. THIS SCROLL SWEEPING INWARD AT
THE FEET IS CALLED ENGLISH. 1690–1700. WADSWORTH ATHENEUM.

1971. SPIRALED, LEATHER BACK. FLEMISH SCROLLS ON TOP RAIL. BEECH. FEET
RESTORED. 47½ x 18½ x 17. 1690–1700. WILLIAM B. GOODWIN.
1972. (Right.) LEATHER BACK. SLIPPER CHAIR. 1690–1700. MRS. F. P. GARVAN.

1973. FLEMISH SCROLL AND STRETCHERS, RAM'S HORN ARM. FIRST OF A CLASS OF CANE CHAIRS, AS THIS WAS ORIGINALLY. 52 x 24½ x 21. MAPLE. 1690–1700. E. B. LEETE COMPANY.

1974. (Right.) SPANISH FOOT, CARVED SIDE. 49½ x 17½ x 14. PAINTED WITH A DESIGN OF LEAVES COVERING ENTIRE CHAIR EXCEPT BACK. CANE VERY FINE. 1690–1700. CLIFFORD S. DRAKE.

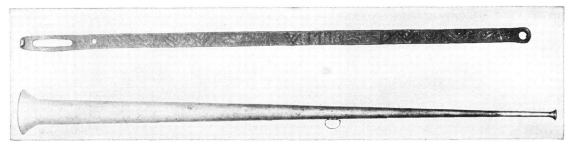

1975. LONG DOOR BAR, DECORATIVE DESIGNS. DATED 1778.

1976. COACH HORN, 18TH CENTURY.

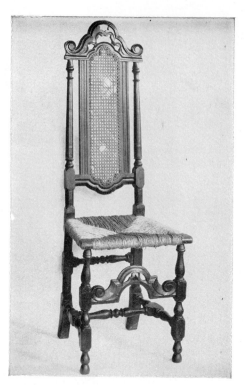

1977. Ball on Foot below the Pear. 1690–1700. Rudolph P. Pauly.

1978. (Right.) Oak, Panel Back. Pennsylvania. 1690–1710. J. Stogdell Stokes.

1979. A Handsome Shape, Ram's Horn Arm, Stretcher Repeated in Crest Rail. Rare. 1690–1700. Helen T. Cooke.

1980. (Right.) Top Turning, English Type, Fine Crest. 1690–1700. Flayderman & Kaufman.

1981–82. A Flemish Side Chair and an Armchair with Flemish Back and Carved Arm. Fruit Wood. This Phrase Covers Apple, Pear, Sometimes Cherry. 1690–1700. Edward C. Wheeler, Jr.

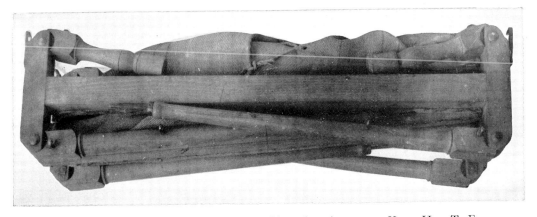

1983. A Complete Full-Sized Bed! It Proves That Our Ancestors Knew How To Economize Room. 18th Century. Adolph Breitenstein, Providence.

1984. Fully Carved Flemish Mode. The Arm Here Is in the Flemish Scroll as Well as the Leg. Crest Rail Similar to, but Not Identical with, Stretcher. 1680–1700. H. W. Erving.

1985. Flemish Chair, Arm Supports Not Carved. Elaborately Carved Stretcher and Crest Rail. 1690–1700. Extremely High, 57½ Inches. Wadsworth Atheneum.

1986–92. Knockers. Palmer Collection.

1993. FLEMISH SIDE CHAIR, FULLY CARVED. IN THE SIMPLER CHAIRS THE BACK PANEL IS NOT CARVED ON THE SIDES. 1690-1700. STANLEY A. SWEET.

1994. (Right.) FLEMISH SCROLL REPEATED ABOUT THE BACK. 1690-1700. EDWARD C. WHEELER, Jr.

1995-2001. KNOCKERS FROM PALMER COLLECTION. COLONIAL AND EMPIRE PATTERNS.

2002. Spanish Foot, Ram's Horn Arm, Turned Stretcher, Shaped Back Panel. 1700–20. Wadsworth Atheneum.

2003. Flemish Side Chair, Fully Carved. 1690–1700. Mrs. John Marshall Holcombe.

2004–10. Knockers from Palmer Collection. Bird and Other Patterns.

2011. English, Flemish Type. Legs Quartered Outward. Crosshatching on Square at Back. 1690-1700. Mrs. Francis P. Garvan.

2012. American Flemish Often Called Charles II. The Crest Rail Is Imposed. It Is Not so Good as When Mortised between the Posts, but It Is More Beautiful. Beech. 1690-1700. Mrs. Francis P. Garvan.

2013-19. Knockers from Palmer Collection. The S Type.

2020. Spanish Foot. Two Cane Panels in Back. Remarkable Outward Rake of Back Leg. 1700. Wadsworth Atheneum.

2021. (Right.) American Flemish Chair. Legs Angle Outward. Molded Seat. 1690–1700. Mrs. Francis P. Garvan.

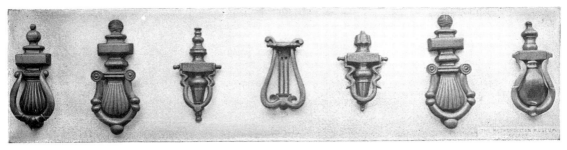

2022–28. Knockers from Palmer Collection. Shell, Lyre, and Pear Types.

2029-30. Pair of Flemish Scrolled, Side Chairs. Were, of Course, Originally Caned
Alike. Good Carving. 1690-1700. Francis Hill Bigelow, Cambridge, Massachusetts.

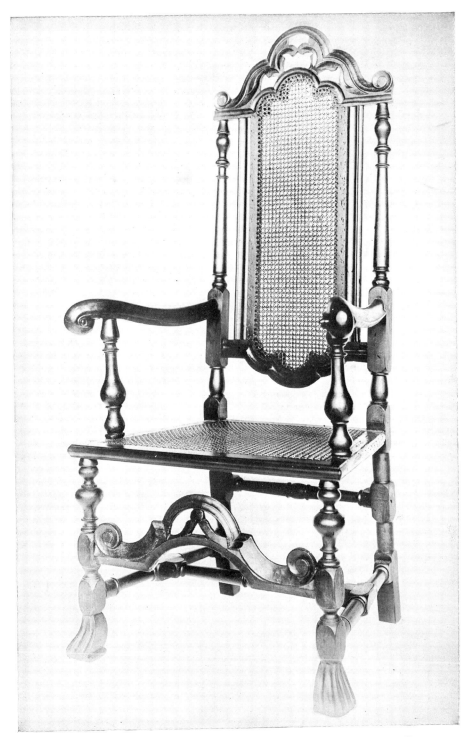

2031. Spanish Foot, Ram's Horn Arm, Shortened so that Post Sets Back from the Front Post. 1700–20. Stanley A. Sweet.

2032. FLEMISH SCROLL ARMCHAIR. ARM SUPPORT TURNED. TOP RAIL MORTISED, IN MORE SECURE AND EARLIER METHOD. FINE RAM'S HORN ARMS. 1690-1700. J. WINTHROP BROWN.

2033–34. A Pair of Beautiful Chairs. The Crest Rail Imposed. The Bottom Stretcher between the Side Stretchers Is Also Scrolled. 1690–1700, Edward C. Wheeler, Jr.

2035. REVERSED SCROLLED FOOT. BACK PANEL WITH REEDS OUTSIDE THE SCROLL. 1690–1700. EDWARD C. WHEELER, JR.

2036. (Right.) A CHAIR FORMERLY IN THE POSSESSION OF THE AUTHOR, IN WHICH THE BEAUTIFUL SCROLL AT THE BACK HAS BEEN RUTHLESSLY COVERED UP IN PART BY AN UPHOLSTERED INSERT.

The material of these chairs, in England, is usually beech. In America it is rarely beech, often maple in the simpler examples, and generally fruit wood in the finer pieces. In construction these chairs are apt to grow shaky in time. Their high backs give a strong leverage. They are not built especially for comfort, but are highly decorative against the wall. They are naturally side chairs. There is a wide difference in the types. Particularly in the front leg, we have it running straight out from the seat and in all degrees of angles, until a full ninety degrees is reached.

2037–38. A Pair of Chairs, Arm and Side, with Reversed Scroll on the Foot. Fruit Wood. The Armchair, as Often, Has the Seat Lower than the Side Chair. 1690–1700. Edward C. Wheeler, Jr.

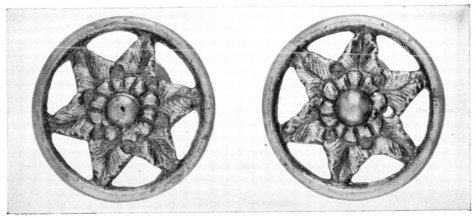

2039–40. Six-Pointed Star Looking-Glass Knobs. c. 1800. William B. Goodwin.

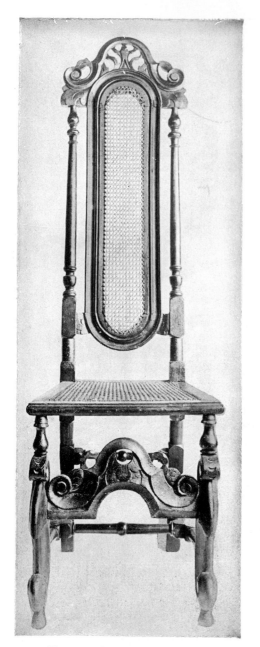

2041. FLEMISH CHAIR WITH OVAL PANEL. A HANDSOME DESIGN. THE STRETCHER BELOW IS A TRUE ARCH. 1690-1700. EDWARD C. WHEELER, JR.

2042. (Right.) SPANISH FOOT, CARVED SIDE CHAIR. PANEL WITH SCROLLS AT THE TOP AND BOTTOM. A VERY GOOD EXAMPLE OF THE FOOT. THERE IS GREAT VARIETY IN THE SPANISH FOOT, AND UNLESS IT IS WELL DONE IT IS UNSIGHTLY. THE STRETCHER IS VERY EFFECTIVE. 1710-20. WADSWORTH ATHENEUM.

2043. FLEMISH SIDE CHAIR, SAID TO HAVE BELONGED TO WILLIAM PENN. NOTICE THE KNOB OR SHOE UNDER THE SCROLL OF THE FOOT. 1690–1700. EDWARD C. WHEELER, JR.

2044–45. A Pair of Spanish Foot Chairs with a Touch of Carving in Interesting Leaf-Like Designs, Reeded Panels, Rolled Crests, Good Front Stretcher. 1710–20. Francis Hill Bigelow, Cambridge.

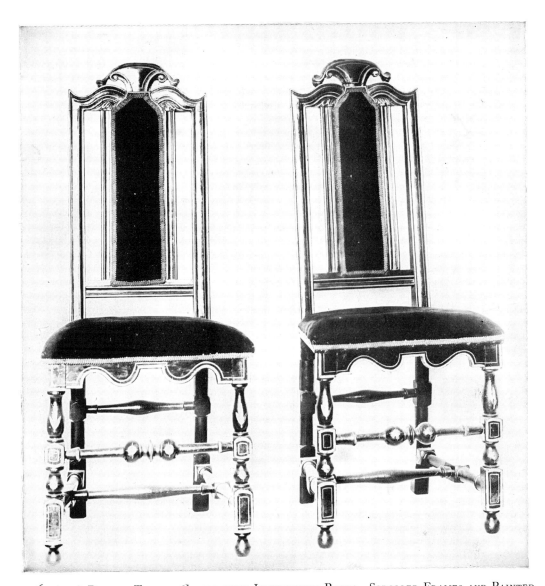

2046-47. A Pair of Turned Chairs with Interesting Backs. Scrolled Frames and Painted Decorations in Bands of Gold. Found at Salem, and Said To Have Belonged to Nathaniel Hawthorne, from Whose Former Residence They Came. The Motive at the Top Is Deftly Handled. The Molded Rails Stop on the Scrolled Panel. We Notice a Transition Here from the Turned Back Posts to a Suggestion of the Dutch Style, Which Is a Little Later. The Bottom Rails and the Side Rails of the Panels Are Reeded. About 1720.

The term side chair has been puzzled over for long. The plausible explanation is that it is a wall chair, to be used, that is, against the side of the room. But as there is no objection to placing an arm-chair against the wall, and no possible objection to withdrawing a moderately low-backed side chair from the wall, the name is not wholly explained. Perhaps it meant a chair readily drawn up against a table, without interference such as arms would offer. Is not that better?

2048. SPANISH FOOT, WING CHAIR. WALNUT. STYLE OF TURNING EARLIER THAN THE DUTCH. 1700–20. KNICKERBOCKER ORIGIN. J. STOGDELL STOKES, PHILADELPHIA.

2049. (Right.) QUEEN ANNE, HEAVY TYPE. WALNUT. MASSACHUSETTS. 1730–50. ESTATE OF HARRY WINTHROP WEEKS, FRAMINGHAM MASSACHUSETTS.

2050. QUEEN ANNE, MAHOGANY. PAD UNDER FOOT. 45 x 29½ x 20½. 1740–60. DR. AND MRS. J. M. BIRNIE, SPRINGFIELD.

2051. (Right.) WALNUT WITH CARVED SHELL, HEAVY. 1730–60. H. W. ERVING.

2052. QUEEN ANNE, WALNUT. LEATHER COVERED. OF COURSE, THE ORIGINAL COVER MAY HAVE BEEN SOMETHING DIFFERENT. NO STRETCHERS. 1730–60. GEORGE S. PALMER COLLECTION.

2053. (Right.) QUEEN ANNE, WALNUT, LIGHTER LEG. WIDTH IN FRONT 29½ INCHES. 1740–60. ROBERT T. SMITH, HARTFORD.

2054. HIGH BACK, ROLLED ARM, NO STRETCHERS. 1740–60. PENNSYLVANIA MUSEUM, PHILADELPHIA.

2055. (Right.) BALL AND CLAW, NO STRETCHER, PLAIN KNEE. NOTE SHAPE OF BACK LEG. 1750–70. HELEN T. COOKE.

2056. Wing or Fireside Chair, Ball-and-Claw Feet, Richly Carved Leg. No Stretchers. Peculiar Break in the Back. 1750–75. Mahogany. 48 x 36 x 24. Francis D. Brinton.

2057. (Right.) Ball and Claw, Carved Knee, Knob Foot Behind. 1750–75. I. Sack.

2058. Acanthus Carved. Leg Simply Swept Back without a Knob. Bell-Shaped Seat, like Most Preceding. 1750–75. William B. Goodwin.

2059. (Right.) Mahogany, Reupholstered in Leather. Plain Edgewise Stretchers. 1760–75. Metropolitan Museum.

2060. HANDSOMELY CARVED. KNOB FOOT BEHIND. WING OR EASY CHAIR. 1750–75. METROPOLITAN MUSEUM.

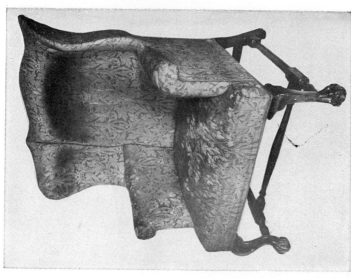

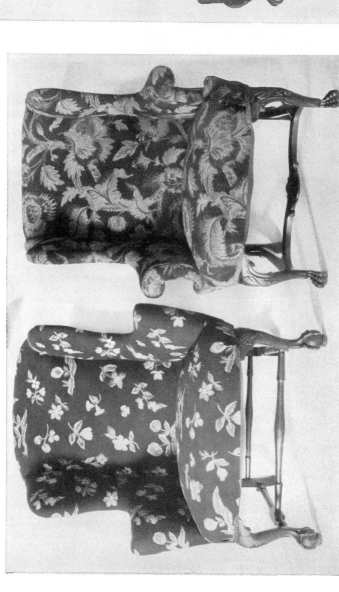

2061-62. A High Ball and Claw Foot with Shell Knee and Stretchers. Also an Animal Foot with Flat Stretchers, One of Which Is Carved as a Shell. One Should Note the Difference in the Arms. The Latter Chair, Supposedly English. 1750-75. F. L. Dunne.

2063. (Right.) Mahogany, Wing Chair with Stretchers. The Method of Breaking the Arm Back to the Whole Width of the Wing Is Here Shown. The Shape of the Arm of the Chair Preceding Is, However, More Fully Carried Out. 1750-75. I. Sack.

2064. Fully Carved on Legs, Front, Sides, and Arms, and Even the Feet Behind. 1750–60. Howard Reifsnyder, Philadelphia.

This is one of the celebrated chairs, of which there are said to be five known, made as samples and bearing the attribution of Randolph, a Philadelphia maker, who showed himself by this work a supreme chair maker.

One notices the so-called animal foot. There is a carved effigy at the center of the skirt, and a diamond-cut background on three sides with dots in the corner of each diamond. The object of this work, like the cross-hatching or stippling, was to overcome the great difficulty of obtaining smooth surfaces in carving of backgrounds. When finished they would not reflect the light properly unless they were as perfect as a lens.

2065. A CHIPPENDALE WING CHAIR WITH STRAIGHT, FLUTED LEG. 1760–75. SANDERSON COLLECTION.

The straight-foot chair is a little later than the cabriole, and was in the later Chippendale manner. As to stretchers, there was variation in usage. Some of the finest chairs had no stretchers, and some of the simpler chairs had them. One notes three classes of arms, perhaps four: That which breaks as here. The earlier type also has a rounded seat and the arm rolls vertically and horizontally. In another type there is an unbroken straight line on the interior, and the arm may or may not roll both ways, but with a double roll vertical and horizontal we get the greatest variety of form.

WING CHAIRS

Otherwise called fireside or easy chairs, are characterized by great depth and are usually upholstered throughout. While we have shown one with Spanish feet, and others exist in that style, the finer types usually appear in the Queen Anne period or the Chippendale time. Perhaps more are found in the Hepplewhite time, but their lines are not so elegant. With the Sheraton there is a shifting of style, and the upholstered arm is omitted and, instead of the wing chair, we have what is often called in this country the "Martha Washington." A few round-back chairs appeared in the Sheraton time. They will be shown in that period, but not in a class by themselves. Of course, the steel spring is never found in old upholstery. Abundance of hair filling and feather cushions made up the depth that secured softness. The best wing chair is built almost like a ship and is a work of art. Nearly all the arms, however, became shaky in time, as their bracing without metal was very difficult. The wing chair and the roundabout, or corner chair, extended together through the same periods, except that in a later time the corner chair was almost an unknown quantity.

2066. A HEPPLEWHITE WING CHAIR. THE FRONTS ARE USUALLY STRAIGHT, AND THE ARM RUNS TO THE BACK AS HERE SHOWN. THE LEG BEHIND HAS NOT SO MARKED A RAKE AS IN THE EARLIER STYLE, AND ALWAYS ENDS IN A PLAIN FORM AS HERE. 1790–1800. WALLACE NUTTING.

2067. (Right.) A HEPPLEWHITE WING CHAIR WITH PEG FEET AND A MOST EXTRAORDINARY HEIGHT. NOTE THE SERPENTINE SHAPE OF THE WING AND THE UNUSUAL CONTOUR OF THE ARM, WHICH IS NOT THICK BELOW THE ROLL. 1790–1800. F. K. GASTON, NEW YORK CITY.

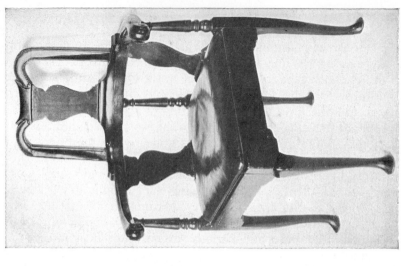

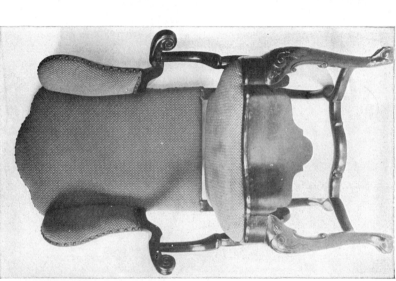

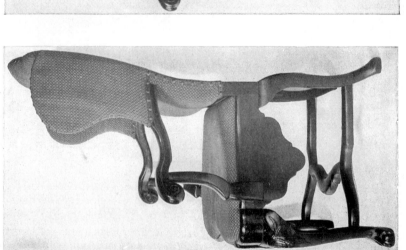

2068–69. A Side and a Front View of the Same Chair with a Scrolled Stretcher and Wide Skirt. The Wing Stops on the Arm. This Wide Skirt Is Found in Philadelphia and Baltimore. The Foot Is a Reduced Ball and Claw, and the Knee Is Carved with the Acanthus Leaf and the C Scroll. Walnut. Rare or Unique. 1730–60. Wallace Nutting.

2070. (Right.) With This We Enter Upon the Corner Chair, Beginning with the Dutch Type. Maple Chairs Have Been Already Shown. All Legs Alike in Their Feet, but Only the Front Corner Leg Is Pure Cabriole. The Back Has the Dutch Splat, and an Unusual Arm Which Rolls Downward Rather than Outward with Slight Carving. On the Back Is Superimposed a Pure Dutch Extension. 1730–50. John H. Buck, Hartford.

2071. A Corner Chair with Four Dutch Feet and Cross Stretchers. The Arm Rolls Outward as Usual, Instead of Downward. Virginia Walnut. Shaped Seat. Compare It with Seat on Bottom of Next Page. c. 1725. New England. H. W. Erving.

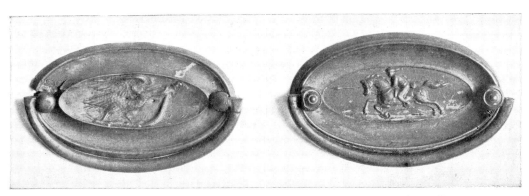

2072-73. Brasses of 1790-1800. Eagle and Serpent, and Post Boy
William B. Goodwin.

2074. FOUR LEGS SHAPED ALIKE WITH BALL-AND-CLAW FEET. TWO PIERCED, INTERLACED SPLATS. GOOD BACK. 1760–75. NATHANAEL G. HERRESHOFF, BRISTOL, RHODE ISLAND.

2075. (Right.) WALNUT DUTCH-FOOT CHAIR WITH WRIST, AND DEPRESSIONS SLIGHTLY RESEMBLING THE DRAKE FOOT. ARMS ROLL DOWNWARD. 1730–50. PHILADELPHIA TYPE. METROPOLITAN MUSEUM.

2076. SHAPE OF ARM AS LOOKED DOWN UPON. SQUARE-SEATED CORNER CHAIR. 1740–70. HELEN T. COOKE.

2077. Three Duck Feet, One Claw-and-Ball Foot, with Acanthus Carved Knee. Square Seat. The Arm of This Chair Appears on the Preceding Page. 1740–70. Helen T. Cooke.

2078. (Right.) Mahogany, Three Turned Button Feet, and One Ball-and-Claw Foot; Acanthus Carving. Cross Stretcher. 1750–75. Formerly the Author's.

2079. Three Straight, One Ball-and-Claw Foot. Ogee Skirt. 1750–75. Flayderman & Kaufman.

2080. (Right.) Walnut, Southern. Three Turned Feet, One Ball and Claw and Marginal Carved Knee. 31¼ x 28 x 27. 1740–60. William B. Goodwin.

2081. Three Ball-and-Claw Feet, with Shells and a Depending Flower. Carved Splats. Cross Stretcher. 1760–75. Wadsworth Atheneum.

2082. (Right.) Mahogany, Three Ball-and-Claw and One Turned Foot. Scrolled Skirt, Pierced Splat, Square Seat. Connecticut. 1750–75. Robert P. Butler, Hartford.

2083. Curly Maple, Straight Plain Legs. Plain Splats. 1760–75. James Fenimore Cooper.

2084. (Right.) Straight Plain Leg, Pierced Splats. Mahogany. 1760–75. Est. Harry W. Weeks.

2085-86. This Page Is an Interlude, To Show a Series of Distinctive Chairs Found in New Jersey. These Two Chairs Have Nearly the Same Turning, and Are Pleasing in Outline, with Strong Local Feeling. Ball and Sausage Turning, Probably Early 18th Century. J. Stogdell Stokes.

2087. Spiral Turned Jersey Chair. Walnut. Cross Wicks. 1699. Described in the Records of the Pierson Family.

A number of these chairs, found in the same vicinity of this type, lead to the belief that they are native.

2088. (Right.) Local Jersey Turnings, About 1720-50. Both, J. Stogdell Stokes.

2089. A Transition Dutch Model with Spanish Feet and Reeded Banisters, Ram's Horn Arm, Feet Partly Worn Away. Unusual Style. 1700–20. Henry V. Weil.

2090. A Leather Back, Side, Transition Dutch. Maple with Stretchers of Beech. 1710–20. Found in Hartford. George Dudley Seymour.

Whether a chair of the period be English is not always easy to declare. A slight difference in value. The wood of English pieces may be Virginian.

2091. A Turned Dutch Chair with an Extraordinarily Wide Splat. Ram's Horn Arms. 1700–20. Katrina Kipper.

2092. Transition Dutch, Spanish Feet, Pretty Well Worn. Decorated in Gilt. 1710–20. Edward C. Wheeler, Jr.

2093–96. Two Pairs of Knobs. The Larger Were for Attaching to Some Piece of Furniture. Henry A. Hoffman, Barrington, Rhode Island.

2097. SPANISH FOOT, CHIPPENDALE BACK. AN INTERESTING COMBINATION OF STYLES FIFTY YEARS APART. 1730–40. J. J. SULLIVAN, WOODBURY, CONNECTICUT.

2098. (Right.) A SIMILAR CHAIR, BUT WITH VARIATION IN THE BACK AND LIGHTLY CARVED EARS. 1730–40. PYNCHON HALL, CONNECTICUT VALLEY HISTORICAL SOCIETY.

2099. SPANISH FEET WITH DUTCH BACK. 1710–30. FRANK A. ROBART.

2100. (Right.) SPANISH FOOT, MOLDED BACK STILES AND TOP RAIL. MAPLE. CONNECTICUT. C. 1720. H. W. ERVING.

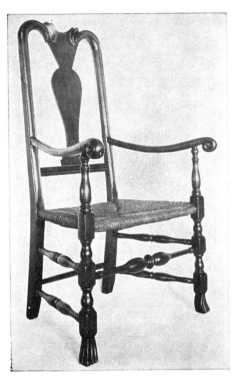

2101. Spanish Feet, with Carved Saddle Back. 1720–30. H. P. Willis, Brookline.

2102. (Right.) Spanish Foot, Too Much Splayed. Ram's Horn Arm with Strong Twist. Carved and Pierced Back. 1710–30. Formerly the Author's.

2103. A Rare Type with Ribbed Arm Ending in a Spiral. Scrolled Skirt, Carved Saddle Back. 1710–30. Henry R. Davis, Everett.

2104. (Right.) A Side Chair of the Same Set and Belonging to the Same Owner.

2105–06. ARM AND A SIDE CHAIR OF A SET FORMERLY THE AUTHOR'S. BOUGHT IN PROVIDENCE. A RARE TYPE OF EARLY AMERICAN DUTCH. ONE SHOULD NOTE THAT THE ARMCHAIR HAS ITS SEAT A GOOD DEAL LOWER THAN THE SIDE CHAIR. 1720–30.

2107. A TURNED DUTCH CHAIR WITH EARS TURNING UP. 1710–30. FRANK A. ROBART.

2108. (Right.) TURNED DUTCH CHAIR WITH LARGE EARLY DUTCH FOOT SUCH AS WE FIND IN PENNSYLVANIA. GOOD STRETCHER, 1720–50. J. J. SULLIVAN, WOODBURY, CONNECTICUT.

2109. A LIGHT TURNED DUTCH, GOOD FEET. 1730–40. FLAYDERMAN & KAUFMAN.
2110. (Right.) CHAIR WITH SOMEWHAT LIGHTER DUTCH FEET AND CHIPPENDALE
SUGGESTIONS IN THE BACK. 1740–50. MORRIS SCHWARTZ, NEW YORK CITY.

2111. AN ARM WITH A DOUBLE BEARING ON SEAT AND FIRST RUNG. A BACK FOUND
IN NEW YORK AND PENNSYLVANIA. 1730–50. T. BELKNAP BEACH.
2112. (Right.) A TURNED DUTCH CHAIR WITH PIERCED SPLAT, REVERSED. 1730–50.
A. D. BARNEY, FARMINGTON.

2113. WE ENTER UPON THE PURER, CONVENTIONAL TYPE OF THE QUEEN ANNE CHAIR, THE LATER PERIOD OF THE DUTCH STYLE. MARGINAL CARVING ON KNEE. 1740–60. FRANK A. ROBART.

2114. (Right.) A QUEEN ANNE ARM, WITH CARVED KNEE. THE ORIGINAL COOPER OF COOPERSTOWN LIFTED HIS WIFE IN THIS CHAIR INTO THE VEHICLE IN WHICH THEY DEPARTED FROM NEW JERSEY. SHE WAS TOO DISCOURAGED TO START. 1720–40. JAMES FENIMORE COOPER.

2115. A CONVENTIONAL DUTCH CHAIR WITH GOOD UNDERBRACING. THIS WELL-SHAPED SEAT IS SOMETIMES CALLED THE BELL PATTERN. RED WALNUT. 1720–40. H. W. ERVING.

2116. (Right.) PROBABLY SPANISH. 1720–40. SOPHIE HARRILL, KNOXVILLE, TENNESSEE.

2117. STYLISH DESIGN, BOLDLY CURVED ARM AND SHAPED SPLAT. THIS TYPE IS CALLED THE PARROT BACK. WALNUT. 42 x 27 x 20. 1725. FRANCIS D. BRINTON.

2118. (Right.) CARVED KNEE, PLAIN STRETCHERS, BACK WITH A MARQUETRY OUTLINE OF AN ANIMAL IN A SHIELD. ENGLISH. 1720–50. KATRINA KIPPER.

2119. A FINE TYPE OF PARROT BACK WITH ACANTHUS KNEE AND SPIRAL SCROLLED. SHAPED SEAT WITH SHELL. WALNUT. 1740–60. HOWARD REIFSNYDER.

2120. (Right.) A PARROT BACK, STRIKINGLY SIMILAR TO NO. 2117 ABOVE, EXCEPT IN THE FOOT. WALNUT. 1730–60. FORMERLY THE AUTHOR'S. METROPOLITAN MUSEUM.

2121-22. A Pair with Carved Drake Feet, Shell on Knee and Back, with Spiraled Scroll
Six Times Repeated. American Walnut. Philadelphia. 1730-50. Metropolitan Museum

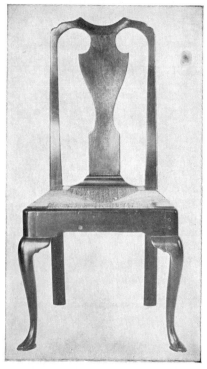

2123. Carved Drake Foot, Handsomely Scrolled Stretcher. Ribbed Arm Support, with
Spiral Scrolled Knuckle. Philadelphia. 1730-50. Ætna Life Ins. Co., Hartford.
2124. (Right.) No Special Merit. Light Dutch Foot with Thin Shoe. 1740-50.

2125. QUEEN ANNE, VIRGINIA WALNUT, BELL SEAT, OVERLAPPING UPHOLSTERY.
29½ x 21½ x 15¾. CONNECTICUT. c. 1750. ROBERT T. SMITH.

2126. (Right.) SLENDER SPLAT, BELL SEAT. CHERRY. 1740–60. J. STOGDELL STOKES.

2127. SHAPED STRETCHER, STRAIGHT FRONT. WALNUT. 1740–60. WADSWORTH ATHENEUM.

2128. (Right.) UNUSUAL BACK SCROLL. THE FULL STRETCHER SCHEME APPEARS HERE
AND IN NO. 2125. 1740–60. E. B. LEETE COMPANY.

2129. Fully Shaped Arm, Concaved Arm Posts, Ogee Skirt. Cherry. 1730–50.
Mrs. Francis P. Garvan.

2130. (Right.) Shell on Saddle Back. Walnut. 1740–60. Katherine N. Loring.

2131. One of Set of Six, Ogee Skirt. Crewel Work, All Different in Design. Painted
Indian Red with Feather Work. Maple. 1712. Made by the Southmeads of Middletown.
William B. Goodwin.

2132. (Right.) Upholstered, Sharply Ramped Arm. 1740–60. Metropolitan Museum.

2133. Transition Chippendale. Maple. New England. 1740–60. Openwork Splat. H. W. Erving.

2134. (Right.) Queen Anne with Panel Back, Caned. Molded Edge Back Post. Slight Carving on Rails. Beech. New England. 1720–40. H. W. Erving.

2135. Leg of Queen Anne Wing Chair. 1750–75. Wm. B. Goodwin, Hartford.

2136. (Right.) Ball-and-Claw Foot in the Queen Anne Type. 1740–60. I. Sack.

2137. RAMPED BACK POSTS, STRONGLY SHAPED SPLAT, BALL AND CLAW, STRAIGHT FRONT. SHELL ON TOP RAIL. 1740–60. GUY E. BEARDSLEY, HARTFORD.

2138. (Right.) FINE LEG WITH STRONG ACANTHUS CARVING. SCROLL IN BOTTOM OF BACK INTO WHICH THE SPLAT ENTERS. CARVED TOP RAIL, RAMPED BACK. 1740–60. SAMSON COL.

2139. OPENWORK SPLAT, CARVED KNEE, SHELL ON FRAME AND BACK. 1740–60. MORRIS BERRY.

2140. (Right.) RAMPED BACK, WITH HIGH SHELL ABOVE SMALLER SHELL ON SPLAT. CARVED KNEE, PECULIAR FOOT. 1740–60. MRS. FRANCIS P. GARVAN.

2141–42. A FRONT AND SIDE VIEW. ANIMAL FEET. FACES ON KNEE. CARVED SADDLE WITH PEND-
ANTS, FOLIAGE CARVED SPLAT. 1720–40. ENGLISH, EARLY GEORGIAN. WALNUT. MET. MUS.

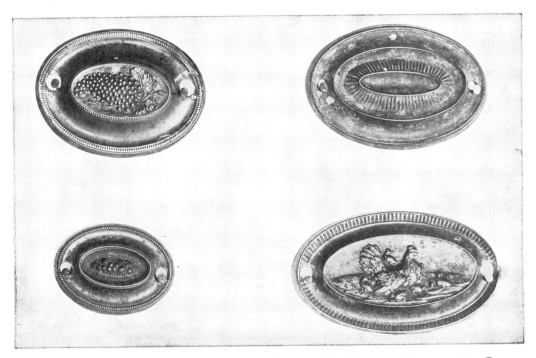

2143–46. A SERIES OF BRASSES OF THE LATE PERIOD. THE HEN AND CHICKENS ARE RARELY
GOOD. RUDOLPH P. PAULY.

2147. Walnut. Queen Anne, Philadelphia Type, with Ribbed Arm Supports, Ball-and-Claw Feet, Shell on Knees and Crest, and Rolled Splat. 1740–60. Pennsylvania Museum, Philadelphia.

2148–51. Brass Belt Buckles. Conventional. 19th Century. Frank A. Robart.

2152. A Philadelphia Queen Anne Arm, with Leg Carving Extending to the Ankle, Ball-and-Claw Feet, Ribbed Arm Supports, Shell on Top Rail, Supported by S Scrolls. Splat Carved. 1740–60. Metropolitan Museum.

The excellence and ornateness of the Philadelphia chairs have never been equaled in America elsewhere, though Baltimore produced some very excellent work, which is scarcely second in quality. The Pennsylvania arm post is somewhat hollowed on the inside, and is cut with two broad flutes which run together at the bottom and leave a rib between. The roll of the knuckle is also characteristic.

A characteristic of the Philadelphia chairs is that the side rail extended entirely through the post with its tenon and is wedged in. The construction was very solid, and is commendable.

2153. Queen Anne Arm, with Acanthus on Knee, and Shell on the Concave Front, and Top Rail, the Latter Supported by S Scrolls. A Parrot-Back Splat, Very Broad. The Arm We Are Accustomed To Associate with a Slightly Later Period. It Is Quite Different from the Philadelphia Arm, Sweeping Down in a Semicircular Curve, and Wrought into a Practically Round Section, and so Meeting at Right Angles the Arm Support. 1750–75. Pennsylvania Museum, Philadelphia.

2154. A Mahogany Side Chair, Queen Anne, with Ramped Back Post, Carved Knees, Ball-and-Claw Feet, and Shell at Top Supported by S Scrolls. Splat Pierced without Carving. Fully Shaped Seat. 1740–60. Metropolitan Museum.

2155. (Right.) Braced, Ball-and-Claw Foot, Queen Anne Side, with Pierced Splat, Ramped Back Post, and Shell. 1740–60. G. W. H. Smith.

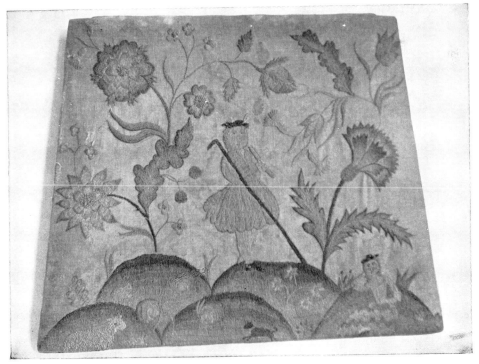

2156. A Seat in Crewel Work on Homespun Linen. A Mrs. Southmead of Middletown, Connecticut, Embroidered the Work. About 1720. William B. Goodwin.

2157. THIS SET IS THE PRIDE OF THE PENDLETON COLLECTION, RHODE ISLAND SCHOOL OF DESIGN, PROVIDENCE.

The class of chairs bearing the great name of Chippendale is the best known to the public as connoting a fine type of antique furniture. While Chippendale made all classes of furniture, he is best known in America by his chairs, his style book having been used largely by American cabinetmakers. Some of his designs were pronounced impractical, and some have not continued popular, as, for instance, those called Gothic, and Chinese. The question has also been raised whether the most intricate of the ribbon backs are in as good taste as the simpler forms. The genius displayed by Thomas Chippendale has never been surpassed, though in a different way Sheraton may rank with him as a designer. There are early types which suggest the growth of Chippendale designs from the Dutch, as, for instance, the celebrated chair above, the side chair of which is on the next page, and a settee of the same set appearing elsewhere. This carving is attributed to Grinling Gibbons, the greatest English name in that art. It seems wise to show a few English Chippendales to fill out and illustrate the style. Details will appear elsewhere. Gibbons died 1720, and if he did this work, the date establishes the earliest possible date of the set, which must, of course, be reckoned as Queen Anne.

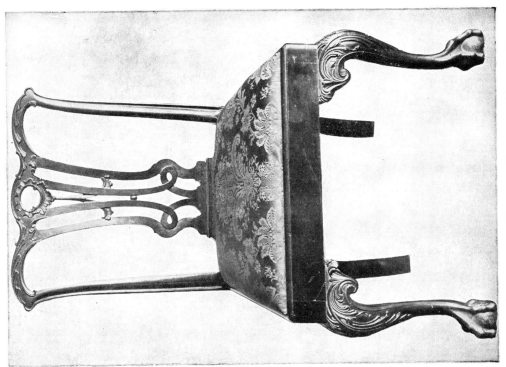

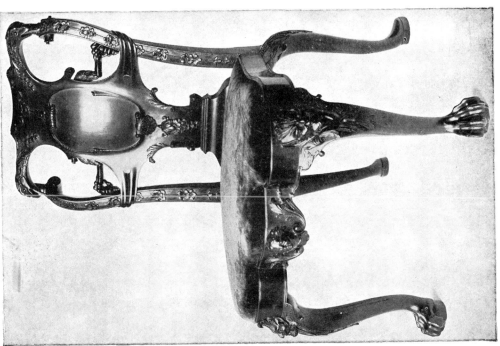

2158. A Side Chair of the Set Mentioned in the Previous Number. Grotesque Faces on the Knees, a Somewhat Mature Cherub on the Center of the Rail (Sometimes Called Benjamin Franklin!), a Large Plaque in the Splat Which Is Tied to the Posts and Held by Bird Claws. The Post with a Repeated Rose Pattern, Varying from Four to Five Petals, Is Rolled in a Fine Spiral at the Top and Grasped by a Bird's Beak, the Neck of Which Connects with the Saddle of the Top Rail. The Other Carving Details Include Shell, Pendants, and Sprays. The Back Leg Is Fully Shaped with a Dutch Foot, Whereas the Front Has the Animal Foot.

2159. (Right.) A Pure Chippendale Type, with Fully Developed Acanthus Knee and Delicate Pierced Splat, Lightly Carved, Dainty Foliage Sprays on the Back Rails and Around a Shield Shaped Opening. Leg Behind in a Plain Sweep. Metropolitan Museum.

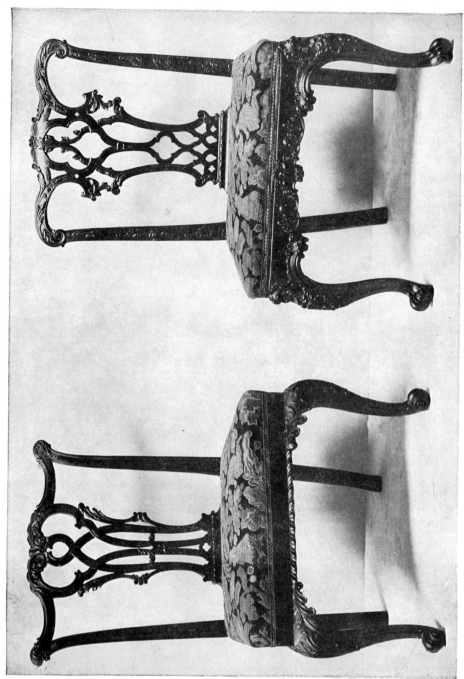

2160-61. Two of the Exquisite Chairs Attributed to Benjamin Randolph. He Worked in Philadelphia and Reached the Climax in American Style. These Two and the Following Have the Spiral Foot Often Seen in France, and Found in Some of the Earlier Chippendale Chairs. Third Quarter 18th Century. Howard Reifsnyder, Philadelphia.

Some exception is taken by English critics to the plain shaping of the back legs. It is a question whether it is any better taste or as convenient to have a knob project like a toe or Dutch foot reversed, on the back leg. The old Latin proverb is pat here, that it is better not to dispute on the question of taste.

2162. ANOTHER CHAIR FROM THE SAME CELEBRATED SET, OF WHICH HOWARD REIFSNYDER HAS THREE. THIS EXAMPLE IS PERHAPS THE MOST ORNATE OF THE WORK ATTRIBUTED TO BENJAMIN RANDOLPH. SOME WOULD CALL THIS FOOT SCROLL A DOLPHIN FOOT. THE OWNER, H. W. ERVING, STILL BELIEVES THESE CHAIRS ARE ENGLISH, AND NO MAN SHOULD KNOW BETTER. IF ROCOCO IS IN ANY FORM ADMIRABLE, IT IS SO HERE. THE EXAMPLE IS SUPREME IN ITS SUPERB CARVING.
MAHOGANY. C. 1750.

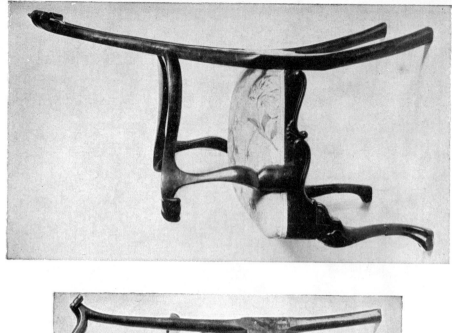

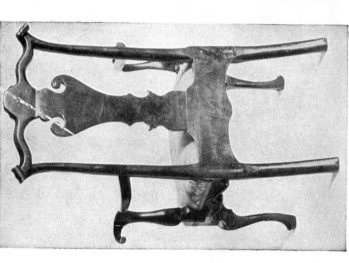

2163-65. THREE VIEWS OF THE SAME CHAIR, PHILADELPHIA SCHOOL. FLUTED DRAKE FOOT, SHELL KNEE, RAISED MARGINAL CARVING, SHELL ON CENTER OF SCROLLED SKIRT AND TOP RAIL, ROLLED EARS, ACCENTUATED PARROT BACK, RIBBED ARM SUPPORTS. MAHOGANY. 1750-75. MRS. FRANCIS P. GARVAN.

Among the particular style marks of the Philadelphia type, is the oval section of the back leg, the long diameter being right and left. The splats also are usually very bold in their scrolled edges. In this example, there is a scrolling on the back rail at the bottom, which is most unusual, and the marginal raised carving extends on the sides, to the back leg. An English suggestion that these chairs are not to be viewed from the rear, is here shown to be without foundation.

Fourteen Chippendale chairs with Dutch feet now to be shown are more or less transitional, some also having a rounded front, showing the hold over of the Queen Anne influence.

2166. Probably Made in Portsmouth or Newburyport. Walnut. $34\frac{3}{4}$ x 22 x $17\frac{1}{2}$. The Seat Is $14\frac{1}{2}$ Inches High, so that One May Say This Is a Slipper Chair. 1740–60. Clifford S. Drake.

2167. (Right.) Straight Front, Dutch Feet, with Stretchers, Lightly Carved Back. 1740–60. Nathan Cushing, Providence.

2168. Always Owned by Fabens-Mansfield Families of Salem, Ancestors of Mrs. Beach. 1740–60. Mr. and Mrs. T. Belknap Beach.

2169. (Right.) Lightly Carved. $38\frac{1}{2}$ x 21 x 17. From Providence. 1740–60. Est. Harry W. Weeks.

2170. ROUND SEAT, MAHOGANY. CARVED KNEE, SCROLLED BRACKET. FROM RICHMOND.
36¾ x 22 x 17. 1740–60. ESTATE OF HARRY W. WEEKS.
2171. (Right.) DRAKE FEET, RIBBED. 1750–70. WALLACE NUTTING.

2172. WALNUT. PHILADELPHIA. DRAKE FEET, RIBBED; SHELL ON CREST. 1740–60.
MRS. FRANCIS P. GARVAN.
2173. (Right.) DRAKE FEET, RIBBED, LARGE HANDHOLE ON TOP RAIL. MOLDED POSTS.
LIGHTLY CARVED EARS. 1740–60. MRS. FRANCIS P. GARVAN.

2174. Carved Back, Straight Front, with Stretchers, Which in All These Examples Follow the Queen Anne Style. 1740–60. T. Belknap Beach.

2175. (Right.) A Well-Shaped Splat, Carved Ears and Shell. $39\frac{1}{2}$ x 21 x 17. 1740–60. Clifford S. Drake.

2176–77. Bases Similar, Backs with Chippendale and Dutch Elements. One Square, One Round Seat. 1740–60. C. Sanford Bull.

2178. Cherry, 1740–60. Straight Front. No Carving. New England. H. W. Erving.

2179. (Right.) Foliage Carving on Splat, Below a Shell with a Pendant; Carved Ears. Walnut, 1740–60. 38 x 21½ x 15½. Dr. and Mrs. J. M. Birnie.

2180. Entering on the Pure Chippendale, We Have a High Ball-and-Claw Foot with a Shoe, and a Light Open Back, Carved Rail and Rolled Ears. 1760–75. I. Sack.

2181. (Right.) Knee Carving Extending on the Frame; Rolled Ears with Rope Molded and Shell Back, Carved Splat. 1760–75. Metropolitan Museum.

2182. CONCAVED ARM SUPPORT, PHILADELPHIA STYLE, WITH DEEP SKIRT. WALNUT. 1760–75. MET. MUS.
2183. (Right.) VERY HANDSOME, SHELL EARS AND FOLIAGE; SHELL AT BACK. 1760–75. MET. MUS.

2184. RED WALNUT, SHELL ON FRONT AND TOP RAILS. ONE OF A PAIR. 1760–75. H. W. ERVING.
2185. (Right.) FLUTED POSTS. TOP RAIL AND SPLAT UNUSUAL IN SHAPE AND IN CARVING.

2186. Quite Unusual in Carving, in Shape of Posts, Splat and Back Rail. 1760–75. I. Saci .
2187. (Right.) English, Mahogany, Fluted Posts, Gadroon Frame, Bell in the Carving of Back. 1760–75. Katherine N. Loring.

2188. Philadelphia, Dutch Underbracing, Carved Ears. 1760–75. Mrs. F. P. Garvan.
2189. (Right.) Philadelphia. Molded Posts, Carved Top Rail. Shaped Frame with Carved Ornament. Good Leg. 1760–75. Henry V. Weil.

2190. Effective, Broad Splat, Beaded Posts. 1760–75. Guy E. Beardsley.

2191. (Right.) Philadelphia, Red Walnut; Large. Shells on Knees, Front Rail and Top Rail. Typical Arm and Post. 1750–75. H. W. Erving.

2192. Connecticut. Cherry. Graceful, Light Stiles, Openwork Splat. Characteristics of an Eliphalet Chapin, South Windsor. Chapin Made Cherry Desks and Highboys Also. 1775.

2193. (Right.) Red Walnut, New England. Shell on Hips, Seat Rail, and Top Rail. Open Splat. 1750–60. H. W. Erving (Both Chairs).

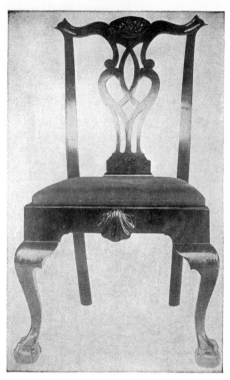

2194. Fluted Stiles; Carved Back. Decoration on Marginal Carved Front Rail. Carved Hips. Hip and Knee Are Terms for the Same Thing. Mahogany. 1760–75. M. A. Norton.

2195. (Right.) Shells on Seat and Back, Fluted Rolled Ears. 1760–75. Mahogany.

2196. Lightly Carved Back, Open Urn Splat, Ball and Claw; Acanthus Knee. 1760–75. Rhode Island School of Design.

2197. (Right.) Fluted Stiles, Foliage Back, Carved Splat, Acanthus Knee. Mahogany.

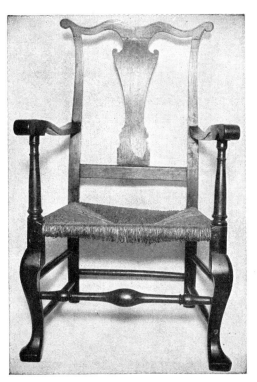

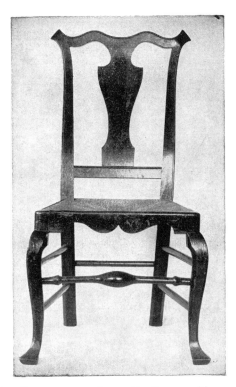

2198–99. PHILADELPHIA. THIS ARM AND SIDE CHAIR ARE SUFFICIENTLY ALIKE TO SUGGEST THEY WERE MADE BY THE SAME PERSON AT AN EARLY DATE. THEY HAVE BEEN ATTRIBUTED TO SAVERY. THEY HAVE SOME DUTCH MARKS. ARMCHAIR 40 x 25 x 18. FRANCIS D. BRINTON. SIDE CHAIR, PERHAPS 1740–60. J. STOGDELL STOKES.

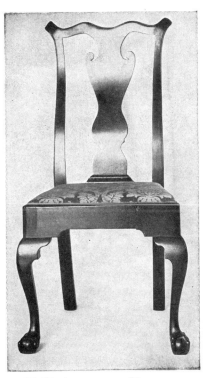

2200. UNUSUAL SPLAT, CARVED SHELL ON TOP. 1760–75. H. H. ARMSTRONG, HARTFORD.

2201. (Right.) NO CARVING EXCEPT BALL-AND-CLAW FEET. 1760–75. SIMPLE CHIPPENDALES HAVE GRACE AND POPULARITY.

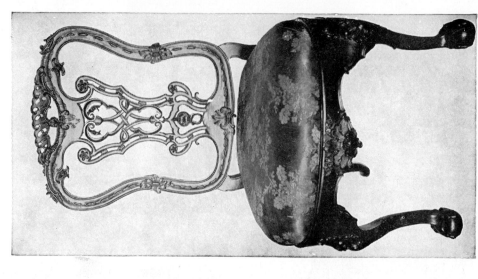

2204. Hispanic. Perhaps Inspiration of the Dutch Chippendale and Hepplewhite. Very Elegant. Walnut. 1740–60. The Misses A. and E. P. Foster.

2203. English, Molded Cross Stretcher, Richly Carved. Ears and Top Rail Very Fine. 1760–75. The Misses A. and E. P. Foster.

2202. English; Mahogany. Engrailed Rail. 1760–75. The Type of Bracket (Which Is Always A Separate Piece) Is a Good Design. I. Sack.

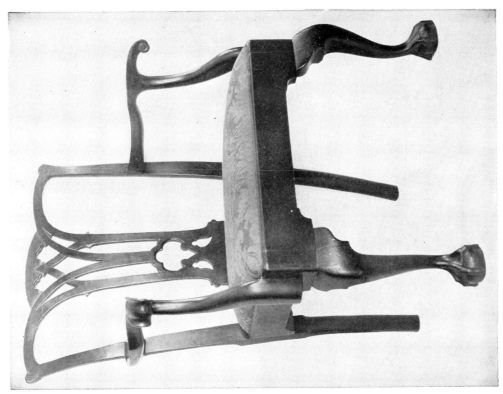

2205. Fluted Stiles, Shells on Top Rail, Seat Rail, and Knees. 1760–75. C. P. Cooley, Hartford.
2206. (Right.) Philadelphia Type, Shown in the Arm and Back Leg. 1750–75. Sanderson Collection.

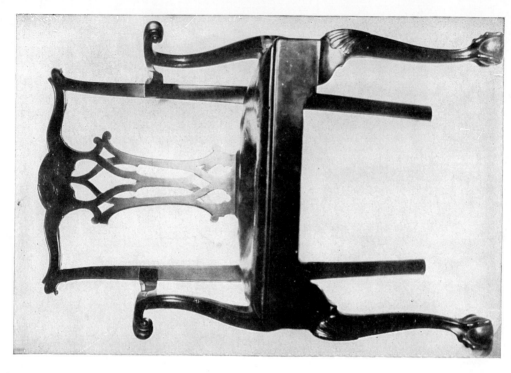

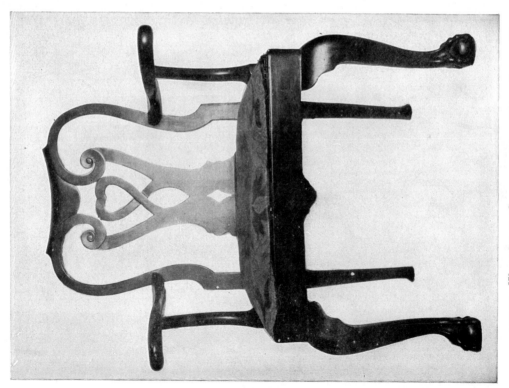

2207. Wide Swept Curve of Arm. Leg a Little Heavy in the Ankle. 1760-75. Morris Berry.
2208. (Right.) One of the Series of Chairs Collected by the Late Morgan G. Bulkeley, for Ætna Life Insurance Company, Hartford. Raised Margins and Rolled Ears on Back Rail. Shells on Knees. 1760-75.

2209. Good Leg. Unusual Motive. Arm Carved without Much Ramp. 1760–75. F. L. Dunne.

2210. (Right.) Shell Knee, Simple Ribbon Back, Sharp Arm Ramp. 1760–75. H. N. Campbell.

2211. Philadelphia; Walnut. Boldly Carved Shells. Good Ears. 41 x 21½ x 16. 1760–75. Francis D. Brinton.

2212. (Right.) Masonic Chippendale, with Many Emblems. Acanthus Knee, Boldly Ramped Arm, Fluted Pillar Stile. 1760–75. I. Sack.

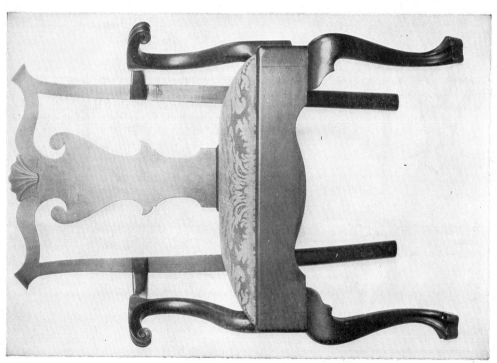

2213. Drake Foot, Philadelphia Arm. Top Rail with Shell and Plain Roll. Wide Splat. Walnut. 1760–75. Sanderson Collection.
2214. (Right.) Broad Splat with Raised Margin Ending in Scrolls. Fluted Rolled Ears, Drake Foot. Walnut. 1760–75. Sanderson Collection.

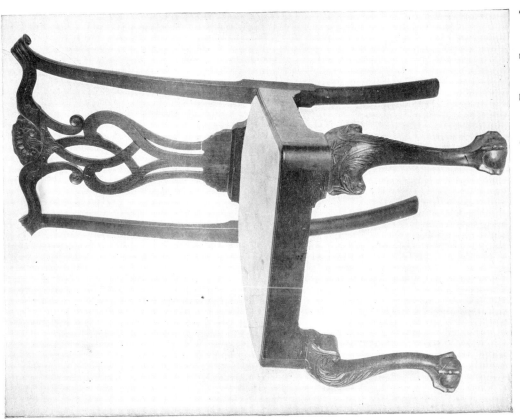

2215. Rolled Ear, Rope Carved Back with Shell. Fully Carved Leg. Philadelphia Type. Mahogany. 1760–75. I. Sack.
2216. (Right.) A Specimen of Considerable Elegance. Mahogany. Stiles with Stop Flute. Rolled Ears, Shell and Scroll Back, and Foliage Carving on Splat. The Tassel Is the Only Element Which Seems Disconnected. Gadroon Mold at Base of Splat. Bought in Charleston, South Carolina. 1760–75. W. A. Hitchcock.

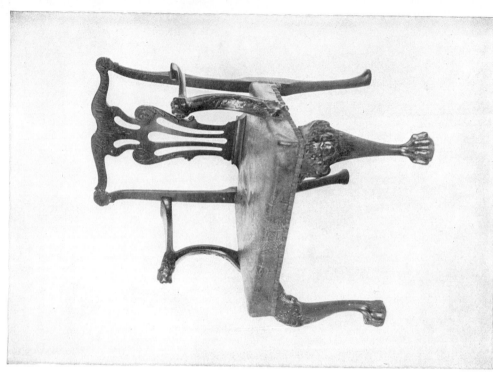

2217. Philadelphia Type. Boldly Ramped Ears. Unusual Shell on Seat Rail. Mahogany. 1760–75. Ætna Life Insurance Company, Hartford.

2218. (Right.) Animal Foot, Elaborately Carved Knee. Carved Arm Support and Knuckle. Shells on Ears, Foliage Carved Splat. Mahogany. English. 1760–75. Palmer Collection.

2219. Philadelphia Type. Ribbed Arm Support and Boldly Contoured and Rolled Arm Ending in a Carved Fluted Spiral. Fluted Stiles, Rope Molding, and Shell on Top Rail; Acanthus Carved Knees and Splat. 1760–75. C. P. Cooley, Hartford.

2220. FLUTED STILES, SHELL EARS AND CENTRAL SHELL; ALSO CARVED CENTRAL FOLIAGE ON CHAIR RAIL. THE ACANTHUS KNEE CARVING IS EXTENDED ABOVE ON THE RAILS, AND SIMILAR FOLIAGE IS FOUND ON THE OPEN SPLAT. PHILADELPHIA TYPE. 1760–75. HOWARD REIFSNYDER.

2221–22. AN OVAL AND A BASKET PATTERN BRASS. 1790 AND 1810. RUDOLPH P. PAULY, BOSTON.

2223. Unusual Scrolled Bracing. Stiles Beaded on Both Sides, and Beading Carried around the Top. 1760–75. Metropolitan Museum.

2224. (Right.) Fluted Stile, Acanthus Knee, Plain Seat Rails, Open Back, Lightly Carved. Mahogany. Attributed to Savery. 1760–75. Mrs. Francis P. Garvan.

2225. Good Conventional Leg. 1760–75. Fluted Ears. Frank A. Robart.

2226. (Right.) Graceful Light Back and Legs. 1760–75. Katrina Kipper.

2227. Richly Carved. The Knee Has Great Elegance, and the Motive Is Carried Up over the Rounded Corner of the Seat Rail. Engrailed Rail Edge. Applied Ornament on Center of Rail Superfluous. Back Rail Carved in a Complex Design. The Splat Is Quite Different in Style from Those with Which We Are Acquainted. Chippendale School. Palmer Collection. I. Sack. The Age Has Been Disputed.

2228. Mahogany, Probably English. Finely Carved. Back Stiles with Carved Rope Molding, "Ribband" Back. 1760–75. H. W. Erving.

2229. (Right.) Simple but Effective Chair with Good Parrot Back. Beading about the Stiles and Back Rail. 1760–75. Charles P. Cooley.

2230–31. Showing the Shape as Looked Down Upon of Two Carved Arms. The Former Is Found in New England and Pennsylvania, but Mostly Through the North. The Latter Has a Very Bold Outward Ramp with Much Grace, and Appears on Chippendale and Earlier Chairs. In This Case a Philadelphia Mahogany Arm, Owned by Mrs. Francis P. Garvan.

2232. A WELL-CARVED CHAIR, WITH LINEN FOLD AND TASSEL IN THE SPLAT, CARVED FOLIAGE ON THE BACK, INCLUDING THE EARS. 1760–75. FORMERLY THE AUTHOR'S.

2233. (Right.) OPEN BACK, SHELL KNEE. MAHOGANY. PHILADELPHIA. MRS. FRANCIS P. GARVAN.

2234. UNUSUAL BACK WITH A SPRAY CARVING AT THE CENTER OF THE SPLAT. RAISED MARGINAL LINE ON THE BACK STILES AND TOP RAIL. 1760–75. FRANCIS D. BRINTON.

2235. (Right.) DUTCH UNDERBRACING, LIGHTLY CARVED BACK, GRACEFUL LINES. 1750–75. I. SACK.

2236. A Carved Rounded Ear. Molded Back Stiles. Graceful Legs, with Acanthus; Ball and Claw; Back Foot Shaped. 1760–75. English. Palmer Collection. I. Sack.

2237. (Right.) Dutch Foot and Underbracing, with Unusual Back, Possibly Dutch. 1740–60. Nathan Cushing, Providence.

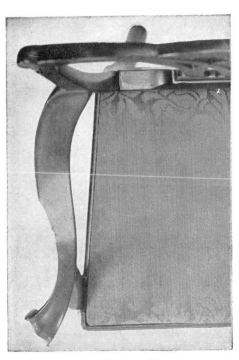

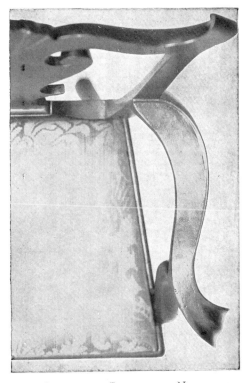

2238–39. Upper View of Two Arms of Chairs in the Sanderson Collection, Nantucket. Raised Marginal Lines. Chippendale Period.

2240. Inward Spiral Scrolled Feet, in Front and Behind. 1760–75. Data Mislaid.

2241. (Right.) Upholstered Chippendale, with Chinese Fret on Legs and Arm. 1760–75.

2242. Interesting Variant. Molded Stiles, Swept in Like a Hepplewhite Back at the Bottom. Delicate Chippendale Ball-and-Claw Leg. 1760–75. Austin D. Barney, Farmington, Connecticut.

2243. (Right.) Transition Chippendale, with Hepplewhite Elements, Spade Foot, Richly Carved Splat. Mahogany. 39 x 20 x 15. 1780. Edward Bringhurst, Wilmington.

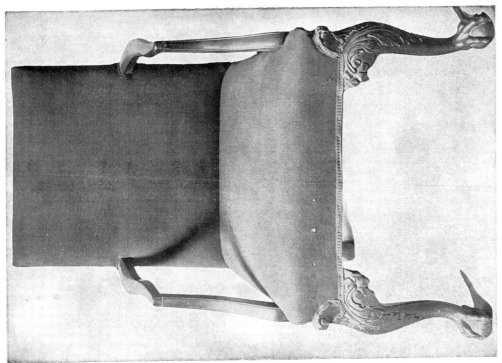

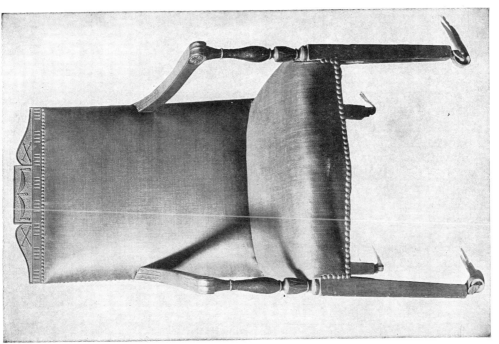

2244. Attributed to McIntire, of Salem. Mixed Elements. Graceful Arm Posts and Arm. 1790. Essex Institute.

2245. (Right.) Unusual Chippendale, Fully Carved Leg, with Extension on the Frame Ending in a Scroll. Back and Arms Much Like Sheraton. 1780. Essex Institute.

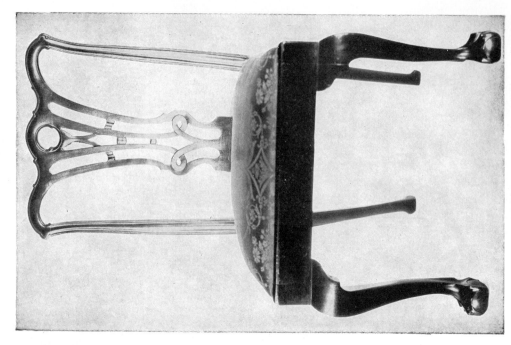

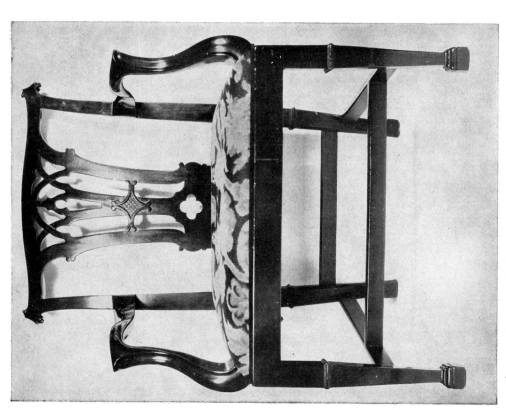

2246. A Transition Chippendale, with Spade Foot and Horizontal Band on the Upper Part of the Leg, Front and Back. Rare but Graceful Arm, Spiraled Rolled Ears. 1780. Charles P. Cooley, Hartford.

2247. (Right.) Molded Back Stiles, Light Open Splat. Plain Seat Rails. 1760-75. Charles P. Cooley, Hartford.

2248. Entering on the Straight Leg Chippendale, a Chair with Light Bracket Is Shown with Molded Stiles and Carved Back. 1760–75. Nathan Cushing.

2249. (Right.) One of a Pair, with Chinese Fret on Legs and Open Fret on Underbracing. 1760–75. Flayderman & Kaufman.

2250. Pierced Ladder Back, Fluted and Lightly Carved. 1760–75. Wallace Nutting.

2251. (Right.) Pierced Ladder Back. Legs, Arm, and Stiles, Fluted. 1760–75. Ætna Life Ins. Co.

2252. Four (Pierced) Ladder Back, Lightly Carved. 1760-75. Ætna Life Insurance Company, Hartford.

2253. (Right.) Three Ladder Back. 26 x 31½ x 18. Ball-and-Claw Foot. Ladder Backs Are Unusual, and Those with Ball-and-Claw Foot Are Very Rare. 1770. Katherine N. Loring.

2254-55. Arm and Side Ladder Backs, Straight Legs with Molded Corner. Hollowed Seat. Lightly Carved, with Spiraled Ears. Part of a Set. 1760-75. F. L. Dunne.

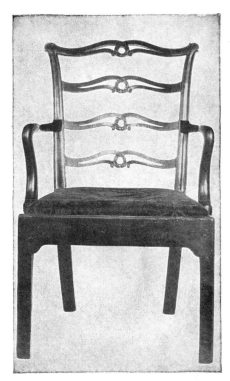

2256. A Three Ladder Back, Cherry, No Carving. Connecticut. 1770. H. W. Erving.

2257. (Right.) Like No. 2252, Except for the Absence of Stretchers, the Slip Seat, and the Brackets. 1770. Frank A. Robart.

2258. A Late Ladder Back, Found at Sherborn, Massachusetts. Maple. 36¾ x 19¾ x 15¼. The Ears Suggest the Date 1790–1800. Estate of Harry W. Weeks.

2259. (Right.) Connecticut. Cherry. Shaped Slats. Back Rather High. 1750–75. H. W. Erving.

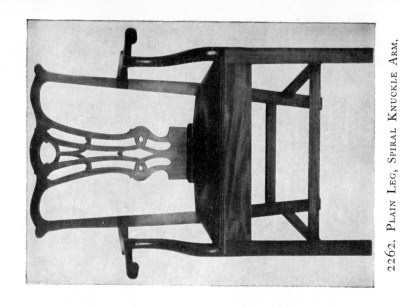

2262. Plain Leg, Spiral Knuckle Arm.
1770-75.
Ætna Life Insurance Company, Hartford.

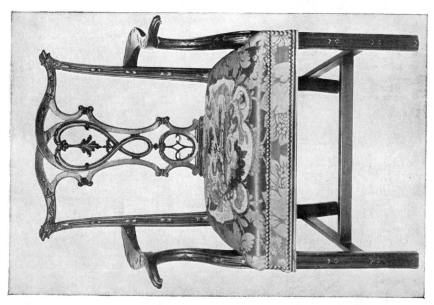

2261. Belonged to Arthur Middleton, a Signer
of the Declaration of Independence.
1760-75. I. Sack.

2260. English Arm, of Which Side Chair Has
Been Shown. A Restrained Arm Knuckle.
Katherine Loring.

2263. CHINESE CHIPPENDALE. MAHOGANY. TRIPLE COLUMN POSTS. ATTRIBUTED TO PHILADELPHIA. c. 1776. 38 x 22 x 21. WILLIAM B. GOODWIN.

2264. (Right.) CHINESE CHIPPENDALE, BAMBOO PATTERN. UNUSUAL AND UNPOPULAR. 1770–75.

2265. BRACKET ON FRAME, CONCAVED ARM SUPPORT. HANDSOMELY CARVED AND SCROLLED ARM. FLUTED BACK. 1760–75. THE MISSES A. AND E. P. FOSTER.

2266. (Right.) NEW ENGLAND. CHERRY. TOP RAIL CARVED. SLIP SEAT. PLAIN LEGS AND STRETCHERS. 1760–75. H. W. ERVING.

2267. MAHOGANY. EARS CARVED; SHELL AT CENTER. FRONT LEGS FLUTED. 1760–75. H. W. ERVING.

2268. (Right.) FLUTED LEGS AND BACK STILES. DELICATELY CARVED BACK. FOUND IN AUGUSTA, MAINE. MAHOGANY. 37½ x 22½ x 18¾. 1760–75. ESTATE OF H. W. WEEKS.

2269. PLAIN LEGS; FLUTED BACK STILES AND TOP RAIL. BACK CARVED WITH FOLIAGE AND TASSEL. 1760–75. MRS. FRANCIS P. GARVAN.

2270. (Right.) CONNECTICUT. CHERRY. FOUR VERTICAL SPLATS WITH A TIE. 1760–75. H. W. ERVING.

2271. Fluted, and with Carved Brackets, Back Delicately Carved. 1760-75.
The Misses A. and E. P. Foster.

2272. (Right.) Fluted Back. Gracefully and Lightly Outlined Pierced Splat. Carved
Back. 1760-75.

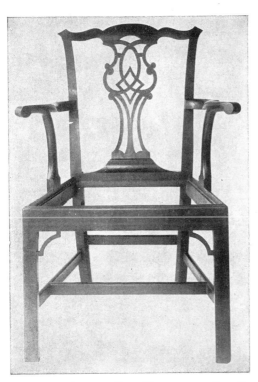

2273-74. Arm and Side Chairs of a Set, Formerly Owned by the Author. Slip Seat Frame,
Showing the Method of Placing the Seat. Open Brackets, Light Pierced Splats. 1760-75.

2275-76. ARM AND SIDE CHAIR OF A SET. BEADED LEGS AND BACK STILES. CARVED BACK. 1760-75. F. L. DUNNE.

Chippendale's later manner was in the straight leg. This style could be quite plain, or ornate.

 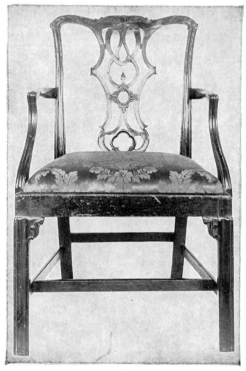

2277. MAHOGANY, WITH FLUTING, AND GOTHIC BACK. 38 x 25 x 21. 1760-75. MRS. FRANCIS P. GARVAN.
2278. (Right.) FLUTED THROUGHOUT WITH CARVED BRACKETS. CARVED TOP RAIL AND DELICATE MOLDED OPEN SPLAT. 1760-75.

2279. (Above.) Fully Carved Legs, with Pendants and Panels. Molded Feet. Carved Brackets. Arm Post Curved but not Carved. Carved Knuckles; Upholstered Arm. 1760–75. Morris Schwartz, New York.

2280. A Brass of the Early Empire Type on a Chest of Drawers in the Sanderson Collection.

2281. Chinese Fret, Upholstered Arm. Plain Stretchers. Upholstered with a Chinese Pattern To Comport with the Style of the Carving. 1760–75. Charles P. Cooley, Hartford.

2283. (Opposite) Chippendale Widely Pierced Slats. 1770. W. Lanier Washington, Westport, Connecticut.

2283 A. Chippendale, Posts of Unusually Rich Design. Seat with Shaped Front and Carved on Three Sides. English. 1760–75. I. Sack.

2282. CHIPPENDALE, CHINESE RAISED FRET ON POSTS AND ARMS. 1760–75. I. SACK.

2284. Plain Rounded Ear, Interlaced Splat, Fluted Legs. 1760–75. Frank A. Robart.
2285. (Right.) Molded Back Stiles; Corner Mold on Legs. 1760–75. Morris Berry.

2286. Arm Scrolled as if One Piece, Carved Bracket, Beaded Corner Post, Fluted Back Rail, Gothic Four-Pillared Back, Connected by Diamonds. Carved Ears on Rail. 1760–75. H. W. Erving.
2287. (Right.) Lightly Built. Molded Back, with Carved Pendant. Rounded Ears, Carved Top Rail. 1760–75. Morris Berry.

2288. VERY DEEPLY SCALLOPED SKIRT. 1760–75. MORRIS BERRY.

2289. (Right.) MAHOGANY. UNUSUAL FRET ON THE LEGS; A CARVED X BACK. CHAMFERED UNDERBRACING. 36 x 21 x 20. 1750–75. EDWARD BRINGHURST, WILMINGTON, DELAWARE.

2290–91. A PAIR OF FLUTED-LEG CHIPPENDALES, WITH A RAISED LINE ON INSIDE AND OUTSIDE OF BACK POSTS, ALSO ACROSS THE TOP. CARVED "RIBBAND" BACK. 1760–75. H. N. CAMPBELL, PROVIDENCE.

2292. Very Delicately Carved Back. Stop Flute on Back Stiles. 1760–75.

2293. (Right.) Back Carved with Raised Margin, Extending Also Down the Open Splat. Carved Foliage and Indented Rounded Ear. Plain Legs. 1760–75. Katrina Kipper.

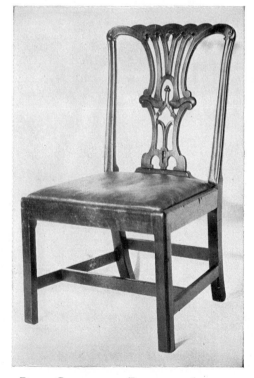

2294. Graceful, Lightly Carved Back, Back Posts Carved and Fluted. 1760–75.

2295. (Right.) One of a Pair, Found in Connecticut. Mahogany. Very Large. Fluted Back. Unusual Splat. 1760–75. James Davidson.

2296–97. Well-Carved Arm. Plain Seat Rail. Chair on Right with Extraordinary Wide Splat, and Deep Scalloped Skirt. 1760–75. Ætna Life Insurance Company.

2298–99. The Former with Solid, the Latter with Open Bracket on Leg. Very Wide Splat on the Former, and Grouped Reeds with a Tie on the Latter. Semicircular Arm. 1760–75. Ætna Life Insurance Company, Hartford.

2300. Daintily Spiraled Ear. Openwork Splat. 1760–75. Estate of H. W. Weeks.
2301. (Right.) A Good Shell. Fluted Ears; Complicated Splat. 1760–75. Wadsworth Atheneum.

2302. No Carving, but a Graceful Pattern. 1760–75. Robert T. Smith, Hartford.
2303. (Right.) Very Unusual Splat, of a Motive Which Perhaps Was Not Intended To Be Analyzed, or with Some Significance Unknown. 1760–75. H. W. Erving,

2304. Upholstered Arm and Back, Fluted Legs and Arm Support. Mahogany. 42 x 26 x 22. 1750-75. C. Sanford Bull.

2305. (Right.) Straight Leg and Plain Curved Arm, Upholstered. Chippendale, as Are All on This Page. Now Upholstered in Leather. 1760-75. I. Sack.

2306. Upholstered Arm. Chippendale Fret on the Foot and Legs. 1760-75.

2307. (Right.) Like the One Above, Except for Bracket on the Frame, and the Width, Which Is a Little Greater. Mahogany. 38 x 27½ x 22. 1760-75. Dr. and Mrs. J. M. Birnie.

2308. A Very Common Chair in America Is the Transition Chippendale-Hepplewhite. The Feature Is the Chippendale Splat with a Back Rail Resembling the Top of a Shield, or with Taper Legs. The First Chair Is Not in That Class, Really Belonging to the Chippendale, with Straight Legs Having No Taper. Fluted Arms. 1760–75. H. W. Erving.

2309. (Right.) Dutch Foot, Chippendale Back. 1750–60. Ætna Life Insurance Company.

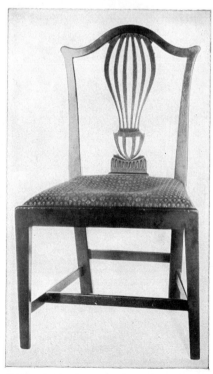

2310–11. Transition, Belonging to Helen T. Cooke and Charles P. Cooley, Respectively.

2311A. A Raised Fret, Chippendale, Upholstered Arms. Molded Feet. 1760–75.
Howard Reifsnyder, Philadelphia.

2312. ONE OF MAHOGANY SET. MASSACHUSETTS. 36½ x 21½ x 19. BELLFLOWER MOTIVE.
2313. (Right.) DOUBLE WHEEL BACK, TAPER LEG. 1780–90. ESTATE OF H. W. WEEKS.

2314. MAHOGANY. CONNECTICUT. 1780–90.
ROBERT T. SMITH, HARTFORD.

2315. HANDSOME URN BACK. 1780–90.
MORRIS BERRY.

2316–16A. Graceful Outlines. Probably Made To Go Together. 1770–80. Mrs. Alexander Armstrong, Baltimore.

2317. From Winthrop, Massachusetts. 1780–90. Estate of Harry W. Weeks.

2317A. Molded Back. Hepplewhite Posts and Top. 1780–90. Morris Berry.

2318–18A. Martha Washington, but Owing to the Taper, Square Feet, Belonging to Hepplewhite Mode. One Molded, One Plain Arm. 1790. Mrs. Francis P. Garvan.

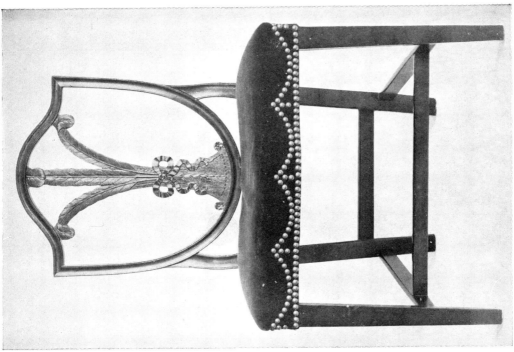

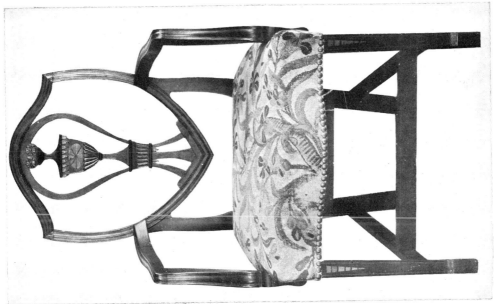

2319. Shield Back, with Inlaid Urn and Carving. Pendant Inlays on Legs and Bands Near the Foot. Fluted Arms and Back and Top Rail. 1790. Metropolitan Museum.

2320. (Right.) Three-Feather Back, from Set Always in the Fabens-Mansfield Families, Salem, Whose Descendant, Mrs. T. Belknap Beach, Owns Six.

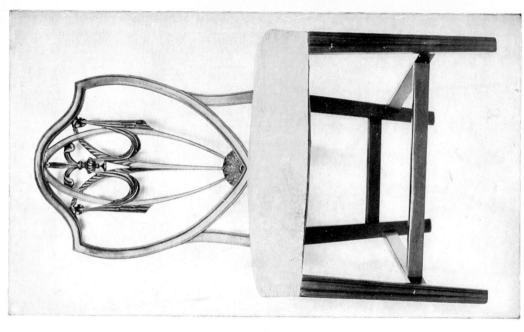

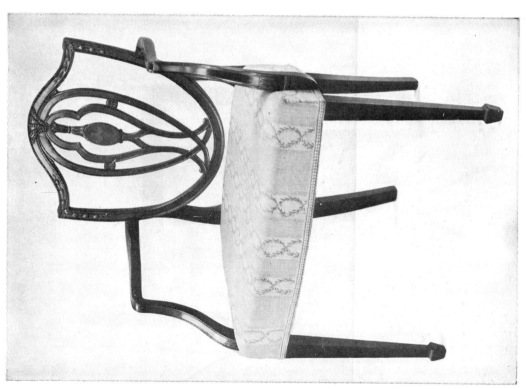

2321. Four Feathers at the Crest, Pendants at the Corners, Inlay on Arm. Raised Edges of Back Laths and Main Frame. Beaded Arm Rails. 1790. Metropolitan Museum.

2322. (Right.) Three Feathers and Graceful Drapery. Fluted Legs, 1790. Sanderson Collection, Nantucket.

2325. Side Chair of No. 2323. 1790.
I. Sack.

2324. Turned and Carved Arm Support. 1790.
Edward Bringhurst.

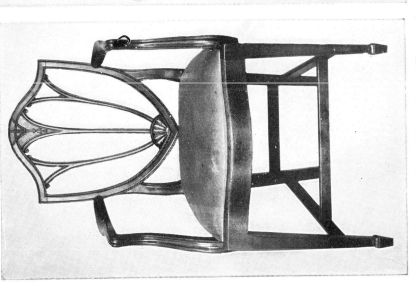

2323. Arm, with Spade Foot, Three-Feather
Back and Inlay. 1790. Shaped Seat. I. Sack.

2326. Inlay at Apex and on the
Three Ovals of the Banisters.
All Frame Members Fluted. 1790.

2327. Five-Sheaf Banisters Tied by
Carving at the Center. Three-Feather
Crest. 1790. Morris Berry.

2328. Three Feathers with Pendant, Frame Fluted Throughout.
1790. F. L. Dunne.

2329. One of Ten, Slightly Carved.
Annapolis. 1790. Joe Kindig, Jr., York,
Pennsylvania.

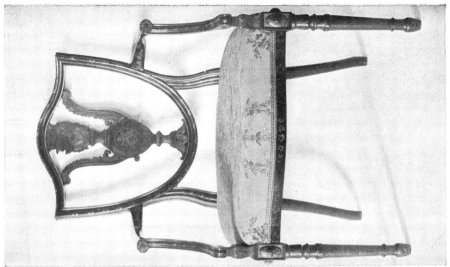

2332. An Elegant Design, Painted. Adam
Brothers' Motives. 1790. F. L. Dunne.

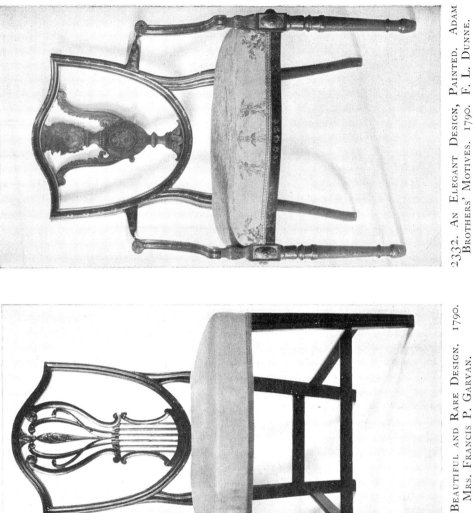

2331. Beautiful and Rare Design. 1790.
Mrs. Francis P. Garvan.

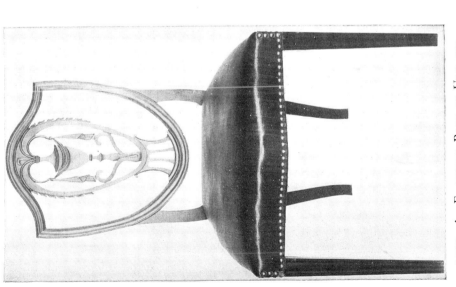

2330. An Exquisite Back of Urn and
Drapery. 1790. Once the Author's.

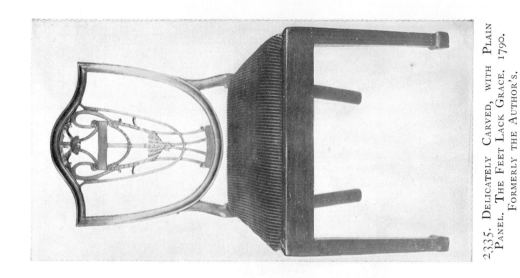

2335. Delicately Carved, with Plain Panel. The Feet Lack Grace. 1790. Formerly the Author's.

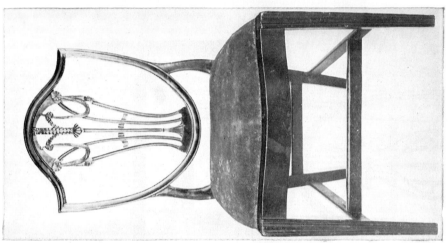

2334. Three Feathers and Drapery. Shaped Front. 1790. Formerly the Author's.

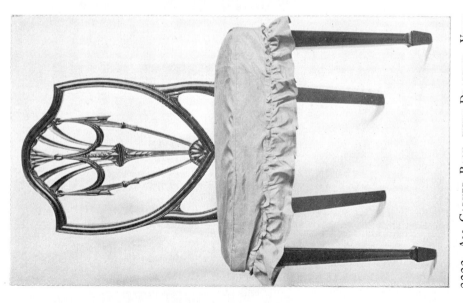

2333. All Carved Back, with Drapery. Very Satisfactory. American. 1790. Mrs. Francis P. Garvan.

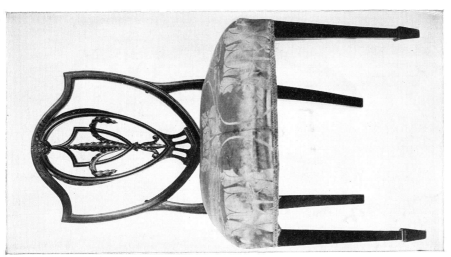

2338. Three Feathers, and Foliage on Top Rail. 1790. Formerly the Author's.

2337. Intersecting Shield, Fluted Legs. 1790. G. W. H. Smith.

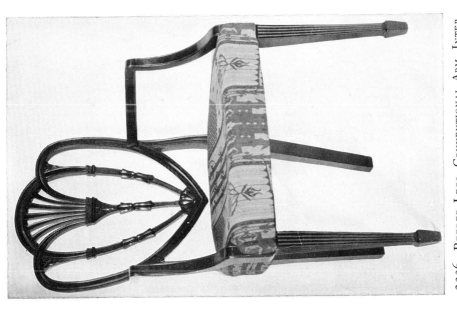

2336. Reeded Legs, Conventional Arm, Intersecting Shield Back. 1790. G. W. H. Smith.

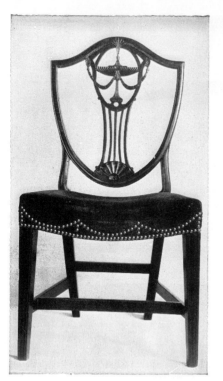

2339. The Rhode Island Type, Attributed to Goddard & Enge. A Considerable Number Known; Some with Hollowed Seat as Here, Others with Flat Seat. 1790. T. Belknap Beach.

2340. (Right.) Finely Carved Urn, All Frame Members Fluted. 1790. Howard Reifsnyder, Phila.

2341. Finely Carved Leg and Arm, with the Same Motives Carried around the Back. Curved Arm Joins the Back with Carved Leaf. Montreal. 38 x 23¼ x 20½. 1790. Clifford S. Drake.

2342. (Right.) Shaped and Molded Front, Graceful Arms, Molded, as Well as the Shield Back. Pierced Banisters. 1790. F. L. Dunne.

2343. Five Feathers. Back with High Ramp. New England. 1790. I. Sack.

2344. (Right.) A Side Chair of the Same Set. These Harmonious Chairs with Their Drapery and Reeded Legs, and Spade Feet Are Very Satisfactory.

2345. One of the Connecticut Senate Chairs. Pendant Inlay on the Legs, Carved Urn with Rosettes Above. Fluted Arm and Back. 1790. Guy E. Beardsley, Hartford.

2346. (Right.) Cane Seat, Carved, Grooved, and Shaped Front Rail; Grooved Back. 1790.

2347. BACK WITH INTERSECTING CURVES, CARVED DRAPERY, AND TIES ON BANISTERS. 1790. THE MISSES A. AND E. P. FOSTER, HARTFORD.

2348. (Right.) ARM CHAIR OF THE SAME SET. DELICATE CARVING, SPADE FOOT, ROSETTE AT INTERSECTION OF ARM WITH POST. 1790.

2349. FIVE FEATHERS, BACK FULLY CARVED, PLAIN TAPER FEET. 1790. PENNSYLVANIA MUSEUM, PHILADELPHIA.

2350. (Right.) THREE FEATHERS AND PENDANT OF HUSKS. 1790. PENNSYLVANIA MUSEUM, PHILA.

2351. Five Curved Banisters, Slight Carving, Molded Frame. 1790. Formerly the Author's.

2352. (Right.) The Curved Banisters Are Done on Their Lower Section with an Imbricated Carving, and Fluted Above. Intersecting Wheat Ears on the Crest of the Shield.

2353. Five Banisters Tied Near the Base and Diverging from That Point. Fully Molded Frame. 37½ x 21 x 18. 1790. Estate of H. W. Weeks (Also Following).

2354. (Right.) Fully Fluted Frame. Inlay at Base of the Shield. 37½ x 21½ x 17½. 1790.

2355. THREE FEATHERS, FLUTING AT BASE OF SHIELD. SHIELD FULLY MOLDED, PLAIN LEG. 1790.
H. H. ARMSTRONG, HARTFORD.

2356. (Right.) FINE SHIELD BACK. AMERICAN. MOLDED LEG AND BACK. MAHOGANY, AS ARE ALL
WE HAVE SHOWN. 1790. H. W. ERVING.

2357-58. ARM AND SIDE. AMERICAN. INLAID AT CENTER, RAISED MARGINS, PLAIN LEG. 1790.
HENRY V. WEIL.

2359. Five Banisters Carved, No Stretchers. Molded Back. 1790. Formerly the Author's.

2360. (Right.) Mahogany. Connecticut. Four Carved Splats or Banisters, or Reeds. Reeded Legs, Spade Foot. 1790. H. W. Erving.

2361. Fluted Legs and Lower Back Stiles, Inlay at Base of Shield. Mahogany. Formerly the Author's.

2362. (Right.) Shield Formed by Intersecting Curves, Fluted Legs, Molded Back.

2363. A Delicately Shaped and Fully Carved Arm and Leg. A High Back. The Chair Usually Going under the Name "Martha Washington." 1795 Estate of H. W. Weeks, Framingham. $47\frac{1}{2}$ x $25\frac{1}{4}$ x 20. Provenance: Groton, Massachusetts.

2364–65. Knobs for Looking-Glass, Dove on Pedestal. Early 19th C. Wm. B. Goodwin.

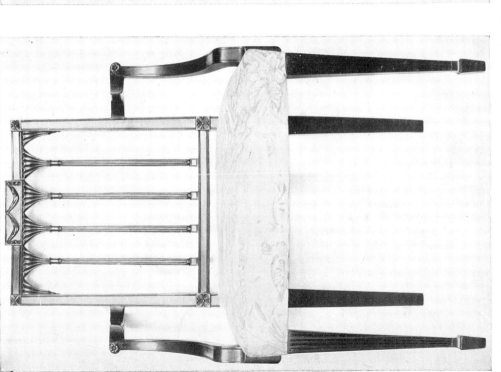

2366. A Chair Which Could Be Classed as Adam. The Banisters Terminate in Fan Carvings, Making Pointed Arches, or What Is Often Called a "Cathedral" Top. Legs Taper More Sharply than Usual. Rosettes in Front on the Arm. 1795. Sanderson Collection.

2367. (Right.) The Sofa Motive Shortened To Form a Chair. It Has the Same Incurve of the Arm, over the Post, That We Find in Many of the Sofas. The Purpose of This Is, in Part, to Conform with the Curvature of the Seat Rail. Reeded Posts and Frame, with Carving on the Post Urn, Straight Back Carved on the Roll. Rare. 1795. Edward Bringhurst, Wilmington.

2368. Four Banisters or Splats, Tied Together by Festoons, and Pointed Arches. 1795. Helen T. Cooke.
2369. (Right.) Handsome Urn Back. 1795. The Misses A. and E. P. Foster.

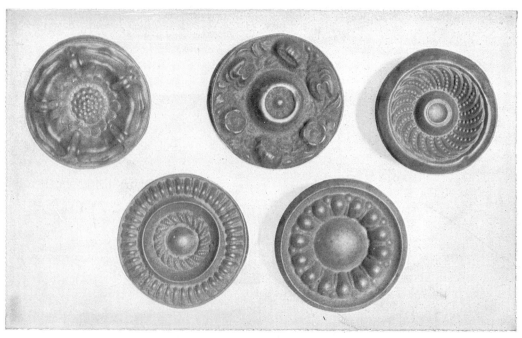

2370-74. Empire Knobs for Chests of Drawers. 1825. F. A. Robart.

2375. The Carving of the Racquet Back Is Too Fine for Effectiveness in a Small Picture. Chamfered Back Legs. 1795. Edward Bringhurst.

2376. (Right.) A Similar Chair, but with Variations. 1795. Pennsylvania Museum, Philadelphia.

2377. "Cathedral" Back Formed of Intersecting Curves. Festoon on Top Panel, Fluted Legs, No Stretchers. 38 x 21½ x 18½. 1795. Estate of Harry W. Weeks.

2378. (Right.) An Armchair with Diamond Pattern Lattice, Very Light. 1795. Frank A. Robart.

2379–80. A Pair of Chairs with Urn and Scroll Back, Set in a Rectangular Form. We Have Here the Turned Leg without Reeding. 1795. Howard Reifsnyder.

2381. American Sheraton. Lightly Carved. 1795. Mrs. Francis P. Garvan.

2382. (Right.) Turned and Reeded Legs, Painted Decoration on the Finely Carved Arm. Carved Diamond Lattice Back. 1795. G. W. H. Smith.

2383. Design of Drapery Connecting the Central Pillar with the Supporting Side Pillars. Husk Pendant. Hollowed Seat. 1795. Helen T. Cooke.

2384. (Right.) One of Six, Which Once Belonged to Benjamin Franklin. 37 x 21 x 18. Delicately Carved. 1785. Francis D. Brinton.

2385. A Delicate and Tasteful Back. Light Chair, No Stretcher. 1795.

2386. (Right.) Gaily and Well Done with Roses and Daisies. 1795. G. W. H. Smith.

2387. "Cathedral" Back, Clustered Column Reeds. 1795. Formerly the Author's.

2388. (Right.) Four Detached Splats, All Carved. Fluted Back and Legs. $36\frac{1}{2}$ x 21 x 18. 1795. Estate of Harry W. Weeks.

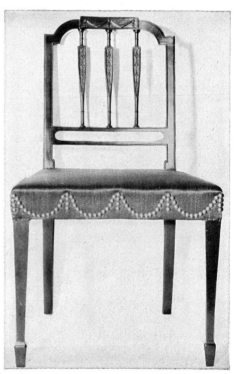

2389. Patera above Urn, Carved Back, Reeded Legs, Straight Feet. 1795. Estate of Harry W. Weeks.

2390. (Right.) Unusual Design. Three Carved Arrow Splats. Festooned Rail. Henry A. Hoffman, Barrington, R. I.

2391. Handsome Back, Carved Urn, Three Feathers. 1795. Helen T. Cooke.

2392. (Right.) Detached, Parallel Reeds, Fluted Frame. 1795. E. B. Leete Company.

2393. Arched Back, No Carving, Very Simple. 1795. Wallace Nutting.

2394. (Right.) Massachusetts Origin, from Wayland. Shuttled Reeds with Carved Ovals. Reeded Back, Fluted Legs. 36 x 15½ x 18. 1795. Clifford S. Drake, North Hampton, N.H.

2395. CENTRAL REEDED BANISTER, FAN SHAPED AT THE TOP, AND CROSSED BY A FESTOON. FLUTED LEGS. STRETCHERS. 1795. · PENNSYLVANIA MUSEUM, PHILADELPHIA.

2396. (Right.) LYRE BACK, TURNED LEGS. 1795. MORGAN B. BRAINARD, HARTFORD.

2397. SIMPLE BACK WITH CHAMFERED CORNERS, THREE SPLATS WITH ROSETTES AND SPREADING CARVED TOP. 1795. THE MISSES A. AND E. P. FOSTER.

2398. (Right.) ADAM-SHERATON. TURNED AND REEDED BACK POST, AND BANISTERS. TURNED AND REEDED AND CARVED LEGS. 1795. VERY HARMONIOUS CHAIR. PENNSYLVANIA MUSEUM, PHILA.

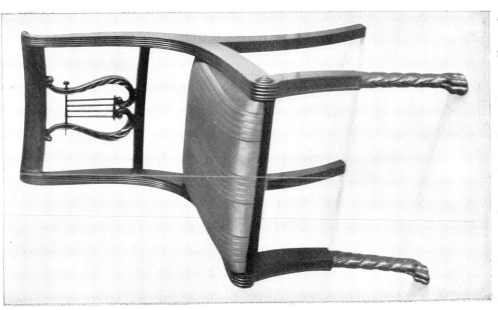

2399. Duncan Phyfe, Lyre Back, Animal Feet, Sweeping Reeded Back Rail Coming to the Front. Above the Foot the Leg Is Carved with a Hairy Shank. 1800–20. Louis G. Myers.

2400. (Right.) Cross-Legged Duncan Phyfe, Animal Feet. Rosette at Intersection of Curve and Single Stretcher Running to the Middle of Back Stretcher and Forming a T. Half-Moon Intersecting Back. Reeded Throughout. 1800–20. Mrs. Harry Horton Benkard.

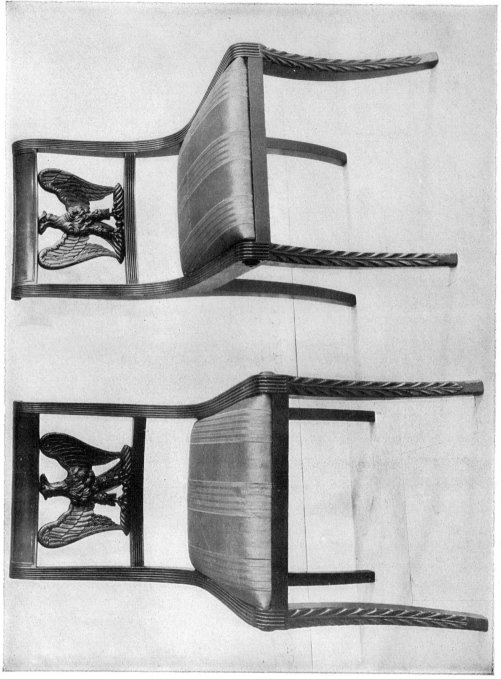

2401–02. A Pair of Phyfe Chairs with Eagle Backs, Carved So that the Eagles Face Each Other. 1800–20. Harry Wilmerding Payne.

2403-C4. Animal Feet Below a Sweeping Line of Leg, Seat Rail and Back. Reeded Throughout. Top Rail with a Carved Lyre; Bottom Rail with Foliage Rosette. 1800–20. Metropolitan Museum.

2405. Sheraton or Adam. Eastern Massachusetts. Painted Decoration. New Cane. 33 x 21 x 18½. 1800–20. Clifford S. Drake, North Hampton.

2406. (Right.) A Very Similar Chair with Variations in the Arm Post and the Feet, and the Decoration. One of Six Bought in Spain by the First United States Minister. Owned by George Gibbons, Grandfather of Present Mrs. J. S. Roosevelt.

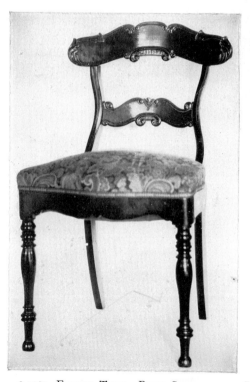

2407. Empire Type. Back Shaped and Carved. 1820–30. Charles P. Cooley.

2408. (Right.) The Detail of Lyre Back from No. 2399.

2409-10. American Empire. Sharply Rolled Backs. c. 1800. Edith Rand, New York.

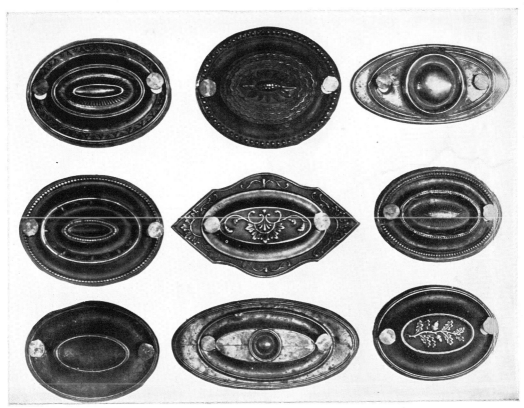

2411-19. Empire Handle Plates from the Collection of Frank A. Robart.

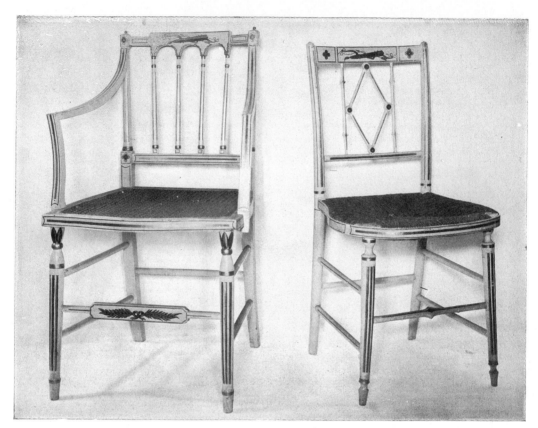

2420–21. Late Sheraton, in White and Gold. Quiver, Bow and Arrow. 1820. Frank A. Robart.

2422. Round-Front Seat, Carved Back Rail. 1800–20. Mrs. Harry Horton Benkard.

2423. (Right.) Late Sheraton. Mahogany. Duncan Phyfe Mode. Carving on Arm, Back Stiles and Top Rail. New England, Probably Connecticut. c. 1800. H. W. Erving.

2424–25. Side and Arm in Late Sheraton. Graceful Lines, Diamond Lattice Back. 1800–20. Frank A. Robart.

2426. Cane Seat and Cane Back Panel, Spiraled Rail and Sections of Post, with Same Effect without Spiral on the Front Seat Rail. 1800–20. Pennsylvania Museum, Phila.

2427. Late Empire with Amusing Cabriole Legs, Rather Overdone. Lyre Back. 1800–20. Samuel Wineck, Hartford.

2428–29. ARM AND SIDE, LATE SHERATON. ENGLISH. LYRE BACK. 1800–20. I. SACK.

2430–31. A PAIR OF HITCHCOCK CHAIRS WITH UNUSUAL DECORATION. CORNUCOPIA BACKS. NOTE THAT A MARK OF THIS STYLE IS THE SLIGHTLY BENT LEG IN FRONT. IRVING P. LYON, M.D., BUFFALO, N. Y.

2432–33. ARM AND SIDE, EMPIRE. BOLDLY CURVED ARM, BACK CARVED WITH ROSETTES AND FOLIAGE. 1810–30. MORRIS BERRY.

2434. LATE EMPIRE, CABRIOLE LEG, CARVED BACK AND KNEE. 1820–40. W. A. HITCHCOCK.

2435. (Right.) CURLY MAPLE, FROM FAMILY OF GEN. HENRY BURBECK, NEW LONDON. IN 1848, AT 95 YEARS, HE WAS THE OLDEST LIVING REVOLUTIONARY GENERAL. 1810–30. JAMES DAVIDSON.

2436-37. ARM AND SIDE, ANTHEMION BACK, TOPPED BY A SHELL. 1810-30. MORRIS SCHWARTZ, NEW YORK CITY.

2438-39. FROM PALMER COLLECTION. THE FORMER CHAIR IS GRACEFULLY CARVED, AND SPIRALED, AND IS THE EARLIER. 1810-30.

2440. Mahogany, Cane Seat. From Virginia. Reeded Throughout, except the Fluted Back. 1810–20. Robert T. Smith, Hartford.

2441. (Right.) American Late Sheraton, Mahogany and Satinwood. 1810–25. Metropolitan Museum.

2442–43. Set of Late Sheraton, from Middletown, Connecticut. Curly Maple. 34½ x 21 x 15. 12 Chairs. By Cabinetmaker Named Bull. His Work Includes Carving, Turning, Bending, and Fretwork. Before 1821. William B. Goodwin, Hartford.

2444. PAINTED LATE SHERATON. HOLLOWED BACK. INTRICATE LATTICE WORK. SEAT ONLY
14 INCHES FROM FLOOR. PAINTED DECORATION. 30½ x 19½ x 16. 1815–25. CLIFFORD S. DRAKE.
2445. (Right.) DECORATED LATE SHERATON OR EARLY HITCHCOCK. MAPLE. 1820. JAMES DAVIDSON.

2446. LATE SHERATON. TAPERED SQUARE ARM POSTS. 1810–20. RUDOLPH P. PAULY.
2447. (Right.) LATE SHERATON, FEET LIKE THE HITCHCOCK. BALL-AND-SLAT BACK AND STRETCHER.

2448-49. Painted Maple Chairs. Plymouth County, Massachusetts. 35 x 18¼ x 15¼.
1810-30. S. Prescott Fay.

2450-51. The Former a Plain Hitchcock, the Latter Decorated with an Eagle Standing on
a Globe. 1830-45. Flayderman & Kaufman.

2452. Late Empire, Carved Eagle Back. 1820–30. The Unsupported Legs of the Late Empire Are an Objectionable Feature. Samuel Wineck.

2453. (Right.) A Very High Chair, Formerly Owned by Nathanael Brookhouse Mansfield, of Salem, Now Owned by His Granddaughter, Mrs. Alec Thayer. 1830–40.

2454-55. Sheraton Windsors. 1810–20. Decorated. Robert T. Smith.

2456–57. Sheraton Windsor and Early Hitchcock. 1820–30. J. J. Sullivan, Woodbury, Connecticut.

2458–59. Late Sheraton. 33 x 17½ x 16. Painted Decoration. New York Origin. Mrs. Francis P. Garvan.

2460-61. Late Sheraton. Painted. Reeded Legs. 1820. Flayderman & Kaufman.

2462-63. Stenciled, Late Sheraton, Early 19th Century. Frank A. Robart.

2464. Late Turned Sheraton, Decorated in White and Gold. Early 19th Century.
2465. (Right.) Painted Sheraton. Turned. Rush Seat. Early 19th Century. Essex Institute.

2466. Late Arrow Back, Windsor Rocker. The Last Style before the Boston Rocker.
Early 19th Century. Pynchon Hall, Connecticut Valley Historical Society, Springfield.
2467. (Right.) The Boston Rocker, with the Famous Roll Seat and Arm. The Most Popular
Chair Ever Made, the Type Which People Use, Antiquarians Despise, and Novices Seek.
Same Owner.

2468. We Class Children's Chairs by Themselves, Going through All the Periods. Above Is the Cotton Mather High Chair. 1640–60. It Is Perhaps the Best Example of the So-Called Brewster Type, in Existence. Worcester Antiquarian Society.

The author recently heard of another just like it, burned up the road for sixty miles to reach it, offering a dealer a sum reaching into four figures, and arrived just after the owner had sawed it up for kindling wood.

2469. A True Carver Child's Chair, with Three Vertical and Three Horizontal Spindles in the Back. The Flattening of the Posts Is Caused by the Chair Being Dragged about by Children. 17th Century. Wadsworth Atheneum.

2470. (Right.) A Pilgrim Slat-Back Baby Chair. Hickory. 17th Century. Beryl De Mott, Millington, New Jersey.

2471-73. Two 17th Century Children's Chairs, Variants of the Carver, and an Early 18th Century Cricket. George McKearin, New York City.

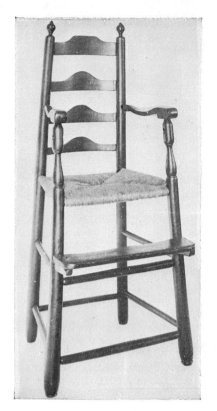

2474–75. Pennsylvania and New England High Chairs. The Former Owned by Chauncey C. Nash. The Latter Formerly Owned by the Author. 1720–50.

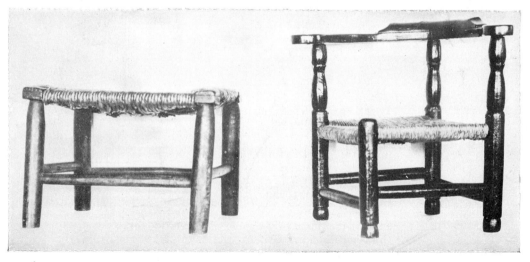

2476–77. A Rush Stool and Baby Corner Chair. Formerly in Ives Collection. 1700–30.

2478-79. A Dutch and an Oxbow Serpentine Child's Chair. The Former 1730. The Latter 1720. Formerly in Ives Collection.

2480-81. The Former a Slat Back with Turned Arms Projecting over the Post. The Latter a Pennsylvania Arched Slat Back. 1720-40.

2482–83. Top Rail of the Former Was Like the Lower Rails. Early 18th
Century. Collection of J. Stogdell Stokes.

2484–85. The Former Owned by Chauncey C. Nash. The Latter by the Author. 1710–40.

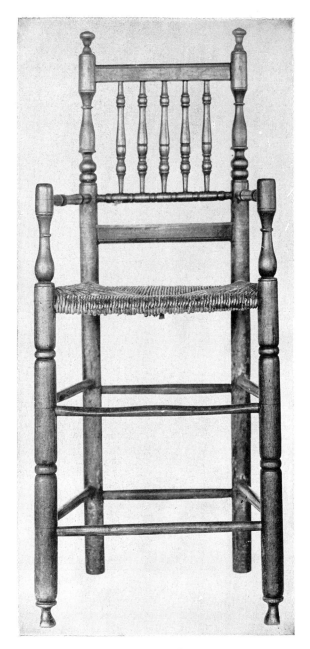

2486. REEDED BANISTER, HEART AND CROWN WITH AN INTERMEDIATE SAUSAGE SPINDLE. 1710–30. PORTION OF THE TOP RAIL MISSING. GEORGE DUDLEY SEYMOUR.

2487. (Right.) A HIGH CHAIR WITH ODD SPINDLES IN THE BACK WHICH DO NOT HARMONIZE. THE AUTHOR DOES NOT UNDERSTAND IT. FORMERLY IN IVES COLLECTION.

Practically all the types of every period up to the latest are found in children's chairs. It seems to be only in the 19th century, that the children are neglected in this respect. There is nothing more appealing than a child's chair, and nothing that can give more delight to a child.

2488. A Child's Chair Decorated with Cutouts of Hearts and Diamonds. 18th Century. T. T. Wetmore.

2489. (Right.) A Reversed Back, Baby Carver, 18th Century. Was B. A. Behrend's.

2490. Child's Wing Chair Extended at Back To Render It More Stable. 18th Century. Wadsworth Atheneum.

2491. (Right.) Child's Chair, with Original Rockers. Finger Holes at Back. 18th Century. Flayderman & Kaufman.

2492–94. CHILDREN'S CHAIRS. 18TH CENTURY. WADSWORTH ATHENEUM. AUTHOR'S COLLECTION.

It was such an easy matter to have saved these chairs! But most have been destroyed. There is room in most attics for a relic. The reason so many chairs are cut down, of all sorts, is that a short person occurs about every third generation. The right and the left chairs above are cut down.

2495–97. A WING CHAIR, A SLAT BACK, AND A STOOL. ALL 18TH CENTURY. WADSWORTH ATHENEUM.

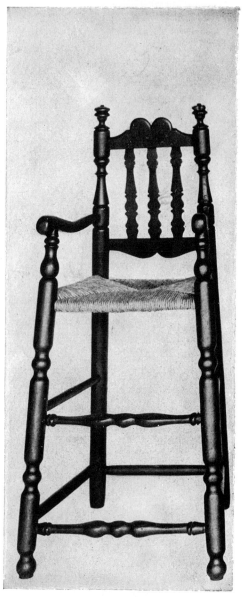

2498. THREE-SLAT BACK, WITH SAUSAGE RUNGS, AND ORIGINAL FOOT REST. 1700–10. WADSWORTH ATHENEUM.
2499. (Right.) BANISTER BACK, CHILD'S HIGH CHAIR. 1720–30. FORMERLY THE AUTHOR'S.

2500–2501. WASHINGTON BRASSES, END OF 18TH CENTURY.

2502–04. BABY HIGH CHAIRS, TWO WITH ROLLED AND ONE WITH TURNED ARM. AMUSING RAKE TO THE MIDDLE SPECIMEN. EARLY 18TH CENTURY. WALLACE NUTTING.

2505–06. A TURNED ARM AND A MUSHROOM ARM. 18TH CENTURY BABY CHAIRS. ROCKERS NOT ORIGINAL. CHARLES P. COOLEY.

2507. The Earliest Type of Windsor Chair, with a Queen Anne Stretcher. Amusing Straddle. 1720. Formerly the Author's.

2508. (Right.) A High Chair with Front Spindle Suggesting the Brewster. 17th or 18th Century.

2509-10. Stamped Brasses. 1700-10. Collection of F. A. Robart.

2511. A Heart-Back Wing Chair, Possibly for Twins. 18th Century.

2512–13. (Right.) High Beaded and Hollowed Turned Stool. 18th Century. J. Stogdell Stokes. Child's Arm Windsor without Stretchers. Cupid's Bow Top Rail. Tenoned Arm. Only Three Back Spindles. Perhaps Unique. c. 1800. J. Stogdell Stokes.

2514–15. Child's Windsors, a Comb Back, and a Side Chair with the Remarkable Number of Seven Spindles for so Small a Piece. 1780–90. Mrs. Francis P. Garvan.

2516. BABY'S BOW BACK HIGH CHAIR. MERITORIOUS TURNING. ARTHUR LESLIE GREEN, NEWPORT.
2517. (Right.) EXCELLENTLY TURNED. THE BOW IS MORTISED INTO THE ARM WITH A SLOPING ELONGATION.
BOTH DATE C. 1770. FORMERLY THE AUTHOR'S.

2518–19. CHILD'S LOVE SEAT AND CHAIR. VERY APPEALING. 1760–80. J. STOGDELL STOKES.

Windsor chairs were as a rule made with hickory spindles, and bent work. Seats were ordinarily of pine, but beyond New England they are often found of other woods. The legs were maple or birch as well as the large front spindles. They were probably first made in Philadelphia, as early as 1720, their Queen Anne stretchers indicating the period. For detailed information, too full even for this work, reference is made to the author's handbook on them.

2520. A SHERATON BACK CHILD'S SIDE CHAIR. PERHAPS UNIQUE. LATE 18TH CENTURY.

2521. (Right.) A COMB BACK CHILD'S CHAIR, ROCKERS, OF COURSE, NEVER ORIGINAL. SECOND HALF 18TH CENTURY. BOTH, J. STOGDELL STOKES.

2522–23. A Bow-Back Arm, Late Turnings. A Low Baby's Chair,
Bow Back. Feet Cut Off. Fourth Quarter 18th Century.
Herbert G. Newton, Holyoke, Massachusetts.

2524–25. Late Baby's High Chairs. Both with Sheraton Influence, and Outside
Stretchers. Probably Early 19th C. Formerly the Author's.

2526. A BABY CHAIR WITH PERFECT TURNING. NOTE THE STRONG BULBOUS BASE LEGS, AND
STRETCHERS. SINGLE PIECE BOW AND ARM. 1750–70. J. STOGDELL STOKES.

2527. (Right.) A LATE COMB BACK. 1800. FORMERLY IN THE STILES COLLECTION, YORK.

2528. A FINE COMB BACK. 1750–60.
MRS. MORGAN G. BULKELEY.

2529. A SIDE BOW BACK. 1770.
THE AUTHOR'S.

2530. A Good Pennsylvania Baby High Chair, but Not Equal to No. 2507.
Formerly the Author's.

2531. (Right.) A Late Sheraton Bamboo. 1800–10. Arthur Leslie Green.

2532. A Good Baby Comb Back, Formerly in the Collection of Samuel Stevens,
North Andover. 1770–80.

2533. (Right.) A Tenoned Arm, Bow Back High Chair with Original Foot Rest. Moderate
Merit. Late 18th Century.

2534–37. LATE CHILD'S CHAIRS. FORMERLY THE AUTHOR'S. ROCKERS NOT ORIGINAL. THE OTHERS ALL SHOW SHERATON INFLUENCE. EARLY 19TH CENTURY.

BEST EARLY SIDE CHAIR

BEST LARGE ARM CHAIR

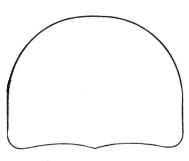

GOOD SETTEE SHAPE
PENNSYLVANIA ARM CHAIR

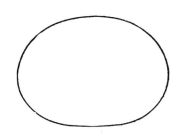

ELLIPTICAL SEAT
ARM CHAIR

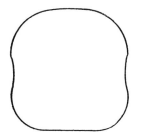

DEGRADED SIDE CHAIR

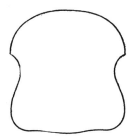

GOOD LATE SIDE CHAIR

2538–43. OUTLINES OF CHAIR SEATS FROM THE BEST TO THE WORST WINDSOR TYPE.

2544. Twin High Chair, Probably Unique. Interest Purely Sentimental. 1800–10.
2545. (Right.) Remarkable Number of Spindles but No Ears. Stiles Collection.

2546–51. Brasses, All but One of Which Belong to the Chippendale Era or Earlier. All the Patterns Are Unusual. A. H. Eaton, Collinsville, Connecticut.

2552–53. Great Windsors, Pennsylvania Type, Shown by the Ball Feet. Queen Anne Stretchers. 1725–60. The Former Arthur Leslie Green. The Latter Formerly the Author's.

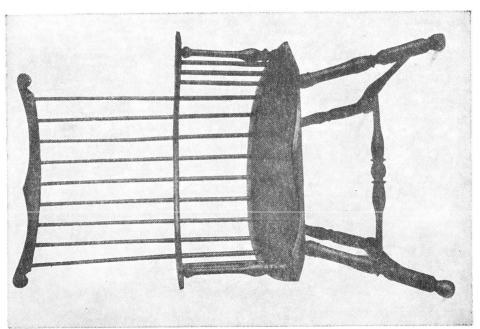

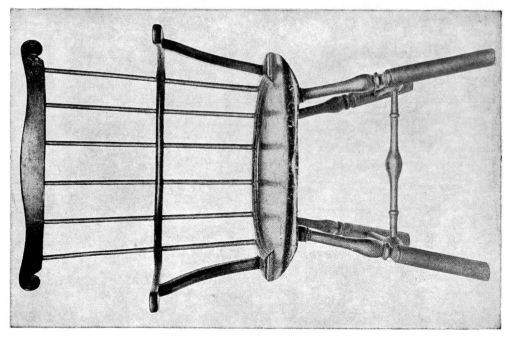

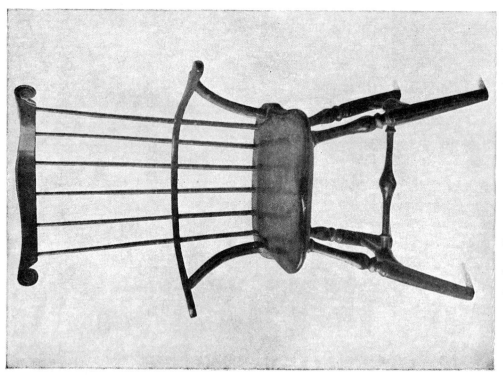

2554. An Odd, Possibly Canadian Type. More Likely American. It Suggests the Goldsmith Windsor. 1770–90. Mrs. Annie B. Hunter, Freehold, New Jersey.

2555. (Right.) A Somewhat Similar Chair, with Curved Arm Supports.

2556. A Very Handsome Windsor with Well-Carved Arms, and Nine
Back Spindles. Pennsylvania Type. Francis Mireau.

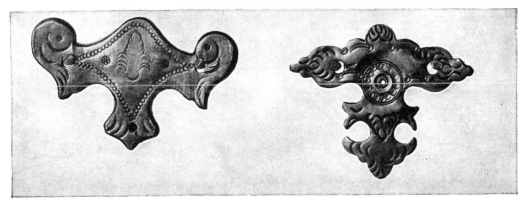

2557-58. Stamped. 1700. Frank A. Robart.

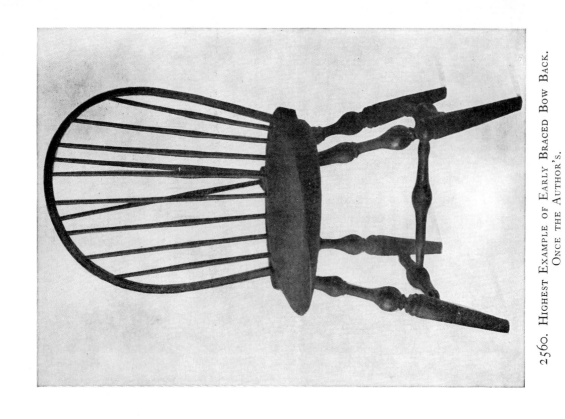

2560. Highest Example of Early Braced Bow Back.
Once the Author's.

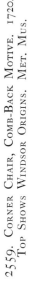

2559. Corner Chair, Comb-Back Motive. 1720.
Top Shows Windsor Origins. Met. Mus.

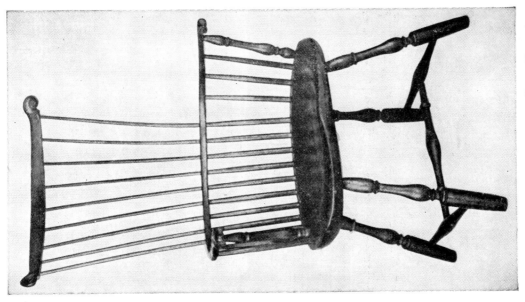

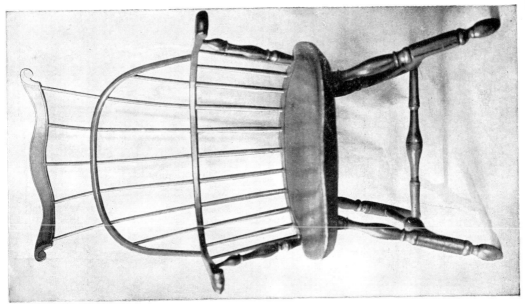

2561-62. The Former a Fine Type of Three-Back Waved Comb. Wm. B. Montague. The Latter Very High Back, Bent Arm. 1760. J. Stogdell Stokes.

2563. An Eleven-Spindle Comb Back. 1760–80. Formerly in
Stiles Collection.

2564–65. Stamped Brasses. 1700–10. Frank A. Robart.

2566. Extra Stretcher in Back. Arm Curved in Strong Forward Sweep. Date Difficult To Fix. This Arm Is Found in Pennsylvania. Arthur Leslie Green, Newport.

2567. (Right.) Early Philadelphia Type, Low Back with Wide Splice. Deeply Shaped Seat. 1740–50. Wayside Inn.

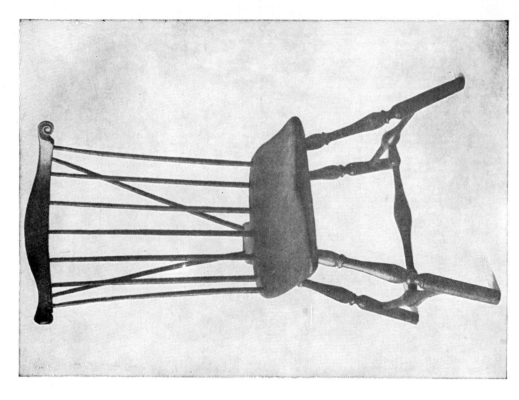

2568. Pennsylvania Comb Back, with Cropped Ears. A Good Shape. 1740-60. Formerly the Author's.

2569. (Right.) Built without Turned Side Posts. A Curious Variant. Late 18th Century. Was the Late J. B. Kerfoot's, Freehold, New Jersey.

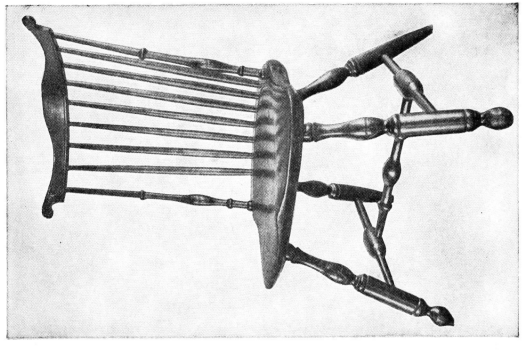

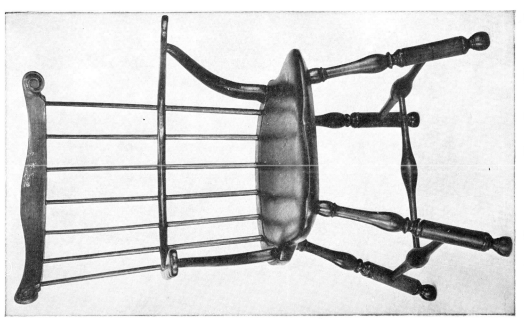

2570. Pennsylvania Comb Back, Moderate Size, Forward Swept Arm Support. Mid 18th Century. J. Stogdell Stokes.
2571. (Right.) Unusual Side Chair in Pennsylvania Turning. The Side Chairs in This Type Are More Rare Than the Arm. Mid 18th Century. Formerly the Author's.

2572–73. A Page of J. Stogdell Stokes' Windsors. These Two Have the One-Piece Bow and Arm. The Former Is the Quainter, and the Latter Has the Better Lines, and Very Excellent Base Turnings, Both in the Feet and the Front Arm Spindle. This Type Is Found in New England and the Delaware Valley. Latter Half 18th Century.

2574–75. The Former a Beautifully Turned Pennsylvania Pattern; the Latter with Unique Side Posts on the Comb. 1740–80.

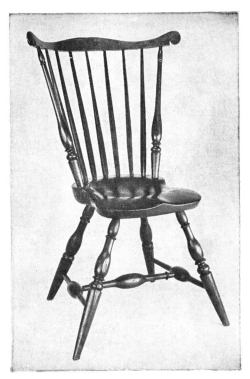

2576–77. Both, J. Stogdell Stokes. The Former the Highest Class Turning in the Fan-Back Chair; the Latter a Less Bold Turning, but with Braced Back and Plain Comb. 1760–80.

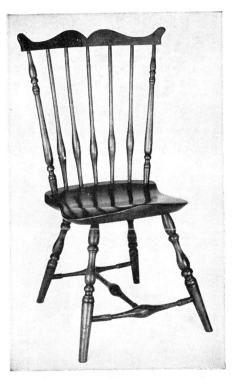

2578. Unique, Fore and Aft Stretcher, and Cupid's-Bow. 1760–80. J. Stogdell Stokes.

2579. (Right.) The Back Stiles Suggest the Dutch Day Bed Pattern. Found in Southern Massachusetts. 31 x 19 x 16. Maple and Oak. Mary M. Sampson.

2580. A Bent Arm with Carved Knuckle, without the Application of the Usual Thickened End. Pennsylvania Turning. 1740–70. J. Stogdell Stokes.

2581. (Right.) A Sport. The Humorous Low Comb Attached to a Secondary Back Applied to a Bent Back. Finger Carving. 1760–80. J. Stogdell Stokes.

2582–83. The Former with Suggestions of the Bamboo Turning. A High Back, and Bent Carved Arm. The Latter a Sawed and Spliced Back, the Arm Ramped Outward. Dates Respectively About 1790 and 1770. J. Stogdell Stokes.

2584-85. Well Turned, Both in Front Arm Spindles and Legs and Stretchers. Latter Half 18th Century. Foster Disinger, Binghamton.

This type of chair has always been popular because it is very light. Great difficulty was experienced by breaking of the arm at the turn, so that those that are whole are much sought for.

2586. A Well-Proportioned, Graceful Comb Back. Pennsylvania. 1740–60. Formerly Stiles Col.

2587. (Right.) Similar to the Preceding, but with Better Stretchers. Same Owner.

2588. A J. Stogdell Stokes' Page. Pennsylvania Chair with Bent Arm Support. Light Knuckle Arms.
2589. (Right.) The First of an Interesting Class, Which the Author Has Named Tenoned Arm.
The Object of This Construction Was To Do Away with the Arm Rail behind the Back. The
Chair Is Handsome, but the Back Post Requires To Be a Good Size. Strong Outward Ramp.

2590–91. Good Comb Backs, the Former Perhaps the More Graceful and Conventional. Perhaps Lost an Inch of Its Feet. The Second Has an Extraordinarily High Comb, and the Amazing Number of Eleven Spindles. Extremely Rare. Date for All 1750–80.

2592. An Eleven-Spindle Back, with No Less than Six Short Spindles on Each Side. The Comb, However, Is a Disappointment, Possibly It Was Intended to Be Finished.

2593. (Right.) A Comb Back That Is an Anomaly, with an Extra but Good Stretcher in Front.

2594. A New Jersey Specimen with Unique Stretcher Arrangement, and Three Legs. Evidently the Comb Was Not Long Enough for the Spindles.

2595. (Right.) Comb Like Back Splice on a Low Back, Spindles Indicate Late 18th Century. Chair Entirely Walnut. All This Page, J. Stogdell Stokes.

2596. A Very Light, Graceful Chair with Dainty Turnings. It Is Probable that Such Chairs Were Not Attempted at First. From Cape Cod. 45 x 23 x 16. Rudolph P. Pauly.

2597. (Right.) A Comb Back with Up-Tilted Ears, and Arm Rail. J. Stogdell Stokes.

2598. Somewhat Heavy Turnings, Perhaps Made Away from Centers. A Very Low Back.

2599. (Right.) Lofty Bow, with a Concave Turn on the Lower Part, Carved Knuckles. Both 1750. J. Stogdell Stokes.

2600–01. Four Chairs of Mr. Stokes. They Are All Fan Backs. The Term Applies to the Side Chairs with Combs. The First Is Well Turned with a Specially Good Back Post, and Plain Ears. The Second Is in the Bamboo Turning, Cross Stretcher, One Running through Another.

2602. A Hollow Seat with Crude Turnings. The Extraordinary Back Is Captivating from Its Odd Design. We Might Call This a Shovel Seat. The Bob Tail or Extension Is One Piece with the Rest of the Seat, as Always in Side Chairs.

2603. (Right.) A Good Braced Fan Back. All, Except the Bamboo, 1750–80.

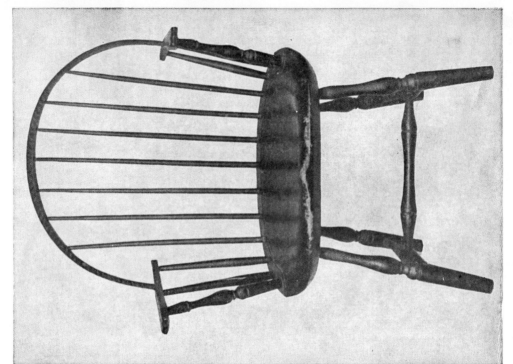

2605. A Cutaway Arm, with Gouge Turning. 1770–90. Wayside Inn.

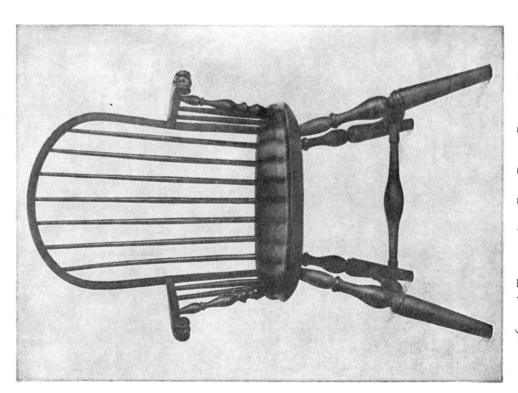

2604. A Tenoned-Arm Bow Back. Rare. 1760. C. C. Littlefield.

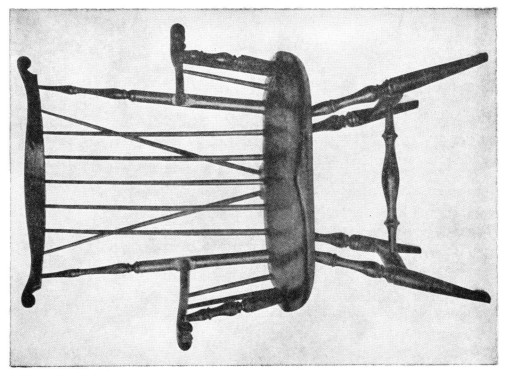

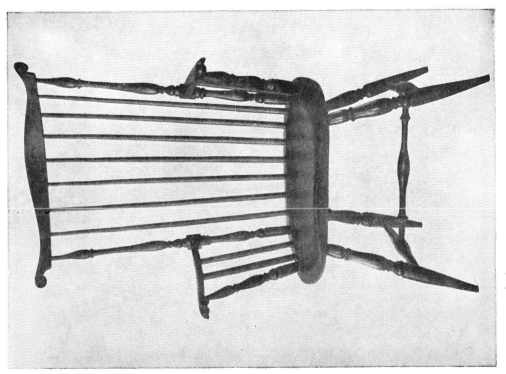

2606-07. Chairs Formerly the Author's, with Tenoned Arm, the Second with a Brace. Very Good. 1760-90.

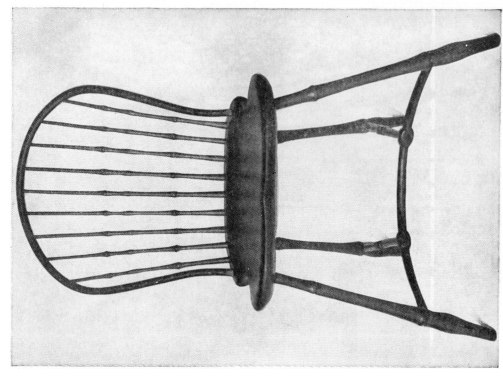

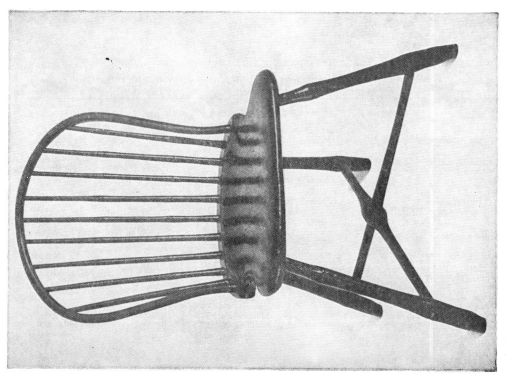

2608-09. The Former with Cross Stretchers, the Latter with Bent or Spoke Stretcher. The Latter Is the Best Chair of the Kind the Author Has Seen. Late 18th Century. J. Stogdell Stokes.

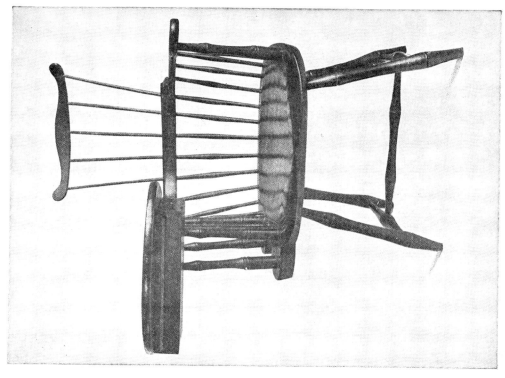

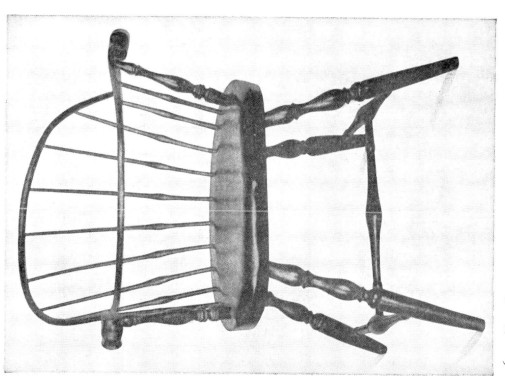

2610. The Commonest Shape in Bow Backs. Seat Shallow. Carved Arms Better than Usual. The Bulb in the Spindles Shows That in Early Times the Spindle Was Whittled, and It Was Natural To Leave This Section Larger. 1770–90.

2611. (Right.) Entering upon the Much-Sought Writing Armchair. Two Horns on the Seat. A Drawer for Stationery. Bamboo Turnings Below, and on Large Spindles. Formerly the Author's.

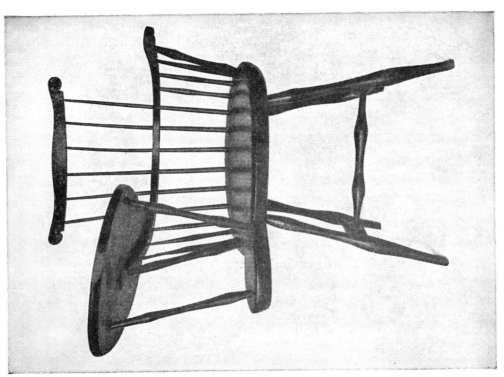

2612. A Writing Arm without a Drawer, Bamboo Turnings. It Shows the Construction Very Well.

2613. (Right.) A Fine Writing Arm. Fat Turnings of the Vase Type. Table Slanting for Convenience. Comb Set to One Side for the Same Purpose. Formerly the Author's.

2614. A Light Writing Arm, with Two Drawers. Not the Best Style, because the Bent Arm Does Not Allow the Table Top to Be Met by the Splice of a Sawed Arm.

2615. (Right.) A Writing Arm, with a Left Leg Larger than the Others. Comb Too Short, Probably Not of Set Purpose. Both Formerly the Author's.

2616–17. Two Views of a Rare and Important Windsor, Tenoned Arm, with a Comb Such as Is Used on a Spliced Sawed Arm. While Not Graceful, It Indicates an Evolution. 1740–60. J. Stogdell Stokes.

2618–19. Heavy Writing Arm with a Bow Back instead of the Usual Comb, Good Drawers, Two Horns. A Remarkable Bracket Toggle Joint Lamp Is Attached to the Arm.

2620. A Fine Writing Arm Showing Distinctly the Shape of the Two Tongues. Extraordinarily High Comb. Found in Connecticut. 48 x 47 x 32. Rudolph P. Pauly.

2621. (Right.) A Writing Arm, Perhaps Unique Since It Is Attached to What Would Otherwise Have Been a Side Chair. Fuessenich Collection.

2622. A Low-Back Writing Arm, with No Less than Three Drawers. Date of All 1760–80. J. Stogdell Stokes.

2623. A Light Bamboo-Turned Writing Chair, with a Good Carved Arm. J. Stogdell Stokes.

2624. (Right.) A New England Writing Arm with an Abbreviated and Scrolled Comb. Hickory and Pine, as Are Most Windsors. Mrs. Francis P. Garvan.

2625. A Light Writing Arm. The Arm Is an Adaptation, Swiveling by a Detachable Thumb Nut over the Ordinary Arm. J. Stogdell Stokes.

2626. (Right.) A Broad-Based Writing Arm, with Candle Slide. Bow Back, One-Piece Arm and Bow. Shallow Drawer under the Seat. W. A. Hitchcock, Farmington.

2627. A Well-Turned Low-Back, Writing Arm, with Sharp Turns at the Back of the Seat. Mrs. Francis P. Garvan.

2628. (Right.) A Writing Arm, with Carved Knuckle, and Three Drawers. The Two Drawers under the Arm Move in Different Directions. Morris Schwartz, New York. Date of the Two 1760–80.

2629. A Writing Arm in the Late Sheraton Style. 1800. Formerly in Stiles Collection.

2630–31. (Right.) Beautifully Turned Specimen, with an Early Brass Candlestick on the Slide, Pulled out Especially To Hold It. Notice the Sidewise Construction of the Comb, as the Back of a Person Would Swing in Its Direction. John H. Buck, Hartford, Connecticut.

2632. A Small Drawer, Perhaps Intended for Smoker's Material. The Arm Perhaps Large Enough To Hold Drinking Glass. Small Three-Spindle Comb. Former Stiles Collection.

2633. (Right.) A Bow-Back Side Chair with Ears. A Very Odd Affair, but not Unique.

2634. A Fan Back, with an Even Dozen Spindles, Including the Turned Posts. Sanderson Col.

2635. (Right.) A Chair with Canadian Suggestions and Three Backs. The Author Has Not Examined It. A Third Back Would Bear Examination, but the Spindles Run Through.

2636-37. The Former, a Bow Back, Unusually Drawn in at the Bottom of the Bow, and with a Straddling Brace. The Latter, with a Quick Change in the Turning of the Legs.

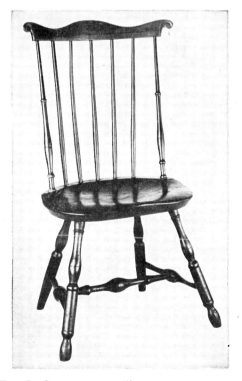

2638. A Fan Back with Small Ears. This Ear Is Occasional in Pennsylvania.

2639. (Right.) A Pennsylvania, with a Seat Rather Wide for the Depth, Lacking a Side Ramp. Blunt Arrow Turnings, Serpentine Back. Small Carved Ears. Only Five Spindles. This Page All 1750-80. J. Stogdell Stokes.

2640–41. The First with an Amusingly High Stretcher. Not a Large Chair. The Second with Its Seat Shaped to the Extreme Saddle Contour. Frank A. Robart.

2642. A Prim High Back. Thick Arm. Legs Raked Less than Usual. 1770–90. J. Stogdell Stokes.

2643. (Right.) Beautifully Turned, Including the Front Spindle. Well-Shaped Bow. Necking to Small Dimensions, and Enlarging Like a Mortise. 1760–70. Foster Disinger.

2644-45. ALL ON THIS PAGE, J. STOGDELL STOKES. ABOUT 1770. THE FIRST FINELY TURNED WITH A HOLLOW TAPER. OFTEN CALLED THE RHODE ISLAND PATTERN. THE SECOND, CARVED EAR, WITH USUAL BLOCK TO ASSIST IN FORMING IT.

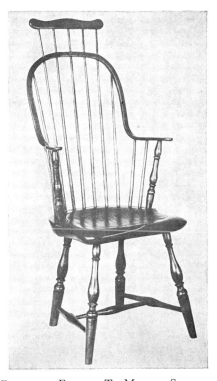

2646. A PECULIAR UPWARD SWEEP TO THE ARM. IT WAS DIFFICULT ENOUGH TO MAKE A SQUARE TURN, AND THIS SPECIAL EFFORT SEEMS SUPERFLUOUS.

2647. (Right.) EXTREMELY RARE. COMB FORMED BY RUNNING THROUGH A BOW. A PRIM BACK.

2648. A Stokes Page. Very Good Turnings. A Slight Widening on the Front of the Arm. 1760–70.

2649. (Right.) A Bow with Sharp Turns at the Corners. This Chair Proves the Widespread Nature of the Chair Industry. Otherwise We Could Not Have So Many Patterns.

2650. A Cupid's-Bow Fan Back. Feet Somewhat Cut Off, Hollow Taper Turned. 1770–90.

2651. (Right.) A Very Low Fan Back. In Case Carving Is To Be Omitted This Is Good.

2652. A Stokes Page. A Low Back. Well-Turned Stretcher, Feet Missing. Pennsylvania. Probably Before 1750.

2653. (Right.) An Extremely Low Comb. Carving on Arm Done without Adding Block. 1770–90.

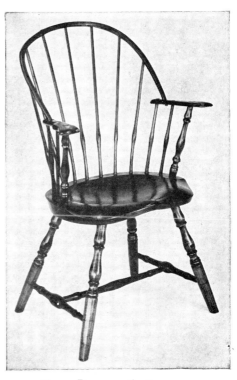

2654. Well Turned. Arm Tenoned into the Bow. Rare. 1760–80.

2655. (Right.) Cutaway Arm. Supposed To Have Made the Back Easier. At the Same Time the Maker Avoided the Necessity of Bending. Note the Deep Cutting Away of the Seat.

2656. A Serpentine Arm, with a Tenoned Bow. Bamboo Style. c. 1800.

2657. (Right.) Very High Stretchers. Purpose Unknown. Late 18th Century.

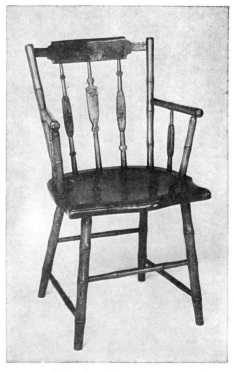

2658. The Bow Was Started as if To Sweep Around to the Arm Rail. An Amusing, but Not Elegant Example.

2659. (Right.) Sheraton Type. Whenever the Rungs Are on the Outside, We Have Lost Real Windsor Character. All on This Page J. Stogdell Stokes.

2660. Sheraton Back with Secondary Comb, the Spindles of Which Are Bent. Unusual. Late.

2661. (Right.) While the Rockers Here Are Believed by the Writer To Be Subsequent to the Making of the Chair, He May Not Be Right. Both Chairs c. 1800. J. Stogdell Stokes.

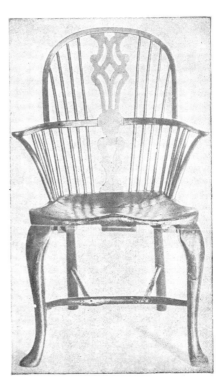

2662. A One-Piece Bow and Arm, with Rolled Knuckle, Bob-Tail Back, Braced. J. Stogdell Stokes.

2663. (Right.) An English Type, with a Pierced Splat, Cabriole Legs, and Spoke Stretchers. This Style Also Found in Canada. Mrs. Alexander Armstrong, Baltimore.

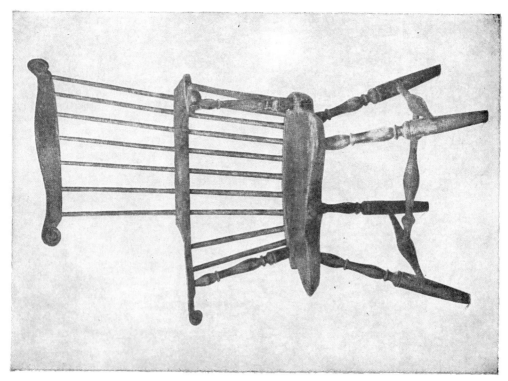

2664–65. New England Comb Backs, One with Well-Shaped Seat, One with a Rounded Seat. The Former, Metropolitan Museum. The Latter, Formerly the Author's.

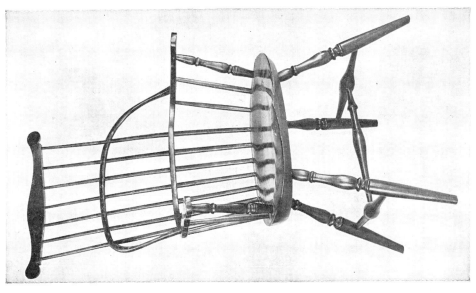

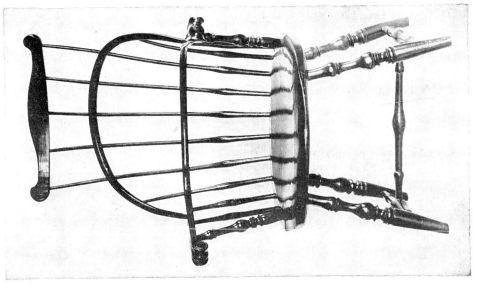

2666. Rare, Three Back. Fine, Boldly Carved Arm. Well Turned. Apologies to the Owner, Whose Name Has Been Lost.

2667. (Right.) Seven Spindles Running through the Three Backs, All without Bending. J. Stogdell Stokes.

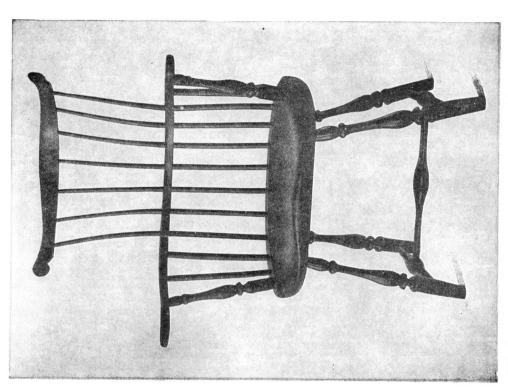

2668–69. Comb Backs, One with Carved Arm, the Other without. Seat Shallow. One Has Flared Spindles in Comb, Whereas the Other Has Straight Spindles. 1760–80. Formerly the Author's.

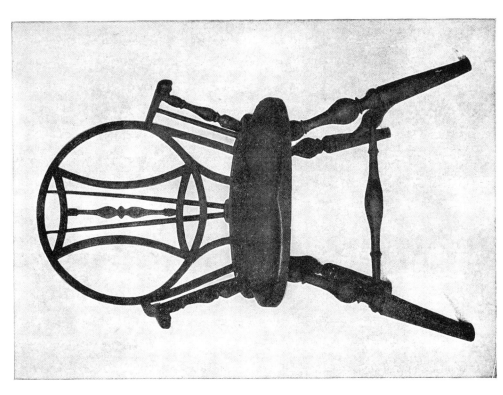

2670. Shown as an Example of the Graceless Arm, and Bow and Leg of the English Windsor. All of These Members Lack Character. The Splat Was Good in Style, but not Comfortable. Formerly the Author's.

2671. (Right.) A Chair with a Round Back, Fine Turning, but with Other Elements Which Put It in a Class by Itself. A Tenoned Arm. William F. Hubbard, Hartford.

2672. A Good Bow Back, with Nine Spindles, the Bulbs of Which Are Long and Obviously Whittled. 1760–70. J. Stogdell Stokes.

2673. (Right.) A Late Turning. Interesting from the Cross Stretcher. 1790–1800.

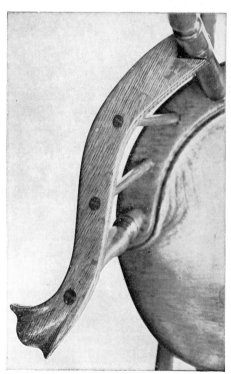

2674. Rockers Not Original. Three Backs with Unusual Comb. Sanderson Collection.

2675. (Right.) Shows the Shape of a Good Arm, and the Method of the Carving on a Tenoned Chair. Henry A. Hoffman, Barrington, Rhode Island.

2676. A Tenoned Arm with a Little Turning in the Middle of the Back, Just Where It Ought Not To Be for Comfort. Perhaps It Might Have Been a Watchman's Chair. 1750–70. Arthur Leslie Green, Newport.

2677. (Right.) A Tenoned Arm with Rockers Which Are Not Original, and Five Spindles instead of Seven, as in the Previous Example. Formerly the Author's.

2678. Small Ears, Odd Turnings, Braced Back.

2679. (Right.) Bold Turnings, Fan Back Braced. Good Example. Both Formerly the Author's.

2680. A, B. Mahogany, Corner Chairs. The Second Is Most Rare, Having Square Enlarged Feet. The First Has a Carved Raised Edge and Drake Feet. Thorpe's Antique Shop, Plainfield, N. J.

2681. A, B. Maple Chairs of the Walnut Period, Molded Backs. The Side Chair Had Spanish Feet Which Are Partially Worn Away. Upholstery New. 1700–10. Benjamin A. Jackson, Wickford, Rhode Island.

2682. A Straighter and Stiffer Back than Usual. Ears Not Carved. It Has Been Suggested that the Ear Was for the Purpose of Hanging a Betty Lamp, While One Read.

2683. (Right.) A Very Rare Chair. Spindles Run through. Wayside Inn.

2684. A Late Chair with Sheraton Influence in the Back. Some Have Called These Openings Dovecotes. Now or Formerly, Wayside Inn.

2685. (Right.) A Boldly Turned Rhode Island Type, with Nine Spindles in the Fan Back. Formerly the Author's.

2686. An Unusual, but Good Turning, Perhaps Rhode Island. The Spiral of the Ear Is a Wide, Hollowed Shape. Formerly the Author's.

2687. (Right.) Attractive Small Bow Back without Carving. It Has Grace and Good Taste. Good Flare of Spindles, but Should Have Had One More on Each Side.

2688. A Large Nine-Spindle Comb Back, with a Waved Stretcher. Not Over-Graceful.

2689. (Right.) Seven Spindles in the Comb, but without Very Much Style. Good Small Carved Arm. Formerly the Author's.

2690. A Light, Small Comb Back with Graceful Comb. Arthur Leslie Green, Newport.

2691. (Right.) A Very Perfect Type for a Light Side Chair with a Fan. A Good Taper of the Legs, and Fine Harmony between Them and the Back Stiles. Mrs. M. E. Welles, Hartford.

2692. A Fine Example of a Bamboo-Turned Armchair. It Is Graceful in All Respects. The Author Challenges, However, the Tenoning of an Arm into so Small a Space.

2693. (Right.) Heavy Carved Arm. Pennsylvania. Both Were Author's.

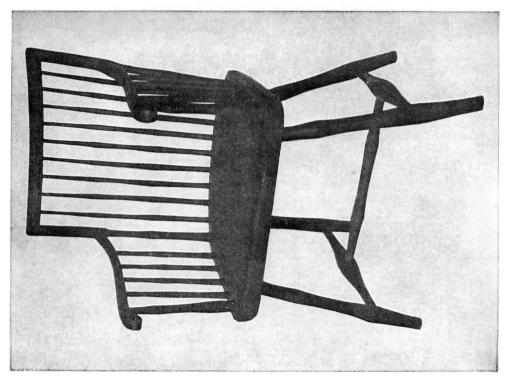

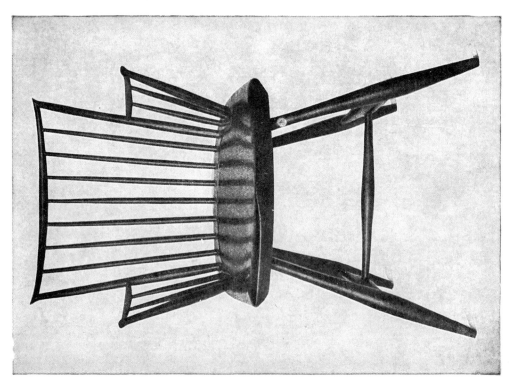

2694. A Duck-Bill Windsor, Which Has Its Name from the Pointed Meeting of the Vertical and Horizontal Members of the Arm. Of Course, the Turnings Are Late, and the Seat Has Not Much Shaping, but the Effect Is Good. William F. Hubbard, Hartford. 2695. (Right.) Sheraton Square-Back Arm. The Seat Is Not Cut Away to a Feather Edge as in Best Examples. The Back Post Is Enlarged Sufficiently To Take a Tenon. All Bamboo Turning. Both These Chairs About 1800.

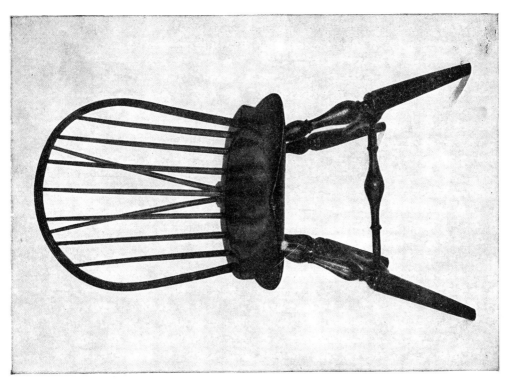

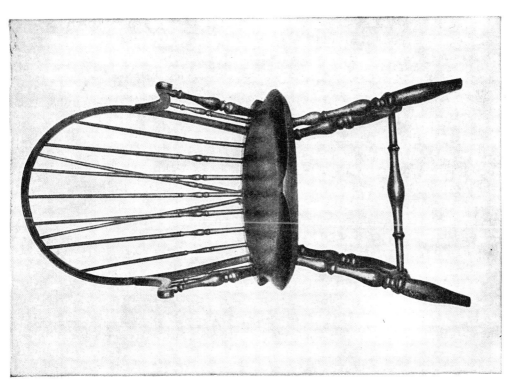

2696. A Mahogany Arm, Rhode Island Chair. An Inch Gone from Feet. Turned Spindles. In Early Chairs Spindles Could Not Be Turned, as the Back Rest Had Not Been Invented for the Lathe. Moderate Size. When Back Is Braced, the Number of Spindles Is Usually Seven.

2697. (Right.) A Well-Turned Bow Back with Brace.

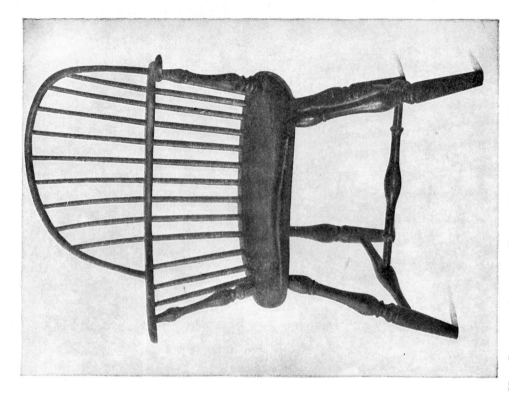

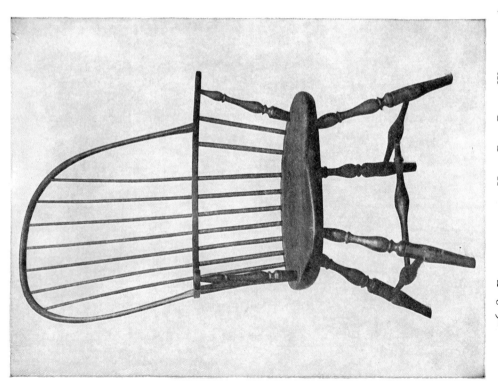

2698. Extraordinarily High Bow Back, Which the Author Has Called a Spinster Chair. Metropolitan Museum. 2699. (Right.) Conventional Bow Back, Which Has a Shallow Seat, Not More than 12 or 13 Inches. Both Formerly the Author's.

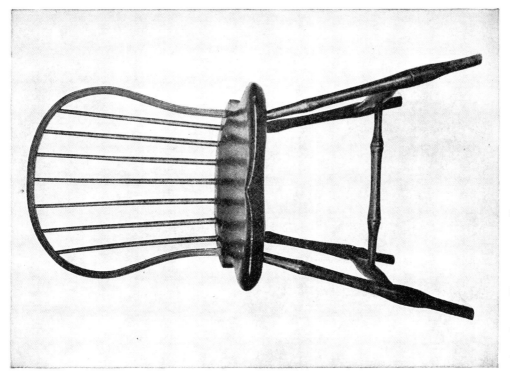

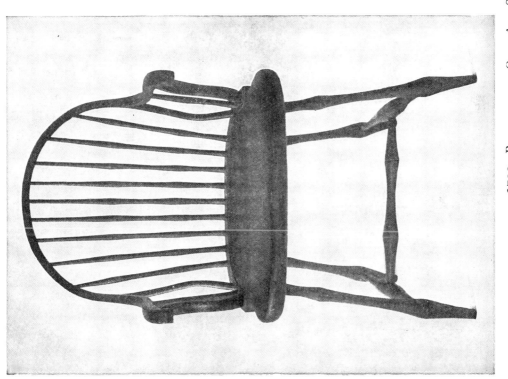

2700. Bamboo, with Ogee Arm Supports. Odd Quick Bent in the Bow.

2701. (Right.) Well-Shaped Seat, Bamboo Turning Below, Plain Above. A Well-Shaped Bow, Bamboo Type. Both Formerly the Author's.

2702-03. ROCKERS ORIGINAL IN NEITHER. THE FIRST HAS THE ARROW
SPINDLES, AND THE PIGEONHOLE BACK. THE SECOND HAS FINE LINES
ABOVE, EXCEPT FOR THE TURNINGS. BOTH FORMERLY THE AUTHOR'S.

2704-05. SHERATON WINDSORS, OF GRACEFUL TYPE WITH BAMBOO TURNINGS EXCEPT FOR THE
OUTER FRAME OF THE BACK. MR. MIREAU, DOYLESTOWN TAVERN, PENNSYLVANIA.

2706. Joint Stool with Drawer, Very Rare. Feet Lost. 1680–1700. Wadsworth Atheneum.

2707. Joint Stool with Vertical Legs. Perhaps American. 1670–90. Wadsworth Atheneum.

2708. (Right.) Stool Raking in All Directions. Feet Lost. Turnings Fine. 1690. Fuessenich Col.

2709. Rare or Unique, American Stool. Feet Lost. Long Enough for Two People. Very Early Turnings. 1660–80. Mary M. Sampson.

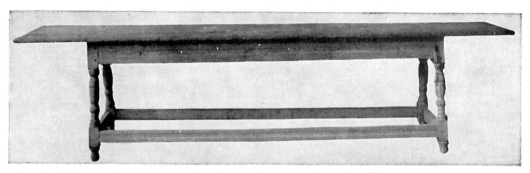

2710. A Long Form. In America the Term Is Bench. 20 x 81 x 11½. The Wide Overhang Would Seem To Have Invited Disaster. Very Rare. 1680–1700. Rhode Island School of Design.

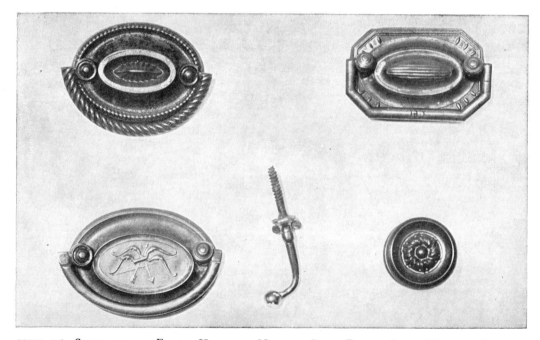

2711–15. Sheraton and Empire Handles. No. 2712 Is an Ear of Corn; No. 2713 Consists of Two Bows and Two Arrows; No. 2714 Is a Brass Hook of the Same Period; No. 2715 Was in Use About 1810.

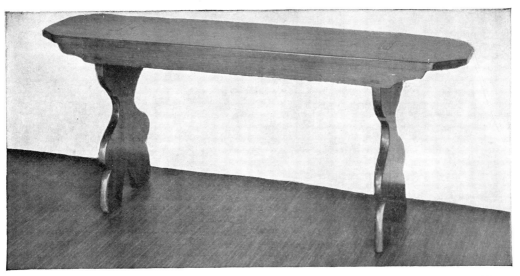

2716. Trestle Stool, Mortised through the Top and Side Rails. Late 17th or Early 18th Century. Howard Reifsnyder.

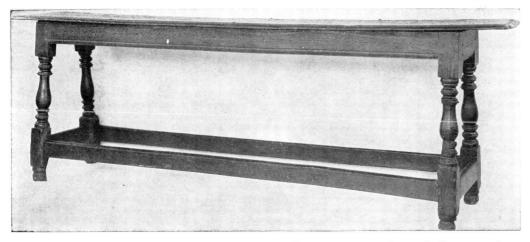

2717. Pear Wood Bench, with Turned, Raked Legs, and Framed Stretchers. Late 17th or Early 18th Century. J. Stogdell Stokes.

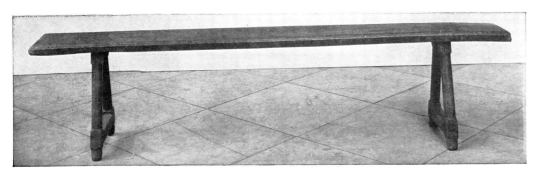

2718. Bench with Stamped Design on the Beaded Rail. A Similar Stamp Is Found on Some Leather Chairs. The Best Long Form Discovered in This Country. 1680–1700. J. Stogdell Stokes.

2719. Joint Stool Found Near Guilford, with Turnings Precisely Like a Wainscot Chair in the Same Town. Height 14 Inches. Legs Vertical. Perhaps Unique. Wadsworth Atheneum.

2720–21. Joint Stools, the Former Lightly, and the Latter Heavily Turned. And with Slight Carving. Both Have Lost Feet. The Second Example Is More Generally Seen in England. 1660–1690. Dwight Blaney.

2722. Neatly Turned Stool, Legs Raking One Way Only. Most Stools Like This Have the So-Called Stone Mold on the Bottom of the Frame. 1680–1700. J. Stogdell Stokes.
2723. (Right.) Stool with Odd Turnings, a Ring Balanced by Two Balls, with a Small Fillet Above. Rare. Maple. 1680–1700. Henry A. Hoffman, Barrington, Rhode Island.

2724. Well-Turned High Stretcher Stool. Double Pinned at Each Mortise. 1680–1700.
2725. (Right.) Joint Stool, Legs Raking One Way, as Usual. 1680–1700. Fuessenich Collection.

2726. FEET LOST, STRONG RAKE ONE WAY. FORMERLY MISS C. M. TRAVER'S, NEW YORK.
2727. (Right.) HEAVY EARLY TURNING. TOP NOT ORIGINAL. 1670–90 FOR BOTH.

2728. MAPLE STOOL, ORIGINAL TOP, WITH OAK PINS. FEET
LOST. 1680–90. WADSWORTH ATHENEUM.

2729. Quaint, in Original Condition. An Article Like This Would Have Been Scorned Twenty Years Ago. Now It Has Large Value. c. 1680. Fuessenich Collection.

2730. (Right.) Walnut "Square" Turning, Scrolled Skirt All Around. Built Like, and Doubtless To Match, a Table. c. 1700. J. Stogdell Stokes.

2731. Gate-Leg Turning. Oval Top. Could Be Counted a Small Table. 1690–1710. Fuessenich Collection.

2732. (Right.) High Stool, Molded, as Often, on the Frame and on the Stretcher. Chamfered Corners. c. 1700. Flayderman & Kaufman.

2733. ALL TURNED STOOL, WELL-WORN STRETCHERS. 1700–1720. HORATIO H. ARMSTRONG, HARTFORD.

2734. (Right.) 17TH CENTURY TURNINGS. WADSWORTH ATHENEUM, HARTFORD.

The American stool is ordinarily in maple. If in oak, it needs careful second inspection, before determining its American character.

2735. A PERFECT LITTLE MAPLE STOOL, RAKING IN ALL DIRECTIONS. FOUND IN MAINE. SIZE OF FRAME AT THE STRETCHERS, 13½ x 16½. 1680–1700. WADSWORTH ATHENEUM.

Stools were usually from 20 to 22 inches high, even when worn down somewhat. For such the term stool-table, is good.

2736–37. Pair of Unique Cross-Stretcher Stools. Newburyport. Basswood. Turning Like That of Chairs of Late 17th Century. Covers Are Old, but Later. Wadsworth Atheneum.

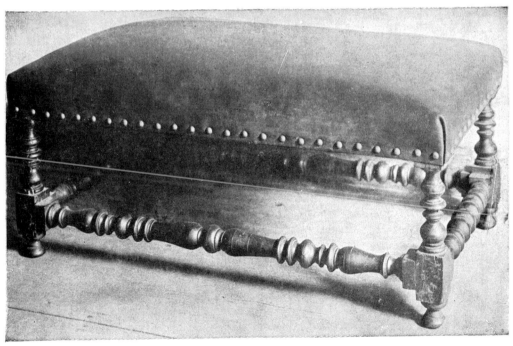

2738. Long, Well-Turned Stool. 1680–1700. Chauncey C. Nash.

2739. High-Stretcher Squab Stool. Designed, of Course, for a Cushion. Note the Stretchers on One Side Only, Leaving the Other Side Free To Draw in the Feet. About the Height of a Chair. 1680–1700. Was Brooks Reed's.

2740. Attractive Stool with Ogee Scrolls on Skirt. Repeated on Stretchers. Small Drawer. 1690–1710. J. Stogdell Stokes.

2741. (Right.) Unusual Turning. Probably Pennsylvanian, About 1690. J. Stogdell Stokes.

2742. PURELY ENGLISH, BULBOUS TURNED STOOL, WITH FLEMISH
SCROLLED STRETCHERS. LATE 17TH CENTURY. I. SACK.

2743-44. OWNED BY BENJAMIN A. JACKSON, WICKFORD, RHODE ISLAND. LEFT: QUEEN ANNE
TYPE, VERY RARE IN AMERICA. WALNUT. RIGHT: CHERRY WITH MIDDLE AND HIGH STRETCHERS.
DATES RESPECTIVELY 1730 AND 1690.

2745-46. MAHOGANY. LEFT: CHIPPENDALE, FLUTED, WITH BRACKETS. VERY RARE. 17 x 20 x 19.
RIGHT: QUEEN ANNE, CARVED KNEE. 18 x 22 x 17, HEIGHTS BEING GIVEN FIRST. 1760 AND 1750
RESPECTIVELY. EDWARD BRINGHURST, WILMINGTON.

2747. QUEEN ANNE STOOL WITH GOOD LINES, PRESUMABLY IN WALNUT.
1730–50. HOWARD REIFSNYDER.

In the early times stools were quite general and chairs were rare. As the 18th century wore on, this condition was reversed. A chair was no longer a seat of special honor. The progress of the position of women can almost be measured by this change. In the 17th century, except in high society, there was often only one chair, that for the head of the house. It is partly for this reason that the Queen Anne, and especially the Chippendale stools are rare. Foot stools of an ordinary character have always, of course, been in use.

2748. A RICH CHIPPENDALE STOOL WITH CARVED KNEE, AND BALL-AND-CLAW FOOT. THESE LEGS ARE FOUND SOMETIMES AS HIGH AS THOSE OF A CHAIR. ENGLISH. 1760. I. SACK.

2749. A Swivel Stool of Very Odd Turning, and a Shaped Seat. 18th Century. Perhaps Unique. J. Stogdell Stokes.

2750. (Right.) A Windsor Stool. Rare. Latter Half 18th Century. J. Stogdell Stokes.

2751-53. Three Windsor Stools, All Good, and Rare. Present Owners Unknown. 18th Century.

2754. Hitchcock, Eight-Leg Bench, Rush Seat. 1840. Rudolph P. Pauly, Boston.

2755. An Empire Stool, Following the Lines of the Most Ancient Egyptian Design. In the Mode of Duncan Phyfe. Rosettes at Intersections of Cross Stretchers. 1800–20. Joe Kindig, Jr., York.

2756. Turned Stool, Perhaps in the 1800's. Straight on One Side and Rounded on the Other, as if To Place against the Wall. Albert C. Bowman, Springfield, Vermont.

2757. A Stump Frame Glass, 17th Century. Initials M. B. Date 1660. Rose, Iris, and Other Floral Forms. Original Beveled Glass. Earliest Type Known. Probably Foreign. L. G. Myers.

2758. A Strongly Featured Burl Bowl. Very Large. Wadsworth Atheneum.

2759. Glass, Said To Have Belonged to Peregrine White. He Was Born on the "Mayflower" and Probably Did Not Bring His Glass with Him. He Lived into the 18th Century.

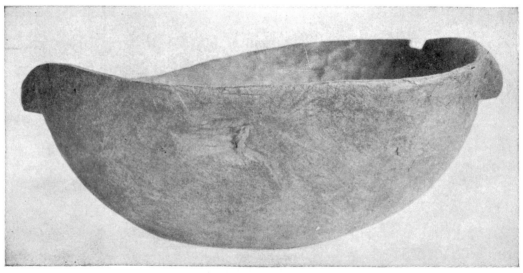

2760. Handmade Bowl. Cocked Hat Shape. Burl. Albert C. Bates, Hartford.

2761. Glass, Which Had Decorative Crest, Now Lost. Original Plate. Shape of Frame Is Convex, and Not To Be Confused with the Victorian Type. 27¾ x 21¼ Outside. Walnut Veneer on Pine, as Usual. Wadsworth Atheneum.

2762. (Right.) A Different Contour in the Border. Decorative Surface. Frame 4 Inches Wide. This Alone Is Indication of Great Age. Inlay in Satin and Tulipwood. Dates of Both, 1690-1700. Francis Hill Bigelow.

2763. Glass Now Cleaned of Quicksilver, and Having the Howe Coat-of-Arms. They Were the Keepers of the Wayside Inn. 1690–1700.

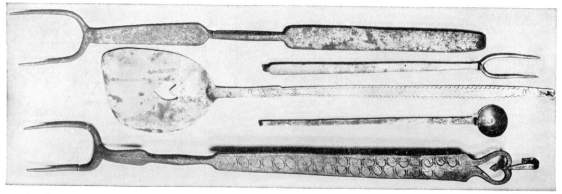

2764–65. Culinary Forks with Hooks. 2766. A Flapjack Shovel with a Heart Cutout and Decorated Handle. 2767. A Copper Spoon Riveted to an Iron Handle. 2768. A Rare and Fine Gift Fork with Handle Decoration Terminating with a Heart and Ending with a Hook. All Pennsylvania. Wadsworth Atheneum.

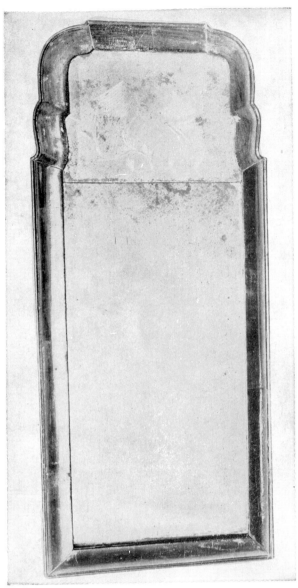

2769. Two-Part Glass, 37 Inches High. c. 1710. Most Early Fine Glasses Were Beveled and, if Large, Were in Two Parts. Francis Hill Bigelow.

2770. (Right.) Upper Section Shows Ship in Full Sail. The Painting Is on Wood, a Background Frequently Used by Great Painters. c. 1710. Chauncey C. Nash.

2771–74. Two Bowls, a Saucer and a Salt, All in Burl. The Use of This Material Was To Prevent Checking. While Walnut Is Frequent, Ash, Maple, and Oak Are Found. Joseph Skinner, Holyoke.

2775. A Scrolled Top in Position, Glass 15½ x 18¼. Walnut on Pine. 1700–20. Francis Hill Bigelow.
2776. (Right.) Glass with Japanese Design. Upper Glass Cut in a Foliage Pattern. 1710–20. L. G. Myers.

2777–80. A Medium and Small Bowl. Toddy Stick for Crushing Sugar. A Mortar and Pestle. All in Burl.

2781. Glass of Great Height in Walnut Veneer. Queen Anne Type. Estate of Harry W. Weeks, Framingham.

2782. (Right.) Queen Anne Glass, Two Part. 20 x 61. Richly Decorated. John H. Buck, Hartford.

2783. RICH VENEER, WITH SHELL IN CREST. CUT-GLASS FOLIAGE ORNAMENTS. 1710–20. I. SACK.

2784. WALNUT, QUEEN ANNE, TWO PART. OPEN FRETWORK AT TOP, AND BAND AROUND THE GLASS GILDED. 24 x 58. 1720–30. JOE KINDIG, JR.

2785–86. CARVED, GILDED EAGLES.

2787-89. Rich Lacquered Mirrors, a Center and Two Sides. Done in Hunting Scenes. The Side Mirrors Have Sconces. Early 18th Century. Flayderman & Kaufman.

2790-93. Beginning of the 18th Century. Drops and Escutcheons. Frank A. Robart.

2794. QUEEN ANNE, FULLY CARVED. ROSETTES, SHELL, AND CARTOUCHE. TWO PLAIN SURFACES ON THE LOWER PART OF THE FRAME, LOOK AS IF THEY WERE INTENDED FOR SCONCES. 1730. MRS. FRANCIS P. GARVAN.

2795. (Right.) FULLY CARVED. SCROLLED TOP GLASS. SHELLS ON CENTRAL ORNAMENT AND LOWER PORTION OF FRAME. 1730–60. 34 x 86. FOUND IN NEWPORT. FLAYDERMAN & KAUFMAN.

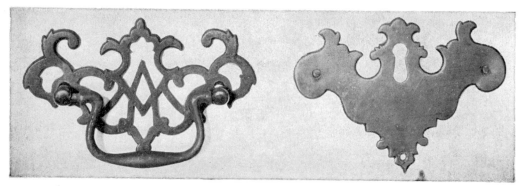

2796–97. AN OPEN AND A SOLID CHIPPENDALE BRASS. 1760–75. FRANK A. ROBART.

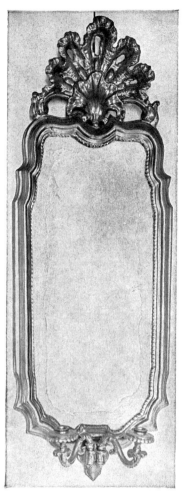

2798. Probably Dutch or French. Fine Double Shell. Carved Sconces. 12¼ x 34. 1770. H. W. Erving
2799. (Right.) A Carved, Three-Feather Glass. 1750–70. Estate of H. W. Weeks.

2800–01. Walnut with Applied Gilded Ornaments. 10¼ x 10½. 1730–50. Flayderman & Kaufman.

2802. A Double Sconce of Quill Work. When Lighted up These Sconce Backgrounds Gave a Very Brilliant Effect. 1710–20. Francis Hill Bigelow.

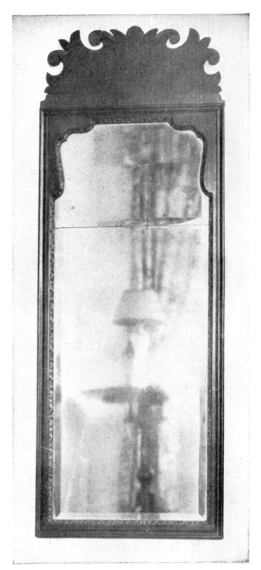

2803. WALNUT, TWO PART. UPPER GLASS CUT. 1710–30. KATRINA KIPPER.
2804. (Right.) UNUSUAL SCROLL. THE TWO-PART GLASSES ARE JOINED ON THE BEVEL, AND THE UPPER
GLASS SETS IN A RABBET A LITTLE DEEPER THAN THE LOWER. 1720–30. SANDERSON COLLECTION.

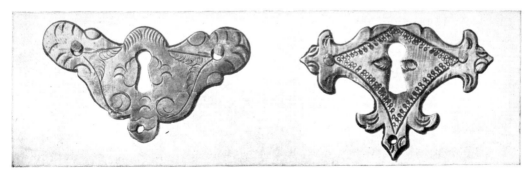

2805–06. HANDSOME STAMPED BRASSES. 1700–20. MUCH MISCONCEPTION EXISTS ABOUT THESE.
THEY WERE NEITHER ENGRAVED, CHASED, NOR ETCHED. THEY WERE SIMPLY STAMPED, WITH A
VARIETY OF TOOLS TO GIVE THESE SHAPES. OF COURSE, THE STAMPING WAS DONE IN SECTIONS
WITH SMALL TOOLS. FRANK A. ROBART.

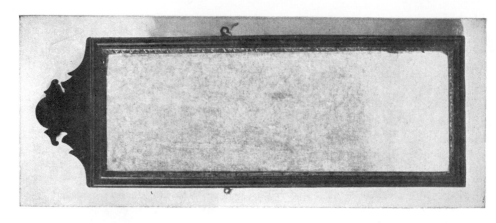

2807. Walnut, Unusual and Attractive. Swampscott. 15 x 36. 1710–30. Flayderman & Kaufman.
2808. (Middle.) One of a Pair of Sconce Glasses. Pencil and Pearl Ornament. Mid 18th Century. Fuessenich Collection.
2809. (Right.) Design the Same Period as the Preceding. Katrina Kipper, Accord, Massachusetts.

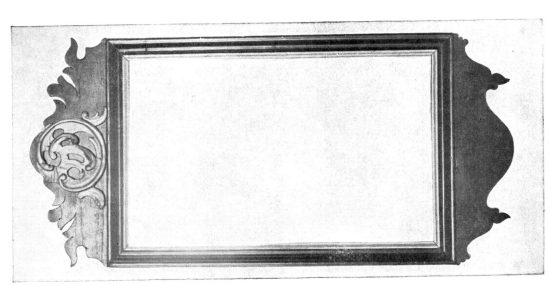

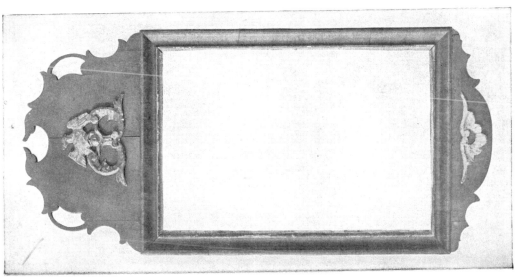

2810. Walnut. Unusual Carved Eagle. 13 x 27½. 1710–30.
2811. (Middle.) With This Mold These Glasses Are Regarded as Much Later in Date. 1785–95. The Author's.
2812. (Right.) Interesting Carving and Decoration. This and No. 2810. Flayderman & Kaufman.

2813–14. Quill Work Sconces. Walnut. Flowers Principally Carnations and Roses, Perhaps Mixed with Mica. Each Petal Edged with Silver Wire. Colors Are Red, Blue, Purple, and White. Made by Ruth Read, Daughter of the Honorable John Read, Distinguished Lawyer in Boston, 1722–49. Brackets Made by Knight Leverett of Boston (1703–53). Engraved R. R. 1720. Supposed To Be Unique. The Purpose of Sconces in Front of Such Glasses, Was To Give a Brilliant Effect of Lighting. Francis Hill Bigelow.

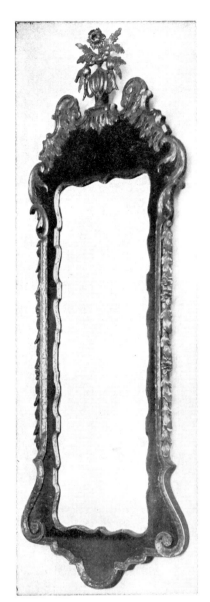

2815. Large Elegant Glass. Fine Central Ornament. 1740–60. I. Sack, Palmer Col.
2816. (Right.) Mahogany on Pine. 26 x 56. Transition Georgian-Chippendale. Early
Use of Mahogany. 1750. William B. Goodwin.

2817–18. Fine Brasses. British Lion with Flag, and Intertwined Dolphins. 1790.
Rudolph P. Pauly.

2819. SCONCE GLASS, WITH JOINTED SCONCE BRACKETS. WALNUT. 1785–95. J. STOGDELL STOKES.
2820. (Right.) GLASS WITH ONE CARVED APPLIED PIECE. OTHERS AT TOP MISSING. 1710–30.

2821–22. BRASSES OF 1790–1805. THE ROSE PATTERN AND THE DOVE OF PEACE.
RUDOLPH P. PAULY.

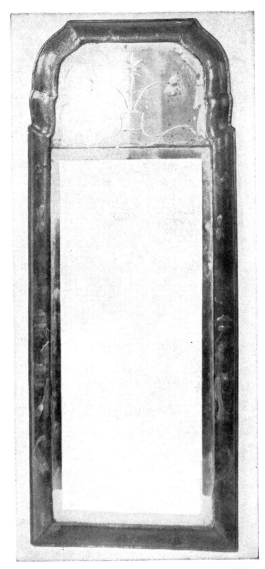

2823. SHAPED UPPER GLASS, CUT WITH POT OF FLOWERS AND STARS. 17 x 35. PORTSMOUTH, NEW HAMPSHIRE. 1710–20.

2824. (Right.) DECORATED FRAME, UPPER GLASS SHAPED AND CUT. PINE BLACK AND GOLD LACQUER. 17½ x 43. IPSWICH. 1710–20. BOTH GLASSES FLAYDERMAN & KAUFMAN.

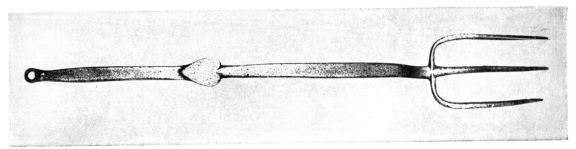

2825. A GIFT FORK, MORE PROPERLY CALLED TORMENTOR, WITH A HEART MOTIVE. 18TH CENTURY. PENNSYLVANIA.

2826. Petit Point Needlework. 17th Century. Frame Like a Looking-Glass. Rich Coloring, Quaint Drawing, Faithful Costume. Frame Pine with Wide Gold Line. To Show Cloud Effect Top Is Made with Double Arch. H. W. Erving.

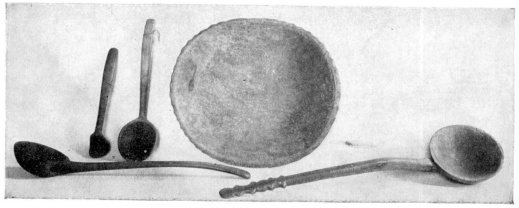

2827-31. Wooden Spoons, Some Decorative. Rare. Bowl with Decorated Edge. Probably 18th Century. Albert C. Bates.

2832. GLASS WITH INLAID MEDALLIONS. SATINWOOD WITH WALNUT OUTSIDE
EDGE. A THREE-INCH MOLD. INLAID WITH THUYA AND TULIPWOOD. 13½ x 16¾.
1710–20. FRANCIS HILL BIGELOW.

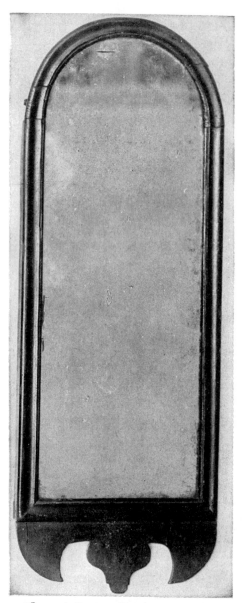

2833. A Sconce Glass, Probably One of Two. Unusual Top. The Mold Should Be Compared with That on Walnut Chairs. 7½ x 20¼. 1710–30. Francis Hill Bigelow.

2834. (Right.) Stained Maple Frame, Ornamented with a Boss. Narrow Portion of the Frame 1⅛ Inches Wide. Glass 11¼ x 17. Francis Hill Bigelow.

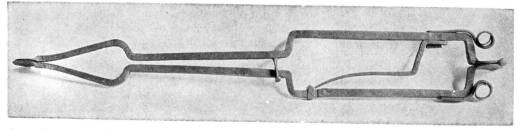

2835. Rare 18th Century Pipe Tongs. As They Open by Squeezing, the Use Must Have Required Some Dexterity. Mrs. DeWitt Howe.

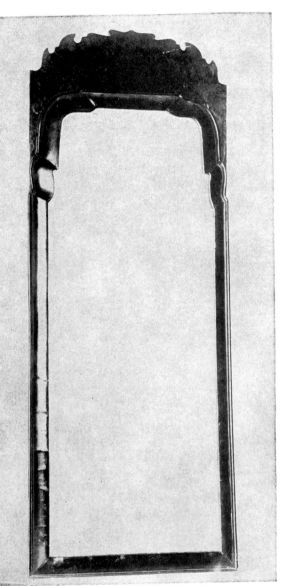

2836. CRESTING IS PART OF FRAME. INLAID DESIGN IN TULIPWOOD. TWO GLASSES ORIGINALLY. 1710–20.

2837. (Right.) WALNUT, WITH CONVEX MOLD. TOP IN STYLE OFTEN SEEN ABROAD. GLASS 11⅞ x 13⅞. 1710–30. BIGELOW COL.

2838–39. BURL BOWLS, THE SECOND WITH HANDLE, OFTEN CALLED INDIAN HEAD. SAMUEL WINECK.

2840. Handsomely Lacquered. 1700–20. Katrina Kipper.

2841. (Middle.) Very Early. Pine. Original Glass. 8 x 13½. Painted. H. H. Armstrong.

2842. (Right.) Walnut. Unusual Top. 20 x 54½. 1720–40. Flayderman & Kaufman.

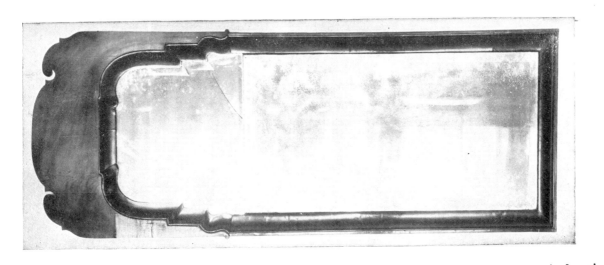

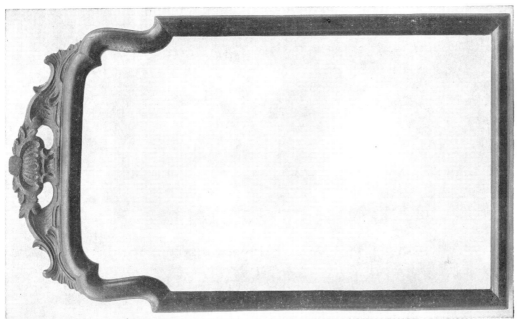

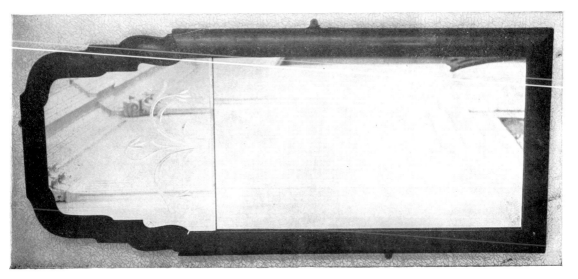

2843. Heavy Frame. 1700–20. Formerly the Author's.
2844. (Middle.) Walnut. Windsor, Connecticut. Glass,
10⅛ x 16⅞. H. H. Armstrong.

2845. (Right.) 22 x 61. 1710–20. John H. Buck, Hartford.

2846. Flat Walnut. Glass Engraved. 13⅞ x 33⅞. c. 1710. Bigelow Col. 2847. (Middle.) Walnut Veneer. Sanderson Col.

2848. (Right.) Frame 2⅛ Inches Wide. 15¾ x 43¼. c. 1710. Bigelow Col.

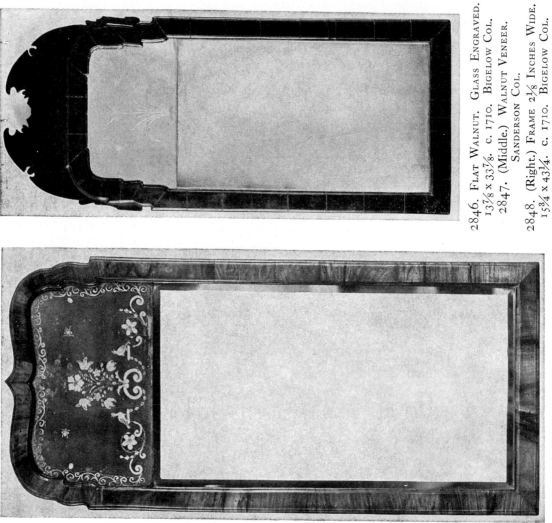

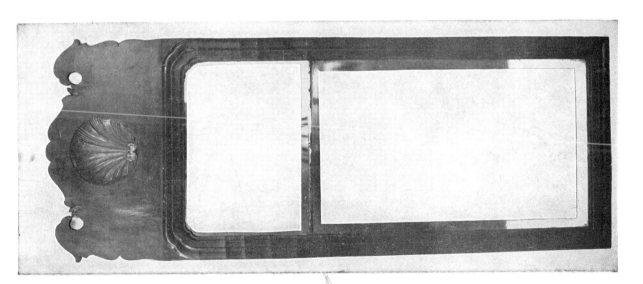

2849 and 2851. (At Each Side.) Walnut. 1710–30. Flayderman & Kaufman.

2850. Rare or Unique. Engraved Glass at the Top in an Irregular Form. Walnut. H. H. Armstrong, Hartford.

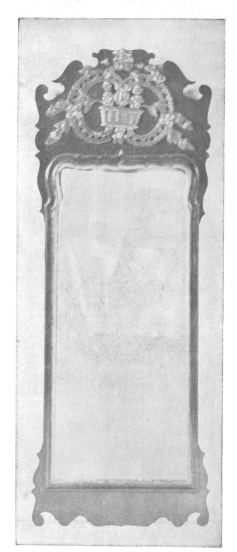

2852–53. Carved, Applied Decoration. Early 18th Century. Left: Katrina Kipper.

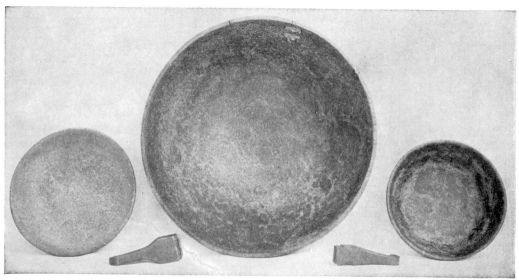

2854–58. Burl Plates or Trenchers, and Large Shallow Bowl. The Knives Are Cutters for Fine Basket Work. Indian Original. Albert C. Bates.

2859-60. Cape Cod. Bright-Hued. 21½ x 9½. Right: Connecticut. Crown Attached by Pegs. Painted. 14 x 8¾. 18th C. Wm. B. Goodwin.

 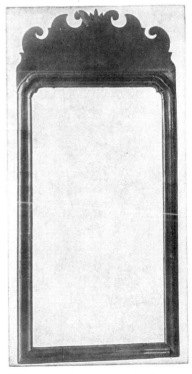

2861-62. Walnut Sconce. Rhode Island. 9 x 24. Early 18th Century. Flayderman & Kaufman.

2863. (Right.) Queen Anne. Indented Corners. Katrina Kipper. 1710-30.

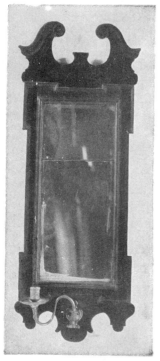

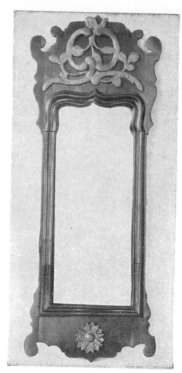

2864. GOOD SMALL SCONCE.
KATRINA KIPPER.

2865. APPLIED CARVING.
FLAYDERMAN & KAUFMAN.

2866. EARLY CHIPPEN-
DALE.

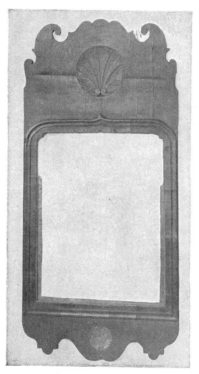

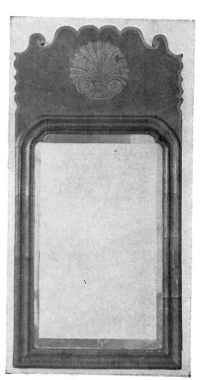

2867. INCISED CARVED SHELLS.
WALNUT.

2868. TWO PART, ENGRAVED.

2869. CARVED SHELL.

ALL EARLY 18TH CENTURY. CENTER: KATRINA KIPPER. OTHERS: FLAYDERMAN & KAUFMAN.

2870–71. Attractive Scrolls. Applied Gilt Carving. 18th Century. Katrina Kipper.

2872. Same Owner as Above.
All Walnut.

2873. Curly Maple, Chippendale.
Charles P. Cooley.

2874. A Small Glass in Pine Frame, Fully Carved. 18th Century. Mark LaFontaine, Springfield, Vermont.

 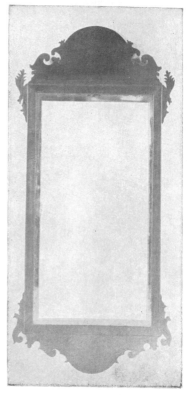

2875. Convex Frame. c. 1700. 15 x 26. Walnut. John H. Buck, Hartford.
2876. (Right.) Sawed Scroll. 1760–75. Katrina Kipper.

2879. Fully Decorated, with Double Shells and Scrolls. Early 18th Century. Shaped Glass. Bigelow Collection.

2878. A French Type, About 1750. Katrina Kipper.

2877. Inlaid Sconce Frame. Unusual Shape. Owner's Name Lost. Apparently Something at Top Lost.

2880. Walnut, Attractive Scroll. A Gilded Dove on an Applied Scroll. 1710–30. John H. Buck.

2881. Scrolled in the Form of Pigeons. Walnut. Flayderman & Kaufman.

2882. A Flower Basket Set in Scrolls Such as Are Found on the Cape. Probably of Foreign Origin. A Carved Pheasant Sits on Topmost Scroll. John H. Buck.

2883. FRENCH. GLASSES ARE INTERNATIONAL, THE GREATER PART OF THOSE FOUND IN THIS COUNTRY OF FOREIGN ORIGIN. PROBABLY MADE IN THE PROVINCES. JAMES DAVIDSON.

2884. (Right.) ENGRAVED AND ETCHED. PINE, PAINTED GREEN, WITH A LANDSCAPE IN THE PANEL AT THE TOP. 12½ x 20½. FROM PORTSMOUTH, DATE UNCERTAIN. FLAYDERMAN & KAUFMAN.

2885. SCONCE GLASS, PINE. 15 x 28. QUEEN ANNE PERIOD. FLAYDERMAN & KAUFMAN.

2886. (Right.) INTERESTING DATED GLASS, WITH FIGHTING COCKS, FACING EACH OTHER, QUAINT DESIGNS AND INITIALS. ANYTHING OF THIS SORT IS IMPORTANT. JOHN H. BUCK, HARTFORD.

2887. DETAIL OF A GLASS DOOR FRAME. RHODE ISLAND SCHOOL OF DESIGN.

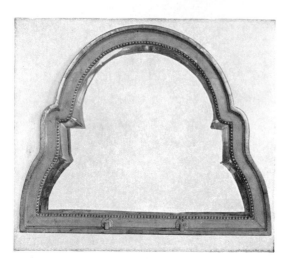

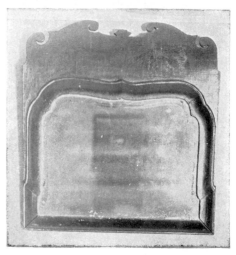

2888. SCONCE REFLECTOR, MADE IN SHAPE OF QUEEN ANNE GLASS TOP. PINE, SHAPED, GILDED, AND BEVELED. NEWBURYPORT. 22¼ x 27½. FLAYDERMAN & KAUFMAN.

2889. (Right.) GLASS TO REFLECT A SCONCE. LIKE TOP OF QUEEN ANNE LOOKING-GLASS. 1710-30. MRS. FRANCIS P. GARVAN.

2890. SMALL PAINTED QUEEN ANNE GLASS. 1710-20. W. F. HUBBARD, HARTFORD.

2891. (Right.) PINE, GILDED. 10 x 15. NEAR WEST POINT, NEW YORK. QUEEN ANNE PERIOD. FLAYDERMAN & KAUFMAN.

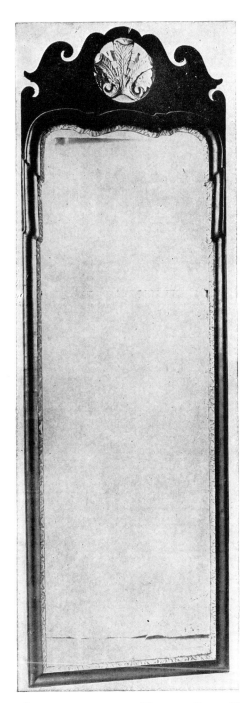
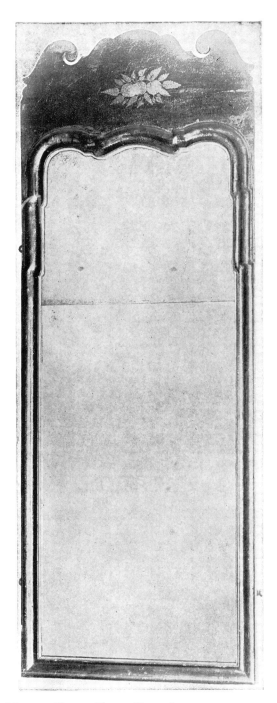

2892–93. LEFT-HAND WALNUT, RIGHT-HAND MOLDED PINE. THEIR DATE IS ABOUT 1720–40.
GLASS IN FORMER, 14¾ x 48¾. GLASS IN LATTER, 16 x 40. THIS FRAME IS GRAINED IN IMITATION
OF ROSEWOOD. IT IS GILT INSIDE. THE STENCILING IN GILT WAS PROBABLY 19TH CENTURY WORK.
BIGELOW COLLECTION.

As to looking-glasses in general it is sometimes difficult to determine whether they are English or American.
The styles also were much the same. It would be impossible, however, to secure a fine and elegant collection
of American looking-glasses covering the various periods. In the notations made, it has been thought best
not to be too specific regarding origins, partly owing to the difficulty of making an authoritative statement.

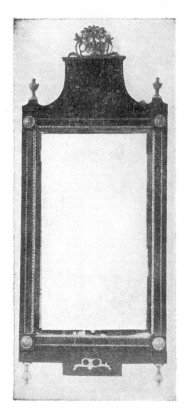
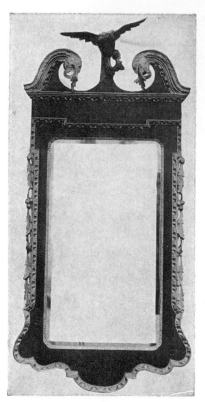

2894. FOREIGN. SOMEWHAT OF BILBAO TYPE. KATRINA KIPPER.
2895. (Right.) SCROLLS TERMINATE WITH DROOPING FOLIAGE. 1740–50. HELEN T. COOKE.

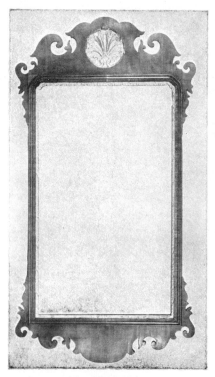

2896. QUEEN ANNE PERIOD, FULLY CARVED. FOUR ROSETTES ON THREE-FEATHER CREST. 1730–60. WE USE THE TERM QUEEN ANNE FOR A STYLE OFTEN AFTER HER DATE.

2897. (Right.) A CHIPPENDALE SCROLL. PERHAPS 1740.

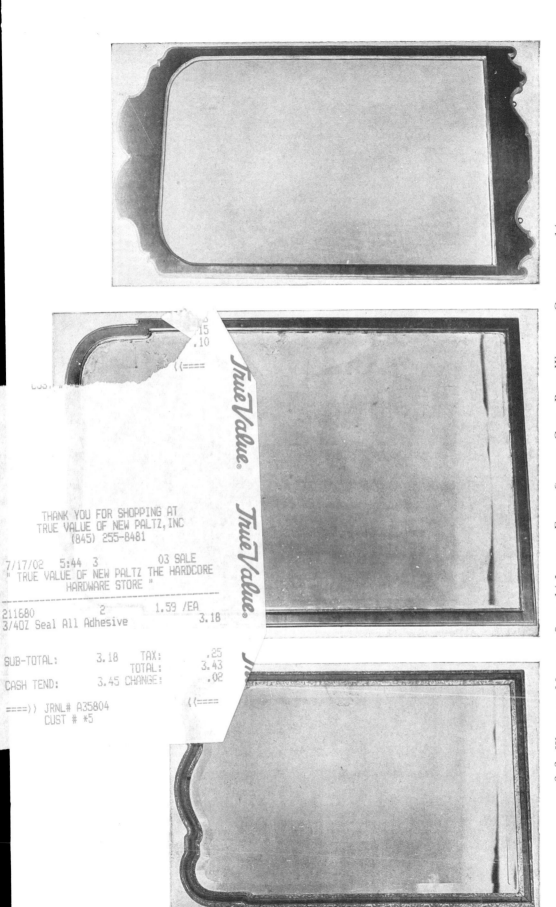

2898. Width of Mold on Side 1¼ Inches. Edges Outside Gilt. Burl Walnut. Glass 21 x 33½. 1720-40.
2899. (Middle.) Walnut, 13½ x 21½. Frame Only One Inch Wide. Gilt Inside and Out. 1730-50. Francis Hill Bigelow. 2900. (Right.) Walnut. 21 x 32¾. Frame 1¼ Inches Wide. Boxwood Edges Inside and Out. 1730-50.

THANK YOU FOR SHOPPING AT
TRUE VALUE OF NEW PALTZ, INC
(845) 255-8481

7/17/02 5:44 3   03 SALE
" TRUE VALUE OF NEW PALTZ THE HARDCORE
          HARDWARE STORE "

211680   2   1.59 /EA
3/40Z Seal All Adhesive   3.18

SUB-TOTAL: 3.18   TAX: .25
                       TOTAL: 3.43
CASH TEND: 3.45 CHANGE: .02

====)) JRNL# A35804   ((====
       CUST # *5

2901. Beautiful Marquetry, 1700–20. Bigelow Collection. 44 x 29¾. Coffin Family in 1732.
2902. (Right.) Glass Painted as Tortoise Shell. The Portion That Has Been Repaired Readily Shows.
Very Rare. 1660–1685. Bigelow Collection.

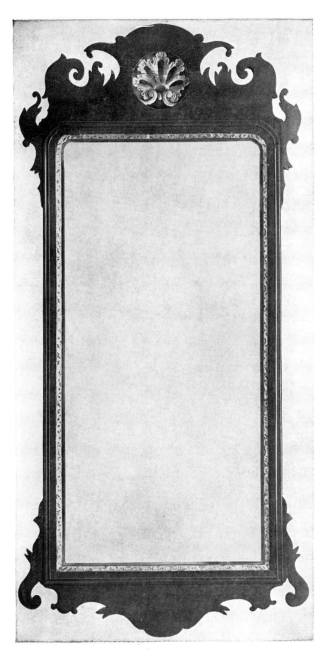
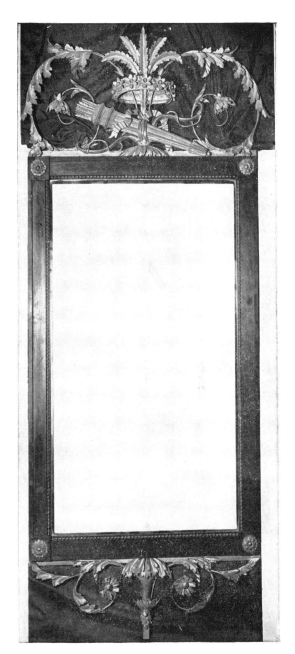

2903. LATE QUEEN ANNE. 1740–60. BIGELOW COLLECTION.

2904. (Right.) BOUGHT BY CAPTAIN WORMSTED IN BILBAO AND BROUGHT TO MARBLEHEAD. THE CROWN, ARROWS, QUIVER, AND THE CENTRAL ACANTHUS LEAVES WERE ALL SYMBOLS OF THE PERIOD. BLACK FRAME, WITH LINE OF GILT BEADING INSIDE; ROSETTES ON CORNERS; DECORATIONS IN CARVED WOOD. 27 x 61. DARK GROUND TO EMPHASIZE DESIGN.

Bilbao was the meeting place of trade. Thence these designs went everywhere; and also they were brought to Bilbao. Thus looking-glasses of all forms were brought by captains returning from Italy, Spain, England, Holland, and China.

2906. William and Mary, 1690-1700.
Bigelow Collection.

2905. Italian, Said To Date from the 17th
Century. Bigelow Collection.

2907. Captain Smith and Pocahontas. H. W. Erving.

2908. Reverse of Same.

17th Century glass, 7 x 9 inside, with frame made double and a picture on glass in the back. Powhatan sits in judgment on John Smith, known by his white color, mustache, and bound hands, while Pocahontas in the rear intercedes for the captive. Frame reeded on one side, broad flutes on the other. It is no wonder that John Rolfe fell in love with such a maiden. Their home near Williamstown, Virginia, as the author is writing, has been bought for preservation.

2909. MARQUETRY GLASS. ENGLISH. PIERCED FRET. C. 1700. I. SACK.

Olive ebony and walnut were the materials of the earliest frames. It is likely that all or almost all of the marquetry frames, and the richer frames in general, were imported. Foliage, flowers and grotesque animals supplied the subjects. The crown of this frame shows two monsters with bodies of oxen and fanciful heads. Only in homes of wealth could such glasses be found. At first glasses nearly square as here were used, because the methods of making plate were expensive.

2910. QUEEN ANNE, CARVED ON WOOD AND GILDED. SHELL, FEATHER, AND LEAF MOTIVE. BIRD HEAD CARVED BELOW THE TOP. 1710–40. BIGELOW COLLECTION.

2911. (Right.) GEORGIAN. CRANE ON BRANCH. THE APPLIED CARVING ON THE TOP SCROLL WAS OBVIOUSLY COPIED FOR THE FINEST HIGHBOY TOPS. THE LITTLE CREST FEATHER AT THE EXTREME TOP IS A TOUCH OF BEAUTY OFTEN OMITTED. MOST GLASSES OF THIS SHAPE IN THE TOP AND WITH THE BIRD GO UNDER THE NAME GEORGIAN, CHIPPENDALE, OR MARTHA WASHINGTON. 1740–60. BIGELOW COLLECTION.

The very earliest frame was convex and broad, even up to four inches, and the glass was almost square. In the next period, about 1700, we get the William and Mary shortly followed by the Queen Anne, with a frame like No. 2910 above, often in walnut, but sometimes gilded, as shown. Then come the frames such as that shown in No. 2914. Then the frame above on the right; then follow at about the same time frames like that on the right, but without any applied decoration, as, for instance, No. 2948, and frames like No. 2915. After that we come to the Hepplewhite, with or without filigree, and the Sheraton or early Empire.

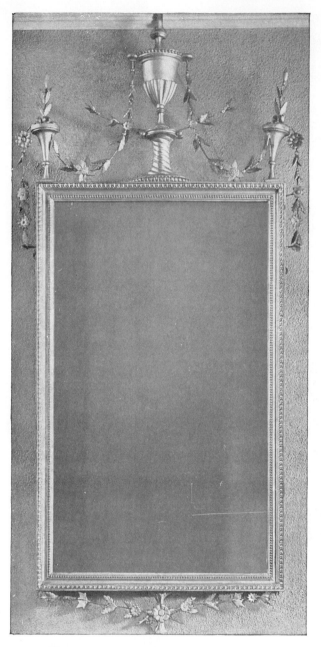

2912. HEPPLEWHITE. 1780–90. BIGELOW COLLECTION.

2913. FILIGREE GLASS. HEPPLEWHITE. 1780–90. ALL ORIGINAL. BIGELOW COLLECTION.

2916–17. (Opposite.) BATTERSEA KNOBS. 18TH CENTURY. CONTINUOUS SINGLE LANDSCAPE. TRANSFER PATTERN. HAND COLORED. UPTURNED FLANGE BEZEL. DIAMETER 3¾ INCHES. HAND TOOLED. CHRISTINE J. STEELE.

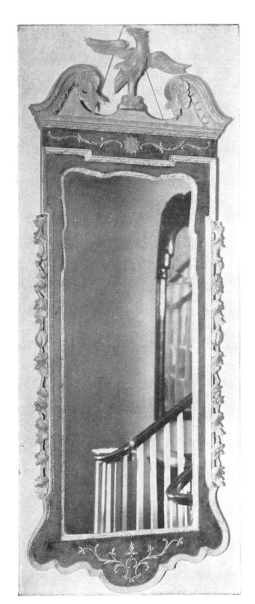

2914. Georgian, Carved on Wood. Gold Leaf and Mahogany. 30 x 76. c. 1760. John H. Buck.

2915. (Right.) Openwork, Carved, Chippendale. Gold. Webb House, Wethersfield, Colonial Dames.

2918. AMERICAN. 1770. MRS. FRANCIS P. GARVAN.   2919. (Right.) GEORGIAN, MAHOGANY. 1750.

2920-21. BATTERSEA. HAND-TINTED ENGRAVINGS UNDER GLASS. 1790-1810. CHRISTINE J. STEELE.

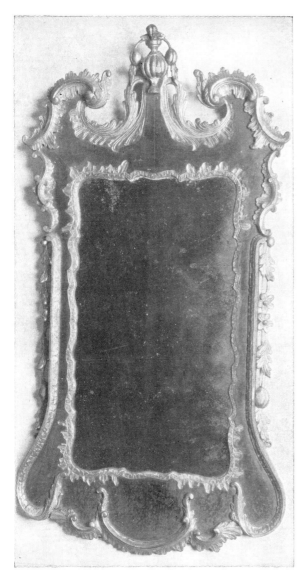

2922. RICHLY CARVED WITH UNUSUAL FINIAL. GEORGIAN. 1740–70. HOWARD REIFSNYDER, PHILADELPHIA.
2923. (Right.) GEORGIAN. MAHOGANY AND GOLD. 1740–70. I. SACK.

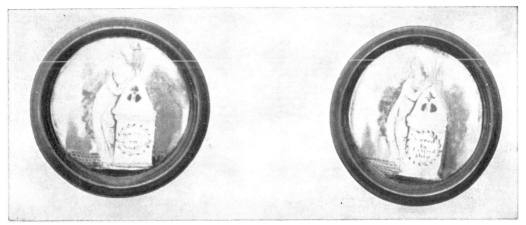

2924–25. "SACRED TO FRIENDSHIP." KNOBS FOR GLASSES. 1790–1810. J. GROSSMAN.

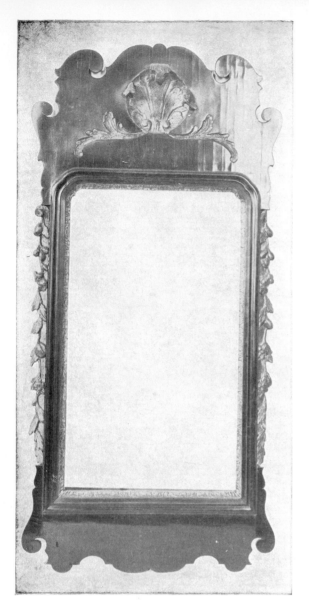

2926. SHELL AND SCROLL, WOOD CARVED AND GILDED. 1740-70. FLAYDERMAN & KAUFMAN.

2927. (Right.) UNUSUAL DESIGN. CROSS BANDING, APPLIED BEADS AND SIDE SCROLLS. BROOKS REED.

2928-29. BATTERSEA. THE FRENCH REVOLUTION; "HOPE." CHRISTINE J. STEELE.

2930. OPEN SCROLL. QUEEN ANNE. 1740–60. APPLIED ORNAMENT. I. SACK.
2931. (Right.) PHEASANT CARVED IN CIRCLE. APPLIED CARVED WOOD DECORATION. 1740–60. H. C. VALENTINE & COMPANY.

2932–35. THE LADY MAY BE A PORTRAIT. AT ANY RATE, IT SHOWS THE COSTUME OF THE TIMES, AND THE SAME MAY BE SAID OF THE GENTLEMAN. THE THIRD FIGURE IN THE STYLE OF AN EARLY ENGRAVING. THE LAST, AN URN. 1790–1820.

2936. Applied Carved Decoration. On Inside the Gilt Is on the Glass. 1740–70. Malcolm A. Norton.

2937. (Right.) Georgian, with a Spray Pending from the Rosette. The Applied Moldings Pine, with Gold Leaf. 28 x 50. 1740–70. John H. Buck, Hartford.

2938–39. Battersea Knobs. Black and Grey, Possibly Mourning. Good Example of Transfer from Copper Engraved Plates. Christine J. Steele.

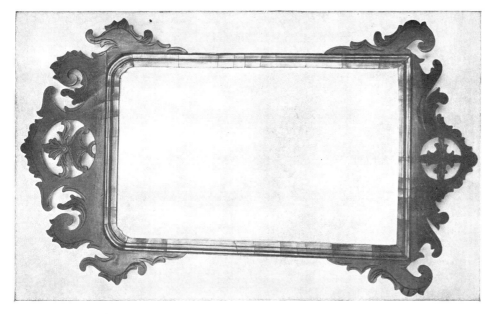

2942. Cross-Banded Frame, with Carved and Sawed Ornamental Additions at Top and Bottom. 16 x 27. 1730–60. John H. Buck.

2941. Handsome Applied Side Carving. Corners Usually Earlier than Chippendale. Three Feathers. 1730–60. Katrina Kipper.

2940. Early Chippendale. The Immediate Frame Is Cross Banded, and the Inside Member Carved and Gilded. Gilded Carved Decoration in Top. 22 x 40. John H. Buck.

2945. French. Gilded. Early Corners. 1780. Katrina Kipper.

2944. An English Chippendale with Coat of Arms Surmounted by an Eagle. Gilded. 1750–70. C. R. Morson.

2943. Walnut, Fine Applied Carving. Salem. Queen Anne. 19 x 43. Flayderman & Kaufman.

2947. MAHOGANY. HERRINGBONE. JAMES DAVIDSON.

2946. MAHOGANY. CARVED. GILDED BIRD. 1780.

2948. (Opposite page.) Rich Chippendale. Carved, Gilded. 1750–70. C. P. Cooley.

2949. (Opposite page; right.) Richly Grained Wood. Carved on the Wood and on Applied Pine Decorations. Gilded.

2951. Carved and Gilded. 17 x 32. 1750–75. H. W. Erving.

2950. Chippendale, Pierced Scroll. 1750–80.

2953. Chippendale, Shaped Corners. Author's.

2952. Late Chippendale. 16 x 24. John H. Buck.

2955. Carved. 1750-75. E. B. Leete Co.

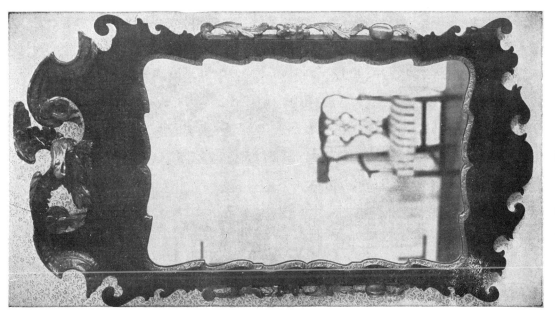

2954. Carved. Gilded. 1750-75.

2958. Carved, Pine, Gold Leafed. 1780. Basket with Flowers. Rococo Outlines. Second Half 18th Century. E. B. Leete Company, Guilford.

2957. Mahogany and Gold. Both Incised and Applied Carving. Second Half 18th Century. H. V. Weil.

2956. Chippendale. Eight Small Glasses Surrounding Large. Gilt Phoenix and Rosette. Second Half 18th Century. Joe Kindig, Jr.

2961. Walnut. Carving in the Walnut and Applied Gilded Decoration. The Effort To Show All the Forms Would Be Hopeless. Second Half 18th Century. N. Cushing, Providence.

2960. Hepplewhite. Swans on Crest, Connected by Filigree Carving with Urn. 1780–90. Formerly the Author's.

2959. Chippendale. Sawed Fret, Enriched with Outlines of Foliage Scrolls. Four Feathers in Oval. Very Popular Type. 15 x 26. Latter Half 18th Century. E. B. Leete Company.

2962. Inlaid with Eagle. 19½ x 30½. 18th Century. Mr. and Mrs. George Shipley, Baltimore

2963. (Right.) Inlaid with Shell. Dainty Scroll. Late 18th C. 24 x 56. John H. Buck.

2964. Label Found on Glass of Late 18th Century. Flayderman & Kaufman.

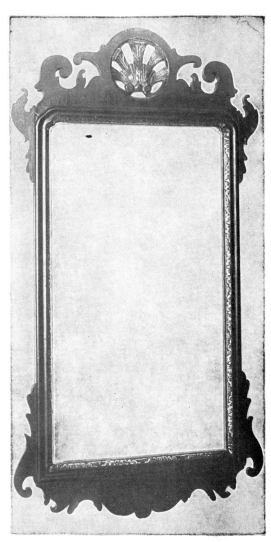

2965. Stooping Eagle on Spiraled Support. Late Chippendale. Stearns Collection.
2966. (Right.) Chippendale. Feathers and Inner Border Carved and Gilded.
Samuel Wineck.

2967. Fully Carved, Chippendale Mantel Glass. Second Half 18th Century.
Metropolitan Museum.

2968. Three-Part Mantel Glass, Fully Carved and Gilded. Second Half 18th Century.
C. R. Morson.

2969. Carved with Crest of Basket and Flowers. Second Half 18th Century.
Howard Reifsnyder, Philadelphia.

2970. (Right.) Carved with Fruit Clusters. These Shapes Are Called Rococo. Second
Half 18th Century. Clifford R. Weld, Rock, Massachusetts.

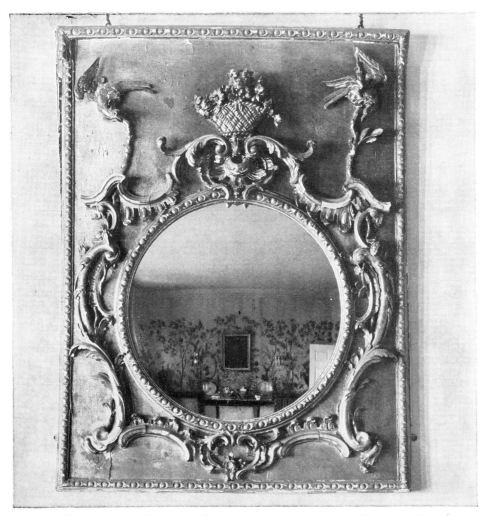

2971. Carved with Birds and Flowers and Scrolls on a Plaque. English. Second Half 18th Century. Mrs. Francis P. Garvan.

2972-73. Silver Candlesticks, Jacobean. Sheet of Hand-Beaten Repoussé. Backed to a Wooden Base. Holder Also of Wood. They Bear Hallmarks. Clifford S. Drake, North Hampton, New Hampshire.

2974. Georgian Glass, Carved and Gilded. Large. Mid 18th
Century. C. R. Morson.

2975-77. GLASS ON MANTEL WITH FESTOONS. 18TH C. STONE MANTEL. EMPIRE CHAIR. FENN COL.

2978-81. GEORGIAN GLASS. DUTCH SETTEE. ENGLISH CUPBOARD. OAK CHEST. C. P. COOLEY.

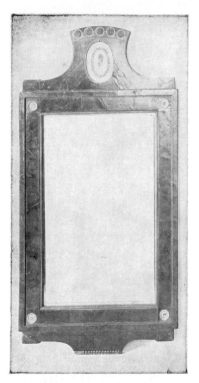

2982. ADAM OR BILBAO. INSET MEDALLION. ROSETTES ON CORNERS. MORRIS BERRY.

2983. (Right.) CHIPPENDALE WITH THE SAME MOTIVE REPEATED ON ALL SIDES. CLIFFORD R. WELD.

2984. MINIATURE QUEEN ANNE. VENEERED AS IF A SLAB OF WOOD WITH BARK. TWO PART. EARLY 18TH CENTURY. BROOKS REED.

2985. (Right.) EARLY CHIPPENDALE. SMALLER GLASSES IN FRAME. 29½ x 53. PINE, GILDED. MID 18TH CENTURY. FLAYDERMAN & KAUFMAN.

2986-87. LARGE CHIPPENDALE. CARVED PINE WITH GOLD LEAF. PLAQUE ON RIGHT BAS RELIEF.

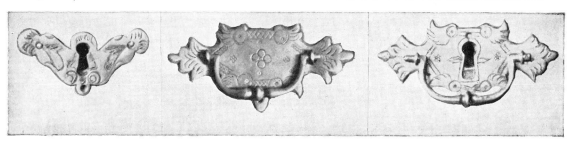

2988-90. EARLY RARE STAMPED BRASSES FROM QUEEN ANNE LOWBOY. HENRY A. HOFFMAN,
BARRINGTON, RHODE ISLAND.

2991. LARGE, DELICATELY CARVED BIRD. SECOND HALF 18TH CENTURY. I. SACK.

These graceful glasses give much dignity to a room. On them seem to be expended some of the best talent of the 18th century. The applied carving of bits of wood wired together and all gilded running down the sides is done in various patterns. The scroll top is practically the same as that used in the Queen Anne and Chippendale time on high cabinet pieces and doorheads.

2992. (Right.) LARGE, WITH AN INLAID OVAL ABOVE AND BELOW. TWO PART. LANDSCAPE IN PAINTED GLASS ON THE UPPER SECTION. CARVED URN WITH WIRED GRASSES. LATE 18TH CENTURY. C. SANFORD BULL, WATERBURY, CONNECTICUT.

2993. Richly Carved, and Gold Leafed. Mantel. 1750–75. C. P. Cooley, Hartford.
2994–95. (Below.) Pine Painted. Bigelow Collection.

2996. An Elaborate and Rich Glass Carved Throughout and Covered with Gold Leaf. Bigelow Collection.

2997. CARVED PINE, GOLD LEAF. SWAN ON NEST AT BOTTOM; BIRDS FACING EACH OTHER ON UPPER CORNERS; BASKET WITH FLOWERS AT CREST; FOLIAGE AND FRUIT AT SIDES. ROCOCO SCROLLS. LARGE. 1750–75. I. SACK.

By Chippendale's time, glass was somewhat cheaper, and larger examples are found. The use of two glasses, in the pier mirrors was merely to save expense.

2998. Butterfly Inlay. Urn with Flowers and Wheat Ears. 1780–90. Charles P. Cooley.
2999. (Right.) Gold on Pine. Scrolls with Flowers. 1750–80. Charles P. Cooley.

3000–01. Two Petal and Thistle Brasses. 1790. A. H. Eaton.

3003. Wheat Ears above Urns Were a Favorite Feature of the Hepplewhite Period. Bead Decoration. 1775. Robert T. Smith.

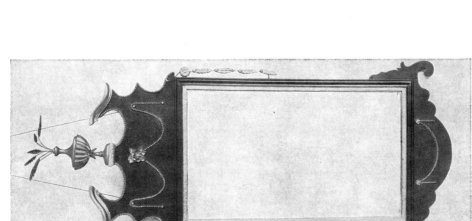

3004. Scrolls at Top with Delicate Ramp, So Sharp as To Reach the Vertical. Applied Decoration, Gilt. H. V. Weil.

3002. Crane, Gilt, as Also All Applied Ornaments. 1770–80. C. R. Morson.

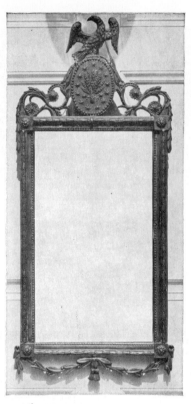

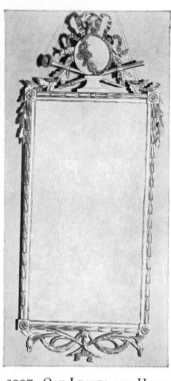

3005. "TABERNACLE." 1790.
WICKFORD ANTIQUE SHOP.

3006. THIRTEEN STAR. 1785–90.
JAMES FENIMORE COOPER.

3007. OAK LEAVES AND HORN.
1790. MISSES FOSTER.

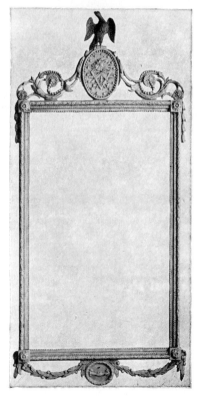

3008. THIRTEEN STAR WITH BIRD. SOME ORNAMENTS GONE. 1790. ALAN WRIGHT.
3009. (Right.) MASONIC GLASS. FIFTEEN STARS AND BIRD. 1790. HELEN T. COOKE.

3010. HEPPLEWHITE. ROPE MOLD, URN AND HUSK. E. F. SANDERSON.
3011. (Right.) 17½ x 20½. GILT INSIDE AND OUT. WALNUT. 1750-75. BIGELOW COLLECTION.

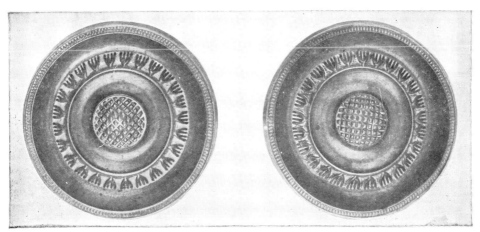

3012-13. LARGE BRASS KNOBS. THIS SORT WAS PRESSED IN A DIE, AND NOT CAST.

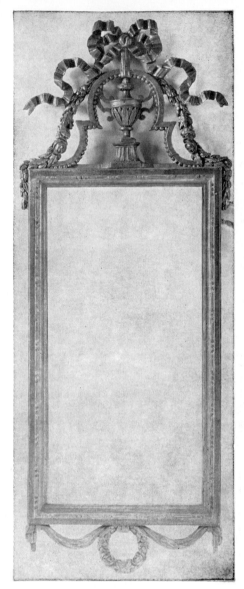

3014. Jutting Squares, Festoons, Urn, Etc. 26 x 61. John H. Buck.

3015. (Right.) Ribbon and Wreath, Urn and Drapery. 1790. Katrina Kipper, Accord.

3016–17. Brasses for Window Draperies. 19th Century. Frank A. Robart.

3018. Italian "Chippendale." All Gold on Wood. 1750–75.
3019. (Right.) In the Style of Bilbao Glass. Landscape in Oval. 1790. Both, C. P. Cooley.

3020–21. Brasses for Draperies. 19th Century. Frank A. Robart.

3022. WHEAT EAR ABOVE URN; HUSK PENDANTS. 1790. SANDERSON COLLECTION.
3023. (Right.) PROFUSION OF ORNAMENT. ALL GOLD ON WOOD. CHAS. P. COOLEY.

3024-25. GILDED EAGLE BRACKETS. RESTS FOR CLOCKS OR VASES.

3026. "Agricultural." Carved on Wood. 1790. The Misses A. and E. P. Foster.
3027. (Right.) Implements and Fruits. Carved on Wood. 32½ x 71. 1790.

3028-29. Knobs for Glasses. Late 18th Century.

3030. Italian. Shows Larger Motives Than Chippendale. 1730.
3031. (Right.) Hepplewhite. Late 18th Century. Both, Chas. P. Cooley.

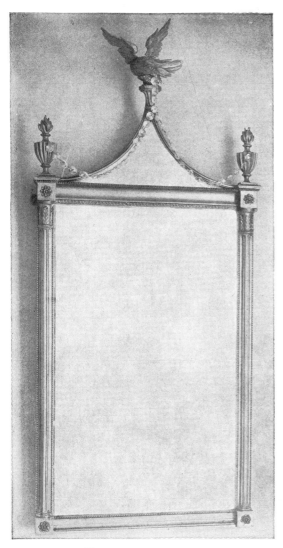

3032. HEPPLEWHITE. 23 X 50. 1790.
E. B. LEETE CO.

3033. 1790.

3034-35. BATTERSEA KNOBS. BRIDGE AND MILL. "ANTIQUES" MAGAZINE.

3038. Top Filled with Decorated Panel. Columns, Capitals, Rope Mold. E. C. Hall.

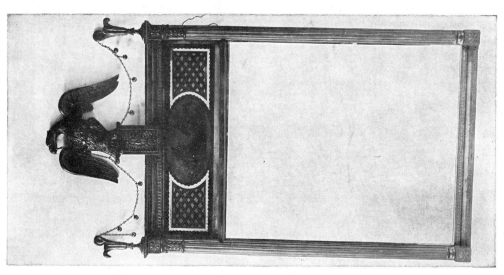

3037. Landscape in Oval. Architectural Half-Round Columns. 1790–1818. Katrina Kipper.

3036. Fully Carved, Gilded. 25 x 54. 1790. John H. Buck.

3039. "Cape Cod." One of Many Types Brought in by Sea Captains. 1760-70. 14 x 32. Carved and Gilded. Newport. Flayderman & Kaufman.

3040. Large, French. 18th C. Clifford R. Weld.

3041. Probably Venetian. "Cape Cod." Gold on Carved Wood. 1760-70. James Davidson.

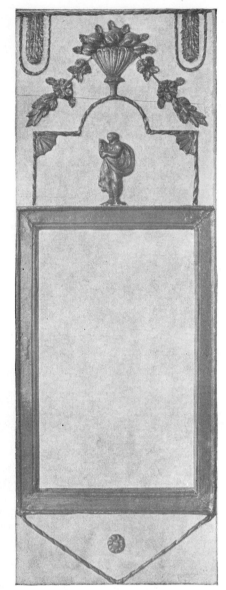

3042. ELABORATE. EAGLE ABOVE MEDALLION. 1790–1800. FRANCIS H. BIGELOW.
3043. (Right.) DIRECTOIRE. 1790–1800. 13½ x 38. FLAYDERMAN & KAUFMAN.

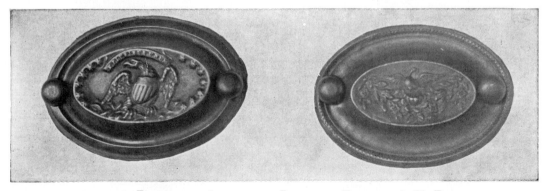

3044-45. EAGLE WITH ARROWS AND BIRD WITH FOLIAGE. A. H. EATON.

3047. Bilbao. Shell at Top. Rosettes and Inlay. Mahogany. 1790. Bigelow Collection.

3046. Seaman's Emblems in the Carving. Lantern, Spy Glass, Bell, Etc. Large. Gilded. 1790–1800. Nathanael Herreshoff.

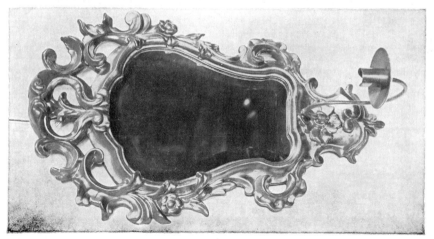

3048. One of Pair. Latter 18th Century. Dutch or French. Carved and Gilded on Wood. Brass Sconce. 12 x 20. H. W. Erving. 3049. (Middle.) Carved on Wood. Gilded. 2nd Half 18th Century. Grotesque Face at Base. 23 x 36. John H. Buck. 3050. (Right.) Carved on Wood. Gilded. Sconces. This and Preceding, Perhaps Italian. 22 x 40. John H. Buck.

3051–53. ALL CARVED IN ONE PIECE. HEIGHT 10½ INCHES. CENTER: HEIGHT 11½ INCHES.
THIS AND THE OTHER TWO, 3RD QUARTER 18TH CENTURY. ALL OF THE SAME PROVENANCE. THAT IS,
THEY ARE CONTINENTAL, PERHAPS FRENCH OR DUTCH. ALL, H. W. ERVING.

3054. CARVED FROM ONE PIECE, NO MITERS. HEIGHT 20½ INCHES. 1750–75. H. W. ERVING.

3055. (Right.) CARVED ON WOOD. OUTSIDE 30½ x 56. MID 18TH CENTURY. THE MISSES A. AND E. P.
FOSTER.

3056–57. Two Italian Glasses. Formerly the Author's. Mid 18th Century.

3058. Carved on Wood in One Piece. No Miters. Height 21½ Inches. 1750–75. Chippendale Type. H. W. Erving.

3059. (Right.) Carved on Wood. Gold. Height 34 Inches. 2nd Half 18th Century. The Misses A. and E. P. Foster.

3062. Carved on Wood, and Gilded. Height 15½ Inches. 1750–75. It Properly Belongs in Style with No. 3052. H. W. Erving.

3061. Carved on Wood. Helmeted Bust over an Oval Boss. Italian. 1740–60. Charles P. Cooley.

3060. Bold Design, Believed To Be Italian. Carved Wood, Gilded. 1740–60. See Other Italian Examples. Katrina Kipper.

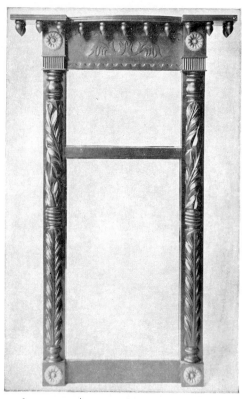

3063. THIRTEEN BALLS. 1800–10. NATHAN CUSHING.   3064. MAHOGANY. 1810–20. JAMES DAVIDSON.

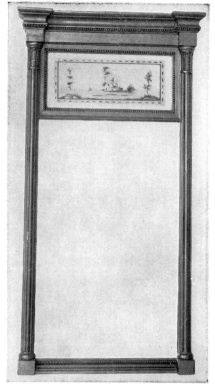

3065. HALF COLUMNS, GILDED. DOUBLE PANEL. PAINTED GLASS. 1800–10. BIGELOW COLLECTION.

3066. (Right.) EMPIRE. MODILLIONS ON FRAME. 1810–20. FRANK A. ROBART.

3067-68. All This Class Called Architectural. 1800-10. Flayderman & Kaufman.

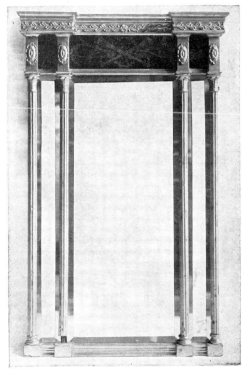

3069. Small Glass Above. S. Prescott Fay.   3070. Three Glasses. 1800. C. R. Morson.

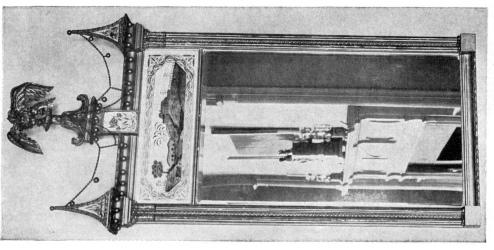

3071. Revolutionary. National Flag and Arms. Belonged to a Continental Soldier. 24 x 43. Gilded. John H. Buck.

3072. (Middle.) Double Columns. Stooping Eagle, Pagoda Corners. Gold. 1800–10. Mrs. Harry Horton Benkard.

3073. (Right.) Pillars Carved in Corinthian Style. Intersecting Arches. 1800–10. G. H. W. Smith.

3074-75. Pine, Gilded. Original Label Shown Elsewhere. 1810–20. Flayderman & Kaufman.

3076-77. Curly Maple. Spindle Columns. 1810–20. McCarthy's Antique Shop, Cheshire.

3079. Four Painted Glasses, in Black, White, and Silver. Reeding Black. Four Pillars with Acanthus Leaf Tops. 30 x 48. Pleasing Effect. 1800–10. Joe Kindig, Jr.

3078 A. Directoire. Figure on Colored Ground. 1790–1800. Bigelow Collection.

3078. All Glasses with Balls Sometimes Called Constitution, as Some Had Thirteen Balls. Architectural Is a Better Name. 1800–10. Charles P. Cooley.

3080–82. Mahogany. The First with a Lyre above the Column. 1820. First and Second, Katrina Kipper. The Third, the Author's.

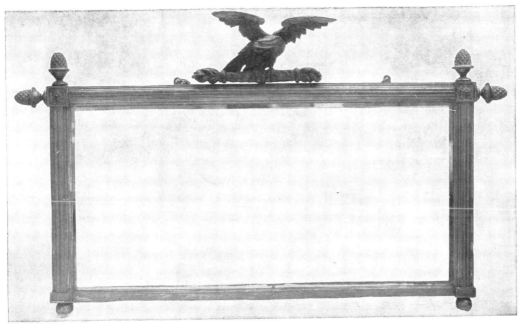

3083. Unusual Design. Pineapples Both Horizontally and Vertically. Really Acorns in Shape. 1810–20. Joe Kindig, Jr.

3084. BALL CORNICE WITH UNUSUAL COLUMNS, CARVED LIKE REPEATED BUDS. 28½ x 36. THORP'S ANTIQUE SHOP, PLAINFIELD, NEW JERSEY.

3085. (Right.) BALL CORNICE. BALLS RECESSED IN COLUMNS. RESTING ON KNOBS. 1800–20.

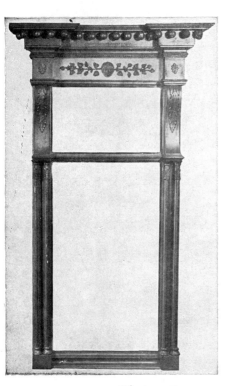
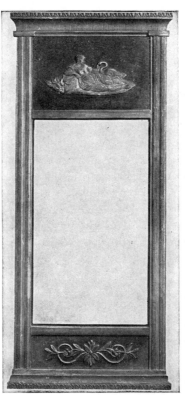
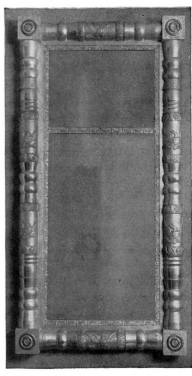

3086. TWO GLASSES, MODILLIONS, BALLS. BIGELOW COLLECTION.
3087. (Middle.) DIRECTOIRE. LEDA AND SWAN. BIGELOW COLLECTION.
3088. (Right). PLAIN. LATE HALF SPINDLE. VERY NUMEROUS.

3089. Half Column. Two Part. Upper Glass with Landscape. 1800–10. F. A. Robart.

3090. (Right.) Eagle in Flight with Scroll and Arrows. 1800–10. Estate of Harry W. Weeks.

3091. Six-Part. Three Upper Glasses, Painted in Five Designs. 1800–20. C. R. Morson.

Mantel glasses of a period earlier than this are very rare. The Chippendale glass scarcely ever seen, though we show some examples. Later than this the mantel glasses are very common.

3092–93. THREE-PART GLASS WITH THREE DISTINCTIVE SHELLS AND A LONG ARRAY OF ACORNS. 1800–20. AN ENGLISH CLOCK. THEY APPEAR IN SLIGHTLY VARYING DESIGNS. CHARLES P. COOLEY.

3094. McINTIRE GLASS, PEIRCE-NICHOLS HOUSE. GLASS PROBABLY MADE FOR ITS PRESENT POSITION. 1790– . ESSEX INSTITUTE.

3095-96. Eight Classical Figures, Dancing, in Central Panel. The Candles in Bronze with Hanging Crystals Are Decorative. 1800–20. Estate of Harry H. Weeks.

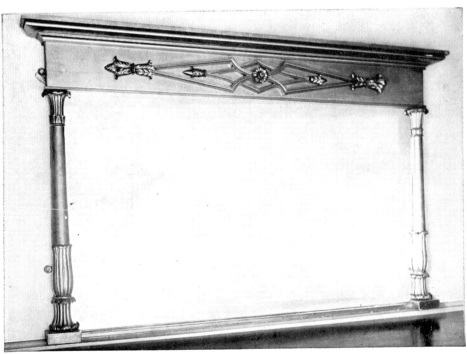

3097. Tasteful Columns. This Specimen Gains by the Simplicity of the Design. 1790–1810. Edward Crowninshield, Stockbridge.

3098. THREE-PART MANTEL GLASS. CLUSTERED COLUMNS WITH LARGE CAPITALS. 1800–10. HELEN T. COOKE.

3099–3100. FOUR-PART GLASS. UNUSUAL DESIGN. MADE BY SOMEONE WHO LOVED TO PAINT ON GLASS. CAPITALS AS MODILLIONS. FIGURES AT SIDES IN DECORATIVE POTTERY. 1800–10. C. R. MORSON.

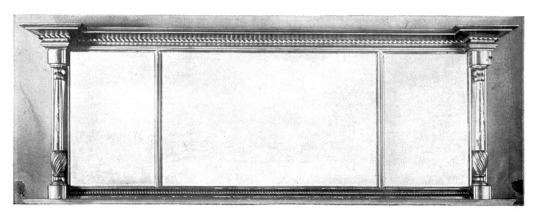

3101. FREE COLUMNS. EXCEEDINGLY RARE. 1800–10. BIGELOW COLLECTION.

3102. THREE-PART MANTEL GLASS. BIGELOW COLLECTION. 1800–20.
3102 A. CLOCK WITH EAGLE. FRENCH ORIGIN.

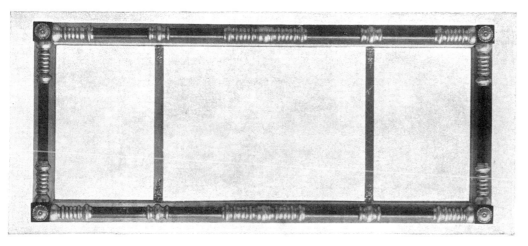

3103. SPLIT-SPINDLE GLASS. $22\frac{1}{2}$ x 53. 1820–30.

3104. CORINTHIAN CAPITALS. SPIRALED BEAD IN HOLLOW MOLD. 1800-10. KATRINA KIPPER.
3105. (Right.) LANDSCAPE OF CONNECTICUT RIVER. 28 x 49. 1800-20. JOHN H. BUCK.

3106-07. BATTERSEA. LATE 18TH CENTURY. DIAMETER 3¾ INCHES. DESIGN APPLIED BY HAND, IN LIVELY COLOR EFFECTS. CHRISTINE J. STEELE. COURTESY OF "ANTIQUES."

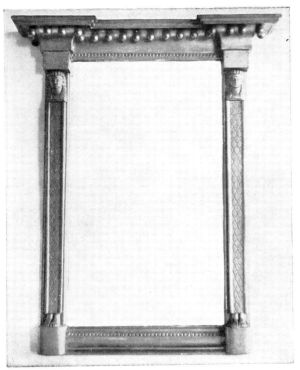

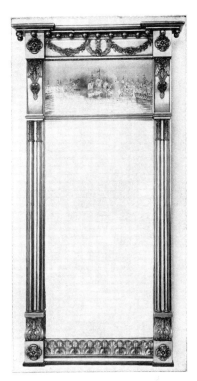

3108-09. Egyptian Mummy Columns. Rare or Unique. 1796. Made in France. 23 x 36. William B. Goodwin. Right: Architectural.

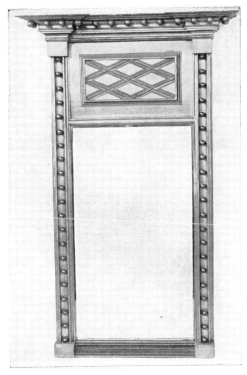

3110-13. Spiraled Column Glass. Mantel: Reading Tavern, Near Cincinnati. Andirons, Old Charts, Admirable Wall Decoration. William B. Goodwin.

3114. (Right.) Ball Glass. 22 x 42. Found in Lynn. 1800-10. Flayderman & Kaufman.

3115. Mantel Glass with Free Columns. A Variant of No. 3101. 1800–10. Bigelow Collection.

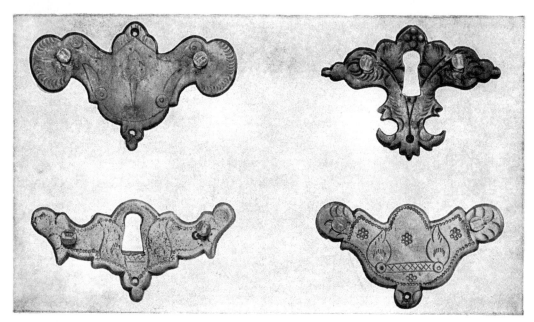

3116–19. Stamped Plates. 1690–1720. A. H. Eaton.

3120–21. Fair Faces on Old Knobs. Collection of A. H. Eaton, Collinsville.

3122–23. Bilbao Glasses. A Rare Pair. Marble and Gold. 1780–90. 22 x 50. Flayderman & Kaufman.

3124–25. Knobs in Black and Grey, Perhaps Mourning. Transfers from Copper Engraved Plates. Courtesy of "Antiques." Christine J. Steele.

3126–27. BILBAO GLASSES, WITH FIGURES ON A BLUE GROUND. UNUSUAL PAIR. 1780–90. MORRIS BERRY.

3128–29. A GIRANDOLE AND A DISK GLASS. PERHAPS BEFORE 1780. 7 AND 9 IN. JOHN H. BUCK.

3130. Mahogany and Marble. Glasses Found at Bilbao, but Possibly from Italy. Suggestions of the Adam Type Do Not Indicate English Origin. Formerly the Author's.

3131. (Right.) Bilbao Glass with Fine Open Scroll. 1780–90. Katrina Kipper.

3132–33. A Knob with the Name of General Steuben. A Second, an Urn with Pendants, and a Fine Border. The Frames of These Knobs Were Often Important as Well as the Picture. J. Grossman.

3134. A Rich Bilbao Glass Nearly Four Feet High. Elaborate Scrolls. 1780–90. C. R. Morson.

3135. (Right.) Mahogany and Gilt, from Portsmouth. 19 x 33½. Carved Gilt Applied Ornaments. Was Owned by Col. Abraham Drake, Who Died 1781. Inherited. Clifford S. Drake.

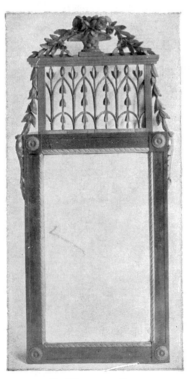

3136. Unusual Fretwork. Gilded Rosettes. 1780–90. Morris Schwartz.

3137. (Right.) Resembling Bilbao Glass, but Wood Frame and No Rosettes. 1790. C. R. Morson.

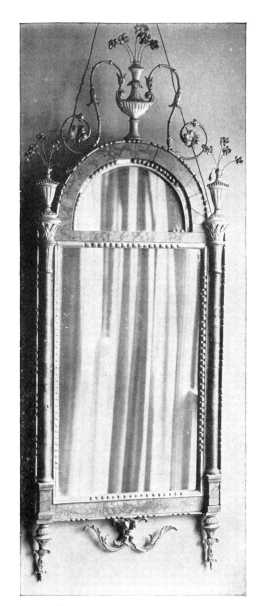

3138. ROUND-TOPPED BILBAO. MARBLE AND CARVED WOOD, GILDED. 1780–90. JOHN H. BUCK.

3139. (Right.) BILBAO GLASS, ORNAMENTS MISSING. MARBLE AND CARVED WOOD, GILDED. 1780–90.
MALCOLM A. NORTON.

3140–41. QUEEN ANNE PLATE, AND ESCUTCHEON. 1690–1730. A. H. EATON, COLLINSVILLE.

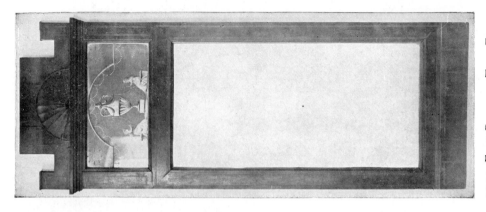

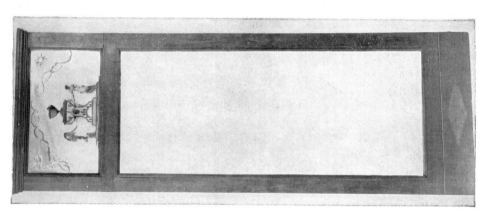

3144. Fine Glass at Top. Frame Inlaid. 18 x 49. Salem. 1790. Flaydfrman & Kaufman.

3143. Daintily Cut Glass. Frame Inlaid. 21½ x 60. 1780–90. Flayderman & Kaufman.

3142. All Continental. Perhaps German. Inlay and Cut Glass. 17 x 44. 1780–90. John H. Buck.

3147. Border Inlay. Conch-Shell. Mahogany Veneer. 20½ x 57¼. W. B. Goodwin.

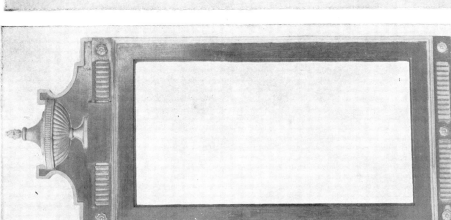

3146A. Gilded Carvings. 26 x 62. Providence. Flayderman & Kaufman.

3146. Well-Shaped Top. Applied Gilded Carving. Mahogany. 17½ x 49. 1780–90. Flayderman & Kaufman.

3145. Inlaid Urn with Flowers and Diamond Inlay Below. 1780–90. John H. Buck.

3148. From Brooks Reed, Boston.

Here begin the courting glasses. They are so-called because they were carried in a shallow box with a cover when ladies went out calling. At the last moment they effected any necessary repairs to their countenances by inspecting themselves in the courting glasses. Their date is about 1800, and, like most glasses, they were brought from foreign parts, probably in the first place from China. The greater part of them are somewhat crude in workmanship. The frames are formed of glass decorated in the Chinese manner, or in other fashions which do not at all suggest that origin. Most of them are small and appropriate for carrying about. Occasionally one like that above is of pretty large size. It would seem that the fancy for them called for a size now and then proper for hanging on the wall.

3149. Unusual Courting Glass in that the Frame Is Mostly Molded. 18th Century.
William F. Hubbard.

3150. (Right.) The Glass at the Top Is Masked. 18 x 26. John H. Buck, Hartford.

3151. Glass in Original Box, Cover Removed. This and the Following, William B. Goodwin.

3152. (Right.) Peregrine White Glass. 7 x 9¼. Pedigree on Back. Peregrine Died
1704. Pedigree Indicates Glass Belonged to His Parents.

3153. Architectural Glass with Doubled Columns. 1800–20. Sanderson Collection.
3154. (Right.) Well Painted and Harmonious. The Art of Painting on Glass Persists. C. P. Cooley.

3155–57. Glasses Owned by Katrina Kipper. Those at the Sides Follow the Conventional Courting Glasses in Design. Center: A Dear Little Piece, Resembling Cape Cod Glasses.

3158. The Usual Type Which Indicates the Close Holding to a Copy. Perhaps Because of Chinese Habit. 12 x 16. John H. Buck.

3159. (Middle.) Beginning the Class of Convex Glasses, Otherwise Called Grandole. It Belonged to the End of the 18th Century, and It Is Said Was Designed so that a Hostess Could Take in at a Glance All That Was Occurring in a Room Full of Guests. Thorp's Antique Shop, Plainfield, New Jersey.

3160. (Right.) Courting Glass in Original Box. The Cover Was Attached by Small Hooks. Estate of Harry W. Weeks.

3161–63. GLASSES AS ARRANGED ON THE WALL OF MRS. CHARLES P. COOLEY, HARTFORD. THOSE AT THE SIDE ARE ITALIAN, AND STRONGLY DECORATIVE. THE CENTER GLASS IS A GIRANDOLE WITH EAGLE. CENTER, 1800. SIDES, 1750–75.

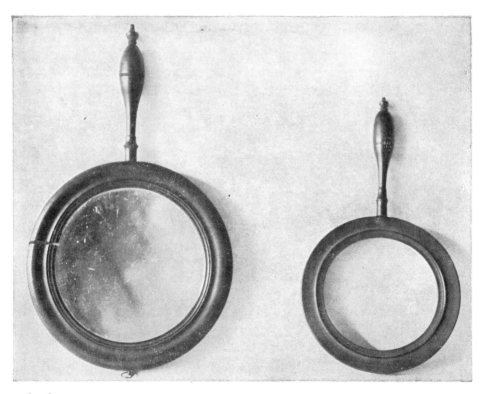

3164–65. BEAUTIFUL LITTLE HAND GLASSES, IN ONE OF WHICH THE GLASS IS CURVED. POSSIBLY THE ATTACHMENT SEEMED FRAGILE, OTHERWISE WE WONDER THAT THE STYLE WAS NOT POPULAR. WILLIAM F. HUBBARD.

3166. A Very Large and Ornate Girandole. St. George and the Dragon. The Sconces Afforded Good Light, Since It Was Radiated at Many Angles. c. 1800. Francis Hill Bigelow.

3167. An Elaborate Glass with Four Sconces Carrying Crystals. Decoration with a Grapevine. Eagle Above and Foliage Below. One Sees Here the Same Balls as in the Architectural Glasses. Rhode Island School of Design.

3168. (Right.) Elaborate and Unusual Glass with Rests for Lights Arranged in an Irregular Form. The Misses A. and E. P. Foster.

3169 and 3171. THE TWO GLASSES, ONE ON EITHER SIDE OF THIS PAGE, ARE A PAIR, BUT THE EAGLES ARE DIFFERENTLY POISED FOR VARIETY'S SAKE. WIRED SCONCES, GILDED. THESE GRANDOLES ARE COMMONLY GILDED. C. R. MORSON, NEW YORK.

3170. (Center.) AN EXAMPLE WITH FOUR SPIRALED SCONCES. THE INCLUSIVE REFLECTION, ALL IN FOCUS, INDICATES THE ADVANTAGE OF THE STYLE. FLAMBOYANT FOLIAGE. CHARLES P. COOLEY.

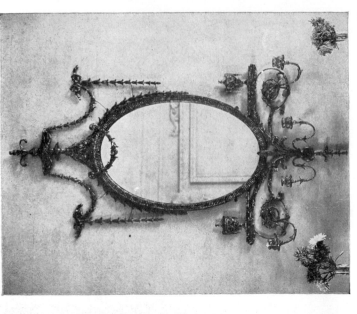

3172. A Four-Sconce Girandole with Foliage Scrolls on the Sconces, and Urns of Flowers on Either Side of the Boldly Carved Eagle. Reeded Black Border Next the Glass. H. H. Valentine Company, Richmond.

3173. (Middle.) Beginning a Class of Glasses of the Hepplewhite Period, Specifically Designated Filigree. Wired Carvings above the Oval Glass, Topped by Three Carved Feathers. English. C. R. Morson.

3174. (Right.) A Glass upon Which the Maker Expended No Little Ingenuity. Four Sconces, Two Good Urns above Them, Surmounted by Large Urns and Festoons.

3175. A High Spike Rising from the Top to a Broad Canopy with Wheat Ears. 1780–90. Katrina Kipper.

3176. (Right.) A Shield-Shaped Glass with Vase, Floral Scrolls, and Sconces. 1780–90. Morris Berry.

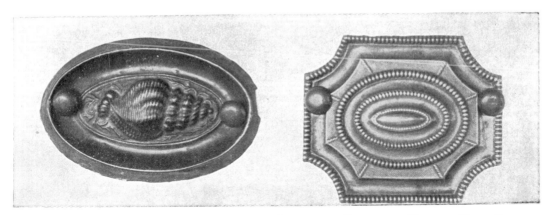

3177–78. A Good Snail Shell Brass, and a Brass with Band upon Band of Pearl-Shaped Ornaments. 1790–1800. A. H. Eaton.

3179–80. Two Glasses from Katrina Kipper, Accord. Such Pieces Are Not Meant To Be Moved Once They Are Placed on the Wall. They Are Most Effective against a Plain Wood or Paper Panel. 1780–90.

3181–82. A Pair of Drapery Holders, 19th C. F. A. Robart.

3183. A Panel or Mantel Glass with Very Sketchy Decoration of Wheat Ears and Festoons. Webb House, Colonial Dames, Wethersfield, Connecticut.

3184. An Unusual Horizontal Glass for Mantel. Three Part, the End Sections Being Cut. Mid 18th Century. Katrina Kipper.

3185-86. Stamped Brass Drapery Hooks. 19th Century. F. A. Robart.

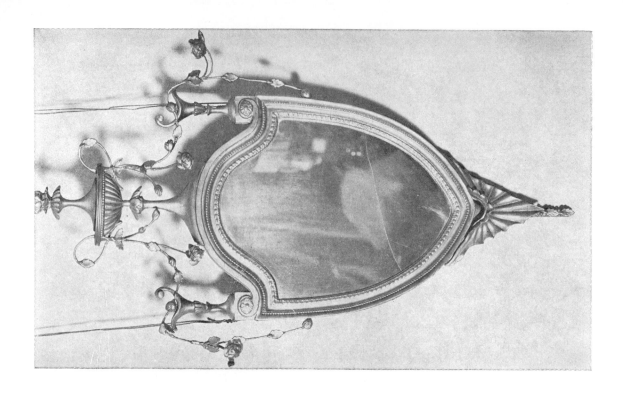

3187 and 3188. (Opposite, left.) 3187 Has Grapevine Decoration with a Knotted Cord and Tassel, Urn and Artichokes. Samuel Wineck, Hartford. 3188. (Opposite, right.) A Shield Glass with Pitchers and Urn Connected by Wired Traceries. 1780–90. John H. Buck.

3189–90. American Glasses, Late 18th Century. Carved, Gilt with Sconces. Metropolitan Museum.

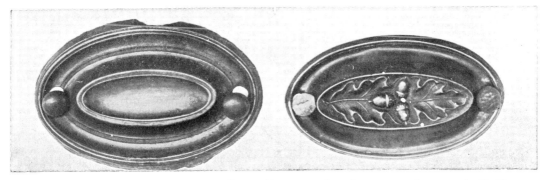

3191–92. Brasses of 1790–1800, the Right Being an Oak Leaf with Acorns. A. H. Eaton.

3193. HEPPLEWHITE, 1780. GILDED, AS ALWAYS. 19⅜ x 32⅜. ROBERT T. SMITH, HARTFORD.
3194. (Right.) PHEASANTS SUSTAINING FESTOONS FROM AN URN. CUPID BELOW. SHELVES AND SCONCES.
HEIGHT 45 INCHES. 1780–90. MISSES A. AND E. P. FOSTER.

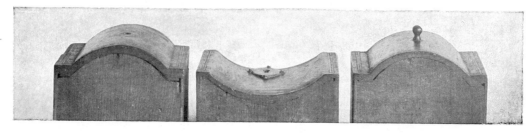

3195–97. DETAIL TO SHOW EDGE OF DRAWERS ON QUEEN ANNE GLASS, NO. 3205.

3198. Queen Anne Glass, Pine. 17 x 12 x 8. Salem. 1740–60. Flayderman & Kaufman.
3199. Queen Anne Glass, with a Curved Base in the Drawers, and Dainty Finials. 1750–70.

3200. A Piece Called by the Owner a Fire Screen, but of about the Height of a Dressing Glass and Obviously Usable for That Purpose. English. 30 x 25. Mahogany. 1780–1800. Inlaid.
3201. (Right.) Another English Glass. Walnut. 22 x 42. All Original. 1730–50.
Both, Mrs. Francis P. Garvan.

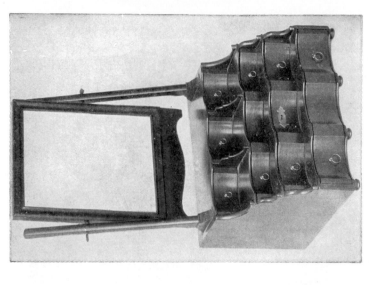

3202. Shaving Glass, Original Condition. 18 x 12 x 7. Mahogany. Connecticut. Very Good Lines. 1750–75. Robert P. Butler.

3203. (Center.) American Empire, Mahogany. Connecticut. c. 1825. H. W. Erving.

3204. (Right.) Shaving Glass with Four Tiers of Drawers, All Concave with Flat Connection. All These Drawers Have Precisely the Same Contour as the Concave Central Drawer in the Next Piece. 1750–70. Frank A. Robart.

3205. (Opposite.) Most Remarkable Shaving Glass. A Recent Find. A Walnut Block Front. The Wood Is Light in Color, like the New England White Walnut. Pine Is Used in the Back and Bottom of the Stand, and Bottom and Three Sides of the Drawers, and Back and Frame of the Glass Itself. The Top and the Front as Well as the Crest Are Crotch Walnut. 6 x 20 x 28. This Piece Indicates Very Early Use of the Block Front, at Least in This Arc Form. Probably Before 1750. A Delightful and Important Piece. Rhode Island. William B. Goodwin.

3206. (Opposite, right.) Kettle Base Glass. Pierced Circle with Ornament, like Chippendale Glass. 1750–75. "Antiques," March, 1923.

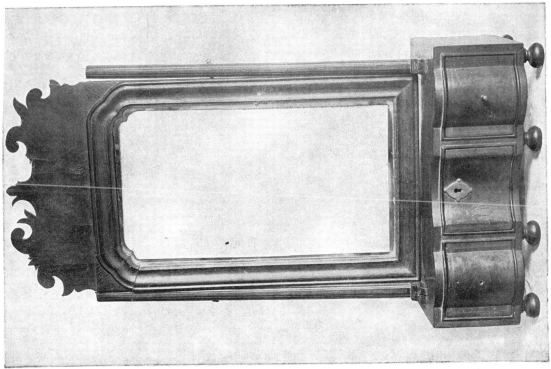

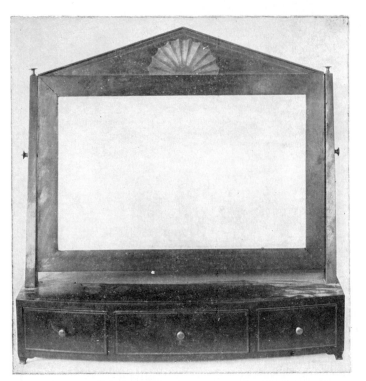

3207. SHAVING GLASS, MAHOGANY, HEPPLEWHITE. INLAID FAN. 21½ x 21. 1780–90. FLAYDERMAN & KAUFMAN.
3208. (Right.) MAHOGANY, INLAID. 1790–1800. JAMES DAVIDSON.

3209. AMERICAN HEPPLEWHITE, MAHOGANY. SLIGHT INLAY. OPALESCENT GLASS KNOBS. SILVER
TRIMMINGS. GLASS 16 x 20. c. 1800. H. W. ERVING.
3210. (Right.) AMERICAN MAHOGANY GLASS, 17 INCHES LONG. SPIRAL CARVED POSTS, AND FINIALS.
KETTLE BASE. FRONT AND ENDS CUT FROM THE SOLID. 1790–1800. H. W. ERVING.

3211. MAHOGANY AND SATINWOOD. AMERICAN. c. 1800. H. V. WEIL, NEW YORK.

These glasses are indiscriminately named shaving glass, toilet glass, also glass with a box. The earliest are in the Queen Anne time, and the latest are degraded Empire.

3212-13. TWO GLASSES, THE FORMER DATING ABOUT 1820, AND THE LATTER ABOUT 1800. MORRIS BERRY.

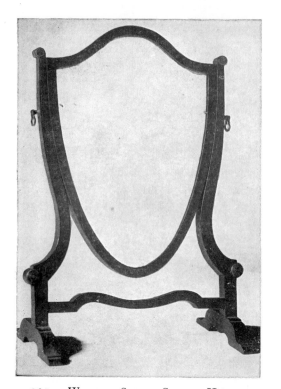

3214. WALNUT, SHIELD SHAPE. HEPPLEWHITE. HEIGHT 16½ INCHES. TRESTLE FEET. IVORY
ROSETTES. STRING INLAY. 1785–95. H. W. ERVING.

3215. (Right.) OVAL, HEPPLEWHITE. THESE STANDARDS LEAN BACKWARD. 1790. SAMUEL WINECK.

3216. DAINTY SIDE SUPPORT. MAHOGANY. 24 x 21. NEW HAMPSHIRE. 1810–20. RUDOLPH P. PAULY.

3217. (Right.) REEDED. IVORY KNOBS. SMALL SPINDLE GALLERIES. 1820–30. FLAYDERMAN & KAUFMAN.

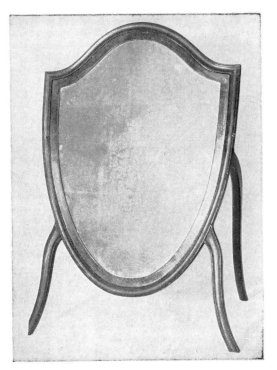

3218. Only Glass Shown without a Base, Suggests the Back of a Hepplewhite Chair. Braces Behind. 1790. Mrs. Francis P. Garvan.

3219. (Right.) Oval. Serpentine Drawers. Ivory Buttons. 1800. Morris Berry.

3220. Mahogany, Reeded Posts, String Inlay. Embossed Brass Knobs and Feet. New York State. Sheraton Type. c. 1800. H. W. Erving.

3221. (Right.) Mahogany, Line Inlay. Connecticut. c. 1800. James Davidson.

JOHN ELLIOTT,
At his LOOKING-GLASS STORE,
the Sign of the *Bell* and *Looking-glass*, in *Walnut-street*, PHILADELPHIA,
IMPORTS and SELLS all Sorts of *English* Looking-glasses, at the lowest Rates.
He also new Quicksilvers and Frames old Glasses, and supplies People with new Glass to their own Frames.

Johannes Elliott,
In seinem Waarenlager (oder Store) wo die Glocke und der Spiegel aushängt, in der Walinuß-strasse, zu Philadelphia,
Hat jederzeit einen grossen Vorrath von allerley Englischen Spiegeln, welche er herein bringen lässet, und um den wohlfeilsten Preis verkauft.
Er macht auch neu Queckfilber an alte Gläser, und setzt sie in neue Rahmen, versiehet auch die Leute mit neuen Gläsern zu ihren eigenen Rahmen.

3222. A LABEL ON THE BACK OF A QUEEN ANNE GLASS.
J. STOGDELL STOKES.

3223. THE WOOL SPINNING WHEEL. OPERATED BY FINGER OR SPINNING STICK.

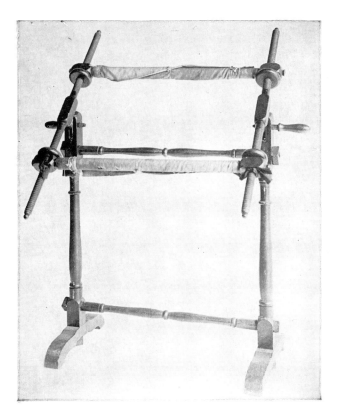

3224. EMBROIDERY FRAME, ADJUSTABLE. 18TH CENTURY. EDWARD C. WHEELER, JR.

3225. (Right.) YARN REEL, WITH CLICKING COUNTER. 18TH CENTURY. WADSWORTH ATHENEUM.

3226. A REEL WHICH REGISTERS THE REVOLUTIONS AND SO MEASURES THE YARN.

3227-28. (Right.) BOBBIN WHEEL AND CARD. THE WHEEL WAS TO PREPARE THE YARN FOR THE LOOM. THE CARD WAS TO PREPARE THE WOOL FOR SPINNING.

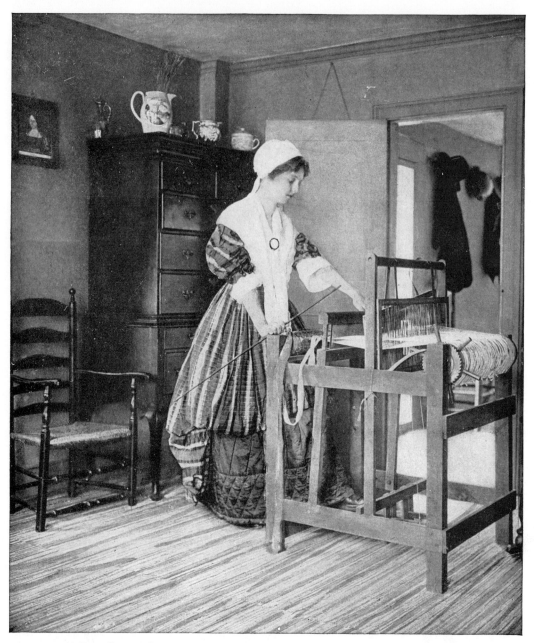

3229–32. A Rag-Carpet Loom in Operation. The Lady Is Wearing One of the Marvelous Old Silk Quilted Petticoats. On Top of Highboy: Washington and Silver Luster Pitcher.

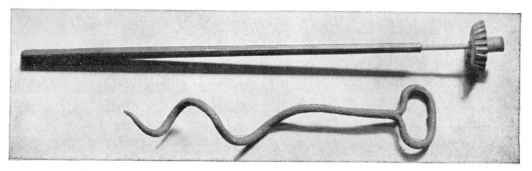

3233–34. A Candle Torch, and a Twisted Article No Longer Used. Fuessenich Collection.

3235. Spinning Jenny or Flax Wheel. Hank of Flax Ready for Spinning.
3236. (Right.) Reel with Adjustable Arms for Shorter Skeins.

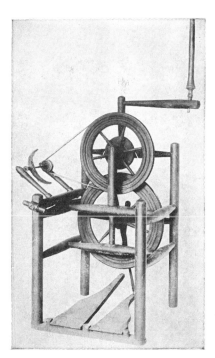

3237. A Double Jenny for Spinning Two Yarns at Once. 3238. Adjustable, Vertical Wheel.
3239. A Jenny of the Connecticut Chair-Frame Type. Adjustment for Tightening Belt.
All: Wadsworth Atheneum.

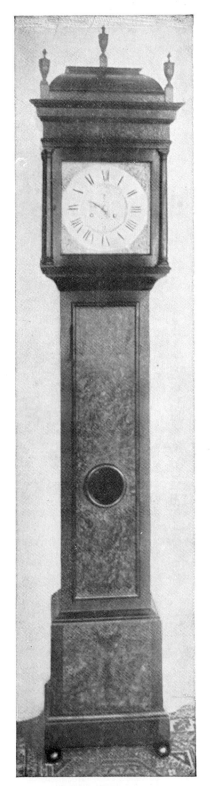 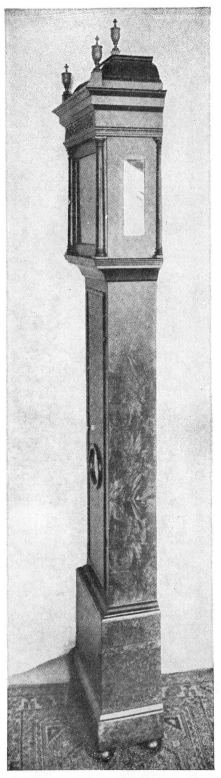

3240. By Benjamin Bagnall, Charlestown, Massachusetts. Burl Veneer on Pine.
c. 1730. One of the Earliest Makers. John M. Miller, Providence.

3241. (Right.) Side View of the Same. Ball Feet. English Influence.

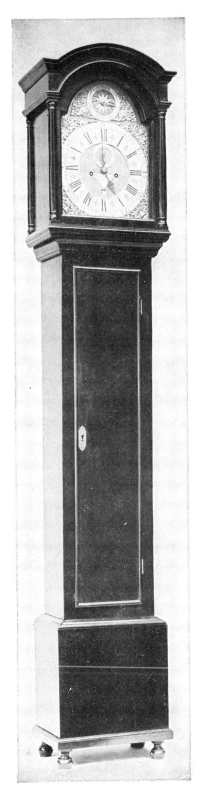
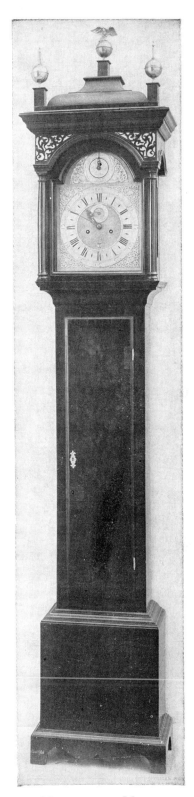

3242. SAMUEL BAGNALL, BOSTON, 1740–60. MAHOGANY. METROPOLITAN MUSEUM.
3243. (Right.) BENJAMIN BAGNALL, BOSTON, 1725–50. WALNUT ON PINE. BEAUTIFUL
FRETS, METROPOLITAN MUSEUM.

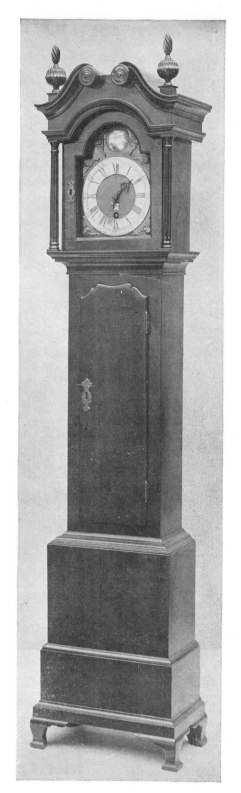

3244. THOMAS CLAGGETT, NEWPORT. 1730–49. MINIATURE, MAHOGANY. METROPOLITAN MUSEUM.
3245. (Right.) WILLIAM CLAGGETT, NEWPORT. 1730–49. CHINESE LACQUER. WALTER H. DURFEE.

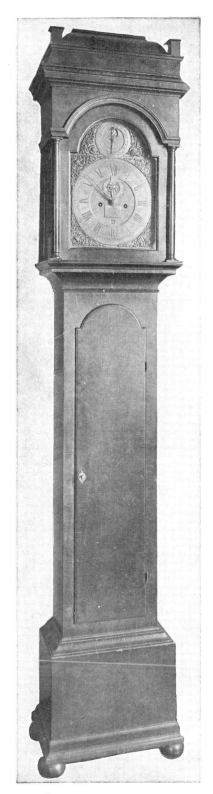
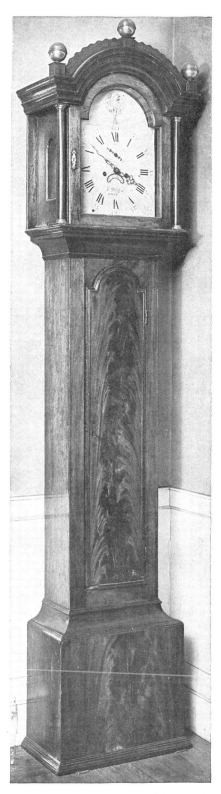

3246. W. Claggett, Newport, 1730–49. Mrs. Stanley Bristol, Newport.
3247. (Right.) "E. Willard Fecit," 1777–1805. Rare. Bigelow Collection.

3248. WILLIAM CLAGGETT DIAL. HE MADE THE BEST. NAME SPELLED HERE WITH T DOUBLED. IN NEXT NUMBER SPELLED WITH ONE T. NOTHING LIKE VARIETY! HEIRS OF WILLIAM G. RUSSELL, LATE OF PROVIDENCE.

3249. WILLIAM CLAGGETT DIAL. CLOCK BURIED AT KINGSTON, R. I., DURING THE REVOLUTION.
G. WINTHROP BROWN, BOSTON, 1730-49.

3250. By Contrast There Is Shown Above a Fromanteel & Clarke. 1710. Name on Outside Edge of Circle. Below on Dial, A. Fromanteel. One of Best Early English. Rhode Island School of Design.

3251-52. Oval and Round Brasses, General Washington. Quite Dissimilar. Bigelow Collection.

3253. E. Willard Dial. Brass; Iron Painted Top, "Boston Light." Important. Clocks of Ephraim Willard Were Rare. Usually Dials Were Painted White on Iron. The Brass Is Better but Not So Legible. W. G. A. Turner, Malden, Massachusetts.

The purpose of the tall clock was to protect the long pendulum. When the short pendulum applied to Willard clocks came in tall clocks soon went out of fashion. But so great is their decorative and sentimental value that a generation ago they again became popular. The ancient short pendulum clock of the 17th century was not a good timekeeper.

3254. FROMANTEEL DIAL. MARSDEN J. PERRY, PROVIDENCE.

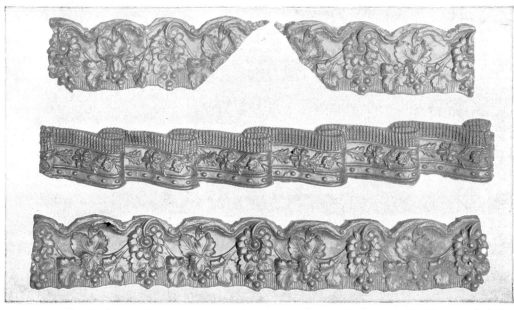

3255-58. BRASS CORNICES FOR WINDOWS. 19TH CENTURY. FRANK A. ROBART.

3259. S. Taber. His Date and Place are Uncertain. S. M. Taber Is Traced to Providence in 1824. Mahogany, Inlaid. 1800–10. Leonard M. Robinson, Providence.

3260. (Right.) Benjamin Willard, Grafton, 1743–1803. Mahogany. c. 1790. Brass Band around Columns Halfway Up. W. L. Mulligan, Springfield.

DIRECTIONS FOR PUTTING UP THE TIMEPIECE.

Drive a brad in the wall where it is to be placed and Suspend the Time piece upon it. Open the lower Door which is unfastened by turning the button a little forward with the key. Loosen the pendulum by which the Timepiece may be plumbed, observing that it hangs free of the case and in a line with the point where it was confined, then screw it to the wall with two screws thro' the back. Put the pendulum in motion. The weight is already wound up. Set it with the minute hand which may be moved backwards or forwards. To make the Timepiece go faster raise the pendulum ball by the screw at the bottom, to make it go slower, lower the ball with the same screw.

These Timepieces are an improvement upon all others, as they go by Weight instead of a Spring, and the pendulum being of a longer calculation than in any other small Pieces, renders it more accurate and has proved to keep better time. The President of the United States having granted a Patent for them, they are made by licence from the Patintee by Aaron Willard Junr. Washington St. Boston! near Roxbury. MASSACHUSETTS.

3261. AARON WILLARD, JUNIOR'S, LABEL.

3262. NEEDLEWORK PICTURE, 21 x 42, IN EARLY FRAME. FRANCIS H. BIGELOW.

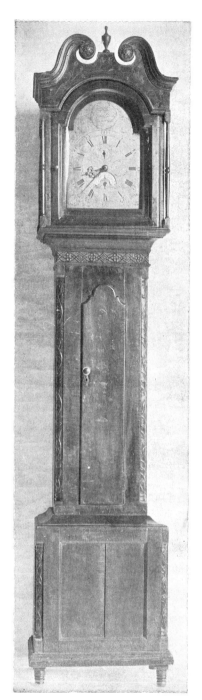

3263. A Block Front with Shell. Scrolled Top, Fretwork and Fine Fluted and Spiraled
Finials. 1760–75.

3264. (Right.) Curly Maple, Connecticut. 84 x 22½ x 12. Asahel Cheney, East Hartford. He
Was Known To Be in Northfield in 1790, but This Clock Is Earlier. Carved Quarter Columns.
Inlaid Spandrels. Both: Mrs. Francis P. Garvan.

A considerable number of block clocks is known. The writer has tallied seven, and has heard of others.
So far as traced they go back to Newport or Providence. They were undoubtedly made by John Goddard
or his father-in-law, Job Townsend. The blocking and the shell are precisely like those found on his secretaries. The same motive is in the hood. They prove that the fret was used on American pieces. It should
be observed that the pillars are not as attenuated as in most clocks. Also that in this fine early period, no
brasses were used for the bases or capitals of pillars, nor for top ornaments. All is in wood. In these clocks
the case is far more important than the works.

3265. (Opposite.) Block and Shell, Stop Flute Quarter Columns, All Wood Including Ornaments. Works by William Tomlinson, London. Before 1760. Metropolitan Museum.

3266. (Right, opposite.) Cherry and Pine, Satinwood Inlay. 111 x 20½ x 11½. Was Capt. Thomas Marshall's, Washington, Kentucky, Son of Col. Thomas of the Same Place and Virginia, and Brother of Chief Justice Marshall. Large Survival about Cincinnati of Cherry, and Inlays of Veneer, Satinwood, Bird's Eye Birch, in Desks, Sideboards, Et Cetera. Weights Left Behind in Virginia. 1775–1810. William B. Goodwin.

3267. (Above.) Beautifully Inlaid and Cross-Band Veneered. Eli Porter, Williamstown, Massachusetts.

3268. (Right.) Mahogany, No Name. 96 x 19 x 10. c. 1790. Mrs. Francis P. Garvan.

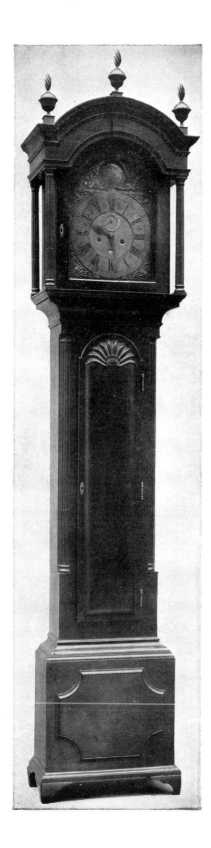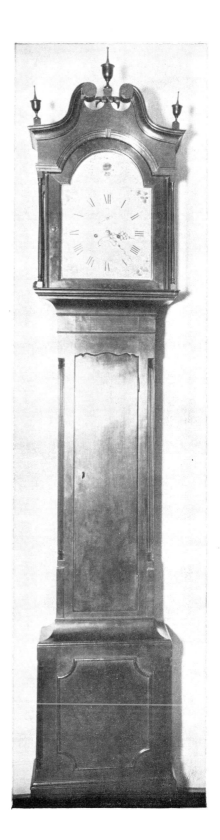

3269. BLOCK FRONT WITH SHELL. JOHN GODDARD. ALL WOOD, NO BRASS ORNAMENTS. NO NAME, AND THE SAME IS TRUE OF SOME OTHER GODDARD CLOCKS. FEET ALWAYS FINE OGEE. 1760-75.
G. W. H. SMITH, PROVIDENCE.

3270. (Right.) BEAUTIFULLY CURLED MAPLE. CLOCKS OF THIS CLASS IN PENNSYLVANIA HAD, USUALLY, TURNED FEET. MADE BY SHEID, PENNSYLVANIA. FRANCIS MIREAU, DOYLESTOWN.

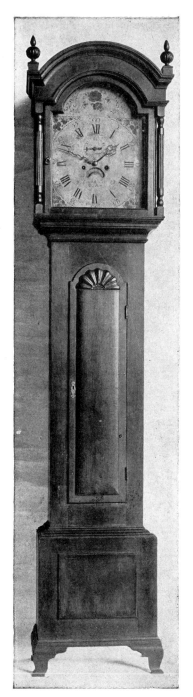

3271. Block Front Shell. Height 84 Inches. Apple Wood. David Williams. 1825, Given as His Date, Is Obviously Too Late. The Shell Is Not Quite Equal to No. 3263, and the Quarter Columns Are Omitted.

3272. (Right.) Very Rare Turned Columns, Repeated on Hood. 1790–1800. Both: Mrs. Francis P. Garvan.

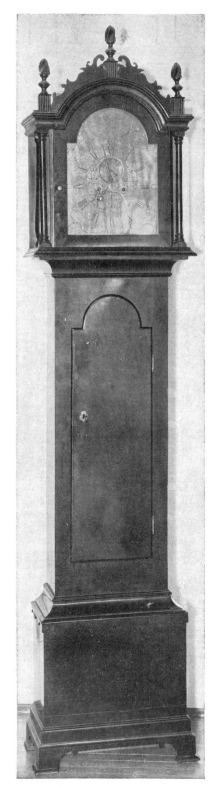
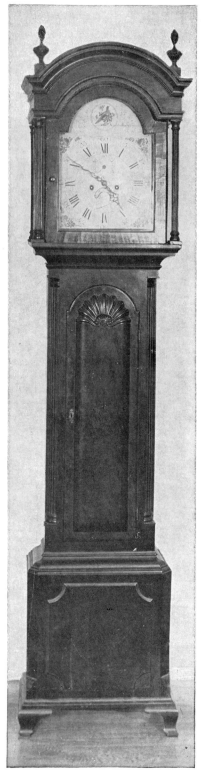

3273. SOLID MAHOGANY. 87 x 18 x 9. BRASS WORKS AND DIAL, ENGRAVED, "TIME FLIES AND DEATH COMES." 1775. BY THOMAS HARLAND, NORWICH, CONNECTICUT. ROBERT T. SMITH, HARTFORD.

3274. (Right.) BLOCK FRONT AND SHELL CASE BY JOHN GODDARD, NEWPORT. CASE VERY SIMILAR TO TOWNSEND'S NO. 3265. WILLIAM H. PUTNAM, HARTFORD.

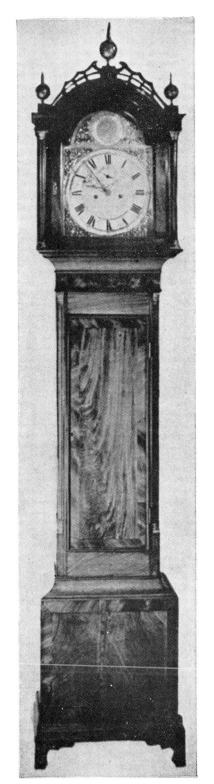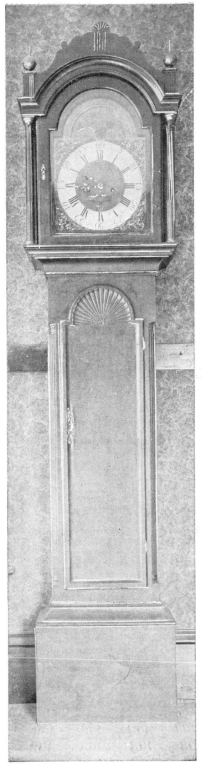

3275. HANDSOME VENEERED CASE. NEW ENGLAND FRET, WITH BRASS BALLS. JOHN H. HALFORD, NORRISTOWN, PENNSYLVANIA.

3276. (Right.) SUNBURST, CONCAVED DOOR. ENOS DOOLITTLE, NEW HAVEN, 1772. OWNED IN PLYMOUTH, MASSACHUSETTS.

3277. (Opposite.) DAVID RITTENHOUSE. OWNED BY DREXEL INSTITUTE AND IN PENNSYLVANIA MUSEUM, PHILADELPHIA. RICHEST AMERICAN CLOCK. CASE OBVIOUSLY MADE IN THE SAVERY TIME, AND IN PHILADELPHIA. THIS CLOCK MECHANICALLY IS A WORK OF GENIUS. OF COURSE, THE CASE, FROM THE NATURE OF THE WORKS, APPEARS TOO BROAD.

3278. (Above.) A DAVID RITTENHOUSE DIAL ON THE GENERAL WAYNE CLOCK. WAYNE'S FIGURE APPEARS DIMLY IN THE BRASS CIRCLE ABOVE. ESTATE OF WILLIAM E. MONTAGUE, NORRISTOWN.

Dav.ᵈ Rittenhouse

3279. David Rittenhouse Was a Great Clock Maker, Astronomer, and Friend. He Shares with Franklin the Features of the Early Ideal American. The Beauty and Quality of His Clocks Are Unsurpassed. He Was a Notable Figure, Politically, Socially, and Mechanically. His Home Was Norriton, from Which Norristown Is Taken.

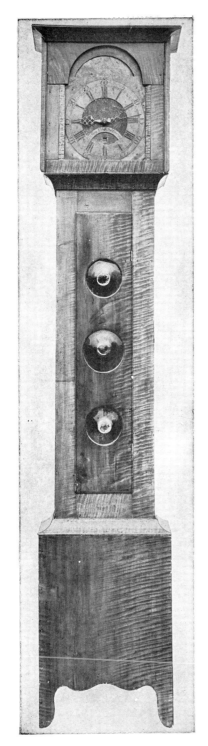
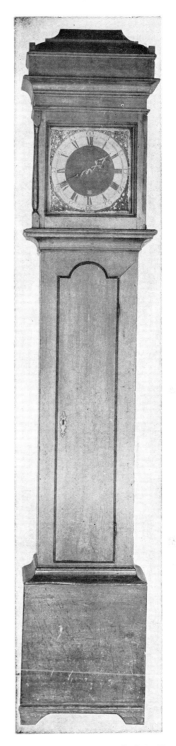

3280. Curly Maple, Three Bull's Eyes in the Door. Plain Top. By Henry G. MolBrow.

3281. (Right.) David Rittenhouse. Case Suggests English Influence. Plain Below. Philip Meredith Allen, Broad Axe, Pennsylvania, Owns Both.

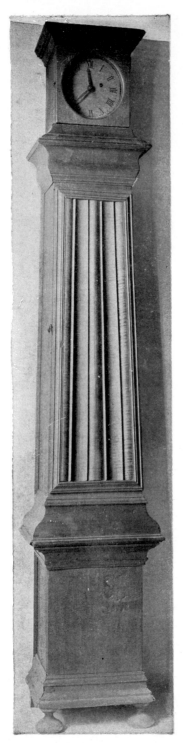

3282. A Rare Pattern like a Monument. Bun Feet, Called in America, Onion Feet. Fuessenich Collection.

3283. (Right.) Unusual Arch with Plain Boss, Finials in Wood.

3284. CARVED BASE OF QUARTER COLUMNS AND FINIALS. DRAPERY UNDER THE HOOD. 1785–1800. MRS. HARRY HORTON BENKARD.

3285. (Right.) CARVED SHELL AND FOLIAGE. REVERSED SPIRAL FLAMES. PLAIN COLUMNS. RICHLY FEATURED GRAIN IN DOOR. W. GEDNEY BEATTY. BOTH AT METROPOLITAN MUSEUM.

3286. By Thomas Harland, Norwich. Good Spiral Flames. Scalloped Mold on Upper Section of Base. Large Ogee Feet. 1773–1807. He Advertised that He Made a Great Variety of Watches and Clocks and Parts "Neat as Is In London, and at the Same Price." Taught Apprentices, among Them, Eli Terry. Wadsworth Atheneum.

3287. (Right.) "S. Willard." Case with Rich Mahogany, Featured, and Inlaid Bands. Fret over Arch, Also Second Fret Immediately over Dial. From E. A. Locke, M.D., Boston.

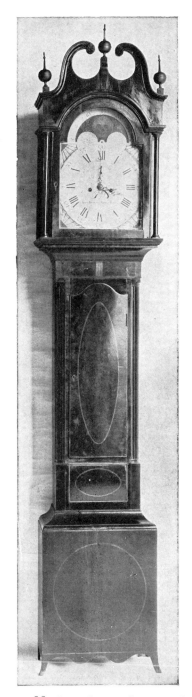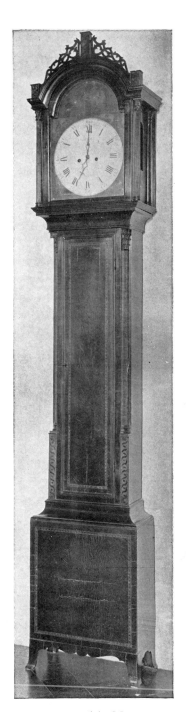

3288. Line Inlay, Slender Arch. Brass Balls. 94 x 19 x 9½. Mahogany.
3289. (Right.) Fine Inlaid Band about Door, Base of Quarter Columns Carved.
By James Doull, Charlestown. Both: Mrs. Francis P. Garvan.

3290. FEATURED GRAIN, CARVED CHAMFER ON BASE. FRET UNDER HOOD, AND OVER ARCH. MRS. FRANCIS P. GARVAN.

3291. (Right.) CARVED DOOR TOP. GOOD LIGHT INLAID SCROLLS IN SPANDREL. BY PETER CLARK, MANCHESTER, ENGLAND. CHARLES P. COOLEY.

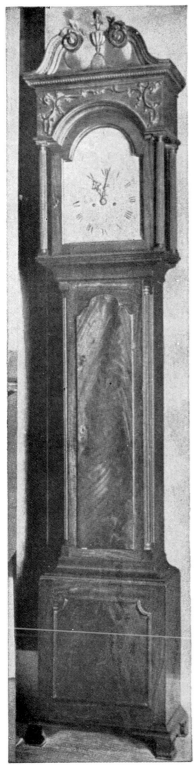

3292. PHILADELPHIA TYPE. BEAUTIFULLY CARVED HOOD WITH DENTILS AND SPIRAL ROSETTES FOLIATED. RICH GRAIN DOOR IN BASE. PENNSYLVANIA MUSEUM, MEMORIAL HALL, PHILADELPHIA.

3293. (Right.) PHILADELPHIA PATTERN, GOOD PIERCED SCROLL WITH DENTILS. MRS. ELLSWORTH SPERRY, EAST WINDSOR HILL, CONNECTICUT.

3294. Daniel Quare, England. c. 1700. He Was a Celebrated Maker. Charles F. Williams Collection, Pennsylvania Museum, Philadelphia.

3295. (Right.) Miniature, Otherwise Called a Grandmother Clock. By J. Wilder, Hingham, 1780–1800. This Maker Specialized on Miniatures. C. Prescott Knight, Providence.

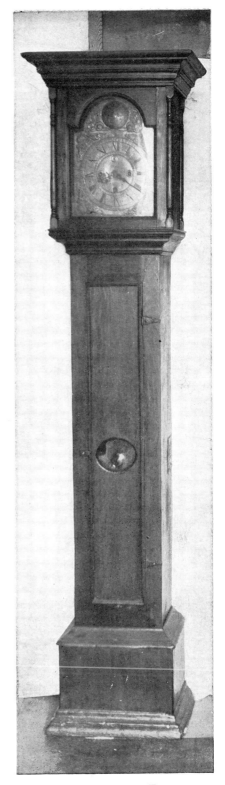

3296. Brass Face, Plain Columns. The Contour of the Hood Is Found in Few English and American Examples. Mrs. Charles P. Cooley, Hartford.

3297. (Right.) Bull's-Eye Door, Engaged Columns Front and Back on Hood, Heavy Cornice. E. S. Macomber, Providence.

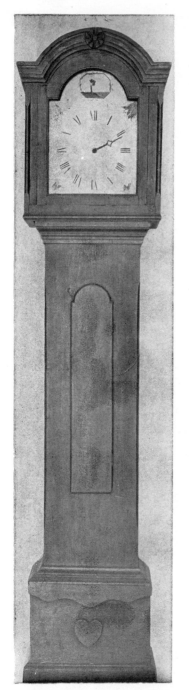  

3298. SIMPLE CASE, APPLIED CARVED HEART IN BASE, CARVED ROSETTE AT CENTER OF ARCH. NATHAN CUSHING, PROVIDENCE.

3299. (Middle.) INLAY ON DOOR AND BASE. REMARKABLE TOP, SQUARE WITH FRETTED GALLERY AND FANS. UNUSUAL HANDS. FOUND BY THE AUTHOR IN PORTSMOUTH. c. 1800.

3300. (Right.) APPLIED HALF SPINDLE, SPOOL TURNED. CARVED ROSETTES. FOUR STAR INLAY. CHERRY AND SATINWOOD, AND MAHOGANY TRIM. BY JACOB COPE, PENNSYLVANIA. NAME ENGRAVED ON PENDULUM. COPE IS AN ENGLISH NAME. THE CASE IS UNDOUBTEDLY AMERICAN. VERY SLENDER WAIST. MALCOLM A. NORTON.

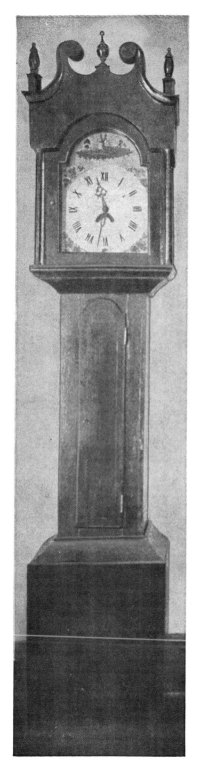

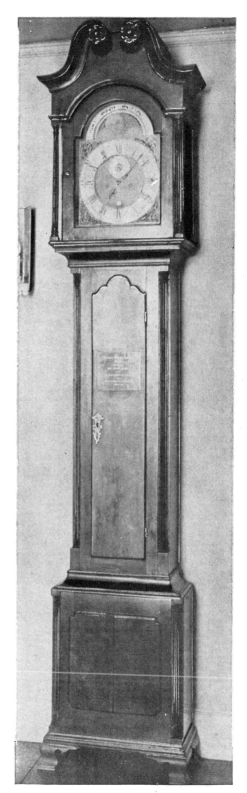

3301. GRANDMOTHER'S CLOCK WITH SHARP RAMP. 1780–1800.

3302. (Right.) COL. WILLIAM TRENT CLOCK, OLD BARRACKS, TRENTON. BY JOHN WOOD, PHILADELPHIA.

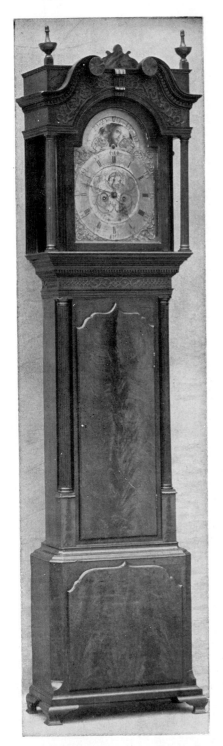

3303. SOLID MAHOGANY. FRONT BEAUTIFULLY MARKED CROTCH. FRET AND DENTIL UNDER HOOD AND OVER ARCH. URNS CARVED, WORKS BRASS. BY BARKER WIGAN. H. C. VALENTINE & COMPANY.

3304. (Right.) BY THOMAS HARLAND, NORWICH. C. 1790. BRASS FACE ON WHICH ARE THE NAME AND PLACE. WILLIAM H. PUTNAM, HARTFORD.

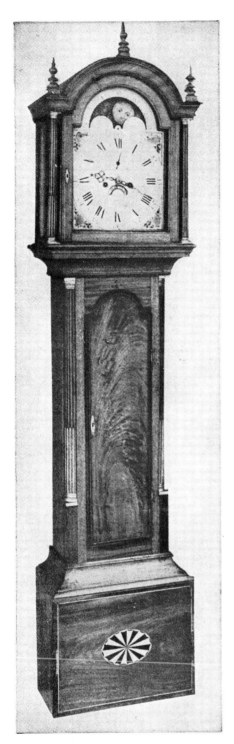

3305. By William Cummens. c. 1825. Flute Stopped with Brass. Crotch Grain Mahogany on Door and Inlaid Patera Below. D. J. Steele, East Milton, Massachusetts.

3306. (Right.) A Dry-Battery Electric Clock, Essex Institute, Salem, Massachusetts.

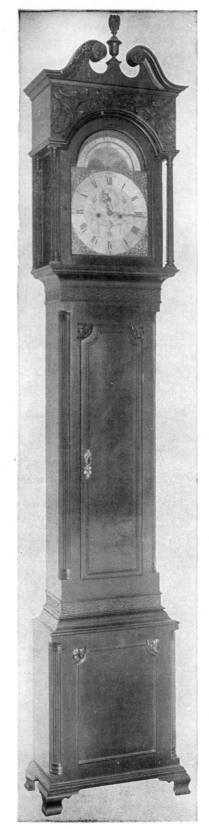

3307. ARCH UNUSUALLY OPEN. VERY LIGHT SPINDLING COLUMNS. PAGODAED FINIALS. ESTATE OF WM. E. MONTAGUE.

3308. (Middle.) QUARTER COLUMN IN BASE AND ON WAIST. RHODE ISLAND SCHOOL OF DESIGN.

3309. (Right.) BY DAVID RITTENHOUSE. EARLY. MARKEDLY SIMPLE AND NARROW. ESTATE OF WM. E. MONTAGUE.

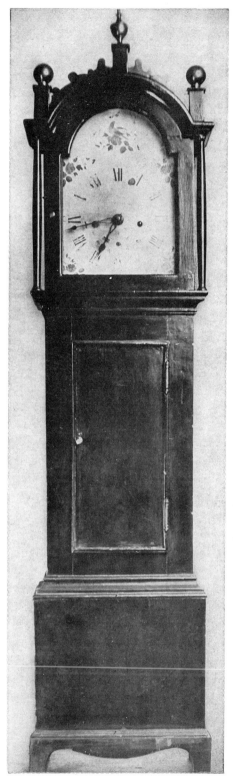

3310. By Henry Flower, Philadelphia. Fine Cabinet Work. Flying Finials.
Mrs. C. Wheaton Vaughn.

3311. (Right.) Miniature, 48 Inches High. Essex Institute. Too Large in Waist!

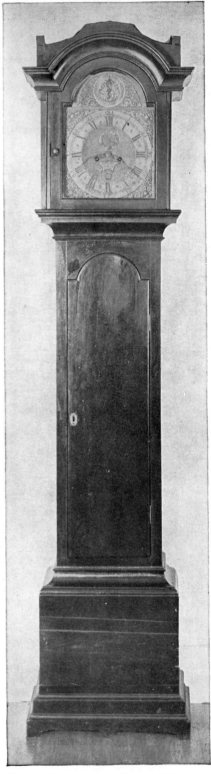

3312. ENGLISH CLOCK WITH PEDIMENT CLOSED. CARVED PENDANTS. GREEK MOLD ON ARCH. CARVED MODILLION. I. SACK, FROM PALMER COLLECTION.

3313. (Right.) BY GAWEN BROWN, OF JAMES STREET, BOSTON, 1750–76, BUT BY RECORD WAS IN BROOKLYN, CONNECTICUT, IN 1742.

3314. The Dial: "Preserved Clapp, New England." Dials Printed from Engravings. Essex Institute, Salem.

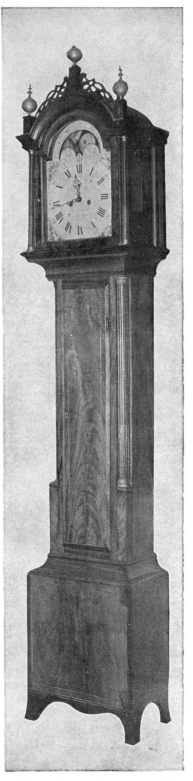

3315. David Rittenhouse, Twenty-Four Hour. The Shell and Door Almost Approach a Block.
John H. Halford, Norristown.

3316. (Right.) Simon Willard, Inlaid Mahogany. 94½ x 19 x 10. Bigelow Collection.
Sometimes Rear Columns on Hood Were Engaged, Sometimes Omitted Entirely.

3317–18. MINIATURE OR GRANDMOTHER CLOCKS, OWNED BY MRS. M. B. COOKEROW, POTTSTOWN, PENNSYLVANIA. THAT AT THE LEFT HAS NO NAME. THAT AT THE RIGHT READS "HY. BOWER." THEY ARE PROBABLY BOTH PENNSYLVANIA CLOCKS. LIKE THE GRANDMOTHER CLOCKS MADE IN PENNSYLVANIA, THEY HAVE A SMALL WAIST, GOOD DIALS WITH A SHIP MOTION, OR OTHER GOOD FEATURES. THE HOODS ARE ARTISTIC, BUT THE FEET ARE NOT ATTRACTIVE.

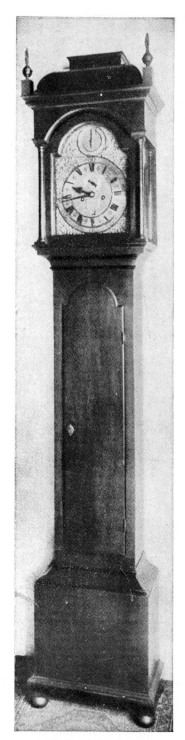 

3319. WILLIAM CLAGGETT, 1730–49, NEWPORT. MAHOGANY. RHODE ISLAND HISTORICAL SOCIETY,
PROVIDENCE.

3320. (Right.) JOSHUA WILDER, HINGHAM, MASSACHUSETTS. C. 1790. PINE. TIME AND ALARM.
THE SHIELD CORNERS ON DIAL ARE COMMON IN HIS CLOCKS. MINIATURE. C. PRESCOTT KNIGHT,
PROVIDENCE.

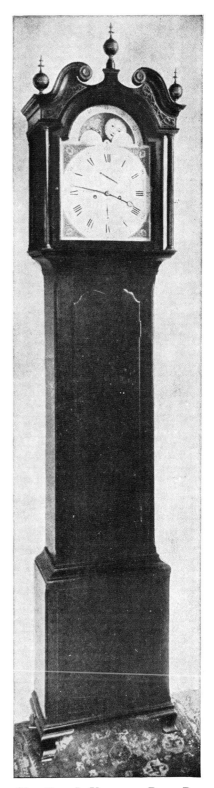

3321. David Williams, Newport. 1800–10. Mahogany. The Fret Is Unusual. Brass Bases
and Capitals and Finials. Dr. Emory M. Porter, Providence.

3322. (Right.) Caleb Wheaton, Providence. c. 1800. Mahogany with Fret on Bonnet.
Mrs. Guy Metcalf Keating, Pinehurst, North Carolina.

3323. By Nathan Edwards, Acton, Massachusetts. Mahogany. Height 88 Inches. Hood 18½ Inches Wide. Waist 17⅝ Inches. Base 17¾ Inches. Warren W. Creamer, Waldoboro, Maine.

3324. (Middle.) Zebra Grain Curly Maple; Spiraled Columns on Hood. Rosettes at Crest of Arch. Unusual Finials. Preston, England. Mrs. Francis P. Garvan.

3325. (Right.) Aaron Willard, Roxbury. Mahogany with Inlay. 76 x 18½. On Back of Dial in White Enamel: "By William Prescott," Who Was a Decorator. Warren W. Creamer.

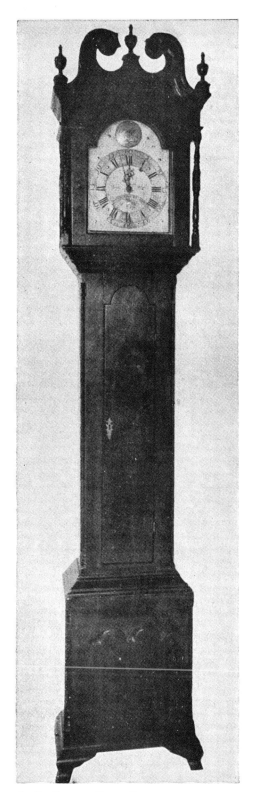

3326. By Daniel Rose, Reading, Pennsylvania. 1820–40. Mrs. M. B. Cookerow, Pottstown.
3327. (Right.) "Richard Simestree, Birmingham." Mahogany, Brass Mounts. Brass Dial with Cast Cherub Spandrels. On Boss, a Flying Mercury. 95 x 21 x 11½. See Britten, p. 745.

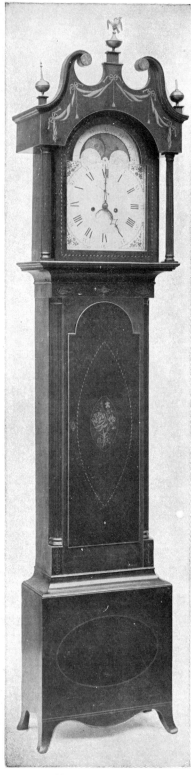

3328. LIGHTHOUSE CLOCK. ROSENBACH COMPANY, PHILADELPHIA. THESE ARE NOW MUCH SOUGHT FOR.

3329. (Right.) MAHOGANY WITH MARQUETRY, CONNECTICUT. c. 1803. METROPOLITAN MUSEUM, NEW YORK.

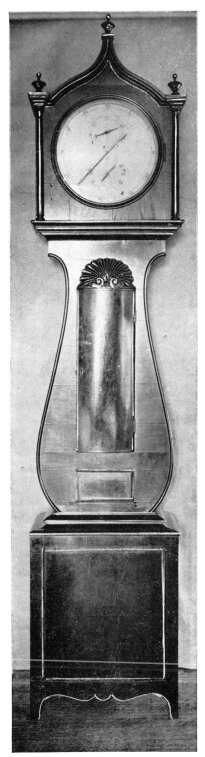

3330. PENNSYLVANIA. A TRUE BLOCK SHELL. BOMBÉ CENTER. GOTHIC ARCH TOP.
ESTATE OF WILLIAM E. MONTAGUE, NORRISTOWN.

3331. (Right.) "BENJAMIN RITTENHOUSE, WORCESTER, FECIT." QUARTER COLUMNS.
CARVED ROSETTES.

3332. "D. H. Salliday, Sy. Town." Glass in Door Not Original. Small Waist, Chamfered. Estate of William E. Montague.

3333. (Right.) David Rittenhouse. It Is Obvious that His Cases Were Made by Different Persons. This Clock Once Sold for Twenty Cents. Same Owner.

3334. By Timothy Chandler, Concord, N. H., c. 1800. Unusual Urn Finials. Essex Institute Salem.

3335. (Right.) By Hoadley, Plymouth, Connecticut. Numerous and Simple Clocks by This Maker. Essex Institute, Salem, Massachusetts.

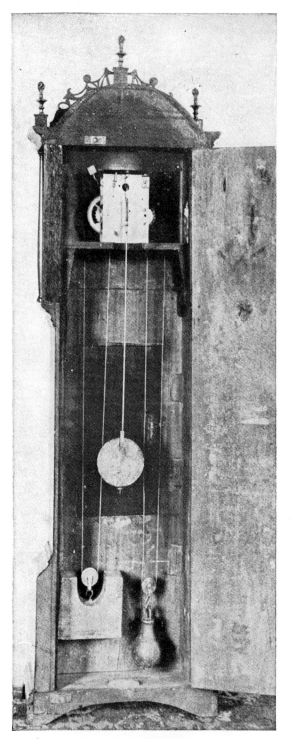

3336. To Show the Movement, Time, and Alarm Weight of Miniature; Joshua Wilder. They Mostly Have a Door in the Back, Running Full Length as Here. C. Prescott Knight, Providence.

3337. (Right.) By Simon Willard. Self Clock Invented by Him. Attractive Case, as of One Piece Imposed on Another. Clarence H. Allen, Portland, Maine.

3338. WATCHMAN'S CLOCK, ANCHOR ESCAPEMENT. BY AARON WILLARD. ESSEX INSTITUTE, SALEM.

3339. (Right.) ENGLISH STYLE, WITH PANELS. SPIRALED PILLARS. BRASS CAPITALS. FRET UNDER CORNICE.

3340. Thomas Harland, Norwich. 1775–1800. A Slight Variant from Those Previously Shown. Metropolitan Museum.

3341. (Right.) Inlaid Curly Maple. E. Storrs, Utica, New York. Very Handsome. Early 19th Century. Metropolitan Museum.

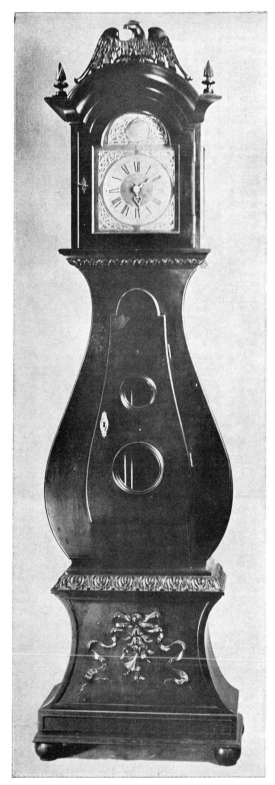 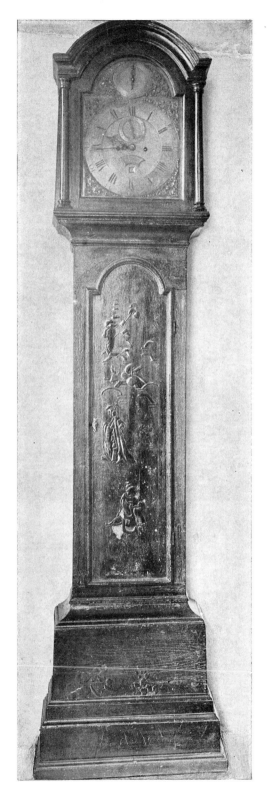

3342. ANCHOR ESCAPEMENT, ONE DAY. 1792. ENGLISH. GOOD OUTLINES, WELL CARVED. FOREIGN. PROBABLY DUTCH.

3343. (Right.) LACQUERED WITH PLAIN DOME. BY THOMAS WAGSTAFF, 1766-94. HE WAS A QUAKER, AND AMERICAN QUAKERS OFTEN BOUGHT HIS CLOCKS. BASE MOLDING SHOULD BE REMOVED. ESTATE OF HARRY W. WEEKS, FRAMINGHAM.

Dr Sir:

Dec 7th 1792

In my Accounts for the Year 1778 as settled by
Committee of Assembly, and printed, you will see how the 35,000
Dollars was disposed of. Whether there was any receipts with the
Contracts I cant say, for I think all the Vouchers are in your
hands. It seems likely that there was one or two receipts, for
my receipt for the money is dated March 28th And I find three
Entries of payments on the 24th and 27th

I am Dr Sir

most respectfully

Your very humble Serv.t

Dav.d Rittenhouse

Comptroller Gen.l

3344. This Letter Speaks for Itself. Rittenhouse Was State Treasurer, Professor of
Astronomy in Pennsylvania University, Director of United States Mint, and President of
American Philosophical Society. His Work Dates from 1751 to Near the End of the Century.

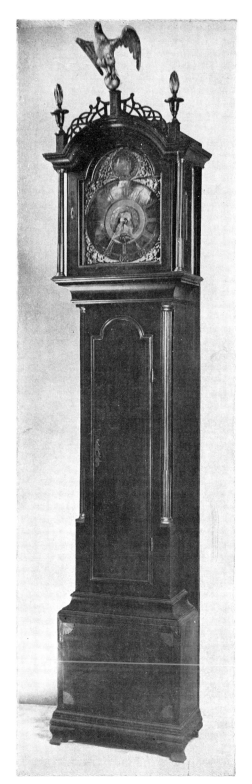

3345. GERMAN, BY JACOB STRAUSSER, NUREMBERG, 1737. NEW ENGLAND CASE, C. 1800.
ESSEX INSTITUTE, SALEM.

3346. (Right.) BY SAM STEVENS, LONDON. SCROLLED BRACKETS ARE VERY UNUSUAL.
ESSEX INSTITUTE, SALEM.

3347. IRISH, BY THOMAS CORNWALL, DUBLIN. WEDGEWOOD MEDALLIONS. ESSEX INSTITUTE, SALEM.

3348. (Right.) BY EDWARD FAULKNER, LONDON, 1710–35. LACQUERED. HENRY FORD, WAYSIDE INN.

3349. By Christopher Gould, London. c. 1695. Burl Walnut. John H. Halford, Norristown.

3350. (Middle.) By Edward East, London. Inlaid Walnut. c. 1690. Rare Month Movement. 54 Inches High. Rapid Beat, Rather Short Pendulum.

3351. (Right.) By Thomas Tompion, Famous Maker. c. 1690. Both: Wetherfield Collection.

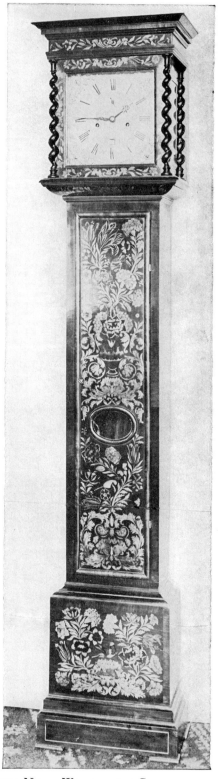

3352. By Charles Gretton, London. c. 1795. Fine Inlay. This 'and Next: Wetherfield Collection.

3353. (Middle.) By Joshua Willson, London. c. 1705. Exquisite Inlay.

3354. (Right.) By George Peacock, England. c. 1700. Owner Is Unknown.

3355. English, Very Early. Movement, Dial, Etc., Next Page. Engaged Spiral Columns.

3356. (Middle.) By Esaye Fleureau, London. c. 1810. Marquetry, Arabesque. Wetherfield Col.

3357. (Right.) By Jonathan Lounde, London. c. 1705. A Good Scroll in Marquetry.

3358. Showing the Dial and Works of No. 3355, Also Two Excellent Hands.

3359. (Opposite.) Beautiful Case, Carved on Base, Fret under Hood, and Interlacing Scrolls above the Arch. Spiral Finials. Pointed Rosettes. Corners Cut Away above and below Quarter Columns. Rhode Island School of Design.

3360. (Right.) By Dieco Evans, London. Cast Brass Feet, and Finials, Very Decorative. Brass Trim Throughout. Fan Inlay, besides Lines and Cross Bands. Rhode Island School of Design.

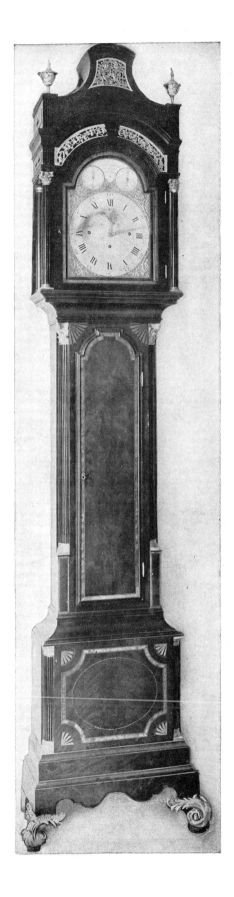

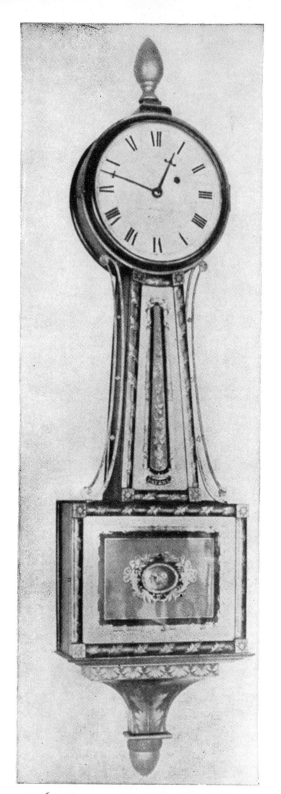 

3361. STENCILED BANJO, BY SIMON WILLARD & SONS, BOSTON. MAHOGANY PERIOD. STENCIL WORK ON THE MOLDINGS, CENTER, AND BOTTOM BRACKET. c. 1820–25. RARE. DR. EMORY M. PORTER, PROVIDENCE.

3362. (Right.) BY L. CURTIS, CONCORD, MASSACHUSETTS. A MAHOGANY LYRE CASE, WITH CARVED BOTTOM BRACKET AND CENTER PANEL, AND LEAF ORNAMENT AT THE TOP. STRIKES HOURS ON TWO PIANO WIRES. J. WINTHROP BROWN.

3363. BY L. CURTIS, CONCORD. FRONT PANELS PINE, GILDED. CASE, MAHOGANY. RARE.
PHILIP A. JOHNSON, NORWICH.

3364. (Right.) BY WILLIAM GRANT, BOSTON. MAHOGANY, PINE PANELS OF FRONT GILDED. 1815-25.
ROBERT C. JOHNSON, NORWICH.

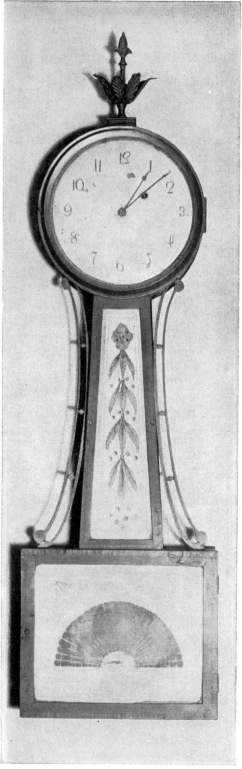

3365. By William Cummens. Spool Banjo. Mahogany; Brass Moldings on Inside of Lower
and Central Panels. c. 1815. Large. C. Prescott Knight, Providence.

3366. (Right.) A Simon Willard. Original Bottom Glass. "S. Willard Patent."
F. L. Dunne, Boston,

3367. Simon Willard, in Pine Case. Banjo Movement. Case Original. Cover Removed.
Estate of Harry W. Weeks.

3368. (Right.) Simon Willard, Picture on Lower Glass, Telemachus. Estate of Harry W. Weeks.
Framingham.

3369. By A. Chandler, Concord, N. H. Mahogany Lyre, Carved Center Panel and Feather Finial. c. 1835-40. A Bottom Door. Striking Movement with Count Wheel. Benjamin A. Jackson, Providence.

3370. (Right.) Similar Clock, with Different Carving and Gilded Panel on Door. Sawin & Dyar, Boston. 1800-20. H. V. Weil.

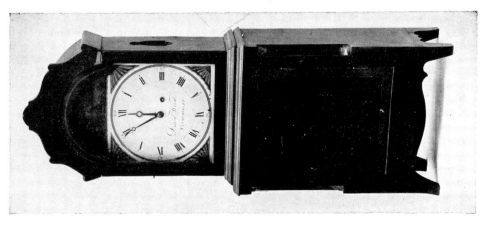

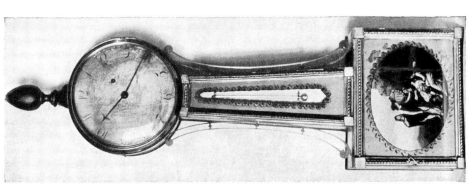

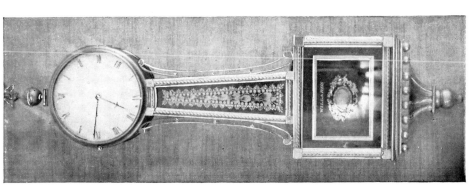

3371. By Simon Willard. Gilded Panel Outlines. Estate of William E. Montague, Norristown.
3372. (Middle.) Simon Willard; with a Barometer. Rare. Estate of Harry W. Weeks, Framingham.
3373. (Right.) By David Wood, Newburyport, Massachusetts. 1800–25. Mahogany on Pine. Metropolitan Museum.

3374. Sawin and Dyar, Boston. This Maker Is Supposed To
Have Originated the Form. Mahogany. 1800–20.
Metropolitan Museum, New York.

3375-78. Beautiful English Clock Hands from Early Clocks. c. 1700. Walter H. Durfee, Providence.

3379. The Works of a Simon Willard Timepiece or Banjo. He Used the Former Name and Possibly Did Not Use the Bracket Below. The Piece Was Made as a Mantel Clock or To Screw to the Wall. This Finial of Gilded Wood Is Probably the Earliest. The Works Have His Peculiar Escapement. Wallace Nutting,

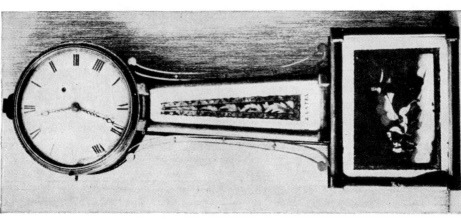

3382. The Ornament Is Used Often.
c. 1802. Estate of Wm. E. Montague.

3381. By Z. Gates. Note the Hands.
Estate of William E. Montague.

3380. Mahogany. Somewhat Late.
Estate of William E. Montague.

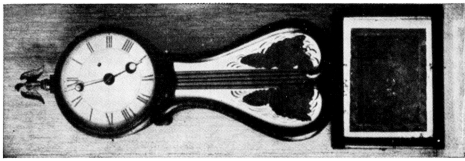

3385. Lyre Clock. Mahogany. A Simpler Form. 1810–20. Estate of William E. Montague.

3384. Aaron Willard Regulator. Mahogany. Early 19th Century. Dish Dial. Banjo Movement. Like "Act of Parliament" Clock. Dr. Emory M. Porter.

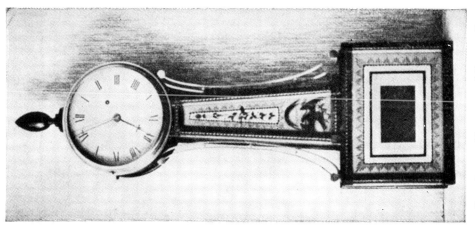

3383. Aaron Willard. "Patent" on Upper Glass. Simon's Invention Was Freely Pirated. Estate of William E. Montague.

3386. Good Design of Lyre. Formerly the Author's. Has Strike. No Name on Dial.

3387. (Right.) The Escapement of a Simon Willard, Showing the Curved Teeth of the Wheel. Simon Senior Invented This Clock, and the Escapement Also Is Peculiar to Him. It Required Great Skill and Was Not Copied. Wallace Nutting.

3390. By Aaron Willard, Jr. Presentation Clock.
36 x 10, Including Eagle. W. W. Creamer,
Waldoboro.

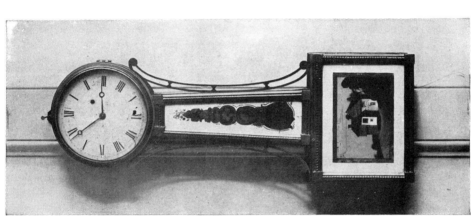

3389. By David Wood, Newburyport. Rare. W. H. Douglas.
1790–1824.

3388. Alarm Clock, Plain Outlines,
John Sawin, Boston. 1823–63. W. H.
Douglas, Plymouth

3391. Carved, Mahogany Lyre. No Gilding. Acorn Top. Estate of William E. Montague, Norristown.

3392. (Right.) "Massachusetts Pattern." John Sawin, Boston. Mahogany with Painted Glasses around the Dial, and Lower Panel. c. 1830. Dial Is Dished, the Usual Term for Convex. Edwin P. Anthony, Providence.

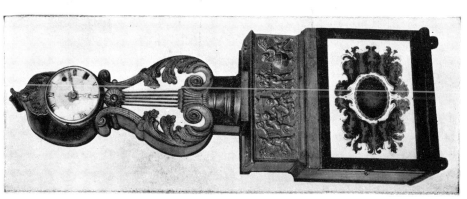

3393. Painted Glass Below, Bas Relief Cupids. Above All a Lyre Pattern. Beautiful and Very Rare Specimen. I. Sack, Boston.

3394. (Middle.) Connecticut. Mid 18th Century. An Immense Number of This Type or Somewhat Simpler Were Made. Charles P. Cooley, Hartford.

3395. (Right.) Rare Pattern. All Gilded, on Pine. 35 x 13½ x 3⅛. Face Diameter 12½ Inches. Early 19th Century. Probably Swiss. Flayderman & Kaufman.

3396. Beautiful Rare Design. Bracket with Doubled Shells. Fine Carved Scroll Above. Old Garrison House, Trenton, New Jersey.

3397. (Right.) By John Winkley, England, c. 1760. Brass, Engraved with Maker's Name. Banjo Works. Cherry. William G. A. Turner, Malden.

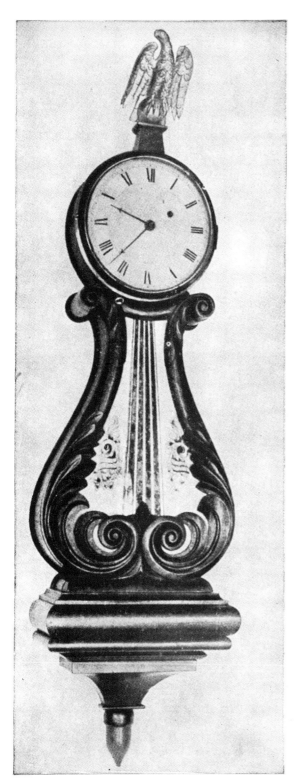 

3398. By John Sawin. Mahogany with Carved Panel. Carved Eagle of Pine, Gilded. 1830–35.
Mrs. Emma A. Taft.

3399. (Right.) Gilded Lower Panel, Painted Glass. Upper Panel Carved and Gilded. Estate
of Harry W. Weeks.

3402. Simon Willard. Paneled Below. Presentation. Charles F. Williams Collection. Pennsylvania Museum.

3401. Miniature. Quarter Columns. Flayderman & Kaufman.

3400. By James Ferguson, London. 1710–76. The Date Seems Doubtful for the Style. Twenty-Four Hour Dial. Essex Institute.

3403. Regulator, by George D. Hatch. Rosewood, Date Uncertain. Unusual Shape. Striking Banjo Movement. Dr. Emory M. Porter, Providence.

3404. (Right.) By J. D. Custer, Norristown, Pennsylvania. 1805–72. Design Suggests Connecticut Pillar and Scroll. Estate of William E. Montague.

3405. Curtis, Girandole. Pine, Painted White.
Bracket, Lower Door, Center Panel and Top,
Gilded. Rare. By Lemuel Curtis, Concord.
1810–18. Mrs. L. F. O'Neil. Auburn, New York.

3406. ENGLISH CHIPPENDALE, CHINESE PATTERN. ELEGANT EXAMPLE.
BENJAMIN M. JACKSON, PROVIDENCE.

3407. BY AARON WILLARD, BOSTON. MAHOGANY, INLAID, FRENCH FOOT, c. 1800.
KIDNEY DIAL. C. PRESCOTT KNIGHT, PROVIDENCE.

3410. By Boston Clock Company. Essex Institute, Salem.

3409. Lyre, Carved. Name Indistinct. Boston. 1820-30.

3408. Familiar Sea Fight Design. Essex Institute, Salem.

3411. By Jerome & Darrow, 1825-30. Mahogany, Black and Gold Stenciled Columns and Top. Quite Usual. Thirty-Hour Wooden Works. Richard E. Wheeler, Providence.

3412. (Right.) Tower Clock from Church in Morristown, N.J. Colonial Date. Washington Headquarters Museum in That Town.

3413. Forestville Mfg. Co., Bristol, Connecticut. Acorn Pattern. Mounted Like a Looking-Glass. 1830. Estate of William E. Montague.

3414. (Right.) By Joseph Ives, New York City, 1818–30. Fine Wagon-Spring Movement, 30 Days. Movement Now in Another Clock. C. Prescott Knight, Providence.

3415. CHIPPENDALE, THREE URNS WITH FLAMES; SHELL BELOW AND
ABOVE DIAL. BALL-AND-CLAW FEET. RICH SPECIMEN. HOSTETTER
COLLECTION, LANCASTER, PENNSYLVANIA.

3416. By E. Taber. Mahogany Inlaid, c. 1800. Kidney Dial; Good Example. Massachusetts Pattern. C. Prescott Knight, Providence.

3417. (Right.) By Simon Willard. Mahogany, 1770–80. Very Rare. Thirty-Hour Movement and Brass Dial. G. Winthrop Brown, Boston.

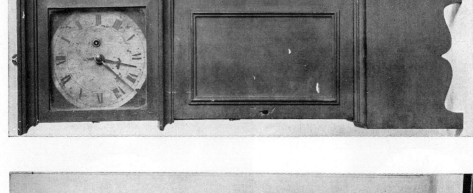

3420. MINIATURE. 29 x 10 x 5. MAHOGANY. MRS. FRANCIS P. GARVAN.

3419. LIGHTHOUSE CLOCK, WITH SUPERIMPOSED BELL. ESSEX INSTITUTE, SALEM.

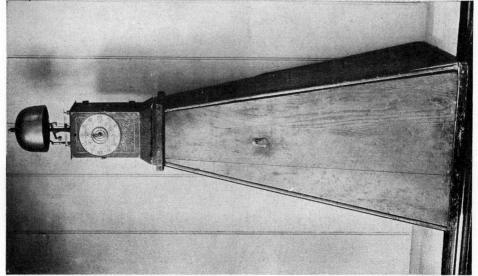

3418. BEAUTIFUL DESIGN, QUARTER COLUMN. OWNER: CLARENCE H. ALLEN, PORTLAND.

3423. LIGHTHOUSE, BALL FEET. APPLIED LEAF. F. L. DUNNE.

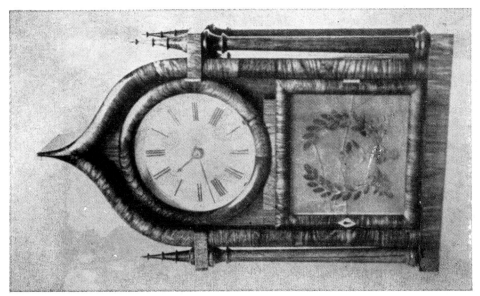

3422. GOTHIC. DESIGNED BY ELIAS INGRAHAM, FOUNDER OF THE FIRM WHO MADE IT, BREWSTER & INGRAHAM. 1843–48. E. INGRAHAM COMPANY, BRISTOL, CONNECTICUT.

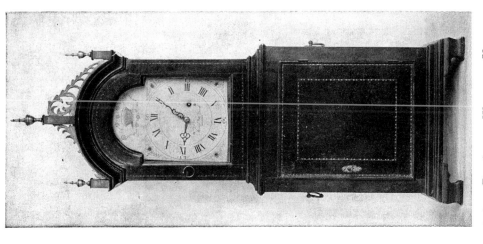

3421. BY AARON WILLARD. UNUSUAL FRET. CASE CARVED. PENNSYLVANIA MUSEUM, PHILADELPHIA.

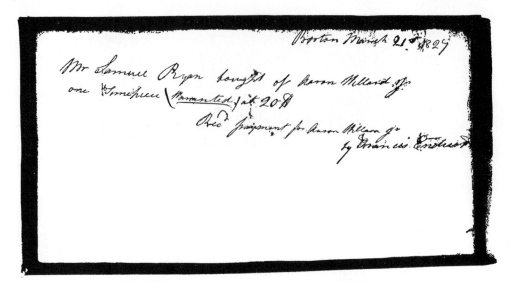

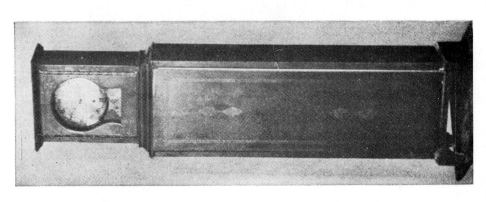

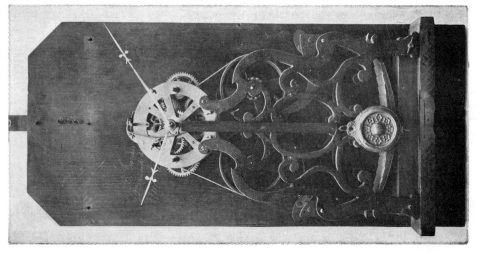

3424. Joseph Ives. Cart Spring Movement. C. Prescott Knight, Providence. 1811-25.

3425. (Middle.) Grandmother Clock, Probably by S. Mulliken. Cherry, 21½ x 10. Dial 5½ Inches, Silvered Brass. Kidney Dial. Pallet Arbor without Suspension Spring. Brass Inlay. P. H. Safford, Fitchburg.

3426. (Right.) Bill of Aaron Willard, Jr., Boston, March 21st. 1829. G. W. A. Turner, Malden.

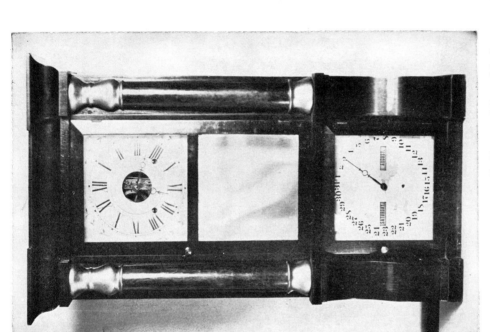

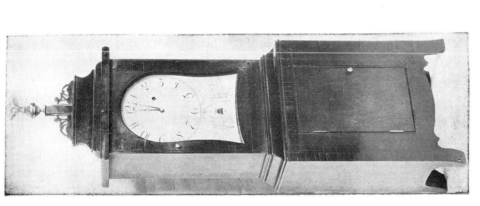

3427. Mahogany, 40 x 12½ x 6½. Probably by E. Taber. Mary M. Sampson, Boston.

3428. (Middle.) By Seth Thomas, Plymouth Hollow, Connecticut, c. 1860. Interest Chiefly in Heavy Scroll of Base, as in Degraded Empire. Essex Institute.

3429. (Right.) By J. Wilder, Hingham. Quarter Columns, Good Fret and Balls. F. L. Dunne, Boston.

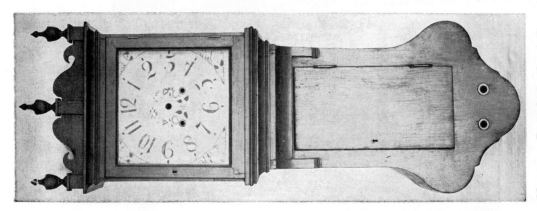

3430. BY DAVID WOOD, NEWBURY PORT [sic]. GOOD DESIGN. KATRINA KIPPER, ACCORD.
3431. (Middle.) PINE, URNS NEW. ODD DESIGN. ORIGIN UNKNOWN. WALLACE NUTTING.
3432. (Right.) BY AARON WILLARD, JR., BOSTON. PAINTED GLASS AROUND THE DIAL. KATRINA KIPPER.

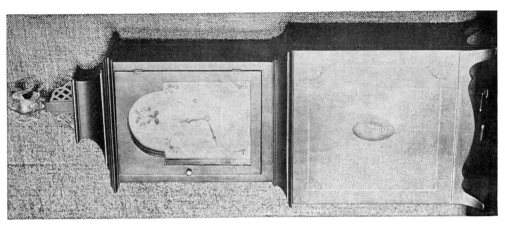

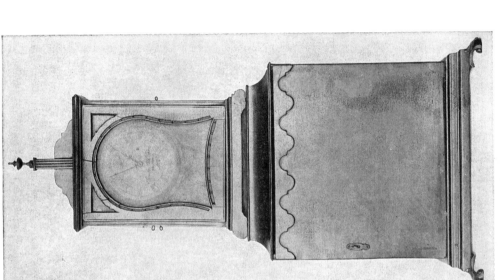

3433. By David Studley, Hanover, 1806–35. F. L. Dunne, Boston, as Also the Others on This Page.

3434. (Middle.) "By Simon Willard, Grafton. N. 2." Probably It Means That This Is the Second Clock of This Kind That Willard Made. Effect of One Cabinet Piece on Another. Kidney Dial. Scrolled Mold on Base Like Those on Harland's Clocks of Norwich. Places Not Far Apart. About 1776.

3435. (Right.) David Wood, Newburyport, Inlaid with Snail Shell and Fan, Inlay on Base,

3436. By John Bailey, Jr., Hanover. Beautiful Fret of Imbricated Leaves. Fine Brass Urns. Rocking Horse above Dial.

3437. (Second.) By Ebenezer Belknap, Boston. 1823. Bigelow Collection. F. L. Dunne, Boston.

3438. (Third). By Reuben Tower, Kingston, Massachusetts. Delicate Finials. 1812–20.

3439. (Right.) Miniature, Benjamin Willard, Lexington. 30 x 9½ x 4½. Mahogany. 1768–1770. Mrs. Francis P. Garvan.

3440. MASSACHUSETTS PATTERN. PINE. THIRTY HOUR. MAKER UNKNOWN. 1780–90.
ELISHA C. DURFEE, PROVIDENCE.

3441. (Right.) WAS OWNED BY MARY WILLARD HAZEN, DAUGHTER OF SARAH WILLARD, AND EDWARD
HAZEN, LANCASTER, THIRD COUSIN OF THE WILLARD CLOCK MAKERS. SHE MARRIED JOSEPH RUGG,
AND HER DAUGHTER JULIA GAVE THIS CLOCK TO MRS. HENRIETTA GATES. OLD FURNITURE SHOP,
WORCESTER, MASSACHUSETTS.

3442. By David Williams, Newport. Mahogany. Kidney Dial.
Well Decorated. Fine Hands. Top Unusual. 1820–30.
Benjamin A. Jackson, Providence.

3443. Beautifully Inlaid, and Fine Shape. Savin Make.
Design Possibly Suggested from the French. Cross-Banded
Border. Ogee Feet. I. Sack, Boston.

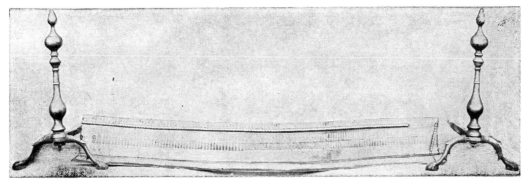

3444. Ball-and-Claw Foot Andirons. Spiraled Tops. Cut-Brass Serpentine Screen.
J. K. Beard, Richmond, Virginia.

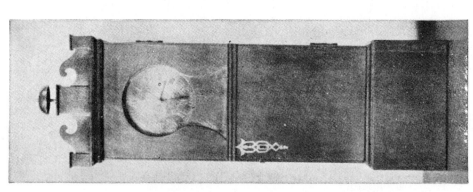

3445-46. Same Clock Open and Closed. Odd Weight To Gain Longer Run. Interesting. Original Ornaments, Kidney Dial. William G. A. Turner, Malden.

3447. (Right.) Grandmother Clock, 48 Inches High. Cherry. Marked by Small Waist, as Often in Pennsylvania Miniatures. Quarter Columns on Both Sections. Good Hood. Philip Meredith Allen, Broad Axe, Pennsylvania.

BENJAMIN WILLARD,
CLOCK and WATCH-MAKER.

BEGS leave to inform his friends, and former cuſtomers, that after eight years abſence from this county, he has again begun his buſineſs at his farm in GRAFTON, eight miles from Worceſter, where he carries on CLOCK and WATCH-MAKING in all their various branches. He would inform the publick, that he has for theſe many years paſt, been with the beſt approved clock and watch-makers on the continent, in order to obtain further knowledge in the different branches of ſaid buſineſs. The publick are often greatly impoſed on, by employing unſkilful workmen ; and many good watches as well as clocks have been almoſt entirely ruined by thoſe pretenders to this art. Said Willard lets no work go out of his hands but ſuch as he will warrant. He is determined to work on the moſt reaſonable terms ; and as he lives on a farm, and his expences are much leſs than if he lived in a ſeaport, he can afford to work cheaper ; it is alſo neceſſary, that his buſineſs (to do it well) ſhould be carried on in retirement. In order the better to accommodate the publick, he has engaged with Mr. Thomas to receive and forward all commands left at his printing-office ; all watches wanting repair, left with him, will be fairly forwarded to me at Grafton, on Thurſdays, and on the week following will be returned, finiſhed, to ſaid office, where thoſe who left them may receive theory, warranted ; and, the expence for repairing, not more than one half as much as commonly charged by watch-makers in ſea-ports.—Said Willard informs thoſe who have purchaſed clocks of him before the war, (as he has finiſhed and ſold two hundred and fifty three eight-day clocks, chiefly in this State,) that thoſe which he ſold, if any, he is ready to repair, and warranted once gratis, if there is any fault in their making, &c. &c. He alſo makes the

New Invented CLOCK-JACK,

for roaſting meat ; ſaid jacks may be had of Meſſrs. S. and S. SALISBURY, merchants, in WORCESTER. This jack was invented by Mr. Simon Willard, who obtained a patent from the General Court for an excluſive right. Said Simon Willard has authoriſed me to make ſaid jacks, which are very uſeful and much approved of by thoſe who have experienced them.—They are much cheaper than imported jacks and more durable.—Country produce will be taken in payment for his work.— Said Willard alſo makes

All kinds of TIN-WARE,

which he ſells wholeſale and retail.

☞ *Wanted by ſaid Willard, two or three active, ſprighty BOYS, about fourteen years of age, as apprentices.*

3448. BY AARON WILLARD, BOSTON. CHARACTERISTIC BALL AND EAGLE, LANDSCAPE WITH CATTLE, SHEEP, DOG, MAN, AND WOMAN. BEAUTIFUL EXAMPLE. F. L. DUNNE, BOSTON.

3449. (Middle.) EARLY ADVERTISEMENT OF BENJAMIN WILLARD, WHOSE CLOCKS ARE RARE. FIRST WORK AT GRAFTON. WALTER H. DURFEE, PROVIDENCE.

3450. (Right.) BY EZEKIEL JONES, BOSTON. FEET QUITE UNUSUAL. GOOD PAINTING ABOUT DIAL.

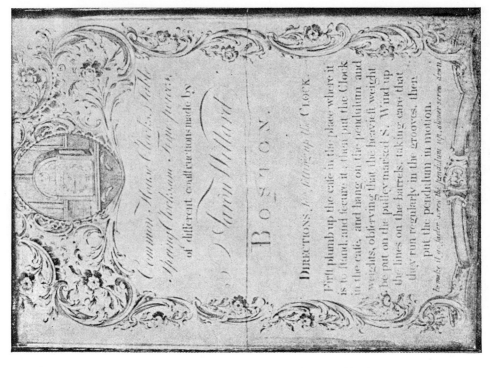

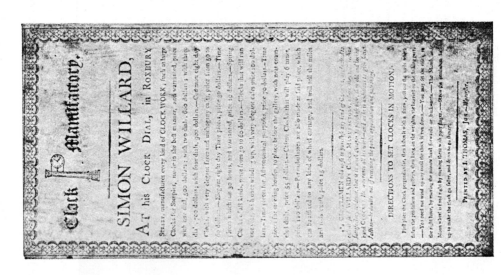

SIMON WILLARD,

BEGS leave to inform the publick, that he has opened a Shop in ROXBURY-STREET, nearly oppofite the road that turns off to PLYMOUTH, where he carries on the Bufinefs of

Clock Making

in all its branches.———Gentlemen may be fupplied at faid fhop on the moft reafonable terms, with CLOCKS of different conftructions, to run either a day, eight days, one month, or a year, with once winding up; common eight-day repeating Clocks, Spring Clocks of all forts, among which are, common fpring table, fpring chime, and fpring tune Clocks, which will play different tunes every hour; alfo large tune clocks which run with weights, will play every hour, repeat the quarters, &c.———Alfo, may be had, faid WILLARD's new conftructed Aftronomical TIME KEEPER, afcertaining the 60th or 20th part of a minute, by a fecond hand from the centre of the large circle;made upon a moft fimple plan, in which the friction and influence of the oil is almoft annihilated; and has proved to keep time with the greateft accuracy, with a new conftructed pendulum, from the centre of the ball, fhews the different degrees of expanfion of the bars, and anfwers, in fome degree, as a thermometor, &c. thofe that ofcilate half feconds are portable,and are eafily moved to any part of the room, or where it is convenient for to make obfervations; to the pedeftal of which is affixed (without obftructing the movement) a perpetual calender, newly engraved, which fhews at one view, the day of the month, the true and comparative time of the fun's rifing and fetting forever; as well as the age, increafe, decreafe, rifing and fetting of the moon, time of high water, &c. the whole globe with its rotation every twenty-four hours, fhewing the longitude, latitude, the hour and minute upon the moft noted places on the globe.—Such gentlemen or ladies as will favour the faid Willard with their commands in the above bufinefs, may depend on having their work done in the neateft manner, and may be fupplied with MEHOGANY CASES in the neweft tafte.—Thofe who live at a diftance may have Clock Work fent them, with direction how to manage and fet them up, without the affiftance of the Clock-Maker.

Watch Work

of all forts is done in the neateft manner, and carefully cleaned and regulated, with Cryftals, Keys, Seals, Chains, Springs, &c. &c. Alfo, is made by faid WILLARD, and COMPANY, a new invented

Roafting Jack,

in which is containe. a compleat apparatus of Kitchen Dripping-Pan, Spit, Skewers and Bafter, &c. which is fo conftructed with tin plates as to reflect back upon the meat all the heat the tin receives, which occafions the faving of almoft one half of that important article fire-wood; it is alfo recommended for its being portable, which can be placed to any fmall fire-place, in any room, and which is made upon fo fimple a plan that it is not fubject to get out of repair, and the friction upon every part being fo trifling, that it will continue for longer duration than any mechanical performances of that kind is known to do.

Roxbury, February 24. 1784.

N. B. The above JACKS may be had of Col. PAUL REVERE, directly oppofite Liberty-Pole, Bofton.

Copied from
THOMAS'S
MASSACHUSETTS SPY, Or
WORCESTER GAZETTE
Thursday, March 11, 1784

3453. SELF EXPLANATORY.

3454. By Seth Thomas, Plymouth Hollow, Connecticut. "Pillar and Scroll" Design. Became Wonderfully Popular. Mahogany, c. 1820. Veneer under Ornaments Is Satinwood. Painting Original and Excellent. Glass Slightly Curved, as in All the Originals. Concave. Mrs. Harrison B. Huntoon, Providence.

3455. (Right.) Said To Be by Simon Willard, but No Name Appears. William E. Montague, Norristown.

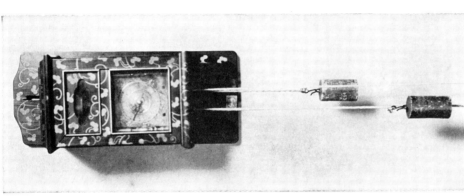

3456. Interior of No. 3458, by Munger & Benedict, Auburn, New York. "A. Munger" on Paster. Carved, with Plaster Top and Painting of Washington.

3457. (Middle.) Japanese Wall Clock. Scrolled Design Carried Over to the Wall Board. Essex Institute, Salem.

3458. (Right.) Stenciled Design, Perhaps Unique. 1833 Engraved on Hammer. Eagle Pendulum Bob. C. Prescott Knight.

3459. By C. & N. Jerome, Bristol. Mahogany, 1830. Heavy Late Empire. Brass, Eight Day. Unusual Dial, Black and Gold. Pierced To Show Movement. Dr. Charles H. Chetwood, Massachusetts.

3460. (Right.) By Eli Terry, Plymouth. Mahogany, 1793–1818. Deservedly Popular. Thirty-Hour Wood Movement.

3461. (Left.) Interior of No. 3459.

3462. (Middle.) An Aaron Willard, with Shields on Spandrels of the Dial.

3463. (Right.) By Atkins & Downs, Bristol, Connecticut, Mahogany Carved Columns, Feet and Top. c. 1830.
Mrs. George L. Shattuck, Providence.

3464. By Eli Terry, Plymouth. Mahogany. c. 1818. Early, with Escape Wheel in Front of Dial. Francis E. Gates, Oak Lawn, Rhode Island.

3465. (Right.) Japanese. Odd Oriental Scrolls and Frets. Essex Institute, Salem.

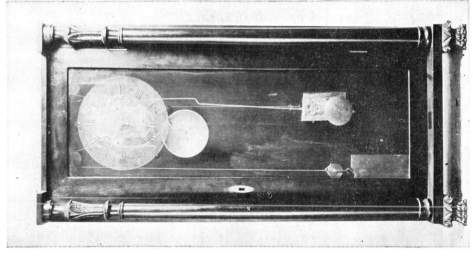

3466. Original Dial Removed. Interesting, Architectural Design Like a Looking-Glass. Essex Institute, Salem.
3467. (Right.) By Burnham Terry. Balance Escapement. Sold by J. J. & W. Beals, Boston, Essex Institute, Salem.

3468. By Joshua Wilder, Hingham. English Type Top. Pine. S. Prescott Fay, Boston.

3469. (Middle.) Line Inlay, Arched Top. James Davidson, New London, c. 1800. Found in a Bristol Factory Some Years Ago.

3470. (Right.) Miniature. Kidney Dial. Unusual Base Scroll. S. Prescott Fay, Boston.

3471–72. Cart-Wheel Spring Movement. Late Empire with Carved Feet and Finials, and Stenciled Scroll. 1830–40.

3473. Kidney Dial. Basket Fret. Data Mislaid. c. 1800.

3474. (Middle.) English Lantern. 1650–90. The First Popular Short Clock. Formerly the Author's.

3475. (Right.) Looking-Glass Front. Maple Leaf Painting, c. 1830. W. F. Hubbard, Hartford.

3476. Movement, Weights, and Center Panel of L. Curtis. 1814–53. C. Prescott Knight.

3477. Chest Lift. Chippendale Brass, from
Philip Meredith Allen, Broad Axe, Penn.

3478. LOOKING-GLASS CLOCK, EIGHT-DAY MOVEMENT AND STRIKE. WHEELS SHOW IN TOP. FROM E. S. MACOMBER, PROVIDENCE.

3479. (Right.) TOBY CLOCK. IT IS SAID THAT A MAN IN GOOD HEALTH CAN TELL TIME BY HIS STOMACH. AN IRON MAN. W. F. HUBBARD, HARTFORD.

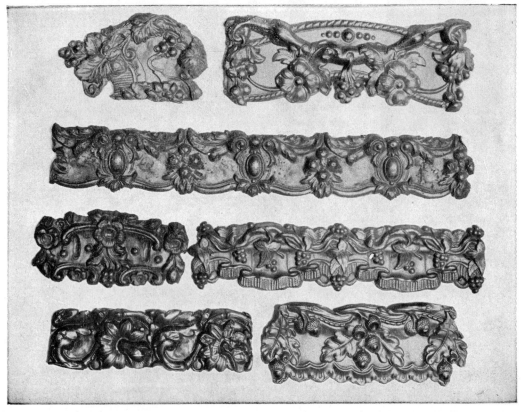

3480-86. DRAPERY CORNICES OF STAMPED BRASS. 19TH CENTURY. FRANK A. ROBART.

3487. American Case, French Works. Fine Ogee Bracket Feet. Good Scroll Top. Francis D. Brinton, West Chester, Pennsylvania.

3488. (Right.) Shows Works through Large Cut-Out. Beaded Ornaments on Side. W. F. Hubbard, Hartford.

3489. Metal Clock, Painted Ornaments. W. F. Hubbard, Hartford.

3490. (Middle.) Curious Small Wall Clock. Pine. 18½ x 8¾ x 4¼. Found by Mrs. Minnie Brown, Rockland, Massachusetts. Wag-on-the-Wall, c. 1820. Flayderman & Kaufman.

3491. (Right.) Small Metal Clock, Painted Decoration. William F. Hubbard, Hartford.

3492. Cathedral Case, Otherwise Called Gothic. Sometimes a Double Decker, or Steeple Clock. By Birge & Fuller, Bristol. Mahogany. 1830–35. Wagon Spring. J. Ives Pattern. Dr. Emory M. Porter, Providence.

3493. (Middle.) Kidney Dial. Shelf Clock. About Same Date as Similar Dials Previously Shown. Essex Institute. 3494. (Right.) Steeple, with Crotchets. E. Ingraham Company, Bristol, Connecticut.

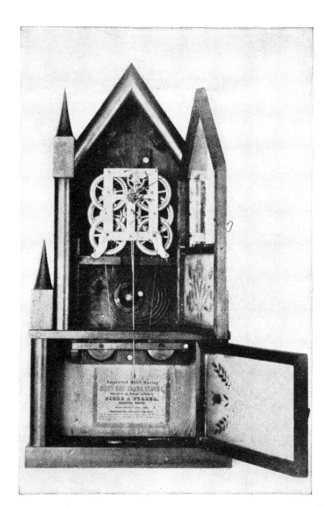

3495-96. Gothic Clock, with Doors Opened and Closed. "Improved Steel Springs, Eight-Day Brass Clock, Birge & Fuller, Bristol, Conn." Glass Is Especially Good.

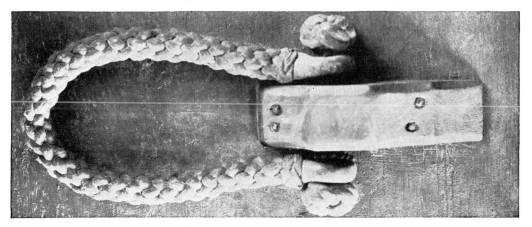

3497. By Way of Surprise, a Becket Is Shown. This Is the Handle Worked by Sailors for Their Chests. The Test of an Antiquarian Is that He Knows the Name of This and a Few Other Things. Sanderson Collection, Nantucket.

3498. A "Solar Time Piece," by Timby, Baldwinsville, New York. Essex Institute, Salem. 3499. (Right.) Late Type by Atkins Clock Company, Bristol, Connecticut, 1820–

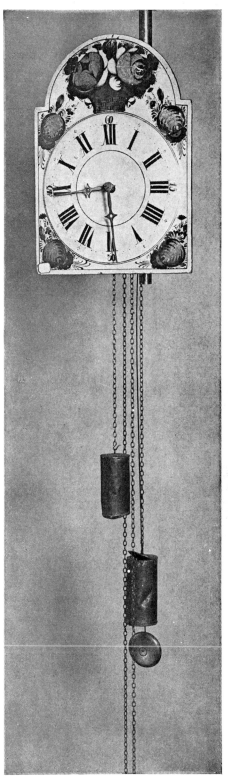

3500. WAG-ON-THE-WALL. DUTCH OR GERMAN. ESSEX INSTITUTE, SALEM.
3501. (Right.) WAG-ON-THE-WALL. GERMAN. ESSEX INSTITUTE, SALEM.

3502. CLOCK WITH A MUSICAL INSTRUMENT IN BACK, A ZITHER. TWO TUNES ARE PLAYED. SPANISH
NETHERLANDS OR SPAIN. 18TH CENTURY.

3503. (Right.) WAG-ON-THE-WALL, PROBABLY GERMAN. ESSEX INSTITUTE, SALEM.

3504. Astronomical Clock. "It Shows the Time All Over the Globe, and the Position of the Stars at All Times." Balance Escapement, Universum Clock Co., Boston. Essex Institute, Salem.

3505. Label in Clock of Henry A. Hoffman, Barrington.

3506. By Peregrine White. 1774– . Dial of Colonial Chime Clock, Plays Tunes Every Three Hours. Different Tune for Each Day of the Week, and a Psalm Tune on Sunday. The Late Ex-Governor Elisha Dyer, Providence.

3507. Bracket Clock. "Jam^s Stevens, London," the Name Being Repeated on Engraved Brass Back. 15¾ x 10¼ x 6¼.

3508. "Jno. Perins, London." Mahogany. Battersea Enamel Dial, Pink Scrolled Spandrel with Birds. Back Plate Engraved. Bigelow Collection.

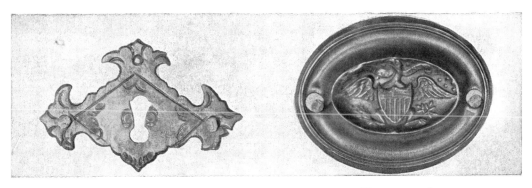

3509-10. Unusual Brass Escutcheon; (Reversed) 1700. Eagle and Shield 1790. Bigelow Collection.

3511. The English Shelf Clock Like the Above Is a Handsome Well-Made Article and Is Likely Always To Be Much Sought for in America. The Works Are Very Good. These Are Largely London Make.

3512. (Right.) Mahogany, Inlaid, Beautiful Open Fret in Ends. G. Winthrop Brown, Boston.

3513. By Alexander Cummings, London (b. 1732, d. 1814).

3514. (Right.) Two-Day, Fusee Movement, by Edward Smith, Dublin, c. 1810. It Is Supposed the Plain Lettering "Two Days," on the Dial Was an Advantage in Selling. Essex Institute, Salem.

3515. (Opposite.) By John Martin, London, c. 1700. Very Rare. Wetherfield Collection.

3516. (Opposite, right.) By Daniel Quare. Ebony, Brass Mounted, c. 1700. Three Chimes and a Quarter Chime on Six Bells. The Maker Invented a Repeating Watch. Wetherfield Collection.

3517. (Above.) By Thomas Parker, Philadelphia. Whether This Means that He Imported It or Not Does Not Appear. But Dealers Had Their Names Placed on the Clocks, as Was Probably the Case Here. Miss Susan P. Wharton.

3518. (Right.) Italian, 17th Century. Pennsylvania Museum, Philadelphia.

3519. T. G. MOORE, WORTHINGTON, ENGLAND. MAHOGANY WITH BRASS FRETS UNDER THE DIAL AND BRASS OGEE FEET,
c. 1830. OWNER UNKNOWN.

3520. (Right.) BY MUMMERY, DOVER, ENGLAND. NAME NOT GIVEN IN BRITTEN. PROBABLY A DEALER. MAHOGANY WITH
BRASS INLAY, FINELY DONE, c. 1830. BEAUTIFUL SPECIMEN. STEPHEN O. METCALF PROVIDENCE.

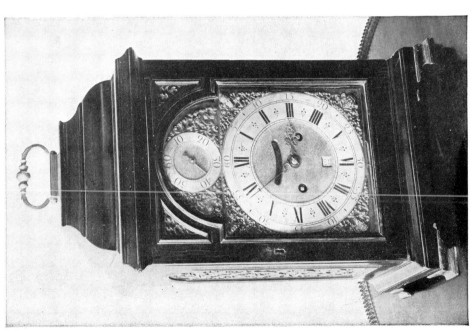

3521-22. Two English Shelf, or Bracket Clocks.

3523. BY STEPHEN RIMBEAULT, LONDON. EBONY, c. 1760–80. SIXTEEN HAMMERS, CHIMES AT THREE QUARTERS, AND PLAYS AT THE HOUR. MUSICIANS IN THE ARCH OF THE DIAL PLAY WITH THE TUNE. MARSDEN J. PERRY, PROVIDENCE.

3524. By J. Smith & Sons, London, c. 1800–10. Case in Red Chinese Lacquer. Picture from Walter H. Durfee, Providence

3525. (Right.) From Soltykoff's "Horologerie," 1858, Plate XVIII. Original Plates in Steel. Soltykoff Says This Piece Has Neither Signature nor Date, but He Believes It German of the Time of Ferdinand of Austria.

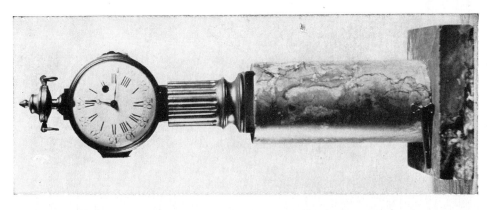

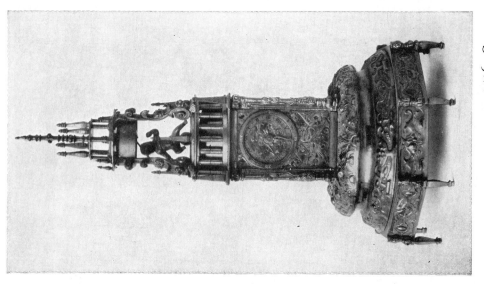

3526. German, 16th Century. Pennsylvania Museum, Philadelphia.
3527. (Middle.) German Sword Clock. Essex Institute, Salem, Massachusetts.
3528. (Right.) By W. Oakes, Oldham, England, Fusee Anchor Escapement. Essex Institute, Salem.

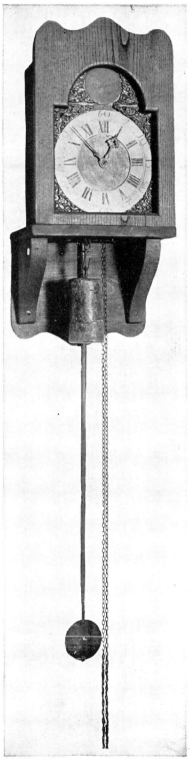

3529. Friesland. These Hooded Clocks, with Pewter or Brass Filigree, All Follow the Same Type. The Figures Often Hint at the Date. Essex Institute, Salem.

3530. (Right.) Wag-on-the-Wall, by R. T. Manning, 1767. Essex Institute, Salem.

3531. ITALIAN, BY ARCANGELO MAYEREFFER, ROME, 1794. ESSEX INSTITUTE, SALEM.

3532. From Soltykoff's "Horologerie," 1858, Plate XX. "The Monogram G. G. Proves that the Beautiful Piece Belonged to Gaston of Orleans, Son of Henry IV."

3533. From Soltykoff's "Horologerie," 1858, Plate XI. By Andreas Müller, in the Reign of Ferdinand, Brother and Successor of Charles V.

3534–35. From Soltykoff's "Horologerie," 1858, Plate I. Constructed by Louis David, Period of Henry III. The Plaque Above Is a Satire of the Huguenot Time against the Papacy.

3536. French. Ormolu and Gilt Bronze, with Sèvre Mounts. Essex Institute, Salem.

3537. Probably English. Pendulum Stimulates the Piston Rod of an Engine.
On the Other Side Is a Barometer.

3538. Perhaps French. Essex Institute, Salem.

3539. Probably Swiss, Possibly German. A Number of Such Clocks Have Been Found. Essex Institute, Salem.

3541. French, Essex Institute.

3540. Japanese, Essex Institute, Salem.

3542-43. French Fusee Clock. They Usually Have White Stone Bases with Ball Feet, and Are Raised on Bell-Shaped Piers. Sometimes There Is an Arrangement for Leveling. Essex Institute, Salem.

3544. EMPIRE, MAKER UNKNOWN, C. 1825–30. AN IMPORTED REPEATING MOVEMENT,
STRIKING ON THE HOUR AND QUARTER, VERY RARE. THE CASE IS AMERICAN.
WARREN R. FALES, EAST PROVIDENCE.

3545. FRENCH, 16TH CENTURY. PENNSYLVANIA MUSEUM, PHILADELPHIA.

3546. From Soltykoff's "Horologerie," 1858, Plate VII. Dimensions in Centimeters: 34 High, 23 Across at the Base, 13 Across in the Main Part of the Clock, and 7 Deep. This Shows the Annunciation, the Adoration of the Magi, and Various Other Scenes from the Life of Christ. A Very Elegant Example. Date, 1521.

3547. French, 16th Century. Pennsylvania Museum, Philadelphia.

3548. French, 16th Century. Pennsylvania Museum, Philadelphia.

3549. From Medici Palace, Via Servi, Florence. Essex Institute, Salem.

3550. HALL CLOCK MOVEMENT, BY JOHANNES A. FROMANTEEL, 1675, LONDON. ALARM DIAL IS ON THE SIDE OF THE MOVEMENT INSTEAD OF IN FRONT. THE WHEEL OF THE WINDING ARBOR IS SEPARATE FROM THE WINDING DRUM. THESE ARE HELD TOGETHER BY THE MOVEMENT PLATES. VERY UNUSUAL.

 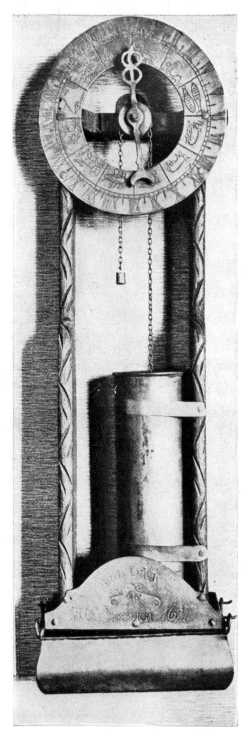

3551. SWISS, OR GERMAN. MOVEMENT OF PENDULUM SEEN IN THE OPENING BELOW. ESTATE OF WILLIAM E. MONTAGUE, NORRISTOWN, PENNSYLVANIA.

3552. (Right.) BY ALBERT DAVIS, NORWICH, 1671. THIS ENGLISH WATER CLOCK WAS ONE OF THE EARLIEST KNOWN FORMS. WATER CLOCKS WERE IN USE IN CLASSICAL TIMES.

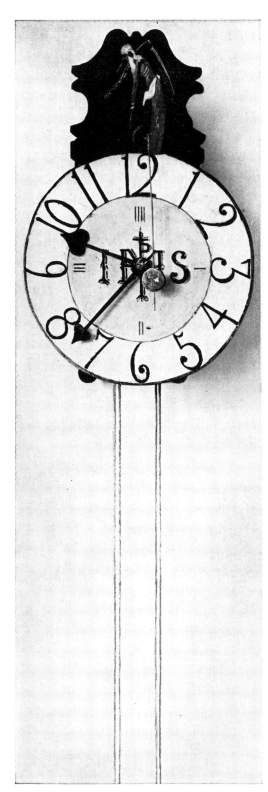

3553. Unknown Origin. Certainly Foreign. The Pendulum Is in Front of the Dial. Father Time in Somewhat Fresh Paint. Possibly Patched Up. Wadsworth Atheneum.

3554. Foreign. The Only Instance Shown of a Base Like a Table Frame for the Support of a Clock. Essex Institute.

3555. NORWEGIAN. THE FIGURES DANCE. THE CARVING OF THE FACE IS SIMILAR TO SPANISH EXAMPLES. ESSEX INSTITUTE, SALEM.

3556. (Right.) SWEDISH. O. I. DAHL, ARTMARK. ESSEX INSTITUTE, SALEM.

3557. WAG-ON-THE-WALL. WINGED HORSE REPRESENTING THE FLIGHT OF TIME. ESSEX INSTITUTE, SALEM.

3558. (Right.) WAG-ON-THE-WALL. CONTINENTAL. SAME OWNERS.

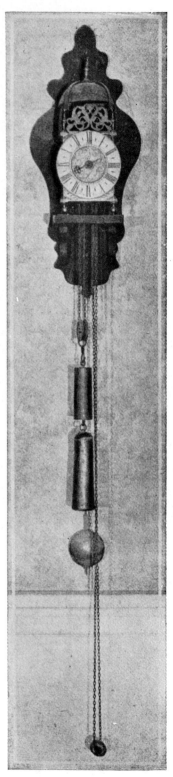

3559. FRIESLAND CLOCK. 18TH CENTURY. FORMERLY OWNED BY L. C. FLYNT, MONSON, MASSACHUSETTS.

3560. (Right.) BY THOMAS MOORE, IPSWICH, C. 1610. THE LANTERN CLOCK IS VERY DECORATIVE AND SHOULD BE POPULAR. JOHN H. HALFORD, NORRISTOWN, PENNSYLVANIA.

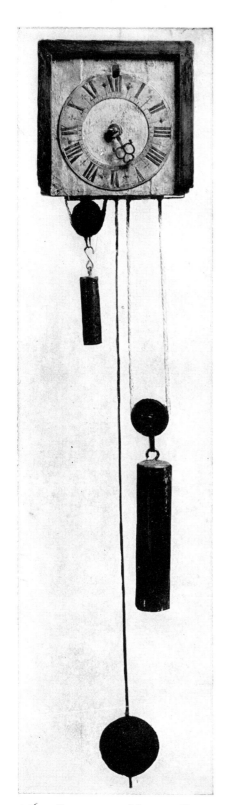

3561. Reported as Made in Bensburg, Prussia, Early 14th Century. Taken to Dalsband County, Sweden. Found in the 16th Century in Ruins of Church Abandoned, 1347-48. This Description Is Not Vouched For. Essex Institute, Salem.

3562. (Right.) Flemish, by J. B. Banderam, Braine-l'Alleud, Near Brussels. Essex Institute, Salem.

3563. "Father Time," Lakeport, California, from a Type Patented in 1808 by John Schmidt
of London, a Dane, Who Was Taken Prisoner in Copenhagen and Brought to England.
He Called It "The Mysterious Circulator of Chronological Equilibrium." This Clock
Is Now the Property of the Essex Institute, Salem.

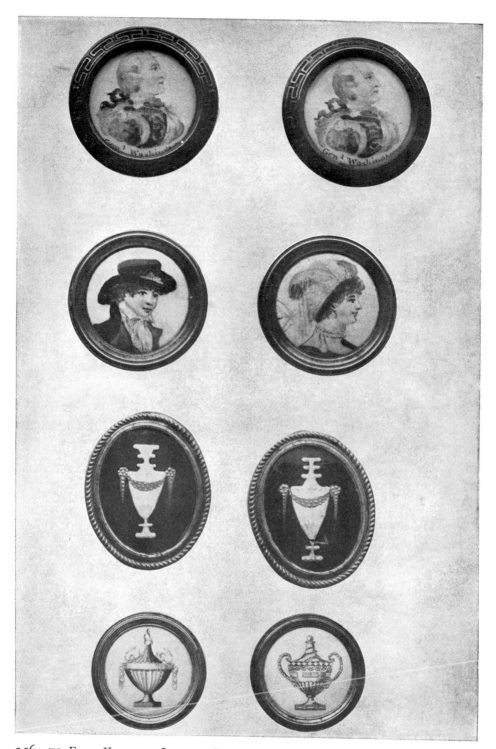

3564–71. Eight Knobs for Looking-Glasses. Picture Supplied by Irving P. Lyon, M.D.
All Belonged to His Father Dr. Lyon, Who Made the First Good Book on Furniture,
Except the Second Set from the Top. They Are from Houses in Newburyport.
The Other Sets Acquired by Dr. Irving P. Lyon in Massachusetts. General Washing-
ton Appears Very Young Here. Is It Possible that Persons Sometimes Had Their
Portraits Made for Knobs, as in the Second Set? They Are in Plain Black, Then
in Sepia, or More Often Painted in Colors. The Greatest Diameter Is
1¾ Inches Inside. About 1800.

3572–77. The Top Pair of Knobs Is Very Beautiful, the Second Pair Are of Huntington, and Governor Morris. J. Grossman, Boston.

3578–91. A Series Supplied by the Courtesy of "Antiques." Nelson's Vanguard Is Dated 1798. Those of Washington Are Next in Importance. The Two Members of the Pair of Knobs Are Not Necessarily the Same. From George C. Flynt, Monson, Massachusetts.

The fashion of these knobs ought to be revived because they supply individuality to a home. Pictures of subjects of special interest to the family or of local importance would enshrine a history and make a permanent record and add a pleasing and useful decorative feature. The same is true of furniture brasses. There is an abundant field for design of modern brasses, which could be made most interesting. Why do we leave to our fathers all such matters?

The author has endeavored to make a representative showing of brasses, partly owing to the intrinsic interest of the subject, and partly in the hope of stimulating the revival of a neglected art.

3592-98. Picture Supplied by Irving P. Lyon, M.D. All Belonged to His Father Dr. Lyon, Except the First Set. These Knobs or Sets Are All Enamel on Copper, Mounted in Brass Frames with Screw Posts Generally about 2½ Inches Long. Most Are Printed on the Enamel from Paper Transfer Prints from Copper Engraving.

3599–3602. Knobs of a Lady Leaning on an Anchor, and of a Lady with
Long Curls. J. Grossman, Boston

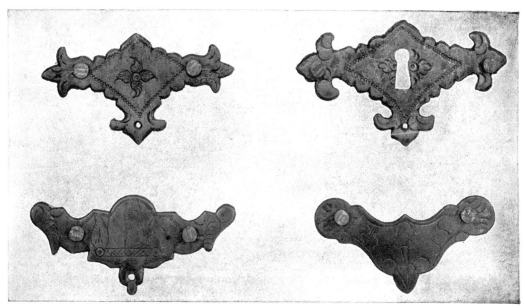

3603–06. Fine Brasses of the First and Second Period, 1690–1710. Rudolph P. Pauly.

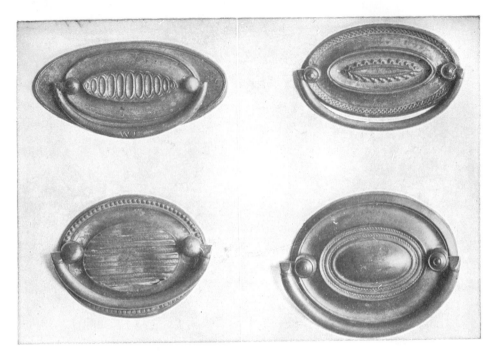

3607-10. BRASSES FROM THE GOODWIN AND THE NORTON COLLECTIONS. THE STAMPED INITIALS W. J. ARE ON THE TOP LEFT BRASS. LATE 18TH CENTURY.

Figure 3611 has been omitted in the numbering.

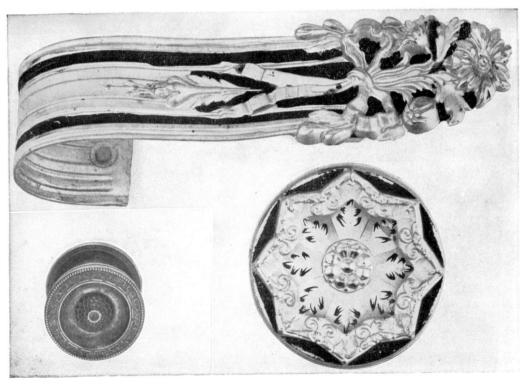

3612-14. THE RICH KNOB AND PULL IN BLUE, PINK, WHITE, AND GILT. KNOB DIAMETER 3 INCHES. PULL 2¼ x 12. THE SMALLER KNOB, AS THE OTHERS, ARE FROM THE WILLIAM B. GOODWIN COLLECTION.

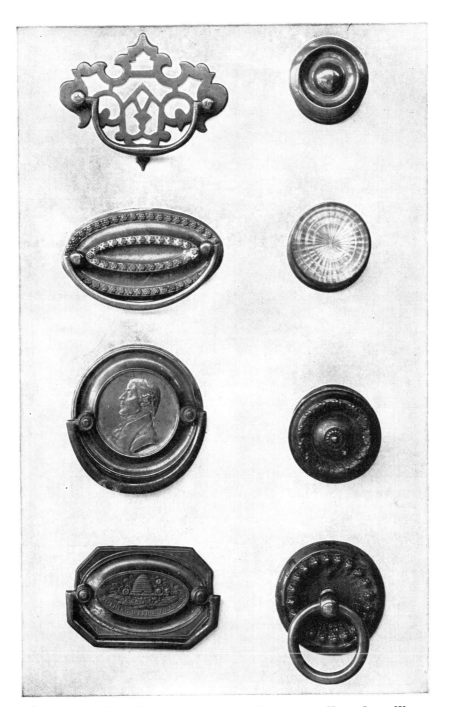

3615-22. The Most Interesting Are the First of the Third Line, Which Is Called Thomas Jefferson, and the Beehive with the Legend "Nothing without Labor." This Set Is One of the Complete Equipment of a Sideboard, Hepplewhite Period. James Davidson Collection.

**3623-31. Fine Chippendale Open Handles, with Three at the Top of an Earlier Period.
Collection of Frank A. Robart**

The teardrop is the earliest brass handle, about 1690. The stamped William and Mary and Queen Anne handles run from about 1700–1730. The open scroll, or the closed scroll handles, usually called willow handles, are of the Chippendale time, ranging from 1740–80. In America the scroll handle like the bottom left example, or at least a handle which is not cut out with interior scrolls, has proved to be more popular. Handles in the first period were attached by wires clinched on the inside. The posts came a little later, with handmade nuts always of irregular form on the outside. Brasses have been, and are, imitated so closely that only an expert, whoever he may be, can detect the difference.

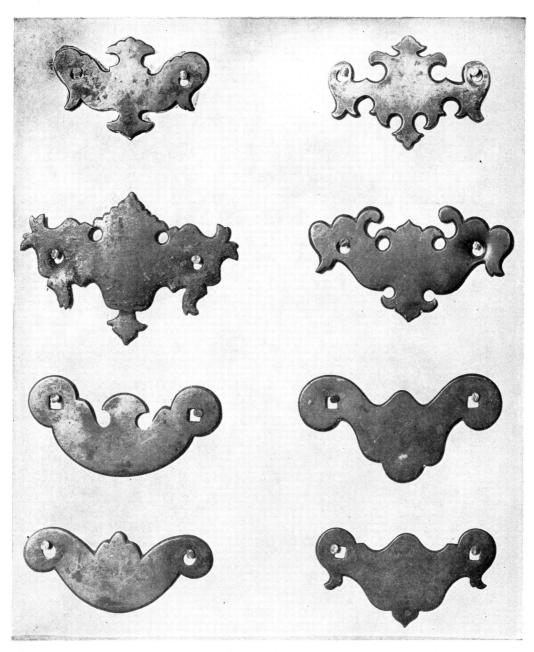

3632-39. Chippendale Brasses. The Lower Ones on the Left Show the Evolution from the Earlier Queen Anne Type. Collection of Frank A. Robart.

These brasses all have a beveled edge, which was cleaned up by a file. They are invariably cast and not cut out by a stamp. They are also very thin, about a 32nd of an inch.

Thick brasses, or brasses with a rounded edge, or a square edge are modern. It is only recently that two American firms have arrived at the skill necessary for the copying of the ancient brasses.

3640–47. All Except the Openwork Brass Are of the Empire Period, and Range from 1800 to 1830. Collection of Frank A. Robart.

By this time the cutting of threads by machine was developed. Brasses before this period had all their threads cut by hand. The detection of the machine-cut thread is the readiest method of learning that the brass is modern. The Empire brasses were all of them stamped in dies. The work on them is not to be confused with the stamping of the Queen Anne time which was done with a series of small tools, each cutting a minute section, and combining in an endless variety.

3648-55. THIS SHEET OF CHIPPENDALE BRASSES, FROM THE COLLECTION OF FRANK A. ROBART, REPRESENTS THE MORE POPULAR AND USUAL PATTERN FOUND ON FURNITURE BETWEEN 1760 AND 1775.

These brasses all had plain surfaces, and it was considered poor housekeeping to neglect the polishing of the brasses. These were highly burnished, and the woodwork about them on old pieces shows a polish where the material used overran the edge of the brass.

3656-63. COLLECTION OF HENRY WOOD ERVING.

The brass most commonly found, and of a design that has appealed to the greatest number of old furniture buyers, are those on the left of this sheet. Messrs. Erving, Goodwin, Bigelow, Norton, Eaton, Pauly, and others have been most kind in allowing individual brasses to be removed for pictorial use. The matter of matching up old brasses is often of great annoyance, and a test of serenity of character. A set of good brasses is now worth, in many instances, more than the piece of furniture to which they are affixed.

3664–71. The Older Specimens Here Are at the Top, Right, and the First and Last in the Second Row. The First in the Second Row Represents a Nude Figure Playing a Fife. The Puffed-Out Cheeks Are Funny. The Creature Has Wings and Appears To Be Sitting on a Cloud Which Consists of Spirals. It May Be Presumed that He Is Supplying the Music of the Spheres. On the Right in the Same Row, Is an Urn with Drapery. The Largest Brass, with the Lion, Shows Also Implements of War. The Lion Was the Most Popular and the Least Attractive of All the Stamped Brasses of the Empire Time. Collection of Frank A. Robart

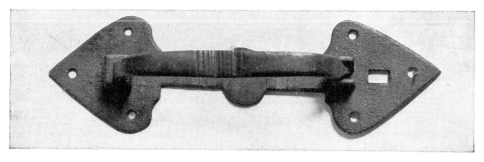

3672. Unique Combined Latch and Knocker. The Author's.

3673–78. The Flying Eagle Carries the Scroll with E Pluribus Unum in the Beak, and a Sheaf of Arrows with the Olive Branch in the Claws. Fifteen Stars for the States, Which Give the Date. In the Second Row There Are Naval Emblems in the Left-Hand Brass, and Fine Shell with Trident and Spear in the Right-Hand Brass. At the Bottom We Have the Acorn Leaf and Acorn Which Appear in Various Forms. On the Right at the Bottom There Is a Small Classical Temple with a Figure. Collections of William G. Goodwin and Malcolm A. Norton.

In these volumes the author has appealed to those who desire compacted information. It is not feasible in the limits of the work to write sketches of notable cabinetmakers, all of which information may be found in any library. The thought is, first, the picture, then the mention of its salient features.

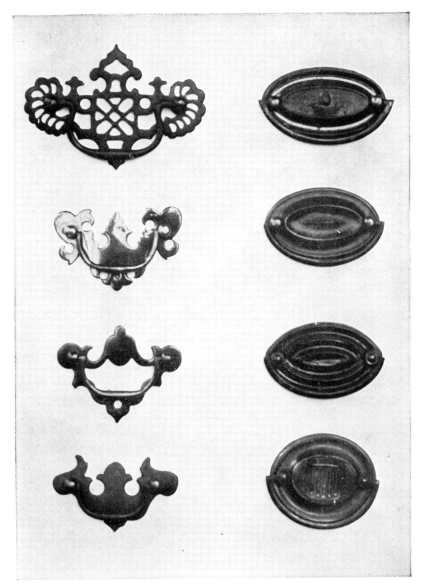

3679–86. Chippendale on the Left, Hepplewhite and Sheraton on the
Right. Collection of Henry Wood Erving, Hartford.

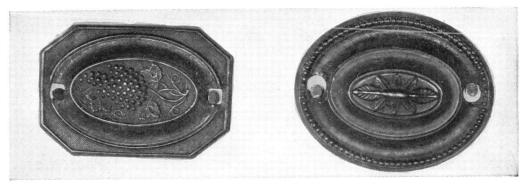

3687–88. An Octagon and an Oval Brass, from Francis Hill Bigelow, 1790–1800.

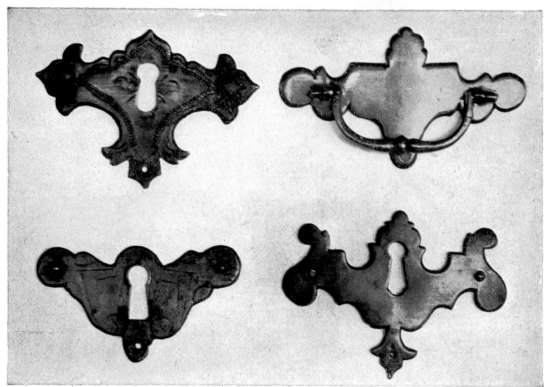

3689-92. Two Queen Anne and Two Chippendale Brasses. Both of the Queen Anne Specimens Are Very Rare. A. H. Eaton, Collinsville.

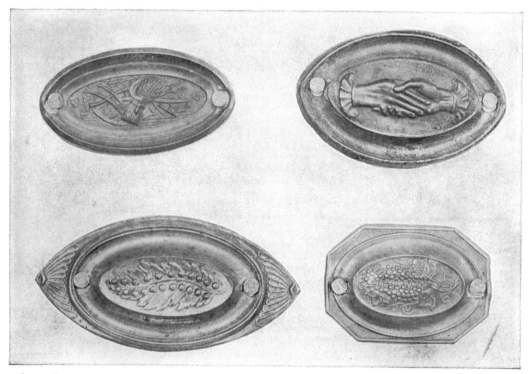

3693-96. Agricultural Brass, Top Left. Clasped Hands on the Right. The Others Are a Leaf and a Grape Pattern. Rudolph P. Pauly, Boston.

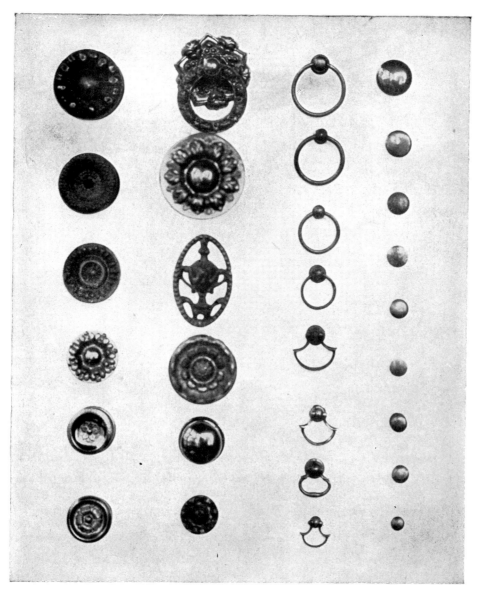

3697–3725. A Sheet of Brasses Prepared by the Patience of Henry Wood Erving.

The first and second columns represent the Empire period. The third column is earlier; the four shaped drops on the right being very dainty and some of them small, used on little cabinet drawers. For the fourth column the knobs were used in the 18th and early 19th Centuries. These small drops are similar to and a hold-over from the first half of the 18th century. They appear in larger form on box locks. In smaller forms we find them on the doors of cupboards. The knobs were used on the sustaining slides for desks and on any small drawer or cupboard door.

Most hardware was imported for old types of furniture and is still imported, but during the last five years American firms have learned to supply all our needs.

3726-30. Late 17th and Early 18th Centuries. All Probably English, but Found on American Furniture.

The teardrops were sometimes flat on the back, and sometimes round, as in the bottom left example. In the top left example, it is easy to see that a round punch mark is used several times in the center of the flower. A second tool was perhaps all that was necessary to complete this brass.

3731-32. A Pair of Knobs Showing an Eagle on a Perch. Unusual. J. Grossman, Boston.

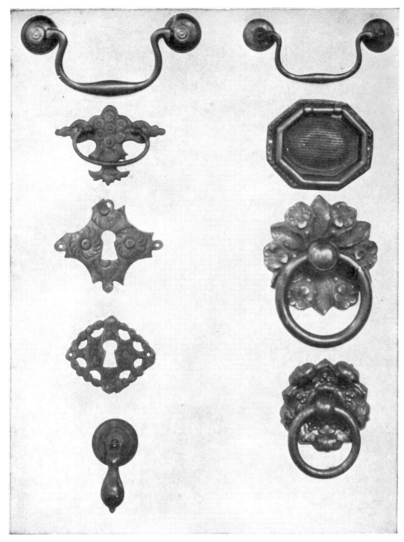

3733-41. NINE BRASSES OF THE EARLIEST AND LATEST PERIODS. THE BAILS WITH PLAIN ROSETTES ARE FOUND ON VARIOUS PIECES AND ON SMALL BLOCK FRONTS. THE ESCUTCHEONS ARE QUEEN ANNE. OCTAGON BRASSES ARE LESS USUAL, AND THEREFORE NOTICED. TWO LATE EMPIRE RING BRASSES COMPLETE THE LOT. H. W. ERVING.

3742-43. LADIES WITH HATS OF THE GAINSBOROUGH TIME, ON LOOKING-GLASS KNOBS WITH BRASS FRAMES. J. GROSSMAN, BOSTON.

3744-50. Seven Brasses from Rudolph P. Pauly. A Cabin on the Lower Left Is Very Rare. Sheaf of Grain Is Good. The Basket and Shell Brass, While Not Common, Were Found in the Empire Period. On the Central Brass Is an Urn with a Wreath. The Others Are Empire Time.

DETAILS

There begin here a large number of detail and turning parts.

3751. A Fine Hepplewhite Bedpost with Spade Foot. J. K. Beard, Richmond, Virginia.

3752. (Right.) A Very Late Post Often Called West Indian from the Fact that So Many Were Imported from That Region. Twisted Reeds. 1820-30. Anne S. Houston, Chattanooga, Tennessee.

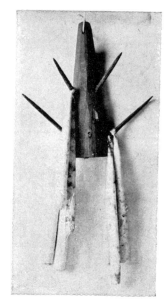

3753. A Curly Maple Trencher, Size of a Large Dinner Plate. Wadsworth Atheneum.

3754. (Right.) A Candle Rack. When the Candle Was Dipped, the Wick Was Doubled and a Small Loop Left at the Top; When This Loop Was Removed from the Stick the Candles Could Be Hung Up Separately To Prevent Them From Sticking Together. Mrs. De Witt Howe.

3755. A Carved Foot Stove. Very Rare. 18th Century. On One Side There Is a Slide To Admit a Box of Iron, for Coals. Wadsworth Atheneum.

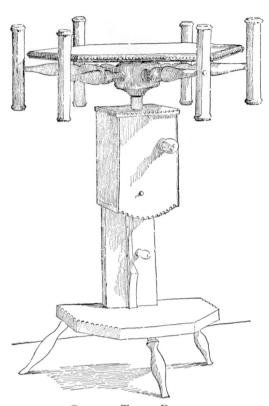

3756. The Head of a Tape Loom, with Pennsylvania-German Tulip Decoration and Inscription. Dated 1794. William B. Montague, Norristown, Pennsylvania.

3757. (Right.) A Combined Table and Wheel. Delaware Valley. Wadsworth Atheneum.

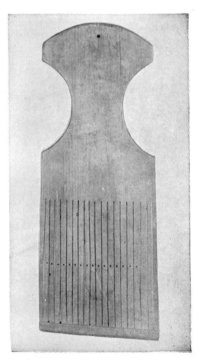

3758–60. Tape Looms. Left: W. F. Hubbard, Right: Wadsworth Atheneum.

3759. (Middle.) A Dish Top Table. Wife of Dr. Samuel Cooper. Bigelow Collection.

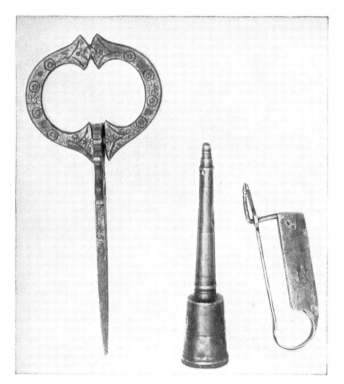

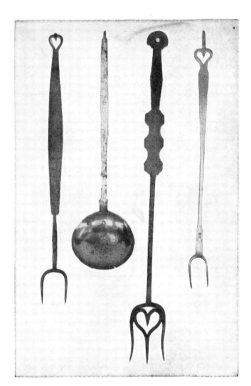

3761–63. A Remarkable Wrought Drop Handle, Stamped. Ink Horn, the Top of Which Unscrews and Releases a Pen. A Miniature Steel for Striking Flint Combined with a Pair of Tongs for Holding the Lighted Material to a Pipe. Wadsworth Atheneum.

3764–67. (Right.) Culinary Articles Decorated. Usually Votive Offerings at the Shrine of a Maiden, and Hung by Her in the Fireplace. All 17th or 18th Century. J. Stogdell Stokes.

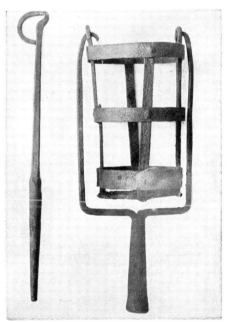

3768. A Smoke Jack, of Which One or Two Others Are Known, Notably That at Mount Vernon. It Is in the Kitchen Chimney of the Wentworth-Gardner House, Portsmouth. The Author Took It Out and Repaired the Fans, Oiled It and Restored It to Its Place, and Made It Workable. It Is Operated by the Draught of the Chimney To Turn the Spit.

3769–70. (Right.) A Toddy Iron, and a Basket for Pitch Wood. Wadsworth Atheneum.

3771. The Finest Burl Bowl at Present Known. There Are Larger, but This Specimen Has the Ears Cut upon It. Diameter 23 Inches. These Bowls Were Made in America, Canada, Ireland, and the Philippine Islands. In Ireland They Are Often of Ash. In America They Are More Often Walnut, Maple, or Other Woods. Cut from the Burl, They Would Not Split. Wadsworth Atheneum.

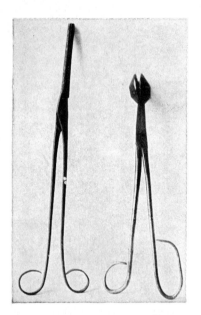

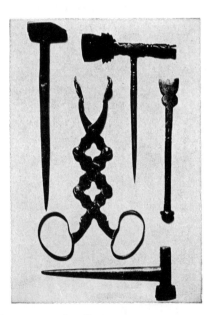

3772–73. Curling Irons. Wadsworth Atheneum.

3774–78. (Right.) An Extension Toggle Pipe Tongs, and Sets of Buttonhole and Eyelet Cutters. Pennsylvania. Mrs. M. B. Cookerow.

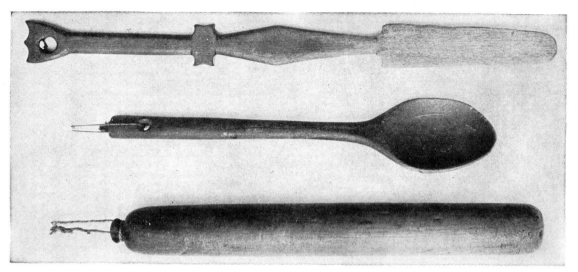

3779–81. Hasty Pudding Stick, Wooden Spoon, Roller. 18th Century. Wadsworth Atheneum.

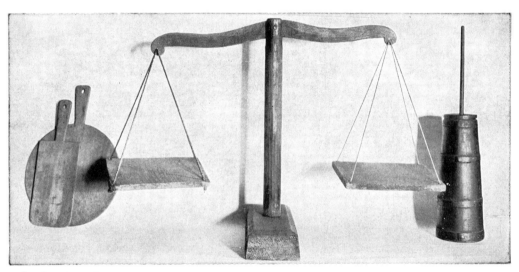

3782–85. Two Butter Pats or Shapers, a Primitive Butter Scale All of Wood, and a Dash Churn. 18th Century. L. P. Goulding, Sudbury.

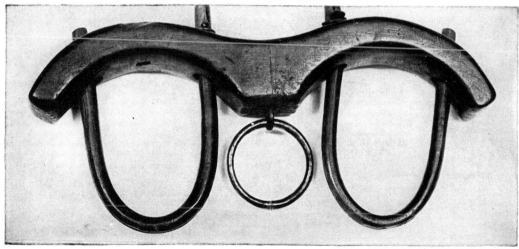

3786. Goose Yoke, Imitated from an Ox Yoke. Nine Inches. 18th Century. Chetwood Smith.

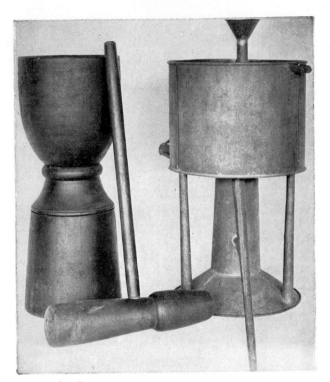

3787–89. FINE LARGE MORTAR AND HUGE PESTLE. 22 INCHES HIGH. AN ANCIENT STILL. WADSWORTH ATHENEUM.
3790. AN ODD INSTRUMENT PROBABLY FOR WORKING DOWN THE NAP OF HATS. WILLIAM B. MONTAGUE.

3791–97. THREE MORTARS, ONE OF THEM ENORMOUS. A HAND-WROUGHT BURL BOWL. A FROE HELD BY THE WOODEN PART, AND STRUCK WITH A SLEDGE ON THE IRON PART FOR SPLITTING CLAP-BOARDS. A GREAT SHOVEL WORKED FROM ONE PIECE OF WOOD, AND A PIGGIN MADE OF STAVES. WADSWORTH ATHENEUM.

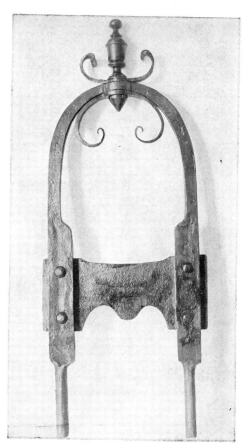

3798–99. DECORATIVE PENNSYLVANIA FOOT SCRAPERS, TO BE SET INTO A STONE AT THE DOOR. FRANCIS D. BRINTON.

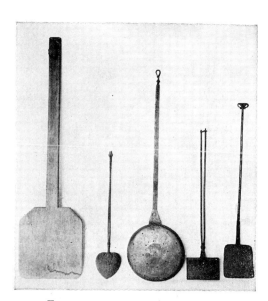
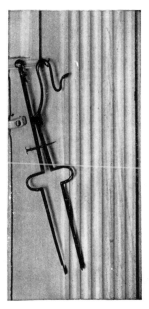

3800. A STANDARD FOR EMBROIDERY WITH A BALL AND SOCKET JOINT, ADJUSTABLE.

3801–05. A WOODEN SLICE FOR THE BRICK OVEN. TWO WAFFLE IRONS, ONE OF HEART SHAPE. A BRASS WARMING PAN, WITH THE EARLY IRON HANDLE, AND AN IRON SHOVEL OR SLICE, DECORATIVE D.

3806. THE BEST PAIR OF PIPE TONGS KNOWN TO THE AUTHOR. TAKEN BY A MEMBER OF THE WILLIAMS FAMILY AT THE CAPTURE OF FORT HENRY, 1756. SOUTH EASTON.

3807-11. A Huge Mortar High Enough To Operate as It Stood on the Floor. It Stands Higher than a Table. A Pestle Which Did Not Go with It. An Ancient Beehive, Which Was Waxed on the Interior by the Bees To Make It Water Tight. The Second Mortar, Hand Worked from a Log, with a Handle, and All in One Piece, Has Also an Enormous Pestle of One Piece. These Are the Finest Examples the Author Has Seen. Left: Wadsworth Atheneum. Right: J. J. Sullivan, Woodbury, Connecticut.

3812-15. An Early Pair of Snowshoes. A Huge Shovel of Quartered Oak. The Author Has Used This in Clearing Paths. An Ancient Churn with a Scheme for Preventing the Overflow of the Cream, and a Log Barrel. It Is Probable that Advantage Was Taken of a Hollow Log, and the Shaping Was Finished by Burning. A Wooden Bottom Was Pinned In.

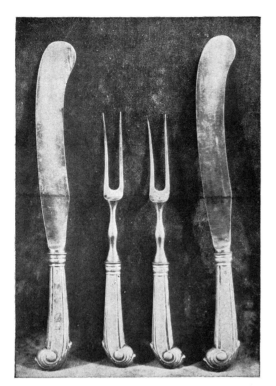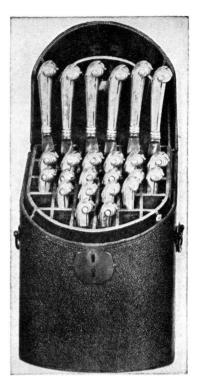

3816–19. KNIVES AND FORKS, SOME SHOWN IN DETAIL, WITH SILVER PISTOL-GRIP HANDLES, SCIMITAR-SHAPED BLADES, AND TWO-TINED FORKS, BEARING THE SILVERSMITH'S MARK. J. L. ATTRIBUTED TO JOHN LE ROUX, NEW YORK CITY, 1732. ORIGINAL SHAGREEN CASE. W. LANIER WASHINGTON, WAKEFIELD, WESTPORT, CONNECTICUT.

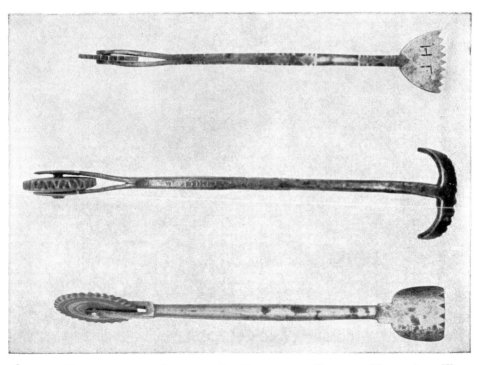

3820–22. DECORATIVE AND INITIALED PIE EDGERS AND CUTTERS. THESE ALSO WERE PRESENTED BY SWAINS TO THEIR SWEETHEARTS. WROUGHT IRON, DELAWARE VALLEY. WADSWORTH ATHENEUM.

3823-24. Sheraton Period Standards, Carrying Respectively a Terrestrial and a Celestial Globe, with a Compass at the Bottom. Joe Kindig, Jr., York, Pennsylvania.

3825. A Heart-Shaped Skewer Holder. The Giver of It Was So Enamored that He Outlined Two Other Hearts with a Punch.

3826. Decorative Scraper of Twisted and Scrolled Iron. 18th Century. Wadsworth Atheneum.

3827. A Burl Bowl with a Turned Cover. These Articles Are Much Sought For, and with a Cover They Are Very Rare. J. Stogdell Stokes.

3828-30. (Right.) A Cork Screw, the Head of Which Opens. It May Have Contained Wafers or Snuff. The Article on the Right Is a Pair of Silver Forceps, Which, When Opened, Disclose in the Cavity a Swathed Figure. Perhaps the Use Was Surgical. Why, However, the Arrangement To Stand It Erect Was Added Is a Puzzle, Unless It Was for Cleanliness. Wm. B. Montague, Norristown, Penna.

3831-32. Combined Spoon Rack and Knife Box. The Hinges Are Shaped from Dowels Formed on the Lid, Which Is Molded as Well as the Other Cross Pieces. The Spoons Are Pewter in Various Patterns. Wadsworth Atheneum.

3833. (Right.) An Ancient Caster, Prettily Turned with a Colonial Drop Handle. The Glass Is of an Early Pattern. Bigelow Collection.

3834. Corner Fireplace in the York Jail.   3835. (Right.) A Cheese Press. L. P. Goulding.

3836. Trammel with a D-Shaped Handle for Adjustment. J. Stogdell Stokes.
3837. (Right.) Brass, Foot Stove, Washington Headquarters, Morristown, New Jersey.

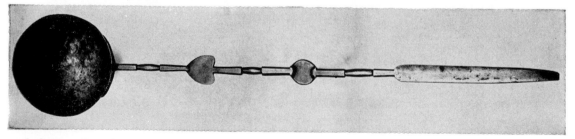

3838. Very Fine Gift Ladle with a Wrought Heart, Copper Bowl Attached by a T-Shaped Welding.
Best So Far Found. Pennsylvania. Wadsworth Atheneum.

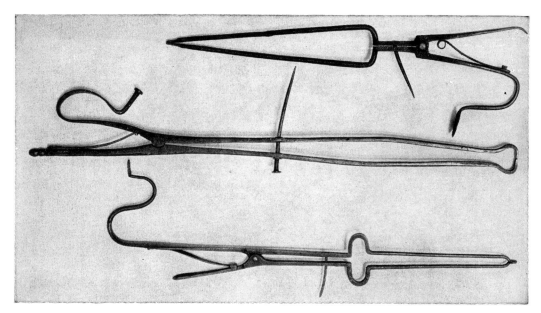

3839-41. THREE FINE TYPES OF PIPE TONGS, WROUGHT. 18TH CENTURY. THE FLATTENED THUMB PIECE AT THE END OF THE SCROLL WAS USED TO PRESS THE TOBACCO DOWN IN THE PIPE, AS THE FINE GENTLEMEN WHO USED THESE ARTICLES HAD NO CALLUSES ON THEIR THUMBS. THE SPIKE WAS USED TO CLEAN OUT THE BOWL. WADSWORTH ATHENEUM.

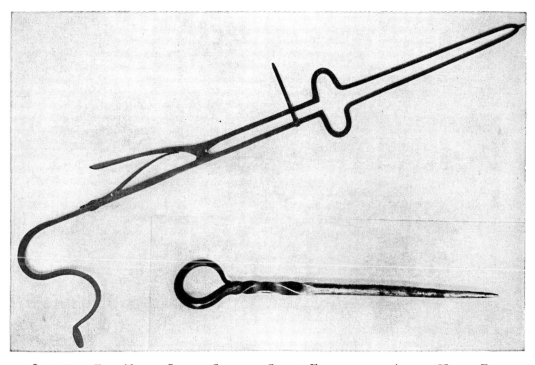

3842. FINE PIPE TONGS, SQUARE SECTION. SPRING ENDING IN AN ACORN. HENRY FORD.

3843. (Right.) ORNAMENTAL SKEWER WITH A DOUBLE TWIST. IT STOOD IN THE JOINT AS IT WAS BROUGHT TO THE TABLE. PRESENTED TO THE AUTHOR BY CHETWOOD SMITH.

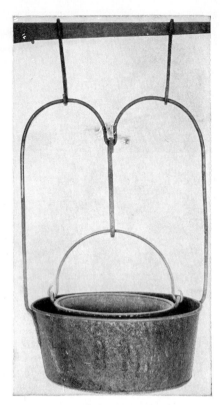

3844. A Double-Ended Trivet. It Had a Wooden Handle. Used over the Coals for a Porringer.

3845. (Right.) A Double Boiler. One of Two Known To Hang on Crane. It Proves that Our Ancestors Worked Out Some of Our Inventions without Patenting Them. Both: 18th Century. Wadsworth Atheneum.

3846–47. A Kettle with a Wrought Frame and Trivet with Wooden Handle. The Top Has Pierced Work. 18th Century. H. W. Erving.

3848. Cast Hessian Andirons. The Mustaches Reach the Ears. Intended To Be Ironical. Cast with Flat Backs in the Early Fashion. 1780–90. J. Stogdell Stokes.

3849–51. Hessian, and General Washington Andirons. The Middle Pair Are Wrought with Square-Turned Brass Tops. Present Owners Unknown.

3852. Wrought Twisted Pipe Tongs, 18th Century. Wadsworth Atheneum.

3853-64. Large Shaped Skimmer, Shovel Handles, Cast Pipe Tongs, Forceps, Trivet, Kettle
Lifter, Tongs, Skimmer, Skewer Post, Small Slice, Pipe Tongs, and Pie Plate Lifter for
the Great Oven. Doylestown Tavern, Pennsylvania.

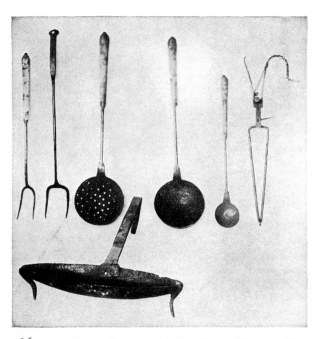

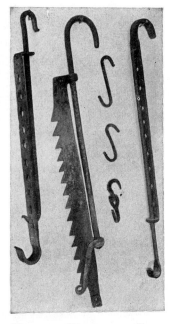

3865-71. In the Foreground Is a Long, Narrow Wrought-Iron Tray for Dipping the Rush.
Very Rare. The Other Articles Have Decorations or Initials on the Handles.

3872-77. (Right.) Trammels, the Second of Which Is the Best, with Saw Teeth. The Other
Articles Are Pot Hooks of Different Sizes, That at the Bottom Being Made with a Swivel.

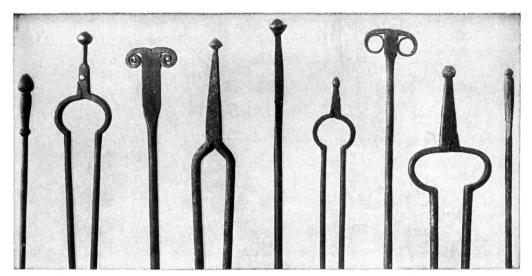

3878–86. Handles of Tongs or Shovels, All Wrought, Showing the Various Designs of Scrolls or Octagons. The Author's.

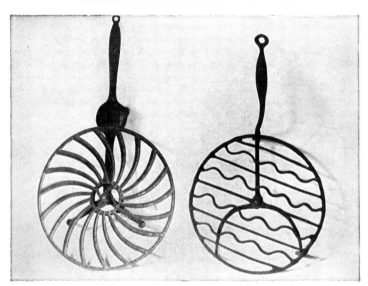

3887–88. Whirling Broilers. The Second Being Wrought. 18th Century. H. W. Erving.

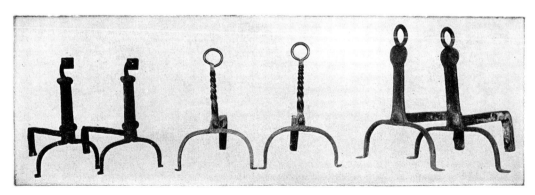

3889–91. Three Pairs of Andirons, the First Having a Goose Neck with Squares, the Second Being Twisted with Rings, and the Third Flattened. Wadsworth Atheneum.

3892–95. Four Broilers, All Wrought. Straight, Serpentine, and Scrolled. The Third Was a Nice Piece of Work. 18th Century. Wadsworth Atheneum.

3896–97. Fine Brass Andirons, Spiraled. Both with Ball Feet. The First Pair Has the Fender Posts. The Second Pair Has Octagon Sections. Bigelow Collection.

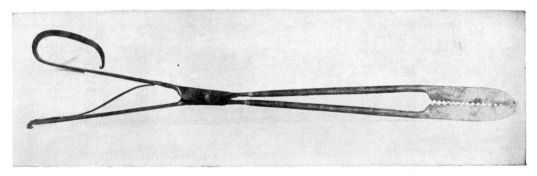

3898. Long, Large Ember Tongs. For Handling Partly Burned Logs in a Fireplace. Mark M. Henderson, Norwalk, Connecticut.

3899-3903. Five Styles of Andirons, the First and Last Being Cast. On One a Bust, the Other a Hessian with a Handle Hat Like a Mitre. The Second Is Wrought with a Brass Cap, the Third and Fourth Are Rare Designs, All Wrought. Rudolph P. Pauly, Boston.

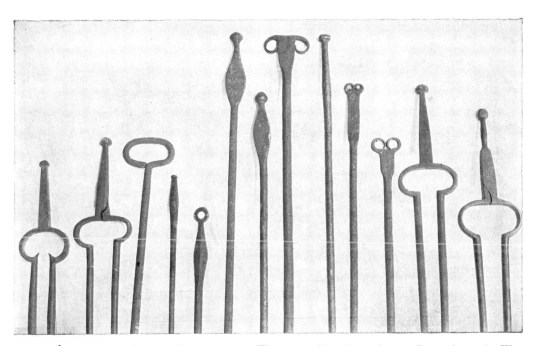

3904-16. Tong and Shovel Handles, All Wrought. The Best Is the Last, Since It Was Decorated with Tool Work on the Handle. 18th Century, The Author's.

3917-54. 17TH CENTURY. L. P. GOULDING, SUDBURY.

The best-furnished fireplace known to the author. Birch broom, carved spoon, gourd, long-handled spider, flapjack turner, S hanger, slice, two skewer holders with skewers, hasty-pudding stick, culinary forks, two kettle lifters, three patterns of broilers, toaster, two trivets, a charcoal stove, andirons with spit rods, swivel teakettle, brass kettle, trammel chain, two trammels, toddy iron, very large skimmer, firkin, dipper, sugar toddy stick, and on the floor the largest toddy iron ever found, hanging spider, bean pot, door for oven, stone fireplace.

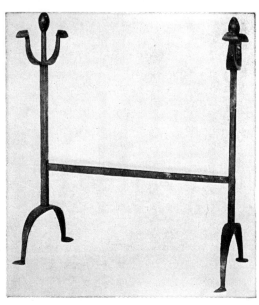 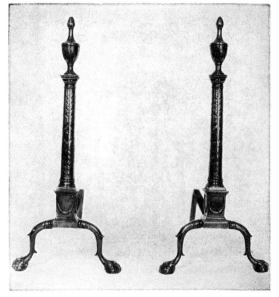

3955. RARE REST FOR SKEWER, OR POSSIBLY FOR SHOVEL AND TONGS. J. STOGDELL STOKES.

3956. (Right.) RARE PAIR OF BRASS ANDIRONS, BALL AND CLAW, DECORATED WITH SEVERAL CLASSICAL MOTIVES. I. SACK, PALMER COLLECTION.

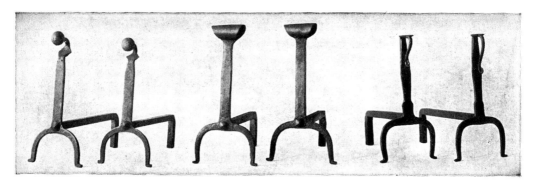

3957–59. THREE PAIRS OF ANDIRONS, THE GOOSE HEAD WITH BALL, THE FLAT SCROLL, AND THE COLONIAL PIGTAIL. WADSWORTH ATHENEUM.

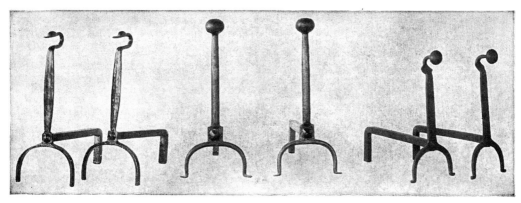

3960–62. THREE PAIRS OF ANDIRONS, A GOOSE HEAD WITH THE BILL, EYE, AND NOSTRIL MARKED, THE STRAIGHT BALL, AND THE GOOSE-HEAD BALL. FORMERLY THE AUTHOR'S.

 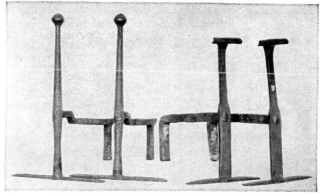

3963–65. THE FIRST A HEART MOTIVE ANDIRON. E. W. SARGENT, PROVIDENCE. THE SECOND AND THIRD TRESTLE-FOOT ANDIRONS, WITH BALL AND SCROLL HEADS. FORMERLY THE AUTHOR'S.

3966. Chiefly Interesting from the Inscription "H. W. Stiegel, Elizabeth Furnace, 1769." Philip Meredith Allen, Broad Axe, Pennsylvania.

3967–81. Fireplace with Equipment. Francis D. Brinton.

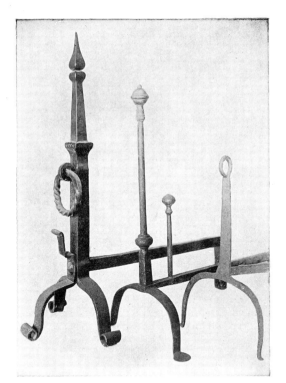 

3982–84. THREE STYLES OF ANDIRONS, OF WHICH THE FIRST IS PROBABLY ENGLISH.
3985. (Right.) A KETTLE LIFTER TO REMOVE HEAVY ARTICLES FROM THE CRANE. VERY RARE.
J. STOGDELL STOKES.

3986–90. BEAUTIFULLY PATTERNED IRON FIRE FRAME, UNUSUAL
FIRE DOGS, BETTY LAMPS, SKILLET, SHOVEL AND TONGS, IRON
TOASTER, LANTERN, PIPE TONGS. E. S. MACOMBER, PROVIDENCE.

3991–99. UTENSILS FROM DOYLESTOWN TAVERN. TWO SPERM OIL LAMPS, TRIVET FOR SAD IRON, A REMARKABLE CAST CHOPPING BOWL, THE EDGED ROLLER MOVING IN THE BOTTOM OF THE TRENCH ONLY, A PADLOCK, TIN NURSING BOTTLE, CANDLE HOLDER, AND AN INK WELL.

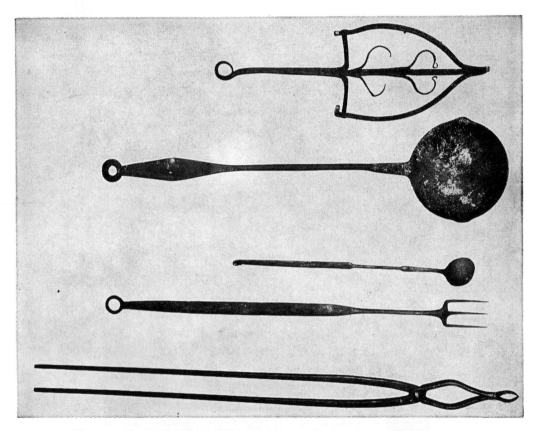

4000–04. WROUGHT FLATIRON HOLDER, DOUBLE-NOSED WROUGHT LADLE, LIGHT WROUGHT SPOON, A FORK LONG ENOUGH TO SUP WITH A CERTAIN INDIVIDUAL, AND ODD PIPE TONGS. WADSWORTH ATHENEUM.

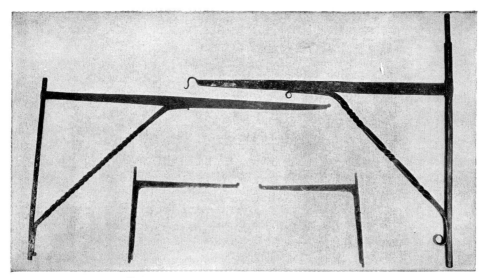

4005–08. Two Unusual Cranes, and a Pair of Cranes.

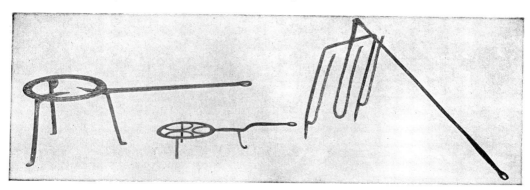

4009–11. A Common and an Unusual Trivet, and a Jointed Bread Toaster. Pennsylvania.

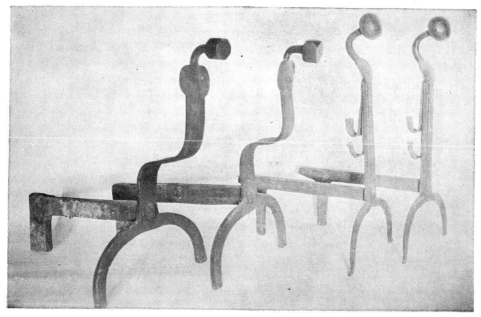

4012–13. Rare Pair of Ogee Andirons, and a Pair with Hooks for the Spit.
All on Page Wadsworth Atheneum.

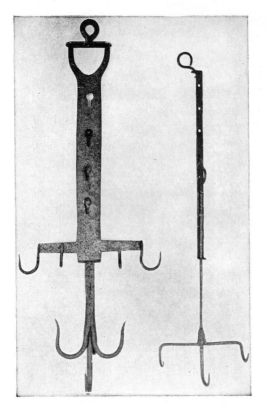
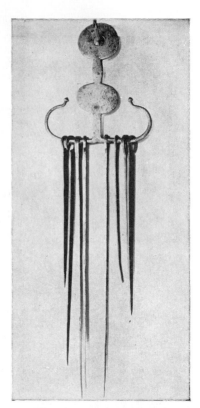

4014-15. Two Trammel Bird Spits, Both Very Rare. Wadsworth Atheneum.
4016-17. An Excellent Skewer Holder with Ball Terminations. L. P. Goulding.

4018. Clockwork Jack with Brass Face and Weight. Wadsworth Atheneum.
4019. (Right.) A Wrought-Iron Beetle Built for a Bootjack. 18th Century. Perhaps the
Original of the Cast, and Late, Jacks. Francis D. Brinton.

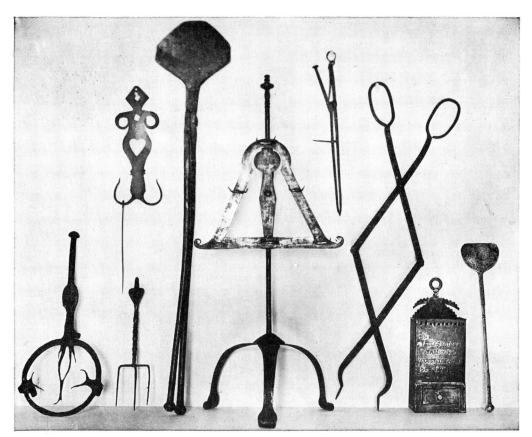

4020–28. Collection of Mrs. J. Insley Blair, Tuxedo Park. The Broiler and Toasting Fork Are Good. The Skewer Holder Is Very Fine. An Odd Waffle Iron, or Perhaps Wafer Iron, an Adjustable Bird Spit, Two Pairs of Pipe Tongs, a Cake Turner, and a Tin Pipe Box, Perhaps Unique, Carrying a Legend.

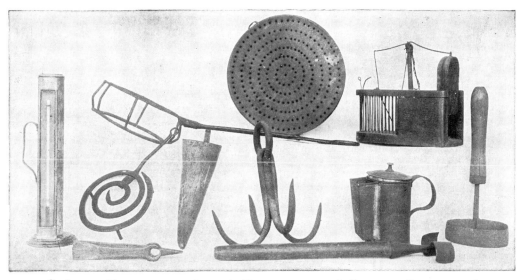

4029–38. In the Foreground a Slater's Hammer and an S Chopper. Behind, an Ancient Thermometer, Spiraled Broiler, Kettle Lifter, Colander, Rat Trap, Milk Warmer, and Chopper. Francis Mireau.

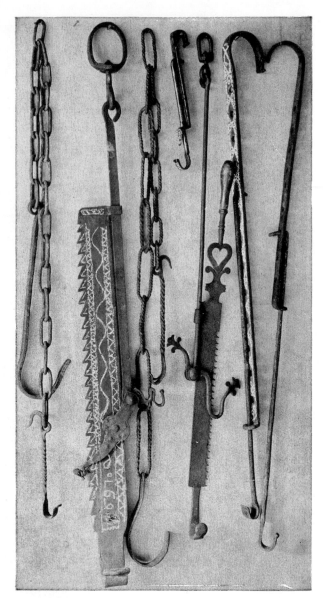

4039–46. REMARKABLE ASSEMBLAGE OF DECORATIVE TRAMMELS. THE FIRST HAS AN ODD SAW TOOTH, WITH PUNCH MARKS AND SCROLLS. THE SECOND AND FOURTH ARE CHAIN TRAMMELS, TWISTED, WITH HOOKS ATTACHED. THE THIRD IS THE OLDEST DATED, NAMELY 1697. THE SIXTH IS FANCIFUL WITH HEART MOTIVE AND WOODEN HANDLE. THE SEVENTH HAS PUNCH MARK DECORATION.

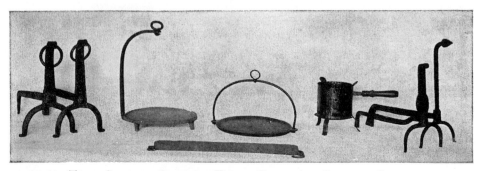

4047–53. THREE STYLES IN ANDIRONS, TWO IN GRIDDLES, A CHARCOAL STOVE, AND IN THE FOREGROUND A SCROLLED FENDER BAR TO LIE ON THE FLOOR. WADSWORTH ATHENEUM.

4054–57. A Good Fireplace, Late 18th Century. A Fender with Brass Turned Ornaments. Very Rare. Fine Pair of Brass Andirons, a Handsome Brass Fire Set. Henry A. Hoffman, Barrington, Rhode Island.

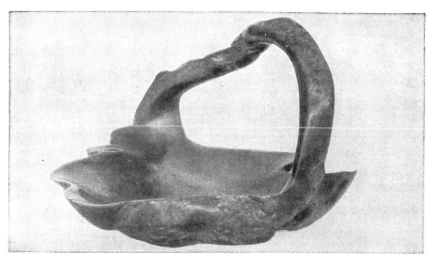

4058. Rare Burl Tray, Wrought from One Piece. A Most Attractive Article in This Material. Joseph Skinner, Holyoke.

4059-64. Fine Scroll Hinge with Scroll Brace, Scrolled Latch Bar. Well-Designed Escutcheon. A Unique Scraper for Attaching to the Side of a Wall, a Fish Held by a Dog, as a Fish Broiler, a Swivel Candlestand. All Wrought Iron. William B. Montague.

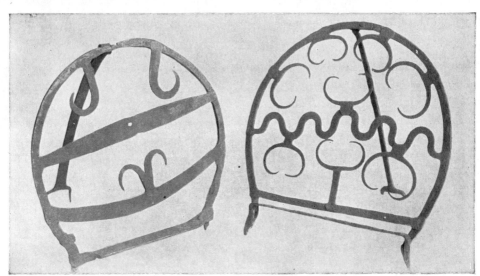

4065-66. Broilers with Swivel Braces To Hold Them at an Angle Against the Fire. Very Rare. William B. Montague, Norristown.

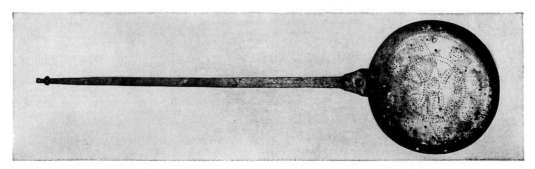

4067. Engraved Brass Warming Pan, Iron Handle, with Crook Top. Earlier than the Wooden Handle. 18th Century. Wadsworth Atheneum.

4068. Rare Pair of Cast Andirons. One Is Welcome to Suppose Them To Be Any Fair Lady of the Olden Day. E. C. Hall, Longmeadow, Massachusetts.

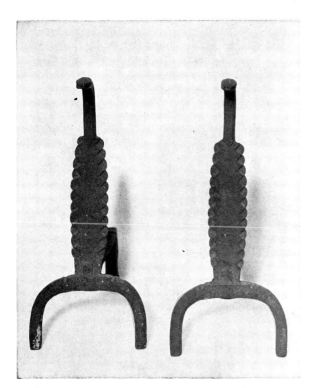

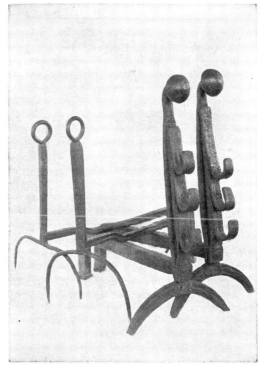

4069. Rattlesnake Andirons, Probably Unique. 17¼ Inches High. 1780. Perhaps These Are All That Is Left To Mark the Recovery of the Blacksmith from Seeing Things.

4070-71. (Right.) Very Light Andirons and a Crude Pair with Three Sets of Hooks for the Spit.

4072. Excellent Design in Andirons. Pad Feet. A Floral Motive Is Worked on the Square above the Branch, the Legs Are Riveted into the Post.

4073. A Camp Kettle, Copper. Iron Scrolled Legs and Wooden Handles. Used by an Officer in the Revolution. Washington Headquarters. Morristown, New Jersey.

4074. Sunflower Andirons. Unique. Formed by Twisting the Sections into One. Bigelow Collection. 18th Century.

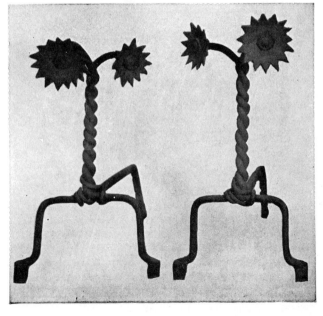

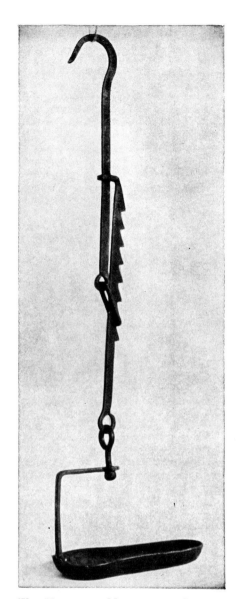

4075. Skewer Holder and Skewers. Such an Article Was Hung to a Nail on the Chimney Girt. Lately Several Fine Ones Have Come to Light. Wadsworth Atheneum.

4076-77. (Right.) Betty Lamp with Trammel. Very Rare. 18th Century. H. W. Erving.

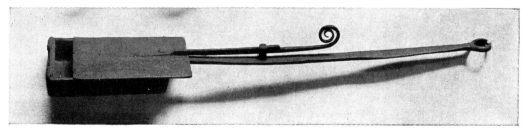

4078. Fire Carrier, in Which the Cover Slides Instead of Lifting. 17th or 18th Century. Fuessenich Collection.

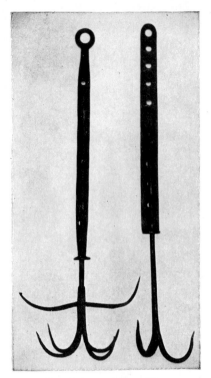 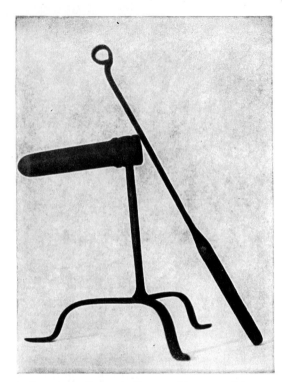

4079–80. Bird or Meat Trammels. 17th or 18th Century. Former: Dwight Blainey. Latter: Mrs. De Witt Howe.

4081. (Right.) A Gophering Iron.

The stick was heated red hot and placed in the sheath, which was then used for ironing ruffles by drawing them over it. The stick was so convenient for toddy that "the profane and the ignorant" have given it the name of a toddy stick. Of course, the toddy stick proper is never carefully rounded. The other name for it is a loggerhead. Yokels at a fireside getting into a quarrelsome discussion would seize these to maintain their positions, hence the expression, "at loggerheads."

4082–86. A Decorative Toaster, Copper Teakettle in Place on a Long-Handled Spider, the Handle To Rest in a Crotch in the Rear, a Charcoal or Invalid's Stove. The Top Lifted. The Pads Were To Hold a Large Dish. Betty Lamp on a Standard for Adjustment. Francis D. Brinton.

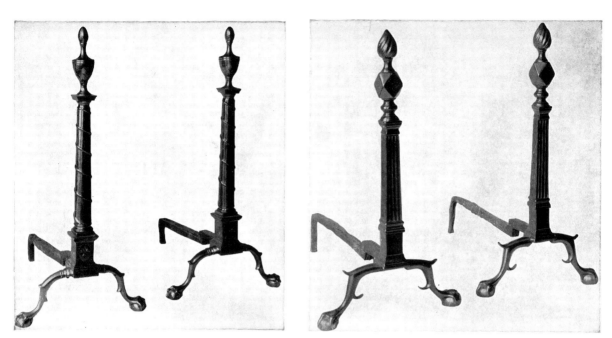

4087–88. Rare, Andirons. Late 18th Century. Rhode Island School of Design.

4089–91. Fire Frame, Brass Urns. Fireback: "F. Pleis." Andirons.
Bigelow Collection.

4092. Charcoal Broiler (Old Handle). 4093. Round Foot Stove. 18th Century. Wadsworth Atheneum.

4094. A Fire Carrier. A Common Convenience in Old Houses, before the Days of Matches. 18th Century. Wadsworth Atheneum.

4095-4100. Six Types of Shutter Fasteners, All Wrought. The Third and Fourth Are the Oldest. Those with Plates Attaching to the Wall Are the Latest, the Last Having a Spring, Being Used in the 19th Century.

4101. Pair of Excellent Shutter Fasteners. Similar Irons Were Used in the Walls of Brick Houses as Headers on Sustaining Rods. William B. Goodwin.

4102. (Right.) A Lantern with Feet and Gables for Ventilation. Sanderson Collection.

4103-05. Ship Lanterns or Binnacles. The First Is Made with Lighthouse Glass. That Is, the Shape Is Designed To Magnify the Reflections. Sanderson Collection.

Since the clipper ship and the sailing ship have gone out of use, ship's lanterns are desirable for porches or doorways or dens, especially in seashore houses.

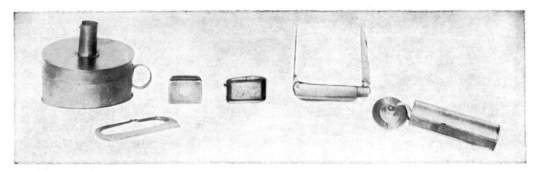

4106–10. A Series of Tinder Boxes or Sparkers. 18th Century. H. W. Erving. The Round Box Contains the Tinder, the Steel and Flint, and the Cover Is Used as a Candlestick. The Next Three Items Were To Carry in the Pocket. The Last One Generates the Spark by the Rapid Revolution of the Wheel. There Is a Pennsylvania Collection of These Articles Running into the Hundreds.

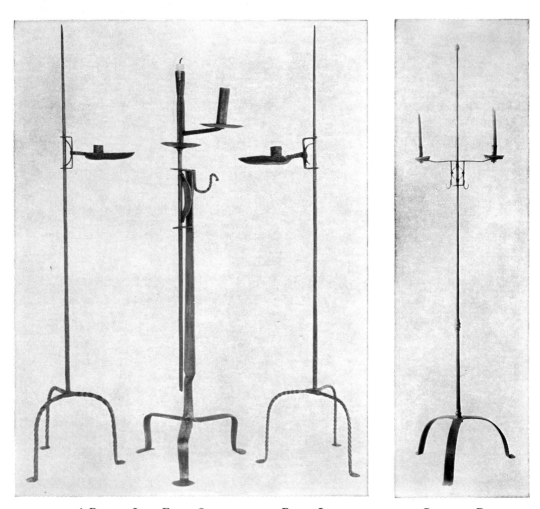

4111–14. A Pair of Iron Floor Standards for Betty Lamps, and in the Center a Rare and Quaint Example for Two Candles. J. Stogdell Stokes. The Last Number Has Brass Mounts. Formerly the Author's.

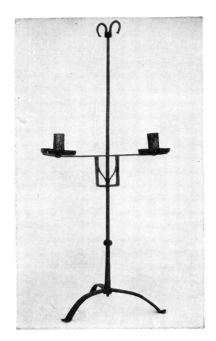

4115. Rare Table Candle Stand, Adjustable. Wadsworth Atheneum.

4116. (Right.) Square Iron Standard on a Weighted Tin Base. Candlesticks and Hood in Tin. Formerly the Author's.

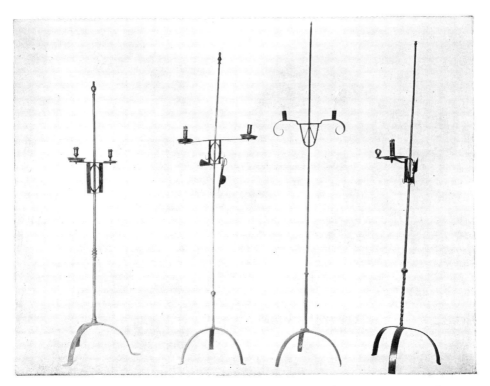

4117-20. Four Stands with Brass Mountings. The Last for a Single Candle. 18th Century. Formerly the Author's.

4121-27. Sconces. The Upper Pair Carry Three Lights Each. The One in the Center Is Very Odd. Those at Each Side Are Also Unusual. All of Tin. Mrs. J. Insley Blair.

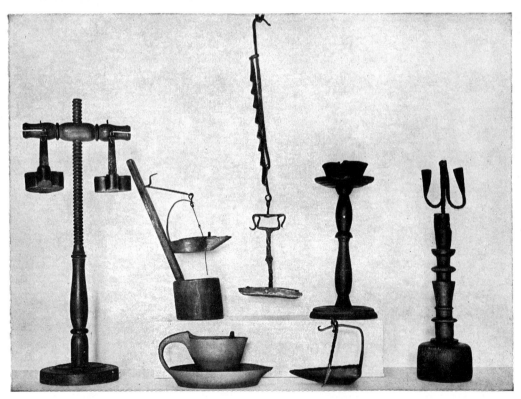

4128-35. The First Is Extremely Rare, a Screw Standard for Two Betty Lamps. That with the Trammel Had Two Candles. The Second in the Foreground Is a Cast Betty. The Next to the Last in the Background Is a Wooden Standard for a Betty.

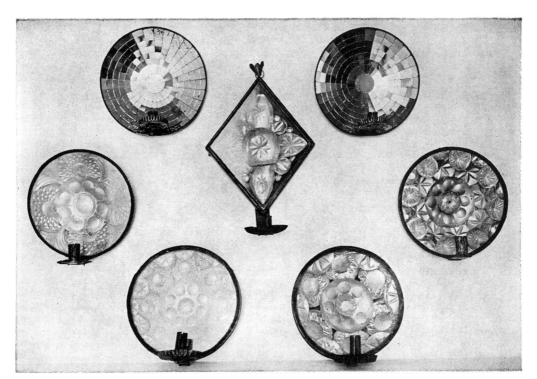

4136-42. SCONCES OF SMALL SECTIONS OF MIRROR GLASS OR OF BITS OF PEWTER AS THIN AS TIN FOIL. A VERY RICH COLLECTION OF RARE AND MUCH SOUGHT PIECES. MRS. J. INSLEY BLAIR.

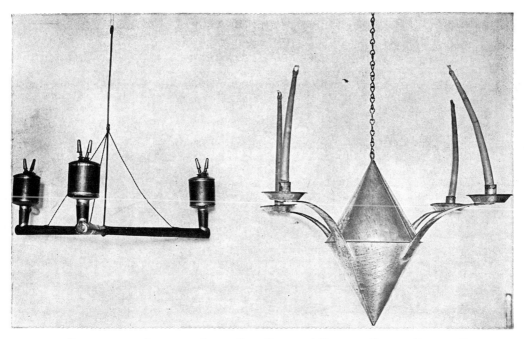

4143-44. CHANDELIERS. LEFT: FOR SPERM OIL. RIGHT: A DIAMOND-SHAPED DOUBLE CONE WITH ARMS FOR CANDLES. MRS. J. INSLEY BLAIR.

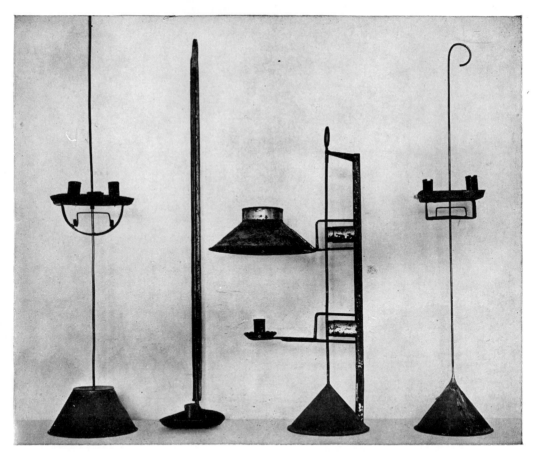

4145-48. Set of Four Standards, Three with Conical Tin Bases Filled with Sand. The Third Is Perhaps Unique. The Second Has a Trammel and Is Sometimes Called a Loom Light.

4149-50. Pewter and a Glass Sconce. All on This Page. Mrs. J. Insley Blair.

4151–53. Five, Six, and Four-Sided Lanterns. The Cut-Outs on the Center One Are Very Laboriously Done, and the Pattern Is Good. The Third Was To Hang against the Wall. Wadsworth Atheneum.

4154–55. Large Ship Lantern and a Lantern with a Reflector Within. Wadsworth Atheneum.

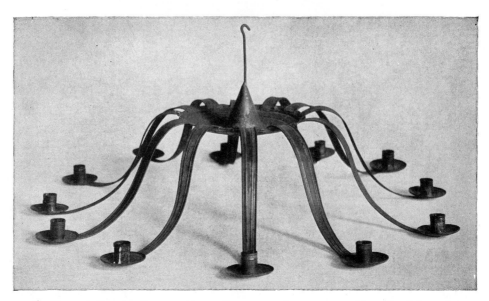

4156. Twelve-Candle Central Light Sconce or Chandelier. This Has More Grace Than Most of the Sort and Presents No Uncouth or Doubtful Lines. The Tin Is Strengthened at the Sides by Being Rolled over Wires. Fuessenich Collection.

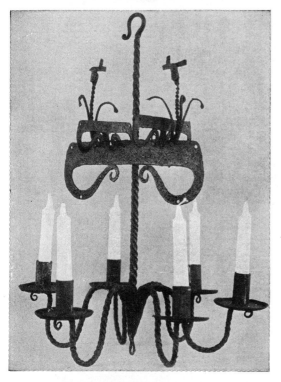

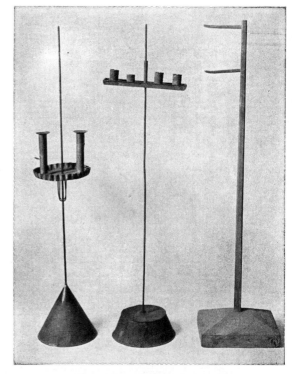

4157. A Unique Iron Chandelier with Odd Motives at the Top, Where Presumably Two More Candles Were Carried. Important. J. Stogdell Stokes.

4158-60. Two Tin and One Wood Stand, the Second for Four Candles, and the Last for Hooking on the So-Called Hog-Scraper Candlestick. Fuessenich Collection.

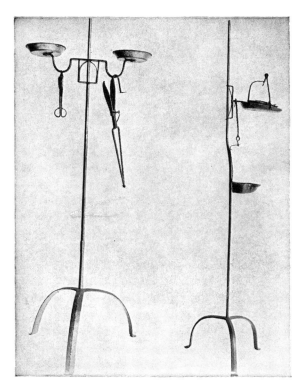
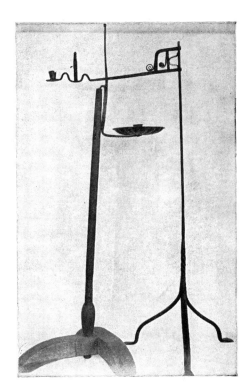

4161–62. Floor Stands, That at the Right for a Betty. The Curving Foot Is Beveled Both Ways. Edward C. Wheeler, Jr., Boston.

4163–64. (Right.) Rare Stand with a T Base Mortised, To Carry a Candle, Which Can Be Lifted from the Socket and Used as an Ordinary Carrying Candle. The Other Example Has a Very Fanciful Arm and Is Probably Unique. Both: 17th or 18th Century. J. Stogdell Stokes.

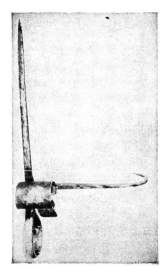

4165. Miner's or a Cooper's Candle with a Spring Catch. The Hook and the Point To Drive into the Wall. Should Be Shown with the Long Line at the Base.

4166–67. (Right.) Lantern and a Sconce. That at the Left Folds, as a Dark Lantern, That at the Right Has a Concave Reflector. H. W. Erving.

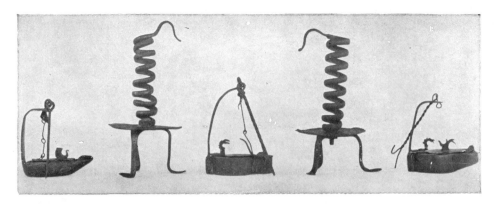

4168–72. Three Rare Bettys, the Left a Rooster, the Middle a Griffin, the Right a Rooster and Griffin. The Pair of Spiral Stands Are Found Abroad, and Perhaps Here Also. J. Stogdell Stokes.

4173–74. Rare Sconce Heads To Be Attached to Shaft. Both Have a Feature We Have Seen But Once Before, Namely Contrivances for Pushing up the Candle as It Burns. Fuessenich Collection.

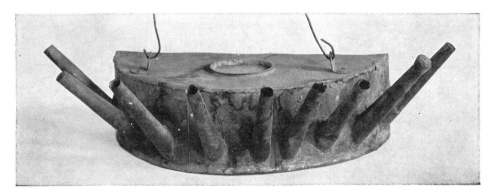

4175. Semicircular Lamp with Nine Outlets for Wicks. Rare or Unique. Fuessenich Collection.

4176–79. Four Rare Pieces. That at the Left Is a Standard for a Betty, and That at the Right Is a Rest for Two Bettys, Adjustable. The Central Pair Remind One of a Fleur-de-Lis. These Are All Pennsylvania Examples. J. Stogdell Stokes.

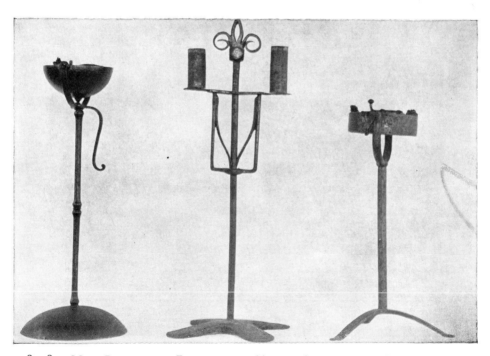

4180–82. Most Interesting Betty with a Turned Standard and Swivel, a Scroll Handle, and Reverse Saucer Base. The Second Has an X Stretcher Base and Top Decoration. At the Right Is a Swivel Betty. J. Stogdell Stokes.

4183–86. THREE OF THESE ARE UNIQUE, AND THE HANGING LOOM LIGHT IS RARE. FAT WAS BURNED IN A BETTY. A. H. RICE, BETHLEHEM. NOW SOLD TO MR. STOKES.

4187–89. THREE RARE LANTERNS, THOUGH THE SECOND IS PERHAPS EARLY 19TH CENTURY, FOR HANGING IN A HALL. THE OTHERS ARE OCTAGON, THAT ON THE RIGHT BEING EXTREMELY QUAINT. RUDOLPH P. PAULY.

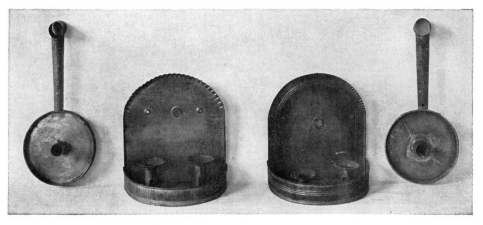

4190–93. RARE PAIR OF CANDLESTICKS, AND TWO DOUBLE WALL SCONCES OF TIN. FLAYDERMAN & KAUFMAN.

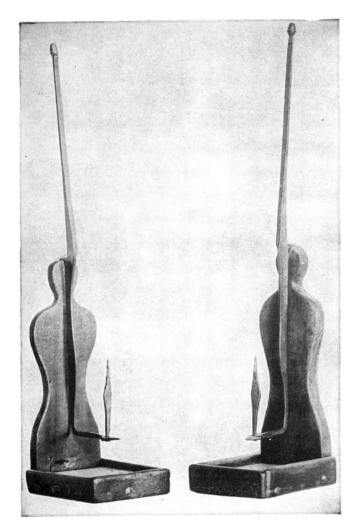

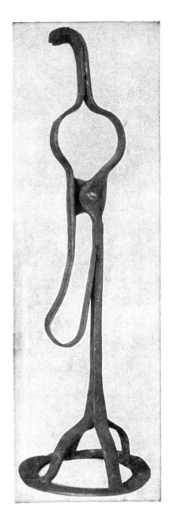

4194-95. Double Purpose Sconces To Remain or To Take Off. E. B. Leete Company.
4196. (Right.) Rare Iron Standard. Benjamin A. Jackson, Wickford, Rhode Island.

4197. A Double Wall Sconce of Tin. Fuessenich Collection.
4198-99. (Right.) A Wooden Bracket To Carry a Tin Lamp, and a Unique Betty, with a D Handle and a Swivel. J. Stogdell Stokes.

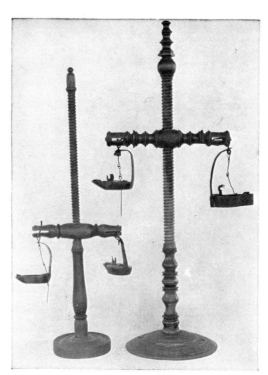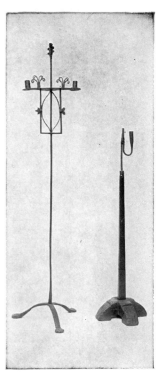

4200–04. The First Is an Adjustable Stand with a Box for Yarn or Other Work. The Screw Stands Are for Attaching Bettys, and Are Rare and Quaint. The Fourth Is a Good Floor Stand of Iron. The Last Is an X Base Wooden Standard for a Rush and a Candlestick. Fourth and Fifth: Owner Unknown. The Others: J. Stogdell Stokes.

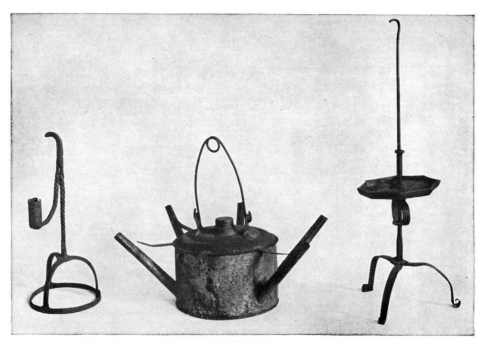

4205–07. A Rare Combined Rush and Candle Standard. A Camp-Meeting Lard Oil Lamp, and a Finely Wrought Standard for Wicks. Fuessenich Collection.

4208. An Elaborate Wrought-Iron Table Sconce with a Ring Carrier, and a Snuffer.

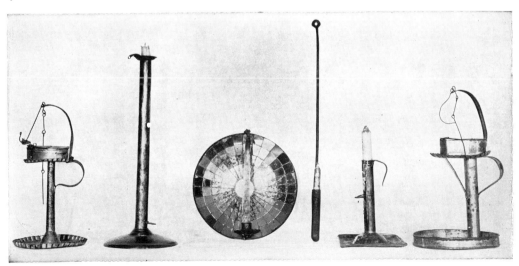

4209-14. Six Lighting Fixtures, the Second Being a So-Called Hog Scraper, and the Fourth a Loom Light. The Fifth Is a Square Base Candlestick.

4215. Combined Wooden and Tin Chandelier. 18th Century. Rare. Anthony T. Kelly, Springfield, Massachusetts.

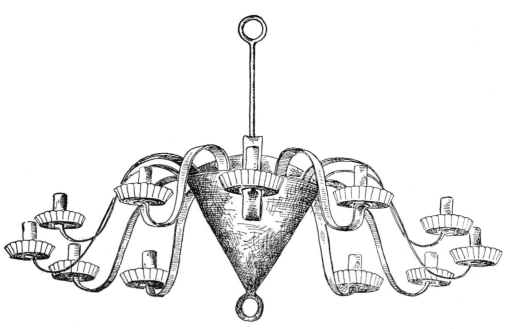

4216. Chandelier of Tin with Scalloped Saucers, and a Cone Center. Drawn by Strickland & Law, Boston, Who Are Acquainted with the Original.

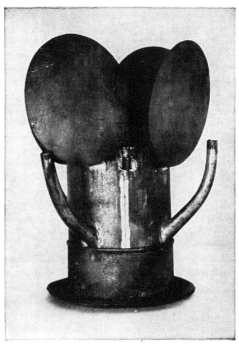

4217. Swinging Wall Bracket for a Beacon.
4218. Camp-Meeting Lamp with Four Reflectors, "Giving Light to Every Quarter."
Both: Formerly the Author's.

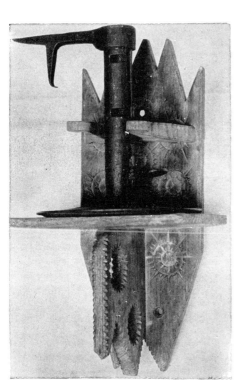

4219–20. Left: North Carolina Carved Standard with a Shelf or Stick Light. Right:
Remarkable Fine Betty with a Brass Escutcheon, Bearing the Maker's or the
Recipient's Initials. This Has a Wick Pick. Both: Formerly the Author's.

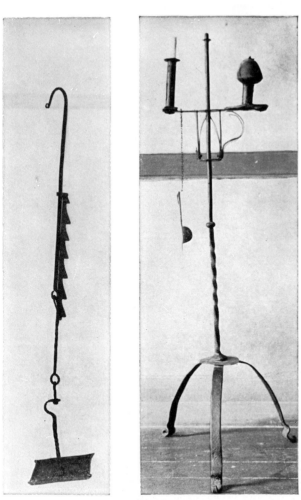

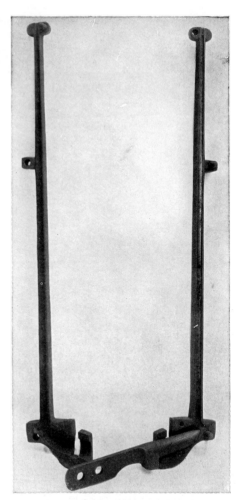

4221. FAT LAMP WITH TRAMMEL. FUESSENICH COL.   4222. LAMP AND CANDLE.
4223-24. IRON MOLDS FOR CHURCH WARDEN PIPES. JOE KINDIG, JR., YORK, PENNSYLVANIA.

4225. FOUR-WICK BRASS. MORRISTOWN. 4226-27. CAST LANTERNS. CLIFFORD R. WELD, ROCK.

4228–30. Sconce with a Glass. Rare or Unique. Above, a Sconce with Blacksmith's Insignia. Unique. A Tin Sconce Decoration. J. Stogdell Stokes.

4231. (Right.) Betty Lamp of the Usual Pattern with Twisted Hook, Which May Be Placed over a Chair Ear or Jabbed into the Wall. Dr. and Mrs. J. M. Birnie.

4232. Lantern of Unusual Design with Ventilators So Arranged as To Prevent Blowing Out the Light. Sanderson Collection.

4233. Sconce with Imbricated Daisy Reflectors of Very Thin Pewter. Author's Collection, Wadsworth Atheneum.

4234-35. Unique Wall Sconces, Quaint Design. Fuessenich Collection.

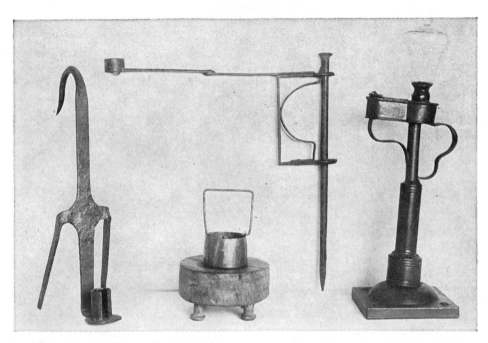

4236-39. Sconce Which Could Be Placed over an Open Barrel, or Any Edge Like a Chair Back, or Hooked. The Second Is a Low Standard Lamp. The Third, a Jointed Sconce for a Reading Chair or Such Purpose. The Last Is a Rare Betty. Mrs. J. Insley Blair.

Dates are not named, as a rule, because many of the lights like the Bettys were made continuously in the 17th, 18th, and even the 19th centuries, up to 1857. Almost universally, however, the specimens are of 18th century.

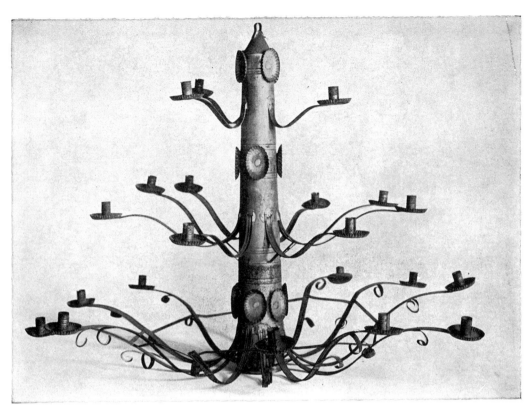

4240. An Amusingly Intricate Church Chandelier with So Many Lights that One Would Be Weary of Counting. Unique. Fuessenich Collection.

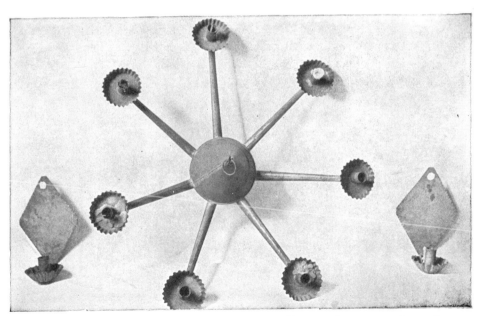

4241-43. Pair of Small Diamond Sconces and a Central Sconce for Seven Lights. Fuessenich Collection.

This collection and the Stokes collection with that of Mrs. J. Insley Blair include many hundreds, perhaps thousands of the rarest and best wrought iron and tin found in America.

It has been thought by some that no rush lights are native. It is hardly believable that simple lights of this kind were not made in the 17th Century in America. Of course, of late, many are brought in from Ireland, France, and Italy.

4244-48. At the Ends Is a Pair of Graceful and Perhaps Unique Sconces. An Odd Betty. A Wall Toggle Light for Two Candles. A Spiraled Gophering-Iron. J. Stogdell Stokes.

4249-53. Lamps for Whale Oil or Lard Oil. James Davidson, New London.

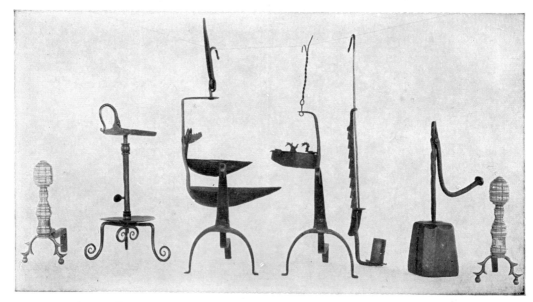

4254-59. At the Extremes a Pair of Doll's Brass Andirons. The Second Is a Rare Betty Stand. The Third Is a Double Betty. The Fourth for a Single Betty. The Fifth, a Loom or Ceiling Light, and Last a Wooden-Base Rush Light. J. Stogdell Stokes.

4260–61. THREE-CANDLE GLASS SCONCE, UNIQUE TO THE AUTHOR. FUESSENICH COLLECTION. THREE-CANDLE COMBINED GLASS AND TIN SCONCE, VERY EFFECTIVE. CHESTER E. DIMICK, GALES FERRY, CONNECTICUT.

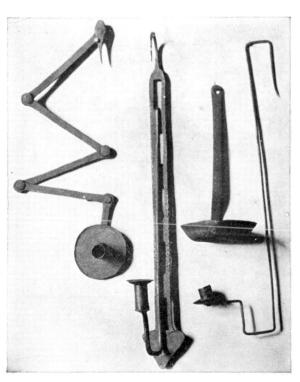

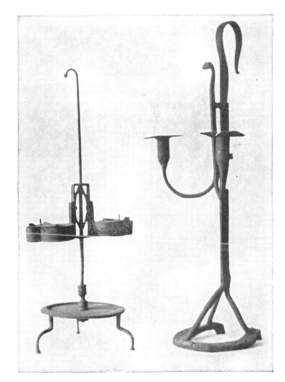

4262–65. RARE OR UNIQUE TRAMMEL CANDLE. THE OTHER SPECIMENS ARE VARIANTS. THE FIRST, HOWEVER, HAS A BRAD WHICH MAY BE DRIVEN INTO THE WALL. FUESSENICH COLLECTION.

4266–67. (Right.) A UNIQUE DOUBLE BETTY STANDARD AND A HORSESHOE BASE, DOUBLE SCONCE, THE ANCESTRY OF THE LATTER BEING OBSCURE. WILLIAM F. HUBBARD, HARTFORD.

4268–71. Four Lanterns, the First Being Called Erroneously Paul Revere, the Second a Tin Dipper, Pierced, for a Candle. Perhaps Unique. The Other Two Are Variants of the Barred Lanterns. All: Rudolph P. Pauly.

4272–77. A Heart Waffle Iron. Below It a Three-Way Pair of Snuffers, Perhaps Unique. They Work Like Scissors. The Two Central Lamps Are of Tin for Whale Oil or Camphine. At the Right Is the Ordinary Brass Candlestick. Wadsworth Atheneum.

4278. Rare, Fine Six-Branch Chandelier with a Wood Hub. Present Owner Unknown.

4279. Four-Armed Tin Sconce with a Glass Globe at the Center. 18th Century. Present Owner Unknown.

4280. Pierced Tin Lantern. It Gave Little Light. Paul Revere Could Not Have Signaled with It.

4281. (Right.) Decorative Lantern To Be Placed on a Post. An Excellent Pattern. Both: Formerly the Author's.

4282–85. Two Pairs of Sconces, All Tin, the Second Pair Perhaps Unique. They Now Contain Bayberry Candles, Such as the Pilgrims Made from Berries Growing among the Sands. Owners Unknown.

4286–90. Piggin, Reading Glass, Triple Sconce, Swivel Pewter Lamp, and Flint and Steel Candlestick. Owners Unknown.

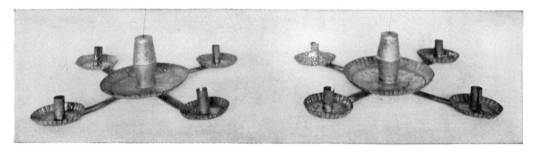

4291–92. Pair of Odd, but Simple Hanging Sconces. Wadsworth Atheneum.

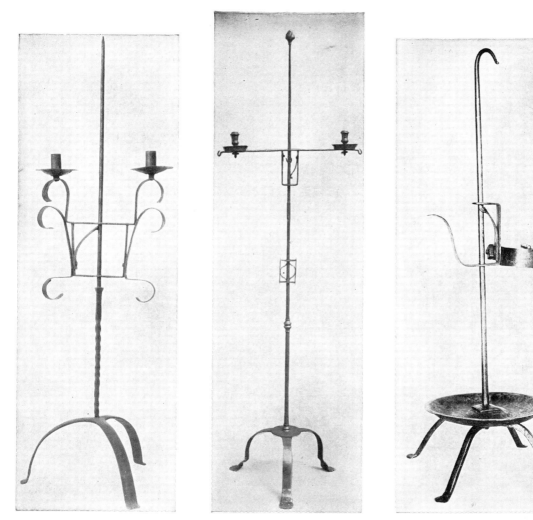

4293-95. The First Is a Very Good Floor Stand. Flayderman & Kaufman. ;The Second Is a Beautifully Wrought Iron Standard Mounted with Brass, the Top Being Spiraled. Metropolitan Museum. The Third Is a Unique Betty with Four Legs, and Drip Saucer. Wadsworth Atheneum.

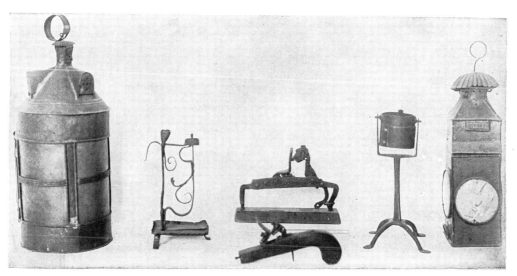

4296-4301. Horn Lantern, a Scrolled Spring Stand, Two Sparkers, One Being a Pistol, a Swivel Betty, and a Bull's Eye. Former Ives Collection.

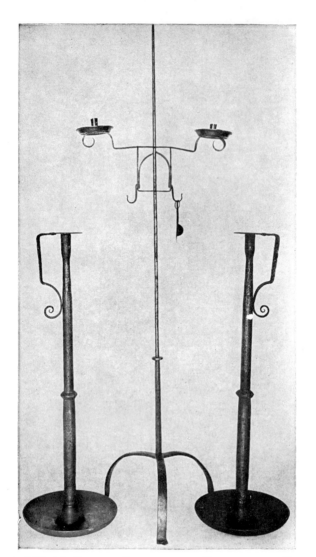

4302–05. Pair of Candlesticks, Found in the Ruins of a Church at Manheim, Pennsylvania. A Floor Stand and a Double Chandelier with Battlement or Crown Ornamentation. All: Mrs. J. Insley Blair.

4306–11. The First and the Fifth Are Rush Holders, the First Also Carrying the Candle. The Second and Last Are Tin Lamps. The Third Is a Fine Sconce. Formerly Anthony T. Kelly's.

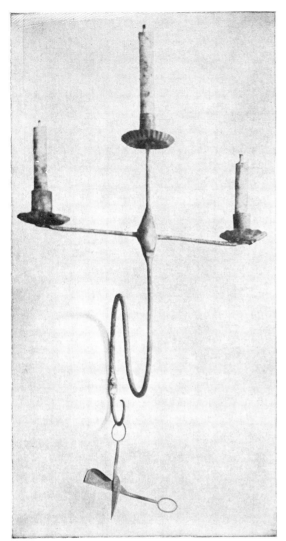

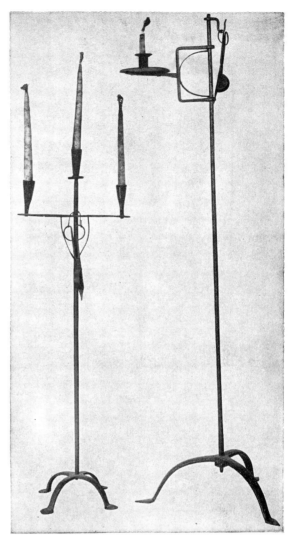

4312–15. The First a Wall Sconce, Sustaining Wrought-Iron Snuffers. Pair of Rare Stands at the Right. Present Owners Unknown.

4316–24. Formerly the Author's, Now Wadsworth Atheneum. The First a Rare Box Light, the Third, a Cooper's Lamp, the Fourth a Wooden Standard for a Betty, the Next a Maid's or Hired Man's Light To Carry to One's Room at Night. It Looks Like a Miniature Pitcher. The Next with a Snout, Is a Whale-Oil Light. Then a Large Saucer-Base Candlestick, and a Miniature Double Candlestick.

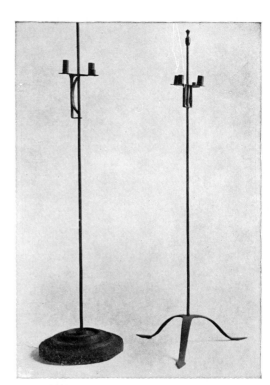

4325–27. The First and the Third Are Standards of Wood, Very Quaint. The Second Is the Usual Floor Candlestick. Formerly the Author's.

4328–29. (Right.) Floor Standards, the Former with a Wooden Base, from Davis Antique Shop, Old Lyme, Connecticut.

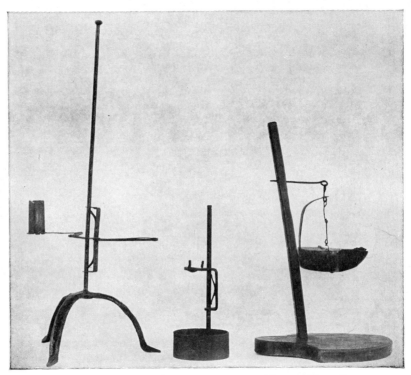

4330–32. An Odd Stand Perhaps for the Table. The Second and Third Are Table Stands of Quaint Design. J. Stogdell Stokes.

4333-36. GOOD SIX-SIDED LANTERN, A RARE LANTERN OF WOOD, A SCONCE LANTERN OF TIN, AND A WALL SCONCE WITH REFLECTOR MISSING. RUDOLPH P. PAULY.

4337-42. SIX LANTERNS, THE FIRST TO CARRY ABOUT THE HOUSE, THE FOURTH WITH A FRAME OF WOOD, THE FIFTH FOR A SHIP, AND THE LAST WAS COMMON FIFTY YEARS AGO. WADSWORTH ATHENEUM.

4343-49. CYLINDER CANDLE WITH FOUR LIGHTS, A REFLECTOR, THREE LARD LIGHTS, A WALL LAMP, AND A RARE, FOUR-SIDED GLASS SCONCE. ANTHONY T. KELLY, SPRINGFIELD.

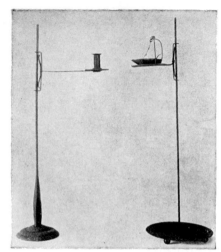

4350–51. PENNSYLVANIA SWIVEL BETTY LIGHTS. HUNDREDS OF DESIGNS ARE KNOWN, AND SCARCELY ANY TWO ALIKE.

4352–53. (Right.) SINGLE STANDARDS, ONE WITH A TOGGLE JOINT, AND THE OTHER WITH THE USUAL ADJUSTABLE STANDARD, AND THE LARGE BASE WITH BALLS. ALL FOUR FORMERLY THE AUTHOR'S.

4354. A TABLE, PROBABLY UNIQUE. TWO DRAWERS, ONE IN EACH END, WITH A KNOT. CHERRY, FOUND IN VIRGINIA. THE AUTHOR HAS NOT HAD OPPORTUNITY TO EXAMINE THE PIECE, BUT BELIEVES IT TO BE OF GREAT IMPORTANCE. MRS. BERYL DEMOTT, MILLINGTON, NEW JERSEY.

4355. Hall Lantern with Cut-Glass Globe. Carefully Worked-Out Design. Bronze Mounts. Flowing Ribbon Band. Bigelow Collection.

4356. A Gate Latch and Lock. Rare. Wadsworth Atheneum.

4357. Rare Standard with Serpentine Jointed Arm and Spring Candlestick. 18th Century. Flayderman & Kaufman.

4358-59. (Below.) Unique Tulip Bud Door Set. 18th Century. The Original Handle Supposed To Be Shown Here Has Now Been Found, And Is Better than This. Wadsworth Atheneum.

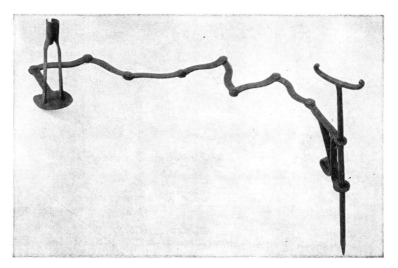

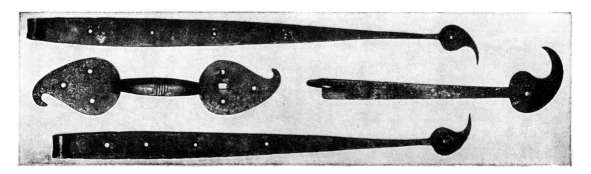

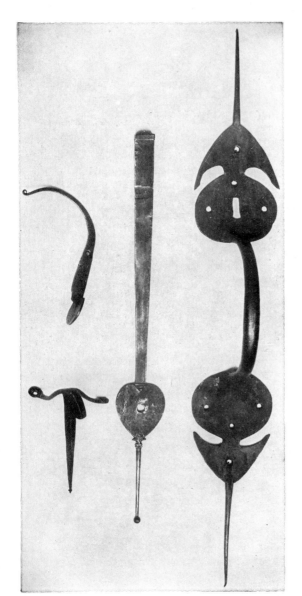

4360–62. Sword Fish Pattern with One of the Two Best Latch Bars Known. Heart Motive. Irving P. Lyon, M.D., Buffalo. Also a Double Brace Wrought Catch.
4363–64. (Right.) Decorative Latch, Spear and Ball Pattern. Latch Bar with a Flat Curled End. Wadsworth Atheneum.

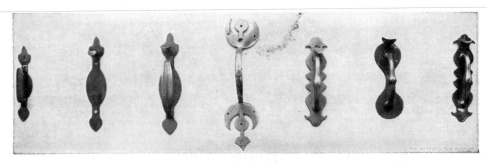

4365–71. Seven Latches. Palmer-Metropolitan Museum Collection. A Part in Brass. Those at the Right are Later.

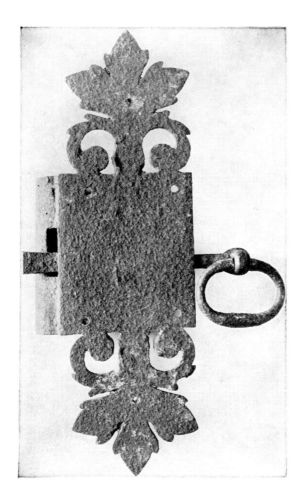

4372. REMARKABLY GOOD CUPBOARD LATCH, WROUGHT IRON, DROP SPRING HANDLE. WADSWORTH ATHENEUM.

4373-74. (Right.) ANCIENT NEW LONDON JAIL LOCK AND HAND CUFFS. JAMES DAVIDSON.

4375. CONESTOGA WAGON AND TOOL BOX LID, WITH DUTCH TULIP DESIGN, AND HASP AND HINGES. PHILIP MEREDITH ALLEN, BROAD AXE, PENNSYLVANIA.

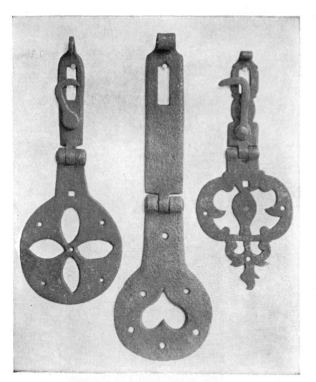

4376-78. The First Three Numbers Are Remarkably Fine Hasps. Probably Pennsylvania-Moravian. William B. Montague, Norristown.

4379-83. (Right.) Four Latches and a Unique Latch Bar. Pennsylvania. It Is Only There That We Find the Latch Handle with a Single Plate, the Bottom Having a Clinch Spur. Same Owner.

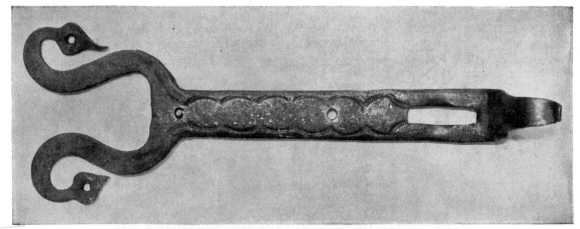

4384. A Scrolled and Stamped Hasp. Late 18th Century. Wadsworth Atheneum.

4385-86. Square Plate Spring Latches. 1750-90.

4387-91. FIVE LATCHES, THE CENTER ONE VERY FINE. ALL WROUGHT. PALMER
COLLECTION. METROPOLITAN MUSEUM.

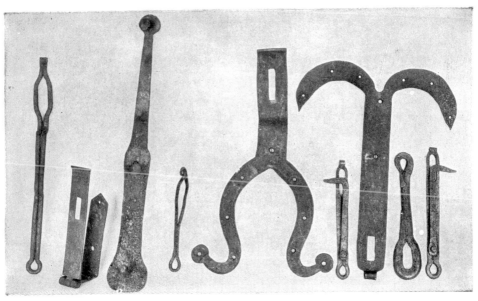

4392-4400. SERIES OF HASPS, ALL WROUGHT, MOSTLY FROM PENNSYLVANIA.
WADSWORTH ATHENEUM.

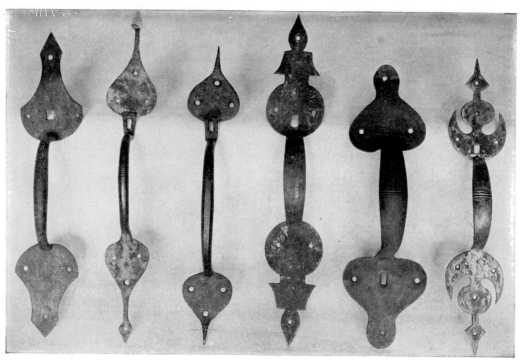

4401–06. Six Latches, the Second and Last Being Very Fine. 18th Century.
Wadsworth Atheneum.

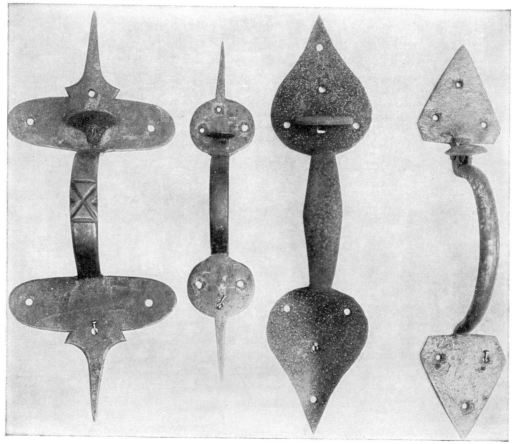

4407–10. Four Latches, the Finest Being the First. 18th Century.
Wadsworth Atheneum.

4411–12. Molded Brass Box Lock. 1730–60. This Is the Elegant Lock of the Best Houses in the 18th Century. North Shore, Massachusetts. Formerly the Author's. Another in the Metropolitan Museum.

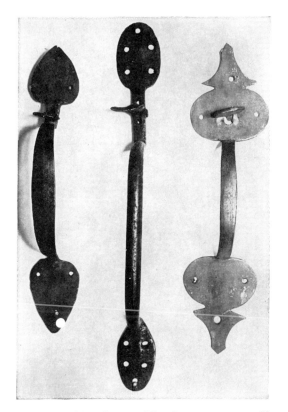 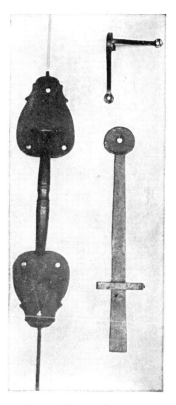

4413–17. The Second Was Intended for a Very Narrow Stile. Heart Shapes or a Modification in Latches Prevail. At the Right Top Is a Double-Braced Catch. A Latch Consists of Five Parts: Handle, Thumb Piece, Latch Bar, Guard, and Striker. Wadsworth Atheneum.

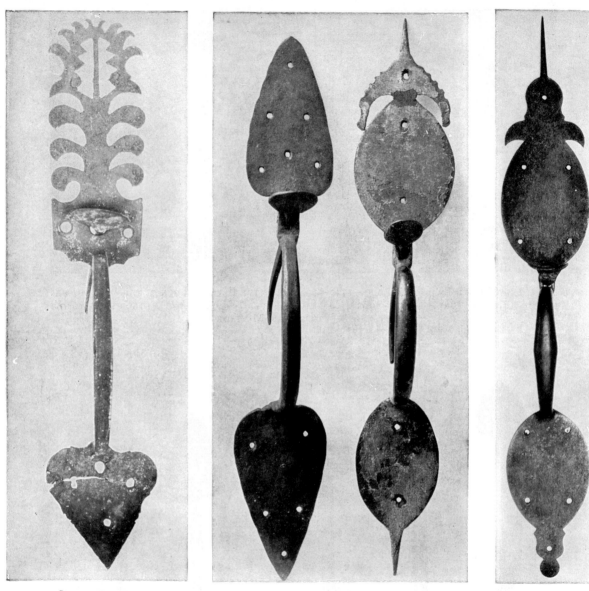

4418-21. Unique Flower Blossom Latch, and Three Church Door Latches. 18th Century. Wadsworth Atheneum.

4422-26. Pennsylvania Locks, All with Springs Except the Middle One. The Last Are Also Found in Germany. Wadsworth Atheneum.

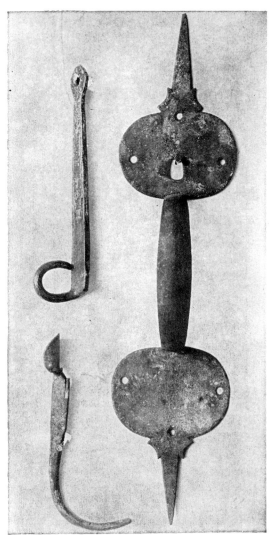

4427. Large Latch, One of Two Found in Connecticut. Wadsworth Atheneum.
4428. (Right.) Ball and Spear Pattern with Rounded Thumb Piece. L. P. Goulding, Sudbury.

4429-36. Eight Latches, Triangle, Heart and Ball Motives. 1810. Wadsworth Atheneum.

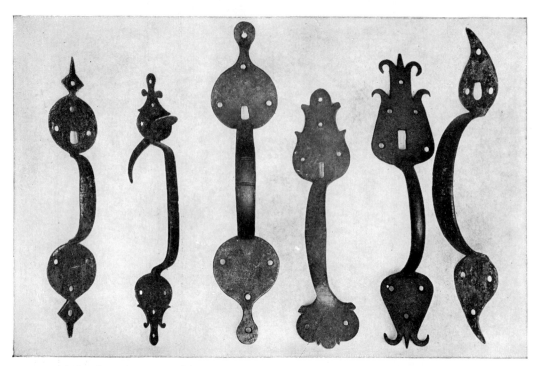

4437-42. Six Latches, the Next to the Last Being a Tulip, and the Last a Tulip Bud. New England and Pennsylvania, Wadsworth Atheneum.

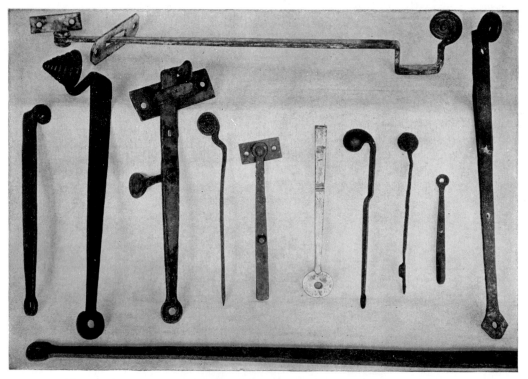

4443-54. Twelve Latch Bars. The Top One and the Second Vertical One Being Unique. The Latter Has a Spiral in the Form of a Cone. Those with the Plate of Early 19th Century. The Others, 18th Century. Wadsworth Atheneum.

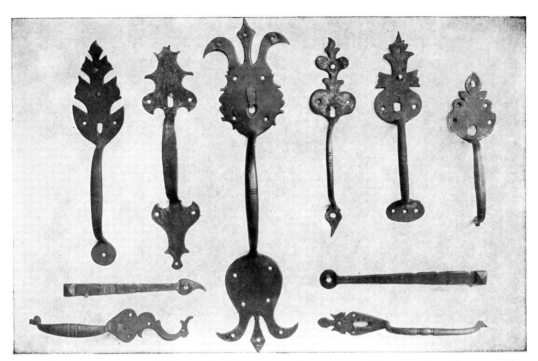

4455-64. COLLECTION OF WILLIAM B. MONTAGUE, NORRISTOWN. SEVERAL ARE UNIQUE. THE LARGEST IS THE BEST TULIP LATCH KNOWN TO THE AUTHOR. THE FIRST IS A LEAF PATTERN BETTER UNNAMED.

4465-67. THE FIRST A BALL AND SPEAR. L. P. GOULDING. THE OTHERS, A RARE LATCH WITH ALL ITS PARTS, AND AN ODD BETTY LAMP. H. W. ERVING.

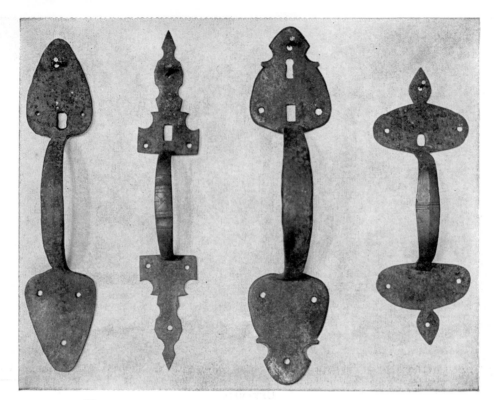

4468–71. Four 18th Century Latches. Wadsworth Atheneum.

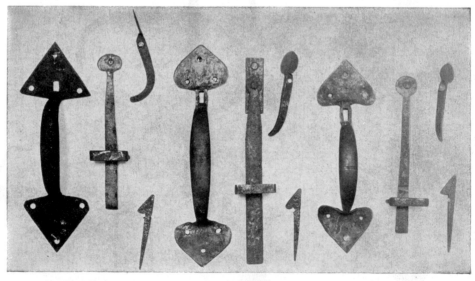

4472–74. Three Latches with All Their Parts. The Triangle, the Heart, and the Fully Formed Heart Patterns. It Shows the Usual Plain Catch. Wadsworth Atheneum.

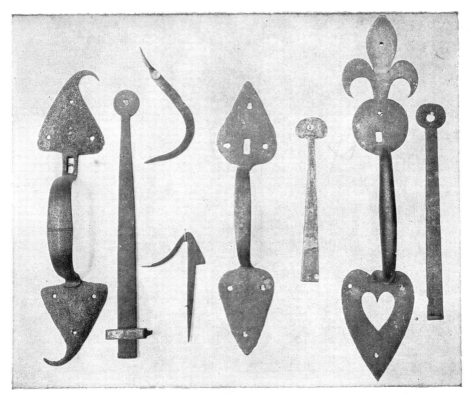

4475-77. Three Latches, the First a Curved Triangle, the Last a Heart,
Ball, and Fleur de Lis, with an Incised Heart. These and Those at the Bottom
of the Page, Wadsworth Atheneum.

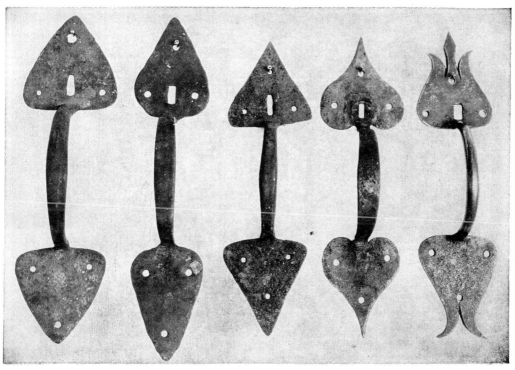

4478-82. The Next to the Last Is a Fine Heart Shape, and the Last Is a Tulip Latch.

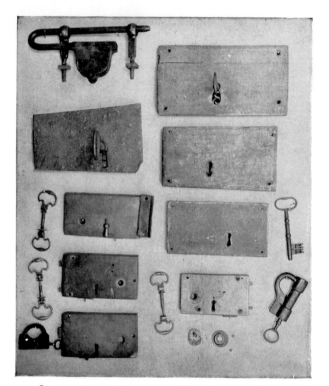

4483–94. Iron, Brass, and Wood Locks. Some of These Are To Be Attached to the Wood by Bolts, and Others by Screws. Interesting Padlocks and Two Early Door Escutcheons.
4495–96. (Right.) A Huge Round Plate Latch with Scalloped Edge. A Bar for a Large Door.

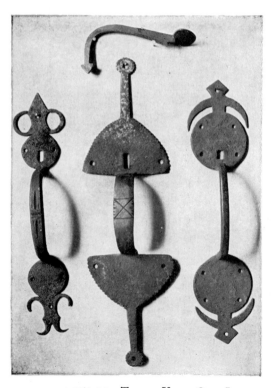

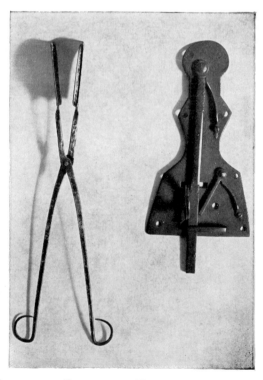

4497–99. Three Very Odd Latches. Fuessenich Collection, Torrington.
4500–01. (Right.) An Odd Curling Iron, and Good Pattern of a Spring Plate Latch.
George S. Palmer, New London.

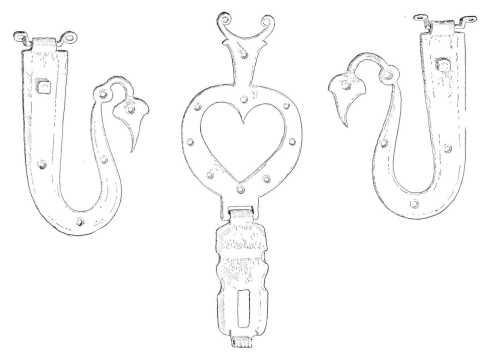

4502–03. Pair of Chest Hinges with Tulip Bud, and a Fine Heart Hasp, Forming a Set. Pennsylvania. Wadsworth Atheneum.

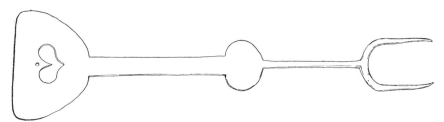

4504. Double Ender with Heart Motive on the Cake Turner, and a Ball at the Center. Pennsylvania. Wadsworth Atheneum.

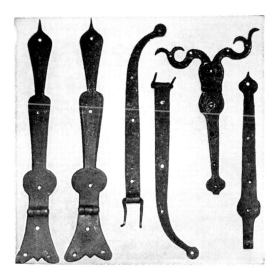

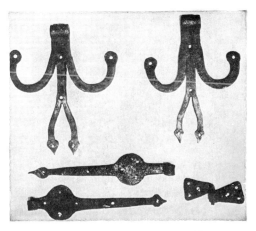

4505–11. Pennsylvania Hinges, except the Last Little Oxshoe Hinge. All Wrought. 18th Century. Wadsworth Atheneum.

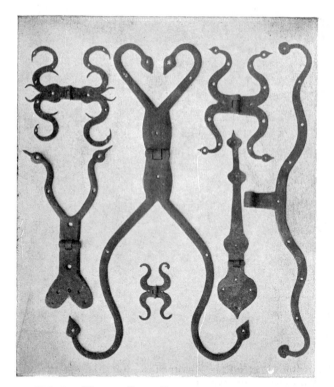

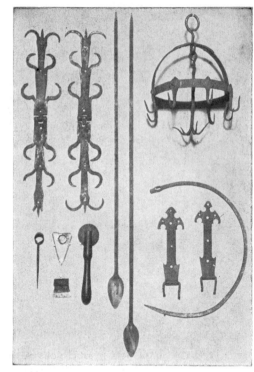

4512–29. Hinges, Stick Candleholder, Triangular Candlestick, Minute Candle Ring, a Pie Cutter, Two Thatching Needles, a Unique Meat Hanger, or Spit, a Curved Thatching Needle, and a Pair of Scrolled Hinges. The Thatching Needles Are Very Rare in America. All Owned by William B. Montague, Norristown, Pennsylvania.

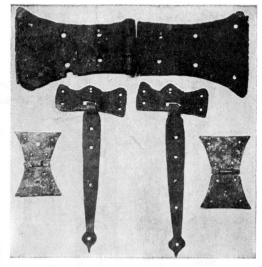

4530–33. Rare or Unique Hinges, One Being a Tulip Blossom. William B. Montague, Norristown.

4534–36. (Right.) An Immense Butterfly Hinge a Foot Long, Two Sizes of Conventional Butterflies, and a Pair of 17th Century Butterfly and Strap. Wadsworth Atheneum.

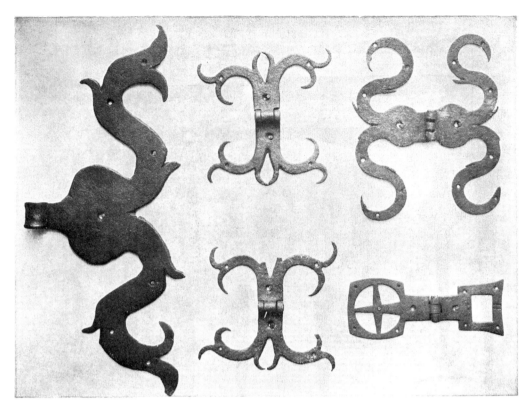

4537-40. Moravian Hinges and a Hasp of the Same Origin, 17th and 18th Centuries. Wadsworth Atheneum.

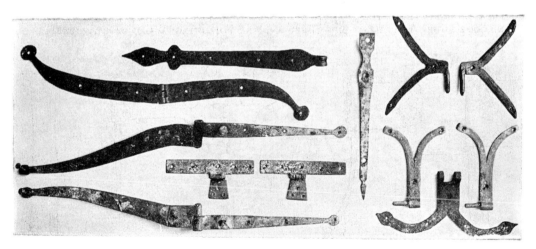

4541-48. Unusual Hinges. The T Pair and the V Scroll Being New England and the Rest Pennsylvania. Wadsworth Atheneum.

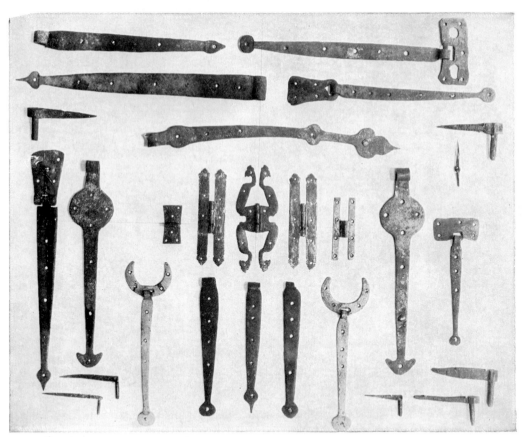

4549–69. SHEET OF HINGES AND GUDGEONS. AMONG THEM THE ONLY CURVED OR FISHTAIL HINGE SHOWN. AT THE CENTER A COCKSCOMB, THE BEST AMERICAN HINGE AND COPIED FROM THE ENGLISH, NO DOUBT. TWO OFFSET STYLES, A RAGGED, A SCREW, AND A CLINCH GUDGEON. THE DOUBLE COTTER-PIN HINGE FOR CHESTS, A SPEAR-HEAD PAIR, AND A HORSESHOE AND STRAP PAIR, AND SOME OTHER VARIETIES. THIS SHEET AND THE FOLLOWING: WADSWORTH ATHENEUM.

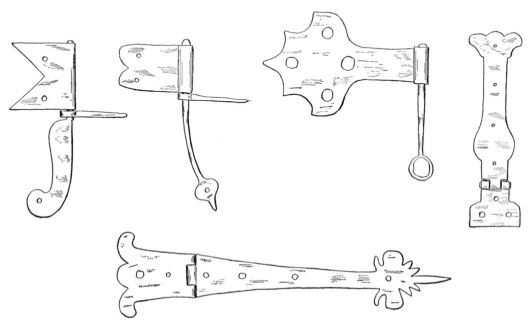

4570–74. PENNSYLVANIA CUPBOARD HINGES, EXCEPT THE LAST, WHICH IS NEW ENGLAND. THE SECOND IS THE DEVIL TAIL. WADSWORTH ATHENEUM.

4575-78. A Door Set with Open Heart Motive. Latch Found in New England and Hinges in Pennsylvania; About 1700. Wadsworth Atheneum.

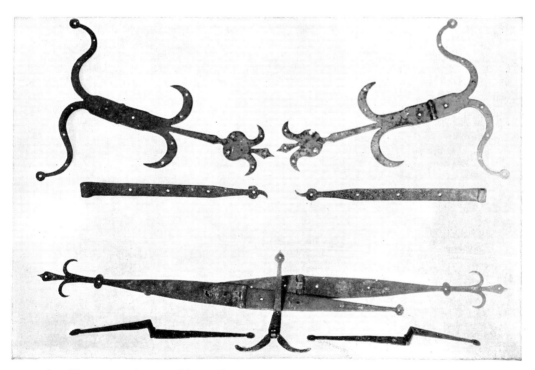

4579-85. Tulip and Scroll, Tulip Bud, Attenuated Tulip, Ram's Horn and Strap, and Simple Chest Hinges. Wadsworth Atheneum.

4586–92. A Scroll Pair, a Fine Escutcheon, Two Chest Handles, a Twisted Kettle Lifter, a Heart Hinge, and a Serpentine. Wadsworth Atheneum.

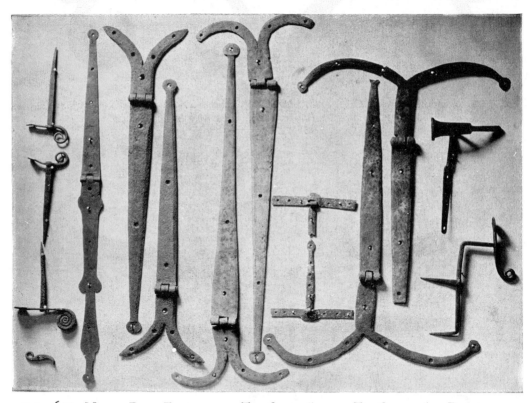

4593–4602. Minute Blind Fastener and Two Other Styles. The Others Are Pennsylvania Type, Except a Pair Which Look Like T Hinges, That Are Wrapped Joints, and 17th Century. Wadsworth Atheneum.

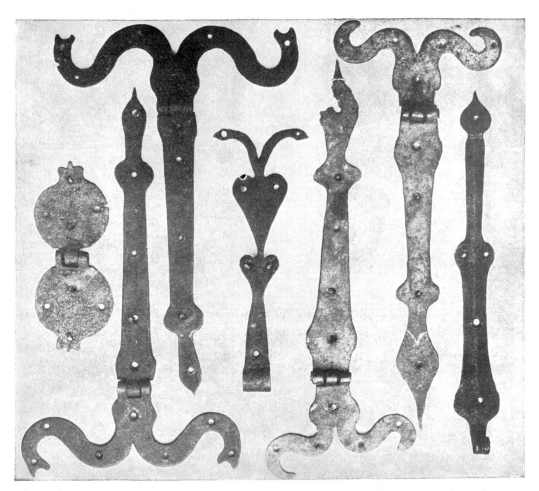

4603–08. Late 17th and Early 18th Centuries. Pennsylvania Hinges, the First Being in the Form of Two Discs. Wadsworth Atheneum.

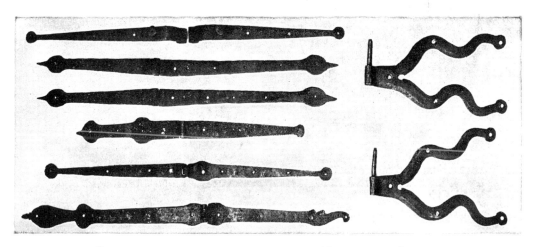

4609–15. Pennsylvania Chest and Door Hinges, 18th Century. Wadsworth Atheneum.

4616. FULLY SCROLLED HINGES, MORAVIAN. PHILIP MEREDITH ALLEN, BROAD AXE, PENNSYLVANIA.
4617. (Right.) WROUGHT CHEST, ELABORATE LOCK. USED AS SAFE. JOE KINDIG, JR., YORK.

4618-21. PAIR OF SPLENDID HINGES, ESCUTCHEON, HASPS WHICH BAND THE TRUNK, AND LIFTERS AT THE END. FOREIGN. 16TH CENTURY. PHILIP MEREDITH ALLEN.

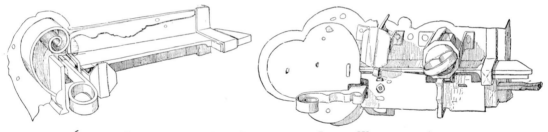

4622-23. DETAILS OF TWO FINE PENNSYLVANIA LOCKS, WADSWORTH ATHENEUM.

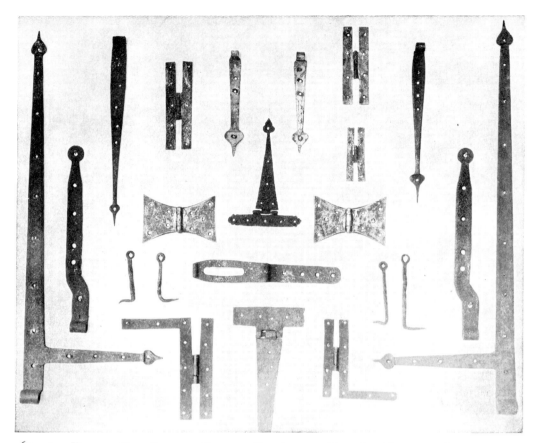

4624-39. Various New England Hinges. The Outside Pair Are Hammered L, as Distinct from the Inside H Hinges, Which Are Cut Out. A Pair of Very Fine Pointed Heart Hinges, a Scrolled T Specimen. An Offset Pair, a Pair of Butterflies, a Common T, Two HLs, and Five Hasps.

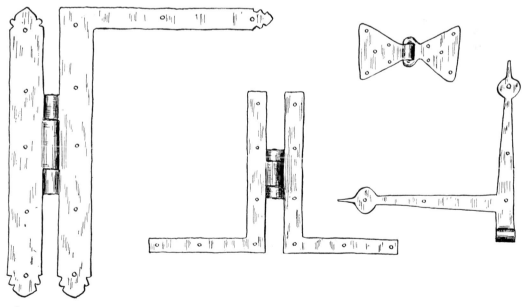

4640-43. Four Rare Hinges. The Scroll HL, and the LL Hinge Are the Rarest, but the Butterfly with the Wrapped Joint Is 17th Century. Present Ownership Unknown.

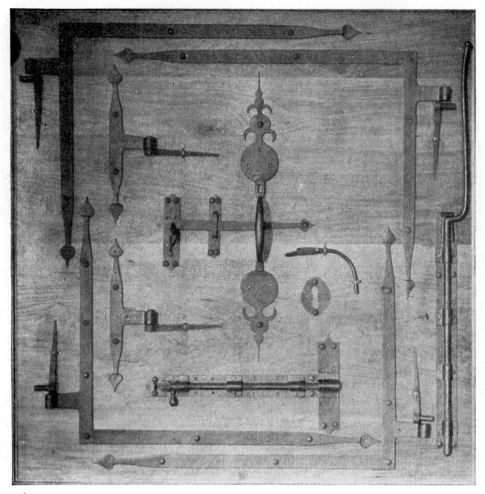

4644–51. CHURCH DOOR SET ARRANGED BY MORGAN B. BRAINARD, AND PRESENTED TO WADSWORTH ATHENEUM. THE LARGE WROUGHT L HINGES HAVE A POINTED HEART TERMINATION. THE LONG BOLT HAS A CURVE TO FREE THE LOWER SECTOR FOR THE HAND, THE OTHER BOLT IS FOR THE FLOOR. A REMARKABLY FINE SET. MADE BY HALL, AN EAST HADDAM BLACKSMITH.

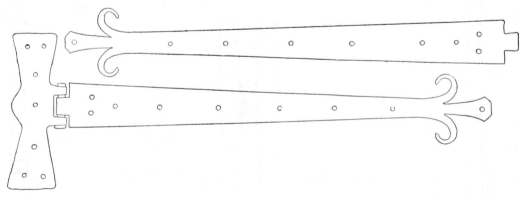

4652. PAIR, BUTTERFLY AND STRAP, FLEUR DE LIS ENDS. 17TH CENTURY. THE AUTHOR'S.

4653-57. COURT CUPBOARD PILLAR TURNINGS. THE FIRST IS THAT OF THE PARMENTER CUPBOARD, THE SECOND AND FOURTH ARE ON A PINE CUPBOARD, THE THIRD IS THE PRINCE-HOWES CUPBOARD, AND THE LAST IS THE SUNFLOWER AND TULIP CONNECTICUT COURT CUPBOARD.

4653, 20⅛ x 4; 4655, 17¾ x 4⁷⁄₁₆; SMALLEST DIAMETER 1⅜; 4657, 3⅞ DIAMETER.

These turnings are always in one piece and are never built up. They are doweled at both ends to fit into the cupboard shelf below and the cornice above. It will be noticed that the middle one is reversible. The material may be maple, or any semi-hard wood like basswood. The smaller turnings have been found in cherry. These large sections often cracked open. They were always painted black, which in process of time has acquired a green tint.

The other court cupboard turnings are, in the case of the urn shape, important, but they are fairly obvious; we show three others. About fifty-four court cupboards have been tallied, and most of them pictured by the author. The greater part are now in museums, and the balance in the hands of collectors or original owners.

4658–60. The Walnut Post of the Durham Cupboard, the Court Cupboard Table Leg, 3½ Inches Diameter, and the Virginia Cupboard, the Central Section of Which Is 6 x 8.

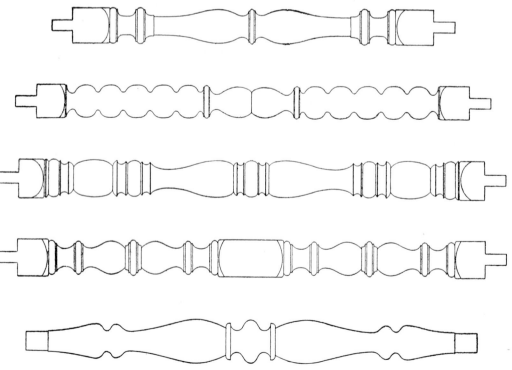

4661–65. Table and Chair Stretchers, Late 17th and Early 18th Centuries.

4666-69. Great 17th Century Table Legs. The Third and the Fourth Represent Communion Tables. The First Is the Bulbous Leg of the Great Andover Table, 31¾ x 4⅛. Note the Extension at the Top, the Tenon Entering into the Mortise of the Top, Which Is Left Loose. The Last Belongs to the Famous Salisbury Table, the First Great Communion Table, Shown under Tables.

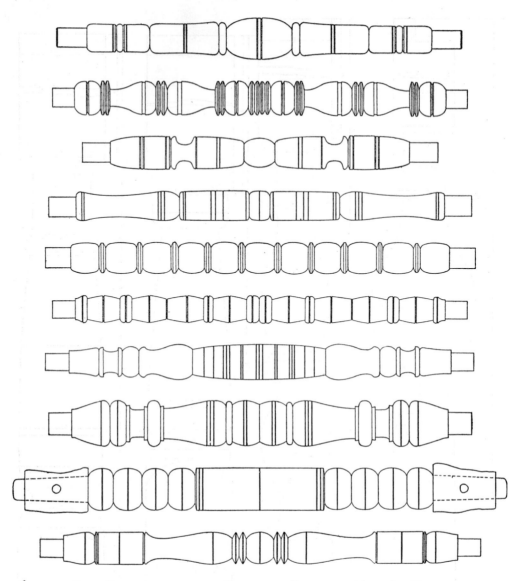

4670–79. Chair Stretchers, 17th and Early 18th Centuries. They Can Easily Be Picked Out From Our Pictures, of the Brewster, Carver, and Other Early Chairs.

These turnings are usually in maple, altogether the best material except birch which is just as good. Ash is slivery and wholly unsuited for intricate turnings. There is no objection to beech.

The period of a chair may be roughly estimated from the size of the turnings. In the earliest examples some of the chairs run to a diameter of 2½-inch posts. Broadly speaking anything less than 2 inch may be set near the close of the century. The author has pointed out what has now become a recognized principle of collectors, that other things being equal, the larger the post, the greater the value. At least one hundred dollars may be allowed for every eighth of an inch up or down of diameter.

4680–86. 17th Century Table Legs with One Couch Leg. All the Legs Shown Are from Pieces in This Work.

4687-91. 17TH CENTURY CHAIR AND TABLE LEGS. ALL SHOWN IN THIS WORK.

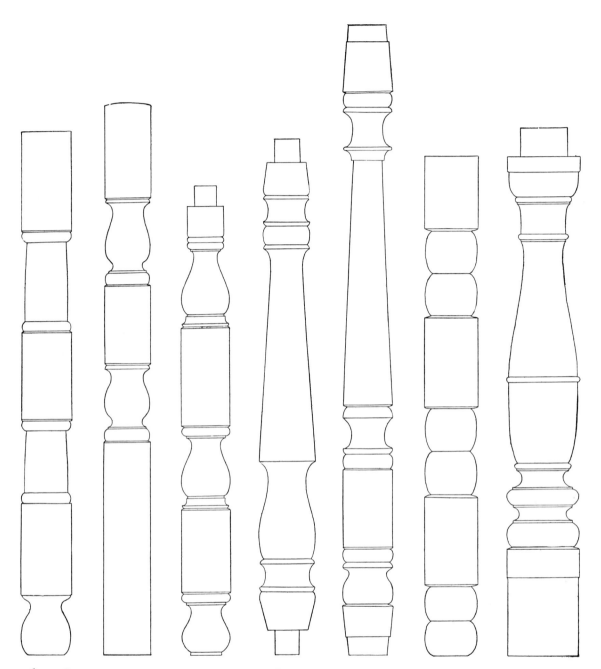

4692–98. First, Fruit-Wood Leather-Seat Chair; Second, Spanish Foot Chair; Third, a Corner Maple Chair; Fourth and Fifth, Banisters from a Carved Banister Back; Sixth, Cromwellian Chair Leg; Seventh, the Shaft of a Simple Maple Table. Richer Tables Shown Elsewhere. The Earliest of These Is the Cromwellian.

We point out again that the banisters must, in the best style, be precisely identical with the back posts. One should note also that the Cromwellian chair is ordinarily made with a right-angle seat, no wider at the front than at the back. The earliest turnings are always the simplest. Elaboration increases as periods grow later. The earliest chairs have no turnings whatever below the seat.

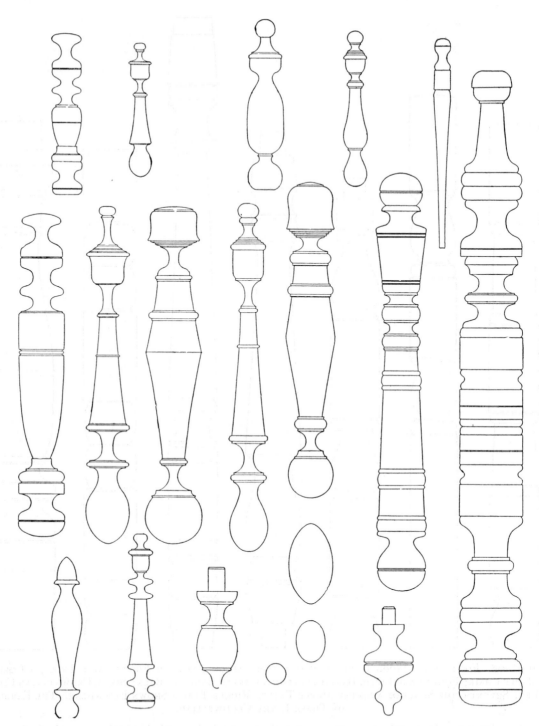

4699–4717. Split Spindle Ornaments Otherwise Called Drops or Bosses on Oak Chests.
The Finer Ones with Bolder Turnings Belong to the Connecticut Sunflower. All the
Pieces Appear in This Work. At the Bottom the Third Piece from the Left Is the Drop
from the Cornice of the Sunflower Chest. The Circle and Ovals Are Outlines of the
Bosses on the Same; and the Last Small Drop Is on the Great Concord Table.

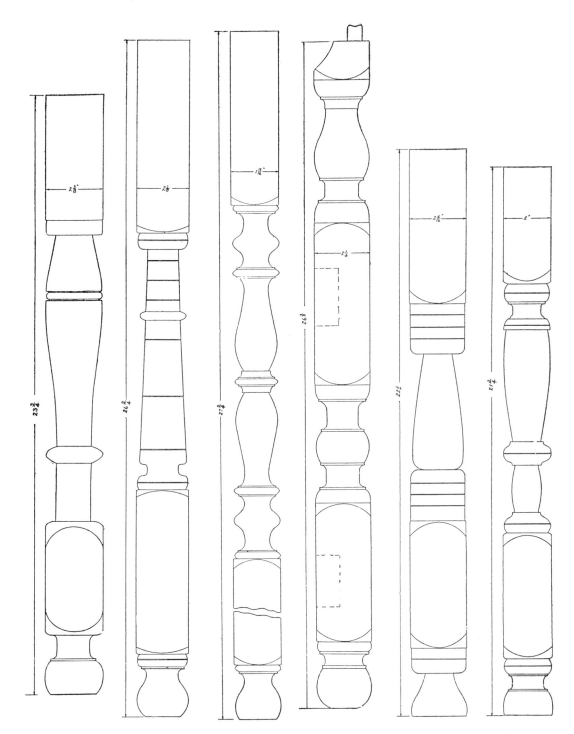

4718-23. 17TH CENTURY LEGS OF TABLES SHOWN ELSEWHERE. AMONG THE EARLIEST ARE THE SECOND AND THE FIFTH.

4724–28. 17TH CENTURY TABLE LEGS. THE FIRST IS THE CHERRY POST OF A TRESTLE GATE LEG. THE OTHER TURNINGS ON THIS PLATE ARE GATE LEGS BEYOND THE FIRST TWO. THE FIRST POST IS 26 x 2⅝.

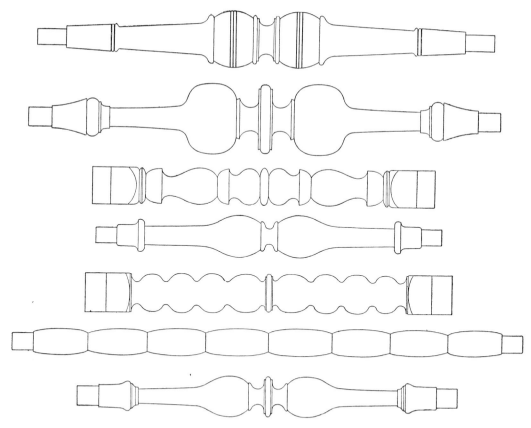

4729-35. STRETCHERS. 17TH AND EARLY 18TH CENTURIES. THE LARGEST ARE THOSE OF SPANISH FOOT CHAIRS. THE LAST IS TYPICAL QUEEN ANNE. NEXT TO THE LAST IS CALLED SAUSAGE TURNING. THE ONE ABOVE THAT IS A BALL TURNING. NEXT ABOVE, ONE OBSERVES THAT THESE TURNINGS ARE THE MEETING OF TWO VASES, AND SO ON TO THE TOP.

4736-38. 17TH CENTURY BREWSTER AND CARVER BACK-POST FINIALS.

4739-41. Brewster and Carver Finials. 17th Century. All the Chairs Are Shown in This Work.

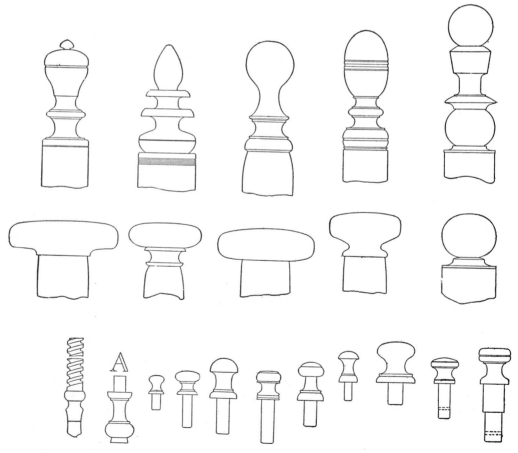

4742-62. The First Row Are the Back Posts, and the Second, the Front Posts of Carver, Brewster, and Slat Backs. The Bottom Row Consists of Chest Knobs. 17th Century.

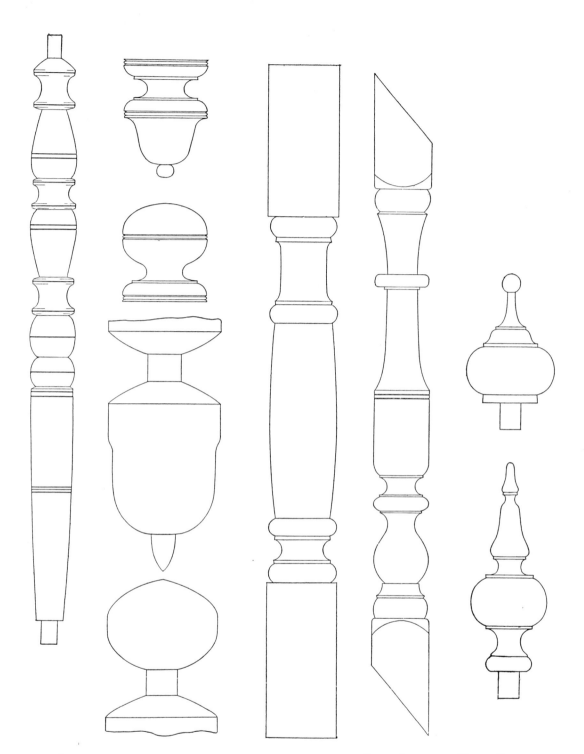

4763-71. Bed Spindle, Stair Banisters and Drops, and Cross-Stretcher Table Finials Such as Are Found on the Earliest William and Mary Lowboys.

Regarding the banisters at the earliest time there was only one on the stair and it was very heavy. The finials of posts were always worked on the posts, that is, they were never doweled on. The best stair in New England was in the old Wentworth House, Portsmouth, and the best in Pennsylvania is now in the Pennsylvania Museum.

4772–76. Legs of Lowboys, Dating from 1690 to 1710. The Last, However, Is the Leg of a Cross-Stretcher Stool.

Regarding critical observations in this work, the reader will understand that there are fads in antique furniture. It is not true, however, that a very rare piece of fine design in any period loses value. For instance, the recent quest for mahogany has not detracted from the value of the finest articles in the oak period. It has, however, lessened the desire for the more ordinary oak pieces. Similarly to-day people having the notion that mahogany is the thing, are too apt to accept inferior specimens merely because they are mahogany. The considerations giving value are: age, rarity, style, condition, fashion.

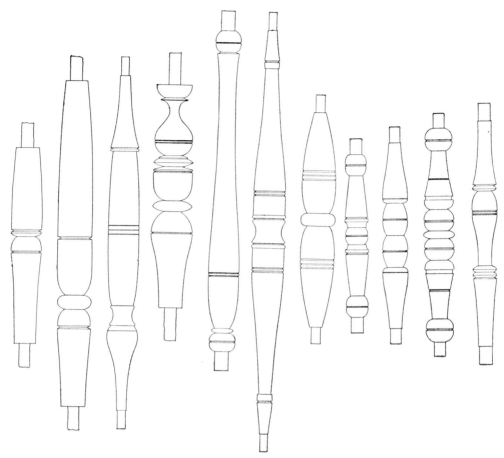

4777-87. 17TH CENTURY CHAIR SPINDLES, ALL BREWSTER OR CARVER. WADSWORTH ATHENEUM.

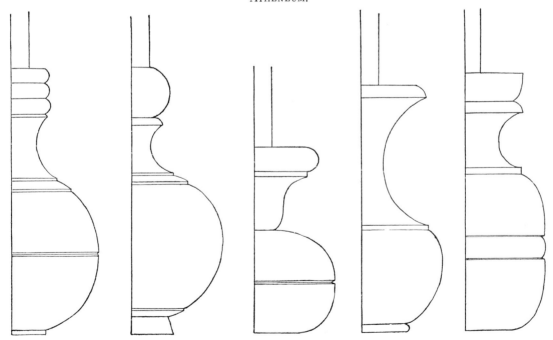

4788-92. FIVE BALL FEET AS FOUND ON OAK CHESTS OF DRAWERS OR CHESTS. ALL 17TH CENTURY.

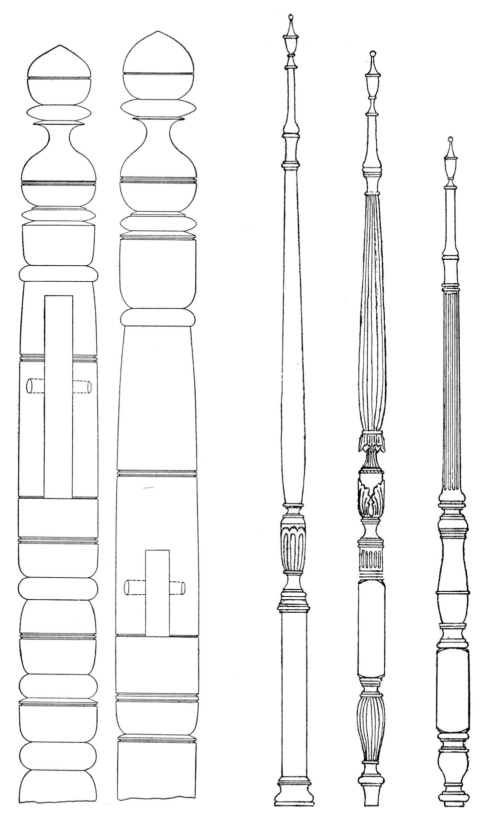

4793-97. Five Bed Posts. The First and Second the Best 17th Century Bed.
The Other Three Are: the First, Carved Maple, 1780; the Second, Carved
Mahogany, 1800; and the Last, Fluted Maple, 1790.

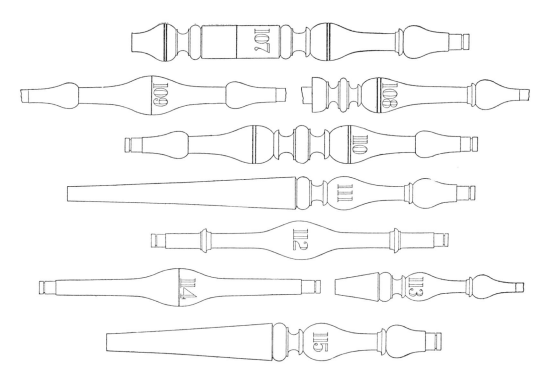

4798–4806. Windsor Chair Turnings. The Numbers Were in a Former Edition. The Four Near the Top Are Pennsylvania Windsors, Front Posts and Stretchers. The Others Are Taper-Turned Windsors, High Chair, Stretchers, Short Posts, and Leg.

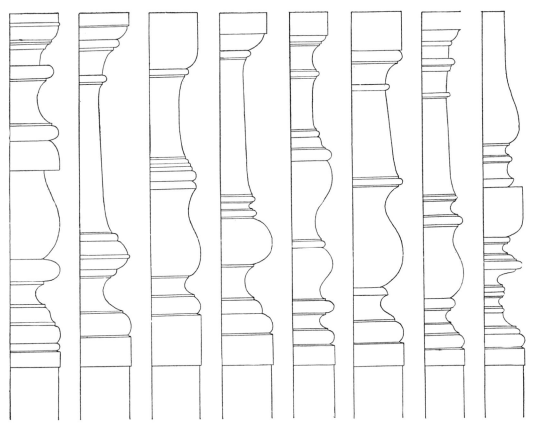

4807–14. Half Posts of Mahogany Tip and Turn Table Shafts. 1750–75. They Range from 4⅛ Inches Down, That Being the Largest Diameter of the Bowl of the Base. All Carved.

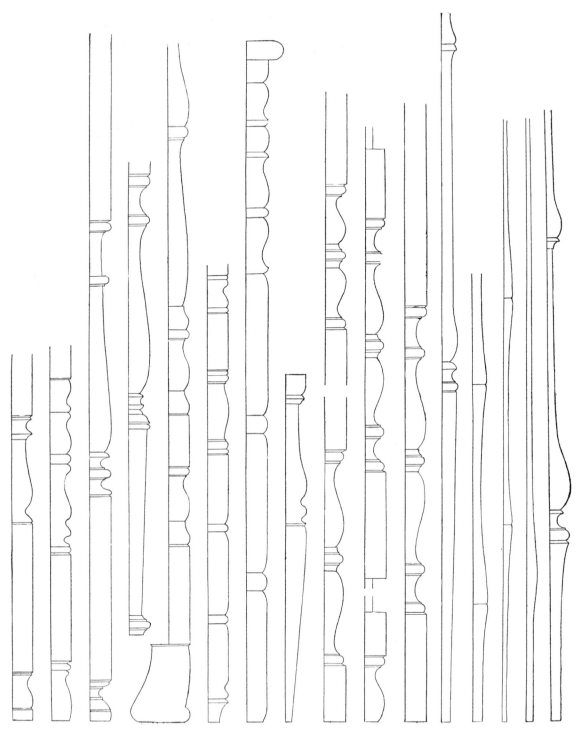

4815-30. Turnings to Centers. On the Left, Back and Small Spindles of Windsors and Stretcher of Bamboo Windsor, and a High-Chair Leg. The Three Following Are from a Turned Crane Bracket, Then the Short Front Spindle of a Windsor Arm. The Next, a Tall One, Is a Mushroom Post. The Rest Are Chair or Table Legs of About 1700. The Diameter of the Large Bulb on the First at the Right Is Two Inches, from This the Others May Be Gauged.

4831-40. THE UPPER SECTION SHOWS THE CONTOUR OF DESK CABINET DIVISIONS. AT RIGHT AND LEFT ARE BASE MOLDINGS OF DESKS, AT THE CENTER ARE CONTOURS OF THREE SMALL CABINET DRAWERS.

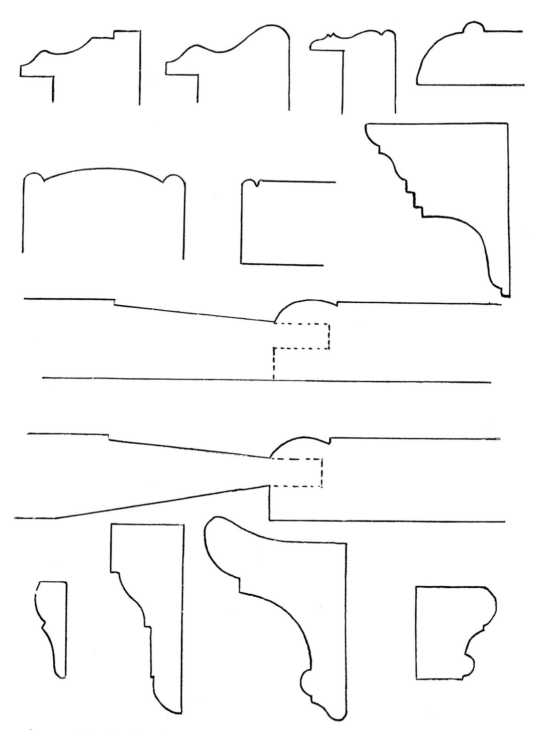

4841-53. The Top Line Shows Looking-Glass Mold, Next Line Left, Molded Dutch
Chair Back; Then a Bead, and the Clock Mold. The Two Matched Portions Show Paneled
Sheathing. At the Bottom, First, an Applied Chest Mold; Next, Pine Cupboard Mold;
Third, Mahogany Dressing Table; Fourth, Oak Mold about Sunflower Chest.

4854–63. Chippendale Period Highboy Moldings, Showing Two Complete Highboys.
The Flat Sections Are Called Fillets. The Quarter Round Is Self Explanatory.
The Ogee Is a Combination of Concave and Convex Mold. The Astragal Is a Very
Small Quarter Round. The Great Single Concave Is Called a Cove.

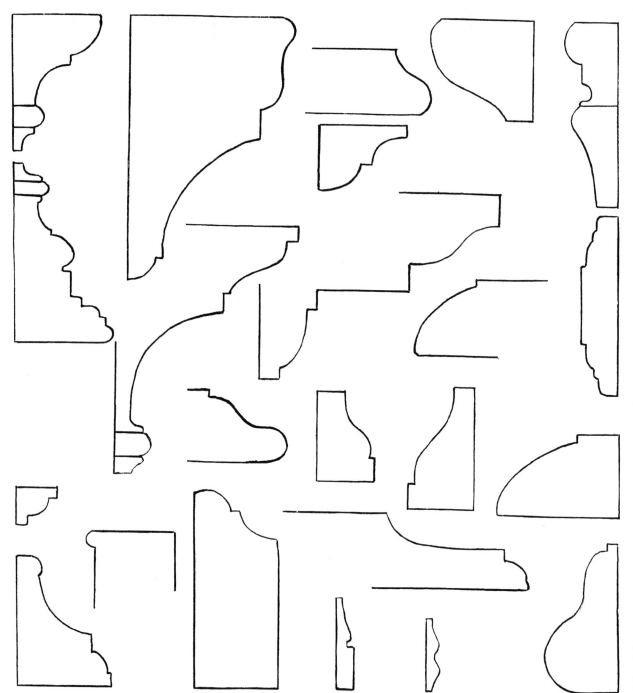

4864–86. Top Left and Thence Downward Are an Upper and Base Desk Mold. A Silver Cabinet Top and Base Mold. Again at Top, the Large Mold Is a Secretary; Next Below, a Maple Secretary, a Mahogany Chest of Drawers Top, and Finally a Mahogany Desk Base Mold. At the Top Again, the Block-Front Chest of Drawers, and under It a Supporting Mold. The Next, Very Large, Is a Dresser Mold, Followed by a Small Base Mold. The Large Horizontal Mold Is on the Splice of a Windsor Chair Arm. Two Small Ones at the Bottom Are a Lining Mold and Channel Mold on the Oak Chest. At the Top Again, Next to the Last, Is an Oak Looking-Glass. At the Extreme Right Top and the One Beneath It Are Oak Molds on a Small Chest-on-Frame. The Third in Line Is an Oak Chest of Drawers Top, and at the Base Is an Oak Bottom Mold on the Same.

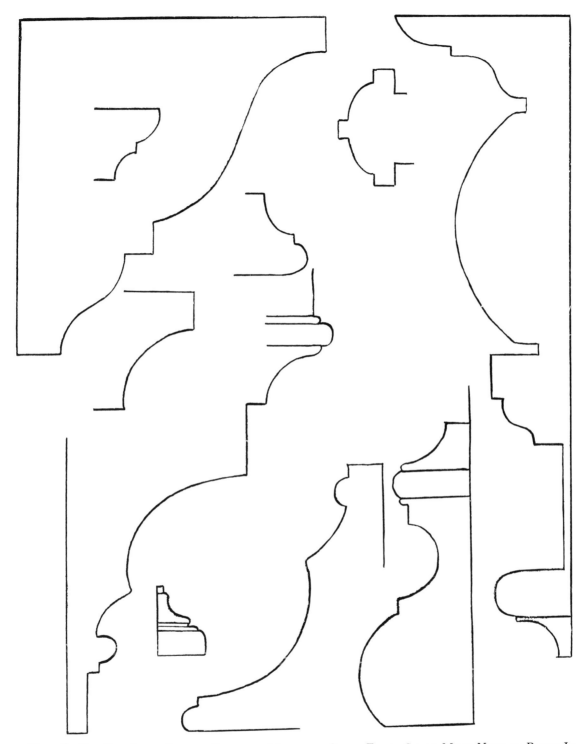

4887-96. The Top Left, Corner Cupboard Mold and Shelf Edge. Small Mold Next at Right Is the Edge of the Small Shelf on the Same Cupboard, and Below at Left a Simple Clock Top, Followed by the Very Large Mold Showing the Full Details of the Elaborate Clock Top. The Little Mold Below Runs Around under the Hood. At the Top the Great Mold Is the Inside of the Corner Cupboard Mold, the Small One At Left Is the Section of a Muntin of This Same Cupboard. At the Bottom the Section at the Right Is the Base of the Pillar of the Corner Cupboard, and Next Left Is a Clock Base Mold.

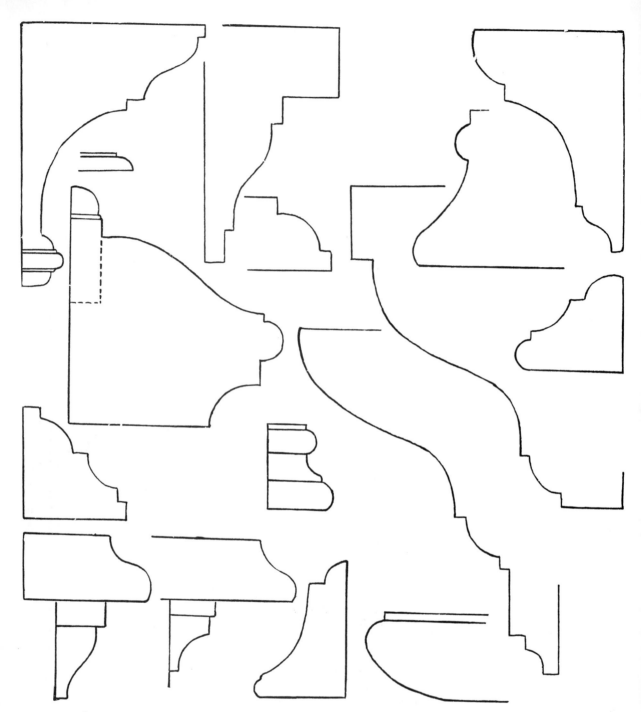

4897–4906. Top Left, Mahogany Chest-on-Chest Top Mold, Then the Thumb-Nail Edge of Drawer. The Next with the Dotted Line Shows the Middle Section Mold, and Below Is the Bottom Mold. Bottom Left Is a Walnut Sideboard Table, and Next Left a Maple Lowboy. At the Top Again, the Second Is a Dresser-Top and Bottom Mold. Below the Smallest Mold Is a Sunflower Chest Band between the Drawers of Oak. At the Bottom, Third from Left, Is a Base Mold of a Small Table Desk. Top Right, a Small Highboy Top Mold, Followed at the Left by a Chest-of-Drawers Base of the Pine Period. Second from Top, at Right, Is the Central Mold at the Division of a Mahogany Highboy. The Two Great Molds Next Following Are the New England Dresser Top and the Welsh Dresser Top; and Finally the Mold on the Shelf of the Welsh Dresser.

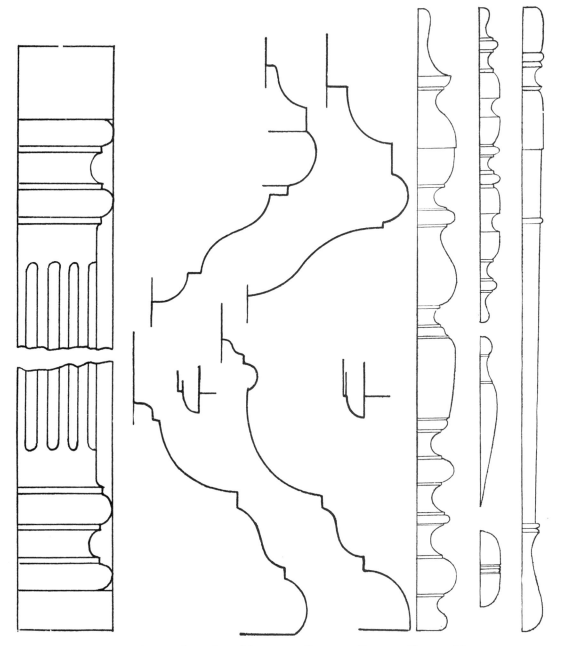

4907–13. At the Left Is a Mahogany Quarter Column, Fluted, Next
Are the Upper and Middle Sections of Two Highboys; and the Thumb-
Nail Drawer Edges.

4914–18. (Right.) Half Spindles from the General Payne Court Cupboard, and Chest. The Little Double Boss Probably Unique.

Of course, no one contends that all, even of the most ancient turnings, are
in perfect taste. They have a charm arising from their quaintness and their
striving after beauty which, in a remarkable number of instances, they attain.
The chief criticism from our modern viewpoint is that they are somewhat too
ornate.

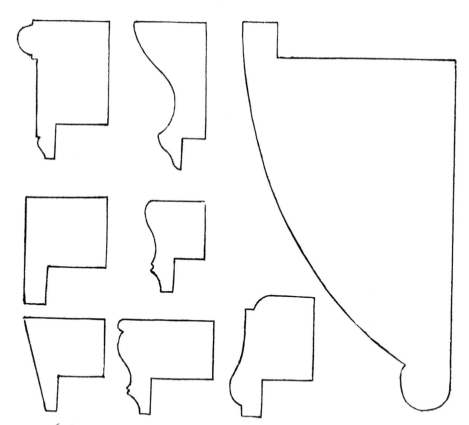

4919–26. Looking-Glass Molds, Largest Being Walnut on Pine, 17th Century. The Other Walnut and Mahogany.

4927–40. Nine Fine Bandboxes, Hat Trees, Twelve Early Poke Bonnets, and a Half Dozen Caps. The Fireplace Molds and Cornice Are 1782. On the Mantel Is a Bronze and Crystal Lighting Set. Old Bonnet Show Stands.

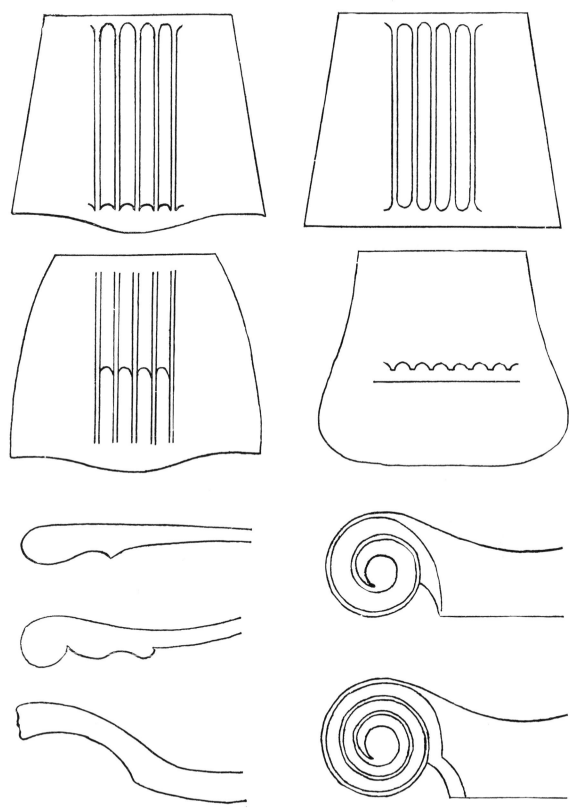

4941-53. At the Top Chippendale Chair Seats, Followed by a Hepplewhite and Dutch Seat, Inside Them Are Shown the Various Forms of Flutes, and the Last Shows a Reeding. The Five in the Lower Half Show Five Chippendale Arms or Ears.

4954-58. THE HEADS OF FOUR SECRETARIES. BEGINNING AT TOP, BIGELOW COLLECTION, FIRST, SECOND, AND THIRD. THE FOURTH FROM SAMUEL WINECK. THE LAST A SECTION OF A FRAME, RHODE ISLAND SCHOOL OF DESIGN.

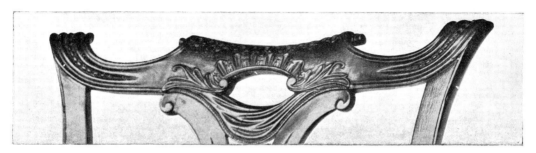

4959–63. Two Chair Backs, Rhode Island School of Design; the Unusual Termination of Blocking on a Desk Front; a Shell on a Knee-Hole Desk, J. K. Beard, and a Chippendale Chair Back. Probably Metropolitan Museum.

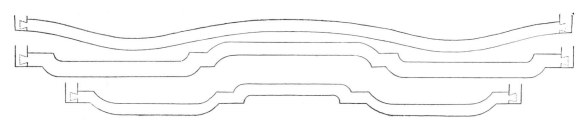

4964–69. TOP: SECRETARY CORNICE WITH A CARVED BIRD AND INLAYS. THIS REPRESENTS THE LAST TYPE IN GOOD SECRETARIES. J. K. BEARD, RICHMOND, VIRGINIA. THE NEXT IS THE TOP OF A HIGHBOY SHOWING DENTILS ON THE STRAIGHT CORNICE AND ALSO ON THE SCROLLED ARCH. THE OPEN FRET IS ALWAYS ATTRACTIVE. MORRIS SCHWARTZ, NEW YORK. THERE FOLLOW DETAILS FROM THE FRAME OF A GLASS DOOR. RHODE ISLAND SCHOOL OF DESIGN. AT THE BOTTOM ARE THREE DRAWER FRONTS. THE DOVETAIL SHOULD NOT SHOW, AS THEY RUN IN FROM THE SIDE. FIRST IS THE OXBOW, SECRETARY OR CHEST OF DRAWERS; THE SECOND IS THE JOHN GODDARD SECRETARY IN THE FULL FORM; THE LAST IS FROM THE SMALL PLAIN BLOCKED CHEST OF DRAWERS.

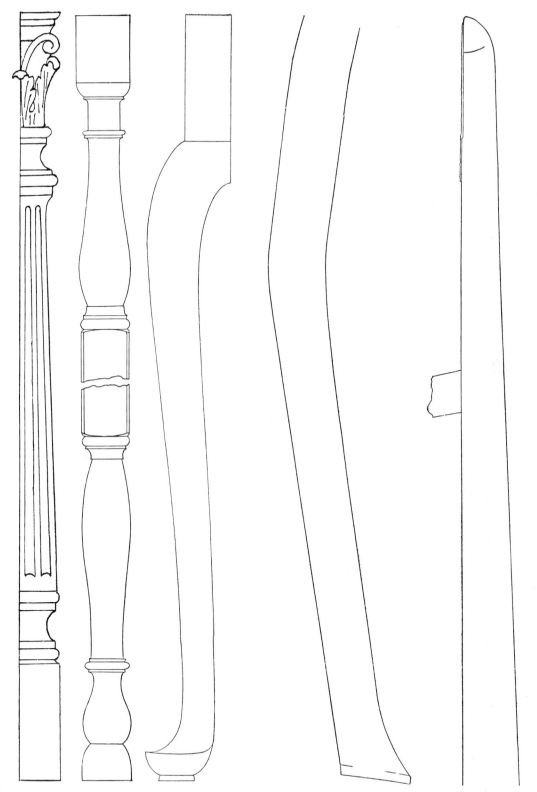

4970-74. SIDE OF A HALF COLUMN ON FRONT OF DOCUMENT DRAWER, HELEN T. COOKE; THE LEG OF A SPINET, OF A DUTCH TABLE, AND THE TWO SECTIONS OF A BACK CHIPPENDALE LEG. THE AUTHOR'S.

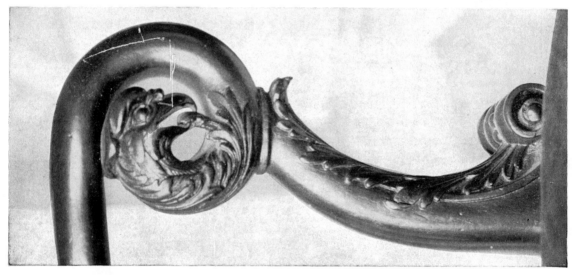

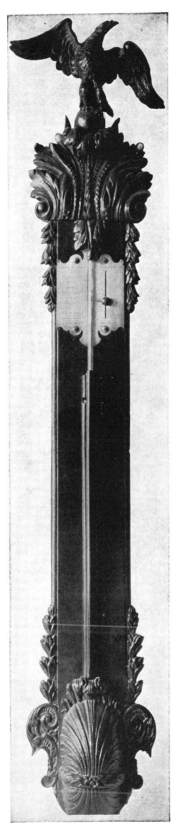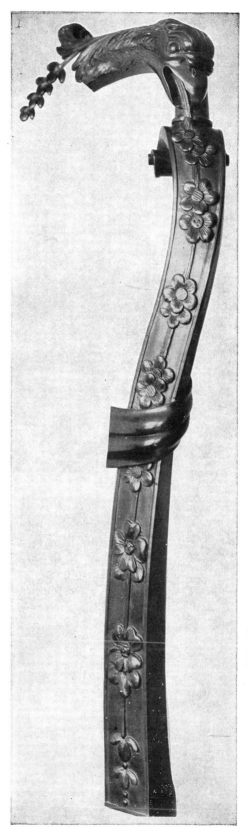

4978–80. Leg of a Sheraton Chair, Estate of H. W. Weeks; Barometer, and Gibbons Chair Post.
Rhode Island School of Design.

4981–83. Spoon Racks, Hudson and Delaware Valleys. Knickerbocker or Pennsylvania German. Above Are the Best So Far Discovered. The First and the Last Bought by the Author Near Hackensack. The Middle One Combines a Knife Box with the Rack, Stars, and Spiral Wheels. The Third Has Most Delicate Tracery in the Central Panel. Also the Inevitable Tulip Above. Dated 1745. Wadsworth Atheneum.

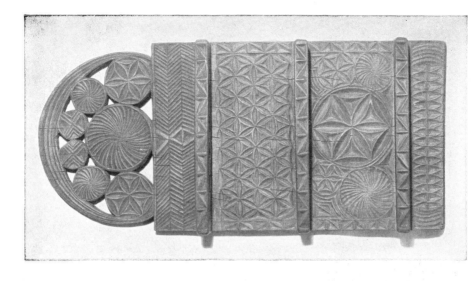

4984. Two Fashions of Wheels, Alternating. Knife Box, Rack Bars Slotted, Not Pierced; Mrs. George R. Fearing, Jr.

4985. Top as if the Kas Were Represented. Wadsworth Atheneum.

4986. Very Fully Carved, Morris Berry. The Maker Indulged Himself in Four Fashions of Wheels, Which He Probably Got Out of His Head. There Is Also a Herringbone Carving.

4987. From A. H. Rice, Bethlehem, Found in Delaware Valley. A Runic Motive.
4988. (Right.) There Are Four Star Wheel Motives. Mrs. Geo. R. Fearing, Jr.

4989. Star and Swastika. The Other Name for a Spoon Rack Was Lepel Bortie. E. B. Leete Co.
4990. (Right.) An Elaborate Pattern, Doubled Heart, and Tulip. 1775. A. H. Rice, Bethlehem.

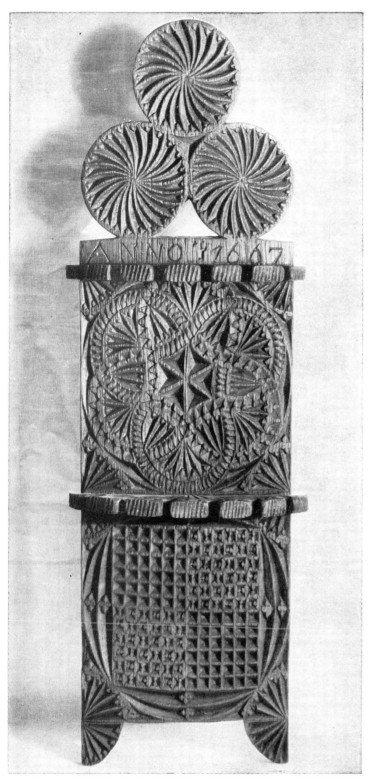

4991. "Anno 1667." This Seems Too Crudely Done, but May Be Correct. The Rack Itself Is in a Pattern Quite Different from Any Other, and Most Interesting. 5 x 17½. P. S. Briggs, Radnor, Pennsylvania.

4992. (Right.) "MH-1763." A Pattern Unique to the Author. Intricate and Careful Carving. Twelve Designs of Wheels, and a Good Endless Band. Very Long. J. Stogdell Stokes.

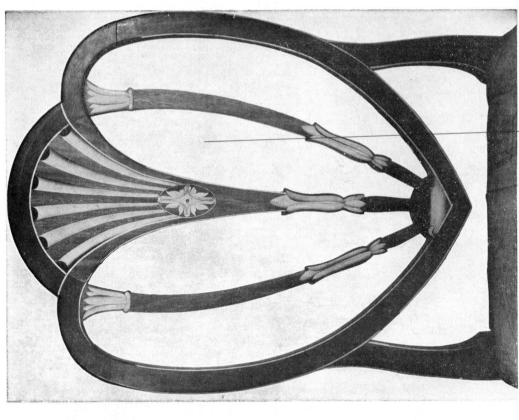

4993. Hepplewhite Back. Unusual in Being So Richly Carved. Three Wheat Ears, and Banisters Appearing To Rise from Petals. 1780–85. Rhode Island School of Design.

4994. (Right.) Finely Inlaid Back, Hepplewhite. J. K. Beard, Drewerys' Mansion, Richmond, Virginia.

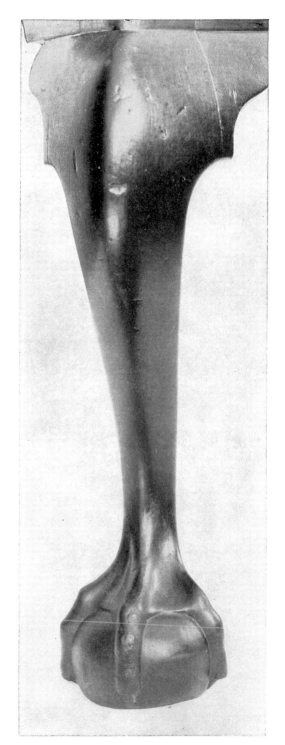

4995. LEG OF CHIPPENDALE CHAIR. 1750–70. SANDERSON COLLECTION.
4996. (Right.) CORNER DETAIL OF HALF COLUMN SET ON CHAMFER OF A SERPENTINE CHEST OF DRAWERS.
ONE OTHER KNOWN, APPARENTLY A MATE TO THIS. CHARLES P. COOLEY, HARTFORD, 1750–75.

4997. LEG OF A TRIPOD TABLE. COURTESY OF "ANTIQUES." 1800–20. METROPOLITAN MUSEUM.

4998. (Right.) SATYR HEAD ON HIP. IT IS UNUSUAL IN RUNNING UP ONTO THE FRAME. TASSEL AND ACANTHUS CARVING. A FOUR-TOED FOOT. 1720. RHODE ISLAND SCHOOL OF DESIGN.

It will be noted that the caster comes in with the 19th century, and that at first it was applied to a turned or decorative brass casting, like that in the Phyfe table above. The presence of casters before late Sheraton or Empire is quite conclusive that the piece originally did not have them. It was very much later that casters were applied directly to the wood. That method belongs to degraded Empire time. The four-toed foot referred to above is often called an animal foot as distinct from the bird, dragon, or rat foot which is more generally found and preferred. The term "rat foot" is used to designate a narrow, very long ball. The ball-and-claw motive is supposed to have come from China, at least there is a chair in China with such a foot, dated from the 8th century.

NOTE: Two errors in numbers are compensated by insertion of many a, b, c, numbers. The total number of objects is much above 5000.

4999. EFFECTIVE HEAD. BASE OF LOOKING-GLASS. THE STAR ABOVE THE FOREHEAD, THE HANDLING OF THE CONVENTIONALIZED HAIR, AND THE BACKING OF ALL WITH A SHELL IS VERY EFFECTIVE. RHODE ISLAND SCHOOL OF DESIGN. BELOW, DETAIL OF LOOKING-GLASS FRAME.

5000. SWAN ON NEST DETAIL. 1760–75. RHODE ISLAND SCHOOL OF DESIGN.

INDEX

The references are to numbers under the figures.

INDEX

INDEX

INDEX

INDEX

INDEX

INDEX

INDEX

INDEX

INDEX

INDEX

INDEX

INDEX

INDEX

INDEX

INDEX

INDEX

INDEX

INDEX